THE VOYAGE
OF
FRANCOIS PYRARD

VIEW OF LAVAL.

Before the construction of the modern Embankment.

THE VOYAGE
OF
FRANCOIS PYRARD
OF LAVAL

TO THE EAST INDIES, THE MALDIVES, THE MOLUCCAS AND BRAZIL

TRANSLATED INTO ENGLISH FROM THE THIRD FRENCH EDITION OF 1619 AND EDITED WITH NOTES,

BY ALBERT GRAY

FORMERLY OF THE CEYLON CIVIL SERVICE

ASSISTED

BY H. C. P. BELL

OF THE CYLON CIVIL SERVICE

IN TWO VOLUMES—VOL. 1

GYAN

Published by

Gyan Publishing House
5, Ansari Road
Daryaganj, New Delhi-110002
Phone: 011-47034999, 9811692060
E-mail: books@gyanbooks.com

Distribution Network
gyanbooks.com
India, USA, Canada, UK, Australia, France

ISBN : 978-81-212-4199-1 (Set)
ISBN : 978-81-212-4771-9 (PB)
First Published, 1887

2nd Impression 2020

Printed at: Gyan Press, Delhi.

The Voyage of Francois Pyrard
Author: Albert Gray

THE VOYAGE

OF

FRANÇOIS PYRARD

OF LAVAL

TO THE EAST INDIES, THE MALDIVES, THE MOLUCCAS AND BRAZIL.

TRANSLATED INTO ENGLISH FROM THE THIRD FRENCH EDITION OF 1619
AND EDITED, WITH NOTES,

BY ALBERT GRAY,

FORMERLY OF THE CEYLON CIVIL SERVICE.

ASSISTED

BY H. C. P. BELL,

OF THE CEYLON CIVIL SERVICE.

IN TWO VOLUMES.—VOL. I.

LONDON:
PRINTED FOR THE HAKLUYT SOCIETY,
4, LINCOLN'S INN FIELDS, W.C.

M.DCCC.LXXXVII.

COUNCIL

OF

THE HAKLUYT SOCIETY.

CONTENTS OF THE FIRST VOLUME.

LIST OF ILLUSTRATIONS.

NOS. 2, 4, 5, 6, 7, 8, and 11 are from photographs by MR. BELL.

"Ὦ ξεῖνοι, τίνες ἐστέ; ποθεν πλεῖθ' ὑγρὰ κέλευθα;
Ἦ τι κατὰ πρῆξιν ἢ μαψιδίως ἀλάλησθε
Οἷά τε ληϊστῆρες ὑπεὶρ ἅλα; τοί τ' ἀλόωνται
Ψυχὰς παρθέμενοι, κακὸν ἀλλοδαποῖσι φέροντες."

Od. ix. 252-5.

"In istâ Indiâ sunt insulæ multæ, et ut audivi, plus quam decem millia habitatæ: ubi sunt multa mirabilia mundi."

Friar Jordanus.

INTRODUCTION.

At the end of the fifteenth century, while the Pope was still regarded as standing arbitrator in the disputes of Christendom, Alexander VI had decreed to Portugal the discoveries of the East. The discovery of the Cape route to India was the first-fruits of that dispensation, and, for the greater part of the succeeding century, Portugal was admitted to hold in lawful possession, not only the territories of her conquest in India, but also the ocean ways which led thither. From the first landing of Da Gama at Calicut in 1498, the policy of the Portuguese was to maintain an absolute supremacy in Eastern waters. Their aim was not territorial dominion, but only command of the seas and of trade routes, in pursuance of which they sought positions of advantage, whether ports or islands, some of which they won by force, others by diplomacy. It was a curious feature of the age that the other nations of Europe in some sense acknowledged their right to the possession of the Cape route,[1] without acknow-

[1] The doctrine that the ocean is the common property of the human race was asserted first by Elizabeth and her bold seamen, and afterwards defended on legal principles by Grotius in his

ledging their exclusive right to Eastern trade. So it was that the Dutch and English navigators, believing they had an equal right to Indian trade, if they could only get at it by some other route, spent long and toilsome years of maritime apprenticeship in their search after the North-west Passage.

The French were the first to set at nought the restrictions of the Papal Bull. Paulmier de Gonville[1] is believed to have rounded the Cape in 1503, and to have reached Madagascar. The brothers Parmentier[2] of Dieppe, following the same route, reached

Mare Liberum. Owing to the disputes with the Dutch as to the North Sea fisheries, the doctrines of Elizabeth were abandoned by James, whose legal champion, Selden, replied to Grotius by his treatise, *Mare Clausum.* It is hardly necessary to add that time has been on the side of Grotius.

[1] He is said to have sailed from Honfleur in June 1503. The evidence upon which his existence and his voyage rest is the statement of the Abbé Binot Paulmier de Gonville, the great-grandson of a female relative of this captain, by her union with a Malagasy named Essomericque, whom de Gonville brought back with him (see Guerin, *Nav. Franç.*, pp. 50-55). M. Estancelin would make out that de Gonville was the discoverer of Australia (*Nav. Normands*, p. 165); but when patriotism comes in at the door, facts fly out of the window.

[2] The voyage of the brothers Jean and Raoul Parmentier is well authenticated. They left Dieppe 28th March 1529, with two ships, the *Pensée*, of 200 tons, and the *Sacre*, of 120. They touched at the Maldives [see App. A], and reached Ticou, in Sumatra, where Jean died of fever, 3rd December 1529. The journal of the voyage remained in MS. until 1832, when it was lent by M. Tarbé to Estancelin, and published by the latter in his *Navigateurs Normands* (pp. 241-312). Jean Parmentier, the gallant leader of this expedition, was born in 1480, or, as some say, in 1494. He was a poet and classicist. Before he started on this voyage, he had translated the *Catiline* of Sallust, and spent

Sumatra in 1526. These, however, were isolated enterprises, and led to nothing. The same national listlessness, which afterwards proved fatal to the schemes of Dupleix, characterised the French at this period. None of their countrymen followed these early pioneers, and the conquest of the East was left to be wrested from the Portuguese by the Netherlanders and the English.

During the last twenty years of the sixteenth century history was made apace. The United Provinces had achieved their independence; Philip II had ascended the throne of Portugal, and the whole conquests of the Eastern and of the Western world were brought under a single sceptre. At this time the distribution of Indian goods throughout Europe was managed by the Dutch merchants, chiefly of Amsterdam, who received them from the Portuguese car-

his leisure on this voyage in working on the *Jugurtha*. He took with him his friend Pierre Crignon, also a poet, who, in the preface to his own works, speaks thus warmly of the discoverer:—"Car quant au regard dudit Jan Parmentier, cestoit ung homme digne d'être estimé de toutes gens savants, et lequel sy les sœurs et déesses fatales luy eussent prolongé le fil de sa vie estoit pour faire honneur au pays pour ses haultes entreprises et belles navigations. C'est le premier François qui a entrepris à estre pilotte pour mener navires à la terre Amérique qu'on dit Brésil, et semblablement le premier François qui a descouvert les Indes jusques à l'isle de Taprobane, et si mort ne l'eust pas prévenu je crois qu'il eust été jusques au Moluques" (see *Le Discours de la Navigation de Jean et Raoul Parmentier de Dieppe*, par Ch. Schefer, Paris, Leroux, 1883, 8vo.). Estancelin identifies Jean Parmentier with the "gran capitano del mare francese del luogo di Dieppa" of Ramusio; and the allusion of Crignon to previous voyages to America goes far to corroborate the suggestion.

racks at Lisbon. One of Philip's first measures, at once revengeful and impolitic, was to prohibit the Dutch from frequenting Lisbon. This was a vital question to a newly emancipated nation of seafaring traders. The Lisbon traffic had given them a knowledge of the products of the East: many Dutchmen were in business houses in Lisbon and Seville. They had ample information at their command, but they hesitated to run the hazards of the navigation of the Cape.

Meantime the English were not idle. The circumnavigation of the globe successively by Drake and Cavendish, and their harrying of the Spanish Main, precipitated a crisis, and the destruction of the Invincible Armada in 1588 was a death-blow to the Spanish and Portuguese theories of property in ocean routes. No longer content with mere fighting and the capture of rich freights, the English were determined to open up a direct trade with the East. The first expedition of three vessels in 1591, under Raymond and Lancaster, was unfortunate.[1] In the year following, however, a fresh spur was given to English enterprise by the capture of the great Portuguese carrack, the *Madre de Dios;* and her "Notable Register and Matricola of the whole Government and Trade of the Portuguese in the East Indies", became in fact the prospectus of our first East India Company.[2]

[1] Two accounts of this voyage are contained in the *Lancaster Voyages* (Hak. Soc.), taken from Hakluyt.

[2] The English voyages incidently referred to in these volumes are as follows:—

Nearly seven years were allowed to elapse after the defeat of the Armada, ere the Dutch began to take its lessons to heart. They pressed on doggedly in their search for the North-west Passage, but it was not till February 1595 that Cornelius Houtman left the Texel with four vessels to reach India by the Cape route. He was at Sumatra in July 1596, and returned to Amsterdam in August 1597.

During the next few years fleets were despatched from the several Netherland ports as fast as they could be built and equipped. By the summer of 1601, when the story of these volumes begins, they had, in a space of six years and a half, despatched no less than forty-nine ships to India by the Cape route.[1]

The *first* voyage (1600-3) under Lancaster; the *Red Dragon*, *Hector*, *Ascension*, *Susan*, and *Guest*.

The *second* voyage (1604-6) under Middleton; the *Dragon*, *Hector*, *Ascension*, and *Susan*.

The *third* voyage (1606-9) under Keeling; the *Dragon*, *Hector*, and *Consent*. Capt. William Hawkins, who commanded the *Hector*, left his ship at Surat and proceeded to Agra.

The *fourth* voyage (1608) under Sharpeigh; the *Ascension* and *Union*.

[1] These include the fleets of C. Houtman in 1595, of C. Houtman, J. van Neck, W. van Warwyk, S. de Weert, and O. van Noort in 1598; of S. van der Hagen and P. van Caerden in 1599; of J. van Neck in 1600. The expeditions which left Holland in 1601 and following years are incidentally alluded to in the text of these volumes. They left as follows:—April 1601, W. Harmansen, 5 ships; J. van Heemskerk, 9 ships; May 1601, J. van Spilbergen, 3 ships; June 1602, W. van Warwyk, 14 ships; December 1603, S. van der Hagen, 13 ships; May 1605, C. Matalief, 11 ships; April 1606, P. Van Caerden, 8 ships;

Instigated at length by the successes of the Dutch and English, some citizens of St. Malo, Laval, and Vitré formed a company, and equipped two vessels for the purpose of "sounding the ford", and showing the French the way to the East Indies. How the merchants of towns so far inland as Laval and Vitré came to take part in the enterprise does not appear. St. Malo was at that time of a commercial importance second only to Dieppe, though its townsmen had for ages enjoyed a wider reputation for piracy than for legitimate trade. The vessels fitted out were the *Croissant* and the *Corbin.* The general of the expedition, and captain of the *Croissant,* was Michel Frotet de la Bardelière; the *Corbin* was under the command of François Grout. Both were men of position at St. Malo. The majority of the crews doubtless hailed from the same town; but the narrative shows that there was a substantial complement from Laval and Vitré; and of the two chroniclers of the expedition, the one, François Pyrard, who sailed in the *Corbin,* was of Laval; the other, François Martin,[1] who went in the *Croissant,* was a native of Vitré. Nor were the crews entirely French; for we find frequent mention of Flemings and Hollanders as having been on board the *Corbin.* Some

December 1607, P. W. Verhoeven, 13 ships. The journals of most of these voyages were published separately soon after their respective terminations, and all, with the exception of the Houtman voyage of 1598 (*v. i.*, p. 30, note 3), are contained in the Dutch collections.

[1] As to his book, see below, p. 2, note 2.

of these received higher pay, in consideration of their skill as gunners or carpenters, or by reason of their having already been to the Indies; and one at least of the crew—viz., the pilot of the *Corbin*—was an Englishman. The ships were of dimensions similar to those employed by the Dutch, the *Croissant* being of 400, and the *Corbin* of 200 tons, the former being less than half the size of a large Portuguese carrack. The plan generally adopted by the Dutch and English, of sending, with the principal ships, a victualler or store-ship, which should supply gaps in the ranks of the ships' companies, and after being emptied of its stores, could be abandoned at the Cape or beyond, was disregarded by the French. This neglect is, at the conclusion of the voyage, remarked by the author as a grievous error.

The ships were officered as follows: each commander had a lieutenant, and each ship carried a pilot and second pilot, a mate and a second mate, a merchant and a second merchant, a clerk, two surgeons, two pursers, two cooks, and two chief stewards. In addition to these were a master-gunner and five or six gunners. A notable omission among the "personnes de commandement" was that of a priest, who by his influence, and by the regular performance of divine service, might have done much to moderate the swearing and blasphemies of the sailors, and to assuage the jealousies and quarrels of the officers and men, to which the author chiefly attributes the ill-success of the voyage.

Let us now turn our attention for a moment to François Pyrard himself, and in the first place to his birthplace.

The chief town of the *Département de la Mayenne*, situate upon the river of that name, and what is more important, on the direct railway line between Paris and Brest, Laval is at the present day a flourishing commercial town of 27,000 inhabitants. The broad spaces of low-lying ground have given the modern town free room for expansion, and have thus left the old town to itself. The principal feature of the latter is the fine old château, whose machicolated round tower dominates the river, and to whose sides cling a mass of quaint, irregularly built houses, the homes and shops of many generations who lived and died under the shadow and protection of the feudal lord. The streets, with their antique appearance, preserve their antique names, and we find here the Rue *du Four*, *du Pin Doré*, *des Serruriers*, *du Jeu du Paume*, *des Orfèvres*, *des Chevaux aux Mesles*, *du Roquet*, etc. The château and old town, viewed from the other side of the river, still present a very picturesque appearance; but within the last few years all the old houses on the river have been swept away to give place to a new and elegant embankment. The woodcut which is given opposite the title-page of this volume shows the town as it was before this modern improvement, and probably very much as it was at the close of the sixteenth century. Laval was a very ancient fief of France[1]; it is said to take its name from *vallum*, —*vallum Guidonis*, as it is called in the old charters, for every Count of Laval was a Guy. These lords, like the Princes of Reuss, are all chronologically numbered. During the youth of Pyrard, Guy XX reigned; and the last of his race, Guy XXV, died in due time before the Revolution, in 1741.[2]

In this old town was born François Pyrard, the author of these volumes. The date of his birth and the quality of his parentage are alike unknown. From his remark at the commencement of the work, that he went the voyage for the purpose of seeing the world, we may assume that he was then, in 1601, a young man between twenty and thirty. His only relative—and, indeed, the only other person of his name—known to fame, is one who was probably his brother, viz., Pierre Pyrard of Laval, who joined the Society of Jesus in the year 1602, being then twenty-one years of age. If François and

[1] The following works may be consulted:—*Annalles et chroniques du pais de Laval*, 1480-1537, by Guillaume Le Doyen, with notes by L. la Beaulueère, 1859, 8vo.; *Documents rel. à l'hist. de Laval*, 1860, 8vo.; *Etudes archéologiques sur la Cathedrale de Laval*, by L. T. Hamard, 1885, 8vo.; *Histoire de Laval*, 818-1855, by St. Couanier de Launay, 1st edit., 1856, 2nd edit., 1866, 8vo.; *Mém. ecclés. conc. la ville de Laval*, 789-1802, 1846; *Notices hist. sur les hôpitaux de Laval*, by Léon Maître, 1868, 12mo.

[2] Laval has given birth to one greater man than any of these five-and-twenty Guys, and has done herself the honour of placing in the principal square of the town a statue of Ambroise Paré, the father of French surgery. The pedestal bears for its legend his own words—"Je le pansay, Dieu le guarist."

Pierre were brothers, the fact that Pierre was a literary and philosophical Jesuit[1] would seem to indicate that François had received, at least, a fair education. Of his youth or life, however, previous to his departure for India, he himself discloses nothing; nor has the diligence of local antiquaries succeeded in gleaning any facts relating either to him or to any descendants of his family.[2]

[1] Pierre Pyrard attained considerable eminence in the Society of Jesus as a professor of theology and philosophy. He was a director at various times of the colleges of Pau and Limoges, and on one occasion represented his province at a General Assembly at Rome. He is the author of a single controversial work, *Responsum ad Jarnacensem ministrum Calvinianum*, Burdigalæ, 1616, 8vo. He died at Pau, 3rd April 1667, aged 87 (*Bibliotheca Sotwelliana*; Haureau, *Hist. Lit. du Maine*, i, p. 193).

[2] Notices of Pyrard, which add nothing to our information, appear in Haureau, *Hist. Lit. du Maine*, tom. i, p. 193; Steph. Couanier de Launay, *Histoire de Laval*, 1856, 8vo.; *Bulletin de la Societé de l'Industrie de la Mayenne*, tom. iii, 1867 (article by Jules Lefizelier); *Annuaire de la Mayenne*, 1841, p. 36 (article by M. Levèque Bérangerie); *Bibliographie du Maine*, 1845, by N. Desportes. MM. Lefizelier and Bérangerie have made every search for traces of the family in the neighbourhood of Laval, but without success. The former adverts to a strange mistake, to which currency had been given by M. Ferdinand Denis, a writer generally well versed in voyages. It seems that one Baron de Saint-Genois, in his *Navigateurs Belges* (1846, 2 vols., 12mo.), claimed Pyrard as a Belgian, born at Stembert, near Verviers, and that his family still existed at the villages near that place. The statement was based upon a supposed claim of descent from Pyrard, made by the Abbé Duval Pyrau, before the Revolutionary Tribunal at Liége. M. Denis fell into the trap, and in the *Magasin Pittoresque* of March 1866, in an article on "Cauris", endorsed the Belgian myth. M. Lefizelier, while preparing his paper on Pyrard, wrote to M. Denis, and appealed from Saint-Genois to

He does not tell us whether he invested any money in the voyage, or merely sailed as one of the crew; nor does he even say in what capacity he shipped. One of his biographers rates him as surgeon,[1] another as supercargo[2]; and though I am aware of no explicit authority for either assertion, I am inclined to think that a probable conclusion may be arrived at by a negative line of reasoning. Besides the captain, Grout, and the lieutenant, Pepin, and one who succeeded the latter, he makes mention of the mate, the second mate, the pilot (an Englishman), and the second pilot. That he was not an officer connected with the navigation, would also seem probable from the fact that he had not been to sea before, and never seems quite at home with nautical terms. Nor was he ship's clerk, for the man who held this office was his bosom friend. On only one occasion does he mention the performance of any duty or task by himself personally, and this was merely to carry a message, on the evening preceding the wreck, from the captain on his sick-bed to the officers on deck. It is not of itself sufficient to lead to the conclusion that he was one of the surgeons; and his allusions to surgery and medicine throughout the book do not exceed the knowledge of a layman of the time. He

Pyrard himself. M. Denis then re-read our traveller, and seeing his mistake, suggested, what is no doubt the fact, that the person with whom the Abbé claimed relationship was not François Pyrard, but Claude Pyraux, another traveller, who died at Bussorah in 1773!

[1] *Sorberiana*, p. 195.

[2] M. Alfred de Lacaze, in *Nouv. Biog. Univ.*, art. "Pyrard".

mentions the merchant and the second merchant, deploring a lasting quarrel between the former and the captain. That he was not a gunner may be inferred from his mention of certain of his comrades as gunners, at times and places when his own skill in that line would most likely have been remarked. The pursers, of whom there were two on board, are the only officers he does not mention personally; and as I think he was an officer, I am disposed to argue, from the remarkable interest which he takes at all times and in all places in matters of trade, and specially in bazaar commodities and their prices, that he was one of the ship's pursers.

The ships set sail from St. Malo on the 18th May 1601. The first omen of misfortune was the breaking of the *Corbin's* foremast at a distance of only nine or ten leagues out. La Bardelière, owing to the rising insubordination of the crews, refused to return to port, and the mast was repaired by the carpenters as best they could. On the 21st they fell in with nine Dutch ships, which may be identified with the fleet of Heemskerk, who left the Texel on the 23rd April. The Canaries were sighted on the 3rd June, and the Cape Verd Islands on the 12th and 13th. On the 14th July they were off the coast of Sierra Leone, and there they saw for the first time the two ships of Joris van Spilbergen. The line was passed on the 24th August, and on the 30th they made land at Annobon. Here the Frenchmen met with a treacherous reception at the hands of the Portuguese and their negro slaves. Thomas

Pepin, the lieutenant of the *Corbin*, was killed, and several others were wounded during the endeavours to obtain fresh provisions and water. Spilberg had been there only a few days before, and had considerable and similar difficulty in obtaining the necessary supplies.

After six weeks spent at this island in fruitless attempts to gain water and fresh food, the French admiral determined to weigh anchor and make sail for Saint Helena, which was reached on the 17th November. The nine days' sojourn here was of great service to the sick, especially to those stricken with the scurvy.

The voyage was continued on the 26th November; the Abrolhos were passed three days later, and on the 28th December the ships had rounded the Cape. There they again fell in with Spilberg's ships, and divers courtesies were exchanged. A short acquaintance, however, gave the Dutch captain an insight into the laxity of discipline on board the French vessels, and determined him not to sail in their company.

Small progress was made during the month of January 1602. In the early part of February a violent storm off the Natal coast scattered and shattered the two small fleets, and on the 19th the *Corbin* found refuge in St. Augustine's Bay, Madagascar. Here she was joined by the *Croissant*, and later by the *Ram*, the Dutch vice-admiral, under Guyon le Fort. This captain, though born in Holland, was the son of a citizen of Vitré, and the three crews foregathered on shore and on board in all friendliness. The author remarks, as an indication of better fortune, or better equipment and discipline, that while the French ships had then a large number of scurvy patients, the *Ram* had not a single man on the sick-list. All three ships required considerable repairs. The Frenchmen remained at St. Augustine's Bay from the 19th February until the 15th May. During this period six of the sailors, lotus-eating truants, deserted the French encampment, and made their way inland to seek refuge among the natives. Their courage had been broken alike by the storm from which they had lately escaped, and by the alarming increase of sickness. "Utterly consumed with sharp distress," they no doubt thought:

> "Surely, surely, slumber is more sweet than toil, the shore
> Than labour in the deep mid-ocean, wind and wave and oar."

A few days of jungle wandering, however, disappointed their expectations. The natives showed no inclination to receive them, and at length, exhausted from want of food and water, they returned in penitence to their comrades. Meantime sickness and mortality made dreadful havoc among the crews, and, in order to supply the needful complement of hands, resort was had to a plan of kidnapping natives. This proved abortive, and, further intercourse being now impossible, the ships were forced to pursue their course.

The state of the crews, owing to sickness and mortality, was now such that it was necessary to seek some other harbour of refuge before attempting to cross the Indian Ocean. Leaving St. Augustine's Bay on the 15th May, the ships arrived at Malailli, one of the Comoros, on the 23rd. A stay of fifteen days here vastly improved the health of the men, and the scurvy almost disappeared.

A course was now laid across the ocean : the line was crossed on the 21st June : on the 1st July some islands and reefs were sighted. The Dutch pilot of the *Croissant* believed them to be those of *Diego de Roys*, a supposed group of islands placed in the charts of the period near the equator, in about long. 70 E. ; but the Englishman of the *Corbin* more correctly recognised them as the Maldives. During the following night, which by order was to have been passed in beating about, the *Corbin* was practically left to herself. The captain was ill and below, the mate and second mate were drunk, the lights of the binnacle were allowed to go out, and the watch were asleep. In these circumstances disaster was almost inevitable : and in the early morning of the 2nd July the *Corbin* struck heavily on the reef of what is now known as *Goidú*, or Horsburgh Atoll. The scene of hopeless panic which ensued is painted in vivid language by the author. All the ensuing day was spent in arduous efforts to get out the galion, and on the morning of the 3rd the crew were landed at the island of Fuladú.

The survivors numbered about forty men. Many, including the captain, were still sick of the Madagascar fever; others, by drunkenness, had fallen a prey to tropical disorders; all were exhausted with fatigue. They were in pressing want of good food and careful treatment. Some, whether from greed or precaution, had, however, supplied themselves liberally with silver money from the ship's chests, which they secreted about their persons or in the sand. The natives raised their prices for the bare necessaries of life, and thus gradually reduced them to the greatest straits. News was carried to Málé of the wreck and of the money landed by the men, and commissioners were despatched to Fuladú to secure the king's rights, the ship with all its contents being, by Maldive law, a casualty of the crown. The Maldivians, on this occasion, as must be admitted, belied their general character for humanity, though their conduct may partially be excused on the ground of the silver question. We may compare the sufferings of the Frenchmen here with the far greater afflictions of the Spaniards wrecked from the Armada on the coast of Ireland.[1] One little band of twelve men, under the mate, stole a boat, and succeeded in making the mainland at Quilon, where they were consigned to the Portuguese galleys. Whether any of them got back to France is uncertain: Pyrard seems to have heard nothing of them in India. The captain died at Málé six weeks or so after the wreck, being treated

[1] See Froude, *Hist. of Eng.;* and also an interesting article by the Earl of Ducie, in the *Nineteenth Century* for September 1885, entitled "An Episode of the Spanish Armada". This story is closely parallel to that of the French at the Maldives.

to the last with the utmost barbarity by his own men. The little band rapidly diminished by deaths and desertions, and out of the shipwrecked crew of forty who were landed at the Maldives only four survived the captivity.

Almost from the first Pyrard obtained exceptional treatment. This was due to his prudence in setting himself forthwith to the study of the native language, whereby he brought himself under the notice of one of the king's commissioners. On removal to Málé he thus was able to interest the Sultan and to obtain favour for himself and his comrades. He was lodged with a lord who was the Sultan's most trusted adviser, and for four years was allowed to go from island to island in company with the islanders, and for his own purposes of trade. With the exception that he was a captive, and deprived of the public exercise of the Christian religion, his term of exile was in most respects tolerable. In February 1607 an expedition arrived at Málé from Chittagong, incited, as Pyrard afterwards heard, by the prospect of obtaining the excellent cannon saved from the *Corbin*. The Sultan endeavoured to escape to the southern atolls, but was pursued and slain, and Pyrard and his three remaining companions, on being discovered not to be Portuguese, were taken to India by the invaders.

The account of the Maldives occupies the greater part of the present volume (ch. v-xxiii). First, we have the circumstances attending the wreck, the escape of the mate and his party, other attempted escapes, and the arrival of the author at Málé (ch. v-ix). Next, a general description of the Maldive islands, details of the religion, manners, and customs of the people, the government and the court, trade and commerce (ch. x-xvii). Thirdly, traditional and current history of the islands, and memoranda of occurrences during the author's captivity, closing with the Bengal invasion, which gave him his liberty (ch. xviii-xxiii). As we shall see hereafter, the greater portion of the Maldive section of the book was not put in writing till long after his return, and four years of varied adventure intervened between his departure from the Maldives and his arrival in France. So vivid, however, was his recollection, so accurate had been his observation, that Mr. Christopher and Mr. Bell, our two modern authorities, writing their accounts of the islands with Pyrard before them, find but little to add and less to amend.

The Bengal ships, laden with booty and carrying Pyrard and his friends, touched first at Minikoy (Maliku) and the Laccadives, and then sailed for Chittagong. Here the Raja endeavoured to induce the Frenchmen to remain with him, but put no obstacles in the way of their departure. After a month's sojourn, they were offered a passage in a ship bound for Calicut, where they expected to be able to put themselves into the hands of the Dutch.

After a three weeks' voyage, they were landed, not at Calicut, but at Muṭṭungal, a port of the Malabar pirates between Cananor and Calicut.

At this and the neighbouring towns, the Frenchmen, as being enemies of the Portuguese, were received with great distinction, and even enthusiasm. His sojourn at the pirate ports enables our author to throw much light upon the relations of the Malabars with the Samorin, and of both with the Portuguese. Although much pressed to remain, Pyrard and his friends proceeded to Calicut by land, arriving there about the end of June 1607.

Their reception at Calicut was no less warm and hearty. An eight months' residence at this famous city gave our author time to observe and admire the conditions of prosperity of a great commercial town under native rule. Unfortunately, they were not the only Europeans at Calicut. Two Jesuits, whom the Samorin found it useful to have at his court for the purposes of his diplomatic intercourse with Goa, induced the Frenchmen to accept their letters of safe conduct to Cochin. One of the party, a Flemish Protestant,[1] who had before found himself in the clutches of the Portuguese, scented treachery, and refused to leave Calicut. Pyrard and his two other friends were kidnapped by a party of Portuguese outside Calicut, and conveyed to Cochin as prisoners.

The description of the Tronco of Cochin, into which our travellers were now thrown, reads as horrible as that of any prison in those dark days of legal cruelty. It may be read, but cannot be para-

[1] Described by Pyrard as a tailor and a trumpeter, and also as a clever carver in wood.

phrased here. The captives, after an imprisonment of nine or ten days, were well-advised in making an application for intercession to the Jesuits' College. Finding them to be Frenchmen and Catholics, the fathers interested themselves in their behalf, and obtained their enlargement. They remained six weeks longer at Cochin, and were then shipped for Goa by the armada of the South, which, after a twenty days' passage, reached the metropolis of Portuguese India in June 1608.

The first volume closes with the author's arrival at Goa. The remainder of his adventures may be allowed to stand over for the present. Suffice it to say that he was pressed into the Portuguese service on shipboard, and visited Ceylon and the Eastern Islands. On his return from the far East he was again at Goa for the latter part of 1609, and got a passage in a carrack, which set sail in January 1610. After a sojourn in Brazil, where the carrack was abandoned, he made his way to Europe. The ship made land at the Bayonne Islands, on the coast of Galicia. Here Pyrard bade farewell to his two companions, who had thus far shared his fortunes, and, after paying his promised vows at Compostella, took ship for Rochelle, and, after an absence of nearly ten years, arrived at Laval on the 16th February 1611.

After a short stay in his native town, Pyrard seems to have proceeded to Paris, where, in the same year, he brought out the first edition of his book. It is in one volume, 12mo., containing twelve chapters,—a Treatise of Animals, Trees, etc., and an

Advice for Navigation in the Indies,—in all, pp. 372. The title-page is as follows :—

"*Discours* | *du voyage des* | *François aux Indes* | *Orientales,* | Ensemble des divers accidens, | adventures & dangers de l'auteur en plusieurs | Royaumes des Indes, & du | sejour qu'il y a fait par dix ans, depuis | l'an 1601 jusques en ceste année 1611 | CONTENANT | la description des pais, les mœurs, loix, facon de viure, Religion | de la plus part des habitans de l'Inde, l'accroissement de | la Chrestienté, le trafic & diverses autres singularitez, | non encore écrittes ou plus exactement remarquees. | TRAITE ET DESCRIPTION DES | animaux, arbres & fruicts des Indes | orientales, obseruees par l'Auteur. | Plus un brief Advertissement & Advis pour | ceux qui entreprennent le voyage des Indes. | Dedié a la Reyne Regente | en France | Par *FRANÇOIS PYRARD* de Laval | A PARIS, | Chez David le Clerc, ruë Frementel, au | petit Corbeil, près le puits Certain | M. DC. XI. | Avec privilege du Roy. | "

The privilege is not inserted.

The book itself is dedicated to the Queen-Regent, Marie de Medici; the Treatise to the President Jeannin. From the former dedication it would not appear that he had obtained any actual assistance from her Majesty. The commencement of the latter, however, intimates that the patronage of Jeannin was of a substantial character. It begins thus: "Ayant esté apres un accueil si favorable induit par vous à mettre par escrit ce qui estoit de mon voyage," etc. Both dedicatory epistles are in other respects worded in the adulatory style of the times.

The second edition was published in 1615. The book was, in great measure, re-written, and now appears in two volumes, 8vo. It was published at Paris, "par Remy Dallin, au mont S. Hilaire, rue de Sept Voyes à l'image S. Hilaire." The first volume, like the first edition, is dedicated to the Queen mother, now no longer Regent; the second to "Monseigneur Messire Leonard Destrappes, Archevesque d'Aux, conseiller du Roy en ses conseils d'Estat et Privé"; and the author acknowledges the great favours he had received from the Archbishop in his house.

The third edition[1] was published in 1619, 8vo. It was the last issued in the lifetime of the author, and contains the Maldive vocabulary, and is thus the most valuable. Its title-page will be found below.

The first volume contains a Dedicatory Epistle to G. du Vair, Bishop and Count of Lisieux, a Table of Contents, pp. 486, and an Index. The second volume has a shortened title-page; a Dedicatory Epistle to Charles Duret, Sieur de Chevry; a Table of Contents; the remainder of the Voyage, pp. 1-361; a Treatise of Animals, Trees, and Fruits, pp. 363-412; an Advice for the Navigation of the East Indies, pp. 413-434; a Vocabulary of Maldive words (unpaged); and an Index.

Pyrard is said to have died in 1621, but it does

[1] An edition of 1616 is mentioned by Ternaux-Compans as having been published at Paris by S. Thiboust; but I believe this to be a mistake, founded upon the error of Boucher de la Richarderie, who, omitting the edition of 1611, and giving the first (wrongly) as of 1615, and the third (rightly) of 1619, says there was a second, of which he does not know the date.

not appear upon what authority the statement is based. For bibliographical purposes the exact date is unimportant, as, in the course of nature, he must have died long before the next edition appeared.

The fourth and last French edition appeared in 1679. This was in one vol. 4to. It is edited by P. Du Val, Geographer in Ordinary to the King, and published at Paris by Louis Billaine, who apparently writes the preface. The book is divided into three parts, with separate pagination:—the first contains the Voyage as far as Goa, pp. 327; the second, the remainder of the Voyage, pp. 218; the third, the Treatise of Animals, etc., and the Advice, pp. 1-48, followed by a discourse on voyages in general—a description of the Coast of Africa, by "M. N. N.", pp. 49-72; Geographical Observations on Pyrard's Voyage, by Du Val, pp. 73-144; and an Index. The added appendices are valueless so far as Pyrard is concerned. That of "M. N. N." has no reference to the book at all; while Du Val merely airs his geographical knowledge, without elucidating the text in any particular. The Maldive vocabulary is ruthlessly discarded, to give place to this trash. The text is a fair reprint, but in some places unneeded polish is given to the style; in others, words and names are corrected according to the superior notions of Du Val; in others, passages excised. Far from being "la plus recherchée", as B. de la Richarderie extols it, this edition is, to the book-lover, a comparatively worthless possession.

Since 1679 the book has never been reprinted as

a whole. Nor, with a single exception, has it been translated. A professedly complete Portuguese version was published at Goa, the first volume in 1858, the second in 1862, by Señor Joaquim Heliodoro da Cunha Rivara. Unfortunately, the text used was that of 1679, and the translation accordingly reflects the demerits of the original. The notes, especially those to the second or Goa volume, convey some historical and local information of considerable value. These have been used in the preparation of the present edition; though, in many instances, where the original authorities are cited, Mr. Rivara's guidance will not be acknowledged. One feature of this and other work from the hand of that eminent Goanese antiquary must not pass unnoticed, viz., the eminent candour with which the evils of the Portuguese system, and the misdeeds of the Portuguese officers, are admitted without exculpation. It is highly to the credit of Portuguese India that the sole translation of a work, which unveils a scene of so much national disgrace and misfortune, should have proceeded from the press of Goa.

While the book has been but once translated as a whole, it has been abridged a score of times. The following may be instanced:—In French: Prevost, *Hist. des Voy.*, 1753, tom. 10; Charton, *Voyageurs Anciens et Modernes*, Paris, 1856, tom. 4; Guerin, *Navigateurs Français*, Paris, 1846. In German: Schwabe, *Allgemeine Historie der Reisen*, Leipzig, 1747-74, vol. 8; *Berliner Sammlung der besten und neuesten Reise beschreibungen*, vols. 13, 14;

Sammlung mehrer Geschichte, etc., Brandenburg, 1783. In English: Purchas's *Pilgrimes*; Harris's *Collection of Voyages*, vol. 1; *The World Displayed*, London, 1774-8, vol. 10; Duncan's *Mariner's Chronicle*, 1805, vol. 4.

A few words are necessary upon the authorship of these volumes. Prone as bibliographers are to the discovery of mare's-nests, it will certainly surprise all readers, who are even tolerably acquainted with the geographical and ethnographical knowledge of the period, to learn that Pyrard figures in the black-list of M. Querard's *Supercheries Littéraires Dévoilées.* On investigation of this charge, it is found to rest upon several authorities of the seventeenth century, though none of them can be assigned to an earlier period than 1650. They would seem to be independent, and are certainly conflicting. None of these *dicta* are dated; approximately, however, they come in the following order:

(1.) Samuel Sorbière [b. 1615, d. 1670] has this note on Pyrard in his *Sorberiana*[1]:

"Les voiages de Pirard, en deux volumes, où l'auteur s'amuse à nous raconter beaucoup de petites avantures particuliéres, que le lecteur lit avec autant de dégoût qu'il les écrivoit sans doute avecque plaisir. Tout ce que j'y apris fut l'histoire du Cocos, dont il parle fort long. On m'assure que le livre avoit été composé par Mr. B. . . . . . sur les mémoires de Pirard Chirurgien, assez idiot, et qui n'eût pas été capable de former un discours de longue halaine" (p. 195).

The two vol. edition referred to, of which Sorbière

[1] *Sorberiana, sive Excerpta ex ore Samuelis Sorbiere.* Toulouse, 1694.

was so unworthy a student, was either of 1615 or 1619. The Mr. B. to whom the authorship is attributed, is either Jerome Bignon or Pierre Bergeron. The number of dots after the initial is one too many for the former, and one too few for the latter. Bergeron was a well-known literary ecclesiastic, and, if he had been intended, he would probably have been designated by a clerical title. I am therefore inclined to think that Sorbière meant to refer to Jerome Bignon.

(2.) The copy of the 1619 edition, formerly owned by Bishop Huet of Avranches [b. 1624, d. 1721], and now possessed by the Bibliothèque Nationale of Paris, contains in the fly-leaf the following MS. note :

> "*Le veritable auteur de ce liure est Pierre Bergeron, qui ayant oui parler des diuerses avantures de Pyrard, lorsqu'il fut de retour à Paris, il le prist chez soy, et se les fist raconter auec toute l'exactitude que l'on peut remarquer dans cet ouurage. Comme Pyrard estoit toujours yure, Bergeron pr̄ discerner la verité de ses paroles luy faisoit dire plusieurs fois et à divers tems une mesme chose, et qd̄ il la rapportoit constam̄m̄ d'une mesme façon et sans varier, il la prenoit pr̄ veritable : sinon, il la rejettoit coē suspecte. Je tiens cela de Mr. Conrart.*"[1]

This note, which I have examined, is not signed, but I have no reason to question its authenticity. The information it contains must be dated prior to 1675, the year of Conrart's death.

(3.) The publisher's preface to the 1679 edition of

[1] Founder of and secretary to the society from which sprung the French Academy.

Pyrard, already referred to, contains the following passage :

" Il y a des avantures si extraordinaires qu'elles passeroient pour les incidents de Roman, si l'on n'estoit pas persuadé de la sincerité de l'auteur, qui n'estant pas homme sçavant, avoit pris la précaution de communiquer ses cayers, et de prendre les avis des plus sçavants hommes de son temps, et entr'autres de feu Monsieur HIEROSME BIGNON, Advocat General ; qui a esté un des premiers hommes de son siecle, et qui a eu la bonté de redresser notre voyageur dans les choses qui surpassoient ses connoissances."

(4.) The last authority is that of Tallemant des Réaux [b. 1619, d. *circa* 1700], in his *Historiettes*, not published till the present century.[1] In *Hist.* No. cccv, on M. et Madame de Blérancourt, he states that this lady was much given to study, and proceeds :

" Bergeron, chanoine de je ne sais où (M. Despesses dont il avoit été précepteur lui avoit fait donner cette prébende), fui celui dont elle se servit pour s'instruire. Elle a fait, dit-on, un *Discours de l'amour conjugal ;* mais on ne l'a point vu. Bergeron demeura avec elle tout le reste de sa vie. Ce bonhomme aimoit fort les voyages ; il tint Pyrard deux ans à Blérancourt[2]; de temps en temps il le faisoit parler des mêmes choses, et marquoit ce qu'il lui disoit, pour voir s'il ne vacilloit point : car Pyrard n'étoit qu'un brutal et un ivrogne. C'est ainsi que le bonhomme Bergeron a fait le livre de *Voyages de Pyrard ;* il prit tout ce soin-là parce que c'est la seule relation que nous

---

[1] Edited by M. Monmerqué. 1st edition. 6 vols., 1834 ; the 3rd edition is published by Garnier Frères. 10 vols. in 5.

[2] This fine château is situate near Noyon, and has been engraved by Israel Silvestre.

ayons des Maldives. Ce bon vieillard n'y mit point son nom, non plus qu'à la première partie de Vincent le Blanc, qu'il ecrivit aussi tout le même, car les autres parties ne valent rien ; et quelqu'un, après le mort de M. de Peyresc, chez qui étoit le manuscrit, y a ajouté le reste pour grossir le volume. Il y a encore un traité des navigations de la façon de M. Bergeron, au bout de la *Conquête des Canaries*, par Bethencourt."[1]

These are the nearest to contemporary records we possess. In the eighteenth century, while the notes of Huet and Tallemant des Réaux were still hidden in manuscript, the Abbé Pérau, in his *Life of Bignon*,[2] was able to assign the book, without fear of contradiction, to his hero. Under the year 1615 we have this passage (p. 88):

"M. Bignon ne donna rien à l'impression depuis ses notes sur Marculfe: on lui est cependant redevable de la relation d'un *Voyage aux Indes Orientales, Maldives, Moluques, et au Brésil*, qui fut imprimé à Paris in 8° en 1615. Mais comme il n'avoit été que le rédacteur de ce qu'il avoit appris du voyageur, il n'eut garde de se l'approprier et il le fit paroître sous le nom de celui qui étoit censé en être le premier auteur. Ce voyageur s'appelloit François Pyrard, originaire de Laval: c'étoit un homme d'assez bon sens, mais peu capable de s'énoncer par écrit. M. Bignon ayant eu occasion de faire connoissance avec lui, l'entendit avec plaisir et trouvant que les découvertes qu'il avoit faites pourroient être avantageuses au public, il lui proposa de les mettre au jour. Cette entre-

[1] Published by the Hakluyt Society in 1872, under the editorship of Mr. Major, who refers in his Introduction to this edition of Bergeron.

[2] *La Vie de Jerome Bignon, Avocat Général et Conseiller d'Etat.* Par M. l'Abbé Pérau, Licentié, de la maison et Société de Sorbonne. Paris, 1757, 8vo.

pris paroissant au dessus des forces de Pyrard, M. Bignon l'attira chez lui, et sur les conférences qu'il eut habituellement avec ce voyageur il en forma une relation qui parut comme j'ai dit en 1615 en deux volumes in 8°. Il y en eut une nouvelle édition en 1679 augmentée de divers traités."

The notices of the bibliographers are not of much value. Before the publication of the Bergeron theory, most of them subscribed to the Bignon authorship; afterwards, *more suo*, they merely stated or tried to reconcile the conflicting accounts. The eighteenth century editions of Moreri attribute the work to Bignon. Niceron follows suit; but Chauffepié, who read the book, doubts whether the book could have come from other than Pyrard's hand :—"Cela paroit un peu difficile à comprendre, quand on lit le voyage même, ou l'auteur parle toujours en première personne. La manière dont la chose est exposée dans l'Avertissement qui est à la tête du livre est bien plus naturelle." He then quotes the passage from the preface of 1679.

Boehman and Zeidler follow the Bignon theory. Brunet and Ebert, Barbier and Querard, merely quote the conflicting notices of Huet and Pérau. M. Cyriès, in his article on Pyrard in Michaud's *Biog. Univ.*, attributes the fulness of detail for which the book is remarkable to the notes taken by Bignon in conversations with Pyrard, and adds :—"Ces matériaux soigneusement transcrits furent confiés à Bergeron, qui les mit en ordre et les publia sous ce titre" (citing the edition of 1615). This reconciliation of the two stories is, I believe, a mere conjecture: there is no authority for the statement that the manuscript notes passed from Bignon to Bergeron; and the notices of Huet and Tallemant des Réaux are express to the effect that the book was made up by Bergeron from Pyrard's lips.

We are, unfortunately, without any data for testing the Bignon theory. As regards Bergeron, we are in a better position to judge. He undoubtedly made a special study of voyages, and in 1629 published an edition of Bethencourt's *Conquête des Canaries*, together with a treatise of ancient and modern voyages. In this latter work reference is twice made to Pyrard. Writing of the caution and provision necessary to be taken in regard to the Indian voyage, he proceeds:—

"De cela on en peut prendre de très-bon aduis du sieur Pirard sur la fin de son liure des Indes Orientales où il donne une bien particulière instruction pour tous ceux qui voudront entreprendre tels voyages; et entr'autres il remarque les defauts tres-grands de nos François, tant pour leur desobeyssance aux chefs, & pour leur querelles entr'eux, que pour beaucoup d'autres fautes & desordres, à quoy toutes les autres nations sçauent mieux pourvoir" (p. 187).

Coming to the mention of particular voyages, he writes:—

"Pour le regard des grands voyages de quelques particuliers és Indes depuis que le pas en a esté ouvert par les Portugais et Castillans, les autres nations, entr'autres nos François, en ont esté assez soigneux, soit pour le trafic, soit par simple curiosité de voir & d'apprendre, comme sont ceux de Pirard, Mocquet, Martin & autres mis en lumière. Quant à Pirard, outre la description assez exacte des costes de l'Inde Orientale, d'Afrique & du Bresil, il en fait une bien particulière des Isles *Maldiues*, qui n'estoient quasi cognuës que de nom auparavant" (p. 195).

This is followed by a note on Mocquet, the well-known voyager whom Pyrard met in India.

In neither of these passages does Bergeron drop the slightest hint that he was personally responsible for Pyrard's book. This omission is by Tallemant des Réaux attributed to modesty, and the voyages of Vincent le Blanc are instanced as an example of like magnanimity. Now the first edition of Le Blanc was published in 1648. The title-page informs us, "Le tout recueilly de ses mémoires par le sieur Coulon." The so-called second edition was issued in 1649, but this is the same as the former in all respects except the title-page, where, in place of the above, we have "Redigez fidellement sur ses mémoires et registres tirez de la Bibliothèque de Monsieur de Peiresc, conseiller au Parlement de Provence et enrichis de trés-curieuses observations par PIERRE BERGERON Parisien." Peiresc died in 1637; and thus the sting of Tallemant's gibe, that Bergeron wrote the real Le Blanc, and that "some one" after Peiresc's death added the worthless matter, is removed. Either Bergeron edited the edition of 1648 under the name of Coulon, or his name was used in 1649 to sell the "remainder" of a book which had not gone off well.

Even assuming that Bergeron did write or edit the Le Blanc voyages, a superficial comparison of that book with Pyrard's will prove, independently of the matter, that the two works did not come from the same hand. The authority of Conrart, conveyed to us by Bishop Huet, is indeed high, and when confirmed by the circumstantial account of Tallemant des Réaux, is entitled to due recognition. But when, in 1679, the publisher of Pyrard makes no mention of Bergeron, and merely alludes to the friendly assistance of Bignon, and, above all, when we read Pyrard's book itself, we must inevitably come to the opinion of Chauffepié, that the matter of these volumes is Pyrard's, and his alone. There can be little doubt, upon the authorities, that, between 1611 and 1619, Pyrard spent much of his time in and about the houses of great and learned men. Some of these, such as Jeannin, Bignon, and Bergeron, must have seen clearly that the book of 1611 contained but a small part of the author's experience and knowledge; and it is probable that by repeated conversation they revived his memories, and induced him to make in the next edition a more ample record. Taking as a test the description of the Maldives, we find that, in the edition of 1611 (the authorship of which has never been in question) this is comprised in 74 pages. The same section of the voyage in the edition of 1619 extends over 223 pages, each of which contains about twice as much matter as one of the earlier volume. And there was not a man then alive (except, perhaps, Pyrard's own fellow-captives, whose names even are unknown) who could have written a single page of this account.[1]

[1] The fulness of the description of Portuguese India in the

If, then, the charge against Pyrard be confined to this, that the proof-sheets were corrected by these learned men, or that by their advice he enlarged his treatment of various portions of his voyage, or amended his arrangement of details, or even that parts of the book were written by others to his dictation,—in any such case, the fact is of no discredit to him as an author, and affords no grounds for a charge of literary fraud.

We may pass lightly, though not with silence, the sad picture of Pyrard's later years, drawn by Huet and des Réaux. Both state that he was a drunkard. Readers of these volumes will not require to be told that, down to the time of his return to France, far from being a drunkard, he had passed unscathed through his great misfortunes and long captivity, chiefly by the virtue of sobriety, wherein many of his comrades were so deficient. With the sole exception of an episode in his Brazilian sojourn, there is not a trace in these volumes of even levity of conduct. He presents himself to us truthfully, so far as we can judge, as a pious Catholic, little used to the world, to whom the drunkenness and blasphemy of his sailor comrades were alike abhorrent, and in whose eyes the one redeeming feature of the Portuguese character was

second volume is perhaps to be attributed to the prior publication of Linschoten's *Itinerary*, which had appeared in Dutch in 1596, in German and English in 1598, and in French in 1610, and had in all probability been read by Bergeron, and used in his conversations with Pyrard.

the sobriety of that race. It would seem that, on his return to France, he failed in striking into the tide of the ordinary civil life of his class. His book of 1611 made him a marked man, and his time was probably spent in shiftless lounging in the ante-rooms and at the serving-tables of the great. Unable to deny the charge as laid, we may at least contend that he probably maintained his former good character till 1615, when his first full narrative had been written. It is in the preface to the edition of 1619 that, for the first time, we find an indication that things had gone wrong with him. If, indeed, he was by this time given over to habits of intoxication, and was without the distraction of trade or business, his health, perhaps still suffering from the effects of Maldive fever and spleen-disease, would soon be broken, and his death in 1621, if not authentically proved, was only a probable consequence.

Whatever may have been the failings of the man, he has given us a book in which each volume possesses a peculiar interest. The first contains his description of the Maldives, on which it is the standard and almost unique authority: the second, with which for this purpose we may include the last five chapters of the first, gives us a picture of Western India at the commencement of the seventeenth century, during those critical years when the Dutch, aided by the Malabars, and at times by the English, fairly grappled with the Portuguese—years which witnessed the sieges of Mozambique and Malacca, the first interference of the Dutch in

Ceylon, and the periodical blockade of Goa itself. The Portuguese were stunned, but they little realised the situation: their great capital was still abandoned to the luxurious habits and official corruption which had characterised the period of undisputed monopoly; and in Pyrard's second volume we have the delineation, by an intelligent and disinterested foreigner, of a scene, which with our present knowledge of the magnitude of the issues then at stake, is not lacking in tragic interest. Nor is the demeanour of the Portuguese without its lesson for us, who are now treading the same stage.

The interest attaching to the first volume is of a different character. The Maldives, even in those days, came little into the current of Indian politics. They are remote in the broad Indian Ocean: of the innumerable little islands of which the group consists, the largest is no bigger than an ordinary English common. Each inhabited island is a little village, separated from its neighbours by sea or lagoon; yet the whole forms and, as far back as we can trace the islands in history, has formed a compact kingdom, with a well-designed constitution, a cabinet of ministers, a body of executive and judicial, religious and revenue officers, all in due subordination. Were not the whole aspect of Maldive civilisation coloured and penetrated by Mahomedanism, that ever-present factor in the East, we might regard Pyrard's description of this little kingdom, so strange and yet so particular, as one which might have come from the hand of Swift or Defoe.

Since Pyrard left the Maldives in 1607, very few Europeans have visited them, and most of these have been shipwrecked mariners. The last detailed account of them is given by my coadjutor, Mr. Bell, in his valuable report to the Ceylon Government of a visit made by him in 1880. The visit was, unhappily, but a short one, but, from his position at Galle and Colombo, he has had frequent intercourse with Maldive merchants and sailors, and he has made a special study of the language. But for the aid he has afforded me, both by his report and by his notes, this volume could not have been edited: and I gladly take this opportunity of stating that most of the notes to the Maldive portion are merely pieced together by me from the very full information on all points which he has placed at my command.

One other modern authority, however, whose name is frequently quoted in the notes, must not pass unnoticed here, especially as he is one of the many noble Anglo-Indians whom untimely death has deprived of what are called the substantial rewards of this world, and whose names should therefore be rescued from oblivion.

Lieut. Willmott Christopher, of the Indian Navy, was a lieutenant on the *Benares*, under Captain Moresby, when the survey of the Maldives was carried out in 1834-5. The crews of the two ships suffered much from illness at the islands, and in June 1835 the survey had to be temporarily abandoned. Lieutenants Christopher and Young, desirous of learning further the language and customs of the islanders, bravely volunteered to remain at Malé. The permission of the Bombay Government was obtained, and the *Benares* left them with a few men in June 1835. Three weeks afterwards, Young fell seriously ill of the fever, and two months later Christopher himself was seized. In the meantime he had been of the greatest service to the crew of an English ship wrecked on one of the atolls. On his return to Malé in August, his friend and the men left, and Christopher, after struggling on for another month, was forced to follow them to Ceylon. The description of the Maldives compiled by the two lieutenants was published in vol. i of the *Transactions of the Bombay Geographical Society* (pp. 54-108), and a Maldive vocabulary, collected by Christopher, appears in vol. vi of the *Journal R. A. S.* The two papers, the result of but a few months' work, in combination with arduous public duties and under the most depressing influences of sickness, form a record of painstaking investigation. They had read either Pyrard or an abridgment, and their papers form a valuable supplement to our author.

After this service Christopher was engaged in the survey of the East Coast of Africa, and there met M. Antoine d'Abbadie, who has in letters to me expressed admiration of his character and abilities. In 1848, *per mare et terram*, the Indian Navy took part in the siege of Mooltan. "During the first siege", writes Mr. Low,[1] "Lieutenant

[1] *History of the Indian Navy*, ii, 218-220.

Willmott Christopher, who, as Assistant Superintendent of the Indus flotilla, had been engaged in transporting men, guns, and stores to Mooltan, took advantage of this opportunity to indulge his love of adventure and unbounded energy, and joined the hastily raised levies of the late Sir Herbert Edwardes, when his intimate knowledge of Mooltan and its neighbourhood was of essential service to that officer." Sir H. Edwardes' own opinion of him may be gathered from the following[1]: "Another volunteer went with me into the field and assisted me greatly in carrying orders—poor Christopher, of the Indian Navy, whose zeal proved fatal to him so shortly after. On this occasion he rode about with a long sea-telescope under his arm, just as composedly as if he had been on the deck of his own vessel."

In the terrible night attack of the 9th September 1848, Christopher received his death-wound. "Captain Christopher", continues Sir H. Edwardes, "had from his first arrival with the steamers at Mooltan shown the usual willingness of his profession to co-operate with his brother officers on shore. On the night in question he had once already conducted some reinforcements to Colonel Pattoun's assistance; but the fighting at the outposts still raged with unabated fury. Another reinforcement came up, but had no guide. 'Will no one show us the way?' asked the officer of the party, looking round on the tired occupants of the trenches. 'I

[1] See Sir H. Edwardes's *A Year on the Punjaub Frontier*.

will,' replied Christopher, and putting himself at their head, steered them with the steadiness of a pilot through ditches and gardens, under a roaring fire of musketry. A ball hit him in the ankle, and shattered the joint to pieces. A few weeks later (9th October 1848), he was borne by the grateful British officers to a rude grave beside a well near the village of Sooraj Khoond, and I myself read the service over him. A better or braver man fell not beneath the walls of Mooltan."

I am far from intending to confine the expression of my obligations to Mr. Bell to the commentary on the Maldive chapters of this book. He has assisted me in all parts of it, more or less, as well by suggestion and original information, as by criticism and answers to queries. I regret that his residence in Ceylon prevented me from profiting by his perusal of the translation and notes in their final form, and that to this cause are due many slight errors in the transliteration of Maldive words, and a few graver mistakes.

I owe a heavy debt of gratitude to our respected President, Colonel Yule, who, regardless of his many other duties and avocations, while not, I am sure, neglectful of them, has rendered me assistance at every turn from his abundant store. While this volume was in preparation, his invaluable *Glossary* was in the press, and he at all times gave me free access to the proofs. In many cases, even where I have appended a reference to his work, my notes were drawn before I saw Colonel Yule's proofs: had it been otherwise, I should frequently have profited by his better choice of quotations. Over and above the aid given by his published work, Colonel Yule has too often spared neither time nor trouble, in my behalf and the Society's, in making searches in reference to obscure or interesting matters occurring in the text. He has put me under further obligation by carefully revising the proof-sheets, to their great benefit.

Lastly, I have pleasure in thanking M. Louis Brière, the well-known antiquary of Le Mans, for placing at my disposal all the information available with reference to the author, and for his kind welcome to me during a short visit to Le Mans. His kindness did not end here, for, being unable at the time to lay his hand on the above-mentioned article of M. Berangerie, M. Brière, after my departure, took the pains to make for me with his own hands a full and careful copy of the whole article of twenty-seven pages. My hope is that the great interest which M. Brière took in the project of this English edition of his countryman's voyages, may not be disappointed by the execution.

A. G.

CHRONOLOGY OF PYRARD'S VOYAGE.

(VOL. I.)

---

18 May 1601, the *Croissant* and the *Corbin* leave St. Malo; 21 May, fall in with 9 Dutch ships; 3 June, sight the Canaries; 12 June, sight the Cape Verd Islands; 14 July, sight Spilberg's ships off coast of Guinea; 29 Aug.—16 Oct., at Annobon; 17—26 Nov., at St. Helena; 27—28 Dec., double the Cape of Good Hope; 6 Jan. 1602, severe storm; 4 Feb., sight Madagascar; 7—11, another storm; 18 Feb., again sight Madagascar; 29 Feb.—15 May, at St. Augustine's Bay; 23 May—7 June, at the Comorros; 21 June, cross the line northwards; 2 July, wreck of the *Corbin* at the Maldives.

July 1602—Feb. 1607, captivity of Pyrard at the Maldives. Aug. 1602, death of Captain Grout; Sept. 1602, escape of the mate and 11 others; Jan. 1604, escape and death of 4 Flemings; 12 Oct. 1605, eclipse of the sun; —, 1606, arrival at the Maldives of Martin Domburgh and another Hollander; also of Adrian de Gouveia, an ambassador from Goa.

Feb. 1607, arrival of hostile fleet from Chittagong, death of the king, and departure of Pyrard and three surviving companions with the fleet; March 1607, Pyrard, after touching at Minicoy and the Laccadives, arrives at Chittagong; *circa* 23 April, leaves Chittagong; May, arrives at Muṭṭungal, on the Malabar coast; May—June, visits Chombaye, Vadakkara, and Kôṭṭakal, and arrives at Calicut. June 1607—Feb. 1608, residence at Calicut. March 1608, taken prisoner to Cochin; May, leaves Cochin for Goa, touches at Cananore; June 1608, arrives at Goa. [End of Volume I.]

ADDENDA ET CORRIGENDA.

Page 23, line 5 from bottom, for "*Formosa*", read "*Tormosa*".

Page 32, line 5 from top, for "some", read "two".

Page 51, line 16 from top, for "he", read "they".

Page 59, line 5, after "Pouladou", add "where we had first landed".

Page 64, line 6 from top, for "hours", read "days".

Page 72, line 17 from top, after "women", read "and had them beaten".

Page 73, line 10 from bottom, for "more highly in his esteem", read "better treated out of consideration for him".

Page 79, note 3, for "*gananawa*", read "*geniyanavā*".

Page 83, note 3, for "*du*", read "*dū*", and for "*duwa*", read "*dúwa*".

Page 90, note 3, for "*miru*", read "*mīru*", and strike out "and is one of the three ministers of the Sultan".

Page 94, note, for "*etula*", read "*atula*".

Page 95, note 2, for "*dolos*", read "*dolos*".

Page 96, note 1, for "Mr. Bell", read "Mr. Christopher".

Page 97, note 1, for "Sin. *hækiri*," read "*Elu hækiriya*".

Page 97, note 2. The following are the numbers of inhabited islands in ten of the atolls in the year 1882, according to information gleaned by Mr. Bell from well-informed islanders: Malosmadulu 32, Mālē 13, Ari 18, Felidu 5, Mulaku 10, Nilandu 14, Kolumadulu 13, Haddumati 13, Suvádiva 21, Addú 7.

Page 127, note 3, for "*namadawā*", read "*namanava*".

Page 160, *dele* last half of note. The corresponding year of the Christian era to A.H. 994 is 1616, not 1677. The tombs so dated are therefore of men who were contemporary with Pyrard, during whose time there was no Portuguese invasion.

Page 184, line 4 from top, for "do otherwise", read "deformed".

Page 202, 10 lines from bottom, for "call", read "called".

Page 248, note, for "Viyadou", read "Viyadoru".

Page 255, note 1, add "or as Mr. Bell suggests, a misprint for *Mauvaye*, the modern *Mává Kilage*, a title, as Kambadi Kilage, confined to ladies.

Page 325, line 12 from top, for "padoes", read "padoes".

Page 339, line 5 from top, for "*Moussey*", read "*Moussez*".

Page 343, note 2, for "*Chastiganes*", read "*Chastaignes*".

Page 355, line 15 from top, for "Moussey", read "Moussez".

Page 375, line 12 from top, for "Goa", read "Cochin".

Page 392, line 8 from bottom, for "parents", read "priests".

Page 393, line 12 from top, for "silver", read "silk".

Page 404. *Auiards* is probably the Morathi *Awar*, a fence enclosing a yard round a house (Wilson).

VOYAGE

DE

FRANÇOIS PYRARD

de Laual.

CONTENANT SA NAVIGATION aux Indes Orientales, Maldiues, Moluques, Bresil : les diuers accidens, aduentures & dangers qui luy sont arriuez en ce voyage, tant en allant & retournant, que pendant son sejour de dix ans en ce païs là.

AVEC LA DESCRIPTION DES PAYS, mœurs, loix, façons de faire, police & gouvernement ; du trafic & commerce qui s'y fait ; des animaux, arbres, fruicts, & autres singularitez.

DIVISÉ EN DEVX PARTIES.

TROISIESME ET DERNIERE EDITION, REVEVÉ

Corrigée & augmentée de beaucoup outre les precedentes.

Avec vn petit dictionaire de la langue des Maldiues.

A PARIS

Chez SAMVEL THIBOVST, au Palais en la galerie des Prisonniers.

ET

Chez la veufue REMY DALLIN, au mont S. Hilaire, ruë de sept Voyes, à l'Image S. Hilaire.

M. DC. XIX.

DEDICATORY EPISTLE

TO

MESSIRE

GUILLAUME

DU VAIR, BISHOP

AND COUNT OF LIZIEUX

And Keeper of the Seals

of France.

MONSEIGNEUR,

At a time when all France hath so much reason to render thanks to God for that in this calamitous age it hath pleased him to call you to the said illustrious office, which you administer so worthily to the well-being and satisfaction of all,—I desire not to be the last, albeit the least of all, to come forward in recognition of that sovereign virtue, which amid the greatest and most important affairs of the estate which it supports, disdains not to admit all the wretched to its protection. Receive then, MONSEIGNEUR, *if it please you of your wonted kindness and humanity, the relics of this living wreck, who, having survived so many strange and luckless adventures, in so many quarters of sea and land, even now in the very port fails not every day to experience all the rigours and violence of his habitual misfortune. And in truth it would be utterly heart-breaking to find myself thus furiously pursued and persecuted of fortune, even on the soil of France herself, my beloved country, were not my last hopes (after God) in your singular goodness, which hath so sensibly affected all that in their necessities have recourse thereto. This it is which hath made me resolve the more willingly to dedicate to you this last edition of the history of my voyages, whose story I have edited in better form than heretofore, with the addition moreover of many facts supplied from my memory. Should it please you,* MONSEIGNEUR, *betimes to cast a glance on this little work, you will see herein the unvarnished and truthful image of all that is most wondrous in nature, as also the most remarkable diversity of events and occurrences in the life of man. For my part, I venture to promise myself with assurance that this my book, with the approbation and favour of your great name, will be better received by all persons of curiosity and virtue, who, already holding in admiration your worthy and laudable deeds in other affairs, will deem it to their credit to esteem that which you have deigned to approve. Thus am I under such obligations to you that in the future I shall have no greater care or desire than to render myself worthy to receive the honour of your commands, and to remain for ever,* MONSEIGNEUR,

Your very humble and obedient servant,

FRANÇOIS PYRARD.

*** Guillaume Du Vair, to whom the first volume of the edition of 1619 is dedicated, was born at Paris, 7th March 1556. At the age of 21 he was Counsellor in the Parliament of Paris. He ranged himself on the side of the Moderates. Henri IV appointed him to important posts in Provence. In 1603 he became an ecclesiastic, and in 1616 was nominated Keeper of the Seals, but was soon afterwards forced to resign owing to his disfavour with the Queen-Regent. In 1617 he became Bishop of Lisieux, and was soon after recalled to official life. He died at Tonneins, 3rd August 1621.

TABLE OF MATTERS CONTAINED IN THE FIRST VOLUME.

THE

VOYAGE OF FRANÇOIS PYRARD.

VOYAGE OF FRANÇOIS PYRARD.

FIRST PART.

THE abundance of all kinds of wealth which France produces, and the favours which the bounty of Heaven hath so liberally poured upon her soil, may have been the cause why the French have so long neglected the sea. And this is so not only in their case, but with most of the nations who have enjoyed that felicity even in a less degree. They have enough to do with the land, which supplies them with a sufficiency of wealth, and take no thought to seek more amid the perils of the treacherous sea. On the other hand, we see that nations whose territory is poor and sterile, or too confined, have sought a recompense in navigation, whereby they have not only supplied their deficiencies, but have also made their cities in all respects rich and opulent. These are the peoples who have excelled in naval science. Yet in truth France, in neglecting trade, deprives herself of riches, which nature offers in addition to her other wealth; for she is washed by two productive seas and furnished with many good harbours, by means of which she might communicate and negotiate with many nations far from her two coasts, as though they were her neighbours, on the east and west, and even with the most distant countries. It must be confessed, too, that the trade of the sea is of the most noble and excellent kind, bringing, amid great risks, the riches and peculiar products of other lands to profit one's own country, and carrying of her abundance to those that are in need. It is like depriving oneself of the use of a limb, for example, cutting off an arm. We are now seeing our mistake, for the French, after neglecting countless fair opportunities (which the Portuguese and Spaniards have not only taken but eagerly sought), are constrained to receive from those nations, in retail, the gold, spices, and the curious things of the East, in place of having fetched them themselves, and distributing them to others. So at present the Portuguese and Spaniards are trying to keep to themselves those elements which are common to all, and by all manner of wrong-doing to chase from the seas the French and other nations who would voyage and traffic therein. This it was which principally induced a merchant company of St. Malo, Laval, and Vitré, in the year 1601, to sound the ford (*sonder le guay*), and seeking a path to the Indies, to show the French the way; in short, to draw from the fountain-head.[1] With this intent, they equipped two ships, the one of 400 tons, named the *Croissant*,[2] the other of 200, named the *Corbin*, which were de-

[1] Pyrard seems to believe this voyage to have been the first undertaken by any Frenchman to the East Indies; and Martin, in his journal of the voyage of the *Croissant*, also so describes it. (See next note.) Both seem to have been ignorant of the voyage of Jean Parmentier of Dieppe, who reached Sumatra in 1529, and, like Pyrard, visited the Maldives. The reason of this ignorance is that no account of Parmentier's voyage was published until 1832, when M. Estancelin obtained a MS. journal, in possession of M. Théodore Tarbé, and included it in his *Discours de voyages et descouvertes des navigateurs Normands* (pp. 241-312); for the Maldive portion, see App. to this volume. There is an excellent new edition of the Parmentier voyages by M. Ch. Schefer; Paris, Leroux, 1883, 8vo.

[2] The fortunes of the *Croissant*, so far as they concern the narrative of Pyrard, will be noted in the course of this work from other authorities, and chiefly from the journal of François Martin, published under the title of *Description du premier voyage faict aux Indes Orientales par les François*. Of this rare book there are two editions; the first published early in 1604 (the privilege bearing date 3rd Feb.), a very few months after the arrival of the author at Plymouth. The second edition, of which is the copy possessed by the Brit. Mus., was pub-

spatched under the command of the Sieur de la Bardeliere,[1] a burgess of St. Malo, with François Grout,[2] Sieur du Closneuf, Constable of St. Malo, as his vice-admiral and captain

lished in 1609. In the title-page of the latter the words "par les François" are an addition—that is, if the title of the first edition be correctly given by Ternaux Compans.

[1] The admiral's full name and title, as given by Martin, was Michel Frotet, sieur de la Bardeliere (*Martin*, p. 13). He was born at St. Malo, 31 Dec. 1549, and was descended of an ancient family of that town, and, like his cousin, Frotet de la Landelle, was one of the most determined supporters of the League. On the 29th March 1589 he was nominated one of the four captains-general of the militia, and throughout the wars of 1589-91 had several important commands and performed many signal services, on account of which his townsmen gave him the name of the St. Malo Ajax (Cunat, *St. Malo illustré par ses marins*, Rennes, 1857, 8vo., p. 77; see also article by Cunat in Lovet, *Biographie Bretonne*).

[2] Grout was of an old St. Malo family, which claimed kinship with the Dutch family of Groot, soon after this time to be made illustrious by the name of Hugo Grotius. Grout's father, also François, was born at St. Malo in 1518, and had his Christian name from Francis I, who happened to be at the town on the day of his baptism. The event is recorded thus: "Le 5e jour d'Octobre 1518 fut baptizé ungn filz à Jehan Grout et Jehanne Brulle sa femme: et fut grand compère noble homme Franczoys Galleaze, grand écuyer de France, et fut nommé Franczoys au nom du roy, lequel est alors présent en Saint-Malo: et petit compère Michel Brulle, et commère Perrine Chenu, baptizé par le vicaire-curé, Maistre Lancelot Ruffler" (Cunat, *St. Malo illustré par ses marins*, p. 369). The date of the birth of the younger Grout is uncertain; he was captain of a ship in 1597, and was appointed Constable of St. Malo in 1600, "en recognoissance des agréables et fidelles services qu'il avoit faicts à Henri IV tant à la réduction de ladicte ville, que ès prinses de l'isle de la Roche-au-vay, Dinan et aultres lieux." (Manet, *Biographie des Malouins célèbres*, St. Malo, 1824, 8vo., pp. 85-6). Whether Grout was married and left issue when he set out on this ill-fated expedition is not known, but it may be mentioned that the family appears again in later days in the person of Grout de St. Georges, who was captain of the French ship *l'Invincible* in the action with the English under Lord Anson on the 14th June 1747. His valour on this occasion won the admiration of Anson as well as of his own countrymen, and when he died at Mozambique, in 1763, in command of the *Fortuné*, Louis XV granted a pension to his brother, M. Grout de la Grassinais. His portrait is now hung in the Hôtel de Ville at St. Malo (Cunat, *ibid.*).

of the *Corbin*.[1] I was of the number, being not less desirous of seeing the world than of getting rich, and embarked in the *Corbin*. This ship had a worse fate than the other, and was lost,[2] and I have at last escaped, after many troubles. Since it has pleased God, contrary to all expectation, to bring me safe and sound to my native land after suffering so many hardships and running endless risks, not only having been borne about to most of the maritime regions and to the Indian islands, making almost a circuit of the world and visiting all four continents, but also having lived for the space of ten years among various races, and in my long sojourn learnt their manners, laws, and customs, perhaps better (as I may say without vanity) than any other Frenchman—nay than even any Portuguese or Hollander,—I have been constrained to put in writing whatever strange things I saw in my long travel, that so my countrymen may share them. My tale may also serve to give warning to those who would make the same voyage, to avoid the troubles into which I fell, or rather which I saw happen to others, so that by learning those mistakes in our navigation which caused our disaster, they may make the enterprise with more circumspection.

[1] Martin adds the name of the chief merchant, Christofle Moreau, sieur du Poisçant (*Martin*, p. 12). This man seems to have taken a prominent part in the League, for he appears at the head of the list of proscribed persons in a decree and ordonnance of the Seneschal of Rennes, 30 April 1590 (Dubois, L. F., *Essai sur l'histoire de la Ville de Vitré*, Paris, 1839, 8vo., p. 141).

[2] He would seem to imply here that the *Croissant* got safely home, but, as we shall see hereafter, she was abandoned almost within French waters, and sank in the sight of her remaining crew, who were rescued by the Hollanders.

CHAPTER I.

Narrative of the Voyage from the embarking at S. Malo to the Cape of Good Hope.

We left St. Malo with a north-east wind to begin our voyage on the 18th of May 1601. When we were but nine or ten leagues to sea the foremast of our ship split and broke in half, and this was a beginning of misfortune. We fired a cannon-shot to give notice to our commander on board the *Croissant*, and to know from him if we should put back to get another mast; but he being resolved to continue his course without delay, sent us the carpenters of his ship, who with ours mended the mast as best they could. The truth was, he was afraid of losing the voyage, for most of the mariners had taken this mishap, trifling though it was, for an evil omen, and said aloud that if we put into any port of France they would be off and give up the business. As for me, I never had a good opinion of our voyage since the embarking, not on account of this chance breaking of the mast, but of the bad order and discipline in the ships; for there was no piety or devotion, but plenty of oaths and blasphemy, disobedience to officers, mutiny and carelessness, and every day quarrelling, assaults, thefts, and the like vices.

On the 21st of the said month we sighted nine large Hollander vessels called "hulks" (*hourques*),[1] which put about to

[1] *Hourque*, "a hulk or huge flyboat" (Cotgrave); "a hulk or double flieboat of the burden of 250 tons" (*Cumberland's Voy.*, in Hak., iii, 774). The name was applied to the old canal-boat, or flyboat, of Holland and Flanders, which was flat-bottomed, with broad buttocks, and with stem and stern much alike. It had originally but one mast and a bowsprit The Dutch sea-going vessels were made on the same model, but squared off at the stern, and when built of considerable tonnage, had three masts and carried seven sails, viz., six square sails and one lateen. The latter ships, preserving the above features of hull, took the same name. They were very similar to the *Marsiliana* of the Venetians. *Hourques* ranged

salute the ships of France. In fact, they passed to leeward of us, which is the greatest mark of submission at sea; and they each fired a cannon, but the gunner of their vice-admiral fired with ball, which struck our ship in the sail and tore it to pieces. When we saw that, we feared that they wanted to fight, and hoisted our ensign or flag on the foremast to inform our commander. This caused him to bring to at once, while we began to barricade the ship all round (these barricades were of red scarlet, with the arms of France worked on cloth of gold),[1] putting our cannon in order, and loading all with shot. We armed ourselves and took up our positions, the captain on the poop and the lieutenant at the bows, and the four gunners with their assistants at the four quarters of the ship. This done, we fired two shots at the sails of the vessel which had attacked us, to know what they would say before we gave them a broadside. But they did not put themselves in an attitude of defence. Our commander, who handled his sails and helm exceeding well, bore down the

from fifty and sixty tons up to 200 and 300, "et il y en a qui font le voiage des Indes orientales, montées seulement de cinq ou six matelots" (Aubin). The words *hourque* and *hulk* are usually derived from the Greek ὁλκάς; but this is contested by Jal (see Aubin, *Dict. de Marine*, s.v. *hourque* and *heu*: Jal, *Archéologie Navale*, i, 141; ii, 216: also *Glossaire Nautique:* Pantera, *Armata Navale*, Rome, 1614: Skeat, *Etym. Dict.*, s.v. "hulk": and Smyth's *Sailor's Word-Book*). From the clumsy build of the Dutch vessels, and its supposed connection with "hull" (erroneous), the word "hulk" has come to be applied to any superannuated ship which is kept moored in rivers or harbours for coaling or other purposes.

[1] These barricades or screens (*bastingues* or *pavois*) were of cloth, stretched all round the upper decks, and also at the tops, of ships of war, to screen the crew from the enemy's sight during combat. At this time they were of a red material, as the author states; in 1670, the king, by an ordonnance, required that in future they should be blue, worked with yellow *fleurs de lis*, and bordered with broad white bands. Sometimes they were strengthened on the inner side so as to resist musket-shot, and this was generally done in galleys to protect the oarsmen (Aubin, *Dict. de Marine*; and Jal, *Gloss. Naut.*, s. v. *pavois*; Cotgrave, s. v. *pavoisade*).

wind, all sail set, towards the Hollander Admiral, and firing a shot, commanded him to strike amain; which he did promptly though much astonished, as he knew nothing that had happened. On being informed, he summoned his vice-admiral, who told him that one of his gunners, being drunk, had made the mistake. The Admiral sent for the gunner and presented him to our commander, begging him to forgive the injury, and offered to give over the offender to be punished as he might wish, or to do it himself on the spot and hang him at the yard-arm. But our General, being satisfied, said that he required nothing more, and prayed the Admiral to pardon the poor gunner. I doubt not he was incontinently punished, for the Flemings and Hollanders never let offences go unpunished on board their ships, keeping better discipline than we do on ours, which is the cause their voyages succeed better. At length we parted, with many mutual excuses.[1] They told us they were bound for the Cape Verd Islands, for cargoes of salt from the Isle de Mayo.[2]

On the 3rd of June following we sighted the Canary Islands, which are in 28°, 29°, and 30° northern latitude, and passed through them.

On the 12th and 13th of June we sighted the Cape Verd Islands. They are ten in number; the first from this side is

[1] This affair has recently been not a little magnified by the patriotism of the St. Malo biographer:—"Apres un combat contre six hourques hollandoises, combat qui eut lieu par la faute de ceux qui les montaient, puisque la guerre n'était pas declarée, le commandant hollandois rendit toute satisfaction à La Bardelière, et les équipages se séparerent bons amis" (*Cunat*, p. 77).

[2] It is probable that the fleet here spoken of was that of Heemskerk, who left the Texel with nine ships on the 23rd April, in company with five others under Wolphant Harmansen. These fleets parted on the 8th May. It is likely enough that the Dutch commander gave out that he was bound only for the C. Verd Islands, as he would not wish it to come to the ears of the Portuguese that he was sailing to the Indies (*Rec. des Voy.*, 1702, ii, 359, *et seq.*). The *rencontre* with the French is not mentioned in the Dutch journals. Martin mentions eight Dutch ships only (p. 13).

Saint Antoine, the second *S. Vincent*, the third *S. Lucar*, the fourth *S. Nicolas*, the fifth *del Sal*, the sixth *De buena vista*, the seventh *de Mayo*, the eighth *Santiago*, the ninth *del Fuego*, the tenth *Bravo.*[1] They begin at lat. 10° N., and reach down to lat. 14°. The Portuguese inhabit and cultivate some of them; the others are only inhabited by animals, such as goats, which are very numerous. They have fruits and provisions in abundance. The principal island, on which the others are dependent, is *S. Nicolas;* it is the seat of the Bishop and of justice.[2] The proximity of Cape Verd on the mainland, only fifty or sixty leagues off, where the Portuguese carry on a continual traffic in negro slaves, causes these islands to be much frequented because of this merchandise, which is carried to the West Indies and to Brazil, as well as to Portugal. In one of the islands, *de Mayo*, there is found such a quantity of rock-salt that one can load as much as one wishes without cost, for the island is uninhabited, and loading and transport are quite easy. You see in another island a mountain which throws out from its summit flames by night and smoke by day. On that account it is called "Isla del Fuego".[3]

On the 29th of the same month we were in lat. 5° N., and

[1] The Portuguese names are more properly as follows:—S. Antão, S. Vicente, Sta. Luzia, S. Nicolao, do Sal, da Boa Vista, Mayo, Santiago, Fogo, and Brava. The C. Verd Islands were discovered in 1456 by the Venetian Cadamosto, under the auspices of Prince Henry of Portugal. The first sighted was Boa Vista, and thence so called (Major's *Prince Henry*, p. 163).

[2] Sir R. Hawkins, who visited the Cape Verd Islands in 1593, says that Santiago was then the chief island, the seat of the Audiencia and the Bishop. This island was sacked by the English under Sir Anthony Sherley in 1596, and the government was then perhaps temporarily transferred to S. Nicolas (*Hawkins's Voyages*, Hak. Soc., pp. 129-30). The established seat of government has always been, as now, Santiago.

[3] "The second island is Fuego, so called, for that day and night there burneth in it a vulcan, whose flames in the night are seene twentie leagues off in the sea" (Sir R. Hawkins, in *Hawkins's Voyages*, Hak. Soc., 130).

saw the North Star very low, and at the same time sighted the Southern Constellation, or Antarctic Pole, otherwise called the *Croisade*, from being composed of four stars in the form of a cross, though it is distant 27° from the Pole. Yet it is the nearest by which the pilots can be guided as to their latitude. Here you see a strange quantity of fish, about as big as those called mullet, which have wings like bats, by means of which, when pursued by the larger fish, they dart out of the water and fly a long way until their wings are dry. So, on the other hand, when they are in the air, the sea birds, of which there is a vast multitude, give them chase and catch them, unless they first regain the sea. Many of them fell on our ships, and when once they fall on something hard where there is no water, they cannot raise themselves again. Thus we got some fresh food (and much pleasure too in watching the chase), for this fish is delicate and good eating. But it was a marvellous sight to see in so deep sea and in this quarter so vast a number of fish, that we might say we saw the whole sea covered with them, and all in a turmoil, though it was calm.[1] There were also big ones, such as bonitos and albachores,[2] and many other kinds, of which we caught with lines enough to supply the ship; and porpoises too, with harpoons attached to pieces of wood, then lifting them by strength of arm. I have seen these flying fish everywhere near the line, both on this and on

[1] For another description of the flying fish see *Hawkins's Voyages*, Hak. Soc., pp. 60, 152. Sir Richard Hawkins likens the pursuit to the chase as conducted by men: "The dolphins and bonitoes are the houndes, and the alcatraces (cormorants) the hawkes, and the flying fishes the game."

[2] Both kinds of tunny, and mentioned by nearly all voyagers. The word *albacora*, as it is written in Sp. and Port., is evidently Arabic. Dozy and Engelmann, however, express themselves unable to trace it in the Arabic dictionaries. It is probably *el-bakra*, "the cow-(fish)", according to the common practice of naming marine animals after those of the land.

the other side of the Cape of Good Hope, and both N. and S. of the line.

On the 14th of July we perceived the coast of Guinea, that is, the land of *Sierra Liona*. We thought we were more than 100 leagues off, but, owing to the calms and the currents, we had been drawn in against our will. We sighted two ships, one of which came near enough to look at us.[1] This coast is very unhealthy and inclement.

On the 24th August we passed the equinoctial line; for on this day, when we took the sun at the usual hour, viz., at midday (which sailors call the observation), there was found to be no elevation, so that we understood that we were under the line. The latitude is taken with the astrolabe from the sun, or from the stars by Jacob's-staff, called by sailors the *arbaleste*.[2] From lat. 7 or 8 N. to the same on the south

[1] These ships were afterwards met at the Cape, and proved to be two Dutch ships, the *Ram* and the *Sheep*, and a yacht, the *Lamb*, under G. Spilberg as admiral, with Guion Le Fort as vice-admiral. Their voyage is described at length in the *Recueil des Voyages*, ii, 421-552. This little fleet was destined to play a great part in the history of India, for Spilberg and his comrades were the first Dutchmen who gained a footing in Ceylon; and it was in that island more than elsewhere that the struggle of the Dutch and Portuguese for Eastern empire was fought and determined (see Tennant, *Ceylon*, ii, 34, *et seq.*). The Dutch chronicler does not mention having sighted the French ships here on the Guinea coast, but Martin, who was on board the *Croissant*, records the meeting thus: "Nous apperceusmes deux navires et une patache que nous jugions estre Flamens : la patache se mist en devoir de nous approcher et voyant que nous ne l'attendions, s'en retourna vers ses navires." (*Martin*, p. 17.)

[2] The astrolabe is an instrument of great antiquity, the treatise on it by Chaucer, written in 1391, being the first on a scientific subject published in England (Craik, *Eng. Lit.*, i, 367). The Jacob's-staff was one of many forms of the cross-staff. In England it was distinguished from the cross-staff proper (see *The use of the two mathematicall Instruments, the Crosse-staffe ... and the Jacob's staffe, set forth Dialogue wise in two briefe and plaine Treatises, etc.*, by Thomas Hood, London, 1596). All the chief authorities as to these instruments are collected by Capt. Markham in a valuable Appendix to his *Voyages and Works of John Davis*, Hak. Soc., 1880. The Portuguese also used several forms of

we were much harassed by the inconstancy of the weather and the bad climate. The heat is violent and stifling in the extreme; it destroys most of the provisions; the water becomes putrid and full of big worms; all kinds of meat and fish go bad, even the most carefully salted; all the butter we had brought was melted to oil, and so were the tallow candles. The ships began to split in those parts which were not under water; the pitch and tar likewise melted; and it was as impossible to remain below as in an oven. Nothing is so inconstant as the weather, but there it is inconstancy itself; in a moment it becomes calm as by a miracle; in half an hour there is on all sides thunder and lightning, the most terrible that can be imagined: this is chiefly when the sun is near the equinox. Suddenly the calm returns, then the storm begins again, and so on. All at once the wind rises with such impetuosity that it is all you can do to lower all sail in time, and you would suppose that the masts and yards would give way and the ship be lost. Often you see coming from afar great whirlwinds, which the sailors call *dragons*[1]; if they pass over ships they break them up and send them to the bottom. When they are seen coming the sailors take naked swords and strike them one against the other, in the form of a cross, on the bows of the ship, or in the direction where they see the storm coming, and they consider that that prevents it coming upon the ship and turns it aside. More-

cross-staff, *e.g.*, *radiometro*, *raio astronomico*, *bordão de Jacob*, *vara de ouro*, and others (Rivara, *Pyrard*, i, 9).

[1] This passage would seem to be the *locus classicus* for the term *dragon*. Jal (*Gloss. Naut.*, s. v. "Superstitions") quotes it from Père René François, *Essay des Merveilles de Nature*, second edition, 1622, ch. xii, who took it and other passages in the same chapter direct from Pyrard: this father, however, does not acknowledge his authorities. The word is used here for a waterspout, and in much the same sense by John de' Marignolli, in his description of a storm: "And such wondrous things we beheld! The sea as if in flames, and fire-splitting dragons flying by, etc." (Yule's *Cathay*, p. 356). Compare the Greek *typhon* and the Chinese *lung*.

over, in this region the rains are very dangerous, for if one is soaked and does not change one's dress promptly, the skin is shortly after covered with tumours and pimples, and worms are engendered in the clothes, so that there is much trouble to those who have a change of clothing, and bad results to those who have none. We were obliged to cover our ships with wax-cloth, and to make awnings to ward off the rain and the sun, and still we had much to bear. It would be impossible for me to relate in detail all the extremities, the labour, the discomforts, and fatigue which we endured for three months owing to these calms and *trauades*[1] (so they call these squalls), which do more mischief than heavy wind or a storm, and ships are soon worn out by them. Ours shook and reeled from side to side from the violence of the great *loüesme*[2] in those seas; but with the wind aft the sails

[1] *Travados*, "gusts of wind which the Portuguese call *Turbades* or *Travades*. These hurricanes, attended with excessive rains, fall on a sudden upon the ships, and toss them so violently that one would think they would perish immediately. But they don't last above an hour and half; and when they are over the air is so calm, that the surface of the sea is as smooth as glass" (*Collection of Voyages undertaken by the Dutch East India Company*, London, 1703, p. 97). The following is from Bluteau:—"Segundo João Jacobo Hofman no seu *Lexicon Universal*, tom. 4, fol. 491, col. 1, derão os Portuguezes este nome a huns ventos do mar Atlantico, que mais frequentemente regnão entre o Brasil e a Africa debayxo do Equador na altura de Guinè, do Cabo de Boa Esperança para o Cabo de Guardafu. Repentinamente sahem de hũa navem e são tão impetuosas que revolvem tudo de cima para bayxo."

[2] This word, which, as will be seen, Pyrard uses frequently in the sense of rollers or swell, as distinguished from a stormy state of the sea caused immediately by wind, is not found in any of the French dictionaries, nor even in Jal's *Glossary*. M. Charton has this note:—"Ce mot ne se trouve dans aucun glossaire. M. Jal, que nous avons consulté, pense qu'il doit avoir le sens de *houle*, ou celui de *grande lame* de fond, ou peut-être enfin de *ras de marée*. M. le docteur Roulin croit que c'est une imitation incorrecte du mot anglais *whelm*, qui signifie 'couvrir d'eau une surface', et que nos marins des bords de la Manche avaient adopté dans le sens de 'spoon-drift', 'embrun', écume des lames chassées par le gros vent, et pendant sa durée" (Charton, *Voy.*, iv,

keep the ship steady, and if she is close to the wind she lies on one side only. These calms try vessels much, chiefly those heavily laden, and too often make their timbers start, so that after one such storm they cannot stand the sea long.

On the 29th August, our pilot, who was an Englishman,[1] being aloft, descried land ten leagues distant. This delighted us exceedingly, for we were in need of fresh water, and yet did not know where to find land, believing that we could not have been driven so near to Guinea, which we intended to pass a hundred leagues off; but the calms and currents had brought us in once more. At the good news our captain quickly hoisted the ensign on the foremast (for only a chief or commander can fly it on the mainmast), and firing a shot to call our General's attention, learned from him that it was the island of *Anabon.*[2] As he was now behind we did not go forward, but put our ship about and waited till the morning, ere we cast anchor at the island: this the mariners call "beating"; it is practised when they want to keep in view of land and to remain in the same part of the sea or coast, first they go one way, and then, tacking about, the other.

Next day, the 30th, after anchoring, we treated amicably with the Portuguese, who are masters of the island. As they had accepted some presents from us, and had also sent us some fruit, we trusted to their good faith, and our General got

243, *n.*). It seems more likely to be a nautical corruption of "lame" than of "whelm", the use of which word does not seem to be correctly appreciated by the Docteur Roulin.

[1] The name of this pilot is not given. English pilots, as Mr. Bell reminds me, were in request in those days, especially when they had been the Indian voyage before. Thus John Davis was pilot to the Dutch voyage of the *Moucherons* in 1598; William Adams to Mahn's fleet of the same year; Mellish, who had sailed with Cavendish, was pilot in Van Noort's fleet.

[2] The island of Annobon, in lat. 1° 30′ S., long. 5° 40′ E., so called from its discovery by Martin Fernandez on the 1st January 1471. It was ceded to Spain in 1778, and is said now to contain about 1,000 inhabitants.

ready his gallion and put in it a number of vessels for the water, fruit, and other provisions, sending for this purpose some sailors and soldiers. With them also six officers of the two ships desired to go for refreshment, and though it was against the General's intention, he did not care to stop them. When they were landed, the six officers were well received by the Portuguese, so that they trusted them entirely, and let themselves be conducted whither they would. They then sent the boat with the sailors round to the other side of the island for the water, as had been arranged. They were led by a party of negroes, who, however, would not enter the boat—a circumstance which was of itself enough to show their want of good faith—but made round the island, they by land, and we by sea. Soon after, the six were surrounded and attacked by a large number of Portuguese and negro slaves in arms, who had been in an ambuscade. One of the six, the lieutenant of the *Corbin,* named Thomas Pepin of St. Malo, began to defend himself, and in fact wounded several of them, but being overpowered by numbers, he was mortally wounded and carried ashore, while the other five were made prisoners. The Portuguese then sent the wounded man on a raft to the ships, accompanied by our General's negro servant, who had gone with the six; but as soon as he was laid on the ship the lieutenant breathed his last. The General at once fired two shots to warn the sailors on the other side to return if they could with the boat, and not to engage in any fighting, which they did promptly. The next day the Portuguese sent on another raft (for they have there no other vessels) one of the five prisoners, to say that they were very badly treated, being kept in chains in the mountains and separate from one another. These mountains are high, and all covered with wood. Moreover, they said that a ransom was put on their heads, which was at length agreed to, viz., 1,500 cruzados, some wine, biscuit, powder, muskets, and other implements, the prisoners being severally delivered up at each part payment. The Portuguese then sent a pig, some rice, fruit, and other provisions, and told us that we might go freely and safely about the island; but we would not trust them any more, though we were in need of fresh water. Therefore we went by night in our boats, well armed, to fetch the water, but got only a little, for the stream is at the bottom of a valley near the sea, and the islanders would not let us have it, but took up a position on the hills above, and attacked us with muskets, wounding in the shoulder one of our ship's boys. They also wounded us with stones thrown or rolled down the hill, so that the work was very dangerous. This continued for six or seven weeks, while we were at the coast.[1] In place of the dead lieutenant, another was constituted, not elected on the spot, but one that had been nominated to succeed by the Company at St. Malo, who had made appointments to all the offices in case of death, so as not to leave that in the discretion of the ship's company, which might give rise to some disorder. And here is to be remarked that one who is promoted to a higher grade, or changes his office, gets no more wages than he had before, because the wages of a deceased officer always run on to the return home of the ship, and are paid to his widow, children, or heirs, just as though he were alive.

This island belongs to a Portuguese lord, to whom the King of Spain has given it[2]: the other Portuguese who reside there are his factors and agents. All the people of the island are his slaves, and with them he drives a great trade as

[1] An interesting cut, representing the attack of the islanders upon the French, will be found in the Dutch journal of Spilberg's voyage, drawn, no doubt, from the description given by the Frenchmen of the *Croissant* and *Corbin*, when they met Spilberg's ships at the Cape and Madagascar.

[2] The Portuguese lord lived at the little dependent island named St. Omer (Martin, *Voyage*, p. 95). Pyrard here, as elsewhere, properly speaks of the King of Spain, Portugal having been subject to Spain since 1580. The island now, in fact, belongs to Spain, by virtue of Art. 13 of the Treaty of 11th March 1778 (Rivara's *Pyrard*, i, 13, *note*).

well in Spain as in the West Indies, exporting every year a certain number, according to their increase. They are all negroes, and go naked, men and women, save that they cover with cotton their privy parts; the women carry their babes on their backs, and give them suck over the shoulder, their breasts being so long that the children grasp and suck them from behind. This island is situate under the altitude of a degree and a half south latitude, and has a circuit of about five or six leagues. It is high, mountainous, and covered with wood, and always green. All the time we were there, not a day passed but it rained more or less. The roadstead on the north-west is very dangerous by reason of the shoals and rocks. Fruits grow there in abundance, such as oranges, bananas (which serve for bread); cocos,[1] which supply the people with wine; sugar-canes, pine-apples, other fruits which they call *Panana*,[2] and also rice and millet. A quantity of cotton is collected, and this forms the sole revenue of the island. The fishery is abundant, and the fish being good, we were greatly refreshed thereby. At a league and a half from Anabon is a little island all burnt up and without any verdure, yet is it so covered with birds that one can hardly walk a step in any direction without treading upon them or their eggs. They are called *Pingui;* they are a little bigger than our pigeons, of about the same plumage, of excellent flavour and good eating, albeit the flesh is very black.[3] We ate many

[1] The word "coco" being applied exclusively to the nut, Rivara is right in pointing out that Pyrard makes a slip here, inasmuch as the wine is drawn from the tree itself.

[2] It is not clear what fruit is here intended; he has already mentioned bananas and pineapples (*ananas*), for which the word might be supposed to be a misprint. In the first edition (1611) it appears as *panaua*; and Martin (p. 22), also writing of Annobon, says: "Et autres fruicts qu'ils nomment *Panama*"; but neither of these various readings help us. The sweet-potato may be meant, or the word may be connected with *pão*, bread, and indicate *cassava*, which grows at Annobon.

[3] As pointed out by Guèrin, in his abridgment of Pyrard, the birds here called penguins were really *manchots* (*Les Navigateurs Français*, p. 218, *note*).

of them, going every day to that little island to take our walks and catch them. One of our fellows, who had been recognised as lieutenant of the *Corbin* in place of him deceased, in pursuing these birds, fell between some rocks and broke his leg, and much trouble we had to get him out at all. We were beset by all manner of misfortunes during our sojourn at this road, for besides this we had many others, and most of them happened to our ship, where arose a great quarrel between our Captain and the chief factor or merchant. They almost came to blows, and were like to have caused a general revolt and mutiny, so that our General had need to come with a competent guard to restore order; nevertheless, this dispute lasted the whole voyage, neither speaking to the other. I leave you to consider how all could go well when the chiefs, who ought to show a good example to the others, themselves created disorder. There was also another mischance, viz.: when the men were getting into the boats to fight for a supply of water, fire reached some powder in one of ours wherein our Captain was, and many were burned and injured. But the last accident was this: on weighing anchor, we were all the morning endeavouring to raise one of ours; and although those on board the *Croissant* came to our aid, we could not get it up, and the cable gave way, though it was as thick as a man's thigh and quite new. The anchor itself was lost—a matter of no small moment at such times.

Having thus sojourned at the anchorage at this island for the space of six weeks, on the 16th October our General gave order to weigh and to hoist sail, and steer a course for St. Helena, because we had not been able to get fitting refreshment here, and we were beginning to have some sick of the scurvy. Those on their way to the Indies do not ordinarily fetch that island (St. Helena), the winds not being favourable, and great risk attending the attempt to make it; indeed, our pilot said that he did not expect we should of certainty reach it. However, on the 17th November, we did at daybreak happily sight the island of St. Helena,[1] situate under the 16th degree toward the Antarctic Pole, and distant 600 leagues from the Cape of Good Hope. We found on the altar of the chapel many letters, which gave notice that the Hollanders had passed there. We looked to find there some timber to refit our foremast, but there was none fit for the purpose. Our sojourn at this island was nine days, and this was of great service to our sick, inasmuch as the water, the flesh, and the fruits there are very wholesome, and the air very pure and healthy: so we were replenished with all the water we stood in need of. I will not tarry here to describe the beauty, fertility, plenteousness, and commodities of this excellent island, postponing a more particular description against my return, because the long stay we then made gave me a better knowledge of it.

On the 26th November 1601, our sick being now recovered, we weighed anchor and set sail, and pursued our route towards the Cape of Good Hope.

Three days afterwards we doubled the *Abroilles*. These are banks and shoals off the coast of Brazil, under the 18th degree beyond the equinoctial line. They stretch a distance of some 70 leagues; the Portuguese call them *Abrolhos*,[2] that is to

[1] St. Helena, in lat. 16° S., long. 5° 50′ W., discovered by João de Nova on St. Helena's day (18th Aug.), 1502, was held under the nominal authority of the Portuguese till 1651, when it was taken by the English. The Portuguese, for reasons stated by Pyrard in his subsequent description of the island, never garrisoned it, nor indeed allowed it to be colonised. It was accordingly used freely for refreshment and as a post-office by Portuguese, Dutch, and English. As Pyrard postpones his fuller description, we may also postpone our fuller notes.

[2] *Abre-olhos!* "Keep your eyes open!" This fanciful derivation was at one time generally accepted. Pyrard was not the first to give currency to it; thus, Sir R. Hawkins writes the word *abreoios* (*Hawkins's Voyages*, p. 171). It is, however, undoubtedly taken from *abrolho*, the water calthrop, which has a secondary meaning, in military use, of a *cheval de frise*, and in nautical use, of pointed rocks or breakers. (See Rivara's *Pyrard*, i, 16, *note; Linschoten*, Hak. Soc., i, 16, *note*.)

say, "Open your eyes", because these shoals are exceeding dangerous, and it is very necessary to keep a good look-out and to give them a wide berth; for if you were to fail to double them, and were to get caught in them, it would be very difficult to get out; and even if you did get out, the voyage would be lost, and you would have to return whence you set out. This is the reason why ships going to the Indies, out of care to keep them at a distance, fall away too much on the other side towards Guinea, where the air is exceeding unwholesome, and where they meet with such calms and currents, that very frequently vessels are lost, or else many men languish and die of grievous ailments; wherefore the dexterity of good pilots lies in not approaching too near the coast of Guinea, and also in not striking these banks of the *Abroilles* on the Brazil side, but in taking their measure, and in so doing they will have plenty of room, for the distance between the coast of Africa and that of Brazil is put down at about a thousand leagues. Having thus doubled these banks, we had a merry-making, and appointed by lot a king to rule during the feast, which lasts a whole day; and there was served out to each a pint of wine more than ordinary. This was in imitation of the Portuguese, who do this, men being always accustomed to imitate rather bad customs, than such as are good and laudable. For my part I nowise approve those feasts and banquets at sea, which result only in consuming the ship's wine and victuals, and in making the mariners drunk and incapable of doing their duties, besides giving rise to quarrels and assaults.[1]

[1] To pass the Abrolhos was with the Portuguese the first crisis of the voyage; the Cape was the second. The same festivities were observed on board the *Croissant*:—" A ceste consideration les Portuguais ayant doublé ces bancs ont accoustumé en signe de regiouissance faire un Roy, eslisant celuy à qui eschet un certain billet, et à leur imitation nous en fismes un, et Dieu voullut que le sort tomba sur moy, et celuy qui est Roy a tout pouvoir durãt ceste solennité, laquelle dure ordinairement quatre

CHAPTER II.

*Of the Cape of Good Hope and the Cape of the Needles.—
Violent storm on the coast of Natal.*

Meanwhile our vessels were daily making their way towards the Cape of Good Hope, and after some days we perceived the signs whereby proximity to the Cape is known. Fifty or sixty leagues out are seen floating in vast numbers the stalks of reeds, with about nine or ten reeds (more or less) attached to each stalk: these are called *trombas*[1];

ou cinq jours, qui ont accoustumé de se passer en festins et joye; le jour de ma promotion je fists deliurer quelques prisonniers qui estoient à la chaine" (*Martin*, p. 32). So Davis, in his Dutch voyage of 1598: "The 10th we passed the Abrolhos, which was the greatest of our feare . . . whereupon our Baase (for so a Dutch Captaine is called) chose a Master of Mis-rule by the name Kesar (*i.e.*, *Keizer*, 'Emperor'). Now the authoritie of riot lay in this disordered officer, who after dinner could neither salute his friends, nor understand the lawes of Reason. And those that ought to have been most respective, were both lawlesse and witlesse. In this dissolute manner we wasted three days, which being ended, and having againe recovered our former discretion, we shaped our course for Cape Bona Esperanza" (*Davis*, Hak. Soc., p. 134). Compare the Whit-Sunday festivities mentioned by Linschoten (Hak. Soc., i, 17), at which some idle words led to a dangerous brawl.

[1] Port. *tromba*. These reeds, together with the various birds, are alluded to by most navigators as signs of the Cape. "The signs and tokens whereby they know themselves certainly to have passed the Cape [homeward bound], are great heapes and peeces of thicke reedes, that alwaies thereabouts drive uppon the water, at least 15 or 20 miles from the land" (*Linsch.*, Hakl. Soc., ii, 250). "Le 31 ils commencèrent à voir floter des *trumbas*, ou poignées de joncs avec leurs racines, ce qui est une marque qu'on n'est pas loin du Cap de Bonne Espérance" (Houtman's voy., *Rec. des Voy.*, i, 211). "There are also other signs of land being near, as those they call *caravels of Brittany*, being weeds, or rather reeds, like the Indian canes, or rather like grass, but as thick as one's finger" (Merolla, 1682, in *Churchill*, i, 665). "These *trombas* are a kind of great canes, about the bignesse of a man's arm, and three or four foot long, which flote upon the water with their roots" (*Mandelslo*, Eng. trans., 248).

also, a multitude of white birds speckled with black spots, which the Portuguese call *mangue de velade.*[1]

On the 27th December 1601, towards midnight, while it was blowing a strong gale with rain, the night being very dark, we suddenly found ourselves close upon land, and but for a mariner, who by accident perceived it, we had been lost, for the seas at that part are passing heavy and stormy, and there are some great rocks projecting out into the sea. As soon, therefore, as this was descried by the mariner, we tacked sails and ship and put about to sea, and fired off a gun to give our General warning. At daybreak it was observed that we had passed the Cape of Good Hope, and that the cape we saw was that of the Needles.[2] This cape

[1] Properly *mangas de vèlludo*, "velvet sleeves". Thomas Stevens, the Jesuit, whom Pyrard afterwards met at Goa, thus writes, in 1579: "Fowles of sundry kindes followed our ship...... The Portingals have named them all according to some proprietie which they have: some they call *Rush-tailes*, because their tails be not proportionable to their bodies, but long and smal like a rush; some *Forked-tailes*, because they be broad and forked; some *Velvet-sleeves*, because they have wings of the coulor of velvet, and boweth them as a man boweth his elbow. This bird is alwaies welcome, for he appeareth neerest the Cape" (*Hakluyt*, i, 161). Linschoten says: "We saw there also divers of the birds called *Mangas de Velludo*, that is to say, Velvet-sleeves, for they have upon the ends of their wings blacke points like velvet, all the rest being white and somewhat grey, which they hold for a certain sign of the land that lyeth within the Cape de Bona Esperanza (Hakl. Soc. edition, ii, 243; so *Mocquet*, edition 1645, p. 227). Rivara points out that Pyrard has misdescribed the "mangas de velludo", which is white with black wings, and has given the description of another and commoner Cape bird, known by the Portuguese as the "Feijão frade" (see *Linsch.*, ii, 250), which is white, freckled with black spots. Dr. Fryer mentions "*Pintado* birds, *Mango faleudos*, *Albetrosses*, the first remarkable for their pointed spots of black and white" (p. 12), without describing the "velvet-sleeve". Mandelslo gives a correct description: "*Mangas de valeudo*, a kind of sea-mews, being white all over the bodies and having black wings" (Eng. trans., p. 248).

[2] *I.e.*, *Cabo das Agulhas*, the name by which it is still known. It is the southernmost point of the African continent. Pyrard places it in 35° S.; Linschoten (Hakl. Soc., ii, 249) in 34½°; it is really in 36° 5′ S.

advances out into the sea further than that of Good Hope by fifteen leagues, and is situate under the altitude of 35 degrees of Southern latitude. It is named the Cape of the Needles, because at this place the compasses or needles remained fixed, pointing directly to the north, without any declination to the east or the west; when it is doubled, they begin to decline to the north-east. On this day we sighted two Hollander ships and a pinnace coming out of a bay that is by the Cape *des Aguilles*, called *Baya Sardeigna*,[1] where they had gone for refreshment. It was, however, impossible for us to approach one another all the day long, because of the wind and of the sea, which was running high and tempestuous; nevertheless, their smaller ship, with great difficulty, ran down the wind toward us and told us who they were. On the morrow we came together, and for two days visited each other and gave mutual entertainment with all friendliness. They were very small ships from Camfer,[2] in Zeeland, their General by name *Spilbert*.[3] They told us it was them we had sighted on the Guinea coast, and that had our General waited until they had sent their pinnace after us, the misfortune that befell us at the island of *Anabon*

As to the non-variation of the compass, see Davis (*Voyages*, Hakl. Soc., p. 136): "We doubled Cape das Agulios, which is the most southerly promontorie of Africa, where the compasse hath no variation."

[1] *Saldanha* bay, called after Antonio de Saldanha, who went to India in 1503. *Baya Sardeigna* is a misnomer, which Rivara accepts by his translation, *Bahia das Sardinhas* (*Viagem de Pyrard*, i, p. 18). As pointed out by Mr. Corney (*Middleton's Voy.*, Hakl. Soc., p. 6) and Mr. Clements Markham (*Lancaster's Voy.*, Hakl. Soc., p. 62), the Saldanha Bay of the Portuguese, Dutch, and English voyagers of this period is our Table Bay. Pyrard's statement that the Dutch were met coming out of a bay near the Needles Cape is incorrect; Spilberg had put into Table Bay and nowhere else, and the two fleets met off the Cape of Good Hope (Spilberg, *Rec. des Voy.*, ii, 438-44).

[2] Veer, Terveer, or Campveer, a small town and fort commanding the Veergat, on the north side of the island of Walcheren. It was taken by the British during the ill-fated expedition of 1809.

[3] Joris van Spilbergen, generally called Spilberg.

had not come to pass. For they related to us how they had landed, and put no confidence in the people of the island as we did; yet they obtained a sufficiency of water, losing, however, two of their men, and having six wounded. They told us, moreover, that if we had been all together in company we should have been strong enough in men to have made ourselves masters of the island: that no great resistance was possible, and so we should have been enabled to refresh ourselves and make provision of water. Thus was our General partly to blame for all that misfortune, because he did not await the Hollanders as he ought. We gave them a mainsail, of which they stood in need, and in exchange they gave us two perriers,[1] or small iron cannon. They were also bound for the Indies, and we should have been glad enough to make the voyage in their company. But this could not be, because they had to go by the passage between the mainland and the island of St. Laurence, in order to meet their countrymen who were awaiting them there, a rendezvous having been appointed at the *Baya Formosa*,[2] on the Melinde coast. Our intention, on the contrary, was to pass outside the island, wherefore we parted and took leave of each other with much cannonading.[3] This done, we took our course outside the island of St. Laurence.

[1] *Perrier*, "the ship's artillery called a fowler" (Cotgrave); "(petit canon de fer), a *pederero* or *petterero*, a fowler, a sort of gun" (Boyer). The word is a corruption of Fr. *pierrier*, Port. *pederero*, and is taken from an engine used for casting stones, which was in use before the discovery of gunpowder. In the sixteenth century there were *pierriers* and *demi-pierriers*, ranging from 35 to 20 quintals. It was a gun proper for use on the main-tops, and in boats (Jal, *Gloss. Naut.*, s. v.).

[2] Near Melinde, in latitude 3° S., longitude 40° 20′ E. In the text it is misprinted *Tormosa*.

[3] The following account of the meeting with the Dutch ships, given in Spilberg's voyage (*Rec. des Voy.*, ii, 444), shows how the laxity of discipline on board the French ships struck the foreigner, and indicates, even in these petty details, the vital difference between the seamanship of the French and Portuguese on the one hand, and that of the Dutch and English on the other:—"Le 27 [Dec. 1604] nous découvrîmes

The 6th January 1602, being Twelfth Night, while all were making merry and crying "le Roy boit",[1] arose a violent

le Cap, et deux vaisseaux François de S. Malo, dont Mr. de Bardelière étoit Amiral, et Mr. le Connétable de Vitré Vice-amiral. Un des Pilotes étoit Flamand, et se nommoit Mayor Wouter Willekens. Après qu'on lui eut parlé, nous fîmes route de compagnie. Le même jour, notre Général aïant beaucoup d'envie de s'entretenir plus particulièrement avec eux, dans l'espérance d'apreudre quelques nouvelles, se rendit à leur bord, accompagné de Corneille Specx : et le lendemain les François passèrent au sien. Ils lui dirent qu'ils avoient aussi relâché à Annobon, où on leur avoient montré des tombeaux de quelques uns de leurs gens, qu'on disoit avoir été tuez en combattant contre trois vaisseaux Flamands. Ces Messieurs les François de S. Malo s'imaginoient être là en grande seureté, parce-qu'ils étoient Catoliques Romains : surtout en descendant à terre, pour aller ouïr la Messe. Mais la Messe leur coûta bien plus cher que qu'ils en eussent paié la façon au Prêtre : car les Portugais en massacrèrent quelques-uns et en retinrent d'autres prisonniers, pour qui il fallut paier de grosses rançons, jusqu'à mille écus en argent, avec diverses marchandises.

"Le 1 de Janvier 1602 les François aïant déclaré qu'ils vouloient aller par l'est de Madagascar, et par conséquent prendre un autre cours que nous n'avions résolu, on se sépara bon amis. Au reste il n'étoit pas à propos que nous fussions plus longtems avec eux. Nos gens n'avoient par semaine que chacun trois livres de biscuit, et tous les dix jours deux pintes de vin ; au lieu que les tonneaux de vin étoient toujours percez dans les navires François, chacun en pouvant aller tirer quand il lui plaisoit. On y avoit le biscuit à commandement : on y jettoit à la mer le stocfiche tout cuit. Chaque ration de vin étoit de six pintes par semaine pour chaque homme, et encore ne s'en tenoient-ils pas à cette règle ; souvent ils alloient plus loin, et s'en faisoient donner davantage. Cet example étoit dangereux, et il ne devoit pas être longtems devant nos yeux, puis-qu'il nous étoit impossible de le suivre, et qu'il auroit pu servir à faire murmurer nos gens, de ce qu'ils n'étoient pas ainsi traitez." The Dutch, perhaps intentionally, misinformed the French as to their route, in order to get rid of them. The course they had resolved to make was first to a point near Cape Sta. Lucia, then across to Cape St. Mary, at the south end of Madagascâr, thence to the Comorro Islands (*Rec. des Voy.*, ii, pp. 432, 433).

[1] In France, the chairman at the Twelfth Night festival was called "Le roi de la fève" (King of the bean). His first act, on taking the chair, was to drink to the company, who responded with a loud shout of "Le roi boit!" The celebration, which in the early Middle Ages consisted of a procession in which the three Kings or Magi took the principal

squall, which required us to lower sail, and one of our mariners, a man of St. Malo, fell into the sea. It was impossible to save him: his messmate,[1] however, would have flung himself after him had he not been restrained; but I think this was more because he had taken too much wine than out of affection, for these sailors have not much friendship. All along this coast we saw all night many fires on the tops of the mountains. Thus continuing our voyage, we passed without any storm the land of Natal, which is on the Ethiopian coast,—an unwonted occurrence, because violent storms are usually met with between the 33rd and 28th degrees.

On the 30th January, in the altitude of 26 degrees, our General asked his pilot[2] on which side of the island of St. Laurence we were; he replied, on the outside; nevertheless, this was not so, for we were between the coast of Africa and the island, contrary to our intention. This was due to the ignorance of the pilot, as well as to our amusing ourselves too long with the Hollanders' ships. Having the weather calm, we let our ships go at their will, carrying generally only lower sails; while the Hollanders' vessels, being better sailers than ours, duly kept their course along the coast of Africa, and we followed them unconsciously. Our General, doubting the fact, demanded to sight the island for his assurance; but after sailing for two days and two nights without sighting it, he gave orders to put about on the opposite

part, had by this time degenerated into a mere jollification; nowadays, in England at least, the sole remaining relic is a cake. The whole history of Twelfth Night will be found well described in Chambers's *Book of Days* (January 6th), where also may be seen a copy of an old French print, exhibiting a party of revellers crying "Le roi boit!" as described by Pyrard.

[1] As the author explains in his Advice at the end of vol. ii, each of the sailors had his messmate: an arrangement made with a view to friendship and mutual assistance.

[2] Probably the Fleming named Mayor Wouter Willekens mentioned by Spilberg (v. s., p. 23, note 3).

course. This done, we sailed on till the 4th of February, when we began to sight the island of St. Laurence on its inner side, whereupon our General was highly incensed against the pilot. Forthwith he gave order to work back out of the strait and to return to the outer course, because he was afraid of not being able to make the passage by reason of the contrary winds which are ordinarily to be met with in the season we were then in.

On the 7th February 1602, while coasting back along Natal to get without the island of St. Laurence, a course we had already made happily without mishap, there arose suddenly a violent squall from the south-west. We had no thought of it; the Portuguese, on the other hand, when they make the passage in this latitude, prepare for these storms, and take precautions in time. Our galleon had been lowered to send a man on board the *Croissant* to confer between the General and our captain on some business concerning the voyage; and just a moment before, I had myself returned from visiting some of my friends that were very ill, amongst others, a young man of our town, Laval, whom I loved dearly. Some of our men who were on board the *Croissant*, seeing the sea wax high, got into the galleon or boat and returned to us. But they made so little haste that they could hardly have been got on board, had we not flung them a cable, which gripping, it was as much as they could do to get on board in safety. It was, however, impossible to hoist the galleon so promptly; it was only lashed, as best we could, with a heavy cable, and this broke, so the galleon filled with water and went to the bottom before we could do anything to save it; this loss was of the utmost trouble to us. I believe it impossible for those who have not experienced it to conceive the horror and fury of this storm, for all we had experienced heretofore was mere child's-play in comparison. It became so dark at high noon that we could not see the sky nor recognise one another. Our two ships got far parted, and in an instant our sails were torn to shreds: the rain and wind were so furious in our faces that we were wounded and bruised as by strokes of rods: the collars of our shirts were torn, and smote us on the face so that we had to wrench them off. The waves also ran so terribly high that you would have said that the ship was at one time tossed up to heaven, at another plunged into an abyss, and all the while rolling from side to side in such wise that it was no easy matter to keep within the ship, and very perilous to remain on deck: for we were continually struck by the heaviest seas, and sometimes by one (roller) *louesme;* more than twenty hogsheads of water were shipped, which passed over the vessel and only partly escaped on the other side. With their violence these would carry away all they met, and so it behoved a man to hold well to the deck. Fortunate was it for us that our ship was so tight and staunch that not a single leak was sprung in her nether timbers by the fury of this storm, and she made no more water than ordinary. All the water she made came in from above when she was struck by these seas and topping waves, which passed over her and drenched not only the men on the deck and those under cover, but also the ship's provisions and furniture. We had hardly hands enough to empty the ship with the pumps, and our captain was foremost at the job. There was nothing that was not soaked and spoiled; and this entailed the greatest hardships; for during the four days and four nights the storm lasted, we were perpetually drenched with salt water, and afterwards had nothing dry for change. We ate nothing but a little biscuit and a little wine, being unable to cook anything; to sleep or get the slightest repose was out of the question. At such a time, all who were wise turned to their own thoughts; as for the mariners, it is then they swear and blaspheme more than usual. At the height of the storm at midnight the question arose of cutting the main topmast. The method of so doing is to cut the standing and running rigging on the leeward side, next to cut the mast half across, then to cut the ropes on the windward side, whereupon it falls of itself without injuring anyone. This was a perilous job, owing to the difficulty a man had in keeping his hold during the violent tossings of the ship. In this task they employed our chief carpenter, a Hollander, and one of the best ship's carpenters living; he received double wages and double portions of wine, but in truth he did as much work as any three men. With great difficulty he managed to cut the mast, and then, unable to keep his hold, fell with it to leeward and beyond the ship's side. By a miracle, however, he encountered the great yard, which being lowered and lashed crosswise, stretched out beyond the ship some nine or ten feet. There were here some ropes, which the poor fellow caught and gripped so firmly that he managed to save himself, though with the utmost difficulty. We thought, too, that another grave accident was to befall us. There were four or five heavy iron cannon, which were dismounted and lashed and belayed below on the first deck. By force of the storm these got loose, but God permitted that some men below should observe it; and these men ran forthwith with mattresses, sacks, and other soft baggage, and cast them on either side to stay the guns, and so to get them re-lashed; otherwise the slightest blow they would have given in their rolling to the ship's side would have driven a hole in her. During this storm our rudder-trunk broke, and this was a great trouble to us, for it deprived us of the necessary use of the helm. Our pilots and the oldest seamen said they had never endured a more violent storm, nor one that had so driven them from their wits and daunted their resolution. But the truth is that they had never before experienced the violence of the sea in those parts, where ordinarily it is much more heavy and stormy than elsewhere. For my part, on my return I came through seas quite as furious, under the same altitude, but not on the same coast.

CHAPTER III.

We anchor in St. Augustine's bay, at the island of St. Laurence. —Of our landing and long sojourn there.—A description of the island, and of the manners and customs of the inhabitants.

The storm lasted until the 11th of the said month of February. When it subsided we were in great trouble by reason we had lost sight of the *Croissant*, our General. What gave us the more anxiety was that we observed a great mast floating on the sea, and believed that the *Croissant* had gone down, and that the mast was hers. By this time the most of our wearied crew were sick and half-dead; wherefore the Captain took counsel whether we ought to make land, and the opinion was to make the nearest we could, which was the island of St. Laurence.[1] Forthwith our course was directed thither, albeit we were somewhat afraid, because we had no pilot nor mariner who had been to the Indies before, saving one Flemish gunner, who was an ignorant fellow.

Approaching the island, at thirty or forty leagues off, we observed the sea to become changed: it was yellowish and exceeding frothy, covered with sea-urchins, canes, reeds, and other floating herbs, and these continued till we reached the island. At length, on the 18th February, we sighted land.

On the morning of the 19th February we cast anchor in a

[1] *I.e.*, Madagascar, first discovered by Soares on the 1st Feb. 1506: it was called St. Laurence, owing to a later discovery by d'Abreu on that saint's day (August 10th in the same year), and was so known all through the Portuguese period.

> "De São Lourenço-vê a ilha affamada,
> Que Madagascar he d'alguns chamada."
>
> (Camões, *Lus.*, x, 137.)

In course of time the native name Madagascar, supposed to be derived from Makdishu (Magadoxo), on the Zanzibar coast, asserted itself (*Linschoten*, Hakl. Soc., i, p. 19, *note*).

bay, surnamed of St. Augustine,[1] situate under the altitude of 23½ degrees south, under the tropic of Capricorn. It is a large and commodious bay, with a good bottom of slime and sand. At midday we perceived a large vessel in the offing. Thinking at the first it was a Portuguese ship, we put on our arms and prepared ourselves, and began to stretch our quarter-nettings for our defence; but when it came nigher we found it was the *Croissant*, from which we had been separated about the space of twelve hours; she brought up close alongside. This was a matter of much joy and comfort, saving that we found her to be in worse plight than ourselves, her furniture in sorry condition, her timbers open, and her crew almost all sick. Towards evening we perceived another ship, without masts or sails, except a single spar fixed amidships, with a little sail for her assistance. She anchored four or five leagues from us, not daring to come closer, and then despatched a boat with three or four hands to reconnoitre us. When they perceived who we were, they approached and came aboard our ship, where they were welcomed and told us who they were. The vessel was one of the two Hollanders we had seen at the Cape of the Needles, and had been grievously dealt with by the gale.[2] Presently the barque returned to inform their captain, who forthwith came and cast anchor alongside of us. He was named Le Fort, the son of a Frenchman of Vitré, but born in Holland.[3] He had

[1] St. Augustine's Bay, in latitude 23° 30′ S.; longitude 43° 35′ E.

[2] It was the *Ram*, one of Spilberg's ships, which got separated from her consort soon after leaving the Cape. The violence of this gale is described in Spilberg's voyage in much the same terms as by Pyrard (*Rec. des Voy.*, ii, pp. 449-53). The *Ram* did not meet the *Sheep* again till the 3rd July, when she joined her at Batticaloa, in Ceylon. Her crew recounted their adventures to their friends, and it is added, "Ils avoient vu dans cette baie [St. Augustine's] deux vaisseaux François de S. Malo, aussi tout-désemparez" (*ib.*, p. 479).

[3] Guyon Lefort, the captain of the *Ram*, the vessel here met with by the Frenchman, had already been to the East in the expedition sent out in 1598 from Middelburg by the Company of the *Moucherons*. The

already been to the Indies, and died on this voyage at Achen. It was said the King of Achen liked him and made much of him. The three ships being now together, our General and our Captain and the Hollander, with the chief men of the three vessels, took counsel what they should do for the common advantage, and, according to the general agreement, a place on shore was chosen, the best we could find, to land such as were sick of the scurvy—a great number on board our vessels, but among the Hollanders not a man. A place was chosen and marked out at the foot of a high mountain, on the banks of a river that falls into this bay; it was enclosed with a palisade of thick stakes, planted and driven in close to one another, and interlaced with big branches and with bastions of the same work, all covered with sails; while for the defence of this fortress we brought ashore some small cannon. Nor could we do otherwise, because there is no stone there fit for the purpose, and no means of making trenches and ramparts, the ground being all shifting sand. We landed there our scurvy-stricken men, and for their

vessels were the *Leeuw* (Lion) and the *Leeuwin* (Lioness), commanded respectively by the brothers Cornelis and Frederik de Houtman. Lefort was on board the *Lion*, in the capacity of Treasurer. In a treacherous attack made on the ships at Achin, Cornelis de Houtman lost his life, and Frederik was taken prisoner. The Dutch lost in all sixty-eight men. Lefort was one of the prisoners, but was subsequently sent back with a message from the Achin Raja; and on the opening of the sealed letters containing the appointment in case of death, he was found to be nominated to the command of the expedition. He brought the ships safely home in July 1600. No Dutch account of this voyage exists; but the story is told in a graphic narrative by our great navigator, John Davis, who was pilot to the expedition. According to Davis, Lefort was the son of "a French merchant, dwelling in Seething Lane" (*Davis's Voyages and Works*, Hakl. Soc., Introduction, pp. lxiv, lxv, and pp. 145, 153; also *De opkomst van het Nederlandsch Gezag in Oost Indie*, door Jhr. Mr. J. K. J. de Jonge, 'sGravenhage, 1864). Lefort died at Achin on the 7th March 1603. Spilberg charged him and his crew with conspiracy, and before his death he was removed from his command (Spilberg's voyage, *Rec. des Voy.*, ii, p. 532).

defence sent some that were able-bodied with arquebuses, muskets, and other arms to keep guard night and day. The Hollanders, not having a single sick man, did not wish to take up their quarters on shore, so they only pitched a tent a hundred paces from our fort, with two small cannon mounted for their protection; thither they sent some of their men for the refitting and re-apparelling of their ship, which they set about with all diligence, and in the morning landed and joined our company. After we had settled everything at the fort for the safety of the sick and sound alike, we sent some arquebusiers into the country to reconnoitre. Having advanced a little way within the island, they perceived some natives, who fled for fear of them. In order not to frighten them they did not follow them further, but returned, according to the orders of our General. The inhabitants, thus apprized that there were ships at anchor and strangers on their shores, came down to the number of fifteen or twenty, armed and accoutred in their fashion, bringing only a cow and a ram. Their design was to reconnoitre us and to try us whether we would treat with them freely and frankly, before they would make up their minds to traffic with us. Wherefore, approaching us, they for some time made signs to us, for neither we understood their language, nor they ours; they then turned away with their two beasts, as though they would not barter, although we had shown them many things whereof they seemed to make much account. Incontinently thereafter (having concluded, as may be believed, that we were men of good faith, forasmuch as we had not done them any violence or outrage, and had not even followed them) they came back in a little while, and frankly gave us the cow and the ram, while we gave them some little knives, scissors, and such like implements as they do greatly prize. Thus did we make friends with them, in such wise that, during the remainder of our sojourn there, they came without fail every four days with good store of animals, fowls, milk, honey, and some fruits, amongst others, *pateques*,[1] as large as pumpkins, excellent eating and highly refreshing. They bartered all these for ironware, and little Flemish and French bagatelles of the most trifling value, insomuch that for two counters (*jettons*), or one copper or tin spoon, we got a cow or bull, or three ewes or rams, for they have neither wethers nor oxen, being ignorant of castration. One day it happened that the pilot of the Hollander ship, who had about his neck the silver whistle which he used, advanced among the islanders while trafficking with them. This whistle took their fancy so much, and they became so enamoured of it, that they thought no more of our little trinkets and merchandises, and would not give us their beasts till we gave them this whistle, so were we constrained to sell it piece by piece, for it was hung upon several little chains: and in like manner we had to sell all the other whistles we had on board our ships. Provisions thus became dear, and a cow or bull that had cost us but one or two sols began to go up to eight or nine. Soon after there came toward us one of their people who had not been seen before, and showed us the buckle of one of these chains and a little piece of wood cut round; we understood thereby that he was asking for reals of forty sols, the piece of wood being of that size, roundness, and thickness, but we would not show him any. He knew quite well the value of silver, wherefore we concluded that further inland were peoples more civilised and better educated than the rest.[2] It was strictly forbidden

[1] *Pastèques*, "water-melons". The word, which Pyrard uses again hereafter for the melons of Malabar, is a corruption of the Arabic *al-baṭṭīkh*. See *Littré*, s. v. *Pastèque*. The word had already been introduced by the Moors into the Peninsula, where it survives in the Port. *albudieca* and Catalonian *albudeca*. After the Portuguese conquests it was re-introduced as *pateca*; but both forms have given way to the modern *melancia*. Fryer speaks of *putacho* "melon" at Bombay (*Fryer*, p. 76); see also *Garcia de Orta*, 141*b*.

[2] The real cause was that St. Augustine's Bay had been frequented

among us for any to buy or traffic on his own account, as well Hollanders as French, so that all provisions and refreshments should be held in common. The Hollander ship received a fourth part and paid a fourth; as between our two ships the proportion had been fixed at St. Malo: that is to say, of all purchases the *Corbin* paid two-fifths and the *Croissant* three-fifths, because the latter had the larger crew. We thought we were arrived at this island most seasonably for our own refreshment, for the benefit of the scurvy stricken, and also for the refitting of our ships, that were sorely in need thereof. But the result was quite otherwise, for they almost all died, and none recovered his health; even those that were whole fell sick of a burning fever, with frenzy, whereof they died at the end of two or three days. The disease was contagious, insomuch that a considerable number of the chiefest among us, and those of gentle birth, to the number of forty-one out of the two ships, died there as well of the scurvy as of the fever; and many that were stricken died full soon thereafter on sea. Our captain also fell sick of that disease, whereof he afterwards died at the Maldives, as we shall relate anon. As it was believed that those sick of the fever had contracted it on shore, they were carried aboard, the air there being fresher than on land, while those sick of the scurvy, which is an ailment proceeding from the sea and its fatigues, were carried ashore. We laid our dead to earth, or rather to sand (there being no earth there), in a spot which we named "The Cemetery of the French".[1] We

previously by Portuguese and Dutch ships, *e.g.*, by Houtman's in 1595, on which occasion tin spoons were in greatest request (*Rec. des Voy.*, i, pp. 231, 233).

[1] Orig.: "Nous enterrasmes, ou pour mieux dire nous ensablasmes (n'y ayant point de terre là) nos morts en un lieu que nous nommasmes le cemetiere des François." At and near this bay Houtman lost a number of his men, who were buried at a little island, which was in consequence called the cemetery of the Hollanders (*Rec. des Voy.*, i, pp. 224, 232).

had much difficulty in digging the graves and laying them therein, for all was moving sand, which filled up again at once; we had to use long pieces of wood, which men bore by the two ends, the body being suspended therefrom with ropes, and thus were they laid in the sand. For my part, during the fourteen months of our outward voyage and the twelve months of our homeward voyage, I was, thanks to God, never at all sick, though I was very ill in the Indies.[1] Certainly the place was very unhealthy, situate directly under the tropic of Capricorn, where the sun was close overhead, and beat upon us perpendicularly, at the foot of a high mountain covered with an infinite number of great lizards, though these were nowise hurtful and gave us no trouble. We had been much more harassed by the heat but for our proximity to a great wood which clothed the river banks, where, by day, those that were well enough went to walk and take the air, besides which we had the benefit of bathing in the river and the sea. Moreover, this wood was so full of apes and little monkeys that nowhere could more be seen. It is vastly pleasing to see these little animals playing together and leaping from tree to tree, as do our squirrels here. There was also a marvellous number of birds of all sorts, principally parrots, some having plumage of five or six different hues; and we had great amusement in listening to the varied music of their cries. Many strange fruits were also to be found there, whereof some were good eating, others not so. At that place and all around was nothing but shifting sand; the river water was unwholesome and salt by reason of the tide, but in default of other we were constrained to use it. The heat was so vehement that many of our men got their

[1] This is inconsistent with the author's statement in his Advice (see vol. ii), where he says that he was twice attacked by fever, the first time being on his arrival at St. Laurence on the outward voyage; though it agrees with his remark in ch. vi. The reference to his illness in the Indies is to a bad fever he had at the Maldives (see ch. ix).

feet burned, for all they had shoes and stockings; thence were generated ulcers, very troublesome to heal, which prevented them from walking. Another thing was that the majority of them, unable to govern their appetites after their long fast at sea, glutted themselves beyond measure with fresh meat, which the excessive and violent heat rendered more difficult of digestion. Furthermore, we suffered vast inconvenience by day from the flies, which persecuted us with the utmost fury, and by night from the mosquitos or gnats, which probe the flesh to the blood and cause the place to swell as by the sting of our honey-bees. In broad daylight they are powerless, and retire within the shady coverts of the woods and dwellings; but at night they swarm abroad. They are in such multitudes, and bite so keenly, that it is impossible to exist without covering the hands and face; while to get any sleep, we were constrained to make a fire well charged with smoke and to lie all around. Many of our sick put themselves in closed sacks, leaving but a small hole for breathing. At the Maldives (whereof I shall treat below), where these creatures are a vast nuisance, they use curtains, made on purpose, of a fine web, which these little flies cannot penetrate. This is a common annoyance throughout all the torrid zone.

The island of St. Laurence is of immense size, being more than 700 leagues in circuit—a fact of which I can speak with assurance, having coasted round both sides, as well on my outward as on my homeward voyage. The one end toward the south is under the 26th degree of latitude; that toward the north under the 14th.[1] It is very abundant in animals; the ewes bear three or four lambs at a time, as I learnt by experience, for we killed some that were big with young, and they had that number in their wombs. The tails of rams and ewes are wondrous big and heavy; one we

[1] Cape St. Mary, the southern point, is in latitude 26° S., and Cape Ambar, the northern, in latitude 12° S.

weighed turned twenty-eight pounds. Bulls, cows, rams, and ewes are so numerous all over the island that they are common property, belonging to any that can catch them. The reason is that the natives eat them but little, being, like the rest of the Indians, not flesh-eaters; they lay more account by fish, fruit, and milk diet. You will see there herds of 300 and 400 of these animals together. And while we were there we witnessed a wonderful habit of these bulls and cows: when they would cross from one side to the other of the said river, which is as broad and deep as our Seine, the larger bulls advanced in front, the cows following and placing their heads on the buttocks of the bulls, and the calves placing theirs on the buttocks of their dams; and when there were more cows than bulls, one cow would lean on the buttocks of another, and so they passed over. These oxen have on their necks a big hump of fat, good and delicate eating, and of the same flavour as the sheep's tails. Nevertheless, the flesh of these animals is neither so good eating nor so nourishing as that of ours here. There are vast numbers of monkeys and parrots, whereof we ate so many that betimes we would have as many as fifty or sixty in the pot together: they are as good eating as large pigeons. There is likewise an abundance of poultry, partridges, pheasants, and other kinds of birds. You see there also many chameleons, large lizards (whereof some are as big as a man's thigh), and bats that are bigger than crows. In the river, hard by which we were lodged, were good store of fish, whereof we took an abundant supply; there were also plenty crocodiles, several of which we killed. Herein we observed a remarkable fact, viz., that on killing one or more crocodiles, and cutting them open and gutting them, the entrails cast abroad a most excellent savour and perfumed most sweetly all the air around.[1] By night we set ourselves on

[1] Vincent le Blanc mentions, with reference to a crocodile killed in his presence at Pegu: "It was flead (flayed), and the flesh distributed

the watch to catch them, having by day cast on the sandy bank of the river a quantity of cows' and sheep's entrails; when night was closed in they failed not to come to the carrion, and then we shot them. Sometimes they were only wounded, and escaped; but even then this same odour as of musk hung about the place all the night long.

The people are of an olive and tawny complexion, approaching red; they are tall, straight, and shapely; clever and intelligent. All go naked, saving that they wear a little bit of cotton cloth about the privy parts; they wear their hair long, arranged in tresses and plaits. For arms they use only darts and javelins, called by them *Azagayes*,[1] which they fling with great dexterity; beyond all things they do fear arquebuses, at noise whereof they flee away. The women have a cloth covering them from above the breasts to the waist, and another from the waist to the knees; they keep the head uncovered and shaven of all hair; their bravery and ornaments consist of bracelets of copper, tin, or iron, of which they are very proud. It is said this island was formerly peopled by the Chinese by the means of one of their ships which was wrecked at this place, the crew taking up their abode there. And in truth the people resemble the Chinese much in face, but not in colour, for the Chinese are white and they olive; that, however, comes from their living under the torrid zone and going always naked. The island at the present is thickly peopled, and contains many kings who wage war one with another. Among the inhabitants are some that hold the Mahometan religion and are circumcised; the rest are pagans and Gentiles.

amongst the courtiers, and is as sweet as musk, which occasioned one of our gang to say he thought ambergris proceeded from these creatures" (Eng. trans., p. 115).

[1] As Dozy has pointed out, the word is the Berber *zaghaya*, with the Arabic article prefixed (see Yule and Burnell, *Disc. Gloss.*, s. v.). It is frequently used by the Portuguese writers, but cannot have been a Madagascar word.

While we were at this island, six of our mariners that were carpenters, gunners, and other craftsmen necessary to the ship's service, were debauched by one of their fellows, a Fleming, who bore a grudge against the mate of the *Corbin.* He persuaded them that it was better to quit the ships, where was nought but trouble, labour, and misery for them, and to escape ashore, where, without doubt, they would be welcomed and received by the kings of the country; and they hearkened to him the more readily because he had already been to the Indies. So it was that one night they went forth of our vessels without the knowledge of the rest, taking with them some biscuit, and each his own baggage and an arquebuse furnished with ammunition, with design to return no more.[1] This being discovered the next morning caused us the utmost vexation, seeing how short-handed we were. We also feared lest they should frighten the inhabitants and hinder them from bringing us provisions—as indeed was the case, for they ceased to come for a time. But at length, constrained by necessity, our men returned. Our General received them back and pardoned them by reason of the great need wherein we were; otherwise they had been punished. They told us they were seven days without finding water, enduring much from the pangs of thirst and the excessive heat, whereby they were compelled to drink their own urine; as for eating, they were in no stress, having taken some biscuit, and meeting with game frequently and fruit sometimes. They often saw numbers of the inhabitants with herds of cattle, but these fled away, so that they could not come nigh them. They also said that they had found a number of little huts constructed of canes and reeds, at which they saw nothing but some cotton nets for catching fish, with some common wood in place of cork, and some big shells and

[1] This is but one of many instances that might be given from actual history of "Lotos-eaters" in the tropics; in fiction see, besides Tennyson's poem, a well-known passage in Kingsley's *Westward Ho!*

periwinkles in place of lead; also heaps of fishbones. Sometimes they found trunks of large trees cut and hollowed, wherein was a little rain-water.

Now to return to the story of my voyage. We endured much hardship at this island during the three months we spent there. Our vessels were in grievous plight, the *Croissant* all open, and ours not better at her forepart. We made a new stem for our foremast from a tree of this island. The Hollanders made some masts of several pieces, and after a six weeks' stay took their departure, without losing a single man. For our part we made the greatest haste, but our men were perpetually falling sick, one dying after another; this caused us to prolong our sojourn. Having thus at length refitted our ships we had to take measures for our departure. To this end we made provision of flesh for the two ships, which was not very good, nor well adapted for preserving; but we were obliged to use it. We cut it in very thin and clean slices while yet quite fresh, then salted it forthwith, and put it in the sun to dry, suspended on ropes; the thicker slices would not dry rightly, and worms were engendered therein. All the viands of that country take the salt less readily than those of our country, and for all we could do, they became spoiled; let alone that they are not such good eating. Our vessels being thus ready, refitted and refurnished, we took in wood and water, re-embarked the remainder of our sick and all our goods that were on shore, and prepared to set sail. But forasmuch as we had lost a third part of our company,[1] and the voyage was still but little advanced, we resolved to take some of the inhabitants of the island for our assistance, for we were too feeble and short-handed in comparison of the size of the *Croissant*. For this

[1] He has said above that they lost 41 men at St. Augustine's Bay, so that the combined crews, including those lost at Annobon, must have numbered about 125 men when the ships left St. Malo. The *Croissant*, having three-fifths of the whole complement, thus had a crew of 75 hands; the *Corbin*, about 50.

purpose our General gave order to go at early morning and hide some carbines, pistols, and swords at a certain spot between the place where the poor natives came to meet us, and the place where they were wont to tarry with us trafficking for their cattle and other goods. At the same time he placed some of our men in two several ambuscades hard by, in order that, when they should come at nine or ten o'clock, as was their custom, and according to their promise expressed on the last occasion by signs, seeing us to be without arms, and not mistrusting us at all (for they were then on very friendly terms with us), they should be easily caught by our men, who were to run speedily for the hidden arms, and by those in ambush. This scheme was thus artfully devised, because out of their great fear of firearms they would never approach us when we were armed; and because, notwithstanding all this familiarity with us, they were yet exceeding cunning and suspicious, regarding all our actions and deportment with the utmost care. Thus did we design to give them a sorry farewell and an ill-requital for their service. But God permitted not this perfidy to succeed. They came not on that day at all; whereupon our General changed his plans, and gave order to make ready to sail on the morrow. It was a great mercy for us on board the *Corbin* that we did not take any of these islanders, for had they been with us when we reached the Maldives, as you shall hear anon, they would have had us all put to death for pirates.

On the 15th May 1602 we weighed anchor. But inasmuch as there were amongst us still many sick, including our captain of the *Corbin*, and three persons having already died since we began to set our sails, we therefore resolved to bear away towards the Comorro Islands.

CHAPTER IV.

We touch at the Comorro Islands.—Our sojourn at the road there, and our agreeable refreshment.

On the 23rd of the same month we sighted the Comorro Islands, which are in 12½ degrees of southern latitude, between the island of St. Laurence and the continent of Africa, distant about seventy leagues from Mozembic. They are five in number,[1] each possessing its own king; the one in the midst of the four others is called *Malailli*, at the roadstead of which we cast anchor. On our arrival, our General incontinently sent a boat ashore to reconnoitre, and to see if we could get some refreshment for our sick, who could not recover their health at the island of St. Laurence; on the contrary, after many had died, the soundest of us fell ill. The boat having taken land on this island of Malailli near a village—one of many we saw there lying close to one another, and of considerable size, the houses being of wood covered with palm leaves—our people were well received. Many of the inhabitants came to meet them with all appearance of friendship, bringing them good store of fruits, in exchange for which our men gave them some cheap ironware, and then

[1] There are four principal islands, Comoro, Mohilla (the *Malailli* of the text), Mayotta, and Johanna (or Anzuan). They were well known to the Portuguese in their intercourse with Mozambique. Davis, who visited Mayotta, mentions five, viz., Mayotta, Ansuame, Magliaglie, Saint Christofero, and Spirito Sancto (*Davis's Voyages*, Hakl. Soc., p. 137). Martin speaks of three only, Malailli, Jonani, and Gonarsige. Dr. Fryer gives views of Mayotta, Mohilla, and Johanna, as seen above the horizon. He visited Johanna, and gives a full description (pp. 15-22). Sir Thomas Herbert also counts five, with two lists of the names, viz.: (*a*) Cumro, Meottis, Joanna, Mohelia, and Gazidia; (*b*) John di Castro, Spirito Sancto, Sancto Christofero, Anguzezia, and Mayotto. He gives a full description, especially of Mohilla (*Travels*, pp. 25-30). For an amusing modern description of Joanna, see W. F. W. Owen's *Narrative of Voyages, etc.*, 1833, i, pp. 177-186.

returned to the ships. The next day we sent again to truck with the islanders, but with great diffidence and circumspection, for we feared to be deceived as we were at Anabon. We had two boats, in one of which was the merchandise for trafficking, with the men to conduct it, and some sailors, two of whom went ashore at the place where the islanders brought their goods: the other boat tarried behind, well equipped with arquebusiers and musketeers, to prevent any harm befalling our men on shore. The islanders also bore their arms, viz., alfanges[1] or scimitars, javelins, bows and arrows. In trucking with them we were not obliged to use signs, as at the island of St. Laurence, for there were some that spoke Portuguese. First they asked us who we were, and we replying that we were French, they asked us if we were friends and allies of the Portuguese. When one of our people said yes, they retorted that we should have gone and anchored at Mozembic. We continued to traffic with them every day in like manner. Three or four days after, they told us we had not quitted us of our duty: that it was customary when a foreign ship arrived at the road of these islands to go and salute the king of the island, who dwelt two leagues inland, with a fair present. Our General, who was in the boat with the soldiers, made answer that he should be held excused, because he knew not the customs of the country, nor that the king dwelt in that island, and that he would give satisfaction in this matter on the following day. Soon after, the General came on board the *Corbin* to visit our captain, who was very sick, and caused to be got ready the present for the king, viz., a pretty piece of gilded glass of Venetian work, and some other little things. So, on the morrow, our General went ashore with his boat to the place where the islanders were assembled; there, after mutual salutations, they were greatly pleased with the present, and offered to conduct those that should land to bear

[1] "Cutlasses", from Arab. *al-khandjar* (Dozy).

the present to the king. But our General, saying that he would send two of our men, demanded two of theirs for hostages. They then began to consult together, and afterwards made answer, that their people were unwilling to enter our boats, being men ignorant of the world; and that he should not fear to land with all assurance, for that they would pledge their word and honour we should incur no damage or incivility. We, who had been once deceived at Anabon out of too much confidence, were careful not to be taken in a second time, so we replied that we would not send our men unless they gave us the hostages. But they added that if none of our men would go and salute the king, at least we might deliver them the present, and that they would salute the king on the General's behalf. To which he replied, that unless he or one of his men should go, he was not minded to send the present, which perchance might be lost and never delivered to the king. This matter did not, however, interrupt our traffic, which was continued as before, each party keeping their guard. I know not why they acted thus, whether their intentions were good or evil, but I know full well that among all the peoples of India there is but little confidence, whether their religion or the humour of the country be the cause, and it is all the same whether they be Mahometans or Gentiles. None of them have any faith, nor respect for aught but profit, taking from those who will give them most; friends now with one party, now with another: even the Chinese are much the same. I know, too, that the Portuguese throughout all the East Indies give counsel to the peoples with whom they are in alliance or friendship, and even earnestly solicit them to do and practise all manner of treachery and surprises upon the ships of the French, English, and Hollanders, and go as far as to promise them recompense for such conduct: so that I would not trust myself in the hands of any of these nations, whether they were allies of the Portuguese or not, unless I had first made an alliance and treaty with the latter; and even then it were better not to have too much confidence, and ever to keep on one's guard with discretion. Now to return to the islands of Comorro. The inhabitants hold the Mahometan religion, for during our traffic with them they told us on a Thursday that the morrow was their feast-day, and that they could not give their minds to merchandise on that day, but would return on the Saturday: this I afterwards found to be the same in the Indies. They are a mixture of several races, as well from the coast of Ethiopia, Caffres, and even Mulattos, as Arabs and Persians; they are also great friends of the Portuguese. I leave you to imagine whether they be wanting in intelligence, counsel, and cunning. I heard afterwards, in the Indies, that they made a design to surprise an English ship that was at anchor in their road. They had become so familiar with the English that they went freely to and fro one with another, and very often budged not from the ship-board for their meals, and sometimes slept there. One night, seeing that they were not suspected, they designed to make themselves masters of the ship, and after waiting till the English were all asleep, they slew twelve or fifteen of them, and would have quite attained their end, had not the rest awakened in time and defended themselves valiantly, and slain a number of these islanders; the remainder escaped by swimming.[1] See how little trust can be placed in these

[1] The ship referred to is probably the *Union*, Captain Rowles, which sailed with the *Ascension*, Captain Sharpeigh, in 1608. The two ships parted in a storm after rounding the Cape early in 1609. The *Union* called at St. Augustine's Bay in Madagascar, and at Comorro, in hopes of finding her consort. Samuel Bradshaw, whose account of the *Union's* voyage is the only one we possess, mentions this attempt made upon her by the natives, but not in the same detail as Pyrard. The incidents mentioned in the text were probably given to Pyrard by Richard Wickham, the merchant of the *Union*, who was afterwards kidnapped near Zanzibar and carried to Goa, where Pyrard met him; he returned to Europe in the same fleet (see vol. ii). See Bradshaw's letter in *Purchas*,

peoples. While we were at this road, and the traffic in fruits continued in the customary manner, our mariners desired to go and make provision of water at the other side of the island, near another village apart from that with which we had been trafficking, because the place seemed convenient for drawing a large quantity. But the inhabitants of that village, who had not been made aware of our arrival, and had drawn no profit therefrom, when our men landed there, assembled all together in arms, and hindered them from taking the water, saying that they would not allow them unless they should give them money: so that our men were constrained to return back empty-handed. Our General hearing this, and not willing to use any violence (the better course, seeing how short-handed we were), gave some money to the mariners to go back withal, and pay the natives. They did so, and on payment of about five or six crowns we were permitted to take as much water as we wanted. These islands are very fertile in fruits; very big bitter oranges and small sweet oranges, citrons of two sorts, cocos, bananas, honey, betel, and rice, which when cooked is of a violet colour. Every day we were at anchor there we bought three or four boat-loads for the most trifling price—to wit, some little ironware and other Flemish bagatelles. Flesh is not so plentiful, for they sell it as dear as in this country, or more so; they have, however, good store of cattle, such as oxen, cows, goats, and sheep. These latter do not resemble those of the island of St. Laurence, because they have the tail large and broad, but not round, and are liker the Barbary

ii, 232-4; *Cal. State Papers, E. I.*, vol. i, p. 639; references to the *Union* in *Lancaster's Voyages*, Hakl. Soc. The *Union* pursued her voyage from Zanzibar to Socotra, thence to Achin and Priaman. On her return she met Middleton at St. Augustine's Bay in 1610. According to the journal of that voyage (*Lanc. Voy.*, p. 147), the *Union* had lost her captain and chief merchants "at *Conggomare*, in the north-east part of the Island of St. Laurence". She was ultimately abandoned near Morlaix in Brittany (*Purchas*, ii, pp. 234-5).

sheep. There is also good store of poultry, partridges, turtle-doves, pigeons, and other birds. I did not learn that these islands had other wealth than that of fruits, wherewith they lade their barques, all made of the coco tree, in the fashion of those of the Maldives, which I shall describe hereafter, and convey the same to Mozembic, a distance of only seventy leagues, getting in exchange what they require, such as cotton, cotton cloth, gold, ivory, and such like things. The Portuguese of Mozembic likewise come and traffic there. These islands are of the utmost convenience to Mozembic and to the Portuguese who dwell there, for the supply of provisions, because the country all around there is exceeding poor and sterile. I also learnt in India from all who had been or resided there that living was very dear.

All the refreshments bought by our people were in the name of the General and at the expense of the ships: the fruits were then divided equally among all; nor was any permitted to traffic on his own account, save that towards the end our General gave permission to everyone to buy for himself what each would, for the space of two days only. But I must not omit to notice a rare sight observed by us. Being in a boat a league from shore, and returning to our vessels that were in the road, we saw appear on the surface of the water a fish of monstrous shape. We only saw the head, which resembled a man's in shape and size, at the chin a kind of beard like a fish's fins, and the head somewhat long and pointed, and covered with scales. But when we would approach it nearer, it plunged its head into the depths of the sea, giving us only a glimpse of its back, which was scaly, and appeared no more.[1]

[1] Probably a dugong or a manatee, one of which animals was also seen here by Sir Thomas Herbert, and described by him (*Travels*, p. 26). Mocquet (1645, p. 231) gives a very fanciful description, representing the animal with its back erect as a pillar, having a shield before its head and a saddle on its back, and making a horrible noise as it passed the ship.

We remained at the road of these islands for the space of fifteen days, and the utility and comfort to us of this sojourn is past belief. All our scurvy patients recovered their health, and the others got an alleviation of their ailments, as well by aid of the good air as of the good water and fruit. I have remarked that for this malady of scurvy, which is so frequent at sea, there is no better or more certain cure than citrons and oranges and their juice: and after using it once successfully everyone makes provision of it to serve him when in need. At length we set sail, the 7th of June 1602.

The 21st of the same month we repassed the equinoctial line toward the North or Arctic Pole; but I remarked nothing more than I have already described of my first crossing, except, however, that we did not fall in with so many calms or *travades*, nor experienced such hardships as we had encountered on the coast of Guinea.

CHAPTER V.

Pitiable wreck of the ship "Corbin", wherein the author was, on the reefs of the Maldives.—How the men were saved at an island with much trouble, and the miseries endured by them.

What I have said of the discomforts and troubles of our voyage up to this point is as nothing compared with what happened after. I shall now describe misery, the greatest that can be imagined, and I am assured there are none in reading it but will deplore an event so sad and lamentable, which ruined and completely overpowered us. This is how it happened.

The first day of July 1602, being 5° N. of the line, with fine weather, neither too calm nor too much wind, we perceived at break of day that the *Croissant* had lost her big boat, which she had towed from St. Laurence, where it had been made use of as a pinnace.[1] It had been arranged at St. Malo, between our commander and the Merchant Company, that we should build a pinnace at the first land we touched on the other side of the Cape of Good Hope, and for this purpose we had brought all suitable timber, a mast and ropes, ready prepared, and requiring only to be put together. It is very necessary on long voyages to have a pinnace to reconnoitre with in unknown places, to land with on occasion, and to enter rivers where a big ship cannot or dare not venture. I mention particularly the loss of the boat used as a pinnace, and our want of the latter, for with it the *Croissant* might have saved our men. Soon after, we sighted at a distance great reefs, which surrounded a number of small islands, amid which we perceived a little sail. We approached our General, and let him know that we no longer saw the boat. But we were told that in the past night it had been filled by a heavy sea, and had broken the tow-rope and had gone to the bottom. After this our mate, who alone spoke on these occasions (the captain and lieutenant being both ill, and our English pilot speaking no French), asked what islands they were we saw. The General and his pilot replied that they were called the islands *de Diego de Roys*.[2] In truth,

[1] "Le 1 jour de Juillet 1602 ayãt cinq degrez d'eleuation, la nuict il fit un orage lequel emplit d'eau nostre gallion qui estoit attaché au derriere de nostre vaisseau ce qui nous retarda fort longtemps ; desirant le sauuer nous abbaissasmes les voiles. Au point du jour nous eusmes la veuë de plusieurs bancs et Isles qui s'appellent les Maldives, ceste perte neãtmoins, fut cause de nous sauuer la vie : laquelle sans miracle nous eussions perduë : si de nuict nous fussions arriuez en lieu si dangereux, duquel nous pensions estre esloignez de quatre vingts lieuës" (*Martin*, p. 45).

[2] There is much confusion as to these *de Roys* islands. In Gastaldi's map of 1561 will be found a group of islands to the south-west of the Maldives, and near them : they are marked "Y^e^ desabitate". There can be little doubt that these are intended for the Chagos. Subsequent maps pushed the group further north, and fixed them on the equator,

we had left the *de Roys* Islands four and twenty leagues behind us in the west. There was great dispute between those of the *Croissant* and ourselves as to these islands and reefs; for our captain, pilot, mate, and second mate held that they were the Maldives, and that we must take care: the General and his pilot thought otherwise. We saw little boats, which seemed willing to approach and pilot us—as, indeed, I afterwards learnt from the natives was the case; but our General would not wait, and imprudently took no notice of them. All day passed in this discussion; we continued our course, keeping near each other till the evening, when our ship went down the wind to bid the General good-night, and to get his orders for the night. Then our mate asked if the passage was open, and the General said it was, and that he was certain they were the de Roys Islands, and no other; nevertheless, as these were unknown parts, and for fear lest there should be other rocks or reefs before us, the best thing was to put about after dark in the opposite course, and sail towards the west until midnight, and after midnight to tack about and get the ship to her previous position, running east to arrive by daybreak where we then

in long. 70° E., and gave them the names of Diego de Roys, de Royz, de Ruiz, or de Rais. The Chagos, being found to be further south, were entered independently. These mythical islands, no doubt, were duly entered in the charts of the *Croissant*. The island of Diego Rodriguez is in lat. 19° 40′ S., long. 60° 45′ E., a long way off; and its name was certainly corrupted into *de Roys*, as Davis (*Voy.*, p. 165) and Mandelslo (p. 246) so use it. How this name got to be used for islands supposed to be near the Maldives is difficult to imagine: there may have been some confusion with *Diego Garcia*, the southernmost of the Chagos, or possibly with *Garayos*, the name of some shoals to the east of Madagascar. However these supposed islands got their names, they maintained their position upon the equator in long. 70′ E. in the maps of Speed (1626), of Hondius (1636), Visscher (1657), Seller (1678), De l'Isle (1723), Vaugondy (1751), and lastly, in Wyld's atlas of 1828. The survey of the Maldives and Chagos by Moresby, soon after this put an end to their existence. The pilot of the *Croissant* was not so far out, if only the islands had been there.

were, or a little further on, so that we should not make any more way in the night, and get lost before we knew where we were. At nightfall we obeyed the orders of the General. The captain, who was very ill, charged me to warn the mate and second mate to keep a good look-out (*bon cart*, as the watch is called which is kept by the mariners every night, each in his turn, as by sentinels), for in his opinion we were in a dangerous part of the Maldives, notwithstanding the opinion of the pilot of the *Croissant*.

Our General intended to pass by the north of these islands, between the head of them and the coast of India; but, on the contrary, we were running right into the midst of them, to our peril. The pilots said they would be careful; for all who have the duty of navigation in those parts must cautiously avoid the dangerous banks and reefs from a hundred leagues off, if he can, otherwise there is great risk in passing through these islands without losing your ship. But misfortune was pressing close upon us, and notwithstanding the foresight of our captain, who could not set right the others' ignorance, that which had not happened once during the voyage now came to pass, viz., everyone was fast asleep that night, even those on watch. The mate and second mate had been carousing, and were drunk. The light usually kept on the poop for reading the compass was out, because the man at the wheel, who had charge of the light and the hour-glass, had fallen asleep, as had also the ship's boy that attended him; for it is customary for the man at the helm always to have a ship's boy by him. What was worse, the ship was steered to the east half-an-hour, or three-quarters at most, too soon. So, while we were thus all asleep, the ship struck heavily twice, and as we started with the shock, she suddenly struck a third time, and heeled over. I leave you to imagine the condition of all on board,—what a pitiful spectacle we presented,—the cries and lamentations of men who find themselves wrecked at night on a rock in mid-ocean, and await a certain death. Some wept and cried with all their might; others took to prayers; others confessed to each other; and far from having a captain to command and encourage us, we had one that aggravated our sorrows. For it was a month and more since he had left his bed; but the fear of death caused him incontinently to rise in his shirt, and, feeble as he was, fall a-crying among us. The ship having half-heeled over, we cut the masts to prevent her going quite over, and then fired a cannon-shot to warn the *Croissant* to keep back. But she was in no danger, as she was well behind us, and was keeping a good look-out. We all thought that the ship must go to the bottom, as we could see nothing but heavy waves going over us; and that, in fact, must have happened if we had struck upon a rock. About three-quarters of an hour after, dawn appeared, and we sighted some islands at not more than five or six leagues distance beyond the reefs, and the *Croissant* quite close to us, but unable to succour us.[1] Our ship remained firm on her side, and being on a reef, could still hold together for a while; for had it been on sand, she must have heeled over altogether, and we should have been drowned to a man. This gave us some consolation, and the courage to endeavour to save our lives and to get to land, although in our present plight there was but little hope of that, seeing what a dis-

[1] "Le 2 jour de Juillet 1602 à l'aube du jour nous vismes le Corbin esloigné d'un quart de lieuë de nous qui auoit perdu son grand mast, incontinent apres au point du jour nous visines qu'il estoit eschoué sur le banc, la Mer passant par dessus le corps du Navire, il avoit encore son mast de mizene, et sa voile haute, lequel tomba peu de tẽps apres; ce nous fut un fort piteux spectacle voir nos compagnons perir sans leur pouuoir ayder, et ne sçauions que esperer de nous, estant encores si proches d'une infinité d'Isles et de bancs, que nous craignions ne pouuions doubler, le vent nous estant plus contraire que fauorable, de façon que nous estions en grand angoisse; sur les deux heures nous apperçeusmes un batteau à la voile entre les Isles et les bancs qui alloit vers les lieux ou s'estoit perdu le Corbin. Nous auions de hauteur 5 degrez trois quarts" (*Martin*, pp. 45, 46).

tance the land was off: and even then we ran the risk of being denied a landing, or of being killed by the natives. We then bethought us to prepare some craft to carry us, as we could no longer expect to get out the galion[1] or the boat. We took spars, rods, and those stout beams called *antennes*, which are at each side of ships, and are useful for spars and rods when occasion demands. And because they are only for use in case of need, they have this name *antennes;* but being in the shape of spars and rods, they are called *materaux, ou verges de beille,*—that is, extra.[2] These we bound together in the manner of a large hurdle, and on to that we nailed a number of planks and boards brought up from below. This kind of raft is called a *panguaye.*[3] This

[1] The use of the word *galion* for a boat carried by a ship is unusual. A *galion* was a mixture of the "round" and the "long" form of vessel. The former was for sails, the latter for oars; the *galion* was for oars and sails; and whereas the proportion of breadth to length in a round ship was 1 to 3, in a *galion* it was 1 to 4 or 5. The name got applied to larger ships of this build, which never used oars. When small, they generally carried three lateen sails (Jal). The *Corbin's* jolly-boat was probably of this build and rig.

[2] *Antenna*, the classical Latin for "yard", has passed into all the Romance languages, but in these, confined to yards of the latin, or, as we say, lateen rig. Such a yard is swung not at its middle, but considerably towards one end. According to M. Rivara, the word *antenna* is used among the Portuguese in the same sense as here; but formerly only for the yards in actual use (Rivara's *Pyr.*, i, 45). There is of course no connection between the word and the sense of spare or extra spars.

[3] As Rivara points out, Pyrard mistakes the use of the word *panguaye*, or, as the Portuguese write it, *pangaio*, which was a small sailing canoe: "hũa pequena embarcação composta de taboas unidas e atadas com cordas, sem prego algum" (Bluteau). Rivara says the word is still used in Portuguese India and Africa for a two-masted barque with lateen sails. It is mentioned in *Lancaster's Voyages* (Hakl. Soc., pp. 5, 6, and 26), where it is described as being like a barge with one mat sail of coco-nut leaves. "The barge is sowed together with the rindes of trees and pinned with wooden pinnes." See also *Alb. Comm.*, Hakl. Soc., iii, p. 60, *note;* and Dr. Burnell's note to *Linschoten*, Hakl. Soc., i, p. 32, where it appears that the word is used so early as 1505, in Dom

was sufficient to carry us all easily, and to save a large quantity of baggage and merchandise to boot. We were working at this raft or *panguaye* all hands, and with all our power, from daybreak until two or three hours after noon; but our labour was all in vain, as it was impossible to get it over the reef and afloat. This made us lose all courage and hope; besides, as I have said, there seemed no chance of getting the galion, which was well forward in the ship below the second deck, and all the masts were cut, and there was no means of fixing a pulley to raise it withal; moreover, the sea was so heavy and stormy that the waves and swell (*louesme*) were going right over the ship to the depth of a pike and more, and we were every moment in danger of having them over us. In addition to this, the sea was so tempestuous (for we saw the waves break for more than two miles distance, with a horrible noise, over the reefs and rocks) that the galion could not have resisted its violence.

Such being our condition, we perceived a boat approaching us from the island, as if to reconnoitre, but it did not come within half a league of us. When we saw it, the best swimmer among us threw himself into the water and made for her, begging the men in her by all manner of signs and cries to come to our aid; but they would do nothing for all his efforts, so that he was constrained at his peril to return. We could not imagine the reason for this inhumanity and barbarism. But I afterwards found that all persons were strictly prohibited from boarding or approaching a wrecked ship,[1] except by command of the king or by leave of the nearest king's officers, who in such case are allowed to save the men, giving information at once to the king. For the rest, I could not sufficiently wonder that, in the midst of our misery, many

Manoel's letter. What Pyrard probably means is *jangada*, the word for raft, which the Portuguese borrowed from the Malayālam *sangāḍa* (see *Linsch.*, Hakl. Soc., ii, p. 181).

[1] *E.g.*, the case of the Ceylon ship, in ch. xxi.

of the sailors and mariners ceased not to drink and eat, and to consume the ship's victuals even beyond the necessities of nature, saying to the others of us who remonstrated, that we were all as good as lost, and that they preferred to die in that fashion. Then they swore and fought, and some broke open the chests of others whom they saw at their prayers (having ceased to think more of the things of this world), and no longer acknowledged their captain, making no more account of him than of their comrades, and saying that, as the voyage was at an end, they were no longer bound to obey him. I was horrified at this; and I make bold to say that seamen of this temper, of whom I have seen but too many, leave their souls and conscience on land, so irreligious, demoralised, and insolent have I seen them to be.

To return to my story. Though we despaired of our lives, we made an attempt to get out the galion, at which we worked our best, as we had done at the raft in the morning. Having got it out with vast trouble, we all did our best to equip it and put it to rights, all broken as it was by the waves; but darkness came on before it was quite ready, and we remained the following night on board in our evil plight, and amid great distress and danger, the ship being very full of water, while the waves frequently passed over our heads and drenched us again and again.

Next day, the 3rd July 1602, in the morning, we got the galion over the reefs with great trouble and risk, ourselves swimming the while. This done, we all got on board, taking with us swords, arquebuses, and small pikes, and pulled towards the islands. Our galion, being heavily laden, made much water, and almost capsized several times by the violence of the winds and waves. At last, after much fatigue, we got ashore at one of the islands called *Pouladou*.[1]

[1] *Fuladu* (in the Admiralty Chart wrongly spelt *Furudu*), in Goidu or Horsburgh atoll, lat. 4° 54′ N. This atoll is a small one immediately

As soon as we reached the shore, the natives who were waiting for us would not permit us to land till we were first disarmed by them. So we having surrendered at discretion to the islanders, they permitted us to land and then pulled up our galion, and took out of it the rudder, masts, and other things necessary for its equipment, and sent them all to the neighbouring islands, whither also they pulled all the boats of their own island, leaving not a single one behind. I perceived from this first view that they were a spirited and quick-witted race. As their island was small (not a league in circumference), and its inhabitants numbered only twenty or twenty-five, they had to fear the arrival with arms of a greater number than themselves, lest we should make ourselves masters of their island and escape by aid of their boats, which would have been easy enough had we known their weakness; but, as I have said, they took the right measures.

On our disembarking we were all led to a building in the middle of the island, where they gave us some fruit, coconuts, and limes. Thither, too, came the lord of the island, called *Ybrahim* and *Pouladouquilague*,[1] who appeared to be of great age. He knew some words of Portuguese, by means of which he put many questions to us; after which his people

to the south of Malosmadolu atoll, and in the division of the atolls for administrative purposes deemed part of it. This explains Pyrard's remark below (ch. x), that he was wrecked on Malosmadolu atoll.

[1] "Lord of Pouladou." The word *quilague* must not be confounded with *calogue*. Quilague, or, more properly, *Kilagé*, has the sense of suzerainty, and is used (i) by itself, meaning the regent of the kingdom (see ch. xv and xviii); (ii) in *renequilague*, "queen", and appended to the name of a queen, as *Manaye quilague* (ch. xviii); (iii) to lords of islands, as here. The word, as will be seen, is common to both genders. *Calogue*, on the other hand, merely implies that the person is of gentle birth, and is used after proper names; in the Vocabulary (vol. ii), Pyrard gives the feminine *camulogue*. The distinction may perhaps be observed even in Ibn Batuta, who calls the grand vizier *Calaky*, and the cadi *Fandayarkâloû* (*Ibn Bat.*, iv, p. 133).

searched us and took away everything we carried, saying that all that appertained to the king, after a ship was wrecked. This lord of the island was a great lord, and, as I afterwards learnt, nearly related to the Christian king of the Maldives, who is at Goa.[1] Seeing that we had a piece of scarlet, he asked us what that was. We replied that we had brought it to present to the king; and although all that was in the ship was his, yet was that brought to be presented to him whole and nnspoiled by the sea water. As soon as they heard that it was for the king, not a man of them dared to take it or touch it, or even to look at it.[2] We were, nevertheless, minded to cut off a piece, about two or three ells, for a present to the lord of the island, in hopes that we should be the better treated. He took it, and thanked us with effusive gratitude, but made us promise not to tell any-one, otherwise he would rather have died than taken it. Soon after, hearing that some officers of the king were coming, he changed his mind, and brought it back, begging us not to tell that he had so much as handled it. For all that, the king heard of it at least six months later, and was wroth against him, and would have sent for him, had he not been then in the last stage of a disease, whereof he died at the age of seventy-five years.

When we had been in this building for the space of a day they took our mate and two sailors away to the king, forty leagues off, in another island, called *Malé*, which is the capital island (all the others being dependencies of it); and there the king resides. Our mate took with him the piece of scarlet and presented it to the king, and was well received, being lodged within the palace. However, this was done

[1] As to the Christian kings of the Maldives, see the text *passim*, and Appendix B.

[2] Mr. Bell, in 1879, took as a present to the Sultan forty yards of red silk, which was highly appreciated, and could not be touched by any inferior person with impunity. In South Sea phrase, it was "tabu".

not so much by way of favour or honour, as to secure his person; for afterwards I came to understand the general distrust.

The king soon sent his brother-in-law with a goodly number of soldiers in barques to go to our wreck and get from it all he could. This was the brother of the chief queen, and was entitled *Ranabandery Tacourou*,[1] his own name being Mouhamede. When he came to the island *Pouladou*, where we were, we were treated better on the occasion of his arrival, and were taken often to the ship to help in getting out the merchandise, baggage, and all the wearing apparel. But they laughed at the advice we gave them, for they knew better than we. As it was impossible for the boats to go over the reef, they fastened a cable to the ship, while the other end was lashed to a big rock of the reef; and so, by holding on to this rope with one hand, we could go and come over the reef to the ship in safety; while so doing, the waves only passed over our heads, and could not overthrow us nor carry us off. For the rest, they had a very pretty contrivance for getting off the cannon and other heavy things, although these were all in the hold, as I shall tell in the proper place.[2]

[1] *Ranabandery*, probably the same as *Ransbandery*, in ch. xv, where it is explained as "Treasurer". *Rana* or *rans* = Sin. *ran*, gold; *bandery* = *bender* or *bandhāra*, treasury; *cf.* Skt. *bhāṇḍārin*, a steward or treasurer; Jav. *Bendárá* and Malay *Bandahāra*, the title of one of the higher ministers in the Malay states. *Takourou* must be Skt. *ṭhakkura*, "an idol, a deity", Hindi. *ṭhākur*, "lord, master". In Pyrard's time it was used only for the greatest lords; in later days it was conferred upon persons of inferior rank, provided they were of good birth. Thus we find it borne by a pilot in 1682 (see *J. Geog. Soc.*, ii, 76). Mr. Bell states that "many persons of respectable birth receive from the Sultan the titular rank of *Takuru-fánu*". He compares with it the common Kandyan name *Tikiri*. He adds that Takuru-fánu is nowadays not so respected a title as *Maniku-fánu* (*Report*, p. 63). As we shall see hereafter, this Ranabaḍéri Takuru-fánu (his correct title) succeeded to the throne after the death of Sultan Ibrahim.

[2] See below, ch. x.

So for several days they got out our merchandise and took it away to the king; but before that, the king's brother-in-law, by virtue of his commission, separated us one from another, and distributed some of us among the surrounding islands (the greater number remaining at *Pouladou*), and on his return took with him our captain, ill as he was, and five or six others. He was presented to the king, and was well received. The king promised to get a ship ready to carry him to Achen, in the island of Sumatra, whither our General had gone; and I know not but he might have kept his word. Our captain, however, died at Malé, the residence of the king, about six or seven weeks after.[1] In all expeditions to the ship they took some one of us in the same way. As for me, the king's brother-in-law, in separating us, took me away from those at *Pouladou*, and put me with two others on a little island called *Paindoüé*[2] (distant from *Pouladou* a league only), where there were no more people than in the other. Here my two companions and I were well received from the very first, and, thanks to the lord who brought us, we had a sufficiency of food.

[1] That is, in the middle of August 1602. M. Manet is, therefore, in error in giving the 10th June 1603 as the date of Grout's death (Manet, *Biographie des Malouins célèbres*, p. 86).

[2] *Fendu*, or *Fehendú*, a small island next to *Fuladu*, in Horsburgh atoll.

CHAPTER VI.

What happened to the men who were saved from the "Corbin", and the miseries they endured.

I have related in detail, as far as I have been able, the circumstances of our shipwreck and our misfortunes down to our reaching land, when it appeared that we had escaped the dangers of the sea; but those I have now to tell of were no less. Bad luck, when long continued, ends in bad health: so those who were rescued from the midst of waves and floods found no alleviation of their ills on land. We numbered about forty persons. Hear now what followed.

While we were still on board, we bethought us to get out all the silver we had, and all our most precious merchandise, and to take on shore most of it, to the end that we might be recognised as good merchants, and not pirates and robbers, and so might get a more favourable reception. This was our captain's advice; but we could not get at any of it, as it was in the *soutes* (which are close-fastened bunkers where the merchandise and victuals are stowed), and right at the ship's bottom, where the sea was so deep that it was all we could do to hold on to the ship's sides. So it remained in the ship with the rest of the merchandise, and in default we took what remained of the silver belonging to the ship's crew, which amounted to about 500 crowns, and what individuals had brought in their chests, which amounted to another 500 crowns. All this was secreted in the men's waistbands. Most of us had these waistbands, but others not, for there were not enough for all. This was not for a present to the king, which it might have been, had we been able to bring away all the silver, but to meet the necessities of us all. Nevertheless, the event showed that it became the occasion of the greatest trouble, and those who took the money turned out the greatest sufferers. The first night we spent at *Pouladou* we buried this silver, for fear lest we should be searched and it be found upon us, and we resolved not to unearth it except for the needs of the whole body. But at length, when our comrades who were left at *Pouladou* found that they got nothing to eat and were dying of hunger, they were constrained to unearth it and offer money for food, and the people indeed gave them food for the silver. The mischief was that the smallest piece of money they had was the twenty sols piece of Spanish money, and the islanders, seeing our men's ignorance, never gave them any change: so that for a thing of the value of two *liars*[1] they had to give one of these pieces, so that at this rate for five or six pieces a man sometimes hardly got a meal. Had our men had the cunning to do as they use at the islands and all over India (where money of every kind and mint is accepted so long as it is of good metal)—that is, to clip it in small pieces, and then to weigh it out when required—their silver would have lasted them much longer. But, as I said, for the smallest commodity they gave a whole piece. So by this waste the silver lasted but a little while to most of those who had it; and to them the natives would give nothing except for money, so they endured all manner of discomforts. Others who had more (for it was not given in equal shares, but handed to individuals for the common use) hid it from their comrades and did not in any way assist them. From this cause many died of hunger, getting no help either from the islanders or even from their fellows, and this was deplorable indeed. On the other hand, those who had money, and who by this means could obtain food, filled their bellies without discretion; and being in a country where the air is very unhealthy for all strangers, even for those of a similar climate,

[1] *Liard*, "petite monnaie de cuivre qui valait trois deniers, le quart d'un sou, et un peu plus qu'un centime" (*Littré*). Its etymology is uncertain. Tavernier says that the Indian *pecha* ("pice") was worth "about two of our liards" (Eng. trans., pt. ii, p. 22).

they fell ill, and died one after another; nay more, in place of receiving aid and consolation from their fellows, those who were without money and in great need came and stripped them, and took their money before they were dead; and for that which was found upon the dead, the healthy who survived fought one with another who should have it, and banded themselves two against two, and finally messmate against messmate,[1] with so little charity, that they would see their comrades and fellow countrymen die before their eyes without giving them any assistance or succour. I have never seen a sight so pitiable and deplorable.

As for me, I was taken by the king's brother-in-law, as I have said above, to the island *Paindoüé*, with two others. We had not taken belts of money, and had nothing in the world. This caused us some trouble at first, but by-and-bye we found we were better off for having nothing. The others who had money were better supplied for a short time, but afterwards experienced the greatest hardships. At first the natives of *Paindoüé* gave us some food, little by little; but when they saw that our companions in the other islands had so much money, and spent it so profusely, they resolved to give us no more subsistence, being concerned that our arrival had brought no profit to their island, as to the others. So, in order to try us whether by extremity of hunger we should not be constrained to give them some of that which they believed we had concealed, they betook them with their boats to the island of *Pouladou*, to sell to our companions their fowls, fish, fruit, and other provisions. This, however, was in secret, for they are strictly prohibited from selling anything to strangers saved from shipwreck, and from taking money or merchandise of them, as all that belongs to the king when once the ship is wrecked (they may, however, give them provisions, and treat them with such humanity as seems good to them): and, in fact, some time after, a strict inquiry was made of those

[1] See p. 25, *note*.

who had taken anything—as I shall tell hereafter. By this conspiracy of the islanders against us, which was to give us nothing more, my two companions and I were reduced to the most terrible straits imaginable. All we could do was to seek for the sea-slugs[1] on the sand, and to eat them; and sometimes perchance we found a dead fish cast up by the sea, which we boiled with divers sorts of herbs unknown to us, salting our food with a little sea water; and if by chance we got hold of a lime we put it in, and days passed sometimes ere we got any such thing. We were in this extremity a good while, until the natives, concluding that we had no money, and having, as may be believed, some pity in them, began to be less shy and barbarous; for before, most of them, and all the women and children, hid themselves from us, fleeing us as though we were monsters, and did not allow us to enter their villages or their houses. They even used us to terrify and frighten their little children withal. At length, discovering that they were becoming less distant towards us day by day, we began to accost them and to offer our services for any job in which they would employ us, which services they accepted. They often took me in their boats to sea and to the neighbouring islands to help them in getting coco-nuts and in fishing, in return for which they gave me a share of fish at the fishing, and coco-nuts, rice, millet, and honey for other work. My companions did their best to win something in the same way, for they took me only to the fishing—for what reason I know not—and then we brought all we got into a common stock and lived on it. Thus were we brought so low, that for fish and coco-nuts we were fain to do the most vile handiwork and the most painful labour—in a word, work which slaves would not or could not do. All this was without force or compulsion: we went ourselves and begged them to employ us; otherwise we should have died of hunger, for they would give us nothing unless we worked for

[1] *I.e.*, *bêche de mer* (M. *ihi*).

it, and then so little, that we were but ill-sustained by what we got; for they fish only in calm weather, their sails being composed of coco-fibre, which they wish not to spoil[1]; and their bodies being naked while at this exercise, they fear the rain, and when they are having a day's fishing they do not return sometimes for eight hours or more. Such was our condition as regards food. As for lodging, during rain by day and for sleep by night we retired to a wooden hut on the sea-shore, which had been put up a while ago for building a boat. We had thus sufficient cover overhead; but at the sides all was open. As it was then winter there—that is, during the months of July and August, when the rains are continuous and heavy—I leave you to imagine the distress we suffered from the wind, the rain, and sometimes the big waves, which were only ten paces off our hut. Owing to these great and grievous discomforts my two companions fell ill. As for me, thanks to God, not having been ill during all our voyage, I held out for a good while.

While I was thus working for my living I was obliged to learn the language of the country as well as I could, though my companions despised it, saying there was no need to learn the language peculiar to these islands, for that they hoped to be sent at length to Sumatra to the General, as the king had promised our captain, and as the islanders told us. I did not despair; but the fear I had that this would not come to pass made me resort to every expedient. I saw, too, the misery in which we were, and I essayed to learn the language to serve my purposes, and got great assistance from it. With this purpose in my mind, an occasion presented itself of learning the language quickly and easily: for the lord of the island *Paindoüé*, where we three were, called *Aly Pandio Atacourou*,[2] who was a great chief and a relative

[1] Mr. Bell says this is literally true of their fishing-boats (*mas-oḍi*) at the present day.

[2] *I.e.*, Ali, lord of Pandio, or Paindoüé (now *Fehendú*). *Atacourou* is a misprint for *Tacourou*. It would now be written *Ali Takuru-fánu*.

of the king through his wife, seeing that I was trying to learn their language, thought more highly of me, and took a liking to me: and in truth I did my best to make myself agreeable to him and his wife, and to all the people of the island, by obeying them in all things. He was a man of great honour and courtesy, knowing and inquisitive. He was also a good navigator, and had possessed himself of the compasses and marine charts of our ship, the use of which he often inquired of me, theirs being made of another fashion. In short, he was at all times well pleased that I should be of his company to entertain him, and to answer all the questions he put to me about our manners and customs. This casual conversation, with the trouble I took, soon made me understand much of the language; and on that account the lord became more and more well disposed towards me, and I began to be not quite so wretched as before, and often received additional provisions through his kindness.

To return to our people who were at *Pouladou*. When their money was spent they were worse treated, and more afflicted with famine than we, inasmuch as their number was greater than ours. The lord of our island, *Paindoüé*, went often to *Pouladou* to visit the lord of that island, who was his relative. One day, after I made his acquaintance, he took me with him to give me the satisfaction of seeing my companions. By this means I became aware of the miserable condition to which they were reduced and the afflictions they had to suffer. When I was with them we all together searched the sea-shore to see if we could chance to find something to eat; for they were dying of hunger, and had to do as we had done at first at *Paindoüé*. We found a very large turtle (for in the Indian Sea they grow to a prodigious size) turned upon its back; it had 500 or 600 eggs, each as big as the yolk of a hen's egg. We were well pleased at our discovery; we cut it in pieces, and boiled it with fresh water in a boiler which they lent to us, and then ate it. The flesh was extremely fat and tasty, like veal, and the eggs were very good; but afterwards we had all such a stomach disorder that we thought we should die, and I was the first seized. I suspect it was because we were famished, and having nothing else, ate that to excess.[1] We had forgotten, too, to cook it in sea water, and so to season it; for, as I afterwards learnt at the Maldives, fish cooked in sea water is more wholesome, and does not go bad so soon, and will keep a long time after being dried. The natives always cook it in sea water. I then learnt the fearful misery to which my comrades, and especially the sick, were reduced by famine, and that they gave no assistance to one another. I slept at this island; next day, the lord of *Paindoüé* took me back with him, and when he returned on another occasion, took me again with him.

Meanwhile, the king's people came day after day to take what they could from the ship, chiefly the lead with which it was bottomed: this they prize highly in that country. They took even the nails, and as much of the timber as they could. And as they came and went they took from time to time some of our men, who were glad enough to go; and those who had silver gave it, to be taken. We were told that the king was to give a ship to our captain, and when it was got ready we should all be taken. Our people died one after another, clinging to this hope. Our captain, chief clerk, second mate, and many others were already dead. The mate had been the first to pay his respects to the king; but he asked leave to return to the ship to get some clothes, which was readily granted to all of us, as the natives had no use for such things. So, when the mate saw that they did not come and look after us, and that the captain was dead, he formed

[1] The turtle was of a non-edible species, probably the "loggerhead"; M. *musimbi (Couanea olivacea).* He relates this incident again in his Treatise (see vol. ii).

a design to escape, which he long revolved in secret and unknown to some of us, to whom he would not discover his mind. The second time I saw him he communicated his design to me, and regretted that he could not include me, as he had not sufficient means. I told him I did not believe that he would succeed, for that the natives were very suspicious of us, and on that account had left [at the island] neither boats nor barques; nay more, the king's people had sent some soldiers, as well to keep watch over us, as to discover what people of the island had received silver from our men, and to make them give it up; nevertheless, the mate conducted his enterprise so dexterously that at length he seized the ship of the lord of *Paindoüé* while he was at *Pouladou* seeing his relative, as on the two occasions when he took me with him. He had well chosen his opportunity, which was just after midday, when the people of the island least suspected anything. So, having stored the ship with fresh water and coco-nuts, of which he had previously hidden a good supply in the wood, he embarked with eleven others, leaving eight of our men (four sick and four sound), without whose knowledge he set sail. The inhabitants soon perceived it, but they had no boats to pursue him. They came to give the news to the men of our island on a raft called *Candouepatis*[1] (of which I shall speak in its place), so that our people had plenty of time to get beyond the reefs before the people had found their boats, and they were already a long way off, out of view and of danger, when the islanders were embarking to pursue. This enterprise was a success so far as they were concerned,[2] but it was the cause of a sea of troubles to the eight who remained; for the soldiers, out of revenge, exercised upon them all imaginable severities. They bound those who were in health, and beat them savagely, and then took from them all the money and victuals they had;

[1] M. *Kadufati*, a raft made of the *Kadu* tree. (See below, ch. x.)

[2] As to the subsequent fortunes of these twelve, see below, p. 80.

then they came to the sick, compelling the healthy to carry them to the shore, and so close to the sea, that when the tide came their legs were soaked, while at the same time they were exposed to the inclemencies of the sky, the sun, and the rain, which was incessant at that season. Moreover, they held them so rigorously that the healthy were not even permitted to carry them fresh water to drink, the only thing which the healthy themselves obtained. So the poor sick fellows died of hunger, and were then thrown into the sea, as the islanders did to all our men who died, not giving us even permission to bury our dead friends. This, however, was done without the knowledge of the king, for he caused some to be buried at the sea-shore, chiefly those who died at the island where he resided. But to return to *Pouladou*,—those who were left told me that the poor sick crawled about in great agony, and lay on their faces, so as to eat the grass beneath them, and so were frequently found with grass in their mouths. The lieutenant of our ship, a man of good family at S. Malo, died in this condition. Of the others who kept their health, there was one who, constrained by hunger to climb a coco-tree by night to try to get some fruit, fell from the high tree-top and was killed, though he had several times before climbed it without accident. His remaining comrades suffered severely; they even ate rats when they could catch them.

As for us three who were at *Paindoüé*, the escape of our friends brought us no other harm than our own fears. The natives of the island assembled together with sticks in their hands (for arms they are not allowed to wear except they be of the gendarmerie, and while they are in the king's service),[1] and came to us in our hut by the sea-shore. There they insulted and threatened us; they even gave us some blows; but as they had never seen us with money, they did not go beyond that, and treated us better than our friends

[1] This rule is strictly enforced still.

at *Pouladou*. The lord of the island, too, a very humane man, prevented them from maltreating us, and gave me proof of his kindness, as did his wife and the elders of the island.

CHAPTER VII.

Arrival of a lord bearing the king's commission to the island of Paindoüé, who at length takes the author back with him.

I have above related our condition during the three months and a half following our shipwreck. Then arrived from the king's island a great lord named *Assant Caounas Calogue.*[1] The first who had been sent was the king's brother-in-law, and, as I subsequently heard, the king had learnt that he had not obeyed his orders, and had retained something from the ship for his own use, and was so enraged that he even boxed his ears, and never sent him again. In his stead he sent one of the highest nobles of his court, whom he consulted on the most important affairs, having more confidence in him than in any other. His orders were to get out of the ship and to convey to the king all he could, chiefly some cannon, and the rest of the lead and iron, and also to make search for the silver which the islanders had received from us. He was assisted by another lord named *Oussaint Rannamandy Calogue*,[2] who had authority over all ships, barques,

[1] *Assant*, no doubt, is *Hassan: caounas*, I cannot explain. It may be the name of his island, as Mr. Bell suggests, and as in the case of *Ali Pandio Tacourou*, and *Misdoue Quilague*. As to *calogue*, v. s., p. 56, *note*. This lord and his family, with whom the author had the warmest friendship, are mentioned several times hereafter.

[2] This would now be written *Husain Ranahamádi Kalóge-fánu*. The title *Ranahamádi* survives, and the holder is still chief of the *Kakísi* or "sailors", but distinct from the *Veláná* (Bell).

boats, captains, and mariners, but not over soldiers; in short, he was chief of the marine, or, as we might call him, superintendent of the galleys and ships of the king, but not admiral. On his arrival he was received as it is the custom to receive the king's officers of high rank who come in his service. I have witnessed a reception of this kind. From a distance the barque or the boat (called *ody*[1]) in which the lord is makes a signal with a red flag, furls its sails, and casts anchor at a gun-shot from the island. Then the lord or chief man of the place sends to inquire who it is, and being informed, gives order for his reception, and goes out to meet him, accompanied by as many men and boats as are available, leaving only the *Catibe*,[2] or curé, with four or five of the *Mouscoulits*,[3] or elders of the island. The boats are laden some with coco-nuts, others with bananas, betel, and other fruits with which the island abounds, everything being arranged in baskets and white boxes made of coco-leaves. These are made for the occasion, and are not used again; for these leaves are so common, and the people so clever in making the baskets, that they never require to use them twice; they also make them so that one cannot get out the fruit or other things from within, without cutting them and breaking them up, and they are then cast aside. On presenting these, the lord of the island enters first and salutes the other, saying *Sallam Alecon*,[4] which is their common salutation; then stooping down, touches his feet with his right hand, which he then raises and puts on his own head, as if to mean that he would put his head under the other's feet. All the others in attendance do the same, and bring all the presents, two at a time, with a rod on their shoulders, at the middle of which the present is suspended. This salutation

[1] M. *oḍi*; Tam. *oḍam*.

[2] M. *Katibu*, from the Ar. *Katib*, "scribe".

[3] *Muskuli*; see ch. xiv.

[4] Ar. *Salaam aleikum*.

and present is called *Vedon à Rouespou.*[1] After this the lord of the island makes his speech, and begs the visitor to land, and to do him the honour to take his lodging at the place prepared. Thither he proceeds, accompanied by his host and his followers. As the great lord nears the island, the *Catibe* and the others who have remained behind are waiting on the strand, and come forward before the guest, wading in the sea up to their waists, and carrying each his cloth or turban on his left arm. This cloth is half silk and half cotton, very well woven, and coloured red, an ell and a half in length, and three-quarters of an ell in width. Then the *Catibe* and his followers salute him in the customary way, and make a speech, offering him cloths and other presents, which are courteously received, and taken in charge by his attendants. That done, as soon as the lord desires to land, one of the chief *Catibes* or *Mouscoulits* comes forward to offer his shoulder—a function much esteemed—and the other gets on his shoulders; and so, with a leg on each side, he rides him horse fashion to land, and is there set down. Great care is taken that his feet do not get wet, for that they hold a great disgrace. He is then conducted in great honour, accompanied by all the residents, to the lodging prepared for him and his suite. There the people salute him again, and he talks with them for half-an-hour or so, and then all take their leave. Then they bring him a bath of lukewarm water, nicely prepared, and after that odorous oils to rub his body withal, after the custom of the Indies. Next they gave him wine of coco to drink, the finest and most tasty to be got, along with many portions of betel, very neatly served, and supplied with all the requisite ingredients, which I shall describe in the proper place.[2] Thus refreshed and rested, he

[1] Chr. gives *wedung*, "present", and *wedung oḍi*, "offering boat". The latter part of Pyrard's phrase is, according to Mr. Bell, a courtly suffix, properly written *aruvaifi*, or *aruvaifu*.

[2] See vol. ii, Treatise, ch. viii.

proceeds to the principal temple, which they call *Oucourou misquitte.*[1] There he says his prayers for upwards of an hour, and then returns to his lodging, where meanwhile his table has been prepared with all the delicacies of the country. While he is upon the island, all people of quality and means send him presents, such as savoury dishes, fruits, and betel, neatly served and borne by the hands of women, with the greatest ceremony and honour possible,—not that he has not always his own kitchen and daily meals: sometimes, indeed, he neither eats nor tastes any of all these things [that are brought]; but such is the custom of all these islands.

This lord having arrived in this fashion, and all these ceremonies being ended, he straightway executed his commission at the ship, and when that was done he went to the island of *Pouladou*, where he made inquiry for those who had had money from our vessel; and to get hold of it he arrested all the inhabitants of the island, even the women, to see if they would confess. Then he had their thumbs put into cleft sticks, squeezed and bound with iron clasps, to the end that by this pain they might be constrained to admit the truth,—as, in fact, they did, and gave up the money; but not all, for the king's people could not discover the full quantity. They also made accusation against those of other islands, to which the king's people were at once sent. In fine, the greater part of those who had touched our money were obliged to give it up, and for a year or two some one was always being discovered in possession of some that had been concealed till then. Even the soldiers who were left there on guard were convicted of it. The people of *Paindoüé* were in no trouble, for we exculpated them; and on that account they always liked me, and sent me presents while I was there; and it was proved that they had taken nothing of us.

All these things happened in fifteen days during which the king's commissioner sojourned at *Paindoüé*, *Pouladou*,

[1] *Hukuru miskitu*, "Friday mosque" (*Bell*, p. 58).

and the neighbouring islands, sometimes at one and sometimes at another, executing the king's commission. The lord of *Paindoüé* and the *Catibe*, as well as the people who took a liking to me, presented me to him, and strongly recommended me, all thinking that I was some great lord from this part of the world [*i.e.*, Europe]; and I did not correct their opinion, seeing that it served me. Owing to this recommendation, the lord sent from the king took me into his friendship, as well as because he saw that I already knew enough of their language to express myself and to make myself understood a little, and that I was taking pains to learn it every day. I have remarked that nothing served me so much, or so conciliated the goodwill of the people, the lords, and even of the king, as to have a knowledge of their language, and that was the reason why I was always preferred to my companions, and more esteemed than they. And so, while he was in those parts, he always desired that I should accompany him and be near him, whether in his boat at the place of the wreck, or at the other islands. Among others, he took me to a little island called *Touladou*,[1] distant ten leagues, whither he had gone to see one of his wives, and he had the greatest pleasure in my conversation. Also, it was on account of this affection that my companions and I were in no want, being more highly in his esteem. The day before he returned, he asked me if I would like to go with him to *Malé*, where the king lives. I told him that I had long desired it. I had, nevertheless, some fear lest he should change his mind, and on the morrow I never went out of his sight; so, when he was ready to start, one of the soldiers of his suite took him on his shoulders, as the custom is, and bore him through the sea to his barque: from there he called me, and got me on board. I was vastly pleased to go; but I was also sad at thus leaving my two companions at *Paindoué*

[1] Tuládu (in the Admiralty Charts spelt *Turahdou*), in lat. 5° 1′ N., at south end of Málosmaduḷu atoll.

and those at *Pouladou*, of whom only four now remained surviving their great calamities. They all, on seeing me depart without them, wept piteously. The lord, perceiving this, asked me, as their interpreter, what caused them to weep; and having the reason of their affliction explained to him, he bade me console them, and tell them from him not to be troubled; that the king would send and fetch them soon; that he himself was desirous of satisfying them, but that he dared not do so without the express command of the king. That did not console them much, seeing that I was going and they were remaining; so that they continued, or rather increased, their tears and lamentations. This distressed me, though I dared not show it, for I had already learnt the humour of the natives on this point, which is that they cannot tolerate in their presence sad and melancholy persons or dreamers, saying that such persons are plotting some treason or mischief in their minds.[1] So one who wishes to be well received among them must be happy and joyous, must laugh and sing if he can, although without occasion or desire, nay, though the contrary be the case. I restrained myself as much as I could, but he, being a man of intelligence, saw well through my disguise the sorrow I bore at my heart. Then he pressed me to tell him what troubled me; this I did, and confessed frankly that besides my sorrow

[1] The Maldivians were of much the same opinion as Julius Cæsar:—

"Yond Cassius has a lean and hungry look;
He thinks too much: such men are dangerous.
. . . .
. . . . . he loves no plays,
As thou dost, Antony: he hears no music;
Seldom he smiles, and smiles in such a sort
As if he mock'd himself and scorn'd his spirit
That could be moved to smile at any thing.
Such men as he be never at heart's ease
Whiles they behold a greater than themselves,
And therefore are they very dangerous."

(*Julius Cæsar*, Act i, sc. 2.)

at leaving my companions and seeing them weep, mourning their condition and the misery they would have to endure, even as they had already suffered, I had, said I, a more particular cause of grief, viz., that one of my two companions at *Paindoüé* and I had, from the day of our coming on board in France, made mutual profession of the warmest friendship; that I had always helped him and he me, in a greater degree than the others, and I could not but confess the great grief I had at parting with him; that, acknowledging the kindness for which I was under daily increasing obligation to him (the lord), that emboldened me to beg him on this occasion to have regard to my affliction, and to give me the satisfaction of taking this man along with us, and to be merciful to those who remained. This speech, and my countenance bedewed with tears, which my extreme sorrow drew forth against my will, affected the lord, whom I ever found in the highest degree kindly and merciful, as well as generous and magnanimous; so much so, that I venture to assert that in disposition and good manners he would yield to no gentlemen of Europe. He at once spoke privily with the other lord, the superintendent of the king's galleys and ships of whom I have spoken, and to the other chief men who were about him, and after consulting with them he told me that to please me he would gratify him, and forthwith caused the man to embark whom I indicated. As for the five who remained, he gave orders that they should be separated, and that they should be placed one in each of the neighbouring islands, enjoining the chiefs and more important inhabitants there present at his departure to treat them humanely, and to take care that they should be in no distress, and to feed them at the public expense until they should receive the king's command to send them. Then I bade adieu to my companions, more easy in mind than before, even as they too were, praying me to keep them in remembrance, that so they might not remain long in these little islands separated one from another. That done, we set sail and made way for the rest of the day.

CHAPTER VIII.

Arrival of the author at the island of Malé, where he salutes the king.—The putting to death of four Frenchmen for attempting to escape.—Arrival of his other companions, and the reasons which prevented the king from sending them to Sumatra.

At nightfall we reached a little island called *Maconnodou*,[1] belonging to the general of the galleys, where we slept: for it is their custom never to sail by night. On the following morning, when it was time to go on board, the lord told me we were within fifteen or sixteen leagues of Malé, where the king was, and that he would not dare to take my companion, not knowing whether it would be agreeable to the king, and that he proposed to leave him there for some days, until he should have spoken with the king about fetching him; that he was sure it would be well with him, and that he had given orders to that end. We arrived at length at Malé, where, on landing, he went at once to salute the king and render an account of his journey, bidding one of his people conduct me to his house. He did not omit, among other matters, to speak about me, the immediate consequence of which was that I was sent for by command of the king. At the palace I remained about three hours in waiting. In the evening I was introduced into a court where the king had come out to see all that had been brought in the last voyage from our

[1] A small island on the north-west side of Málé atoll, in lat. 4° 31′ N., now called *Makunudu*. Mr. Bell visited it in 1879, putting in there for the night, just as Pyrard did. He describes it as being about a quarter to half a mile in circuit.

vessel—*i.e.*, the cannon, balls, arms, and other implements of war and navigation, which had been brought to his magazine there. I was bidden to approach, and then I saluted the king in the language and in the mode of the country—which I had carefully studied the moment I was admitted, and had been particularly instructed in beforehand.[1] This pleased him, and induced him to inquire of me the uses of some of the things brought from the ship, which he did not know; these I explained to him, expressing myself as best I could. It being now night, he bade the lord who had brought me to give me lodging and entertainment, and me to come every day to see him along with the other courtiers. This done, we retired.

On the following days I was entirely occupied in attendance upon the king, in answering all his questions concerning the manners and customs of the people of Europe and of our France, the dress, arms, and estate of the kings, of whom he made particular inquiry. While I discoursed upon the greatness of the kingdom of France, of the generosity of its noblesse, and their dexterity in arms, he said he was surprised that they had not conquered the Indies, and had left it to the Portuguese, who had given him to understand that their king was the greatest and most powerful of all the Christian kings. The king also let me see the queens, his wives, who in like manner kept me many days replying to their inquiries, being especially curious to hear of the figures, dress, manners, marriages, and customs of the ladies of France; and often they sent for me without the king's knowledge, a thing not allowed in the case of others.

As I have already said, fifteen or sixteen of our people had already been brought to the island of Malé, where the king dwells. When I arrived there I found no more than three—

[1] This would imply some customary mode of obeisance. Christopher, however, states that, at the Durbar, no salutation is expected (*Trans. Bomb. Geog. Soc.*, i, 67).

two Flemings, and a Frenchman who was in the last stage of sickness, and died eight days after. At first, when our people came there, a Portuguese ship[1] of 400 tons was at anchor in the roads, having come from Cochin with a full cargo of rice, to take away *bolys*,[2] or shells, to Bengal, where they are in great demand. The captain and merchant were Mestifs, the others Indian Christians, and all habited in Portuguese fashion. They showed much enmity towards our men, and spoke evilly of us to the king, who believed them; and this was in part the cause why we were not so well treated as we had been. They asked the king to let them take us all to Cochin, whereto he consented—in fact, asking our captain and chief clerk if they wished to go, and telling them that they might. They made reply, with all the others who were present, that they would rather die than go. In truth, they had good reason to fear them, as it was not to do us any good, nor for our advantage, that they wished to take us; so our men trusted always that the king would send them in a barque to Achen in Sumatra, as he had promised. Soon after, the captain and chief clerk died; the others followed one by one, worn out by the fatigue they had already endured, and by the bad climate and water of that island, which make it impossible for most foreigners to live there. Moreover, when the news came to the king of the escape of the mate and the other men from Pouladou, he was so enraged, that he swore a solemn oath that he would not let one of us go. I was assured by several of the lords that otherwise he would have provided us with a barque, as we desired. The pilot, hearing this resolution, which confined him for life to these islands, designed to get a barque and escape, like his friends of Pouladou. To this end he conspired with three of our sailors, and hid in a wood all that

[1] This ship is again referred to in ch. xvii.

[2] *Boli*, "cowries"; Sin. *bella*. The traffic in these shells is more fully described below.

was required. Their design was discovered by the islanders, who had remarked their goings to and fro the wood by the shore, and played spies over them. They then gave information to the six elders, called *Mouscoulis*, who rule the highest affairs of state, and they in turn informed the king. Careful observation was made of the carriage of these four, and on the night on which they were to embark they were taken in the act by the soldiers, who put their feet in irons. Two days afterwards the soldiers took them in boats, feigning to take them to some other island; and when they were upon the sea they cut off their heads with blows of the *caty*,[1] which is made like a large bill-hook of this country, and of excellent steel, well-polished and highly worked: it comes from the Malabar coast, and cuts exceedingly well. They felled them by many blows; and one who dealt only one blow was esteemed no good soldier [of the king]. Thus do they always when they execute their king's orders, and so would they to their near relative, even their own brothers, to testify their zeal in the king's service. So, when the king likes anyone, all the world likes him; and if the king wishes one ill, all the world hates him, and no one associates with him, nor even looks at him. The four corpses were flung into the sea.[2] After all, it is no wonder that the king was enraged at these attempts to escape on the part of our men, for it is high treason to steal a barque or boat and to depart beyond the realm: that may not be done without passport, and a special and precise permit of the king, even though the boat were one's own. Without that, it is death and unpardonable, and no one need hope for the king's mercy if convicted. This crime is called *odican anpou*.[3] I heard this sad news, and

[1] M. *Katu*, a bill-hook = Sin. *Kætta*.

[2] This unfortunate pilot, as above observed, was an Englishman. His name is not given.

[3] This would have been nearly right if he had written *odi-ganan-pou*. The modern M. is *oḍi gengosfu*, "having taken away a boat". As to *ganan*, *cf.* Sin. *gananawa*, "to take away".

that of the natural death of our other comrades, as soon as I arrived at Malé, where the Cochin ship still was; it took away the greater part of the equipment of our vessel, which the king sold to it, consisting chiefly of things he could not use. At the same time one of the king's pilots told me that the twelve of *Pouladou* who escaped with the mate of our ship had arrived at Coilan, on the coast, and had been put in irons on a Portuguese galley, where he had seen them, and would be taken to Goa.[1]

I was then one of three at the island of Malé, along with the two Flemings. I petitioned the king to send for my comrade who had been left on the way at the island of *Maconnodou*, which he did at once, and we were only parted from one another for ten days; thus we mustered four, he, I, and the two Flemings. Two months afterwards, I managed to get the five brought who were left scattered among the little islands near the scene of the wreck; this done, we numbered nine, four Frenchmen and five Flemings, all kindly treated by the king and his lords. But we had no good understanding betwixt us, and this was due to the Flemings, who all five held themselves apart from us, and ever through interpreters spoke evil of us to the lords and to the people. The cause of this discord was that they were jealous of seeing me more courteously received than they were, and well liked and esteemed by the king, always at his side, and in consequence graciously entreated by the nobles. Thus they persuaded

[1] Referred to again in ch. xviii: these men succeeded in reaching Quilon, but received an unfriendly welcome at the hands of the Portuguese. They were the only party, according to Pyrard, who did escape from the Maldives, besides himself and three companions. Martin, however, writing of the 22nd Oct. 1602, says that some Portuguese arrived at Achin from Pedir, and assured the crew of the *Croissant* that they had seen twenty-five men saved from the *Corbin* in two boats, one containing fourteen and the other eleven men, and that they had made land between Cape Comorin and Ceylon, at the pearl fishery (*Martin*, p. 59). Pyrard is more likely to be right.

themselves that my three French companions were more welcome than they, and that I favoured these more than themselves, who were strangers to me. Nay more, because I spoke the Maldive language with some facility, while they understood it not at all, they imagined that I spoke evil of them, and that I was the cause of their being less at their ease: yet verily the truth was far otherwise.

The king's oath in his anger was the cause why his promise to give us a barque was not carried out; and, moreover, all our people were dead, saving nine; so there was no glimpse of hope that we should ever leave the place. This was a grievous affliction for us to think of, and we sought consolation of God and of each other. I have mentioned the reason given by the king for not treating us with courtesy; for, in truth, in the case of all the other ships which were in like manner wrecked during my sojourn there, he gave the men the means of departing, retaining only the money and merchandise. But, besides the reasons mentioned, I have thought that he had yet another, viz., the money which had disappeared, which one may say was the chiefest cause of misfortune, and of the death of the greater part of our crew; inasmuch as the king, being informed that some money was taken from the ship, and imagining that what our folk had concealed was a large sum, perhaps as large as that he found in the ship, he would not that this money should go out of his country; and while he searched for more than he had, most of our men died. I believe that, coming after that, the escape of the mate and the attempt of the pilot nettled him still more. It had been proposed not to take any of the silver at all, or to convey it all to the king, like the piece of scarlet. On one occasion he told me plainly that my companions had concealed the silver, and had made him a present of the piece of scarlet only because they could not hide it like money, and that they had all acted wrongfully in that matter, and were unworthy of his favour.

CHAPTER IX.

Grievous sickness of the author, which left him in evil plight.—Escape of four Flemings, and the ill-favour of the king towards those who remained.

I was for about four or five months in fairly good health, and, except for the want of the free exercise of my religion and liberty, was comfortable, well housed, fed, and treated by the lord who had brought me, my lodging being in a little apartment within the enclosure of his house. One of his servants waited upon me at all hours, and brought me my food with separate utensils, for they never eat with one who is not of their religion. He loved me as one of his own sons, of whom he had three, of nearly the same age as myself, and they loved me as their brother. This lord was in favour with the king, who placed all confidence in him; they had been attached to each other from the time they were four or five years old, and each was now fifty. Such being my condition, I fell ill of a severe burning fever, very common there and very dangerous, especially to strangers, so much so that few get over it; still less the Christians, for whom there is no sort of cure, for they are not disposed to obey the sorcerers, and get cured by charms and enchantments, as the islanders use. I was ill and in great danger for more than two months, and it was ten months before I was quite well. Not a day passed but the king and the queens sent to get news of me and my condition; he sent at all hours the choicest dishes and the most delicious morsels from his own table; and in order that I might be treated more at my ease, and might the better ask for what I wanted, he sent one of my own comrades, whom he charged with the care of me, in addition to the house servants. The sickness was severe and very troublesome; it is known through all the Indies under the name of Maldive fever: they call it *Malé ons.*[1] It is the sickness of which most of my companions died, as all strangers fail not to be soon attacked; and when one gets over it one may be sure he will recover from the other maladies to which the climate will subject him; for a man changes by habit with the climate and manner of living, and this malady, as it were, makes him a new body, and he feels quite inured. And, indeed, if a stranger, whom in their language they call *Pouraddé*,[2] recovers from it, they say that he is *diues*,[3] as who should say naturalised, and no longer a stranger. For this kingdom in their language is called *Malé-ragué*,[4] the kingdom of Malé; but by the other Indians it is called *Malé-diuar*, and the people *diues.*[5] To return to my illness. I was eight days without swallowing anything but water, and that too is a bad thing. The country people refrain from drinking

[1] M. *Málé hung* (Bell); Sin. *una*, "fever". The Maldivians also use the word *homan* (Ar. *hummā*); see ch. xiii, and Vocabulary (vol. ii). All travellers bear witness to the baneful effects of this intermittent fever and ague. Ibn Batuta says, "In the midst of all this a fever seized me, and I was very ill. Every one who goes to that island must inevitably catch the fever" (App. A). The Indian Navy Surveyors of 1834-6 suffered severely (Taylor's *Sailing Dir.*, pt. i, p. 569; *Journ. Geo. Soc. Bom.*, i, 55, 67; *Bell*, 7, 8). I have also had an account of the difficulties which constantly recurred during the survey, in supplying fresh crews owing to this cause, from the lips of Capt. Chas. Campbell, one of the few survivors of that meritorious service.

[2] *Furadi míha*, "voyage man" (Chr.).

[3] *Dives*, or more properly *divehi*, is the adjectival form of *diva*, or *du*, "island"; Sans. *dwípa;* Sin. *duwa*. In modern times "islanders" is expressed by *divehi míhun* (*Bell*, p. 3), and the "island letters" by *divehi akuru; cf.* the *divi* of Ammianus Marcellinus, as to which see App. A.

[4] More commonly *Divehi rájjé;* see Sultan's letter of 1795 (*Bell*, 78).

[5] There seems some little confusion here. He has already said that *dives* was the Maldivians' name for themselves, and I believe he means *Malé divar* as the continental name for the Maldivian people, not kingdom; the form *divar* would seem to be Dravidian. The Sinhalese usually call the Maldivians *gundara-kárayo*, "the *gundara* (boat) men", and the islands *Mála diva*, or *Máladiv dúpat* (*Bell*, 3).

anything but lukewarm water, with a little powdered pepper in it; this prevents the inflammation, which would otherwise ensue when the fever passes off. I could not, however, take this beverage, which does nothing to quench the thirst. After the fever left me my legs and thighs swelled greatly, as if I had the dropsy. All foreigners suffer in the same way. Besides, I could not see for more than ten or a dozen paces before me, and I was afraid I should become blind. The fever also left me an obstruction and inflammation of the spleen, which caused me great difficulty of breathing. This spleen disease is very common among them, and they all have it rather large; they call the disease *ont cory*[1]; and, in fact, it so remained with me all the time I was at the Maldives. About the same time the king fell sick, and on this account I could not see him when I was on my feet again—until, on his recovery, as he was going to the mosque, I saluted him. He was much surprised to see the state to which I was reduced by this inflammation, and said that his illness had prevented him doing more for me. He at once bade his attendants see to it, and sent to find men who were skilled in curing this ailment, and told them to take the unguents from his own stock; for the king always keeps a quantity of drugs, medicines, and recipes of all sorts for the sick, even charms. The people would go and ask for them, and he was well enough pleased to do this kindness to all comers; and by this means also to know who were ill, who recovering, and who dying, and so to provide for the burial of those who died. It was his wont to do this for the poor and for such as were without means, in manner suitable to the degree of each. Thus did many busy themselves with my illness; but I did not get well until my legs burst and the water which caused the swelling escaped; my eyes then recovered their former power. But the mischief was that the ulcers in my legs became very large and deep, and so painful that I got no rest

[1] Below, ch. xiii, spelt *on cory*, properly *huṇ-korhi*.

by day or night, and the humours taking their course by this channel, it was difficult to close the wounds up. In this condition I remained for four months; the king causing me to be attended to and cared for to the best of his power. There was a little island within sight of Malé called *Bandos*,[1] where dwelt a man esteemed expert in that line. The king sent for him, and bade him cure me if he knew how, and he would reward him handsomely. The man promised to do so; but he added that if it should please the king to permit him to take me with him he could cure me much sooner, for the air was much better and more bracing, and the water better at that island than at Malé. The king permitted him, and gave word to his officers to serve out to him everything he asked for my support; so I was indeed well treated and cared for by this man. But meanwhile happened an accident to my comrades, which grieved me much and entailed much discomfort to me. This was, that of the five Flemings that were at Malé, four made resolve to escape from the islands by stealing a boat, seeing the desperate position to which we were reduced by being unable to depart with the king's permission. Two of the Flemings had arrived at Malé with our captain and the others brought with him; and having been with these men when they died, they succeeded to the money which they had kept concealed; thus they had every means of procuring the requisites for embarking. See now how they pursued their enterprise. The factor of the Christian king of the Maldives kept a banquesalle,[2] or storehouse, on the sea-shore at Malé. He was an Indian of Cochin, of the race of Canarins, and a Christian, though a bad one, as I afterwards came to understand. These Flemings

[1] *Baḍos.* There are two islands of this name in lat. 4° 15′ N. *Boḍu-* and *Kuḍa-Bados* (big and little); the former only is inhabited, and is, therefore, probably the one intended here. The Adm. charts give the names *Burrah Bunduse* and *Coorah Bunduse*.

[2] As to the history of this word, see Yule and Burnell, *Disc. Gloss.* and *New Eng. Dict.*, s. v. "Bankshall".

made friends with him, and so plied him with money that he let them put and keep in his store the provisions and baggage which they required. It remained only to await an opportunity for seizing a boat, which was a long time in coming. At length it happened that one of the followers of the lord who brought me to Malé left his boat near the place on account of the rain; and as he was hour by hour expecting the fine weather, he did not take out the rudder as usual. The boat was all equipped for the fishing, but very small, being no more than eight times the length of an arm, which is the most common measure used (it is called *Riens;* another smaller measure is used for cloth, viz., from the elbow to the tips of the fingers, this is called *Moul;*[1] all this by the way). The boat was called *Donny*,[2] *i.e.*, "bird", because it was a quick sailer, and it was equipped with provisions and water for several days. Our people having made this discovery, embarked at nightfall with their goods, and made off; but bad luck had it that this night and the day following there raged the most violent storm imaginable, not a whit less than that we came through off the coast of Natal. Even the islanders said they had never seen so many coco-trees blown down in four-and-twenty hours. I leave you to imagine whether it be possible that our poor fellows could have saved themselves in such a storm, in a little frail bark, not knowing the channels and passages which they ought to take in the midst of so many rocks and reefs. So it was that afterwards there were found upon the beach some pieces

[1] More correctly *riya* and *murhe.* The Sin. *riyana* is a cubit; the Maldivian *boḍu riya* (big riya) = length of the arm; *kuru riya* (little riya) or *murhé* = cubit; and *baya murhé* (half murhé) = span (*Bell*, 119).

[2] Rivara identifies this word with the Tam. *tóṇi*, "boat"; but the author distinctly says it was called *donny*, *i.e.*, "bird", because it was a good sailer: the word is repeated in the Vocabulary as the equivalent of "birds". Correctly written, as by Christopher and Bell, it is *dúni.* Pyrard may have confused *doṇi*, "boat", with *dúni* "bird", but there is not enough to forbid us taking the passage to mean that "Bird" was the name of the boat.

of the boat's equipment, which led to the belief that they had perished—as, in fact, they had; for nothing was ever heard of them again, neither at the islands nor on the mainland. The king was greatly incensed at this third escape, as well on the account already stated, that it is high treason to steal a boat and depart without leave, as because one of the four Flemings was a good gunner, and he liked him for that. This gunner was engaged at S. Malo for the voyage. Having received some money as an advance, he married, and was no longer willing to come, and offered to return what he had received. This our captain would not agree to; on the contrary, he had him seized and carried on board, neck and heels, by four men, on account whereof he was never afterwards well disposed, and even on several occasions when some of the ship's crew were offended at the captain for some punishment, conspired with them to make a wrong course, and to wreck the ship, and so get ashore. This he confessed to us at the Maldives. He also behaved with barbarous inhumanity towards our captain while he lay at the point of death at Malé, for he took off him by force a night-shirt which he was wearing; nor was he dissuaded from the act by all the prayers of the poor sick captain, only saying that he wanted it, and that he no longer recognised the captain after the loss of the ship. This disaster happened to these poor Flemings about eighteen months after our shipwreck. I reflected that by God's assistance, amid so many tribulations, I had never engaged in these attempts at escape, which all turned out ill, as I have related.[1] Two days afterwards, my comrade with whom I had vowed so warm a friendship died after a long illness. This was to me an intolerable affliction. He was from Vitré, and in our vessel had the office of clerk. I believe that he was at length brought down with vexation and melancholy, having

[1] The mate and his eleven friends did indeed reach the coast of India, but were there consigned to the Portuguese galleys.

left a wife and children to make this voyage, and now saw no hope of return. To come back to the Flemings who had gone off. When it was discovered, and the king was informed, messengers were sent to our people's lodgings to see for a fact who were left. They found two Frenchmen, one Fleming, and the man who was dying, as I have said. The six elders assembled at the king's palace, the accustomed place, and summoned our three men, whom they kept there by the space of four or five hours, telling them that they were accomplices in the others' treason, and threatening them with death. At length, seeing that they were not guilty, they let them go; but the king gave orders not to give them any more rice as provision from his store,—not however, preventing those who would from giving them victuals: for his part, he would never again believe a Frenchman. And, in fact, they did not by reason of that order fail to get a livelihood.

All these things grieved me excessively: my long and tedious illness, the loss of our men, the death of my friend, and the anger of the king, which waxed against those of us who were left. On my recovery, which was at the end of two months after I was taken to the little island of *Bandos*, I desired to tarry there, thinking thus to avoid the wrath of the king, which by this delay might be appeased; but at length I was advised not to add by contumacy to my transgression (for so they referred to our friends' mishap), and to return at once to the king. I took the advice, and on arrival, as the custom is, I put myself in the way of the king before going to my lodging. He happened to be going out at one of the lower courts, next to his sleeping apartments. I saluted him in the usual way, without any difference. Then he spoke to me, and asked if I had been well treated, and was quite well, and even wished to see the place of my sore. This gave me good hope that I was again in his favour as before; but I was greatly deceived, for he forbade them to give me anything from his house, any more than to my comrades. I was vexed—not, however, for the victuals, for the lords let me not want for aught; but for this cause, that, there, a man to whom the king does not give food is of no account, and has no position. And even the great lords accept rice of the king, and it is a high honour, too; so, on the contrary, is it a kind of infamy to be deprived of it. My especial friends did not, however, cease to favour me and help me, as they saw that the king did not speak ill of me, and that he acted thus to inspire me with fear for the future; otherwise, when the king is in good earnest incensed against anyone, that man would not find a single friend, and those who had been his friends would abandon him.

Two months passed in this disgrace, but for all that I did not cease to go regularly to the palace to present myself to the king. I was warned that by the custom of the country one should not absent oneself when the king is angry, nor cease to go to the palace regularly, until by long patience the king speaks and again receives you into his favour.[1] I again fell ill of a fever. The lord with whom I lodged apprised the king of it, and he bade him treat me well and spare nothing. Nor did he; and to give me better hope, he assured me that the king was not at all angry with me, but on the contrary was solicitous for my health: and, indeed, the king bade them give me the ordinary provision of rice, and to my three companions, too. The illness was short, and I was soon well again. Six weeks afterwards I was fairly astonished to be summoned to the palace by the six elders, and to be told that they were informed that we had a design to escape. They gave me orders, on the part of the king, not to have any dealings with my companions, nor to speak French to them; and that I was to give them the same order. It was very diffi-

[1] This custom is quoted from Pyrard, with approval, by Montesquieu, as "disarming the prince's indignation" (*Esp. des Lois*, liv. xii, ch. 30).

cult, lodged so near each other, to obey this order and not to speak or communicate with one another,—which, indeed, we did in secret. For all that, fifteen days after, it was reported to the king, who was much offended, and commanded that my three companions were to be taken to an atollon named *Souadou*,[1] which is eighty leagues to the south of Malé. You have to pass the line to get there. That is the place where the king exiles those who displease him; it is an island far removed from his court, where foreign vessels never touch, whose inhabitants are very unmannerly, rude, and boorish. This order was given to the master or Intendant of the royal ships, who is called *Maé dau da elle*[2]; this person had conceived an ill-will towards me, out of jealousy of the lord who had brought me from *Paindoüé*, with whom he was there, for he had made me promise on the journey that I should lodge with him, and I could not do it, for the king made me lodge with the lord who had brought me. By way of revenge, he sent word to me by one of the royal sergeants, who are called *Mirvaires*,[3] that I was to come to him to be embarked for Souadou with the others. I could not refuse

[1] The atoll *Suadiva*, or *Huadiva*, is here probably intended to include the smaller atoll Addú, and the island Fua Mulaku. This remote portion of the Maldive kingdom was treated as a sub-kingdom, the exiled King Dom Manoel describing himself as "rei das ilhas de Maldiva e de tres Patanas de Cuaydu" (Letters Patent in *Arch. Port. Or.*, Fasc. 3). As appears here and elsewhere in the narrative, Suadiva atoll was the place of exile for political offenders and a place of refuge for unsuccessful conspirators; and, as Mr. Bell informs me, contains at this day the descendants of several occupants of the throne.

[2] This office was that of captain or superintendent of the king's private ships, and must not be confounded with that of *velannas*, or admiral. The duties are described above at pp. 69-70, where the name of the officer is given. The title *Múdaḍahelu* is still in use.

[3] M. *miru baharu* (Bell); Ar. *Emir-el-Bahr*. In Pyrard's time (see below, ch. xv) there were two of these officers, having the duties of harbour masters, in subordination to the *velannas*, or admiral. Nowadays there is one *Miru Baharu*, who is port surgeon at Málé, and is one of the three ministers of the Sultan.

nor resist this order, and in great sorrow went to embark, when one of the sons of the lord with whom I was, well knowing that the king had given no such order with regard to me, promptly informed him of it; the king at once ordered that I should be disembarked, saying that he did not intend that I should be elsewhere than near himself. By this means I was freed. Some of the lords begged of the king to let one of the three others also remain, or that he should go at another time. This was because they liked the man for being a good tailor and a trumpeter: and this gave him much custom and acquaintances in all ranks. The king consented, so that only two were embarked, a Frenchman and a Fleming, and we two remained; for after the departure of the others there was no word of sending him, as they thought that we could not effect our escape. The king sent for me and reprimanded me for our disobedience; adding that he was annoyed that I had entertained a design to escape, and that he did not wish me to go and drown myself as the gunner had done. I humbly excused myself, and assured him that I had not participated in any such enterprises. It was then that I began to be in the greatest favour with the king. Two years afterwards, my two comrades who had been banished to Souadou were recalled on this wise. One of them, the Fleming, was a very clever cutter of soft wood with the point of a knife; and having more leisure than he cared for, took it into his head to make a little vessel in the Flemish fashion, no longer than an arm's length, but so neatly done that it had all its proper sails, ropes, utensils, and equipment, no less than a big ship of 500 tons. He sent it to the king, who admired the little work so highly that he sent orders that the workman should be sent back at once, and out of esteem for him, his companion too. So we were again all four together for the space of fifteen months.[1]

[1] As will be seen hereafter, Pyrard left the Maldives in February 1607; the date of the return of his two comrades from Suadu would,

The king gave me a lodging close to him, and every day I had rice and other provisions brought from his house. He also supplied me with a servant to wait upon me, besides some money and other presents; by means of which I became somewhat rich, according to the notions of the country, to which I conformed in every possible way, as well as to their habits and customs, so as to be the better received among them. I trafficked with the foreign ships which arrived there, and with so much address, that they put entire confidence in me, and left large quantities of merchandise of all kinds for me to sell in their absence, or to keep against their return, and gave me a certain share. I remained also in the king's favour, whom I went to salute every day, and

therefore, be about Nov. 1605. No more deaths occurred, and these four, besides the twelve who escaped from Pouladou, were all who reached India out of the *Corbin's* crew. This will be a convenient place to summarise the misfortunes of the whole party. About forty survived the wreck (p. 60). The mate and two sailors were the first taken to Malé (p. 57); then the captain and five or six others (p. 59). Pyrard and two others were taken to Paindoüé (*ib.*). Many at Pouladou died (p. 61), and his own two companions fell sick (p. 64). The king's officers take others to Malé, where the captain and second mate die (p. 66). The mate and eleven others escape from Pouladou, leaving eight, of whom four were sick (p. 67). Of these latter, four die, one falling from a coco-tree (p. 68). Pyrard goes to Malé, with one of the two at Paindoüé, leaving four at Pouladou (p. 76). Fifteen or sixteen had already been brought to Malé, of whom P. found only three surviving, two Flemings and one Frenchman, the latter dying eight days after P.'s arrival (pp. 77-78). The pilot (an Englishman) and three sailors had been put to death for an attempted escape (p. 80). P.'s companion, who had been left at Maconnodou, is now brought to Malé, making four, two French and two Flemings. Two months later he gets the five brought from Pouladou, *i.e.*, nine at Malé—five Flemings and four French (*ib.*). Four Flemings escape and are drowned (p. 86), leaving four French and one Fleming. His great friend, a Frenchman, dies (p. 87), leaving two French (besides Pyrard himself, who was then at Bandos) and one Fleming. These four were taken to India in 1607 by the Bengal invaders. It is not known whether the mate or any of his eleven friends got back to Europe.

was consequently well received by the grandees, and treated with the warm friendship of many.

I had a number of coco-trees of my own, which are there a source of riches. I had them tended by labourers, who give their services for hire. In a word, I wanted nothing but the exercise of the Christian religion, and I was much grieved to be deprived of that, and to lose all hope of returning to France. So it is that my long sojourn in these islands gave me a great knowledge of them, of the people who inhabit them, and their manners and customs, and I am now disposed to leave on record, with some particularity, the information I thus acquired.

CHAPTER X.

Description of the Maldive islands, of their situation, and the people who inhabit them.

The Maldive isles[1] begin at 8 degrees from the equinoctial line to the northward, and terminate at 4 degrees to the southward. Their length is thus great—about 200 leagues; their breadth is only 30 or 35 leagues. They are distant from the continent—that is, from Cape Comorin, Coilan, and Cochin—about 150 leagues. The Portuguese account it 4,500 leagues by sea to reach them from Spain.

They are divided in thirteen provinces, called by them *atollons*,[2] which is a natural division, according to the situa-

[1] The Maldives extend from latitude 7° 6′ N. to latitude 0° 42′ S., and from longitude 72° 33′ to longitude 73° 44′ E., a space 470 miles in length north and south, and seventy miles east and west. Ihavandiffulu, the northernmost atoll, is distant about 350 miles from Cape Comorin, and Málé atoll about 400 miles from the nearest port of Ceylon (Bell, *Rep.*, 1; Taylor, *Sailing Dir.*, 1874, pt. I, pp. 567-9).

[2] The Maldive is *atolu*, and is perhaps the only word which that language has given to European vocabularies. The word used by Ibn

tion of the places. For each atollon is separated from the rest, and contains in itself a great number of little isles. It is a marvel to see each of these atollons, surrounded on all sides by a great bank of stone, and no human device could so well wall in a space of land as it does. These atollons are either round or oval, each thirty leagues, more or less, in circumference, and all in a line, end to end from the north to the south, without touching each other. Between every two there are channels, some broad and some narrow. Standing in the middle of one of these atollons, you see around you this great reef of rock, as I have said, which surrounds and defends the islands from the impetuosity of the sea. But it is a fearful thing, even to the most hardy, to approach this reef, and to see the billows from afar come on and break with fury all around; for I assure you, as a thing which I have seen an infinity of times, that the crests and foam of the breakers rise higher than a house, of the whiteness of cotton, so that you see around you, as it were, a wall of exceeding whiteness, chiefly when the sea is high.

Batuta is *aklīm*, κλίμα; while the exiled Maldive king at Cochin, in his letters patent of the year 1561, describes himself as "King of the Maldive islands and of the three *patanas* of Suadu, and of the seven islands of Pullobay" (*Arch. Port. Or.*, Fasc. 5, No. 350; see also Barros, *Dec. III*, liv. iii, c. 7. Rivara's *Pyrard*). The word *patana* is a Sinhalese word, meaning in Ceylon a patch or stretch of mountain land on which jungle does not grow. As there were three atolls, Suadu, Addu, and Fua Mulaku, which, being distant from the rest and near each other, ordinarily went under the name of Suadu, the word *patana* would seem to be synonymous with *atolu*. Colonel Yule (*Enc. Brit.*, article "Maldives") finds the word *atollon* in Zeidler's *Univ. Lex.*, published in 1732, and I am not aware of an earlier use of it as a borrowed word. Mr. Bell considers the word to be connected with the Sin. *étula*, "within"; and Mr. Burnell, who had suggested the Malayâlam *adal*, "closing, uniting" (see *New Eng. Dict.* s. v.), was satisfied with this derivation (Yule and Burnell, *Disc. Gloss.*). Mr. Bell is of opinion that Pyrard's *atollon* is a misprint for *atollou*; but the word appears so frequently in the former form, and never in the latter, that it is more likely Pyrard intended by the soft French final *n* to give his notion of transliteration.

Within each of these enclosures are the islands, great and small, in number almost infinite. The natives informed me that there were as many as 12,000[1]; but my notion is that there is not the appearance of so great a number, and that they say 12,000 to indicate an incredible number, which cannot be counted. Yet, true it is that there is an endless number of little ones which are mere sandbanks, altogether uninhabited. Moreover, the king of the Maldives puts this number among his titles, for he called himself *Sultan Ibrahim dolos assa ral tera atholon:* that is to say, "Ibrahim Sultan, King of 13 provinces and 12,000 isles."[2] However that may

[1] The number of the islands has been variously stated. According to Ptolemy, there were 1,368 islands in the vicinity of Ceylon. Moses Chorenensis increased the number by four:—"Taprobane insularum omnium maxima......atque insulas minores circumjectas habet, ad mille trecentas septuaginta duas" (Whiston's edition, 1736). The following also have reference to the Indian islands generally:—John of Montecorvino puts the number at over 12,000 (*Cathay*, p. 215); Friar Jordanus had heard of 10,000 or 12,000 inhabited (Hak. Soc. ed., pp. 28, 53); and Marco Polo asserts as a fact that there were 12,700 inhabited and uninhabited. To come now to those who speak more definitely of the Maldives. Suleyman, in the ninth century, gives the number 1,900 (Reinaud, *Relation*, etc.). Masudi says "there are counted of them 2,000, or more exactly 1,900" (Sprenger's edition, i, 335). Hieronymo di Santo Stefano says seven to eight thousand (*India in the Fifteenth Century*, Hakl. Soc., p. 8). De Barros derives the name "Maldiva" from *Mal*, the Malabar (?) for 1,000, and *diva*, "islands" (*Dec. III*, liv. iii, c. 7); while Garcia de Orta, by way of correcting him, says they are not called Maldiva, but *Naledica*, "because *nale* in Malabar signifies '*four*', and *diva*, 'island'; so in the Malabar tongue they are said to be 'the Four Islands'" (*De Orta*, 11; see also *Mandelslo*, pp. 62, 116). Padre Lucena says "11,000 inhabited" (*Vida de S. Franç. Xav.*, liv. ix, c. 20), and he is followed by Bartoli (*Asia*, lib. iii, p. 201), by Philippus a Sant. Trin. (French edition, p. 226), and by other clerical writers. Mandelslo (Eng. trans., p. 116) says "near upon a thousand". Valentyn heard that they numbered 13,000. Captain Owen believed the total number was three or four times 12,000 (*J. R. G. S.*, ii, p. 84).

[2] *Dolos*, "twelve", Sin. the same; *assa*, "one thousand, or ten times 96", according to Pyrard (see Vocabulary, vol. ii), Sin. *dāsa*; *ral*, "country" (see Vocab.); Chr. has *rag* (*g* mute), "island"; *cf.* Sin. *rața*; *téra*, "thirteen"; the old Sin. is *tera* or *teles*, the mod. is *dahatuna*.

be, the currents and heavy seas are continually diminishing the number, as I was told by the natives, who also said that the inhabitants were decreasing in proportion, and are not so numerous as in ancient times.[1] One would say, in looking at the interior of one of these atollons, that all the little islands and the sea between them form but one continuous shoal, or that it was of old but one island, afterwards broken and divided into many. And in fact those who sail near the Maldives perceive the interior to be all white, by reason of the sand of that colour which covers all the shoals and reefs. The sea is calm and of little depth, at the deepest place not being twenty fathoms, and there are but few such places, for nearly everywhere you see almost to the bottom. This bottom is everywhere stone reef, rocks, and sand, so that when the sea is low it would not come up to the waist, and in most places only to the knee; so it would then be easy to go without a boat to all the islands of the same atollon, were it not for two things which prevent that: first, the great fish called *Paimones*,[2] which devour men, and break their arms and legs when they meet them; in the second place, the rocks at the bottom of the sea, for the most part, are sharp and pointed, and these give countless wounds to such as walk thereon. Moreover, one meets also a mass of branches of a thing whereof I cannot say whether it be tree or stone, only it is like white coral, and is also branched and pointed, but not polished at all; on the contrary, it is very rough, and all hollow and pierced with little holes, and

[1] Mr. Bell notes the prevalence of this notion, that the islands are wasting away (p. 2), and mentions in confirmation that the black soil of the islands is in some places to be seen below low-water mark; but adds that it is admitted that additions are made to the inhabited islands. Valentyn states that, according to Sinhalese tradition, Ceylon and the Maldives were formerly one island.

[2] M. *Femunu* (Chr. and Bell). In his Treatise (see vol. ii), Pyrard mentions a smaller kind, called *tuberons* (tuberão) by the Portuguese, which may be identified with the M. *miyaru* (Chr.).

quite porous; nevertheless, it is hard, and in weight like stone. In their language the natives call it *aquiry*,[1] and use it for making honey and sugar of cocos, bruising these with little stones and boiling with coco-water: thus are their honey and sugar prepared. That substance (*madrepore*) greatly incommodes those who bathe or wade in the sea; and it was therefore difficult for me to go from isle to isle without a boat; those, however, who are accustomed to it often do so.

Of the islands, an infinite number—that is, as I believe, a large majority—are entirely uninhabited,[2] and have only trees and herbs; others have no vegetation, and are merely shifting sand, some being for the most part submerged at high tides, and laid bare when the sea is low, the remaining part being covered with large crabs, called *cacouué*,[3] and crayfish, or else with numbers of birds called *pinguy*,[4] which lay there their eggs and young, and in quantities so prodigious that one could not (and I have often tried it) plant one's foot without

[1] Madrepore, M. *hiri* (Chr.). Mr. Bell compares the Sin. *hækiri*, also the Sin. *hirigal*, "coral stone". Chr. gives *hiri*, "white coral", and *mudu*, "madrepore".

[2] It would be a difficult, if not an impossible task, to attempt to count the uninhabited islands, even with our very excellent Admiralty charts. The number of inhabited islands is as follows:—

Atoll.	Inhab. Islands.	Atoll.	Inhab. Islands.
1. Tiladummati . .	17	9. Mulaku . . .	8
2. Miladummadulu .	32	10. Kolumadulu . .	11
3. Fádiffolu . .	2	11. Haddummati . .	12
4. Málosmadulu . .	30	12. Huvadú . . .	17
5. Ari	13	13. { Addu / Fua' Mulaku } .	7
6. Málé	8		
7. Felidu	5		
8. Nilandú . . .	13	Total .	175

Colonel Yule has numbered 602 islands with names on the Admiralty Chart.

[3] M. *Kakuni* (Chr.); Sin. *Kakuluwa*.

[4] There are no penguins at the Maldives; he means probably *manchots*.

touching their eggs or young, even the birds themselves, for they fly not away at the sight of men. For all that, the islanders eat them not, good eating though they be; they are as large as pigeons, and of a black and white plumage. These islands, which I have said are uninhabited, appear from a distance as white as if they were covered with snow; this is from the exceeding whiteness of the sand, which is as loose and fine as that of an hour-glass, and so warm that these birds' eggs are easily hatched in it. These islands but rarely have fresh water; the others which are covered, whether inhabited or not, have it, excepting some, whose inhabitants have to go to the neighbouring islands to fetch it; they have also contrivances for catching that which falls from heaven[1]; and though they have water on these islands, it is not all alike, being better in some places than in others. All their well water is not good and wholesome. They make their wells in this fashion: by digging for three or four feet, more or less, they find fresh water in abundance, and what is a very strange thing, at four paces from the beach, even in places that are often washed by the sea. I have observed that the water was quite cold by day, especially at noon, and at night was quite warm.

But to return to the thirteen atollons. Hear their names,[2] commencing from the most northern, which is at the head of the rest, and on that account called by the Portuguese *Cabexa de las ilhas*, and in the Maldive language *Tilla dou matis*, with the same meaning, that is, "the highest point"; it

[1] Mr. Bell informs me that the natives use two simple contrivances for catching the rain: (1) a cloth is stretched horizontally, with a stone in the centre of it, under which vessels are placed to catch the water as it filters through; (2) coco-nut leaves are tied tightly round coco-tree trunks near the ground, and the rain as it runs down is conducted into vessels.

[2] The names of the atolls, according to the more correct modern system of transliteration, will be found above, p. 97, *note*. Compare the names given by Ibn Batuta, see App. A. The termination *dou*, *dous*, or *doue*, also written *diva*, is the Sansk. *dwípa*, Sin. *duwa*, "island".

is under the eighth degree from the line to the northward, at the same altitude as Cochin,[1] and no more. So the first atollon is called *Tilla dou matis;* the second, *Milla doue madoue;* the third, *Padypolo;* the fourth, *Malos madou;* the fifth, *Ariatollon;* the sixth, *Malé atollon*, which is the principal one, having in it Malé island, the capital of all the others; the seventh, *Poulisdous;* the eighth, *Molucque;* the ninth, *Nillandous;* the tenth, *Collo madous;* the eleventh, *Adoumatis;* the twelfth, *Souadou;* the thirteenth, *Addou* and *Poua Molucque*, which are two little ones, distinct and separate like the others, but so small that they are only counted as one. Generally *Addou*, being the chief, gives its name to the other. During my sojourn I was in all the atollons, and sailed about them with the natives.[2] Each of these atollons is separated from its neighbour by a sea channel, and these vary, some being narrow and some wide; but whichever they be, you cannot pass them in large ships without disaster. Albeit, there are four much wider than the others, which the largest ships can pass; but even these are very dangerous, and it is hazardous to go by them, especially by night; for then you are infallibly lost, as we were, for you must meet with some shallows and reefs, which ought to be avoided. I have seen at the Maldives many marine charts, in which all this was very precisely laid down.[3] The people

[1] The northernmost island of the Maldives is in 7° 6′ N.; Cochin is in 9° 55′.

[2] This statement may be taken generally. He does not describe any trips made round the atolls.

[3] These charts (M. *muruba*, Chr.; *mouraban*, Pyr., Voc.) have been seen in Ceylon (Tennent, *Ceylon*, i, 612, *note*). Sir A. Johnston, a former Chief Justice of Ceylon, obtained two of them, which he presented to the Royal Asiatic Society (Christopher's paper in *J. R. A. S.*, vol. vi); but these appear to have been lost. Mr. Bell has in his possession several charts of the coasts of India and Ceylon; but he never saw among them any of the Maldives themselves. From the photographs of these charts most of them seem fairly good copies of European originals: the one of Ceylon and the Coromandel coast given here is the worst of the lot, *i.e.*, the most purely native production.

also were wondrous clever at avoiding them and in getting out of the most dangerous passages without harm. I have often seen them pass through the midst of reefs, shoals, and rocks, by channels so narrow that there was room only for the boat, and sometimes so tight was the fit that she would scrape both her sides on the rocks, and for all that the natives would go with confidence through these hazards, and with all sails set, while I, travelling under their conduct, suffered the gravest apprehensions: this often happened to me. But I was never so afraid as on one occasion when I was with some of them in a little boat of not more than four arm-lengths, in a sea towering above me two pikes high, more stormy and swollen than ever was. Every moment it seemed that a wave would carry me off the boat, wherein I had much trouble to hold myself, while they recked nothing of it, and only laughed; for they fear the sea not a whit, and are exceedingly adroit in managing their barques and boats, being brought up to it from their youth, as well the great lords as the poorest of the people: not to understand these matters would be esteemed a disgrace. So it would be impossible to tell the number of barques and boats upon all the islands, for the poorest will have a boat of his own, and a rich man will have many. They never navigate by night, wherefore they fetch land every evening; they steer only by eyesight and without compass, except when they go beyond their own islands on a long voyage. For the same reason they take not much provisions, buying from day to day whatever they require at the several islands. A great number of the islands within an atollon are also surrounded by a shoal, with only one or two openings, very narrow and difficult to notice, and therefore much need for them to know how to manage their barques dexterously; otherwise, if they made the least mistake in the world, their barque would be upset and their merchandise lost. As for the men, they can swim so well that in these sea passages they always save themselves; and, in truth, they are half fish, so accustomed are they to the sea, in which they pass their days, either swimming or wading or in boats. I have seen them many a time within the reefs where the sea is calm—I have seen them, I say, swim after fish, which they have suddenly caught sight of while bathing, and catch them in their course. That is quite a common thing. And yet they often lose their barques, with all their dexterity. They are most troubled by the currents *oyuarou*,[1] which run now to the east, now to the west, through the island channels, and in other parts of the sea, six months one way and six months the other; and not six months for certain either way, but sometimes more and sometimes less, and this is what deceives them, and usually causes the loss of their vessels. The winds are often steady, like the currents from the east or the west; but they vary even more, and are not so regular, sometimes veering to the north or south; while the current always keeps its accustomed course until the season changes. This, as I have said, is variable, and is the cause of disasters to the shipping. I shall note some instances hereafter.

In connection with this there is also a feature well worthy of note. It is that the atollons, which, as I have said, are all in a line and end to end, separated by the sea channels, have openings or entrances opposite each other, two on one side and two on the other, by means of which you can go and come from atollon to atollon and have communication at all times: in which thing is to be observed an effect of God's providence, which leaves nothing imperfect. For if there were only two openings in each atollon—that is, one at each end—it would not be possible to pass from atollon to atollon, from opening to opening, owing to the strength of the currents, which run six months to the east and six months

[1] M. *oyivaru* (Bell); Sin. *oya*, "river". As to the plural form, *varu*, see Professor Childers, in *J. R. A. S.*, New Series, vii, 35. According to Mr. Bell, however, this form is used for singular as well as plural.

to the west, and suffer you not to cross, but carry you down. And in cases where the two openings were not opposite each other, but one on towards the east and the other towards the west, you could easily get across and enter, but you could not return until after the six months were past and the current changed.

As the entrances are disposed, you can go from one atollon to another, notwithstanding the current, at all seasons, and traffic and communicate freely, as in fact they do. For each atollon has an opening at four places, corresponding to its two neighbours; for example, there is an opening toward the east, which is almost directly opposite the entrance to the other atollon; and on the western side there is another, which is likewise over against that of the neighbour on that side; so that if the current is running from east to west, you cannot cross direct from opening to opening; but in this case you set out from the eastern opening, which is the higher up the current, and over-thwarting it, enter the other atollon by the western opening. And so you can speedily return at all times without awaiting the change of season; but then you must set out from the eastern opening, which is opposite the one you started from, and, over-thwarting the current, make the western opening of the other atollon. When the current changes, and runs from west to east, you must do the opposite to what I have said: that is, set out from up the current, and enter by the opening of the other atollon, which is down the stream, that will be towards the east. The utility and necessity of these openings further appear in this, that notwithstanding them, barques and boats are very often lost, being carried out of their course by the currents, and chiefly when they are caught by calms or contrary winds on their passage; but if these openings were not where I have described them, it would be much worse, and you could not navigate frcm atollon to atollon.

For the rest, these entrances to the atollons vary in size,

some are broad, some narrow; the broadest is not more than two hundred paces or thereabouts; while some are hardly thirty, and even less. At each side of these entrances to each atollon are two islands, and you might say that they were for the very purpose of guarding the entrance; for, in fact, it would be easy with cannon to prevent ships from entering in, seeing that the broadest is no more than two hundred paces.

As for the channels, called by them *Candou*,[1] which separate the atollons, four of them are navigable for large ships passing the Maldives; all sorts of foreign craft use them, but not without danger, and many are lost every year. It is not that men choose to pass through: on the contrary, they avoid them as much as possible; but these islands are so situated in the midst of the sea, and are of such extent, that it is difficult to avoid them; the currents, more than anything else, carry the ships out of their course during calms and contrary winds, when sails are of no avail to escape the currents. The first (channel) to take from the north is that at the entering in whereof we were wrecked on the reef of Malosmadou atollon. The second, nearer to Malé, is called *Caridou*,[2] in the midst of which is the largest of all the islands, surrounded by reefs, as I have described. The third is beyond Malé, to the south, and is called *Addou*. The fourth is called *Souadou*, which is directly under the equinoctial line, and is the widest of all, being more than twenty leagues broad.[3] The islanders, while going among the islands

[1] M. *Kaḍu* (Chr. and Bell). The same word is used for "channel" and for "sea" (Chr. and Pyr., Voc.). In the former signification, *cf.* Tam. *kaḍi*, "to cut"; in the latter, Tam. *kadal*, "sea".

[2] So named from the island *Kaharidú*, or *Karhidú*. If the latter be correct, it would seem to mean the "Coco-nut Island", from *karhi*, "coco-nut".

[3] Mr. Bell understands the first of these to be the Moresby Channel (M. *Dekuna Kaḍu*); the second, the *Kaharidú*, or channel of Cardiva island; the third, the *Ariyadú*. The *Souadou* is generally known in

and atollons, do not use the compass; but only on long voyages beyond, and on crossing this wide channel, they use it. All the other channels between the atollons are quite narrow, and full of shoals and flats, and can only be crossed in small barques; and even then a good knowledge of the ground is required to escape danger. I have been surprised, while sailing with the islanders on the channel which separates Malé and Poulisdou (it bears the name of Poulisdou,[1] and is seven leagues broad or thereabouts), to find the sea as dark as the anchor; and for all that, if you put it in a pot, it was just like other water: I saw it ever bubbling in dark eddies, like water over a fire. The sea does not flow at this place as elsewhere, and this was fearful to behold: it seemed I was in a whirlpool, as I did not see the water flow one way or the other. Nor can I assign a cause for this; but I know well that the natives are afraid of it: they often meet with storms there.

As I have said that these islands are so near the equinoctial line on each side, you may imagine what is the quality of the air (viz.), that it is very intemperate, and the heat excessive. The night and the day are of equal duration at all seasons; the nights are quite cool, and bring an abundance of dew. It is on account of this coolness that this country may be lived in without inconvenience, and herbs and trees abound, notwithstanding the heat of the sun. Winter begins in April, and lasts six months; summer, in October, and likewise lasts six months. There is no frost in winter, but continual rain. The winds then are stronger from the west; on the other hand, the summer is extremely hot, and there is no rain; the winds are then from the east.

English charts as the One-and-a-half Degree Channel. But Pyrard omits two others, the Véimandú, or Kolumaḍulu, and the Equatorial Channel, south of Suadiva atoll, both of which are regularly used by large ships (*Bell*, i, 4; Taylor's *Sailing Directory*, i, 567–9).

[1] M. *Fuḷidú Kaḍu.*

It is believed that the Maldives were formerly peopled by the Cingala (for so they call the people of Ceylan); but I find that the Maldivians do not in any way resemble the Cingala, who are black and ill-shapen, while the former are of good form and proportion, and differ but little from ourselves, saving in their colour, which is olive.[1] Yet it may be believed that the climate and lapse of time have rendered them more fair than were those who first peopled the islands. Add to this, that a large number of foreigners from all parts meet there and make it their home; besides many Indians who from time to time are wrecked there, as we were, and remain at the islands. This is why the people living at Malé and the neighbouring parts toward the north are more polished, genteel, and civilised, while those toward the south are ruder in language and habits, and also are less well-formed in body, and darker; and you see many women, chiefly the poor, go about naked, without any shame, with nothing on but a little cloth to cover their private parts.[2] The northern parts, therefore, are more frequented by foreigners, who usually marry there. There, too, pass all the ships, which enrich the country and tend to civilise it, and so people of quality and means go there more willingly than to the south, whither, as I have said, the king sends those whom he would punish with banishment; albeit the people of the south are no less well-informed and clever than the rest, perhaps more so in some ways; but as for the

[1] See further below, ch. xix. The Maldivians may, as a rule, be fairer than the low country Sinhalese, but are, I believe, no fairer than the Kandyans. As will be seen in his chapter on Ceylon (vol. ii, chap. x), Pyrard knew little of that island, and probably nothing of the interior. Mr. Bell is distinctly of opinion that our author is wrong in his contrast, and that the Maldivians compare badly with either the Kandyans or the low country Sinhalese, whether in face or figure.

[2] In all parts of the Maldives, nowadays, the women are decently attired.

nobles, they are all in the north, where, too, the soldiers are obtained.[1]

In short, the people are exceeding adroit, much given to the manufacture of all kinds of things, and excelling therein, even in letters and science, according to their notions; but more especially in astrology, of which they make great business. They are a prudent and circumspect people, very cunning in trade and in social life. And while they are valiant, and courageous, and skilled in arms, they live under a complete system of law and police.[2] As for the women, they are pretty, for all they are of an olive complexion; and yet you find some as fair as in Europe, albeit their hair is always black; but that they esteem a beauty, and many make it come so by keeping the girls' heads shaven up to the age of eight or nine, only leaving them a little hair all along the forehead,[3] to distinguish them from the boys, who have none at all, except the eye-brows; and from the time the children are born they shave their heads every week, and this makes the hair very black, though it would in some cases have been otherwise, for I have seen some children with it almost fair.

[1] Our knowledge of the southern atolls is, unfortunately, very limited. One authority, however, the captain of the s.s. *Consett*, wrecked on Suadiva atoll in 1880, gives a pleasant picture of the islands there. He describes the people as "very obliging, kind, and friendly", not ignorant, having books in their own language, and carrying on manufactures of coir yarn and rope, fine rush mats, fans, and tatties. The children are taught to read; the women are prettily dressed, and morality is good (*Bell*, 19).

[2] The following character of the Maldivians, given by Barros, shows the unjust notions current among the Portuguese: "A gente destas ilhas, com quem os nossos tem communicação, é baça fraca e maliciosa, cousas que sempre andam juntas, não somente com a natureza dos homens, mas ainda nos brutos animaes, donde se pode verificar uma paradoxa, que todo fraco de animo é malicioso em cautellas" (*Dec. III*, liv. iii, c. 7).

[3] Or, as the practice now is, leaving a rim of hair all round the head.

Their hair, then, is in general black, and the blackest is the most admired, as well in men as in women. This blackness, as I have said, comes from their being shaved every week from their birth. It is a beauty among women to have the hair very long, thick, and black; they dress and bathe it often, and clean it with water and washes made on purpose; and after bathing and cleaning their heads and hair, they let it all float in the wind (that is, within their own house-yards) until it be perfectly dry, then they apply oils, very odoriferous, in such wise that their heads are always soaked and oily.[1] For they never wet their bodies, men or women, but after they have oiled,—*i.e.*, two or three times a week for the hair, and for the body sometimes oftener than once a day. They are not obliged to wash their hair except when they have company, and especially every Friday, which is their Sabbath, and on all the other great feasts; the men on the Fridays, and the women on the great feasts only, and besides then as often as they like or require.

The women also perfume their heads, however small their means, and so, after washing, oiling, and perfuming the hair, they dress it, and that is by taking all the hair from the front behind, and drawing it as tight as possible, so that not a hair strays hither or thither; then they tie it up behind and make a large knotted bunch; and in order to enlarge that they use a perruque of man's hair (but as long as a woman's), in form like a horse's tail; to hold this, they fix it in the thick end of a kind of thimble, to which all the rest of the hair is fastened. This thimble, of gold or silver, is set with pearls or precious stones, according to their means; and some of them wear two of these false tresses, which serve to form the knot of hair behind, and to enlarge the bunch. Some-

[1] They use, as Mr. Bell informs me, at least four descriptions of hair oil: (1) plain coco-nut oil; (2) the same, scented with jasmine; (3) the same, with champak; and (4) a fish oil.

times, but not always, they insert the sweet-smelling flowers of the country, which are never wanting.[1] And all this is so well managed that not a single hair stands out beyond another.

As for the men, it is only allowed, as I have said, to the soldiers, officers of the king, and nobles to wear their hair long, as these do for the most part, and as long as the women. They take just as much trouble, too, as do the women, in washing, cleaning, oiling, and perfuming it with flowers; and there is no other difference except that the men tie theirs on one side or on the top of the head, and not behind, as the women use; moreover, they never wear a false perruque. Nevertheless, they are not obliged to wear their hair so, but short or long, as they think fit, as moustaches or whiskers are worn with us.[2] I have seen there the king and the princes and most of the lords and soldiers wear their hair short, and some of those who generally wore it long, when they got tired of it, or when it ceased to grow, cut it off and sell or give it to the women; for the false perruques are only those of men; the women never have their hair cut, alive or dead. Most of these false tresses come from the mainland, from Cochin, Calicut, and the Malabar coast, where all the men grow their hair long, and then cut it and sell it to the women of their own country and to foreigners. Their hair grows much faster than ours, because, as I fancy, they wash and oil it so often; also by reason of the excessive heat, which makes the hair grow more thick and strong: never, however, curly,

[1] No false perruques are now used; but where the hair is insufficient for an ample *koṇḍé*, or chignon, a pad of a certain root is inserted, and the hair dressed over that. No gold or silver hairpins are used, nor other ornaments, except flowers; and these, in the atolls as far south as Málé, must be concealed by the head-kerchief, of which, by the way, Pyrard says nothing.

[2] Whether in obedience to the custom of Indian Mussulmans, or to convenience, as the author's subsequent remarks seem to indicate, the universal practice of Maldivians at the present day, from the Sultan downwards, is to shave the entire head.

as among us. The men are very hairy in their bodies: one could not imagine a covering more thick; they pride themselves in it, as in that in which the strength of a man is. This is not, however, true of them all; and if a man be not thus hairy, they say he is more like a woman than a man, and despise him accordingly. The women are not so, and have hair only on the ordinary places. There are in that country no regular barbers, and every man knows how to shave himself, as well men as women. They use a razor only for that, and they have no combs; but they have scissors of copper and of iron, and mirrors also of copper, which they use for guiding the razor, which is of steel, but not made like ours, which they do not value.[1] They shave themselves in the same way (as we do); but the king and the great lords have men who are proud to do this for them,—not for gain, but from affection, being men of quality; albeit the king makes them some presents at the end of the year.

So, throughout all the islands there is no person, man or woman, rich or poor, gentle or simple, who after the age of fifteen has not a private set of implements for treating the hair, which they are very careful to brush aside when it teases them but a little. As for the girls, they are shaven in youth every week; but to distinguish them from the boys, they have a small fringe left. They wear no clothing up to the age of eight or nine, save only a cloth reaching from the waist to above the knees, and this is first worn when they begin to walk; the boys, however, do not wear it till the age of seven, and until they have been circumcised. They say, with regard to their daughters, that there is no need for them to wear clothing before the time mentioned, for it is then that the breasts begin to swell and rise, and it behoves them to cover them, as parts which they take as much shame in

[1] It need hardly be said that copper scissors and mirrors and Maldivian razors have long since given place to the wares of Sheffield. Glass mirrors, combs, and brushes are in common use.

exposing as we here other parts. Then, too, they let their hair grow, and cut it no more. They are dressed and decked out, as being then eligible for marriage. Before that they are considered children, and no one, man or boy, may talk to them of love, inasmuch as, up to that time, they are not recognised nor attired as girls.

The men, when they grow old, are covered with hair, as I have said; not being clothed from the waist upwards, they shave only as far as the chest and stomach, but in such fashion betimes, cutting it in one place and leaving it in another, that it looks like a slashed doublet. They wear their beards in two styles; the one, which is allowed only to the Pandiares, Naibes, Catibes, and other clerks, and to all who have made the journey to Mecca and Medinatalnaby[1] in Arabia (where is the sepulchre of Mahomet), is to wear the beard as long as possible, and only to shave it under the throat, and above and below the lips: for they would not for the world have anything that they eat or drink touch their hair, that being one of the most disgusting pollutions: therefore they have no hair around the mouth; nay, I have sometimes observed that when they found a single hair upon a dish of meat, they would not touch it, and would rather remain fasting, and give the food to the birds and other animals, no one else caring to touch it. The other kind of beard for all other people and the commonalty is to wear it small, in the Spanish style, shaved round the mouth and under the throat, but without moustaches; on the cheeks they cut little spaces with the scissors, quite close to the skin, but so, however, that some hair is seen. At the chin it is pointed, as with us at present.[2] Moreover, they keep with care the cuttings of their hair and nails, without letting any drop; these they are careful to bury in their cemeteries with a little water; for they would not for the world tread upon them nor cast them in the fire,

[1] Medinat-en-Nabi, "the city of the Prophet".

[2] These two styles are still observed.

for they say that they are part of the body, and demand burial as it does; and, indeed, they fold them neatly in cotton; and most of them like to be shaved at the gates of temples and mosques. They are very handy in this matter, and use no warm water for shaving; their razors cut exceeding ill. They only pass a little cold water over the surface, and however bad a business they make of it, they make no complaint, and aver it gives them no pain. I used to take greater precaution, and had the water warmed, and soaked my hair a long while; but sometimes I thought they would rasp all my skin off and tear up my hair by the roots. It is a matter of habit with them, for otherwise they would be as sensitive as we. But it is time to come to a particular description of these islands.

The Maldives are very fertile in fruit and other commodities necessary for human life. There is millet in abundance, which they call *Oura*, as well as another small grain called *Bimby*,[1] which is like millet, except that it is black like turnip-seed. These grains are sown and reaped twice a year. They make of them a kind of flour, whereof they concoct a gruel with milk and coco-milk, and also cakes and fritters, and many other comfits. There grow there also roots of divers kinds, on which they live; among others, one called *Itelpoul*,[2] which is plentiful without being sown; it

[1] M. *urá;* Sin. *tana hál* (Setaria Italica); M. *bimbi;* Sin. *kurakkan* (Cynosurus corocanus). Mr. Bell mentions the former as grown in the southern, the latter in the northern atolls. He also mentions a second kind of millet—M. *kudibai;* Sin. *menéri* (Panicum miliaceum)—as found in the south (*Report*, 84). "All the Maldive islands are destitute of grain, except that in the province of *Souweid* (Suádiva) there is a cereal like the *anly*, which is brought thence to Mahal (Málé)" (*Ibn Bat.*, iv, 112).

[2] M. *hittala-fu* (*fu* = "flour"); Sin. *hiritala* (Dioscorea oppositifolia). From it, as Ibn Batuta says, "the natives prepare a flour, with which they make a kind of vermicelli, and this they cook in coco-nut water; it is one of the most agreeable dishes in the world. I had a great taste for it, and ate it often."

is round, and as large as the two fists, or thereabouts. They crush it upon a very rough stone, then they put it on a cloth in the sun to dry; it then becomes very white, like starch or flour, and keeps as long as is desired. They make it into thick soup, cakes, and biscuits, which are very good eating, except that they are too filling for the stomach, and must be eaten fresh, to be wholesome. There are also other kinds of roots called *Alas*,[1] good to eat and plentiful, which are sown and cultivated; one kind red, like beetroot, others white, like turnips; they are in general larger than a man's thigh. They are cooked and served in several ways; and to preserve them the year round (for they are ripe only at the end of winter, in the month of September), they mix them with honey and coco-sugar, and that compound forms a great part of the food of the people. Wheat, which is called *Godam*,[2] and rice, called *Andoue*,[3] do not grow at all; but plenty of rice is brought from the mainland by the merchants, and therefore they use it much, and it is cheap. It is served and eaten in divers ways: it is cooked by itself in water, and eaten with other viands in place of bread, or else mixed with spiceries; sometimes with milk and coco-sugar; sometimes cooked with chickens or fish, which dishes they serve with great neatness and propriety. They also cook it, and then dry and pound it; and with this flour, along with eggs, honey, milk, and coco-butter, they make tartlets and other very excellent cates. Herbs and trees abound everywhere in the islands; a large number bear fruit, others not at all; yet of these latter the leaves are eaten, being sweet

[1] M. *alu*, Sin. *ala*, "root". He particularises the two common kinds of yams, the red and the white. *Ālu* is now in Hind. the common name for the potato; originally that of an esculent *arum*. Yams in Hind. are called *rakt-ālū*, *i.e.*, "red ālū".

[2] M. *godaṇ*; Sans. *godhama*; Tam. *kothumei*.

[3] In the edition of 1619 printed *Indoue*, but corrected as above in edition of 1679. The M. is *haḍu* or *haṇḍu*.

and delicate[1]; others are applied to every sort of use. I shall describe them in detail in another place: it will suffice to have made this mention of them here. As for fruits, there are limes, pomegranates, and oranges, in the greatest possible abundance; bananas, which the Portuguese call Indian figs,[2] but the Maldivians *Quella*.[3] It is a large fruit, which multiplies fast, tasty and very nourishing, so much so, that they feed their babes upon it in place of pap. There are ever so many more which I cannot name, some of which resemble our plums, pears, figs, cucumbers, and melons, though they grow on trees. None, however, is more useful than the coco or Indian nut, which they call *Roul*,[4] and the fruit *Caré*,[5] which is more plentiful at the Maldives than elsewhere. The islands supply many neighbouring countries, and the natives there know better than others how to extract its substance and the commodities it yields. It is, indeed, the most wondrous manna imaginable; for this single tree can supply everything necessary to man, furnishing him in plenty with wine, honey, sugar, milk, and butter. Besides, the kernel or almond is good to eat with all kinds of viands instead of bread: there, they neither make bread nor ever see it; indeed, I was five years or more without tasting it, or even seeing it, and I got so accustomed to that style of living that it seemed not strange to me. Moreover, the wood, bark, leaves, and nuts provide the greater part of their furniture and utensils. But I had rather not tarry in its description here: that were too long a tale, and would take

[1] Mr. Bell states that they eat the leaves of the *manga* and the *kul̤l̤o-filá* trees.

[2] *Figos da India*; see *Garcia de Orta*, fol. 95.

[3] In orig. (and here only) misprinted *qualla*; M. *keyo*; Sin. *kehel*; Hind. *kelā*; Skt. *kadalī*. There are many sorts.

[4] M. *rú*; *cf.* Sin. *ruka*, "tree".

[5] In orig. *cate*, an evident misprint for *caré*, as the M. *karhi* is printed in the Vocabulary, in vol. ii.

me from the course of my story. In another place[1] I will more conveniently give a particular description of this marvellous tree, which will perhaps be more ample than any previous accounts; for I knew it thoroughly; I lived upon it, and had a large number in my possession for a long time. As for firewood, there is so much that it is not bought and sold, the country being quite covered with all kinds of trees, which give capital shade, and a pleasant freshness to the air. People are free to go and cut such trees as are only fit for firewood, at their pleasure. Some of the islands, too, are entirely covered with such timber, which people send their servants and slaves to fetch for their use. With all this abundance of fruits, as I have said, it is a remarkable thing that each of the thirteen atollons yields different produce: for though all are under the same sky, yet each hath not everything needful, and the growth of products cannot be spread from one to the others. You would say that God had willed that these people should visit each other, such diversity is there; what is plentiful in one island is rare in another. I have often wished that some plant which grew abundantly in one place should grow elsewhere; but it will hardly do so, and is not so good or so natural as is grown in those atollons and islands proper to it; in other places it is a forced production. The people, too, in their domiciles have followed a similar rule, for the craftsmen are collected in different isles—for instance, the weavers in one, the goldsmiths, the locksmiths, the blacksmiths, the mat-weavers, the potters, the turners, and the carpenters in others; in short, their craftsmen do not mingle together; each craft has its separate island.[2] But they communicate

[1] See vol. ii.

[2] This is, to some extent, the case still; thus, two islands of Nilandu atoll, Ribadu and Huludeli, are exclusively occupied by men of the jeweller caste and craft. Three islands of Tiladummati atoll, Uligan, Berimadu, and Tiffardu, are occupied by toddy-drawers, and Takandu,

with the other islands in this way. They have boats covered with a little deck, whereby they go from isle to isle, working and dealing in their goods, and it is sometimes more than a year ere they return to the island of their home. They take with them all their male children from the age of four or five upwards, to teach them the business. At their halting-places they always sleep, eat, and drink in their boats, and generally work there too. I remember seeing the tinkers' boat thus going from village to village. I might here specify the atollons and islands which produce peculiar fruits and commodities, but that would be superfluous.

Among their animals are poultry in great plenty, which cost only the catching, for they are wild; and in the market they are sold at a sol apiece, and about thirty-six eggs for the same price. It is the flesh they use the most, next to fish. There are also quantities of pigeons, ducks, rails, and certain birds[1] most resembling sparrow-hawks, spotted with black and grey, which do not, however, live on prey, but on fruits; there are other different species, all wild and undomesticated. The crows annoy the natives much, for they are so bold that they will enter houses to take anything, though people are there, and are not a whit afraid; this seemed very strange to me, and at first I thought they were tame. They are so numerous as to be beyond counting, and the people do not kill them. The bats there are as large

in the same atoll, by tinkers. Mat-weaving is confined to the islands of Huvadú, and the manufacture of cotton-cloth is carried on chiefly in Máḷosmaḍulu, Aḍḍú, and Huvadú atolls. In the remoter parts of Ceylon, villages are exclusively peopled by distinct castes; all are now cultivators of the soil, though they to some extent also pursue their hereditary calling. There, a potter or a blacksmith village would be but a few miles off. At the Maldives, where the island of a particular craft was probably leagues away beyond the channels of ocean, the segregation of trades is remarkable evidence of the endurance of caste after four, and now nearly seven, centuries of Muhammadanism.

[1] The spotted *koil* of India; M. *diṇḍi-koveli*.

as ravens. Much annoyance, too, is suffered from the mosquitos or gnats, which bite keenly. They are as much or more of a nuisance there than at the island of S. Laurens, or anywhere in the Indies. But what trouble the people most are the rats, mice, and ants, which are everywhere, with other kinds of animals and vermin, which come into their houses, and eat and spoil their grain, provisions, fruit, and soft goods; so that they are constrained, in order to obviate this, to build houses and granaries on piles in the sea, at 200 to 300 paces from shore, and thither for safety they convey in boats their grain and fruit. Most of the king's magazines are built in this wise.

There are no venomous animals, except some snakes. There is one kind of snake in the sea which is very dangerous.[1] One sees numbers of cats, polecats, and ferrets.[2] That is all I have to say of the animals native to the islands. I have seen others of all kinds, but they came from abroad. There are no beasts of burden, nor other large animals, either wild or tame. It is true there are about four or five hundred cows and bulls, but they belong to the king, who keeps them at his island of Malé. They had been brought from the continent as a curiosity, and had multiplied to this number, as they are never eaten, except four or five times a year at the great feasts, when the king has one killed, and sometimes to give to foreign ships which the king desires to gratify. I have also seen some sheep, which also belong to the king.[3] He has no dogs: the people have a horror of them. While I was there, the Portuguese of Cochin sent him two, as a

[1] Two kinds of water-snakes are much dreaded by the natives, the *veṇ-harufá* (Hydrophis spiralis), and the *máridá* (Pelamis bicolor) (Bell, *Report*, 85).

[2] By "polecats and ferrets" he evidently means the mongoose (M. *mugari*).

[3] The few sheep and cattle at Málé all belong to the Sultan or great men, and are still kept for the purposes stated. Mr. Bell was presented with a kid on the occasion of his visit.

curiosity, which he incontinently drowned. If a native had been touched by one of them, he would go and bathe at once to purify himself.

The sea yields fish in wondrous wise, of all kinds, great and small: chiefly on account that it is shallow and calm within the atollons, and for other reasons peculiar to those shores. The fishery is of great yield, and it is the chief employment of the islanders; so their principal food is fish, either fresh, with rice or other viands, or fried with coco-oil, or cooked in sea-water and dried as a preserve; and they are daily despatching ships with cargoes of this to Achen, in Sumatra, and elsewhere. Among the fish are some large ones which trouble them, seeing that they devour men when they come to bathe or fish. I myself was within an ace of being devoured by them. One sees many people who have lost arms and legs, or are otherwise maimed.

This great abundance makes living easy, and everything is cheap. You get 400 coco-nuts for a larin,[1] which is of the value of eight sous; 500 bananas also for a larin; for about the same price, 100 large fish, a dozen fowls, or 300 pounds of roots, and so on; so that there is not a country in India where foreigners enrich themselves so fast, for the trade is good, and living costs but little. So they have a proverb, that they themselves will never get rich, but only the foreigners. In my opinion, it is the easy means of living which renders them indolent and negligent, and this prevents them getting rich; for most of them care only for the wherewithal to live, without ambition, desire, or trouble for aught beside.

The principal island, as I have said, is called Malé, which gives its name to all the others; for the word *Dives*[2] means a number of little islands collected together. It is about the

[1] In recent years the price has been 90 coco-nuts for 1 rupee.

[2] M. *divehi*, applied to the whole Maldivian group. They call themselves *divehi-mihun*, "the island men".

middle of the other islands, and is about a league and a half in circumference. It is the most fertile of all, and the emporium both for them and for foreigners. It is the residence of the king and of the court: for this reason it is the most thickly peopled; but it is also the most unhealthy, for which they assign this cause, viz., that, time out of memory, the kings have resided here, and there have died a vast number of people, who have been separately buried, so that the whole island is full of corpses, and the sun, beating down upon the soil, has caused noxious vapours to arise. The water, too, is very bad,[1] wherefore the king is compelled to send, for the use of himself and his house, to a neighbouring island,[2] where it is better, and no one is buried. The nobles and people of means at Malé do the same.

Throughout the islands there are no walled towns—not even in the island of Malé; but over the whole island are scattered here and there houses and buildings, both of the lords and of the commonalty; and so at the other islands. Sometimes the houses are separated by streets and into quarters, with neat arrangement; and everyone knows his own parish.[3]

The houses and buildings of the common folk are of coco-wood, cut from the trunks of the trees; they are thatched with the leaves of the same tree, plaited together double. The nobles and the rich build houses of stone, raised from the

[1] Mr. Christopher states, with reference to this passage, that there are wells all over the island of Málé; but he never heard that the natives entertained this bad opinion of the water (*T. B. G. S.*, i, 58). Mr. Bell, on the other hand, informs me that the water is not good. He does not know of any neighbouring island from which a pure supply could be obtained; but the Sultan and great men do occasionally have it brought from Kurendú, in Fadiffolu atoll, where it is of excellent purity.

[2] Probably *Bados;* above, at p. 85, he says that the water was better there.

[3] M. *avaru*, of which Málé now has four; other islands are similarly divided.

shallows of the sea, where they get as much as they want, both as to length and thickness.[1] It is polished, and of good grain, very white, but a little hard in some cases for cutting and working; in time it loses its natural hardness and whiteness, and at length becomes quite black, after being beaten with rain or soaked in fresh water. The manner of drawing up this stone from the sea is remarkable. There grows, in these countries, a kind of tree called *Candou*,[2]

[1] The general use of stone has not been maintained. Mr. Bell, in 1879, found only one house built of it at Málé, besides the Sultan's. The dwellings of the well-to-do natives are now of wood; those of the poor of coco-thatch, or wattle and daub, with thatched roofs, resembling the "lines" of Tamil coolies (*Report*, 56). Pyrard may be going too far in saying that the houses of the nobles were built of stone; if this were so, some of them would probably be standing still. Ibn Batuta states that stone was used in his time for the foundations, and the Indian surveyors of 1835 found only the ruins of a few houses built of madrepore. The following account is still true: "Their houses are ill-built and dark, having at most only one small window, and frequently none at all; in fact, they are but large-sized huts with a peaked roof, in general about 28 feet long by 12 broad, and 15 feet high to the top of the roof. They are made of a substantial frame-work of wood, thatched all over with coco-nut leaves; the floor is plastered, and the sides are sometimes boarded; a partition near the middle divides the house into two rooms, one of which is private and the other open to visitors. In this public room there are two ranges of seats; the one on the right side on entering is considered the most honourable, and the other on the left (carried across the house) is appropriated for the common people" (Chr., in *T. B. G. S.*, i, 59). Mr. Bell supplies the Maldive names for this description. The inner or private room is the *eteri-gé* or *maval-gé*; the outer, or public room, is *béru-gé*; the range of seats on the right is *kuḍa-arhi*; the other is *boḍu-arhi* (*Report*, 56).

[2] M. *kadu*, pronounced *kandu*. It is now used precisely as Pyrard describes. There are two kinds, *mas kadu* and *varu kadu*. Only the former is sawn into planks; it has a larger leaf, and is the heavier. *Varu kadu* (which Pyrard evidently intends to describe) has leaves like the *suriya*. The fruit is small; the nut is not eaten, but is useful for furnishing an oil with which the native boats are caulked. The timber, light as cork, is used for rafts, etc. The species is certainly identical with the Sinhalese *kenda*, of which Moon, in his Catalogue (pp. 10, 160), gives the following five varieties: *Aṇ-* (horn), *alu-* (ashy), *lunu-* (salt), *savu-* (sago), and *ul-* (pointed) *kenda* (Bell).

which is as large as the walnut here, with leaves like the aspen, and as white, but extremely soft. It bears no fruit, and is not even good for burning; when dry, it is cut into planks, which are used as deal is with us. It is the lightest wood possible, more so than cork. On espying, in the sea, a stone which they would have, they make fast a cable to it. That is a common thing for them; for, as I have said, they are half-fish, and very adroit swimmers; their women even swim as well as, or better than, the men of these parts: so that any will, at the slightest need, dive to the bottom of the sea, be it fifteen

Málé Harbour, showing the Breakwater.

or twenty fathoms of water, and will remain there a long time surveying the bottom, very often to see if it is a good place for an anchor; and sometimes, in place of throwing an anchor, they choose some big rock at the bottom of the sea and belay a cable to it. So, when they have chosen the stone they want, and made fast their cable to it, they take a piece of this Candou wood, and fasten it to the cable close to the stone, or if the wood is pierced, run the cable through it, and above that they add as many more like pieces of wood as may be necessary. That wood being marvellously light and buoyant, floats up the stone or other heavy substance, even though it may be of the weight of 100,000 pounds. I have seen this done nearly every day. The cannons of our ship, which were at the bottom of the sea, also the anchors and other heavy things, were got up in this way, in the presence of all of us, who thought to give the people some advice, but they knew how to do it much better than we. By the same means, which is common and ordinary with them, I have seen the harbour of Malé, which was formerly so full of big rocks that ships could not sail nor anchor there in safety, to be cleared and improved and rendered navigable, with a good anchorage, in less than fifteen days.[1] With this floating wood they drew the stones ashore and took them out to a deeper place, and then, cutting the cables, which are made of a certain fine bark,[2] let them fall to the bottom. Stones for their building are got in the same way; but when the wood is soaked with water it must be dried in the sun, otherwise it would not float. I will add two other uses which this Candou wood serves, since I have said so much about it. This is one: they take five or six large pieces of wood, and lash them together in a row, and then place upon them sawn planks of the same timber, so that it makes a level and well-fitted raft; all around the surface they put little benches in front, behind, and at the sides and in the middle, to sit upon. This serves them to go upon the sea, and to pass from island to island. I have been one of ten on board, and it is chiefly with this craft that they do their

[1] Mr. Bell thus writes of Mâlé: "An unbroken reef, just awash, renders its south side inaccessible; but the rest of its circumference has a lagoon or harbour, formed by an artificial bank of coral, 3 to 4 feet above water, and 6 to 8 feet in width, roughly renewed from time to time, which serves as an effective breakwater against the monsoon storms. As the depth of the water inside is from 6 to 14 feet, this harbour gives excellent shelter to both the trading and fishing boats of the natives (*Report*, p. 12).

[2] M. *digga-vakka*: *i.e.*, the bark of the *digga* tree (Bell).

big fishings. Each man has his own, for it is very handy, and requires only one to manage it, whatever the weather may be,—I mean within the atollons and channels, and not upon the high seas. No need to fear that it will capsize, for that wood always floats; and, moreover, in making the raft, they know the proper measurements of wood, and the ordering and balancing of the pieces, so that it never is upset; all they have to fear is lest the pieces should become detached. This (raft) is in their language called *Candoupatis*,[1] from the tree of which it is composed. The Candou tree has another property, viz., that by rubbing small pieces of it one against another, fire is generated, and so they light their fires, using it as we do steel.[2] Thus is their stone for building obtained from the sea in the manner described; as for lime, it is made from the shells found on the sea-shore, and binds exceeding well.

But, since I have spoken of the people, it is meet, before going further, to add a word about their language and what it is.

There are two languages in use. The first is peculiar to the Maldives, and is a very full one. In the five years and more which I spent there, I had mastered it as though it were my mother tongue, and was quite familiar with it. The second is the Arabic, which is highly esteemed, and learnt by them as Latin is with us. It is also used daily in their prayers. There are, besides, extraordinary languages, such as those of Cambay, Guzerat, and Malaca, and even Portuguese, which some learn for the sake of commerce and of the intercourse they have with that nation. In the Sou-

[1] M. *Kadu-fati* (Bell), still made and used as above stated. It is provided with benches, and worked with an oar at the stern, but without sails, and will carry ten persons. As to *fati*, *cf.* the Sin. *pata*. It is used in compounds, as *giléfati*, "necklace".

[2] Only the *mas kadu* is used for this purpose, the *varu kadu* being too soft (Bell).

adou atollon, and towards the south of the Maldives, a language is spoken difficult to understand, rough and barbarous, but still it is the common tongue.[1]

CHAPTER XI.

Of the religion of the inhabitants of the Maldives, and the ceremonies which they observe.

The religion which they profess is that of Mahomet, and there is no other throughout the islands,[2] save among the

[1] The language of the Suvadiva group still preserves more of the Sinhalese character than that of the northern atolls (Bell, *Report*, 69), and the natives of the north have considerable difficulty in understanding those of the southern atolls; but Mr. Bell considers the difference to be no more than exists between our own provincial dialects.

[2] Pyrard does not class as a religion the worship of Nature and of the elements, which undoubtedly existed in his day, and indeed still survives: all such observances he ranks as superstitions. Apart from all these remains of a primitive faith, there lies the question whether Buddhism ever ruled at the atolls. In his time, Buddhism was but little understood, and he himself seems to know nothing of it, so that we need not be surprised to get little or no information from him. We may bear in mind, too, that in India, except where Jainism prevails, traces of Buddhism are to be found in ruins and sculpture, but hardly at all in the religious observances of the people. Further than this, Mahommedanism has in all cases made a cleaner sweep of all pre-existing forms of worship than any other missionary religion. Yet it seems likely that further investigation will justify the conjecture already made by me (*J. R. A. S.*, vol. x, new series), that there was an intervening Buddhism at the Maldives. The Sinhalese chronicles and sacred books are found to contain no reference either to the Maldivians or to their religion. Christopher, however, notes that at the Maldives the body is buried in the posture of the recumbent Buddha—*i.e.*, on the right side, with the right hand under the right ear, and the left placed along the thigh. But this was the mode used with Muhammad himself, and adopted throughout all Islam (Burton, *Pilgrimage, etc.*, vol. ii, ch. 2). Christopher was also informed by a learned Buddhist priest that there were formerly on

foreigners who land there; albeit of these the most frequent are Arabs, Malabars, and Indians of Sumatra, who hold the same faith. Their temples are called Mesquites,[1] which are

the Maldives two noted temples of Buddha. He gave the names of the islands, but Christopher "could not recognise them as perpetuated to the present day". The name of the priest is not given, and no Sinhalese priest now knows anything of the matter. Mr. Bell, however, has it on the assertion of trustworthy natives, that there are on the island Fua Mulaku "jungle-covered ruins of a tope or dagaba, and amid them the stone image of a Buddha in the *sthánamudrá*, or standing position." The tope is described as resembling the solid bell-shaped dagabas, rising from platforms, usual in Ceylon. Such ruins the islanders of the southern atolls term *astabu* (Aḍḍu atoll), *havitta* (Fua Mulaku), and *vére* (atolls further north), in which it is easy to recognise the Sanskrit *stúpa*, *chaitya*, and *vihára*. One of the islands in Ari atoll is called *Vihama-furhi*, and one in Málé atoll *Vihamaná-furhi*, meaning "the island of delightful Viharas". Mr. Bell notes an island called *Muñña-furhi*, perhaps = *Munipura*, "Buddha's city"; and another, *Huludeli*, Sin. *saladala*, "Bo-tree island". He also mentions that the term applied by the Maldivians to their first sovereign converted to Muhammadanism is *Darumavanta*, *i. e.*, *Dharmmavanta*, "religious", "just". Christopher further states that the Bo tree (*Ficus religiosa* or *Pipal*) is said to be "still suffered to stand alone in the vicinity of mosques, when all other shrubbery is cleared away for the burial-ground." As to this, Mr. Bell remarks that only two Bo trees (M. *bói gas*) are known to be growing at the present day on the Maldives: one in Suvadiva atoll, the other at Málé, near the palace, but not within the walled enclosure or burial-ground of any mosque. So little is known of the islands individually, that it is rather premature to conclude that there are not more Bo trees, or that it is not held in some veneration. The evidence of names is not of great value, unless coupled with other testimony; but the existence of actual dagabas, witnessed by any European who knows a Buddhist building, will settle the question (see Christopher, *Trans. Bom. Geo. Soc.*, i, pp. 313-14; Bell, *Report*, pp. 59, 74, 75). Since the above went to press, a pamphlet on the island of Minicoy has appeared, from the hand of Mr. O. Bartholomeusz, the medical officer who served there during the erection of the lighthouse. He states that "the general belief of the islanders is that their ancestors were Buddhists"; and that there still exist, in close proximity, the ruins of a Buddhist temple and of an artificial tank. But whether the temple be a *dagaba* or a *vihara*, and upon what evidence its Buddhist character is determined, he does not indicate.

[1] M. *miskítu*.

well built of fair worked stone, and well bonded; they have thick walls, and stand in the middle of a large walled square, which is their cemetery, where they bury their dead,—or rather, some of them: for they choose burial-places where they will, and everyone likes to have a place for his own. The temple is square, facing the west, for that, they say, is the direction of the sepulchre of Mahomet. It has three doors, and at the entrance to each, on the outside, there is a large well, descended by steps, the bottom and sides of which are paved and fitted with flat stones, well polished and neat, to accommodate them at their ablutions; and thence to the door is a paved way of the same stone (for all the rest of the close or cemetery is only sand), so that they may not be soiled after bathing, and then they must mount eight or nine steps to the elevation of the temple. The paved floor of the temple is covered with pretty mats and carpets; and they are careful to keep it neat and clean; none durst even spit or blow his nose there; and if they have no handkerchief, and have a mind to spit, they must go to the door-step and spit outside. The superstructure is of wood, the carpentry of which I admired much, for it could not be better polished or worked. The walls are wainscoted with wood, worked and fitted in the same way; and the whole of the woodwork, outside and in, is put together without nail or bolt of any kind, and yet holds so fast that one could not take it to pieces unless one knew the artifice. You see large slabs, either of stone or wood, fixed to the walls in divers places, on which are engraved letters and inscriptions in the Arabic language. At the end of the temple, towards the west, there is a little enclosure, like a chapel in the choir of a church (that is, in the temple of Malé), where the king sits along with his nearest relative, who carries his sword and shield, the Pandiare, one of the Catibes, and the four Moudins.[1] Next to this enclosure are two large galleries, where the

[1] M. *Fadiyaru*, *katíbu*, *mudímu*.

soldiers and their captain sit with their arms. And generally throughout the temple, which is spacious and of large extent, there are partitioned spaces for certain persons—not, however, for a single person, but for those of a certain order, estate, age, or quality.[1] And this order is so well observed, that no one would dare to set himself in a place ordained for one of another condition, otherwise he would be fined in a penalty prescribed in this behalf; so there is no jealousy or dispute about places, and a commoner could as easily get a great lord fined on the spot for taking his place, as the lord the commoner. In this temple are lamps kept burning continually; there are coco-trees set apart as an endowment for this purpose by every man and woman householder, who help to keep it up. These temples, or mesquites, are very numerous in all the inhabited islands, and in some islands one sees as many as nine or ten; but their festival is celebrated in one only, which is ordained for the purpose, and is in consequence greater than the others, the latter being like chapels or oratories for praying in, founded by the devotion of individuals. The principal one, in which the festival is held, is built and maintained at the common expense, and is called *Oucourou mesquite*.[2] It is also to be remarked that the festival is not celebrated in any island unless it has forty persons above the age of fifteen years, not counting the Catibe; consequently, in such an island there cannot be a Catibe, who is the principal officiating minister in the ceremony. In such case the inhabitants go to a neighbouring island; albeit, they have one or more mesquites in their own

[1] I am indebted to Mr. Bell for the accompanying plan of the chief mosque at Málé, and the interior arrangements at present. He has obtained this from his Maldive pandit, who, on hearing Pyrard's account interpreted to him, bore witness to its substantial accuracy. The walls of the partitions are said to run to the roof, or at least above a man's height. They are loopholed or trellised, so as to allow of hearing, and, to some extent, of seeing through.

[2] M. *Hukuru miskítu*, *i.e.*, Friday mosque: *Jamu' Masjid* of India.

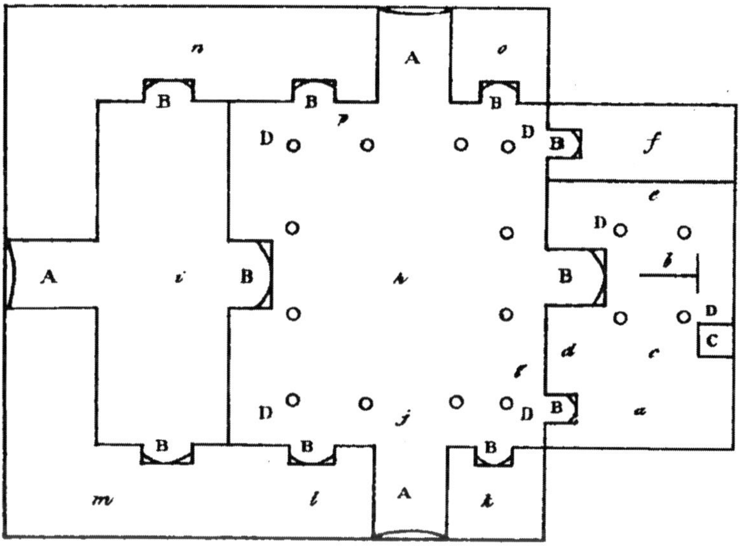

GROUND PLAN OF THE INTERIOR ARRANGEMENT OF THE CHIEF MOSQUE

(*HUKURU MISKITU*) AT MÁLÉ.

A. Principal doors.
B. Entrances to partitions.
C. Pulpit.
D. Pillars (16).
a. The Sultan.
b. Katību (officiating).
c. Mudimun (priests).
d. Vazirun (ministers of state).
e. Dari-kalun (Sultan's children).
f. Kilagé-fanu (lords).
g. Sáhibun (nobles).
h. Laskarun (soldiers).
i. Rayyetun (commonalty).
j. Askaru-muskulin (?).
k. Kudi-bé-kalun (palace guard).
l. Dorhun, special attendants of Mosque.
m. Miskitu mīhun, attendants of Mosque.
n. Abudálun (fakirs).
o. Majalis-bé-kalun (?).
p. Askarun (?).

island for their daily prayers. Each mesquite has its own priest, called a *Moudin*,[1] who receives the revenues and takes charge of it as a chaplain does of his chapel. The islands which have a sufficient number of people have also a Catibe, or rector, who is a superior priest of their religion, and says the public prayers, and delivers sermons and homilies, having under him the moudins of the several mesquites. All work together in teaching the people the law of Mahomet, and especially the moudins, who teach the children to read and write the language of the country, and that of Arabia, in return for which the parents give them some fitting reward.

Every day of the week they go at daybreak to the temple, and for this they give a reason according to their belief, viz., that the world is flat, and not round, and that there is a wall of copper all around which prevents the world from being submerged by the waters which encompass it[2]; and that the devil, the enemy of the human race, is at hand all night trying to pierce and undermine this work, and when the day breaks he must nearly have worked a hole. By reason whereof all the men from fifteen years of age upwards go at break of day to the mesquites to make their orisons, for without prayers the world would perish. Four other times during the day they enter it,—at noon, at three in the afternoon, at sunset, and at ten at night, remaining in the mesquite each time for about half-an-hour. The women never enter the temples, but remain at home and say their prayers there. Nevertheless the men need not go to the temples on week days if not so disposed, but may say their prayers and perform the ceremonies called *Namandé*[3] at their own

[1] M. *mudímu;* Ar. *muaḍḍhin.*

[2] The Arabs believe the earth to be flat and surrounded by the ocean (el-Bahr el-Mobeet), which is surrounded by a chain of mountains called Kaf. The latter are described by El-Kazwini as composed of green chrysolite, like the green tint of the sky. These mountains are the abode of the Jinn (Lane, *Ar. Soc. in the M. Ages*, pp. 100, 104).

[3] M. *namādu*, Sin. *namadawā*, Pers. *namāz.*

houses or elsewhere; and what is more, no one is compelled to say prayers. If, however, it were known that a man did not say them at all, no one would eat or hold intercourse with him: that is all the punishment that would befall him; and such a one, they would say, was not a good Mussulman; and for this reason they nearly all do it; yet it is a heavy tax upon their time, whether they are busy or not. They also use beads, as we do, but without crosses.

Before entering the temple they wash their feet, hands, ears, mouth, and eyes, using the while certain ceremonies and prayers, which vary according to the hour, festival, or other occasion; for example, when they have performed the offices of nature, or touched their privy parts, they have to wash and to say prescribed prayers; so also, after sexual intercourse they must bathe the whole body,[1] and say other prayers; if it has been with his own wife, they must be of another kind, for they hold themselves polluted by it, and they would not omit this ceremony for anything, believing that by this means they are purified of their sins and defilements. What I considered indecent, besides the superstition of their damnable and abominable errors, was their washing and bathing all in the public gaze, and many together, and saying their prayers quite loud, whereby from their various prayers one became aware of their most secret doings,—when they had slept with their wives, and when not, and when with other women.

All are circumcised (they call circumcision *Seunat*[2])—that is to say, the male children—when they reach the age of seven; then they hold a feast for all comers, which lasts for ten

[1] The references here are to the greater and less ablutions, *ghusl* and *wuḍû*, the former being used after such pollutions as he mentions, the latter on every occasion before prayer (see Sale, *Koran*, Prel. Disc.).

[2] Ar. *sunnah*, "the duty". Christopher gives the M. verb *gebaindang*, "to circumcise". The age varies between six and sixteen among Mahommedans, but the rite is not performed until the boy can distinctly pronounce the profession of faith (Sale, *Koran*, Prel. Disc.).

days, according to their means, and there is dancing to the music of flutes and tambourines, and other rejoicings. For circumcision there are operators who only circumcise, and do nothing else. This is the manner of the proceeding. Six or seven hours before the circumcision, the child is bathed in the sea, and kept there till the hour arrives, for they say that this causes the member to shrink, and renders the skin more soft. A shed is constructed on purpose in the yard of each man's house, covered all round with cloths, or silk stuffs; the floor of it is covered with fine white sand. The child is then brought into the shed, where, to prevent him struggling, two or three moudins are stationed, who meanwhile chant the proper verses and prayers. The operator, taking a little white lime, marks all round the member the line where he has to cut, then draws the prepuce as far as he can and ties it with a little cord, and then performs the operation with a razor used only for that, and very keen and sharp. The boy is tended and doctored by the operator himself, until he is recovered. Meanwhile, the relatives and friends of the parents come to visit him, bringing presents for the operator, who also receives payment from the father. Recovery takes about fifteen days, and then the operator takes the circumcised boy to the sea and bathes him, saying prayers and performing ceremonies the while; then he puts into his hand a little palm or coco-branch, fixing at the end of it a little piece of white taffetas, cut to a point like a little pennant, and called *dida*.[1] This they offer, with all their vows and offerings, as we do wax candles; but they offer divers other things, as I shall describe. Before a child is circumcised they say that he is innocent, and cannot sin; and, indeed, most of them before this time wear no cloth to cover their private parts, for they say that one who cannot sin has no shame; but after circumcision they fail not to cover them. For their daughters, there are no feasts or ceremonies, except

[1] M. *dida*, Sin. *dada*, "a flag".

that for their circumcision they draw two or three drops of blood when they reach the age of two years. When the children grow up they hold in great respect the man who circumcised them, and call him their master.

Throughout the year they celebrate many festivals. In the first place, the Friday of every week is kept solemn. They call this festival *Oucourou*,[1] and in Arabic *diu matil*,[2] and all the people join in it—*i.e.*, the men and youths, but not the women, nor the boys until they have attained the age of fifteen, or are at least proficient in the faith, and have been through the whole of the Alcoran, which they call *Couroan*.[3] On Thursday evening, the eve of the festival, some have vespers said at home: this they call *Saluat*[4]; others have prayers made for the dead, and with this view prepare some food and drink, sending the same to their priests or Moudins of the mosques near which the deceased are buried; or else they bid them to come and say the prayers at their houses (this prayer is called *Pastia*[5]), and entertain them; so that often the Moudins cannot partake of the repast, and put off saying prayers for some, for fear lest they should be obliged to eat when they cannot. All this evening they use quantities of perfumes, as well in their temples as in their own houses.

This Friday festival is celebrated with great ceremony and in great style, as I have seen it done at Malé. In the morning, the man whose duty it is to make public proclamations on behalf of the king, goes round the island, bearing in his hand a kind of metal bell called *coly*,[6] which resembles the cover of an alembic, with a wooden mallet, with which he strikes the bell; and at every cross-road he stops and admo-

[1] *I.e.*, "Friday". M. *hukuru*, Sin. *sikura-dā*.

[2] Ar. *juma*.

[3] *Kurán:* in Maldive, *guruán* or *guruván*.

[4] M. *salátu;* Ar. *salah*.

[5] Ar. *fátihah*.

[6] M. *Koli*.

nishes the people that it is their *Oucourou* festival. He is assisted by three persons carrying straight trumpets, in their language called *Tarapilly*,[1] which are blown at the same moment. The people, on receiving notice of the festival, cease from their labours, which they may not resume for the rest of the day. They go to bathe and wash, saying certain prayers, which vary according to the occasion or feast at which the ablutions are made; everyone puts on his best clothes, and dons the finest he can, according to his means and quality, and all from the age of fifteen upwards are obliged to be present. Meantime, over the gateway of the king's palace, the players of instruments, different kinds of drums, flutes, hautbois, fifes, etc. (for they have no stringed instruments[2]), play continuously from morning to mid-day. The trumpets, too, are blown; all these have certain single notes, which harmonise very well. The four royal Moudins also are there; they are men of quality, of birth and education, their office being one of honour and dignity; and no one can become Catibe of the king's island unless he has previously been one of these four. They are not like the Moudins of the mosques who minister to the people on all occasions; for they perform service only on the feast day and at other solemnities. These four Moudins all together ascend a stone building of great height, which adjoins the mosque, and putting their hands to their ears, cry out three times in unison, with all their might and in fearful tones, these words in Arabic, "*Alas, alas aquebar*,"[3] that is, "Great God," and add something about Mahomet. Afterwards they go to the king's palace and do the same; and then the king, if he wishes to attend (as, indeed, he seldom fails), sends a carpet of silk

[1] M. *tála fili*.

[2] *Beru*, "tomtoms" or "drums"; *dummárhi*, "flageolets" or "hautbois"; *tára*, "tambourines", are instruments mentioned by Mr. Bell (*Rep.*, 62).

[3] *Allahu Akbar!* "God is great!"

to be put at his place: if he does not so, it is a sure sign that he is not coming. Thence the Moudins proceed to the house of the Catibe, and do the like. On receiving the notice, he attires himself in a long vestment of white cloth, putting over it a cassock, or gown made in the Arab style, with slippers of gilded leather. The Moudins attend him, as he attends the king. If the king is going, all the lords, gentlemen, captains, and soldiers proceed to fetch him at his palace, and accompany him in line, all with their arms, and to the sound of trumpets and drums, in great magnificence.

Minaret and portion of Mosque at Mâlé.

If he does not go, he comes out at his usual hour at mid-day. The Catibe also has his head veiled with a white veil, and over that a large white Turkish turban, which covers him completely, so that he cannot see, and one of the Moudins leads him by the hand, and conducts him to the mosque, where he is the last to arrive. By this time all the people have assembled, and the king is there, and has said his prayers; but as soon as the Catibe enters he must begin at once. So the Catibe (who is a kind of parson), taking his place at the end of the temple, ascends a pulpit of wood, constructed for the purpose, six or seven steps from the ground. There, holding a naked sword in his hand, pointed downwards, he brandishes it to and fro, and recites his usual prayers. During this, all the people are at their prayers, and do their Namandé unceasingly, putting themselves in divers postures, sitting, standing, kneeling, with foreheads to the ground, hands raised and lowered, and then crossed, heads and eyes turned hither and thither. It would be hard to describe all their gestures and antics during this interval. At that time they lay down their arms, and even their knives, and they would not dare have anything upon them but their clothes, which, however, must be of the cleanest. The Catibe changes the prayers every Friday until the end of the year, and then begins afresh. He repeats them all by heart; yet for all that, one of the Moudins holds the book (before him), and if the Catibe haply were to miss a single word, nay, even a syllable or a letter, the Moudin would correct him loudly and distinctly; for they hold that if there should be the slightest fault the festival would be null and void. I have seen them in anxious discussion, one with another, upon this point. In the island of Malé there are two Catibes,[1] who relieve one another, and celebrate the festival in turn, week by week: the other islands have only one. The service lasts about two hours. Sometimes the grand Pandiare, who is the religious superior of all the islands, gives a sermon or homily, according to the occasion, and adds a prayer for the health of some one, or for the downfall and destruction of their enemies, as the case may be. This done, everyone salutes his neighbour, taking hands, and saying, *Salan à lescon*,[2] which is the ordinary salutation of all Mahometans.

When the king returns from the temple he has a finer

[1] So at present.
[2] *Salaam aleikum!* "Peace be with you!"

retinue than on his going thither, for the Pandiare, the Naibes, Catibes, Moudins, and gentlemen of quality, besides those who conducted him thither, like to accompany him to the palace in the same ceremony wherewith he came. Then he thanks them, and sends them so fine a repast, that they spend the rest of the day enjoying themselves with good cheer at the king's expense. This is never omitted when he goes to the mosque; but the order of their eating is that those of the same rank and quality are together, apart from the others, as I have said above.

On new moon days throughout the year a like festival is held, and a general rejoicing as soon as the new moon is observed. They put in order their houses, courtyards, and all the streets; while at the entrances of the mosques, and at all house doors, as well without as within, they place on each side coco-nut shells cut in half, like wooden bowls, full of white sand, upon which they lay embers, and throughout the night they burn thereon aromatic gums, scented woods, and perfumes, and inside their houses in like manner, at the corners of their beds and elsewhere. On all feast days they daub and decorate their doors and furniture with sandal and other aromatic woods and paste of perfumery; but above all they solemnise four new moons in the year more than the others.

In the month of December, about the new moon, they observe a fast, called in Arabic *Ramedan*, and in their language *Rodet*.[1] I say about the month of December, for I cannot with certainty designate the time, seeing that their month and year are lunar, and are not fixed as ours are. This solemn fast begins at the new moon, and ends at the new moon of the following month. It does not, however, commence exactly at the time of the new moon, but when they first observe it; so that in some atollons and islands it begins a day sooner or later, according as they descry the

[1] *Ródá*, the Maldive form of the Pers. *Rózu*, "fast".

crescent. The months are reckoned in the same way; it is not counted a new month till the moon is seen, which is very uncertain when the sky is thick and cloudy. Sometimes the months are different in different places. In order to observe the moon, everybody betakes him to the highest eminence in the island, and each one is very keen to be the first to discover the moon, and show it to the others. Forthwith the king has volleys of cannon and musketry fired; and trumpets, drums, and other instruments are played. This takes place at all the new moons; but at the four above mentioned, more of it, and at that one (Ramedan) most of all. Forthwith they say their prayers, and take each other's hands, giving their ordinary salutation; then put their hands over their eyes, and cover their faces for a long space, and so continue their devotions throughout the following day. This happens at the beginning of every month; but at the month of Ramedan the ceremony is much more grand. On that night, men and women go separately to pay visits, regale themselves in company at banquets, dances, and amusements, and retire not till it be nearly dawn. Before it be day, all go to bathe and perform ceremonies peculiar to this night alone, whereby they hold themselves to be purified of all their past sins, and prepared for the fast ensuing. They dress themselves and wash their teeth well, and put aside their betel, though so used to it that they can but ill afford to want it; then they go to bed. Thenceforward they fast all day long until the night, and with so much scruple, that not only do they taste nothing, but they would not even wash their mouths, nor put their fingers in them, nor swallow their spittle; so they are obliged to spit frequently: and this is very inconvenient, especially when they go to the temple, where, it not being lawful to spit within, they have on every occasion to go to the door. The men may bathe, provided they do not immerse the head, for fear lest a drop of water should enter by the mouth or the ears; but the women may not, for they might admit water elsewhere, so great is their superstition. Half an hour before sunset all the men and boys above fifteen years betake themselves to the temple, so as to be there exactly when the sun disappears. During the half-hour they wash and clean their teeth and their mouths very thoroughly, and for this purpose the Moudins of the mosques throughout the fast supply large packets of toothpicks,[1] scrapers, and little coco-wood implements expressly made for cleaning the mouth and teeth. This done, the Moudins cry out three times, and enter the temple. One of the Moudins then advances as far as possible in front, no one being at either side of him, but all behind. So it is they make their prayers at the temple, while the women make theirs at home; and afterwards they make good cheer with their friends, entertaining each other in turn. Nobody does otherwise; all are fond of entertaining their friends. And for a long time before, they make the necessary provision by laying up a store of meats and luxuries. You would be surprised to see how curious and exact they are in all this; how careful they are to scour and clean all their kitchen and table utensils, their furniture, and their houses, too, in such wise that I think I have hardly ever seen such cleanliness and neatness. Even the poorest do the like, and save all they can to make good cheer during Ramedan with their relatives, friends, neighbours, and those of their own class; and they spend more in that one month than in the six preceding. On some days the king entertains large numbers of persons,—on one day the lords, on another, the soldiers, on another, the Pandiare, Catibe, Moudins, and other clergy, and so on through all the people of the island, never inviting but one class on the same occasion. This he does with great magnificence and at great expense, in the style of the country, and with perfect order and propriety; the lords, too, do the same with their friends

[1] M. *dai-konna-karhi.*

and equals: for it is a rule which they scrupulously observe, not to eat with persons of a different order. The captains entertain the soldiers, and so everyone in his own rank of life, from the lowest to the highest. This supper is called *Rodet pillauay*,[1] as who should say "breaking the fast". Only the men and boys feast in this wise: the women are never present; yet true it is, that by night they send each other presents and eatables, and they bathe every evening, when the men are not allowed to do so. They say that throughout Ramedan men abstain from their wives during the fasting days, but not during the night; and when they do indulge, both are bound to go and bathe, and say certain prayers the same night and before daylight. Every day during this month, until the new moon following, they fast in the manner described, and abstain all the time as far as they can from committing any sin, more so than at other times, and are very zealous in good works. If haply they have broken their fast any one day or more by some slight act, they add at the end as many days as they have missed. This happens often, for they are very superstitious, as I have said, and even believe that the fast is null if they have lost blood at any part of the body; moreover, they will none of them do any work during the month of the fast, how poor soever they may be; and they make up their minds neither to go out of their island, nor to send any thence. Nevertheless, they are not forbidden to work: they prefer not to do so. The Pandiare gives a sermon every day at three in the afternoon, lasting two hours, either at the king's palace, or at the temple, or at his own house, which all the inhabitants of Malé are careful to attend; it is given in the native language, sometimes in Arabic, and thence interpreted. They employ the rest of their time in the exercise of arms and in divers games, such as the game of ball, of which they have three kinds; it is kicked with the feet, and they

[1] M. *róda villán*, "to keep the fast".

assemble in bands and companies to play it.[1] On their part the women and girls pay visits at each other's houses, and play little games suitable to their sex and to their bringing up; and of these they have many kinds and varieties.

In this month you see boys and girls caressing and making love of their own accord, more than at other seasons.[2] Then they send songs, sonnets, and verselets, written on coco-leaves, which are as white as paper, the letters being graven with bodkins. The boys cull the fairest and sweetest flowers, and arrange them in garlands very prettily, and send them to the girls, who in return send some betel, nicely ordered and prepared. This is their way of making love. They are not allowed to marry by day in this month, but must await the night. In short, during this month they seek out every means of passing the time gaily. So the fast of Ramedan lasts from one new moon to the next. The women and girls are obliged to fast eight days longer than the men at the close of the month, on account, as they say, of their courses.

Three days before the close of Ramedan, the bell, or *coly*, and the trumpets go round the town in the usual way, as when a festival or a royal command is announced, and warn the people on behalf of the Pandiare (whom the Arabs call *Cady*), that all the Maldive islanders should bring or send in writing the names of all, both great and small, men and boys, women and girls, to be registered; those of Malé to the Pandiare, and those of the other islands to the Naibe of their atoll. When they do this, they have to give in for each person an offering of half a larin, equal to four sols of our

[1] The game of football, not practised by the Sinhalese, was probably introduced from the Malay countries, where it is a favourite amusement.

[2] Though, according to the above description, the Maldivians observed Ramadan in strictness, the youths would appear to be somewhat lax, it being unlawful even to touch a woman during the fast (Sale, *Prel. Disc.*, sec. iv).

money, or its equivalent in goods; this is done quite voluntarily and faithfully, for they believe that without it their fast would be of no effect. It is called *Pitourou*,[1] as being the tribute which they pay to God and Mahomet; and those who have not wherewithal to pay this offering, beg it of the rich, who willingly give for that purpose. Those who wish not to be obliged to others, nor to have the shame of being paid for (as indeed it is a badge of shame and of poverty; the king pays for everyone who asks him, as do the lords and the rich), and those who have not at the time a half-larin or its equivalent, make a written declaration that they cannot pay till after the festival, and thus make a debt of it. Fathers and mothers pay not only for themselves but also for their children, as soon as born, until they marry or cease to live with them, and also for their servants and slaves. The money collected is divided into three parts, which amount to a great deal according to the country notions. For receiving and guarding this *Pitourou* there is a very good system, for there are four receivers chosen for this office alone from among the men of means and the officers of the Pandiare. One of these officers represents the king, another the clergy, the third, those who are only recently of their religion, and the fourth, the poor. There are also eight persons who make entries in writing of everything presented, refusing nothing that is brought, be its value or price what it may. All the money and goods are put aside until after the festival, when all is received, for a fair and proper division. The first part belongs to the priests—*i.e.*, the Pandiare, Naibes, Catibes, Moudins, Deuanits[2] (who are the sergeants), and other like functionaries;

[1] M. *fituru*, Ar. *al-fiṭr*, "the breaking of the fast", used elliptically for *ṣadaḳatu'-l-fiṭr*, "the alms of the breaking of the fast". According to *Qanoon e Islam*, p. 57, the alms portion is said to be two-and-a-half seers of some grain or fruit, payable by all but wives and grown-up sons.

[2] M. *dévâni.*

the second is given to those who have recently become of their religion; and the third is for the poor; and if anything remains over to be paid, that is the priests' concern, for they are responsible for it, as being church money; but they never lose any.

The fast ended, they celebrate a grand festival, and one of the greatest solemnity with them, called *Ydu.*[1] The day is no more certain than the commencement of Ramedan, for it is the day of the new moon following,—*i.e.*, when it is seen; and this renders it somewhat uncertain year by year. They hold the same festival and solemnities at the sight of this moon as of its predecessor; the bell and trumpets make a round of the island to announce the festival, as also next morning early, in like manner. All rise very early, wash and bathe the whole body, with ceremonies peculiar to this occasion. It must be noted that their fast is not over until the service and prayers are performed, and they go forth of the temple; then they come out with scents and perfumes, and put on the finest clothes they have, which are made expressly for this day and the festival following, and after that are preserved with great care, in order to be placed after their death upon their coffins when they are borne to the grave. They are early at the temple—that is, about seven or eight o'clock, and not at mid-day, as on Fridays. The service lasts an hour and a half, being shorter than usual; and afterwards, when the king goes forth, he returns to his palace with a braver retinue of grandees than on other days; cannon are fired, and the air resounds with the noise of drums, flutes, and musketry. When the king enters the second court of the palace, a bullock and a ram are brought forth

[1] Ar. *'íd.* The festival which celebrates the close of Ramadan is known as the *'Ídu-l-fiṭr*, or the *'Ídu-s-saghír*, i.e., "the minor festival"; in India, the *choti*, or little, *'Íd.* As it is in some parts celebrated with more rejoicing than the "great festival", it has sometimes been so called by travellers and even eminent Orientalists; never, however, by the Arabs (Lane, *Ar. Soc.*, p. 22).

and slain in the presence of him and his retinue, as a kind of sacrifice; they are cut up into pieces and distributed among the grandees of the island, or others to whom the king is pleased to send, for he gives his directions there in person. The recipients esteem it as high an honour as among us it is to receive the consecrated bread. Those who get a good share call together their neighbours to participate, if they are so minded, for it is a mark of friendship so to do; and those who can get a morsel to eat think themselves in luck. This done, the king retires to his apartments, whence he goes not forth until, after dinner, he comes to see the games and amusements. Meanwhile, he provides a banquet of all the luxuries of the country, for all classes of people in his island, according to their rank and quality, in separate rooms and sheds, which are hung with pretty cloths. The festival lasts two days longer. The nobles and captains entertain their friends, soldiers, and servants; after dinner there is nothing but games, dancing, and rejoicings, which take place in front of the king's palace only. On the third day these are held in front of the houses of the nobles and persons of quality, who are greatly honoured thereby. The chief sports[1] are with arms, the buckler and naked sword. They fence with

[1] Mr. Bell gives the following picture of these sports, which are still observed:—"On fête days at Málé, sports (M. *kuli jahan*) are exhibited, under rules and restrictions, to prevent injury to the performers. The arena is simply a portion of one of the main streets, with thatched buildings on either side, from which the Sultan and ladies of the harem may view the sports. All the male spectators stand round in a ring. The sports consist entirely of mimic hand-to-hand combats between successive sets of performers, two at a time, armed with sword (M. *kaḍi*) and targe (M. *addana*), lance (M. *daḍi-haliya*), or quarter-staff (M. *kuli jaha daḍi*). The players do little more than posture at each other *ad nauseam*, and show but little skill in managing their weapons. The Sultan and by-standers alike appear to evince no real interest in the proceedings, which are conducted from first to last in gravity and silence, and repeated for days together with wearisome monotony. It is not considered beneath the dignity of the principal men to take part in these games (*Rep.*, p. 62).

dexterity, but suffer no harm, all the blows being received on the buckler. They use also pikes, hung with bells, in which case they receive the thrusts in like manner upon the buckler. All join in this mimic warfare with good temper, dancing and leaping to the music of drums, trumpets, flutes, etc., which play incessantly. The king comes to view the scene, but he remains not long. The queens, too, and their ladies

Arena for the Sports at Málé.

look on; but they are concealed by jalousies and curtains, so that they cannot be seen. There is no other kind of dancing, nor at any other time, neither on the part of the men nor the women, save it be of some good-for-nothing creatures, who play the buffoon by night to make their neighbours laugh. Some folks disguise themselves in foreign dress, and construct large and roomy ships, which they run along the streets and highways with armed parties on board, and when the ships approach one another they have a fight; and this affords great amusement. The king gives betel and areca to his whole court, both small and great (this is much thought of), as also do the chiefs and captains to their followers, soldiers, and subordinates.

At the last quarter of the moon following this festival they have another, called *Mas Ydu*, *i.e.*, "grand festival", lasting three days, when they observe the same ceremonies. It is the holy day upon which the Mahometan pilgrims assemble at Mecca to visit the sepulchre of Mahomet.[1] More ceremonies are then performed than during all the rest of the year: on that day they come from all parts of the world, and sometimes when they have arrived too late, and it is over, they have to await the return of the festival for ten or eleven months.

About the month of April, or May, at the full moon—a day before and a day after—they have a festival, called *Poycacan*,[2] that is to say, "full moon". It is more of a rejoic-

[1] The festival referred to is the *'Idu-l-kurbán*, or *'Idu-l-azhá*, the "feast of the sacrifice", commonly called the greater Beiram. It is generally regarded as in commemoration of the sacrifice of Ishmael, whom the Moslems substitute for Isaac. The great day is the 10th of the month Zu'l Hijjah, when the pilgrims, halting in the valley of Mina, on their return from Mount Arafat to Mecca, perform their sacrifice. This festival continues three or four days (Lane, *Ar. Soc.*, p. 21; Burton, *Pilg.*, vol. ii, ch. 5; Sale, *Prel. Disc.*, sect. vii).

[2] M. *foi-kakkaṇ*; *cf.* Sin. *poya*, a change of the moon, and *kanavá*, to eat. This festival is evidently not Mahomedan, and is probably the Buddhistic celebration of the full moon (Sin. *depoya*) of the month *Wesak* (May), when the Sinhalese commemorate the attainment by Gautama of Nirvána. Whether its introduction to the Maldives had anything to do with that of rice, we are likely never to know. The description of the observance is, however, a true picture of the Kandyan festival at this day. Many a time have I been present at these nocturnal festivities, made weird and fantastic by hideous disguises and pantomimiç gestures, displayed to crowds of gaily-dressed Kandyans. The whole scene is lighted by flaring torches, amid the sombre shadows of the temple trees, while here and there groups stand or sit round little fires at which coffee and *appas* are being prepared for the

ing than a (religious) festival. When it is evening, the neighbours assemble, gentle and simple (I bethought me it was like St. John's with us[1]), each bringing his portion of rice; they make a big fire at the nearest cross-roads, and there cook their rice. While they are all around the fire, instruments of music are played; and betimes some merry-andrews, disguised as birds, wild beasts, or such like, come and dance, indulging in lascivious and indecent gesture, even in the presence of women and girls, who are there along with the men. This goes on throughout all the islands, but at the palace the king gives rice to the soldiers for doing it. They say it was at this moon that rice was brought to the islands for the first time, and on that account they have from time immemorial kept this holiday, which lasts three days.

In the month of June, or thereabouts (for, as I said, their months do not accord with ours), they keep a festival of the dead, with many superstitious observances. On the day, the king, with all his wives (who have not permission to go without their houses but on this day only), pays a visit to the sepulchres of his predecessors, and to those of persons held to be saints in their religion; there he makes offerings, burns perfumes, and presents some *dida*,[2] as we should candles.

sustaining of exhausted nature. No indecent gestures or behaviour are now to be observed, though these were characteristic of some of the Ceylon festivities too, until they were suppressed in Knox's time. That traveller, however, expressly says that the orgies he describes were never performed in presence of women (*Knox*, p. 97).

[1] The Nativity of St. John the Baptist, June 24th. The reference is, however, to the Eve or Vigil, to the celebration of which all the popular ceremonial was confined. This consisted in bonfires, torchlight processions, dancing, etc., the celebrants adorned with garlands, ribbons, and other gewgaws. It was a superstition of the Middle Ages, probably transmitted from pagan times, that it was advisable to keep watch through this night, to prevent a temporary wandering of the soul from the body. An account of the festival will be found in Chambers's *Book of Days*.

[2] *I.e.*, flags; see p. 129.

Everybody, too, goes to visit the graves of his kindred and friends, and presents as many portions of food as he has dead relatives and friends. The food is laid aside by the Moudins of the neighbouring temples, who offer as many separate prayers as there are portions. All the graves of those who have kinsmen and friends living are visited, and replenished with white sand on that day, and perfumes are burned while the prayers are said.

Next day there is a general almsgiving at the king's palace, the king giving to all the poor with his own hand; and they, well aware of the day, come up from the most distant islands for it. He makes inquiry first what people they are, and if they be indeed in want: for to those who are not he gives only a little silver ring worth half a larin, of which he has a large number made against this day to give to folks of the lowest estate, who bring there all their children to receive of the king each his ring. On this same day all householders likewise give alms, according to their means, being bound to give to the poor the fifth part of their goods, provided they are worth at least 100 larins; and those who are not worth 100 larins are not obliged to give anything in alms.

About the month of August or September, for two days the king has a large quantity of rice cooked very thin, or half mixed with honey and coco-milk; this is carried about the island in tubs containing about a hogshead apiece. The bearers of it have cups and ladles to serve out to all they meet, and no one declines, be he beggar or lord. Everyone does the same on his own account, and even the poorest must cook some rice and send it to his neighbours. They told me that they keep this festival in remembrance of a miracle which Mahomet did as on this day, while he was at the wars, and they call it *Candis cacan.*[1]

[1] M. *Kandi-kakkan*, "kanji-eating"; Sin. *kenda*, "kanji" (rice gruel), and *kanavá*, "to eat", past tense, *kakā*.

There is yet another very solemn festival about the month of October, which takes place at night, and is called *Maulude*[1]; they say it is the night whereon their prophet Mahomet died. This is the ceremony: they begin a month before the festival, by meeting to elect officers to make arrangements and to supervise; these number at least fifty, all men of quality, and act as our "valets de feste". Their duty is to go from house to house collecting from every man the sum at which he is rated, according to his means; they go also to ask people to take part, and to arrange everything; though, indeed, the people of the parish fail not all to assist at this festival, which is diligently observed in all the islands. At Malé I have seen it performed at six places. The king bears the expense of one celebration, which takes place at his palace. At the four corners of the island it is celebrated by the people in their several parishes, and one general celebration for all the people is held in the middle of the island, in front of the principal temple. At each of the six places is erected for the occasion a wooden house, sixty feet long by forty broad, or thereabouts; the roof is of coco-branches; the wood of which it is constructed must not have been, nor may in the future be, used for any other purpose, not even for the festival of the following year. The ground is covered with fine white sand to the depth of half a foot. This house within is hung with cotton or silk cloths of all colours, and of the finest and richest description available. Above, to serve for a ceiling, they stretch pieces of cotton cloth, very white and very fine, and to support them they run cotton cords, dyed black, from side to side at right angles and aslant, so cleverly that the white above seems to

[1] M. *maulúdu.* Moolids, or, more properly, Mólids, are great periodical or annual festivals held on the anniversaries of saints (Lane, *Ar. Soc.*, 71). Mahomed died at noon on the 12th day of Rabia el Awwal of the 11th year of the Hejira. The 1st, 4th, 8th, and 12th of this month are observed as maulúdu at the Maldives.

be cut into squares and lozenges of exactly the same size: it is very neat.[1] On the sand wherewith the ground is covered they spread pretty new mats, on which each one sits, and there are no other seats. On all sides are hung copper lamps to the number of about thirty; each is large and has two wicks, so that it is almost as bright as daylight. By contrivances with air-holes, odorous perfumes are introduced within, though burnt without, for the heat of the place of itself is well-nigh insupportable: only the fumes and the odour come within. There are other conduits, too, for the introduction of water, which is very necessary, for they often wash their mouths by way of refreshment after chewing betel, which they do the whole night long.

In the middle of this hall there is a table of the height of the knees, whereon are arranged little wicker baskets, and polished lacquer vessels containing divers kinds of cates made of rice flour with coco-sugar, like little macaroons, of the thickness of the thumb: these are excellently well served with all kinds of native fruits. The table is covered with sweet-smelling flowers, while all around are jars containing drinks of different mixtures, chiefly [flavoured with] amber[gris] and musk. The whole is covered over with a large cotton cloth worked with a coloured pattern. The people rig themselves out in their bravest style; but only the men and boys are present, and no women. The men of quality of the parish do not go, for it would be beneath their dignity; it is a feast of the common folk. They assemble at eight o'clock in the evening, and sit in places assigned to them, according to their rank, by the stewards of the festival. All night long the Pandiare, Catibes, Naybes, and Moudins, with all the rest of the clergy, and other good singers, cease not to chant with all their might in alternation like a choir; nor is their chanting without rule, for some of them who know not how

[1] This description will be well understood by all who have enjoyed the hospitality of the native Sinhalese.

to sing have to take lessons from a master: so the harmony is good, and the singing far from disagreeable. They call this chanting *Zicourou*,[1] and say that they are the Psalms of David.[2] On the stroke of midnight everybody with one accord lies down at full length with his face to the ground, and so remains for a space of time. Then of a sudden the Pandiare or the Catibes stand up, and all the rest after them, and set a-leaping upon each other as they were madmen or lunatics, crying, at the top of their voices, "*Aly alas Mahomedin*", again and again; this lasts for some time. I have inquired of them why they did this, and they asking "What?" and I replying, "These mad leapings and dancing," they told me they knew nothing of having danced or done any such thing, but only remembered that for a space of time they had been rapt with ecstasy and had been partakers of heaven and the joys of their paradise. Sometimes the Pandiare remains for an hour or more like dead; they say then that he is transported to heaven, and that it is a mark that he is a righteous man. The king does not take part in this festival the whole time; he comes to see what is going on for an hour or two, and then returns. In this manner I have many a time seen it in his

[1] Ar. *zikr.* These performances consist of chorus chanting at night, the name of God being perpetually repeated, accompanied by motions of the head, hands, and whole body. The munshids at intervals sing religious odes or love-songs to the accompaniment of a kind of flute. (Lane, *Ar. Soc.*, p. 72.)

[2] The Psalms of David are well known even among remote Mahomedan communities (Mungo Park, *Travels*, c. xi). Compare the quaint account of Lancaster taking his leave of the Sultan of Achin:—"And when the general tooke his leaue, the king said vnto him: Have you the Psalmes of David extant among you? The generall answered: Yea, and we sing them daily. Then said the king: I and the rest of these nobles about me will sing a Psalme to God for your prosperitie, and so they did very solemnly. And after it was ended the king said: I would heare you sing another Psalme, although in your owne language. So there being in the company some twelue of us, we sung another Psalme: and after the Psalme was ended the generall tooke his leaue of the king" (*Lanc. Voy.*, Hak. Soc., p. 97).

company. Fifty persons are elected to minister to the rest; this is a great honour, and there is no one but is glad enough to accept the office, for none but distinguished men and scions of good families get the offer. These officers distribute during the night to all ranks of the people, seated in their proper order, a portion of betel and areca, arranged and prepared in a different style from their ordinary (I mean of the common folk, for the king and the great lords always use it prepared in the same way). They give as many as a dozen portions to each person, whoever he may be; in like wise they present to all who have a mind to drink, beverages of the country brew, in large copper bowls, exceedingly well fashioned and worked, and with a cover on the top. Now and then are brought like bowls full of water, with basins, for washing the mouth and hands; they would not for the world let a drop of water or any refuse fall to the ground. The people are arranged in lines, and at intervals are vacant spaces for passing between them.

Towards the close of the night the chanting ceases and the Pandiare and Catibes say prayers, after which they proceed to the midst of the hall, where the aforesaid table is spread; this they uncover, and all crowd around, and each one receives a portion; this they take great care of, and carry it home to show that they have been to the festival. At the same time the officers, taking some aromatic waters in vases placed there, sprinkle it upon the bodies of all present, touching them with their hands; and this is received by them as a benediction of great efficacy. This done, they must lay to the eating, for they have no celebration of solemnities without that. So the officers bring basins of water for washing their hands and mouths, they having done nothing but chew betel the night long; then they make a circle of nine or ten together, but always of the same class, and grouped according to the prescribed order. Viands are brought upon large heavy dishes, each of which contains other small ones, in which are divers meats, well served, and these are placed in the midst; it takes three to carry them. And when they have done eating, they go home to bed.

CHAPTER XII.

More of their ceremonies,—at betrothals and weddings, at obsequies and funerals.

At their weddings, which are called *Caueny*,[1] they also use formalities and ceremonies not a few: it is the Pandiare or the Naybes to whom alone they address themselves on this occasion; these send their *deuanits*,[2] or sergeants, to make the inquiries I shall speak of. If everything is settled, the girl or woman sends her father, or in default, her next of kin on the father's side, and gives him the power to represent her. This person and the future husband present themselves before the Pandiare or Naybe, who being certified on all points, takes the bridegroom's hand, and asks him if he wills to take the woman on the conditions proposed, and then of the father or kinsman he demands the same; and if they answer yea, he goes through the prescribed formalities, taking the attestation of the witnesses present—namely, the kinsfolk, sergeants, and others—to the promise of marriage, and to all the proceedings. Thereupon they go to the woman, who is waiting at her house, and assure her of all that has passed. That done, they all sit down to a banquet at the expense of the bridegroom, according to his means, music being played all the day long. Many people come to visit and salute them, the visitors receiving betel, which is their token of respect, as we should give refreshment here. To the Pandiare or Naybe are sent two larins, a dish of food, and a box

[1] M. *káveni*.

[2] M. *dévani*.

of betel. Likewise, those who marry are wont to give presents to the king and the queens, to the great lords and ladies,—that is, the bridegroom to the king and lords, and the bride to the queens and other ladies, as well as to their own kindred and friends. On the other hand, when the king marries, he receives presents from all his subjects, as well lords as commoners, men as women, who present themselves in good order, each with those of his own quality, class, parish, and sex, with their offerings of cloths, robes, turbans, meats, flowers, etc., according to the means of the giver. The people of Malé appear in person, those of the other atollons and chief islands generally by deputies; the great lords tarrying awhile to have the pleasure of saluting him in person. For all that, the king goeth not forth nor showeth himself on these days, but hour by hour his attendants come and tell him what persons have arrived at the hall, of what quality, how arrayed, and with what presents, and at the last these are laid before him. They amount to a great deal, and all appertain to the newly married queen.

A man may have three wives at once,[1] but no more, and these only if he is able to support and maintain them. If all three wives live in the same island, the husband is obliged by their law to sleep as many nights with one as with another; but they do not observe this. It is but an ill-considered law for these countries, where three husbands would not suffice for one wife, so lewd are the women.

The women have no marriage portion; it is for the husbands to provide them with everything necessary, and to bear the expense of the wedding in manner suited to their rank. So they settle for them a jointure, called *Rans*,[2] according, not to the means and quality of the husband, but to the

[1] Mahomed allowed four (*Koran*, Sura iv), but Maldive usage may have limited husbands to three, which seems to have been the number kept by the Sultan.

[2] M. *ran*, "gold", and the same in Sin.

quality of the wife, and to what her mother and grandmothers had: for she must have no less. For this cause the Pandiare or Naybe full often sends them away without marrying them, when he finds that the bridegroom's means suffice not for such a jointure; even though both parties ask to be married without thought for the jointure. Most of the women take this *Rans* for the traditional honour of their house, and most of them of their own accord give up a part or all of it a few days after marriage. If the husband dies, she is allowed to take her jointure with her own goods; but the husband's heirs will make a composition with her; whereas, if she has parted with it during the life of the deceased, she can ask none of it back.

The impediments to marriage, of which the Pandiare or Naybe informs himself before he marries anyone, are the being brother and sister, or cousins-german, or foster-brother and sister, or having formerly called each other in token of friendship by the name of son or daughter, father or mother, brother or sister: in such cases they may not marry together.[1]

Youths may marry when they list, but girls may not till they have attained the age of fifteen years,—I mean, when they are orphans, or rather, bereft of their father,—for a mother would have no authority, neither any of the kindred on the mother's side. In default of a father, their brother gives them in marriage; if no brother, the nearest male relative on the father's side. Fathers, however, give their daughters in marriage as soon as possible after the age of ten years, thinking it a great sin to let a girl want a husband; wherefore they hand them over at the age of ten or eleven to the

[1] See *Koran*, Sura iv, where the actual relationship of brother and sister, or foster-brother and sister, is a bar; but no mention is made of the fictitious brother- and sister-hood of friends. This latter is, however, a well-established Sinhalese relationship. It is common to hear a man say, "M. is not my brother, but I call him brother."

first that asks them, without making any bother, be he old or young, man or boy: provided only there is little difference in their quality, that is all they think of.

A man can leave his wife when he will, provided that she agree (they call divorce *Varicor*[1]); otherwise, if she do not consent, the man may still leave her, but would be obliged to pay her jointure. But this does not happen, for what displeasure soever the wife may feel, she will not ask for her jointure, for that would be to her a reproach among women. They would despise one of their sex who was so mean-spirited and unworthy as to fear she could not get other husbands; and, indeed, no one would court such a one: so that public opinion prevents them enjoying what the law ordains. The wife, too, can separate from her husband, provided he consents; otherwise not. This divorce, which is very common among them, must be made in the presence of witnesses, all or some of whom must be present when either of the parties expresses a desire to marry another, otherwise the Naybe would not perform the marriage. This is the source of many quarrels, for full often, in a sudden choler, they divorce each other by consent, and soon after one of the parties rues it, and the other does not. Thus do they frequently come before the judge, bringing their witnesses to prove their divorces and marriages.

When the divorce is effected, the parties may marry again when they like; and they can marry each other again as before; but only three times, and no more, save when the woman after three marriages has married another man, and he has left her.[2] As they are flighty in their notions about

[1] M. *vari-kuran*. As to the Mohamedan law, see *Qanoon e Islam*, pp. 145-7; *Hughes*, p. 182.

[2] "Ye may divorce your wives twice. . . . . . But if the husband divorce her a third time, she shall not be lawful for him again, until she marry another husband. But if he also divorce her, it shall be no crime in them if they return to each other, if they think they can observe the ordinances of God" (*Koran*, Sura ii).

marriage, it often happens that, after three marriages and three divorces between the same parties, they wish to come together again, and are prevented by the law. But hear now the means they contrive. Vile and abject beings are found who, for a money consideration, contract a marriage with the woman, and sleep a night with her, but without touching her (for she would not suffer him, and it is so understood); next day he swears that he has had her company, and then two or three days after he quits her in the presence of witnesses. By this means the letter of the law is obeyed, and, three months after, the former pair are married afresh. The highest ladies in the land are constrained to go through the same business in like case. These middlemen are called *Medu piry*,[1] as who should say "middle husband"; they are held in great contempt even of the common people, as infamous creatures without honour or conscience. It is a grievous slander even to be called *Medu piry*. Even if it happens by chance that a man marries a woman already divorced three times, and after awhile he leaves her, and her old husband takes her to wife again, he would be greatly offended, as having been got to take the part of a *medu piry*, and his honour would be gone, did he not avenge himself. For the rest, they cannot make use of a *medu piry* more than twice[2]: after that they cannot marry together again; and it is to be noted that there is no expense in the wedding or in presents when the same parties are remarried. So it is, by these frequent

[1] If such a custom were known in Ceylon, the "middle husband" would be called by an almost identical name, viz., *mada pirimi*. That he was designated by a Maldive, and not an Arabic, term, shows, as the fact would seem, that the feigned marriage was a legal fiction invented at the Maldives.

[2] As the *medu piry* marriage was the fourth, after three marriages with the first husband, a second *medu piry* marriage would imply that the lady had gone through the marriage ceremony at least eight times; she could then be married three times more to her first husband, and only then would the law step in and put an end.

divorces they marry many a time, and change marvellously often. A man may in his life have had eighty wives and more; among others, the Pandiare, who died shortly after I resided at the islands, had as many as a hundred. In like manner the wives have a vast number of husbands; but, far from that being imputed to them for any kind of blame, they are prouder the oftener they have changed husbands; and when they are courted they tell the number, names, and quality of their former husbands as a high recommendation. Nor are they less esteemed by their gallants, but rather more; and less is thought of one who is still a virgin than of one who is no longer so, except it be by the king and the great lords. Yet, notwithstanding this common changing, you will find men and women who remain for a long time together, by reason that they love and cherish each other more than all the world.

After the dissolution of the marriage by divorce or death, the women cannot marry again quite so soon. When a husband dies, four months and ten days are ordained for the widow to mourn him; and then, to marry again, it suffices not for the woman to say off-hand that her husband is dead, for she must prove his death by three witnesses, who speak to the time, manner, and cause thereof. If, however, the husband were absent from the kingdom, and the wife had nothing of his, she could remarry a year after. So in divorce is there a time prescribed: for the woman must certify that since the separation she has had her courses three times, and she must wait till then ere she marries again. This is done to avoid the uncertain status of the issue, if she should be with child. Wherefore the Pandiare or Naybe informs himself particularly of this, and has the woman who desires to marry examined by three other women of the same parish and of good repute; and in addition he makes her swear that she has had her courses three times.

Burial is with them called *Calbalolan*,[1] and is a matter of much consideration, as to which they are highly superstitious. First of all, the dead body is washed by six men; if it is a woman, by six women. They use more than a hogshead of water in the washing, and say certain prayers the while; this done, they cover it with cotton, and shroud it with two cloths of white cotton, the one over the other, placing the right hand upon the ear and the left along the side. They place it in a coffin of Candou wood, laid upon the right side, until the time for burial comes.[2] The women of the family and of the neighbourhood assemble and bewail the corpse, telling all the praises of the deceased. The six men and six women are public officers, and they must be good people and without reproach; for if they were proved to be otherwise, they would lose their offices. These they buy for money of the king, and they have besides to give a sum of money to their comrades, which is divided among them. Their earnings are for the common stock, and are equally divided among the six men and six women, whether it be a man or woman (who is dead), and whether the men or the women have had most work. When the body is taken away these women set up the most fearful crying and yelling, and continue their wailing throughout the obsequies. The body is borne to the grave by six of the kindred or best friends, the place having been chosen and arranged by the deceased in his lifetime; for these people take such thought for their burial, that from

[1] M. *valulin*, Sin. *valalanavá*, "to bury".

[2] As will be seen, he says of the actual burial only that the body is laid with the face toward Mecca: the posture of the body here described would, of course, be unchanged. "The Prophet's body, it should be remembered, lies, or is supposed to lie, stretched at full length on the right side, with the right palm supporting the right cheek, the face fronting Mecca, as Moslems are always buried, and, consequently, the body lies with the head almost due west and the feet due east" (Burton, *Pilgr.*, vol. ii, ch. 2). At the Maldives the body would thus be laid with the head to the north, the feet to the south.

the time they marry and have the means, they make ready with great care all the requisites for their burial—the place, the coffin, stones for the tomb, folding sheets, and so on. They even put aside and collect little by little the money required for that occasion, and would sooner die of hunger than touch it. This fund they call *Capon.*[1] Each of them, too, has two suits, of the richest he can afford, according to his quality, which are worn at the festival *Ydu*, and then preserved in their boxes, as I have said, against the day of their burial, to be then placed upon their coffin. These suits are afterwards divided among the priests of the temple. The relatives and friends accompany the corpse, together with a large number of people not invited, who walk on all sides of the body confusedly, and without order. From the house to the place of burial they scatter over the road *bolys*[2] (which are little shells, of which I shall speak in their place), to the end that the poor may collect them and make a profit. They bring also a quantity of packages of rice and millet, which they distribute on the way to the poor. They cut also a large number of small bits of gold and silver, according to the wealth of the deceased and his heirs, who put their several shares in little pieces of cloth and give to the chief officiating minister, whether Pandiare, Naybe, or Catibe, to distribute among all the others who have assisted in praying for the deceased; but all do not share in this, for it belongs, say they, to the clergy only. Sometimes others take it if they like: this depends upon the wealth of the deceased and his heirs. Before the body walks a man with a bottle full of water, scented with aromatic flowers; this he sprinkles over all he meets along the road, which is neatly swept and brushed from the house to the mosque at which the burial is to be. For this duty this person receives a piece of silk or new cotton, according to the means of the deceased; as also

[1] M. *kafun.*

[2] M. *boli*, "cowries".

do the six who bear the body.[1] The burial of the nobles and the rich is usually in the cemeteries around the mosques, where ground is bought dearly enough: except when they have themselves built the mosque, in which case they are wont to reserve a site for themselves and their family adjoining the mosque; and this is the most honourable place. This money is distributed, with other like profits, among the priests of the mosque; for besides the Moudins, every mosque has a certain number of other priests called *Quiauany*,[2] who are maintained for the service of the temple and cemetery out of the funds settled by the builders of the temple. These incumbencies are very honourable, and are even bought. Only those of that temple can perform the funeral service at a burial there, not those of another. Yet some people desire to have a large number of priests at their funeral, and then those of the temple call in as many as are wanted from the neighbouring mosques. These priests chant continually during the three hours the ceremony lasts. Over the hole of the grave a large coverlet of silk or cotton is stretched, until it is filled up and the interment completed; it then goes to

[1] Christopher witnessed the funeral of the grandmother of Sultan Muhammad 'Imád-ud-dín, who ascended the throne in 1835, and thus describes it:—"The body was conveyed to the mosque, where prayers were read over it. The men who carried her coffin walked on cowries, which (to the value of 100 rupees) were strewed on the road from the house. As the procession moved on, handfuls of the small copper coin (50 of which go to a rupee) were scattered, for which the lower orders of the people kept up a scramble, very much out of character with the occasion, and ill-according with the rest of the scene. All the men were attired in full costume, consisting of a red waist-cloth with black and white borders, and a head-piece corresponding to it, both of native manufacture. At the burial, a gaudy canopy of various colours, supported on four poles, was elevated over the body, and the Fatha was read. After a temporary hut had been erected over the grave for the readers of the Koran, the company adjourned to the Sultan's palace, to partake of a dinner prepared for them" (*T. Bo. Geo. Soc.*, i, 63).

[2] M. *kiyaveni* (*bé-kalun*), *i.e.*, "readers"; *kiyavāṇ*, "to read".

the Moudin. Upon and around the grave they strew a quantity of fine white sand. When they lay the body within, they turn the face in the direction of the sepulchre of Mahomet, and then cover it with white sand, and sprinkle it with water from a bottle, by way of refreshing it, and over the grave they lay a large cotton sheet. After that, the relatives, who have brought a quantity of food, give to all the assistants to eat thereof.

When it is a great lord, there is no more ceremony, save that the chanting continues longer, even for the space of a year; and day by day dishes of meats are sent to the place, along with some betel: these are taken by the Moudin. If it be a king or queen, this continues during the life of the heir. For the rest, prayers are said for the deceased night and day until the third Friday after the burial; and most frequently the priests chant and eat their meals at the tomb itself, where there is a hut erected for the purpose: this is taken away at the conclusion of the service, on the third Friday after the funeral. At the close they have a great feast, to which they invite all the kindred and friends, along with the priests and Moudins, saying that they are then despatching the soul of the defunct to Paradise. On that day they place at the two ends of the grave, two stones of the same size, and fixed upright, high or low, according to the quality of the dead person. Upon these they engrave the name of the deceased and his praises. Every year, on the same day, they have a similar feast, with the same ceremonies, in the courtyard of the dead person's house, or in that of his principal heir, in a hut just like the former one.[1] In short, the expense in all this is often so great that their means are exhausted. Every year, at the festival of the dead, they

[1] "They are careful, in erecting tombstones over their lost relatives, to preserve the date of their death, the anniversary of which is observed by almsgiving and prayer on the part of the surviving members of the family" (*T. Bo. Geo. Soc.*, i, 63).

place some fresh white sand on the grave, and burn a quantity of perfumes and incense. Such as have the means, leave funds in the hands of certain persons in trust to keep their graves covered with white sand, to tend them every morning, and to keep them enclosed with little wooden posts and rails, so that none may tread thereon; for they have a horror of treading on ground wherein anyone is buried, and take care not to do so, deeming that the dead would feel insulted, and that it is a great sin. Some sepulchres they hold sacred, and at them keep many lamps burning continually.[1] Moreover, they hold in great reverence the bones of the dead, and when they are digging a grave, or on other occasion discover any, no one, not even the Pandiare or the Catibes, would dare to touch them but with a cloth; wherefore they never bury two bodies in the same place.

I have never observed that they used any mourning garments, or other than their ordinary; only this, that the kinsmen, on the way to a funeral, take off their turbans and walk bareheaded, and so continue for that day and some

[1] "A remarkable object on the island is a tomb erected over the remains of a person who is regarded by the natives as the most eminent of their saints. The building, which is surmounted by a cupola and a short spire, is thirty feet high; the gate, over which a lantern is placed, is of copper network" (*T. Bo. Geo. Soc.*, i, 63). Christopher also mentions tombs at the S.E. point of Málé island as being specially sacred. They are said to be of certain Persians who came in search of a countryman (Tabriz, or from Tabriz), who is believed to have reintroduced Mahomedanism after the expulsion of the Portuguese. Only two out of about sixty tombs were legible, and these were dated A.H. 994 (A.D. 1677), more than a century after the Portuguese conquest, and more than forty years after the last abortive Portuguese attack, viz., under Ferreira Belliago in 1632. They might possibly be the tombs of some heroes who took part in the repulsion of the Portuguese on this last occasion. That anyone buried in the seventeenth century had anything to do with the re-establishment of Islam is, of course, palpably absurd; for although one at least of the Portuguese armadas contained a *posse* of padres with missionary intention, the faith of Mahomed was never in peril. Possibly Pyrard refers to some of the older tombs in the same locality.

days thereafter, if so minded; for there is no fixed time; and, moreover, they abstain from chewing betel.

Such as are slain in battle against men of a contrary faith are buried without ceremony, in their own clothes, on the spot where they have been slain. No prayers are said for them, for they are deemed sanctified and blessed, and are called *Chaydes*,[1] and in fact are invoked in time of affliction.

They never transport a corpse from one island to another; even were it the king, he is buried where he dies.[2]

If, haply, one of them dies at sea, the body is washed and prepared for burial, with all the ceremonies aforesaid; it is placed in a coffin fixed upon three or four pieces of Candou wood, so that it may continue afloat, and then is cast into the sea. In the coffin they put some money, according to their means, with a writing mentioning the religion of the dead man, and entreating those who may meet with it to take the money and to bury the body honourably: this have I seen done many a time.

CHAPTER XIII.

Of the form of their apparel, of their manner of living, ordinary exercises, and other peculiar customs which they observe in their conduct.

As for their garments, see how they apparel themselves. First, the men bind all round their private parts a broad band of cloth, lest in coming or going, or in doing some work, these should be discovered. Over this they wear a small cotton cloth, dyed blue or red or some other colour, reaching only as far as the knees. Above this they wear a large cloth of cotton, or silk, if they be at all rich and well off; this reaches to the ankles, and is belted with a fine square ker-

[1] Ar. *Shahíd* (*i.e.*, "martyrs"); M. *Sahídu*. [2] See *infra*, ch. xxiii.

chief, embroidered with gold and silk; this is folded in three, drawn round the loins, and tied in front. Then, for braver adornment, they add a little piece of silk of divers colours, fine as crape or gauze, and short, not reaching further than the mid thigh; and after all this they gird themselves with

Young Girl and old Man.

a large silken sash, like their turbans, with pretty fringes, the ends whereof they let hang down in front.[1] In this

[1] Compare Mr. Bell's description of the Maldivian male attire at the present day:—"The ordinary dress of the men consists of short drawers (M. *haruválu*), a cloth wrapped round the waist, after the Sinhalese fashion (M. *mundu*), and a plain handkerchief twisted over the head (M. *rumá*). On board their vessels, and in foreign parts, some don a

girdle, which serves them for a purse, they keep their money and their betel on the left side, while on the right they carry their knife, by which they lay great store; every one carries it, not excepting even the king himself. These knives are exceedingly well made, all of excellent steel,—for they have not the invention of blending iron with steel. Men of means have the haft and sheath all of carved and worked silver. At the upper end of the sheath is a silver buckle, from which hangs a little chain, also of silver, to which is attached a tooth-pick and an ear-pick, and other little implements. Other folks, who cannot afford to have them so costly, use a sheath of carved wood and a haft of fish-bone, either of whale or other marine animal: for they like not to wear the bone of any land animal. They are careful of these knives, and would not consider themselves to be properly dressed without their knife at the waist; and there is none, how vile or mean soever, but wears it: it is their means of defence.[1] Other arms none is allowed to bear. It is only the soldiers and

thin shirt, generally white (M. *kuru libás*), and Turkish waistcoat (M. *saduriya*), which, with the peculiar coarse blue waistcloth edged with red, and the red handkerchief, mark a Maldivian at once among other races. The upper orders, and those who have been the Haj, wear, besides the waistcloth (particularly on Fridays, when attending mosque), a kind of long dressing gown (M. *digu libás*), reaching to the ankles, somewhat similar to those worn by Mahomedan priests in Ceylon. The dress of the men, as minutely described by Pyrard, must formerly have been richer and more elaborate, including the use of turbans, silk scarfs, silver chains, and fancy knives. No Maldivian not of the priesthood now ventures to wear a turban (M. *fagudi*) in the royal presence or island, this head-dress being retained by the Sultan exclusively" (*Report*, 55). See also Christopher (*T. Bom. Geo. Soc.*, i, 58). For Ibn Batuta's description, see App. A.

[1] "Ordinary Maldive waist knives (*vali*), chastely inlaid with silver and mother-of-pearl, leave nothing to be desired in portability and serviceableness, whilst for shape and handsome finish the larger silver-mounted knife-dagger with ivory handle (*fiyohi*), worn exclusively by grandees and soldiers, is unique. Knife handles are carved from *kuradi* wood, black coral (*endiri*), and whale's teeth (*bodu-mas dai*)" (Bell, *Report*, 88).

king's officers who may; nor they, indeed, save when they are in the service of the king at Malé, or elsewhere on his commissions. These have usually at their side a waved dagger called a *Cris*, which comes from Achen in Sumatra, from Java, and China. When they walk in the street they also bear a drawn sword in one hand, in the other a buckler or else a javelin. The soldiers have another peculiar mark, and that is, they wear their hair long, done up all together and tied in a large bunch.[1] Their chief bravery is to wear all around their waist many silver chains; and every person of any substance, be he man or woman, boy or girl, likes to have them, but always in number according to their means and quality. In these they lay out all their treasure, and usually destine them to pay the expense of their obsequies. But it is only the great nobles or foreigners who may wear them above their clothes and let them be seen: all others wear them concealed beneath; yet they must needs have them to talk about and to display in private. The rest of the body from the waist upwards is left naked,—I mean by the common folk; for the gentlemen of quality do not so; and yet on festival days they put on their doublets and gowns of cotton or silk, fastened with buttons of gilded copper; for they durst not have them of gold, that being for the king only.[2] These gowns are of divers colours, but all have borders of white and blue. The sleeves reach only to the elbow; for they say that if they were to come to the wrist, as with us, they would not have the free use of their arms. Along with these are worn coloured drawers, close-fitting and covering the body from the waist to the ankles, where they are fastened also

[1] Mr. Bell states that the men now, without exception, shave the head (*Report*, p. 55). The long hair of the soldiers described by Pyrard would seem to be a relic of Sinhalese custom. Every Sinhalese man, even at the present day, wears his hair long, and tied in a bunch at the back of the head.

[2] The wearing of gold ornaments is still confined to the Sultan and those of royal blood.

with gilt buttons. The nobles don these doublets and gowns every day. There are others, a great number, who on festival days wear no doublets, but use another sort of bravery, which is this: they pound some sandal and camphor, or other odorous wood, on very smooth stones brought from the mainland; that they mix with distilled essence of flowers, and then with the paste so made cover all the body from the waist upwards, describing with their finger all sorts of patterns, according to their fancy. They appeared to me like slashed and patterned doublets; and the scent was very pleasing. Sometimes they paste on themselves flowers, the fairest and sweetest to be found. It is their wives and lady friends who deck them in this sort, figuring upon their backs such designs and flourishes as they fancy. This kind of bravery is exceedingly common; but they dare not present themselves in this guise before the king nor in his palace.[1]

Those who have been to Arabia, and have visited the sepulchre of Mahomet at Mecca, are held in high respect by all the world, whatever be their rank, and whether they be poor or rich; and, indeed, a great number of the poor have been there. These have peculiar privileges: they are called *Agy*[2]; and in order to be recognised and remarked among the others, they all wear very white cotton frocks, and on their heads little round bonnets, also white, and carry beads in their hands without crosses; and when they have not the means to maintain themselves in this attire, the king or the nobles supply them, and fail not to do so.

All wear on their heads turbans of red, or chequered of divers colours. Most people have these of silk; but such as cannot afford silk, of the finest cotton. The soldiers and officers of the king wear them arranged in a style not per-

1 This practice seems to have died out. See below, ch. xxvii, where it seems this mode of adornment was practised by the Samorin of Calicut.

2 According to Professor Robertson Smith (Yule's *Glossary*, s.v. "Hadgee"), the correct Ar. for one who has made the pilgrimage is *ḥājj*; but the incorrect form *ḥājji* is used by the Turks and Persians, and, as appears here, by the Maldivians.

mitted to others, most frequently tying round their heads the broidered kerchiefs of which I have spoken, and other things which the rest may not wear. Their hair, which is long like the women's here, is not concealed by the turban.

All go barefooted, and most often barelegged. Nevertheless, at their homes they use a kind of slippers or sandals[1] of wood; and when a person of greater quality comes to visit them, they put off these sandals and remain barefooted.

Maldive Woman.

As for the women, first of all they have a large coloured cloth of cotton or silk, which covers them from the waist to the ankles, and serves as a petticoat. Above this they wear a robe of taffetas, or of very fine cotton, but very long, reaching to the feet, and with blue and white borders. To give a notion of its shape, I cannot better describe this robe than

[1] Called *mara váli*.

by comparing it to the chemises which the women here wear. It is a little open round the neck, and fastened with two little gilt buttons, and likewise open at the throat in front, but no further at the breast; so that when they want to give suck to their babes, they have to lift these robes, without, however, making any exposure below, which is saved by the petticoat cloth of which I have spoken. Their arms are charged with heavy bracelets of silver, sometimes from the wrist up to the elbow; some of them have them mixed with tin, chiefly the poor, while the rest have them of fine and massive silver, in such sort that some of them carry as much as three or four pounds of silver on their arms. In addition, they have the silver chains round the waist, which are not seen, save sometimes when the robe is very transparent. Around the neck all women of means and quality have a number of gold chains, to which are threaded some pieces of gold money from Arabia or the mainland.[1]

Their hair is plaited, and sometimes they add a false peruke to make the bunch seem larger: this is of men's hair, for the women never cut theirs; it is covered with a gold netting, which the great ladies stud with precious stones. At their ears they wear as rich pendants as they can afford, but of a different sort from those worn in these parts; for mothers bore their daughters' ears at a tender age, not only at one place in the lobe, but at several places all along the cartilage, and insert cotton thread to keep the holes open, in

[1] "Like the Sinhalese, the women wear a waistcloth, generally of native manufacture, coarse in texture, the ground of a chocolate colour, relieved by black and white stripes (M. *féliya*). The upper part of the body is covered by a loose-fitting, red-coloured jersey reaching to the knees, short sleeved, and edged at the neck with silver tinsel lace (M. *libás*), whilst round the high-worn *kondé* is twisted a handkerchief matching the *libás* in colour, the *tout ensemble* forming a very becoming and picturesque costume. A profusion of bangles, with necklace, ear-rings, and other ornaments, deck the person. The use of gold trinkets is no longer rigidly restricted to women of quality" (Bell, *Report*, 55).

order, when they grow up, to fix therein golden clasps, to the number of twenty-four in the two ears. The front of the clasp is commonly adorned with a precious stone or a pearl. Besides these, there is in the lobe of the ear another pendant of a peculiar shape. When the women walk in the street by night or day, though it is but rarely they go forth by day, they wear a veil over the head. This, however, they take off in the presence of the queens and princesses, or even of ladies of higher quality than themselves,—not, however, before men, nor even before the king: on the contrary, that is the time to conceal themselves, when they think they are observed of men.[1]

I have said that they wear gold chains at the neck and precious stones in their ear-pendants; but it is to be remarked that no one, be it man or woman, saving a prince or a great noble, would dare to wear either rings or precious stones, bracelets or necklets, ear-rings or gold chains, without the permission of the king in the case of men, or of the queens in the case of women, and granted by letter. This permission is bought for ready money, unless given gratuitously, as is often the case to women. Only the queens and princesses may wear bracelets and rings of gold on the arms or legs; but other ornaments they may use of gold: and although the toe-rings and anklets may be of silver, such may not be worn but on payment of a certain sum, saving by those of high quality and birth; nor may any but the queens wear rings except on the thumb. The princesses and great ladies may wear them on the middle finger and the other two, with permission, but the men only on the thumb. So each knows his own rank and quality, and what he may use in

1 "The liberty enjoyed by the women is remarkable. Though their apartments are considered strictly private, they are not kept from the view of strangers, nor now debarred from openly walking abroad unveiled in the daytime. Even now (however) Maldivian ladies of the upper classes do not walk, but pay their visits in closed palanquins" (Bell, *Report*, 62).

the way of ornament, himself and his wife, and there is no confusion in these matters. For instance, if any man's wife who was not aforetime accustomed to much finery began to adorn herself more, or a man were to wear finger-rings,—albeit in this they were not exceeding their rights,—they would be taxed more heavily for that, excepting the officers of the king and of the queens, who pay no tax, and excepting also the inhabitants of Malé.[1] These, however, are subject to other charges and to many extraordinary expenses. Strangers and their wives have the privilege of dressing as they please, and of wearing any ornaments or bravery without permission, in like manner as the great princes and the king himself; and in many other things I have remarked that strangers have many rights and privileges denied to the natives of the country. So, too, the Pandiare, the Naybes, and Catibes, as well of Malé as of the other islands, many dress and adorn themselves as they will, and are not constrained by laws as others are in this respect. But to return to our discourse: the women are careful in dressing and adorning themselves with propriety, in bathing every day, in anointing their hair with scented oil, and in perfuming themselves. They have also a custom of colouring their feet and finger-nails red. It is the country notion of beauty. It is done with the sap of a certain tree,[2] and endures till the nail grows again, and then they do it afresh. And in truth they seemed to be pretty and engaging enough, as much by reason that they are neatly dressed as that they are well formed, of good figures, and winsome ways; albeit they are of an olive skin, for the most part, although you will find many brunettes, and many quite fair, just as in these parts.[3]

[1] The people of Málé are still free of taxation (Bell, *Report*, 67; Christopher, *T. Bom. Geo. Soc.*, i, 60).

[2] The juice of the Eastern privet, *Lawsonia* (M. *híná*), taken from the leaf; Pyrard mentions it later as *innafa* (*híná-fai*); *fai* = "leaf".

[3] "The women are short, usually of a more olive colour than the men, much resembling, in this respect, the fair-skinned Kandyans, with

The people at large, as well men as women, have many peculiar customs in their ways of life and deportment. First, they never eat together unless they are of the same quality and condition: it is dishonourable even to be at the same table with an inferior: so they never meet to feast together except at the religious festivals already described. If, however, they wish to entertain their friends, they cause to be prepared at their houses a large dish containing many courses, which is served up on a large round table with a cover of taffetas, and sent to the house of the person to be entertained: this is esteemed a great honour. When they are at home, they like not that others should see them eat, wherefore they retire to the back of the house, and let down all their screens and curtains towards the front, so as not to be seen. They say prayers before meals, and likewise before going forth. They have no other table but the floor of the house, covered with a neat little mat, on which they sit cross-legged. Linen they use not at all; but, to avoid soiling their mats, they use large banana leaves, whereon they place their food, and others in front of these to serve as ashets.[1] They take their food so nicely that they spill nothing, not even a drop of water, though they wash the mouth before and after dinner in basins served on purpose. The vessel used is of earthenware like that of Fayance,[2] fashioned in the native style, and imported from Cambaye; or else it is of China porcelain, which is very common, and used by almost all. But they use not any plate of earthenware or of porcelain, saving one kind of round box, polished and lacquered, with a cover of the same; it is manufactured in the island. When closed, this box is covered with a square piece of silk of

oval-shaped faces, regular features, and shapely figures. Clean and healthy in appearance, they are generally good-looking, some decidedly pretty" (Bell, *Report*, 55).

[1] I may be permitted to use the common Scotch form of the French *assiette*.

[2] *I.e.*, the coloured ware called after Faenza, 18 m. S.W. of Ravenna.

about the same size, which is worked in various styles of needlework and of all colours.[1] Even the poorest use these covered dishes, for the boxes cost but little. Their use is by reason of the ants, which exist in such wondrous multitude that they swarm everywhere, and it is difficult to keep anything from being incontinently covered with them. The people are so careful in their feeding, that they would not taste any food upon which has dropped a fly or an ant, or any other little creature, or the least dirt; in such case they would give it to the birds. They would not think of giving it to the poor, for they give to them nothing but what they would care to eat themselves, and prepared as for themselves. On this subject I have remarked that when the poor come to their doors, they make them enter the house and enjoy the same cheer as themselves, holding them to be as much the servants of God as they are. But to return to their ways of life, and to the utensils used at table. The greatest nobles have no other vessels, nor more costly than the rest, and use only the one already described. Although they could well afford vessels of gold and silver if they liked, yet their law forbids it, and for that reason they use them not. If haply their vessel should be a little cracked, they eat no longer thereout, putting it aside as polluted. No spoons are used either for eating rice or honey, nor even for liquids such as broth or gruels, neither there nor in the rest of India, but everything is taken with the fingers, which they are accustomed to do so neatly and dexterously that nothing is soiled. It is with them the greatest possible incivility, and very blameworthy, to let drop anything while

[1] These lacquered wooden dishes (*kurandi*) are mentioned by Mr. Bell (*Report*, 88). He has had a set of cups, saucers, and plates of this work presented to him, and reports them pretty. Although Pyrard (*v. s.*, p. 114) mentions a potter caste, the Maldivians seem to have done little in this line, earthenware being among the imports from Portuguese India (Correa, *Lendas*, i, 341; Bell, *Report*, 97). See also Ibn Bat., App. A.

eating. During the meal none present would dare to spit or cough: he must rise and go out to do that. Nothing they abhor, or consider so indecent and undignified, as spitting. In eating they never use the left hand, by reason that it is used for another purpose. They like to eat a half-ripe coco-nut when they begin their meal, and to drink its water, deeming it very healthy, and a laxative for the bowels. For the rest, all eat with much greediness and in great haste, holding it the best manners not to tarry at their food. Moreover, if they are (eating) in company they utter not a word one to another. To drink during a meal is bad manners: they never do so, and mock us for the habit; but after eating their bellyful, they drink once. Their commonest beverage is coco-milk, or coco-wine drawn the same day. They have also two other sorts of a more choice nature; the one is a warm drink composed of water and coco-honey with some pepper (much used in their other food, and called *Pasme*[1]) and another grain called *Cahoa*[2]; the other is cold and more delicate, being made of coco-sugar dissolved in water. But these drinks are for the king and the great lords, or for the solemn banquets at their festivals. They drink out of copper cups, exceeding handsome and craftily worked, which also have covers. After meat, when they have washed, a portion of betel is served in place of dessert, for fruits are served along with the meat. Most part of them have no fixed hour for their meals; they eat at all hours of the day when the fancy takes them, even the great lords and ladies.[3] The

[1] The M. is *asé-mirus;* the Sin. for pepper, generally, is *miris*, the variety being shown by an affix. Mr. Bell thinks Pyrard's initial "p" is an error; he cannot otherwise account for it.

[2] *I.e.*, coffee; Ar. *kahwa*. For the varied history of the word, see Yule's *Glossary*. Coffee does not grow at the Maldives; this would therefore be the real berry of Mocha or Yemen, where alone it was grown in quantity in those days, and not Ceylon coffee reshipped from Aden, as the most genuine of our Mocha is said now to be.

[3] Mr. Bell confirms this, and adds: "The usual meal of the natives consists of rice, often only half boiled, mixed with a few chopped

women and girls prepare the meals and look to the cooking, and not the men. The greatest insult that can be passed upon a man is to call him *cisdy*,[1]—that is to say, "cook"; and if any are found to be addicted to it (and there are some, chiefly among the grandees, who find that they can cook better than the women), they are mocked and despised of all men, in such sort that they are looked upon as women, rather than men: they even durst not associate but with women, nor engage in other exercises; so no difficulty is made in leaving them with the females.[2]

When they require to slay any animal for food there is much mystery in the matter. They cut the throat, turning themselves towards the sepulchre of Mahomet, and say their prayers, and after quitting their hold of the animal, or throwing it down, they touch it not again till it be quite dead; and should any touch it sooner, they would cast away the flesh and would not eat of it. Nor is this all: the throat must be cut at a certain place only, otherwise none would eat of it; nor does everyone know of that place, but chiefly it is known to the priests and Moudins. They who take in hand to slay an animal should be elders, and not boys: they should be fathers of children themselves. I have been amused to observe, at the common business of killing a

chillies, a little fish, 'fish sugar', and scraped coco-nut. This they consume in silence, even when eating in company, and with a haste that savours of greediness. A draught of water closes the repast" (*Report*, 56).

[1] "The contemptuous term *sídí*, applied to men who descend to this menial service, retains its old force" (Bell, *Report*, 56). The word is not to be derived from a Sinhalese source; Mr. Bell is inclined to think that it means merely "negro slave", the term "Sídí" being applied generally in Western India to East African negroes. The Zanzibar negroes on our men-of-war are still known as "Sidi-boys". See Yule and Burnell, *Glossary*, s. v. "Seedy".

[2] The suggestion here, which is obvious, seems to confirm Mr. Bell's derivation; the negro slaves at the Maldives would be generally, or at least frequently, eunuchs.

fowl, how they run about a whole island to find a man who knows how to do it,—ay, and who will be willing, for they refrain from the job as much as they can.[1] When they skin a fowl they throw away the skin, neck, back, and entrails, and eat the rest.

In all their actions they are scrupulous and superstitious, even in the smallest matters. After sleeping, whether by day or night, they fail not, as soon as they awake, to bathe their eyes and face, and rub them with oil, putting some black stuff[2] upon the eyelashes and eyebrows ; nor would they dare to speak or to say good-day to anyone ere they had done all that. They are very particular in cleaning their teeth, and are further of opinion that the red colour of the betel and areca, which they are continually chewing, is good for them ; so that they all have red teeth by reason of the betel-chewing, and they deem it a beauty. They carry betel always on them in the folds of their waist, and it would be a dishonour to a man to be found wanting it ; it is the custom, when they meet one another on the road, each to give of his own. They bathe many times a day, not only when they list, but as their religion requires ; and when they enter a temple they bathe the extremities, as I have said : this, in their language, is called *voulos*.[3] So, too, after making water, or otherwise obeying nature, they wash their parts with the left hand, or else bathe the whole body (this is called *Innan*[4]), with divers forms and ceremonies proper to the several festivals. So, when they bathe in public, as is their wont, it is well seen why they are bathing,—as, for example, when they have had the society of their wives, whether by day or night, you see them plunge the head three times under water : this is exceed-

[1] A probable, though very slight, trait of former Buddhism.

[2] See also Ibn Bat. They call it *galadun*.

[3] Ar. *wuḍu* or *wuzu*. "This consists in washing the hands, mouth, nostrils, face, arms, as high as the elbow, the right first, each three times ; and then the upper part of the head, the beard, ears, neck, and feet each once" (Lane, *Ar. Soc.*, 11).

[4] M. *hinán*, to bathe ; Sin. *nánda*.

ing indecent. When they are seated in any place, others must take care to pass behind them, for to do otherwise would be held a great indignity, and would bring about some untoward result; but if it is necessary to go in front of another, the one who does so crouches full low, and holds his hands down to the ground, saying *Assa*,[1] as who should say, "Be not displeased." It is a grave indiscretion for one seated in the presence of others to swing the legs; they are much offended at it, and hold it to be a sign of bad luck and a piece of bad manners. So, when they set out on any voyage, they like not to meet or touch any person; and if aught untoward or unfortunate should happen, they will lay it at the door of him who touched them. Above all, when they go a-fishing, one must not salute them nor give them good-day.[2] From sunset on Thursday until three or four o'clock on the following day, they suffer none to take anything from their houses; should it be their greatest friend or their father who would borrow anything, they would not lend it then, nor would they give up anything which another had sent to demand, even if it did not belong to them; nevertheless, they make no business about receiving anything or admitting anything to their houses at that time. I have noted as worthy of praise that when they have disputes and quarrels, or are at enmity, they refrain above all things from abusing the food and drink which they may have received from one another; if any should do so, all would vent their anger upon him.

When at sea, if they are caught by contrary winds, by calms, or by storms, they make vows to him who rules the winds, who is called not God, but King; and there is no island

[1] Probably a contraction of the Sin. *avasara*, "leave" or "permission", which word is used on precisely similar occasions in Ceylon. Mr. Bell says the expression seems to have died out, at least in the northern atolls, the modern phrase being *amuru-devvá*, "grant leave".

[2] See the interesting collection of Sinhalese omens on commencing a work or a journey, given by S. Jayatilaka Mudaliyar in *Ceylon As. Soc. Jour.*, vii, 147-161; and Mr. Bell's paper on Sin. customs connected with Paddy cultivation, in the same journal for 1883.

but has a *siare*,[1] as they call it, which is a place dedicated to the King of the winds, in a corner of the island remote from the world, where those who have escaped from danger

[1] The title of "king", in place of "god" of the winds, is, no doubt, a concession to the monotheistic principles of Islam; and the passage gives a curious insight into the primitive worship of the islanders. It may first be observed that the powers of wind and sea are separately worshipped, the Maldivian sailors having to contend not only with monsoons but with currents; next, that the stage of culture when the sea and wind are themselves the objects of worship has been passed, and personal, if not anthropomorphic, deities have been conceived. As to the character of the worship of the two kings, the author is not so precise as might be wished. The proceedings at the *siare* (M. *Ziyára*, Ar. *Ziyarat*, "visitation", in orthodox Mah. usage meaning, the visiting of sacred places, as opposed to the Haj, and vulgarly the place so visited) are by way of thanksgiving for safety, offered, it would seem, exclusively to the king of the winds; the worship of the king of the sea is deprecatory, and it does not appear whether it is paid at the *siare* or elsewhere.

The worship of wind and sea is ancient and extensive. Cicero writes: "Ergo imbres, nimbi, procellæ, turbines Dii putandi. Nostri quidem duces, mare ingredientes, immolare hostiam fluctibus consueverunt" (*De Nat. Deor.*, iii, 20). Thus would a successful voyage be secured while the elements were still uncertain. Both this method, and the propitiatory ceremonies as employed by Mahomedans during a storm, are well exemplified by Père Dan in his description of the Barbary pirates of the sixteenth century. The pirates' wives would light a little fire, in which they burned incense and myrrh; then they cut the throat of a cock, sprinkling the blood in the fire. They scattered the feathers to the wind and tore the body to pieces, casting most of it into the sea (Dan, *Hist. de Barbarie*, 1637, liv. III, c. iii). The pirates themselves appeased a storm as follows: first they sacrificed a sheep, disembowelling it alive, casting one-half the body into the sea on the starboard side, the other on the port. If this were unsuccessful, they would next pour two barrels of oil on the water, one on each side of the ship. This, as recent experiments have proved, would be efficacious for a time; but when the storm again prevailed, they placed lighted candles on all their cannon, allowing them to burn out. This failing, one resource only remained, never resorted to but in the last extremity; they constrained the wretched Christians, chained to the galley-benches, to make vows to the Virgin, St. Nicholas, or some other saint, they cared not which! (*ib.*, liv. III, c. vi). In no part of the world has this sea-worship been so strongly marked as on the Guinea coast of Africa. Bosman says: "When it rages, and hinders us bringing our goods on

come to make offering daily of little boats and ships fashioned on purpose, and filled with perfumes, gums, flowers, and odoriferous woods. The perfumes are set on fire, the little boats are cast upon the sea, and float till they are

shore, when no ships have been there for a long time, and they impatiently wait for them,—on these occasions they make great offerings to it, by throwing into it all sorts of goods. But the priests do not much encourage this sort of sacrificing, by reason there happens no remainder to be left for them" (*Pinkerton*, vol. xvi, p. 500). Snelgrave describes the sacrifice of an old woman, who was fortunately picked up by the English boats before the sharks got her (*New Account of Guinea*, pp. 101-105). The same practices survived to our own day: "In Dahome the Ocean has a special priest, who, at stated times, repairs to the beach, and there begs the Ocean god not to be boisterous, throwing in rice and corn, oil and beans, cloth, cowries, and other valuables. Occasionally the king of Dahome offers a human victim, who is carried in a hammock to a canoe, and thence delivered to the sharks" (Burton, *Dahome*, i, 141). The races of India proper are so little addicted to navigation, that they contribute few instances of this worship; we find, however, that at Carwar, on sight of the new moon in August, the effigy of Ganesa "was carried in procession to the river's side and thrown into the river, upon which all rivers which have bars are opened for navigation" (Alex. Hamilton, *New Acct.*, i, 274-5). Further east, among the Lampongs of Sumatra, we find the most ancient and simple adoration of the sea itself. When the inland natives behold it for the first time, they make it an offering of cakes and sweetmeats, deprecating its power of doing them mischief (Marsden, *Sumatra*, 250).

The sacrifice of a model boat, filled with perfumes, gums, etc., and set on fire, described by Pyrard as a thank-offering, is, with the Malays of Larut, resorted to, in almost identical form, as a means of enticing away the evil spirits from a sick person (see *Medical Hist. of the Laroot Field Force*, by Surgeon-Major Davie, in App. to *Army Med. Dep. Rep.*, 1876, quoted in *J. R. A. S.*, new series, vol. x, p. 202, note 2.

The sacrifice at the launch of a new ship still survives at the Maldives, as described by Pyrard. "On such occasions a small vessel, three or four feet long, being decked out with flags, and having samples of the various fruits of the island, is set adrift; should it be a boat newly built, other ceremonies are observed, accompanied with feasting, music, etc. The miniature vessel is decorated with flowers, and her gunwales are hung with fruits, for which, as soon as she enters the water, there is a general scramble" (Christopher, in *T. Bom. Geo. Soc.*, i, 75). Exactly the same offering of a miniature canoe is made to Ganga Bandera, a

burned, for they too catch the fire, and this, say they, that the king of the winds may accept them. So, when they have any difficulty in launching their ships or galleys, they kill some cocks and hens, and cast them into the sea in face of the ship or boat which they desire to launch. Likewise they believe in a king of the sea, to whom in like sort they make prayers and ceremonies while on voyages; or when they go a-fishing, they dread above all things to offend the kings of the winds and of the sea. So, too, when they are at sea, they durst not spit nor throw anything to windward for fear lest he should be offended, and with like intent they never look abaft. When I was in their boats, they were concerned to see that I observed not these superstitions. All boats, barques, and vessels are dedicated to these powers of the winds and of the sea; and, indeed, they treat their boats with as much respect as their temples, keeping them exceeding clean, and abstaining from all filthy or indecent actions on board. Likewise they hold in honour the kings of the other elements (as they call them), as him of war, and pay them all great ceremony.

They lay great store by certain charms, called *Tauide*,[1]

malignant river-demon in Ceylon (*Pridham*, p. 165; *cf.* translation of the poem "Gangárohaniya", in *Ceylon Friend*, 1879-80, p. 282). And generally, see *Qanoon e Islam*, pp. 31, 99-101; Barbot, in *Churchill*, vol. v, pp. 143, 344, 375).

Since writing the above, Mr. Bell informs me that some of this demon worship exists in the southern atolls, though the natives are loth to give him information on the subject. He has, however, obtained the names of the following ten devils:—1, Gharaguginni Rannamári (the "king of the winds"); 2, Nabajaháge; 3, Aku-isanja' javija; 4, Lajjígavisanavi; 5, Gálígóti; 6, Jajjálu; 7, Habbóráza; 8, Dihabórajañí; 9, Kosmoyázabadu; 10, Laggitúḍí. One of the last nine is probably the king of the sea.

[1] M. *tavídu*, Ar. *ta' wíz*. Sorcery is, with the Maldivians, *fadita* (Sin. *paṇḍita*), "the learned (science)". Mr. Bell (*J. Ceyl. Br. R. A. S.*, vii, 119) gives two examples of these *mantras* from the southern atolls, remarking that they come under the Sanskrit category of *Stambhana*, or of *Vibhíshana*, *i.e.*, intended to procure illicit intercourse and effect discord. The

which they carry under their dress, enclosed in little boxes, which the rich have made of gold or silver. They wear these either on their arms, neck, or waist, or even at the feet,

first runs as follows: "Gada istiri vari tura' kurákan haivakaru abaku de míhunge rúfa kurahai *hadduru harruli nuvá gihí badili elagodí* abu gahani." Translation: "To completely estrange a desirable woman (from her husband), make a teak nail (and) an image of both persons, (mutter) 'hadduru harruli nuvá gihí badili elagodí' [unintelligible], and drive in the nail." The second is as follows: "Gada istiriye' liame karhi male' fari nuvanís kadágen au valie' hanulaigen mi malu effurhu *Al Kadr Sura* lie ane' furhumati *Vajahatu* lie mi malu rúfa kurahá váhaka vará olun lie *Al Rahmán Sura* huswáden lie' vá' rónu' fas tan bede rakas bode' Katiláeige lein kaliko' dumarhí bávvai hikkai tin duvas véinái nagaigen gos múdu alani kakú fenu eli nama balai fonavani fúlu fenu eli nama audei." Translation: "Write (the name of) a desirable woman; pluck an unopened bud of the screw-pine flower; sharpen a new knife; on one side of this flower write *Al Kadr Sura;* on the other side write *Vajahatu;* make an image out of this flower; write particulars of the horoscope; write *Al Rahmán Sura* from beginning to end; tie (the image) in five places with left-hand (twisted) coir; cut the throat of a bloodsucker (lizard); smear its blood (on the image); place it on a loft; dry it for three days; (then) take it and enter the sea—if you go in knee-deep (she) will send a message; if you go in to the waist (she) will come."

The *tavídu* of the Maldives correspond in all respects to the *huniyam* of Ceylon. In the *Jour. Cey. Br. R. A. S.*, vol. vii, p. 116, Mr. Louis Nell gives a photograph (actual size, about two inches) of a *huniyam* image, which was discovered in a little tin box in a hollow tree. A most valuable account of them is given in the same journal for 1865, by Dandris de Silva Mudaliyar, under the title "Sinhalese Demonology". The Mudaliyar there writes:—"*Kodivina*, or *Huniyam*, is the name given to evils of whatever kind inflicted by the agency of charms. . . . There are said to be 84,000 (charms) of every degree of malignity, most of which, more or less, contribute to bring to an untimely death the person affected by this influence, though that event may be deferred for many years."

Of the Maldivians' skill in charms, Barbosa writes:—"As gentes dellas nao tem armas, e sao homens fracos, mas muito engenhosos, e sobre tudo grandes encantadores" (*Noticias das Naçoes Ultramarinas*, tom. ii, p. 352, Lisbon, 1812). This passage, unfortunately, appears in Lord Stanley's *Barbosa*, Hakl. Soc., p. 164, in this disguise: "The inhabitants are ill-formed and weak, but are very ingenious and charming."

according to the subject of distress; for they serve all purposes, as well offensive as defensive, as well for loving as for gaining love, for raising hatred, for making well or making sick. The magicians and sorcerers sell them for money, and say that they bring good luck, and will heal or preserve one from many a sickness; and in their sicknesses they have but few remedies, and then by recourse to these magicians and sorcerers, who are their only doctors; they have none other. Likewise they all believe that evil is brought by the devil to harass them withal, and that he is the sole cause of death and sickness. They invoke him, accordingly, and offer him flowers, and prepare a banquet of all sorts of meats and drinks, which they place in a secret spot and leave to be wasted, unless peradventure some poor folk take them away. With the same design, they kill some cocks and hens, turning themselves towards the sepulchre of Mahomet, and then leave them, praying the devil to accept them, and to take himself off and leave the sick person at ease: they call this sorcery *Cauuery*.[1]

But since I have spoken of their cures by sorcery, it seems needful to tell what are their sicknesses, and then I shall add something of the natural remedies which they practise. Fever is very common there, and is called by them *homan*[2]; but it is most dangerous to strangers sojourning there, whom it does for in but a few days. I have already spoken of it from my own experience, having seen many of my comrades die of it, and having had it myself. It is

[1] In ch. xix, more correctly *Quennery* (M. *Kanvcri*). "This is the savage theory of demoniacal possession, which has been for ages, and still remains, the dominant theory of disease and inspiration among the lower races. Disease being accounted for by the attack of spirits, it naturally follows that to get rid of these spirits is the proper means of cure" (Tylor, *Prim. Cult.*, second edition, ii, 124, 125; see, too, p. 127, and the authorities there given; also Knox, *Ceylon*, p. 78).

[2] Ar. *hummá*; yet at p. 83 he calls Málé fever *Malé ons* (M. *hung*, Sin. *una*).

known throughout all the Indies under the name of "Maldive fever". Every ten years there comes a sickness called *cariuadiri*,[1] in the presence of which they abandon one another as if it were the plague. It is like the chicken-pox which our children have, and of this malady many die. The eye-sickness[2] is common enough, and you see great numbers of people blind by it, and most of them have short sight. Often, too, when they have been for long in the sun during the heat of the day, when the sun sets they cannot see at all, though they are near a fire or a light, even were it a hundred torches: it does not otherwise harm them. This evil or ailment is called *rosnans*.[3] To cure it they cook the liver of a cock, writing over it certain words and charms, and swallow it at sunset. My comrades and I were much troubled by it at times, till at length, being apprised of this recipe, we took a cock's liver, rejecting the charms, to see if it would serve us, and found that it cured us as it cured them, without the use of their sorceries. They suffer much from the itch, which they call *caz*[4]; but they cure it with coco-nut oil. They are also greatly troubled with ringworm, and have no cure for it, for there are some whose bodies are nearly covered with it. These diseases come from the quantity of salt fish they eat, and by reason that nearly all their food is salted only by being steeped in sea-water. In winter, when the rains are continuous, they still go barefooted, and then there attaches to their feet and between the toes a kind of worm, generated in the mud, causing pustules and tumours; and these, when they burst, raise ulcers, which impede their walking. These worms are called in their

[1] *I.e.*, small-pox; M. *karhivaduri*. Mr. Bell relates that on small-pox breaking out among the crew engaged at the wreck of s.s. *Seagull*, on the island Gaufaru, in 1879, the natives fled *en masse* to another island (*Report*, 8).

[2] Ophthalmia.

[3] M. *róná* (Bell). This is night-blindness, a well-known tropical ailment. The *roshuwandu* of Chr. is the appropriate medicine.

[4] M. *kas*, Hind. *khaj*, Sin. *kushta*.

language *Quillapanis*,[1] that is to say, "dirt worms". In the other parts of the body, too, they are much troubled with worms. All alike have the spleen enlarged, and besides that, they are subject to having it obstructed, with the abdomen distended and tight, whereby they are much troubled. They are of opinion that this comes from the water of the islands, which is not good; and from the same cause they get the fever. This malady they call *Oncory*.[2] The cure they use for this, as for all other kinds of inflammation or local pain, is to apply large button-cauters to the swollen or painful part. This makes an issue and wound passing large, to which they apply cotton steeped in oil of cocos, whereby they get much relief. I have seen men thus burnt and cauterised in five or six places. As for me, when I was sick, I declined to let them practise this remedy upon me. As to ulcers, to which they are greatly subject, and chiefly on the legs, they cure them by putting over them copper plates, which entirely heal them, as I found by experience. Besides these remedies I have described, they have some recipes and compounds of their herbs and drugs for divers ailments, most of all for wounds, which they cure with great dexterity. Yet are they ignorant of the art of using bandages and linen for wounds, for they apply ointments only, as we do here to horses. Catarrhs and rheums annoy them betimes, as also gout in the bones. Venereal disease is not so common, albeit it is found, and is cured with China-wood,[3] without sweating or anything else. This disease they call *farangui baescour*,[4] from its coming to them from Europe, whose

[1] M. *kila fani* (kilá, "earth", *fani*, "worms"); *cf.* Sin. *panuwa*, "worm".

[2] See *supra*, p. 84.

[3] *Bois de la Chine*; elsewhere he writes *bois d'Eschine*. It was formerly called *China radix*, but latterly *Smilax China* (Linn.); also vulgarly *chine* and *squine*. "A red and spungious Indian root, good against the gout" (Cotgrave); Linschoten has a long chapter upon it, and asserts its virtues for both these diseases (*Hakl. Soc.*, i, 239; ii, 107-12).

[4] *Cf.* Ar. *bāsūr*, "piles".

inhabitants they call by a common name, *farangui*, or *frangui*, from the French, the most renowned people of the West.[1] I have remarked that they know not what it is to suffer from toothache: and this seems to be caused by their habit of chewing betel, which strengthens the gums; and, indeed, by adopting their practice, I never had toothache there, though I have always suffered much from it elsewhere.

In nursing their babes, they have some peculiar customs and habits, which I have not observed elsewhere. As soon as their children are born, they bathe them in cold water six times in the day,[2] and then rub them with oil, which they continue a long while; moreover, as often as they obey the calls of nature they bathe their parts with water, just as if they were grown persons. Mothers nurse their children themselves, and would not think of letting them be suckled by others, not even the queens, for they are wont to say that all animals suckle their own young; yet they keep servants to tend, carry, and manage them. Besides the breast, they give

[1] Rivara (*Viagem de F. Pyrard*) is sarcastic :—"O auctor devia saber que tambem na Europa o nome desta molestia traz a sua derivação da mesma origem, privilegio que as outras nações não invejam por certo aos Francezes." Dr. Burnell (*Linsch.*, Hakl. Soc., i, 239, *note*) cites the evidence which goes to show that syphilis was not introduced into Europe by Columbus's crew *circa* 1493, that it was an old disease known both in Europe and Asia, and that only a fresh and notable outbreak occurred towards the end of the fifteenth century. He quotes the statement of Varthema, that he found the Samorin of Calicut suffering from it in 1505, and argues that he could not have got it from the Portuguese,—*sed quære*. Whether it existed in India before the Portuguese period I will not examine here; the name given to it at the Maldives shows that the natives there attributed it to the Portuguese; and this opinion is universally entertained in Ceylon and elsewhere in the East.

[2] *Cf.* Virg., *Æneid*, ix, 603 :—

> "Durum ab stirpe genus, natos ad flumina primum
> Deferimus, sævoque gelu duramus et undis;"

and Claudian (*in Ruf.*, ii, 112), of the Germans—

> "Et quos nascentes explorat gurgite Rhenus."

them gruel of rice or millet, pounded and soaked, and then cooked with coco-milk and sugar[1]; most of them—that is, the poorer folk—give them bananas. They never swaddle them, but let them go free; nor have I ever seen them do otherwise. They put them to bed suspended in the air, in little cord beds, or little cradles, in which they are swung and rocked. About the age of nine months they begin to walk; at nine years they begin to be taught the studies and exercises of the country.

Their studies are to read and write, and to learn their Alcoran, and so to know how they have to live. Their letters are of three sorts[2]: the Arabic, with some letters and points

[1] This particular kind of kanji they call *furahani*.

[2] In other passages (*supra*, pp. 138, 142, and vol. ii, Introduction to Vocabulary) he speaks of the languages at the Maldives; this is the only reference to the characters used. The letters thirdly mentioned are perhaps the Tamil, those only being common to Ceylon and India. But there is little or no evidence of intercourse between the Maldives and the Tamil country; along the Malabar coast, with which the Maldives had so much to do, the language and alphabet used are almost universally Malayâlam; this latter, however, is not used at all in Ceylon. The matter must be left in doubt. The second character referred to is, doubtless, the *Divehi akuru*, or *dives ákuru*, "island letters", the more ancient alphabet of the Maldives. Christopher (*J. R. A. S.*, vol. vi) gave a plate showing the principal consonants and vowel-signs, which I reproduced in my paper on the Maldives (*J. R. A. S.*, new series, vol. x); but Mr. Bell says the alphabet has never been published in full, and M. d'Abbadie, who met Christopher on the Nubian coast, and had from him his own copy of the letters, tells me that this is so. "It consists of twenty-five letters", says Mr. Bell, "not counting duplicates, capable of some hundreds of vowel-mutations." "One peculiarity", says Christopher, "in the alphabet is, that some of the consonants change their form according to the various vowel-sounds with which they are united, the construction of the letter being altogether different." This character is clearly a modification of the old Vaṭṭeḷuttu of S. India, the parent also of the Sinhalese (see Dr. Burnell, in *Ind. Ant.*, i, 229; and *Elements of S. Indian Palæography*). It is largely used in the old Maldive tombstones and walls, and, from the appearance of these inscriptions, must have been in use long before the Arabic. It is not known now in the northern atolls except by the Faḍiyâru, and a few of the

which they have added to express their language; another, whose characters are peculiar to the Maldive language; and a third, which is common to Ceylon and to the greater part of India. They write their lessons on little tablets of wood, which are whitened, and when they have learned their lesson

learned at Málé, though said to be still prevalent in the south. In Christopher's time all orders for the southern atolls had to be transcribed into it, but, according to Mr. Bell, this practice is now discontinued. Like the Sinhalese and other Indian writing, it was written from left to right.

What form of writing Pyrard exactly means by the Arabic, "with some letters and points which they have added", is somewhat difficult to say. That the Arabic character in its entirety was, and is, used, is proved both by Mr. Christopher and Mr. Bell, and the former states that it is written in two different ways, the old and the new. Somewhere about Pyrard's time, however, a change was introduced, and an alphabet called the *Gabuli tána* came into vogue. It consists properly of eighteen letters, nine of which are the first nine Arabic numerals, the other nine being adopted from the *Divehi akuru.* It has also some auxiliary letters borrowed from the Arabic and Persian. Vowels are not inherent, but are supplied by diacritical strokes common to the Arabic. Unlike the *Divehi akuru*, these letters do not admit of being joined in writing. This alphabet will be found in *J. R. A. S.*, vol. vi; *J. A. S. Beng.*, v, p. 784; and *J. R. A. S.*, new series, vol. x. The mode of writing this character is from right to left, following the Arabic, as appears by the facsimiles of Maldive letters given by Christopher (*J. R. A. S.*, vol. vi), and by Mr. Bell (*Rep.*, plate, App., 78). Mr. Prinsep, however (*J. A. S. Beng.*, v, p. 784), gives a few words written by a Maldivian nakodah in this character, which are written from left to right, so it may be that in or for the southern atolls the modern character was then used in the old direction. A similar change was made by the Tagals of the Philippines, who formerly wrote from top to bottom, and after the Spanish conquest adopted the left-to-right method (see *De Morga*, Hakl. Soc., p. 295, *note*). It may be added that there are several kinds of *Tána* writing; Mr. Bell mentions the *Harha tána* and the *Defo' tána*, "but these are awkward and rarely employed." As, according to Christopher, the modern Arabic form and the *Gabuli tána* were introduced about the same time, after the expulsion of the Portuguese,—a date which is, I believe, fixed only by tradition,—and as it does not appear whether Pyrard knew Arabic writing, it must for the present remain doubtful whether the Arabic which he refers to was really Arabic or the mixed *Tána* alphabet.

they efface what they have written, and whiten them afresh, unless the writing is required to be preserved[1]; in that case, they write upon parchment made of the leaves of the tree *Macare queau*,[2] whose leaf is a fathom and a half long and a foot broad. They make books of it, which last as long or longer than ours, without decaying. In teaching their children to write, they use wooden boards made on purpose, well polished and joined, and spread thereon some fine, powdered sand; then they make the letters with a bodkin and bid them imitate them, effacing betimes what they have written, and using no paper for this purpose.[3] They all treat their masters with the same respect and honour as their own fathers, by reason whereof they may not contract marriage together, as though related in affinity. Among them are men who make a pursuit of study, and are esteemed vastly learned in their knowledge of the Alcoran, and in the ceremonies of their law: these are chiefly the Moudins, Catibes, or Naybes. These two offices are compatible; the Catibe may be a Naybe, and the Naybe a Catibe.

Mathematics are taught and much cultivated, especially astrology, which is studied by many, seeing that the astrologers are consulted at every turn. None would care to engage in any enterprise without previously taking their advice. And not only do they like to know their nativities and have their horoscopes taken, but also when they have to do any building, whether in wood or stone, they must go

[1] They whiten boards with a kind of clay (*marhi*), and write on this surface with ink of native manufacture; the whole washes off.

[2] M. *má-karhikeyo*, the "pandanus". Paper has now almost entirely superseded these leaves as writing material (Bell, *Report*, 70, 84). Pyrard gives a further description of this tree in his Treatise, in vol. ii.

[3] The Maldive children are still taught in the same manner; it is called *vorhufilá liyaṇ*. The Sinhalese use the same, calling it *vëllé-liyanavá*.

and inquire of the astrologer at what hour it were better to commence it, that so it may be done under a good constellation; and the same if it be the building of a ship, but with differences proper to the different uses which the vessel may be building for; thus, they choose a different day or hour for a ship of war, for a merchantman, and for a fishing-boat. Moreover, when they undertake a voyage or any other enterprise, in like wise it is not without first inquiring of the astrologer what will be the issue of it, and whether the day be good or bad, and the planet favourable or unfavourable; and so, if anything untoward befalls them, they attribute it to the day, and accept it with patience, saying that the will of God has been done. The king at all times keeps a number of these astrologers about him, as well as other mathematicians, and ofttimes employs their services. They also study magic and sorcery.

These islanders practise themselves greatly in arms,—how to use the sword with the buckler, how to draw the bow with ease, how to fire the arquebuse and handle the pike; they also have schools of arms, whose masters are highly honoured and respected, they who take this office being in general great lords.[1] They have no other games but ball (large and small), which they catch and throw with much address, though they use the feet only.[2]

[1] *Vide* ch. xix.

[2] They have two ball games, as Mr. Bell informs me, in which the feet are used, but not entirely, viz., *suvá* and *lubómaṇdí*. These games would seem to have been introduced from the Eastern Archipelago, whose natives are very expert at them. "They have a diversion similar to that described by Homer amongst the Phæacians, which consists in tossing an elastic wicker ball from one to the other in a large party. They arrive to a great degree of dexterity in the sport, receiving it with equal facility on the foot or hand, the heel or the toe, from whence it is thrown either perpendicularly into the air and caught again, or obliquely to some other person of the company, who stand in an extended circle" (Marsden, *Sumatra*, p. 239; see also Crawfurd, *Ind. Arch.*, i, 117).

They employ themselves also in manufactures, and are exceeding apt and adroit therein, in such sort that there are among them a great number of different crafts for the making of furniture, utensils, and other commodities.

Their chiefest and most common employment is fishing, wherein all the people indifferently in all parts of the Maldives take part; nor are there only certain persons of this employment, as elsewhere, nor certain places for it, reserved from the public. Natural freedom prevails, and every man may fish where he likes and as much as he likes.[1] It is deemed an honourable employment, even the greatest lords joining, and taking great pleasure in it, as they do here in the chase; but they care not otherwise to profit in the takes. On the contrary, all men of honour and quality, when they go a-fishing and catch any, send them to their friends or give them to any who come and ask of them, or else they have a quantity cooked with green bananas, called at the Maldives *quella*,[2] and call all their neighbours to come and eat; this they do without other ceremony, by way of merry-making. The kings themselves have officers to wait upon them when they would enjoy this sport. Being islanders, with but a small extent of land, with them fishing is what the chase is to other nations. Twelve persons are appointed to work and man the king's boat, and to do the needful when he goes a-fishing. They are all great lords who are appointed to these offices; they think themselves highly honoured, and purchase them dearly. Over them is a captain, one of the highest grandees, who must work the rudder of

[1] Owing to the abundance of the fishery, no restrictive rules or limits were necessary. Very different is the case in Ceylon, where the utmost jealousy exists between the coast hamlets as to their respective fishing grounds, and local feuds have as long a duration as those between the British and French fishermen of the Newfoundland banks, which have for so many years exercised the highest diplomatic talent of London and Paris, and are still unsettled (1885).

[2] M. *kéu*, and in the southern atolls, *kéki*; Sin. *kehel*; Hind. *kelá*.

the vessel. The king gives each of the twelve a heavy silver ring or bracelet,[1] to put on his right arm, of the weight of a quarter of a pound (which is called a *gaux*,[2] and is like our weights), and to the captain one of gold: these they wear when the king goes to fish. Nevertheless, the king who reigned when I was there went a-fishing but rarely.

Fishing is done at the Maldives in several ways. The chief fishery, that of the fish in which is the greatest trade, is pursued beyond the reefs and atolls in the deep sea, six or seven leagues out, where that kind of fish always lies. A marvellous quantity of large fish are caught there, of seven or eight sorts, which are all of the same race and kind, though not of the same appearance or size; for example, *bonites, albachores, daurades*,[3] and others, which are very like each other, and of the same taste, and have no scales, no more than mackerel; they are all found together in the same grounds, and are caught in the same manner,—that is, by a line of a fathom and a half of thick cotton cord, fixed in a big cane, which is a wood of great strength. The hook at the end is of a different sort from ours. It is not bent, but is longer, and pointed at the end like a needle, without barb or tongue, resembling in all respects the letter "h" written

[1] A badge adopted, perhaps, from the Malabar coast. "The principallest or chiefest of those Nayros, which are leaders or captaines of certaine numbers of Nayros, weare a gold or silver bracelet or ring about their armes, above their elbowes; as also their Governours, Ambassadours and Kings, whereby they are knowne from other men" (*Linsch.*, Hakl. Soc., i, 282). Compare the use of the *annulus aureus* among the Romans (Smith, *Dict. Gr. and R. Ant.*). See also below, ch. xix.

[2] M. *gau*, or *galé*; *cf.* Sin. *gala*, "stone"; now also = ¼ lb. A *Cypræa mauritiana* shell, bearing the Sultan's seal in wax, is the regular "Imperial *gau*" in the southern atolls (Bell, *Report*, 118).

[3] *I.e.*, *bonito*, the *Thynnus pelamys* (Day); *albacore*, a kind of large mackerel, *Thynnus albucora* (Lowe), perhaps the same as *T. macropterus* (Day); and *dorado*, or "gilt head", the sea-bream (often called "dolphin"; see *Hawk. Voy.*, Hakl. Soc., p. 148); the *Coryphæna hippurus* (Day).

in the French running hand. No bait is attached, but the day before, they provide a lot of little fish of the size of little roach or whitebait, which are found in great abundance on the reefs and shallows; these they keep alive in net-bags of coco-nut cord of small meshes, and let them drag in the sea at the stern of their barques. When they get out to the deep sea to the fishing ground they cast abroad these little fish, and at the same time put in their line. The big fish, seeing the little fish—a rare sight in the deep sea,—rush up in numbers, and are caught at the hook, which is whitened and tinned on purpose,—for this kind of fish is exceeding greedy and foolish, so to be taken by a white hook, which it mistakes for a small white fish.[1] They have then only to draw the line into the boat, where the fish drops at once, being hardly hooked; the line is speedily put back into the sea, and thus a marvellous quantity are taken, in such wise that in less than three or four hours their boats are nearly full: and this, be it remarked, while they are going full sail. The fish which is taken there is commonly called in their language *Cobolly masse*,[2] that is to say, "black fish", for they

[1] This is equally true at the present day both of the Maldivian and Ceylon fish: they have learned neither wisdom nor self-restraint.

[2] M. *kaḷu-bili-mas*, *i.e.*, *kalu*, "black"; *bili*, "bonito", Sin. *balayá*; *mas*, "fish". It is vulgarly pronounced *komboli*, or *kommala mas*, and is known in Ceylon as *umbala kada*. Ibn Batuta calls it *koulb al más* (see below, App. A). Pridham (*Ceylon*, 605) writes *komblĕmas*; the Hindustani form is *kumbala*.

With the *komboli mas* of the Ceylon and Indian bazaars, though chiefly bonito, pass several other kinds of fish, such as the *godá*, *kanneli*, and *rágoḍi*. There are several methods of cutting up the fish for curing, all of which are fully described, with diagrams, by Mr. Bell (*Report*, pp. 93-5). The preparation is then as follows:—"The pieces are washed with salt water, then thrown into a cauldron of boiling salt water and allowed to remain a few minutes only, to prevent the flesh becoming too soft. It is said to be important that the water should be boiling from the first. On being taken out they are placed on the wattle, loft, or shelf (M. *mehi*, Sin. *messa*) above the fire. There they are left three or four days till well blackened and dried, after which, if necessary, they

are all black. They are cooked in sea-water, and then dried in the sun upon trays, and so when dry they keep a long while; wherefore there is great traffic in them, not only in the country, but throughout the rest of India, where they are in great request. For the rest, the largest and finest fish caught must go to the king, and as soon as the boat lands, one of the chief men takes the fish and reeves a cord or osier through his gills, and then carry him with a rod over the shoulder to the king's kitchen. Next, they give some to the clergy, to the poor, and to their friends, and the remainder are divided amongst themselves; but however small the catch, this division must always be made.

There is another kind of fishing, which is done at night on the reefs around the atolls, and only twice a month, when the moon is in conjunction and again when it is full, three days each time.[1] It is done from these rafts, called *candoue patis*, of which I have spoken above.[2] Long lines of fifty or sixty fathoms are used, of thick and strong cotton, blackened with the bark of a tree, which serves them in place of charcoal or pitch: this is to preserve the line for a long time from rotting. At the end are hooks to which baits are attached, in like manner as with us. With these lines they catch a quantity of fish, of a kind I have not seen elsewhere; it is three or four feet long, and broad in proportion, and all red; but within quite white and firm when cooked. It is most excellent and delicious eating, by reason whereof these people—who, in the names they give to things, full nearly express their nature—call this fish "the

are exposed to the sun to be finished. Thus dried, they are, as is well known, of the appearance and consistency of blocks of wood" (Bell, *loc. cit.*; also his paper in *Ind. Ant.*, xi, 196).

[1] This is called *fö'-mas*, or *föi-mas*, Sin. *poya-mas*, the fishing of the *poya* or festival days.

[2] At p. 122.

king of the sea".[1] They eat it fresh, and salt it not at all. Likewise they catch many other kinds of fish in marvellous quantity; it would be impossible for me to distinguish them, so great is their variety: fishes unknown to us in these parts, and by me not seen in any other region of the world. It will suffice here to mention them thus generally, to give a notion of the principal source of the wealth of the country; and if there be aught else to remark in particular, I will reserve it to speak of elsewhere. Also they have all kinds of nets, lines of cotton thread, weels, and implements of fishery, as we have, for catching fish in various ways in the shallows of the sea; but these are only for eating fresh, and there is no traffic therein. On the seashore, where it is but shallow, they for a pastime take pleasure in fishing for little fish resembling sardines, and exceeding delicate eating, with a net of cotton twine of large extent, having all over it little pieces of tin to keep it taut; this they cast with great art when they perceive a shoal of these little fish, which are caught in the width of the net by means of the tin, which draws the net over the bottom and encloses them all.[2] But see one other manner of fishing, which I have noted, a manner most strange and laborious.

For twice a year, at the time of the equinoxes and the high tides, they have a general fishing, and a great number of people assemble at certain places on the sea. To understand the manner of this fishing, you must know that then the tide not only flows and rises higher than during the rest of the year, but also ebbs proportionally, and on so going back discovers shoals and rocks which are seen at no other time. In such like places, when the sea is gone back, they note some convenient nook, and plant all around large stones

[1] *Rat-veri-mas*, *i.e.*, "the red chief of fish"; Mr. Bell identifies it with the Rangoo (*Lutianus*).

[2] This net is called *ellá-dá*, "cast-net", corresponding to the *baru-dæla*, "weighted net", of the Sinhalese.

one upon another, in such wise that it seems like a round wall or a ravelin. This enclosure is forty paces round or thereabouts, and an entry is left of two or three paces wide. They assemble thirty or forty men, each of whom carries fifty or sixty fathoms of thick coco-cord, at every fathom of which is attached a piece of dried coco-husk to keep the cord always floating, just as cork is used with us. The cords brought by each are tied together, and the whole stretched round the shoal. I leave you to imagine the extent of the circle. The marvel is that the fish within this cord are all caught, though there are neither nets, nor gins, nor line depending, but the cord only. Yet the fish fear the cord and the shadow of the cord, in such sort that, instead of escaping away under it, and not letting themselves be thus encircled, they flee before it, thinking there is a line beneath it which would arrest them. The men all come round towards this stone enclosure of which I have spoken, drawing the cord little by little, some in boats, others in the water; for in these shallows the sea is of little depth, and reaches no more than to the neck, or mostly short of that. Thus, as they draw the cord, the fish flee and crowd towards the enclosure, so at length the cord being nearly all drawn in, the fish enter within; then at once the men fill up the entrance with bundles of coco-branches and leaves, tied end to end, twenty or thirty fathoms, and of the thickness of a man, so that when the sea goes down the fish are left on dry land.[1] Then it is great sport to see the fish struggling and leaping, and in such quantity that sometimes there are ten or twelve thousand or more caught. They fill sacks and net-pockets of small meshes with them, placing these at the opening and chasing the fish from within, in such wise that they lose not one. And some of them I have seen so huge that it

[1] This mode of fishing seems a combination of the *má*, or *boḍu dá*, Sin. *má dœla*, and the *mas-hifá-korhi*, Sin. *mas korotuva*. It is a fish-kraal, and may be seen on the rivers and sea-shore of Ceylon.

was all a man could do to carry one. I have been often at this fishing, and have had for my share more than a hundred large fish, although I was a stranger, and of the least account among so many, where all had their full share; yet in truth I had to endure more than they, for they were accustomed to go barefooted on the reefs and rocks, and I was not, and on some occasions I had to go nearly half a league in this fashion, and always in the sun. All this fish is used for their food in banquets and treats, there being no traffic in this kind; yet they cook and dry it on trays, else they could not keep so great a quantity for a length of time without rotting. This fishing is practised only once in six months in each shoal, and each time for fifteen days; they change the place every day, and do not often return to the same place for the same mode of fishing, except it be at the other equinox.

The fish found on these shoals or within the reefs of the atolls is called in the Maldive language *phare masse*, as who should say "shoal" or "reef fish"—from *phare*, that is to say, a reef or bank, and *masse*, "fish".[1] The other sort taken in deep sea, as I have said, is called *combolly masse*, that is, "black fish", in which they have their great traffic, supplying therewith all the coasts of the main. The fish of which I speak is cooked in sea-water and dried, for other mode of salting they have none; and when betimes they salt some of it, it is left in the brine till wanted. But it is not this kind that they send abroad. No salt is made at the Maldives: what they use comes from the coast of Malabar, and would not suffice for the quantity of fish they catch every day, both for the food of the people and for trade; for in truth there is no place in all the Indies, nor elsewhere (in my belief), so rich in fish and abundantly supplied therewith.

I omitted, before closing my discourse of the manners and exercises of the islanders, to say a word of their behaviour, which, though it might easily be gathered from their conduct

[1] M. *faru mas*; *cf.* Sin. *para*, in *galpara*, "reef".

as I have represented it, yet may conveniently here be somewhat touched upon. This people is quick and apprehensive, subtle and crafty in most part of their actions. Courage also they lack not, and love arms and exercises. They are industrious in arts and manufactures, and polite of manners: a people superstitious beyond measure, and much devoted to their religion, yet, in their indulgence of women, lascivious and intemperate. Adultery, incest, and sodomy are common, notwithstanding the severity of the law and penalties. As for simple lewdness, nothing is more common; they think it no sin, neither wives nor unmarried girls, and make no work about submitting themselves to their male friends and afterwards (a most execrable practice) voiding their fruit, or bringing about abortion, or making away with their bastard babes. The women are strangely wanton, and the men are no better; but they have less of force and spirit. Their chief desire is to find, if they can, some recipe wherewithal to satisfy their wives, and to get themselves greater strength to practise their lechery; and I believe they would give all their substance for such a thing. They have often asked me if I knew of any such means, even the highest nobles, and so often, in fact, that I was quite sick of the subject. They talk thereof continually, even in the presence of their wives, of whom they have as many as three, as I have said, so that they are unable to satisfy each. Then the air is exceeding sultry, and causes some part of the natural force to evaporate; moreover, their manner of life is against them in this matter, their nerves becoming slack by being continually in the water; add that the most of them eat opium, or, as they call it, *aphion*,[1] which intoxicates and stupefies them.

Notwithstanding this, they are all given to this vice without moderation, as well men as women, not to say more of their abominations.

The women conceal their nipples and breasts as carefully

[1] M. *afihun*, Ar. *afyún*.

as the private parts, and there is the same modesty and shame in showing or uncovering them. Even to speak of a breast is with them most lewd and shameful. Kissing is made as much of as sleeping together, and is as improper to speak of. For the rest, though they be exceeding lewd in their conversation, they restrain themselves before their kindred and respect their presence. If a word such as I have spoken of should escape a man in talk with a woman before one or more of his kindred, they would retire and be highly offended at him; he would have to make his excuses, and say that he was not aware he was among his kindred, otherwise, if they should think he said it of design, they would complain to the judge, to have from him that uttered these shameful words in their presence an acknowledgment that he held them for men of virtue and honour.

A man durst not enter a place where a woman is bathing, or even where she has cast off her robe, though she might still have the cloth which serves them for a petticoat: for, as I said, they deem their breasts and bosom to be private parts. When a man and a woman are seen together and are met by other people, you must not ask of the man if the woman is his wife, his daughter, or his sister; for if she was his daughter, and you asked if she were his wife, he would be insulted as much as if you had accused him of incest. You must only ask if she is related to him, and he will tell the degree of relationship. While the women have their courses they bathe not at all, neither wash, save their hands and mouth, nor change their robes while these last: also they sleep not with their husbands, nor eat or hold converse with anyone. I have said above that the women go forth but rarely by day: all their visits are made by night; but I have omitted to mention something peculiar in their customs which I may without inconvenience add here. In their visits by night they must have a man to bear them company, to walk before them, and when he hears anyone coming, he says three times, *Gas*,[1] that is to say, "Beware"; men warned by this signal leave that side of the road on which the women are coming, without seeming to see them or wishing to be accosted by them, so great is their respect. And if other women should meet them, each takes her own side, and gives no salutation unless they be intimate acquaintance. You do not knock at a door, for there is no knocker; and you do not call to anyone to open the door, for the chief gate of the courtyard is always open to a certain hour, that is, till eleven at night, when all have retired; wherefore, you enter the courtyard, which is close to the house, and that is also open, saving only that it has a curtain of cotton, or other stuff, hung in front. As you approach this door you only cough, at the sound whereof those within come forth to see if they are wanted for anything. In like manner, when men walk in the streets by night, they frequently cough on purpose to put others on their guard, for fear of running against, or wounding one another, for all (I mean the soldiers and king's officers at Malé) carry drawn arms. Whatsoever remains to be said of their manners will be better understood by what I shall describe hereafter, and by the history of what passed at the Maldives during my sojourn there.

CHAPTER XIV.

Form of the government of the state, of the magistrates, of justice and the laws.

The government of the Maldive state is royal, very ancient and absolute; the king is feared and dreaded, and everything depends upon him. I have said that the islands are divided into thirteen atollons,—a natural division, which

[1] Probably a misprint for *gos*, "having gone", *i.e.*, "begone!"

has been followed in government; for of these are constituted thirteen provinces, over each of which is a chief called a *Naybe.*[1] These Naybes, or chiefs of provinces, are priests or doctors of the law, who have an eye as well to all matters of religion and education, as to the administration of justice in the province, giving their orders to the priests under them. For the atollons are again divided into many islands, and in each one containing more than forty-one men, as I said, there is a doctor called a *Catibe*, the religious superior of that island, who has under him the priests incumbent of the mosques. All these see to the instruction of the people in the law: they are supported in part by fruits, which everyone is bound to yield, and in part from certain endowments assigned to them by the king, according to their degree. But the Naybes, besides their duties and authority in religion, are also appointed to administer justice, each in his own government. They are the sole judges in the land, as well in matters civil as criminal; and if one wants to go to law, he must go find the Naybe or attend his coming to the place. For the Naybes four times a year go the circuit of the islands in their several governments, and hold visitations as well ecclesiastical as judicial.[2] This brings them in great revenues, for it is then the people pay their dues, besides which they receive many presents from a multitude of people, and of such they are very greedy. Be it remarked that throughout the Maldive islands there are no judges but these thirteen Naybes, for the Catibes and the priests of the mosques are overseers only. Over these Naybes is a superior, who resides at Malé, and is always near the person of the king; he

[1] Ar. *naib*. The Naibs are only the ecclesiastical and judicial chiefs of the atolls. No doubt, in Pyrard's time, they were superior to the collectors of revenue, *atoḷu-veri*, but the latter are much the bigger men now.

[2] It is said that the Naibs "travel the circuit" only twice a year now.

is called the *Pandiare*,[1] and not only ecclesiastical superior of the whole kingdom, but also sovereign judge. Wherefore, if any, after pleading before the Naybe, is loth to obey his judgment, be it in a matter civil or criminal, he appeals to the Pandiare, who decides all matters brought before him, taking the advice of some Naybes who are about him, of the Catibes, and of certain personages called *Moucouris*,[2] that is to say, doctors or learned men, who for all that are not officers: and he gives no judgment but by the assistance of four or five of such persons at the least. These Moucouris know the whole of their Alcoran by heart (all others read it only), besides having a knowledge of other sciences. They are invited in state to all feasts, preachings, and ceremonies, and are greatly respected and honoured of all men. There are but few of them, not fifteen in all the islands. The Pandiare is called *Cady* in the Arabic tongue. And yet after the judgment of the Pandiare some will plead to the king himself, who gives order for justice to be done and executed, and this by six lords, his chief officers, who manage the most important affairs of the realm. They are called *Mouscoulis*,[3] as who should say "elders".

The Pandiare, assisted by the two Catibes of Malé island, and by the Naybe of the atollon, along with some of these doctors, also makes his visitation throughout the island of Malé, just as each Naybe in his atollon. He is also assisted by his officers, who carry a long whip, of which I shall speak hereafter, for correcting the delinquents: he makes what inquiries he thinks fit, with especial regard to all matters of religion and justice. All he meets without exception he causeth to say their creed, and some prayers in Arabic, and

[1] M. *Faḍiyaru*, or *Faṇḍiyáru*; derivation uncertain, but perhaps connected with the Tam. *paṇḍaram*, "religious mendicant, monk, or friar" (Winslow).

[2] *Mugari-bê-kalun*; *bé-kalun* is the ordinary ending of all class-terms.

[3] M. *Muskuḷi*, "elders". They are now called *vazíru*.

then asks them the interpretation of the same in the Maldive language. If they know it not, he hath them whipped and scourged on the spot by his officers. The women durst not show themselves while he passes along the street, and if he should meet one without her veil, he would have her head shaved. So it is ordained by their law, and the Naybes do the like.

Besides the Naybes, there is in each province or atollon a man appointed and employed by the king to collect and levy his dues and revenues, and those of the Christian king at Goa, to carry out his orders, and, in short, to manage his affairs. These are called *Varuery*,[1] and they are highly honoured and respected. Such as come with any commission from the king address themselves to them, and they furnish whatsoever is needful in the way of attendants and guides for the islands of their atollon.

All the islands have each its separate wards and parishes, in like manner as Malé, where there are five wards, each with its headman, called *Mouscouly auare*,[2] the alderman of the ward, and nothing is done there but he knows of it; and if anything in the ward is required, whether for the use of the king or the people, he must be applied to, and no other, as having charge of everything there; and if anything

[1] M, *atoḷu-veri*, or *Váru-veri*; i.e., *váru*, "tax", and *veri*, "man". Mr. Bell thinks that *váru* may be connected with the Sin. *varuva*, a paddy-heap, and may be traced to a time anterior to the separation of the races, when taxes were paid in kind. These collectors are appointed to an atoll, or part of an atoll, by the Sultan on the recommendation of the *Hadégiri*. They do not necessarily reside in their districts. The majority reside at Málé, and employ sub-agents (*rarhu-veri*). The emoluments of the office are considerable, and it is frequently held by relations of the king, and by the ministers themselves. It is held for life or during the sultan's pleasure, and at the decease of an *atoḷu-veri* his estate is held liable for any balance due to the treasury (Bell, *Report*, 67).

[2] M. *Muskuḷi ava'*; *cf.* Sin. *avadhi*, "limit", "division". There are only four of these wards now.

is missing, it must be sought of him. The people of the ward treat him with great honour and respect,—not that he can do nothing without the counsel and advice of the other elders and counsellors of the ward, but when he has any project in view, he summons them to his house or other place as it pleaseth him, to consider together of what is to be done; the same goes on at the other islands, for each one has a superior unto whom the folk of the ward give ear.

Law in their language is called *Sacouest*,[1] and is administered at the house of the Naybes, or at Malé at the house of the Pandiare, with the assistants above mentioned, and betimes also at the king's palace when the case is of grave importance.

When one willeth to commence a suit, he applies to the judge or Naybe, and he sendeth one of his sergeants, of whom each hath a certain number, called *Deuanits*,[2] to cause the party appealed to appear; and if he be not in the same island, he is entitled to a writ of the Naybe, whereby he is directed to come to where the Naybe is, provided it be a place within his jurisdiction. For if it be in that of another, the Naybe has no power therein, and in such case he is served with a writ of the Pandiare, who may summon a man from any part of the realm to the king's island where he resides. The writ is delivered to the Catibe, the headman of the island, who in presence of all delivers it to the person appealed, straitly warning him to go. In the which he dare not fail, for as many as disobey the behests of the law are not admitted to the company of the others, to go to mosque, or to eat or drink with them, and are treated as outside the pale of their law. If a man, for example, some grandee, will not obey, the king sendeth his soldiers to constrain him. And if one liketh not to plead before the Naybe, whether

[1] M. *Sakuvá*; probably connected with the Sin. *sákiya*, "evidence"; *cf.* Skt. *sākshin*, "a witness".

[2] M. *Dévâni*. Now six in number (Bell, *Report*, 65).

for cause that he is ill-disposed towards him, or that he favours him overmuch, then the plaintiff or the defendant who is appealed applies to the king, who makes order that justice be done by indifferent judges; the cause is then heard at the palace of the king, in the presence of all the grandees of the island.

The parties plead their own causes. If it is an issue of fact, each brings three witnesses; and if they have none, the defendant is believed upon his oath, which he takes by touching with his hand the book of their law, the judge presenting it; and the plaintiff, if he be at all a man of the world, scrupulously observes whether his opponent really touches the book, and at the proper place. If the issue be one of law, it is adjudged by the law. The judges receive nothing for their judgments, and nothing is due, save that the deuanits or sergeants get a twelfth part of the judgment debt or penalty.

Slaves may not be witnesses, and their word is of no avail as evidence; and in like manner that of three women is taken as of one man. The slaves are such as have become so, or have been brought from abroad and sold, for strangers wrecked there lose not their liberty if they had it before; if they were slaves, they remain so. In good truth, the slaves, who are call *Allo*,[1] are of much more sorry condition than the rest. They can have but one wife, while all [others] are permitted to have three, and they can put them away and take them back but once only. The penalty for beating a slave is only half that for beating or assaulting a free man.

Debtors are obliged, if they have no means of paying, to go into servitude, not as slaves, nor treated as such, but as natives of the country; they serve only their creditors or others who pay the money for their redemption. These

[1] M. *ala*; *cf.* Sin. *vàlà*.

bondsmen are called *Pemousseré*,[1] which is to say "bondsman on loan", and this lasts till they be acquitted, and their

[1] M. *femuséri*. The custom of debt slavery, evidently of great antiquity, is mentioned by Ibn Batuta (see App. A), and exists at the present day. Christopher states that the men of Málé become "dependents of any of the chiefs, most of whom retain as many followers as they may be able to support, a large retinue being considered a sign of rank and power" (*Trans. Bom. Geo. Soc.*, i, 60). Mr. Bell says, "A curious custom, still surviving, permits an insolvent debtor to work off his debt as his creditor's servant. These bondsmen are called *Femuséri*" (*Report*, p. 65).

In Ceylon the custom was in full force in Knox's time (*Knox*, 102), and lasted until some time after the British occupation. The following account is given in Sir J. d'Oyly's MS., *Laws and Constitutions of the Kandyan Kingdom*, a copy of which is in my possession:—"If the debtor have no property, the chief sometimes delivers him to his creditor, who is thereupon authorised to confine him in his house, and if he cannot obtain satisfaction, to employ him as a servant, or rather as his slave, treating him as such, and supplying him with victuals and clothing" (p. 180). The author proceeds to say that the creditor could also, by leave of the chief, enter upon and cultivate the debtor's field, and that he sometimes (illegally) seized his child. In times of great scarcity people voluntarily became bondslaves, and sold their children (p. 235). In some cases the king paid the debt by way of largess out of the royal treasury, in others it was raised by public subscription (p. 395).

It is in the Eastern Archipelago, however, that the practice obtains most widely and persistently. The best account is that given by Marsden:—"When a debtor is unable to pay what he owes, and has no relation or friends capable of doing it for him; or when the children of a deceased person do not find property enough to discharge the debts of their parent, they are forced to the state called *mengeering*, that is, they become a species of bondslaves to the creditor, who allows them subsistence and clothing, but does not appropriate the produce of their labour, to the diminution of the debt. Their condition is better than that of pure slavery, in this, that the creditor cannot strike them, and they can change their masters, by prevailing upon another person to pay their debt and accept of their labour on the same terms. Of course, they may procure their liberty if they can by any means provide a sum equal to their debt; whereas a slave, though possessing ever so large property, has not the right of purchasing his liberty" (*Sumatra*, 214; see also pp. 190-2, 335; also Crawfurd, *Ind. Arch.*, iii, 98; Raffles's *Java*, second edition, i, 394, *note*).

Debt slavery was found to be in full force, with its attendant abuses,

children continue to be so for ever if they do not pay. Sometimes, when they are badly treated, they can get released by binding themselves to another, who pays for them; all their hire is their food and maintenance, and when they die their master takes all they had; and if that is not enough for the debt, the children remain in bond till the whole be paid. A great number of the people seek to be the *Pemousseré* of grandees and men in office, and so to gain support and favour, for while they belong to nobody they are tormented by one another.

In the matter of crimes a man must plead for justice to be done, and he must be a person of capacity to sue, except it were a crime punishable by the law, otherwise there is no public process in case of crime or injury committed on the person of another—unless, as I say, it is a crime against their law. A wife cannot appeal in the court for the murder of her husband, but only the children or kindred; and if the children are of young age, time is given till they attain the age of sixteen years, to see if they desire to be avenged for the death of their father. In the meantime, the judge condemns him that is suspected of the murder to support the children of the deceased, and to teach them some art or craft; then, when they come of age, they may demand justice, or release and pardon the murderer; if not, he may be accused at any time thereafter. For there, in the matter of an injury done to any private person, the person injured must be the complainant, otherwise the crime is annulled; nevertheless, if the king wills, he has justice done, without any other party to the cause; but that happens rarely.[1]

in the Malay states of Perak and Selangor, on the assumption of the British protectorate a few years ago. It has now been abolished by a scheme of compensation from and after the 31st December 1883. See *Parliamentary Papers*, C. 2410 (1879), C. 3285 and C. 3429 (1882), and C. 4192 (1884). The custom was abolished at Sarawak by Sir James Brooke, but is still in use in the native states of Borneo.

[1] We have here, succinctly stated, the same double modes of prosecu-

The usual penalties are banishment to the desert islands of the south, as I have already said, mutilation of a member, or the scourge,[1] which is the most common, but infinitely cruel. It is of thick leather straps, as long as the arm and as broad as the four fingers, and as thick as two; of these, five or six are fixed together in a haft of wood. With this, malefactors are chastised, and so cruelly beaten that full often they die of it. It is the usual penalty for great crimes, such as sodomy, incest, and adultery. Women taken in adultery, besides the said penalty, have their hair cut off.[2]

False witness and perjury are punished in the same way, the guilty party being also amerced in a money fine, which is given to the poor.

If a wife or a daughter be ravished, the guilty party is punished as an adulterer, and in addition is obliged to settle a portion upon the wife or daughter.

A thief who has stolen any article of value has his hand cut off.[3]

tion which obtained in English law for many centuries, viz., the prosecution by the king, in which case the charge was called a "plea of the crown", and the prosecution by the injured party, called an "appeal". The intricate technicalities with which the latter procedure was incrusted may be studied in the pages of Bracton, Britton, and Hawkins. As lawyers are aware, this mode of prosecution, after being for long deemed obsolete, was revived by an "appeal of murder" in the year 1818, with due "wager of battle", and was only then abolished by statute. The main difference between the English and Maldive appeal was, that in the former the right was primarily confined to the widow, and only passed to the heir when there was no surviving widow.

[1] Below, in ch. xxii, he calls this scourge *gleau*. Christopher states that flogging is done with "two or three rattans held together in the hand". He confirms Pyrard as to the severity with which it is inflicted, adding that "sometimes death ensues" (*Trans. Bom. Geo. Soc.*, i, 78).

[2] According to Christopher, if the woman has not given encouragement, the man is severely flogged, the injured husband being the administrator (*Trans. Bom. Geo. Soc.*, i, 78).

[3] This is the punishment prescribed by the Koran: "If a man or woman steal, cut off their hands in retribution for that which they have committed: this is an exemplary punishment appointed by God, and

In the matter of injuries a prosecutor is not free to hush up the charge; the penalty is exacted when there is proof of heinous wrong.

If a man has committed some offence against the law, he must do penance in a public manner, as a public apology. For the rest, they hold it for certain that they could never enter Paradise did they not pay and perform whatsoever the court has ordered. For the execution and scourging of malefactors they have no executioner: that office is performed by the *deuanits* or sergeants.

As for the penalty of death, though their law ordains it for a homicide, the judges never pass the sentence.[1] All the time I was at the Maldives, I never saw one condemned to death by the ordinary judges. They would not dare to do so, but by the express command of the king, which is given but seldom. Moreover, it is a common saying with them, that they could not afford thus to lose their men; and that if all were put to death that merited it, in course of time the islands would be dispeopled, and so that the human race in other parts would not suffice to pay the penalty, and that the world would come to an end. Yet true it is that the king sends some of his chosen soldiers, and condemns, and puts

God is mighty and wise" (*Sura*, 5). Ibn Batuta (below, App. A) mentions that this penalty was unknown or unpractised before his arrival at the Maldives, and states that when he, as Cadi, had a thief's hand cut off, the bystanders all fainted! Christopher was shown a stone block on which offenders' hands were chopped off in former days (*T. Bom. Geo. Soc.*, i, 78). The real humanity of the islanders had reasserted itself, in defiance of the Koran. Mutilation is unknown and forgotten now (Bell, *Report*, 65). Note in the above passage, "any article of value", as indicating, perhaps, a similar distinction to that which obtained in English law, between "grand larceny", where the thing stolen was of the value of one shilling or over, and "petty larceny", where it was under; our law was the more cruel, the penalty of the former being death, of the latter, whipping.

[1] Murder is now punished by flogging and banishment to the southern atolls (Chr., in *Trans. Bom. Geo. Soc.*, i, 78; Bell, *Report*, 65).

to death such as merit it, or have offended him. For though the processes of justice are in the hands of the doctors of the law, and they are the judges, yet the king is the sole arbiter and dispenser of it; he alone has the power of life and death. Appeal is made to him, and he gives his orders for justice to be done as he wills it, as well to the judges and doctors, as to his lords and officers. And to speak generally, he is absolute throughout his whole realm, and disposes all things according to his pleasure, and that in most tyrannical sort at times, though chiefly in his dealings with the vulgar, a most abject and caitiff herd. Among other kinds of chastisement, he maketh use of one peculiar to the lot of such as have incurred his displeasure, for he causeth them to lie upon their bellies on the ground, their four limbs held by four persons; they then receive some stripes upon the back with a rod or kind of cane, which is called *Rotan*,[1] and comes from Bengal: this takes off the skin, and the weals and scars remain ever after to mark such as have displeased the king. I have also observed, as a matter pertaining to the forms of their judicature, that they put not the process or the pleadings in criminal causes into writing, nor the indictments, nor the depositions, nor the judgments: all is very prompt and summary. And it is the same in civil actions, except in suits for hereditaments, or coco-trees (which are immovable property), wherein judgments are delivered by the Pandiare or the Naybes. In such case they grant writs [of possession], sealed with their seal in ink,—for I have never seen them use wax for sealing,—and these serve for evidence to their posterity, to the end that thenceforth neither he that hath gained the cause, nor his heirs, may be disquieted in their possession.

[1] *Rattan*.

CHAPTER XV.

Orders of the people,—of the nobility, the great offices and dignities, and their rank.

As for the orders and distinctions of the whole people, according to their condition and quality, be it remarked there are four sorts of persons.[1] In the first are comprehended the king, called *Rasquan*,[2] the queen, called *Renequillague*,[3]

[1] It will be observed that the first, third, and fourth classes are distinctions settled by birth; the second so-called class includes all dignities and titles of honour granted by the king. 1. Persons of the blood royal are termed *Baṇḍára*, or *Baḍára*, the term applied also to the children of the Sinhalese kings. By including the "great lords" in this first class, Pyrard probably refers to the titles of *Manipul*, assumed only by the nearest relations of the sultan, and *Dídí*, applied to remoter scions of the royal house and descendants of former sultans. 2. The second class of dignities, viz., those conferred on individuals, include the officers of state and titles conferred out of court favour or bought. The highest is that of *Kilagé-fánu* (Pyrard, *quilague*), formerly confined to the regent acting in the absence of the sultan, but now given to several grandees. Among titles independent of office are *Kalege-fánu* and *Takuru-fánu*, the former of which can be purchased for a few rupees. Masters of vessels get the titles of *Nákhudá*, *Néví*, and *Málimi*, as implying skill and experience in seamanship. 3. The third class is that of the aristocracy generally, viz., the *Maniku*. The wife of a *maniku* man is termed *manike* (*cf.* the common Sin. name, *meṇika*). When a *maniku* man receives a title of honour, he is called *maniku-fánu*. Some of this class preserve the relics of Portuguese influence, and call themselves *Don Maniku*. Either Pyrard is wrong in stating that children's status comes from the mother, or the law is now changed. Mr. Bell is informed by the highest Maldive authorities that the status of the father governs; *e.g.*, a *maniku* woman marries a *Dídí*, the children are *Dídí*. It may be noted here that Pyrard also states (ch. xviii), that nobility comes "from the mother as well as from the father". 4. The common people are termed *Kalo* (fem. *Kamulo*). He does not here speak of the slaves, *alu* (see p. 202); nor does he refer to the handicraft castes.

[2] M. *raskan* or *rasge-fánu*; *cf.* Sin. *rajan*, *radu*, and *rada*.

[3] M. *rani-kilage-fánu*. This would seem to be the title of a reigning queen or princess regent, as of the queen Aminá (1754). The sultan's wives are called *Rasge-fánu Abi-Kabalun* (Bell, *Report*, p. 76).

and those who are of his race and of the lineage of former kings; princes, called *Calans*,[1] princesses, *Camenaz*,[2] and great lords. The second is the order of dignities, offices, and rank granted by the king, in the which precedence is likewise carefully observed; the third is the nobility; the fourth, the common people. I will begin with the third, that being the rank conferred by birth, and separating its possessors from the common people. Dignities and offices are casualties independent of this rank. There are a great number of nobles here and there throughout the islands. Such as are not nobles durst not sit with them, nor even in the presence of a nobleman so long as he is standing; and should they see one how far off soever coming behind them, they must needs wait and let him pass before them. So, if one has a cloth or anything else thrown over his shoulder, he takes it down.[3] Noble women, though married to men of inferior condition, lose not their rank: even the children the issue of such marriages are noble by virtue of the mother's estate, even were the father of the lowest order. So women of low quality married to nobles are not ennobled by their husbands, but retain their former rank; everyone keeps his own place, and there is no confusion on this subject. But besides the nobility by birth, the king ennobles whom he will. When that happens, the king, besides a grant of letters (patent), sends one of his officers, specially appointed for this duty, to make publication thereof throughout the island to the sound of a kind of bell, which is a plate of metal struck with a hammer. As for the dignities, hear which are the principal, and the rank of them. After the king come the princes of his blood, and such as are descended from other

[1] M. *kalá-fánu*, Pers. *kalán*, "great". Mr. Bell informs me that the Sultan of Pyrard's time is still known by this title, specially applied.

[2] M. *kamana-fánu*; *cf.* Sin. *hámini*, "lady".

[3] The Sinhalese hardly ever omit these marks of respect when they meet a chief or a European in the road.

kings, his predecessors; these, though of a different line, are all held in honour and respect. Next, the great officers of the realm,[1]—to wit, the *Quilague*, whom we might call the king's

[1] We are fortunate enough to possess tolerably full lists of the ministers composing the "Cabinet" of the Sultan, at periods covering the last five hundred years; and it will be seen that the offices and their respective status have been altered, probably from the like causes of the necessities of the times, as our own high offices of State. The authorities as to those offices are the same as for other events of Maldive history, viz., Ibn Batuta (A.D. 1344), Pyrard (1602-9), Christopher (1835), and Mr. Bell at the present day.

I. Ibn Batuta (see below, App. A) gives the following offices:—

1. *Calaky*	... ...	Grand Vizier or Sultan's Lieutenant.
2. *Fandayarkalou*	...	The Kádi.
3. *Hendidjéry* ...	...	Preacher.
4. *Fâmeldâry* ...	...	Chief of the Treasury.
5. *Mâfâcalou* ...	...	Receiver General of Revenue.
6. *Fitnâyec*	... ...	Minister of Police.
7. *Mânâyec*	... ...	Admiral.
8. *Déherd*	... ...	General of the Army.

After describing the offices of the first seven, he says, "All these have the title of Vizier." The eighth is mentioned incidentally in his subsequent narrative as a Vizier.

II. Pyrard's list of dignities is as follows:—

1. *Quilague* (*Kilagē*). Same as Ibn Bat.

2. *Parenas* (*Fáruná*, and in southern atolls, more correctly, *Fárhiná*). Not traced in other lists; no distinctive duties assigned. The title is now given to the Regent or Lieut.-General.

3. *Endequery*. The same in title, but not in functions, as Ibn. Bat., 3.

4. *Velannas* (*Velánâ*). Admiral: under him—
   (*a*) two deputies called *Mirvaires* (*Míru Baharu*).

5. *Dorimenaz* (*Dorhiménâ*). General of the Militia.
   (*a*) *Acouraz* (*Hakurâ*), his lieutenant.

6. *Manpas* (*Máfai*). Chancellor; *cf.* Ibn Bat., 5.

7. *Carans* (*Karani*). Secretary.

8. *Mas bandery* (*Má badēry*). Intendant of Finance; probably corresponding to the Auditor-General of British colonies.

9. *Rans bandery* (*Ran̦ baderi*). Treasurer.

III. Christopher, in 1834, found a Cabinet of six Viziers, whose titles are given here according to the more correct spelling of Mr. Bell:—

lieutenant-general, because, next to the king, and in his absence, he is the most powerful in the government of the state,

1. *Dorhiméná.* Chief or General of the Army. See Pyrard, 5.
2. *Hakurá.* See Pyrard, 5 (*a*).
3. *Veláná.* See Pyrard, 4.
4. *Fámudéri.* Pyrard mentions (ch. xviii) a *Pammedery calogue* as a great lord, but does not place him among the ministers,—but see Ibn Bat., 4.
5. *Máfai.* See Ibn Bat., 5, and Pyrard, 6.
6. *Dáhará.* See Ibn Bat., 8. Pyrard (ch. xix) mentions a *Darade Tacourou* as a "Count" or "Duke", but does not place him among the ministers.

IV. Lastly, Mr. Bell (1879) finds that the Sultan now employs only three chief ministers, viz.:

1. *Hadégiri*, or *Boḍu Baḍéri*, "Chief Treasurer of the realm". See Ibn Bat., 3, and Pyrard, 3.
2. *Dáhará.* See Ibn Bat., 8, and Chr., 6.
3. *Míru Baharu* (Ar. *Emir-el-Bahr*). See Pyrard, 4 (*a*).

The *Hadégiri* (preacher in Ibn Batuta's time, a lord privy councillor in Pyrard's, and now chief treasurer), though not placed by Christopher among the six ministers, was a high officer in his day, as he says he "is vested with authority to enforce the payment of revenue when complaint is made to him by the *Atoḷwari*". Mr. Bell says, "He seems to rank above the other two ministers, and to possess greater influence in the community. A staff of accountants and clerks are employed to assist him in the revenue duties at Málé."

The *Dáhará*, Mr. Bell observes, "has no specific department of public business to supervise. But for a certain voice in the military and municipal affairs, his office would be a titular sinecure."

The *Míru Baharu*, according to the same authority, "is the Port Doctor and Master Attendant of Málé. He visits all vessels that arrive, and refuses permission to land until it has been ascertained to his satisfaction that there is no sickness on board. Generally speaking, the entire management and control of all public business not falling within the province of the *Hadégiri*, and distributed a few years back among the six Viziers, devolve now on the *Míru Baharu* and the *Dáhará*."

It will be observed that the *Pandiare*, or Kadi, is included in Ibn Batuta's, but in no subsequent list. Although in Pyrard's time, as at present, he was supreme in ecclesiastical and judicial affairs, he was not supposed to interfere in the executive government.

Mr. Bell considers that a good many of the offices mentioned above may be traced back to the offices in the ancient Sinhalese monarchy,

and without his authority nothing is done. So, if the king wills to do, observe, or execute anything, he is the first to be

which occur in the *Mahawanso:* thus, he traces the *Hadégiri* to the *Bhándágáriko amachcho*, the Lord High Treasurer of Ceylon (Turnour's *Mahawanso*, pp. 231-3); *Dorhiméná* to the *Dvára-náyaka* (*ib.*, 260); *Fámudéri* to the *Amachcha Pámukha* (*ib.*, 69), Sin. *pámok, déta; Máfai* may be derived from *maha*, "great", and *pati*, as in *Senápati*, *Chamupati* (Mah. *passim*); the *Dáhára* would seem to be the *Dovárika* (*ib.*, 117); the *Mánáyec* of Ibn Bat. is clearly enough the Sin. *maha náyaka*. (See Ibn Batuta; Christopher, in *Trans. Bom. Geo. Soc.*, i, 70-72; Bell, *Report*, 66, 78.)

Departmental Government.—(i). *Ecclesiastical and Judicial.*—These formed one department under the Pandiare, who was and still is chief priest and chief justice. Under him were the Naibs, thirteen in number, one for each atoll. These, according to Pyrard, were the sole provincial judges. Under them were the Catibs, of whom there was one in each island containing upwards of forty inhabitants. They were the religious superiors of their respective islands, but in judicial affairs they were "overseers" only. There were at Málé a Naib and two Catibs, who assisted the Pandiare in both departments. Subordinate again to the Catibs were the *Moudins*, or incumbents of mosques: every mosque had its Moudin. At Málé there were four "king's Moudins" (p. 147), who were of much greater consequence than ordinary Moudins: they were, in fact, royal chaplains, and the Catib of Málé was chosen from among them.

Christopher states that the Naibs were also called Catibs, and intimates that residence in their atolls was not obligatory, six or seven being usually at Málé (*Trans. Bom. Geo. Soc.*, i, 70). He states, in corroboration of Pyrard, that the Naibs were supported by the islanders; but he seems to be wrong in asserting that the Naibs and Catibs were identical, for Mr. Bell confirms the distinction of Pyrard, and states that at Málé the Pandiare is now assisted by four Naibs and two Catibs (*Report*, p. 65).

The last officers to be mentioned in this department are the *devanits* (M. *déváni*), who performed, as they still do, the functions of peons, process-servers, and executioners. They are assigned to the Naibs as well as to the Pandiare. Mr. Bell states that the Pandiare has six, "who for their general services receive a small monthly allowance of rice, and one-twelfth share of the awards and proceeds of sale" (*Report*, p. 65).

(ii). *Revenue.*—Pyrard does not state specifically what officer presided over this department; he may have been the *Pammedery calogue* mentioned by him as one of the great lords,—and Ibn Batuta's list would lead to this conclusion,—or he may have been the same officer as at the

deputed and to receive his commands. There is next to him another of great authority, called the *Parenas;* then an *Endequery,* whose office is to be ever by the king, and to counsel

present day, viz., the *Hadégiri* (Pyrard, *Endequery*), who embraces the functions of the Treasurer (Pyrard's *Rans bandery*), and probably also those of the *Mas bandery* (Bell, *Report*, p. 66). Each atoll had, and still has, its collector, called by Pyrard the *Varuery*, or, as correctly given by Mr. Bell, *Váru-veri*, or *Atolu-veri*. They are now appointed by the Sultan on the recommendation of the Hadégiri. "They do not necessarily live in the respective atolls assigned to them. The majority remain at Málé, and employ sub-agents, *varhu-veri*, who are frequently Catibs. Each atoll has a storehouse (*váru-gé*), where the Government revenue is temporarily warehoused until required to be transmitted to Málé. The emoluments of this office must be considerable, as it is held by the relations of the Sultan and chief ministers, and frequently by the ministers themselves. Its tenure lasts for life, or during the Sultan's pleasure; and at the decease of an atolu-veri his estate is held liable for any balance due, or alleged to be due, for his division. The revenue of the different atolls, usually paid in native produce and manufacture, is collected into the treasury (*bodu-badéri-gé*) at Málé, whence it is shipped in the Sultan's and private vessels, on Government account, to different parts of India and Ceylon" (Bell, *Report*, p. 67).

It would seem from Christopher's account that the revenue officers have acquired in some measure the judicial powers formerly exercised by the Naibs and Catibs.

(iii). *Admiralty.*—Pyrard calls the High Admiral, *Velannas;* and says that he had two subordinates, *Mirvaires* (*Emir-el-Bahr*). Christopher calls him *Wilono Shabander*, and mentions also one Emir-el-Bahr, whom he describes as Master Attendant of Málé. Mr. Bell, as stated above, finds the *Veláná* gone altogether, and the Emir-el-Bahr (M. *Miru-Baharu*) elevated to a seat in the Cabinet.

(iv). *Military.*—The Maldive militia was under a general, called by Ibn Batuta the *Deherd*, and by Pyrard, *Dorimesna* (*Dorhiméná*). His lieutenant, not mentioned by Ibn Batuta, is by Pyrard called *Acouraz*. In Christopher's time the second Vizier retained his title (*Hakurá*), with no distinct duties. The gendarmerie of Málé (there appears to have been no military force in the other islands) was divided into six companies, raised in the six wards of the town. The company of each ward (*auare*) was under one of the six *Mouscoulis* or Viziers. Mr. Bell finds the militia still divided into six companies, with a nominal strength of 100 men each. The Sultan's body-guard of forty men is under a separate officer (*Report*, p. 68). The officer entitled by Ibn Batuta *Fitndyec*, or "Minister of Police", cannot be traced in later times.

him on all occasions and in all matters. Next, he that hath charge of the marine, called the *Velannas*, as we should say the admiral: I have said something of him above. He it is who keeps watch over all ships which arrive, and what merchandise they carry, having the care of lodging strangers, and representing their wants; in general, he hath an eye to all that concerns the shipping, and what comes by the sea. He is wont to board ships as they arrive, even the smallest barques, to take their rudders and have them borne to the king's house, for fear they should depart without leave. Under him are two sergeants, called *Mirvaires*, who keep watch over ships arriving, and render him an account of them, and otherwise carry out his orders and those of the king among the country people. These sergeants are known by reason that they carry in their hand a thick bâton of Bengal cane, which others than they durst not bear. There is also a general over all the militia, called the *Dorimenaz*, who has a lieutenant, called the *Acouraz*.

Besides these, there is the Chancellor, called *Manpas*, who applies to all letters the king's seal, which is nothing but his name in Arabic, graven in silver, dipped in ink, and pressed upon the paper. The secretary is called *Carans*[1]; the director of finance, *Mas bandery;* the treasurer, *Rans bandery;* and besides these are divers other minor offices which it were superfluous to describe in detail. Be it noted that all these above-mentioned great officers are often summoned to give counsel to the king, when he desires it, along with six persons of age and experience, and of the highest rank and learning, called *Mouscoulis*, that is, elders, of whom I have already spoken. They are nominated by the king, chosen

[1] From the Skt. *kάran*, "a doer"; *cf.* Sin. *karanavá*, "to do". The word may have reached the Maldives from any part of India, where it was in general use for "a clerk". Ibn Bat. twice, at least, uses *kiráni* for a ship's clerk, and *cranny* is modern Anglo-Indian for a clerk or copyist. (See Yule and Burnell, *Gloss.*, s. v. *Cranny.*)

and deputed by the other grandees to assist the king, and give advice on all occasions, to avoid the necessity of calling together the whole council on every matter; in short, they manage all kinds of business, and are ready at all times to carry out the king's pleasure. It is the six elders, too, who administer justice in the palace to such as have appealed to the king, not being satisfied with the judgments of the Naibes and the Pandiare. They have command of six companies of men-at-arms, each his own.

Many other dignities there are of divers degrees, which the king grants unto such of the nobles as he hath a favour to, assigning to them certain islands for pension and salary, as he doth to all the above named, more or less, according to the rank and quality of each; we might say they are like the dignities of Count, Marquis, Baron, etc., with us. But besides the revenues of certain islands apportioned to these officers, the king also gives them rice for their maintenance, as he doth to the soldiers for their pay, with the tolls and dues from the barques and vessels that come to traffic at the Maldives: these the king allows to them for their support, besides some little presents which he gives them on certain days. The highest honour in that land is to eat the king's rice, and to be of the number of his officers; wanting that, a man is but little thought of, noble though he be; insomuch that, after the office bearers, the soldiers get the most honour and privilege, and a gentleman is of but small account if he be not enrolled in the militia.

This militia[1] consists of soldiers of the king's guard to the

[1] The Maldivians have never been a warlike people. Ibn Batuta says of them, "In body they are weak, and have no aptitude for combat or for war, and their arms are prayers." As will be seen hereafter, the military organisation described by Pyrard was totally unfit to meet the Bengal invaders, who slew the king and gave the author his liberty. Here is Mr. Bell's description of the present state of things:—"The sole military force consists of a nondescript militia (*Hagu-bê-kalun*) at Málé, divided into six companies, numbering nominally 100 men each, but

number of six hundred, divided into six companies, and commanded by the six Mouscoulis or elders; ten other great companies are also kept up. These ten companies have each for its captain one of the greatest lords in the kingdom. These latter do not keep the guard, but serve the king when he requires them, not only as soldiers to march and fight, but also to do whatsoever he bids them, as to launch a ship, or to haul it ashore, or to do other heavy labour wherein many hands are needed, even to build the king's palace, if occasion required, or to construct any other work or building for the king. They are called out by the sound of the bell of which I have spoken. They are divided into two regiments, for there are five companies which are more honourable, the nobles only being admitted to them; they also get more pay than the rest. As for the other five, they are of all sorts of people, and are less esteemed. The revenue of many islands is set apart for the payment of these companies. They have many privileges; among others, none durst strike them; and it is permitted to them to habit themselves differently from the rest, to wear a thick gold ring on the finger to assist them in drawing the bow, which others may not wear; in a word, to be more brave and fine in their dress. So there are few men of means but choose to

with an actual strength at the present day of probably not less than 1,200 all told. These companies were formerly under the command of the six viziers as captains (*Boḍu-bé-kalun*). The soldiers bear no arms, and are under no sort of discipline beyond that which results from the habit of assembling, without much order or arrangement, when called together. Their duties, according to Christopher, are so anomalous that they often serve as sailors on board the public boats. A body of forty men (*Kudi-bé-kalun*) is required to mount guard in rotation at the Sultan's palace, and is in charge of an officer called *Má Baḍéri Takurú-fánu*. These men have certain privileges, and are distinguished from the *Hagu-bé-kalun* by their head-herchief. A small body-guard (*Dagedetere-bé-kalun*), bearing muskets, escort the Sultan whenever he appears in public" (Bell, *Report*, 68; also Christopher, in *Trans. Bom. Geo. Soc.*, i, 72).

join; albeit, they must have the permission of the king; and it costs them sixty larins to enter, whereof twenty go to the king for permission, and forty to be divided among the company which one desires to join. Slaves cannot enter them, nor may those whose business it is to gather and draw the produce of the coco-tree, nor other sorts of mean labouring men, nor such as know not to read or write, nor those who serve others. For the rest, most of the offices are bought of the king, and are much sought after by the rich for the sake of the honour, power, and authority which they get thereby over their fellows; but they may not sell them again, or transfer them to others.

All the islanders have but a single name apiece, without any surname or family name, those in most common use being *Mahomet, Haly, Hussum, Assan, Ibrahim*, and the like; but for the sake of distinction the name of their rank is added to their name: for instance, the nobles in blood add to their names *Tacourou*,[1] which shows who they are, and their wives, *Bybis*[2]; and besides that they add the name of the island which belongs to them. Such as are noble only by office or rank are called *Callogues*,[3] and their wives and daughters, *Camullogues*.[4] This name is used not only by the officers whom I have named, and others in actual service and pay, but also by many others who obtain sinecure rank from the king, so as to be distinguished from the common herd, and so to have a certain position and be respected accordingly. This is bought of the king dearly enough, yet such names and qualities are limited in number, to the end that the honour, being granted to but a few, may be more prized nor soon degraded. The common folk are called by the name

[1] As pointed out above, the title of *Takuru-fánu* is, in these latter days, sold. Takuru is probably the Skt. *Thākur*, which survives in Bengal as *Tagore* (see Yule's *Gloss.*, Supplt., s. v. *Thakoor*).

[2] *Bibi* (see Yule's *Gloss.*, s. v. *Beebee*).

[3] *Kaloge*.

[4] *Kamulo*.

Callo,[1] along with their own names, besides which is added the craft or condition of which each is. Their wives and daughters are called *Camulo.*[2]

CHAPTER XVI.

Of the king's palace,—a description of it; of his manner of life, and of the queens, his wives.

To come now to a description of the king's palace.[3] It has been mentioned several times above, that the king resides ordinarily at Malé, which is in consequence the chief of all the other islands, his palace being there.

It is built of stone, and consists of several houses well constructed, yet without much ornamental architecture, and of a single story. All around are orchards and gardens, with fountains and ponds of water, enclosed within walls, and paved with large polished stone. These places are guarded perpetually by men appointed to that duty; for it is there the king and his queens bathe, and it is strictly forbidden to all others to bathe there.

In the close of the palace, called in their language *gan-*

[1] *Kalo.* [2] *Kamulo.*

[3] The Sultan's palace seems to have been rebuilt or enlarged since Pyrard's time. Chr. gives the following description of it:—"The Sultan's palace is a large, upper-roomed house, with a peaked roof, covered with thick sheet-copper, in a walled enclosure, which is surrounded by a shallow moat, comprising an area of about a square mile. Within this space there is also a well-built magazine, besides several other houses, and a neat building raised on stone arches, from which the ladies witness the games exhibited before the court on festivals. One of the above-mentioned buildings is said to contain a variety of arms and relics taken from wrecked vessels; and it is currently reported and believed that there is a tank near the palace filled with ambergris" (*T. B. G. S.*, i, 53). Christopher was not admitted to view the interior, nor was Mr. Bell.

doyre,[1] which is of great extent, there are many buildings, and also courtyards, in each of which is a well, set off with fine white stone. In one of these courtyards are the two royal magazines; in the one the king keeps his cannon, in the other all his other sorts of arms.

At the entering in of the palace there is a guard-house, where you see some pieces of cannon and other arms. The gateway is made like a square tower, on top of which

Principal Entrance to the Palace.

the musicians play and sing on feast days, as I have described.

[1] M. *gaḍuvaru*, or *ganḍuvaru*. The meaning of the word is not quite clear. *Gaḍu* is "piece", or "part", as in *mas-gaḍu*, the best cut of fish; *re-gaḍu*, "the night (part of the day)". It also has an honorific sense, as in *alu-gaḍu-men*, "I", when used as our royal "we"; *fen-gaḍu*, water for the Sultan's use; *vedun-gaḍu*, said of the present annually made to the Governor of Ceylon. The *varu* is, perhaps, only a plural suffix, as in *oyivaru*, "currents"; cf. *váru-veri*, above.

Proceeding thence, you come to the first hall, where the soldiers attend; further on, another great hall for the lords, gentlemen, and qualified persons: for nobody, be he lord, gentleman, or commoner, man or boy, woman or girl, durst go further than this, saving only the domestic officers of the king and queens, and their slaves and servants. Hear now how these halls are built. The floor is raised three feet above ground, and is laid with wood nicely joined and highly polished. It is for a precaution against the ants that the floor is thus raised, and it is the same in all the houses of the country, except that, as you may suppose, if builders' work can be done better at one place than another, it will be at the king's palace. The floor is all covered with little mats made at the islands, interlaced of divers colours, with figures and other patterns prettily worked, and marvellously fair to see. The walls are hung with silk tapestry; while above, the ceiling is covered also with silk tapestry from which hang pretty fringes as those of a curtain. In the hall of the soldiers and strangers the king had spread upon the ceiling the great ensign and banner of our vessel, which was blue, with the arms of France in gold, beautifully worked. He was greatly proud of this, showing it off as a curiosity to strangers; and ofttimes he made me explain what was represented in the arms, as indeed I did, not without causing him to wonder at the greatness of our king. In these halls, over the place where the king sits, there is another kind of ceiling and curtain of a richer character, under which is a large space raised two feet, and covered with a large carpet, on which he seats himself cross-legged, for they use no other seats. On the mats throughout the hall, the lords, when they come to court, sit in the same fashion.

At this court[1] the order of ranks is strictly observed; for

[1] According to Christopher, "the customs and etiquette observed in the Durbar are remarkable for their simplicity. The courtiers and officers take stations according to their respective ranks" (*T. Bo. G. S.*,

those of lower condition remain standing, unless the king, or in his absence the grandees who may be there, bid them to be seated. The places next to where the king is wont to sit are the most honourable, and so on in proportion to the distance. For the gentry of Malé, and other regular courtiers, who are bound to come and salute the king every afternoon, tarry sitting in this second hall, and may not proceed further; there they amuse themselves conversing with one another until the king comes forth, or some domestic officer shows himself, whom they bid tell the king that they have come to pay their respects, or convey some special request to him. Such is the manner of holding court in that country. Sometimes, while they are sitting there, the king sends them dishes of fruit and betel, which they esteem a great honour and favour. Once a week, or fortnight, as he pleases, the king comes to sit in this hall to take part in their deliberations, and to take counsel with them on affairs of state or other. The nobles of the other islands, who are very numerous, often come to court, and observe the same procedure as do those of Malé and the ordinary courtiers; but they never come for a fresh visit without bringing a present: for no one, whether noble or merchant, is admitted to salute the king unless he brings an offering. Likewise, those lords who hold islands of the king, bring the tribute due to him. By this manner of offering presents a man is soon aware whether he is in his good graces or not, for if the king accepts his present, he is assured of his goodwill; but if not, or if the king says not a word to the messenger who announces his arrival and conveys his respects, it is a certain sign of disfavour and disgrace. When the king receives strangers, it is in the first or large hall, where the guards attend.

The king's private apartments and the corridors are also much adorned, and are hung with silk tapestry, worked richly

i, 67). A court regulation requires that all persons wear dress of native manufacture when they come into the Sultan's presence.

with flower and branch patterns in gold and divers colours; this dazzles the eye, as well with the richness of the gold and the colours, as with the wondrous work of it. These hangings come for the most part from China, Bengal, Masulipatan, and St. Thomas, and are also made at the Maldives. The (common) people use cotton hangings, composed of pieces of cotton cloth of all colours, arranged together in various ways, and upon them figures and patterns in needlework, or other pieces applied and sewn on. From Bengal comes also another sort of hanging, of fine linen painted and ornamented with colours in a very agreeable fashion: these they call *Iader*.[1]

The beds are suspended in air by four cords from a bar supported by two posts; the pillows and sheets are of cotton and silk, the whole covered with precious curtains of silk and cloth of gold. The beds of the king, the grandees, and the wealthy are in this style, as they are thus more comfortably rocked to sleep.[2] They are also accustomed, when they go to bed, to have their bodies handled and chafed, and gently rubbed by their attendants, and to be patted with both hands; they say this is good for their spleen disease, and that it cures the pain; it also puts them to sleep sooner, and makes them forget the pain in the part patted and rubbed. The ordinary domestics of the king sleep on cotton pillows laid on boards fixed on four posts four feet high.

The ordinary habit of the king was a gown, of exceeding white and fine cotton, or rather a cassock, falling to the waist or rather lower, with a border of white and blue, and fastened in front with buttons of massive gold. With this he wore

[1] Probably the Hind. *chadar*, "a sheet", the Anglo-Indian *chudder* (see Yule and Burnell, *Gloss.*, s. v.)

[2] Marco Polo, bk. III, ch. xvii, states that the wealthier people of the Coromandel coast had bedsteads of light canework, in which they were drawn up by cords nearly to the ceiling, in order to escape vermin during the night.

a piece of red taffetas, edged, reaching from the waist to the heels. This taffetas was girt with a long and large waistband of red silk with gold fringes, and by a heavy gold chain, fastened in front by a fine buckle larger than the hand, set with the rarest gems known. He carried also a knife, after the manner of his country, but richly ornamented. On his head he wore a little bonnet of red scarlet, which is highly prized in that country and permitted to the king alone: this bonnet was trimmed all round with gold, while on the top was a big button of solid gold with some precious stone, signifying in a way his royalty, the whole bound round with a turban of red silk like the waistband. And although the greatest lords and the soldiers like to wear their hair long, as has been said, yet he was wont to shave every week. He went always barelegged, like the rest, and wore on his feet only gold-sewn leather slippers,[1] brought from Arabia, and made like sandals. These no person in the kingdom, of whatever rank, would dare to wear, saving the queens and the princesses of his house. As for the princes, though they might, or could easily get permission, yet they care not to use aught but certain wooden sandals,[2] and those at home only, leaving to the king this mark of distinction between them and him, though he has another by which he may easily be recognised: for when he goes forth, a white umbrella or parasol[3] is borne over him. This is the chief mark of royal majesty; neither is it, nor would it be allowed to any other person whatsoever, except to foreigners, who are permitted to dress as they please, and carry what they like. Walking by the king on all occasions are pages, one carrying a fan, another the king's sword drawn and a buckler, a third his box of betel and areca, of which he partakes every hour.

[1] *Fai-rán-koḷu; koḷu* is a royal suffix, like *gaḍu*.

[2] *Maravali-koḷu.*

[3] *Hudu-hai-koḷu*; *hudu* = Sin. *hudu* or *sudu*, "white"; *hai* = Sin. *sat*, "umbrella".

A doctor of the law also follows, never losing sight of him, reading a book in his presence and admonishing him of his religion.

At table, where he eats alone, he is served by the chief of his household in the same manner as I have related of his subjects, except that he is served with greater care, honour, and reverence. His plate is neither gold nor silver, for that is forbidden by their law; but of porcelain, or of other China fabric, or of copper, neatly fashioned and worked at the Maldives; he also uses the boxes of polished and lacquered wood.[1]

His exercise and ordinary pastime was not to go forth frequently, or to go a-fishing, as I learnt from the islanders was the habit of kings that preceded him, but to tarry most of his time shut up in his palace, entertaining his queens, seeing his courtiers, and superintending numbers of workmen and artisans, such as painters, goldsmiths, embroiderers, cutlers, bead-makers, turners, joiners, armourers, and divers others, whom he kept at his palace, supplying them with materials, and paying them for their work as it was finished; he then stored the articles with care in various places in the palace, and sometimes made presents of them. In this occupation he took much delight and spent much of his time; he also used himself to work, and would say it was a sin to be idle. He was of quick and ready wit, knowing something of most things; he worked at several crafts and trades, and was ever anxious to learn; he sought out such as excelled at anything; and if he met with any foreigner who knew something that neither he nor his islanders knew, he paid him great attention, to the end that he should teach him his art.

When he goes out he is accompanied by his soldiers, of whom a hundred are on guard daily. On Fridays, when he goes to the mosque, it is in fine array and in grand pomp, as

[1] See above, at p. 170-1.

I have to some extent described above, for the soldiers march in order, one company before and the other behind, his ordinary officers beside him, along with the greatest men of his court, while drums, flutes, trumpets, and other instruments are played with a harmony most pleasing to the ear.[1] The service done, he returns to his palace in the same order, the soldiers marching to the sound of the instruments, and dancing and capering in front of the king with their arms, and with their swords striking the shields of one another: in this they show their address, for to avoid confusion they strike not all together, but two at a time only, and one after another continuously. The residents of the island who have taken part in the festival escort him back, and it would be a shame for any not to go. Arrived at his palace, the king keeps the Pandiare, the Naybes, Catibes, and Moudins, as well as the chief lords, gentlemen, and soldiers, or such as he selects on each occasion to dine at the palace, and after dinner he sits to administer justice. When the king used to go out, he went always on foot (since on none of the islands are there any horses or other beasts for riding), except when he was carried in a chair on the shoulders of his slaves; but that happened rarely or never, for, being strong and healthy, he liked better to walk afoot; besides, the island is of but little extent. At Malé the streets and roads are not paved, and still less elsewhere, wherefore the inhabitants, to prevent weeds growing upon them, are obliged to sweep them; this they do principally at the festivals, for then they know that the king or the queens must come and walk about the island, and on that account they are careful.

When the king walks in the street, the people quit that side and leave it free, and go to the other, so that there be none where the king goeth; for the king never passeth between two persons, and great care is taken not to touch

[1] See Ibn Batuta's description of the Vizier's procession to the mosque, App. A.

him. The great lords are treated in the same way in their own islands by their inferiors.

It is also to be remarked that when one speaks to the king or the queens or their children, or to the princes of the blood, or when one speaks of them to others, it is in terms applied only to them, and such as one durst not apply to others; as, for example, when you say of a man that he sleeps, of the king you would say he slumbers, or takes rest; and these terms are never used but with respect to the king.[1]

The king's wives are habited in the same style as I have described the great ladies, save that they are more profuse with gold, pearls, and gems, in the richness of their ear-pendants, gold chains, and bracelets, and in their carkanets on the neck, arms, and legs.

The ladies that are wives or daughters of the grandees of the island are expected to go and visit them in the evening, to pass the time with them and to take them presents.

Sometimes the queens go abroad, but that is rarely, and then they have women and slaves who go far ahead to warn men to keep out of the way, and not show themselves on the road: only women are allowed. Indeed, the women assemble from their several wards, and come forward with little offerings, such as flowers and fruits. Four chief women bear over the heads of the queens a silk curtain reaching to the ground, in such wise that they cannot be seen.

When they are with child, they also go out to bathe in the sea, like all the other women, for it is a custom of the country, and esteemed healthy. For this purpose a little shed or enclosure of posts and sticks is erected in the sea, and covered all round with cloths. There the queens and grand ladies bathe at their ease, after which they come out into

[1] So in modern Maldivian and Sinhalese; of an ordinary person it is said, *nidáoti*, "he sleeps", Sin. *nidágannavá;* of the Sultan or other great person it is said, *avahárafụla*, "he slumbers", Sin. *sætapenavá*.

another little house built on purpose, where they have another bath of fresh water nicely served.

In the apartments of the queens, princesses, and great ladies, no daylight is admitted, but only lamps are kept burning continually. They withdraw to a part of their chamber where they are shut off by four or five several curtain-hangings, which have to be raised one by one before a person gets to where they are; but no man or woman, domestic or stranger, whoever it might be, would dare lift the last, although they might not be asleep, taking their meals, or doing anything. One must first cough and say who it is, and then the ladies call to him, or send, according to their pleasure. By the way, I omitted to say that all women and girls when they go to bed take off only their robe, and wear their waist-cloths; but these are cloths solely for night use, and men have the like, and they would not think of doing otherwise.

CHAPTER XVII.

Of the revenues of the king, money, traffic, and commerce of the Maldives; and of the merchandise imported and exported.

The revenues of the king consist of his domains, many islands being held of him in seignory; next of the dues[1] paid by his subjects of the produce of the land, that is to say, the fifth part of all grain sown; a certain share of the cocos

[1] "Each atoll is bound to pay yearly a certain portion of its produce, said to be levied as a poll-tax upon every male or female over twelve years of age, at the following rates :—1 *koṭṭa* of cowries, 12 *cadjans* (M. *fan̥*), and 1 *tula* (28 lb.) of coir for every woman and girl, and for each man and boy the same, with the addition of 50 dried fish, 100 coco-nuts, and 50 *adubá* of jaggery" (Bell, *Report*, 67). "Native money is now occasionally accepted in lieu of produce" (*ibid.*).

and lemons has also to be paid; but they compound with him by a fixed annual contribution of honey[1] or fruit. Besides these dues, the king imposes on his subjects an ordinary tax, according to their means, consisting of coco-cordage, of shells called *Boly*, of which I have spoken, and of dried fish in those islands where it more abounds and the fishing is best,—for they never pay him these dues and taxes in money, except when they buy rank or office, or the permission to don their braveries. Also he requires the inhabitants of the islands to make and furnish annually as much cotton-cloth as he delivers to them of raw cotton: this is for the use of the soldiers, to whom he gives these cloths three times a year, besides their pay.[2] The king's revenue consists also of merchandise; for all ships that put in there in the first instance report themselves to him and declare their cargo; then he compounds with them at a certain price for what he wants to take, and this is most often the greater portion: afterwards the people buy the rest at a price fixed at higher rates than the king has paid, and then the king distributes his merchandise abroad among the richer islands at such prices as he pleases, though they have no need of the goods, while he takes from them in exchange such merchandise as he wants at no more than half its value.[3] Ofttimes, too, he despatches ships to foreign parts, laden with the merchandise of his island, insomuch that his revenue cannot with any certainty be told, for it is variable, now more, now less; and sometimes he has a loss, chiefly when his ships are wrecked, or fail to make a good port.

[1] *I.e.*, jaggery or palm-sugar.

[2] "A payment of cloth and mats is also exacted from atolls where these are manufactured" (Bell, *Report*, 67). Christopher says that the Sultan makes an annual distribution of red cloth to the Viziers for the soldiers under their command, each man receiving a piece of cloth and 30 pice in money (*T. Bom. Geo. Soc.*, i, 72).

[3] The Sultan still asserts a right of pre-emption at low rates on all cargoes imported from foreign parts (Bell *Report*, 67).

Besides these revenues, the king has certain dues appurtenant to him—for instance, all that is found on the sea-shore belongs to him: a man dare not touch such a thing with a view to keeping it; he is bound to collect it, and bear it to him, whether it be wreckage, timber, chests, or other casualties; or ambergris, called by them *gomen*, and when prepared, *Meuuare*,[1] of which more is found there than in

[1] *Goma*, the Maldivian name for ambergris, is also the Sinhalese for cow-dung, which it somewhat resembles in appearance and consistency. No doubt they thought it was whales' dung, as did the Japanese, according to Kœmpfer. *Meuuare* is for *mávaharu* (= *maha*, *vaharu*), the "very sweet smelling" substance. Ambergris, the origin of which was so long obscure, is now known to be a secretion formed in the stomach or intestines of the *Physeter macrocephalus*, or spermaceti whale. It is found chiefly in those whales which appear torpid and lean, whence it appears to be the product of disease (McCulloch's *Dict. of Com.*). It is opaque and soft, and when heated gives out a peculiarly agreeable perfume. It is now used only for perfumery, but was formerly employed in medicine as a cordial and an aphrodisiac (*G. de Orta*, f. 14).

The first notion as to the origin of ambergris seems to have been that it was a kind of fungus, produced at the bottom of the sea (see Reinaud, *Relation des Voyages par les Arabes*, i, p. 4). The knowledge that it came from the whale is, however, found in *Mas'udi*, i, 335. Marco Polo (Yule's edit., ii, 341) states the same, and that in his time whales were killed with harpoons, for the possession of their ambergris. Friar Jordanus, in the fourteenth century, mentions it as *embar*, and says it is like wood (p. 18). Barbosa, who says that large quantities were found at the Maldives, relates (p. 165) that the Moors informed him that it was the droppings of birds, which, torn from the rocks by storms, floated on the sea, and was afterwards swallowed by whales. Kœmpfer (*Hist. of Japan*, Eng. trans., i, 111-12) says it is chiefly found in the intestines of whales, but retails the current stories of its nature, as birds' dung, a sea-sponge, and also a bituminous substance, or a kind of earth or clay. Garcia de Orta (f. 13) does not believe that it comes from the whale. Sir R. Hawkins states that some think it to be found in the bowels of the whale, or voided by him, "and maintaine for certaine that the same is ingendred by eating an hearbe which groweth in the sea. This hearbe is not in all seas, say they, and therefore, where it wanteth, the whales give not this fruit" (Hawkins, *Voyages*, 155). P. Vincenzo says that it is produced at the bottom of the sea, and afterwards refined in the whale's belly (ed. 1678, p. 242). Though so much

any of the East Indies; it, too, belongs to the king, and he that would dare appropriate it would have his hand cut off. It is the same with a certain nut, cast up by the sea from time to time, and as big as a man's head, which one might liken to a couple of large melons joined together: this they call *Tauarcarré*,[1] believing that it comes of certain trees

was known, Tavernier thinks its origin still an open question—"there is no person in the world that knows either what it is, or where or how it is produced" (pt. II, ch. xxi).

Ambergris is of several descriptions. Barbosa (*loc. cit.*) mentions the white (*ponabar*), the greyish (*puambar*), and the brown (*minabar*). The lightest in colour is the best, though Herbert (4th edit., p. 372) says the grey is better than the white. It was always rare, and fetched high prices, and being a product of the sea, was generally (but not in Japan, according to Kœmpfer) regarded as royal property. It may be superfluous to note here that the *'anbar* of the Arabs, and of all these travellers, was solely the whale-secretion. The application of the word to the yellow amber, as we now use it, is modern. Large pieces of ambergris were occasionally found. Kœmpfer speaks of a piece found in Japan, weighing 100 *cattis*, or 130 lb. Dutch, and of another weighing 185 lb., sold by the King of Tidore to the Dutch E. I. Company for 11,000 rix-dollars, or about £2,000. Tavernier mentions two pieces of 33 and 42 lb. respectively as being large. Capt. Hamilton saw a piece belonging to the Raja of Cananore "as big as a bushel, and valued at Rs. 10,000, or £1,250 sterling" (*New Acct*., etc., i, 298). But these are small compared to that recorded by J. los Santos as having been found on the coast of Melinde, which was so big that a man could hide behind it! (Fr. trans., p. 105).

Tavernier states that the Governor of Mozambique was in the habit of getting 300,000 pardaos of ambergris during his three years' term of office, one pardao being equal to about 2*s*. 6*d*. Its value in the Portuguese time is difficult to determine, owing to its variety of quality; some information will be found in the *Livro dos Pesos*, etc. (p. 13), and the *Lembranças* (p. 46), contained in *Subsidios para a Hist. da Ind. Port*.

Ambergris is found throughout all the tropic seas, and, in former times at least, was occasionally washed ashore in Spain and England (Hawkins, *Voy.*; Tavernier, *loc. cit.*).

[1] This is the celebrated sea coco-nut (*coco de mer*), *Lodoicea Seychellarum*. From the mistake as to its habitat it was termed *Cocos maldiricus* by Rumphius, and, from its fancied medicinal properties, *Nux medica* by Clusius. The species *Lodoicea* grows only on the Seychelles; the trees being close upon the sea-shore, the fruit is floated across the

under the sea: the Portuguese call it "coco des Maldives"; it is an article of medicine, and fetches a high price. Often at the season for this *Tauarcarré*, or for grey and black amber (as this too is found there), the king's servants and officers harass the poor people when they suspect them of having found any; nay more, when they have a grudge against a man, they impute to him this charge, as they do here that of false money, to the end that he may be searched; and when

Indian Ocean, and being occasionally picked up at the Maldives, was supposed, at first, to be a product of these islands, and afterwards, when the tree was not forthcoming, of a species which grew under the sea. See, as to this tree, Sir W. J. Hooker, in *Bot. Mag. and Reg.*, vol. xii; Macleod (L.), *Eastern Africa*, i, 224-7; G. de Orta, 69-71; Sonnerat, *Voy.*, Eng. trans., pp. 2-6; Thunberg, *Travels*, 3rd edit., iv, 133, 159; Labillardière's *Voyage in Search of La Pérouse*; and Yule's *Glossary*, s. v. "Coco de mer".

Like many other products, the sea coco-nut was a remedy for all manner of ailments, such as the flux, epilepsy, and apoplexy (Thunberg), colic, paralysis, and nervous infirmities (G. de Orta). Above all, it was an antidote to poison; and Faria-y-Sousa says it is "a greater antidote against poison than bezoar stone"; while de Orta, with greater medical experience, believed the bezoar to be better. The shell was made into goblets for kings of the East and West, and set in gold and diamonds, and it was supposed that those who drank a poisoned draught out of those marvellous cups would escape unhurt. According to de Orta, the Queen of Portugal sent every year for these nuts. The Emperor Rudolf II is said to have offered 4,000 florins for a single specimen (*Malte Brun*, iv, 420). It is thus described in the *Lusiads* (x, 136):

"Nas ilhas de Maldiva nasce a planta
No profundo das aguas, soberana,
Cujo pomo contra o veneno urgente
Hé tido por antidoto excellente,"

The name *tavarcarré* is given in Piso's *Mantissa Aromatica*, and also by Sonnerat and Thunberg; and no doubt they borrowed it from Pyrard. Sonnerat says the meaning of the word is "treasure", but it is clear that he has mistaken the passage following, where Pyrard says that when a man becomes suddenly rich, he is said to have found *tavarcarré*, or amber, "as though it were treasure". The Maldivian word, as Mr. Bell informs me, is *tâva' karhi*, or *tava karhi*, *i.e.*, the "hard (shelled) nut"; M. *tava* = Sin. *tada*.

one becomes suddenly rich, it is commonly said that he has found *Tauarcarré*, or amber, as though it were treasure. There is also a plentiful fishery of black coral,[1] which belongs to the king, and he keeps numbers of men employed at it.

The coin of the realm is silver only, and of one sort. These are pieces of silver called *larins*,[2] of the value of eight sous

Maldive Larin.

or thereabouts of our money, as I have said, as long as the finger, but doubled down. The king has them struck in his island, and stamped with his name in Arabic characters. All other coins are foreign, and though they are current, they are only taken at their just value and weight, and they must be

[1] M. *endiri*.

[2] This coin takes its name from the city Lar, in Persia. The earliest mention of it by a European writer is, so far as I am aware, in the *Lembranças das Cousas da India* (*Subsidios*, iii, 53), that is, in 1525, and the following table is given :—2 *fules* =1 dinar; 12 dinars =1 tanga; 3 tangas 10 dinars =1 new larin; 3 tangas 9 dinars =1 old larin. At Cambaye, the same writer says (p. 38) that 1 *tanga larin* = 60 reis, and that 45 of these larins weighed 1 Portuguese marco, *i.e.*, 50 grammes each (*Subsidios*, i, 61). We get the following values from Antonio Nunes (1554), in his *Livro dos Pesos*, etc.: "At the port of Bengala, 80 cowries =1 *pone;* 48 *pones* =1 larin" (*Subsidios*, i, 61). The editor of the *Subsidios*, taking a *marco* of silver in the reign of João III as being equivalent to 2,500 reis, notes that the larin would then be worth 51.012 reis.

The early Portuguese writers do not mention the shape of the larin, but there is no reason to doubt that it was as Pyrard describes it, that is, in the form in which it was current all over Western India in the seventeenth and eighteenth centuries.

The earliest Dutch authority describes it as current at Goa and the Malabar coast:—"Ils usent aussi une monnoye venant de Perse nommée *Larrin*, du nom de la ville *Lar*, où on les forge; elle est longue comme gros fil d'argent, doublé: ayant à l'un costé un signe ou caractère du Roy de Perse; elle est de pur argent sans aucune mixtion: valent la pièce 105 ou 108 Basarucos selon que le change va" (*Premier*

gold or silver; all others are rejected. For in India and the adjacent parts, where there are many kingdoms and lord-

Livre de la Nav., p. 53, f. *b*). In Pyrard's time the larin was worth a little more than the tanga; he says a larin was worth 8 sous, and a tanga 7½ sous. The author of the *Premier Livre, loc. cit.*, likewise gives a pardao as being 6 tangas or 5 larins.

Mendelslo, in 1637, in describing the money of Persia, indicates that the larin which was formerly coined by Shah Ismail was then no longer minted (Eng. trans., p. 299); but Tavernier, about the same time, states that the Arabian merchants coming to Persia take nothing but larins for their goods (Eng. trans., pt. ii. p. 1). Chardin, at the end of the seventeenth century, states that the larin was no longer minted, but was still current all along the Persian Gulf (*Voyage*, 1711, p. 92).

In Ceylon, the larin is traced almost into the present century. Valentyn says that the cinnamon and cardamoms of Ceylon were exported to Persia, and paid for in ready cash: this cash was in all probability larins. Tennent (*Ceylon*, i, 463) says that the Ceylon larins are stamped with Persian characters; but this cannot be true of them all, for Knox (1660-79) writes: "The shape is like a fish-hook; they stamp what mark or impression on it they please" (*Knox*, 98, mispaged 97).

Thunberg was informed that larins were struck by the king of Kandy; he describes them thus:—"It consists of a silver cylinder, hammered out, which in the middle is bent together, the ends being afterwards turned up like a hook, and the upper end distinguished either with certain letters or stars, or else with engravings. One of them which I procured by barter cost 12 Dutch stivers, and another, of a smaller size, 9; both of them were of fine silver" (Thunberg, *Travels*, iv, 210-2). Fra Bartolomeo thinks the larin was introduced by a modern king of Kandy, and describes it as "a piece of silver wire rolled up like a wax taper. When a person wishes to make a purchase, he cuts off as much of this silver as is equal in value to the price of the article." According to Davy, it had a definite value equal to 7*d.* English.

There are some interesting papers on the *larin* in the *Numismatic Chronicle*, viz., by Mr. W. B. Dickinson, in vol. xi, at p. 161; vol. xii, p. 82; vol. xiii, p. 61; and by Prof. H. H. Wilson, in vol. xvi, at p. 179. The first-named writer gives some excellent illustrations of various forms of the larin in vol. xi; and Prof. Wilson gives a plate of some specimens of a parcel of 397 larins found at Sangameswara, in the Ratnagiri collectorate, in 1846. These latter seem to have been all of the straight variety, *i.e.*, bent only once. The legends of most were illegible, owing to the silver being too narrow for the stamp; but, by collation of various specimens, Prof. Wilson read the legend of one

ships, there is a great variety of money, both as to form and stamp, not only of gold and silver, but also of another

side as "Sultan Ali Aadil Shah", and of the other, "Zarb Lari—Dangh Sikka", *i.e.*, "Struck at Lari" (or rather, "a Lari", as Mr. Thomas suggests)—"stamped tanga", and of date A.H. 1071, *i.e.*, A.D. 1659. Notwithstanding this legend, the probability is that the coins were struck at Bijapur. Mr. Vaux read, on some larins of the British Museum collection, the legend, "Mohammad the prophet of God", and the word "Melek" (king). There is no sufficient proof of the currency in India of the larin in the eighteenth century, as Prof. Wilson believes, in reliance upon a Sattara document of 1711, wherein is mention of "Dabul larins", as, long before this time, the word had become a mere expression in the territories where Portuguese influence prevailed.

The cut given on p. 232 of a Maldive larin obtained by Mr. Bell (it has long since gone out of use) shows that it was identical in shape with the Persian coin (see the cuts in Tavernier, and in the *Premier Livre*, etc.). The Ceylon coin, as will be observed from Thunberg's description, was first doubled flat, and then bent in the shape of a fish-hook, as stated by Knox. To the present day it is known in Ceylon as the "fish-hook" coin. Cuts of it will be found in Davy's *Ceylon*, p. 245, and in *Tennent*, i, 463, as well as in the *Num. Chron.*, *ubi supra*, and in Mr. Rhys Davids' article in *Numismata Orientalia* (part iv, p. 34). The British Museum possesses between twenty and thirty specimens, most of them presented by Mr. Marsden, but, unfortunately, it is not known where any of them were found, and the characters of but few are legible; I am therefore unable to say whether the Ceylon hook-form is common to the larins of other countries.

Ceylon Larin (fish-hook).

Although, as stated above, the silver larin is now obsolete at the Maldives, the name has passed to copper coins of the ordinary shape.

Bodu lári.

Kuda lári.

These are of two kinds, the *bodu lári* (big lari) and the *kuda lári* (little lari)—25 of the former and 100 of the latter going to a rupee. Mr.

metal called *Calin*,[1] which is white like tin, but harder, purer, and finer, and much used in the Indies: coin is also made of iron. But this kind of money is only current in the territory of the prince that coins it; so that in this matter there is great diversity, by reason of the multitude of duchies, in such wise that the Portuguese at Goa struck coin of calin or of iron, which would be of no use in Portugal, nor even at the town of Cochin, which also belongs to them, in India, and is not far from Goa; so that there they likewise employ a peculiar coinage. But gold and silver, of whatever form or stamp, is taken in all the kingdoms at its proper value, which nevertheless is very different from ours, seeing that silver is in greater demand, and is dearer than here, and gold cheaper. Spanish reals fetch a high price, the silver being very good. Now to return to the Maldives: the king coins larins only; other pieces of less value he coins not at all; insomuch that for the uses of trade they cut the silver and pay by weight for the value of the goods bought: but this is not done without some loss, for in cutting the larin they lose a twelfth part. They take no silver without weighing it and trying it in the fire to prove it; and everybody

Bell has specimens of these larins dating from 1716 down to 1877 (*Report*, 118, 121).

[1] This was, in fact, Malayan tin. The word is originally Malay (*kalang*); it appears in Arabic as *ḳala'i*, and in the Portuguese writers as *calaim* (*Livro das Monçoes*, ii, 181; *Subsidios*, i, 6; ii, 17, 256; iii, 54; Correa, *Lendas*, ii, 256). The form *calin* seems to have been adopted by French writers from Pyrard (see Marsden, *Sumatra*, 22). As to the history of the word, see, further, Yule's *Glossary*, s. v. *Calay*, where it will be seen that other writers of the period, like Pyrard, conceived it to be a distinct metal. Tin coin was in use at Malacca long before the Portuguese conquest (Correa, *Lendas*, ii, 256; Da Cunha, *Indo-Port. Num.*, p. 16). A *calaim* there was worth 100 caixes, or 11 Port. reis (*Dalb. Comm.*, Hak. Soc., iii, 78, *note*). The metal was introduced into the Portuguese coinage by Albuquerque, but chiefly as an alloy with lead, and the name *calaim* as a coin then disappeared.

has weights in his house for this purpose. Then, in place of copper and small change, they use the shells of which I have said somewhat above, and will presently say more; 12,000 of them are worth a larin. For the rest, all the gold and silver comes from abroad; there are no mines in the islands. In all the public markets and in their private traffic they most frequently barter one thing for another.

There is a great trade at the Maldives, and they are much frequented for their commodities. You see merchants from all quarters, as Malabar men from Barcelor, Onor, Bacalor, Cananor, Calecut, Tananor, Cochin, Coilam, Cael[1]; Guzeratis from Cambaye, Surat, and Chaul; Arabs, Persians, men of Bengal, St. Thomas, and Masulipatam, Ceylon, and Sumatra, who bring goods that are in demand there, and take away what the Maldives produce in abundance. First, of the coco tree, which grows naturally at the islands without any cultivation, they make many sorts of goods in demand with the foreigners: for instance, cordage, with which all the vessels of the Indies are equipped; the coco fruit, which is carried in such quantity to the coasts of Arabia and Malabar and throughout India, that more than a hundred ships are laden with it every year, as well as with the oil and honey of the same tree; and the leaves which serve for sails: but the greatest trade is in cordage.

There is another kind of wealth at the Maldives, viz., certain little shells containing a little animal, large as the tip of the little finger, and quite white, polished, and bright: they are fished twice a month, three days before and three days after the new moon, as well as at the full, and none would be got at any other season. The women gather them on the sands and in the shallows of the sea, standing in the water up to their waists. They call them *Boly*,[2] and export to all parts an infinite

[1] These Malabar ports are mentioned separately hereafter.

[2] The cowry, *Cypræa moneta*, M. *boli*; *cf.* Sin. *bella* (*animate*), and pl. *b.li*, "shells" (*inanimate*); well known as a very ancient and still the

quantity, in such wise that in one year I have seen thirty or forty whole ships loaded with them without other cargo. All

most widely used shell-money. Pyrard writes it here *boly*, and elsewhere *bolli*. The earlier geographers, the two Mahomedans of the ninth century, Masudi in the tenth, and Edrisi in the twelfth (*vide infra*, App. A), all describe the cowry as being taken by casting wood or branches into the sea, the creatures fastening themselves thereon in great numbers. The same method is stated by de Barros (*Dec. III*, liv. III, c. iv), and by Capt. Hamilton early in the eighteenth century. Ibn Batuta (see App. A) does not say how they are taken, but mentions that they are placed in pits in the sand in order to rot. According to Pyrard, corroborated by Mr. Bell, they are taken by men wading up to the waist.

In the Arab *Relation*, i, p. 5, they are said to be called on the islands *al-kabtaj;* Edrisi writes *el kendj;* and Albiruni refers to the M. as *Diwa kandha, i.e.*, Cowry Islands. Ibn Bat. calls them *wada'*, a frequent Arabic word for them. The Portuguese, Dutch, and English have all adopted the word cowry from the Hind. *kauri*, though the Portuguese commonly referred to them as *buzios*, "shells".

All these quoted writers state that a large trade was carried on from the Maldives in these shells, that they formed the king's treasure, and in fact were used as money. Ibn Batuta is the first to give measures and values. He describes them as sold by the *syah* (100), *fâl* (700), *cotta* (12,000), and *bostou* (100,000). At the Maldives the market value ranged from four to twelve *bostou* to a dinar of gold, probably = 10*s*. 6*d*. As to the value of the *dinar* in Ibn Batuta's time, see *Cathay*, 439. Even then it seems cowries were current all over Africa, distance adding greatly to their value; for Ibn Bat. adds that a dinar of gold, which would purchase four to twelve *bostou* at the Maldives, was given in the Soudan for only 1,150 shells. It is somewhat strange that, though these shells have been for so many centuries current coin in Bengal and all over Africa, they seem never to have been adopted for monetary purposes on the neighbouring coast of Malabar (see *Varthema*, p. 131, *note*), nor even in Ceylon. The Portuguese bought cowries at the Maldives by the *cotta* (spelt *cota*, *Subsidios*, i, 35), 4½ cottas being taken as weighing a quintal: the price in Portuguese currency is not stated. Nunes, the author here quoted, however, gives the value at the ports of Bengala, where of course the price has always been much higher. There, in 1554, cowries were current coin, 80 = 1 *pone* (=*paṇ*, which is still used in Bengal for 80 cowries), and 48 *pones* = 1 larin ; and a quintal was worth 700 reis (*ib.*, 37). In Bengal, therefore, a larin purchased only 3,840 cowries, while at the Maldives it would purchase 12,000.

go to Bengal, for there only is there a demand for a large quantity at high prices. The people of Bengal usė them for

Pyrard gives the current price as 12,000 = 1 larin = 8 sous, which would, at the then rate of exchange, equal about 7½d. English.

The period of Dutch supremacy in Ceylon, which included the suzerainty of the Maldives, was also the great period of the African slave trade, and large quantities of cowries were exported *viâ* Ceylon to the European markets, to be thence employed in purchasing human beings on the Guinea coast. In 1740 the Dutch Governor fixed the price at 2½ rix-dollars for a cotta of 24 lb. The annual home demand was then 400,000 lb., which, he says, would sell for fl. 1,100,000 (£8,300), but even then was not a profitable business (Lee's *Ribeyro*, App., p. 175). If the price so fixed was what the Dutch paid the Maldive Sultan, it results that the impetus given by the slave trade had sent up the market for cowries. But the most interesting account of these shells in connection with the slave trade occurs in the narrative of an anonymous Dutch gentleman, published in English in 1747 (*A Voyage to the Island of Ceylon*, etc., by a Dutch gentleman, London, 1754):—"The Dutch drive a considerable trade with the inhabitants of the Maldives for those little shells called *cowries*, where are prodigious quantities of them, and not only on the shore, but in the very ground, being probably deposited there at the time of the Flood, and left there when the ocean receded from the land. What we call money being arbitrary, and its nature and value depending on a tacit convention betwixt men, these shells, in several parts of Asia and Africa, are accounted current money, with a value assigned to them. This is established by a reciprocal consent, and those who are pleased to show a contempt of them don't reflect that shells are as fit for a common standard of pecuniary value as either gold or silver; they certainly forget that they themselves are obliged to do what they ridicule, and take them for ready money. In 1740, 2,400 *cowries* [probably 24,000, or 2 cottas] were equal to a *rupee*, or about a crown at three guilders of our money.

"But their great currency is on the coast of Africa, particularly *Guinea*, where the negroes value them as much as gold and silver, and call them *bougies* [Port. *buzios*]. An instance of the great consumption of these shells, that the French merchants of the kingdom of *Whydah* usually give forty pounds of these *cowries* for every piece of common linen manufactured by the natives, and proportionably for the products of the country, as wax, ivory, gold, etc. The company it is which supplies the European nation with the far greater part of this negro money, if I may be indulged the expression. The esteem in which these shells are on the coast of *Guinea* must appear surprising. They are not only, like gold and silver, the measure and instrument of commerce betwixt

ordinary money, although they have gold and silver and plenty of other metals; and, what is more strange, kings and great lords have houses built expressly to store these shells, and treat them as part of their treasure. All the merchants from other places in India take a large quantity to carry to Bengal, where they are always in demand; for they are produced nowhere but at the Maldives, on which account they serve as petty cash, as I have said. When I came to Malé for the first time, there was a vessel at anchor from Cochin, a

the negroes, but worn as ornaments in necklaces and bracelets, strung in one or more rows, which looks something odd, yet not amiss, by the contrast of the whiteness of the shells with the blackness of their skins.

"Formerly twelve thousand-weight of these *cowries* would purchase a cargo of five or six hundred negroes; but those lucrative times are now no more; and the negroes now set such a value on their countrymen, that there is no such thing as having a cargo under twelve or fourteen tons of cowries.

"As payments in this kind of specie are attended with some intricacy, the negroes, though so simple as to sell one another for shells, have contrived a kind of copper vessel, holding exactly a hundred and eight pounds, which is a great despatch to business. However, the *Maldives* must not be thought the only place which affords these shells; they are also found in the *Philippine* islands, but they don't come up to the *Maldivian*, either in colour or clearness. The chief European market for these shells is Amsterdam, where there are spacious warehouses of them, the French and English merchants buying them up to send to Africa."

The rate of exchange in Bengal at the end of last century, given by Fra Bartolomeo, was 60 to the pice, or 3,840 to the rupee (*Fra Bart.*, Eng. trans., 86). In 1820 the Bengal rate was 6,000 to the rupee, *i.e.*, Rs. 2 the cotta (*Prinsep. Ind. Ant.*); the same price obtained at Málé in 1835 (*T. Bom. Geo. Soc.*, i, 85). In 1843 the exchange in Bengal was at 64 cowries to the pice, which would now purchase about six times the number. At Málé the price in recent years has generally been R. 1.50 the *cotta* = 25 lb., or Rs. 5 the cwt. It is a far cry from Masudi to Mincing Lane, but I may conclude this note with the following extract made by Mr. Bell from a recent Produce Market Report:—"Cowries, Maldive small, 15*s.* to 18*s.* per ton; medium, 10*s.* to 12*s.*; large, 6*s.* Very dull. Bombay large common Maldive, 8*s.* to 10*s.* per cwt.; medium Calcutta, 20*s.*"

town of the Portuguese, of 400 tons burthen; the captain and merchants were Mestifs,[1] the others Christianised Indians, all habited in the Portuguese fashion, and they had come solely to load with these shells for the Bengal market.[2] They give 20 *coquetees*[3] [? kegs] of rice for a parcel of shells: for all these *Bolys* are put in parcels of 12,000, in little baskets of coco leaves of open work, lined inside with cloth of the same coco tree, to prevent the shells falling out. These parcels or baskets of 12,000 are negotiated there as bags of silver are here, which between merchants are taken as counted, but not by others: for they are so clever at counting, that in less than no time they will take tally of a whole parcel. Also in Cambaye and elsewhere in India they set the prettiest of these shells in articles of furniture, as if they were marbles or precious stones.

The Maldives have also an infinite abundance of fish of all kinds, as I have said before. And so rich is the fishery, that not only have they always enough to fill their own bellies withal, but they also sell a large quantity, both cooked and dried, to foreigners. This commodity is in great demand in all parts of India, notably in Sumatra, whither whole shiploads are carried.

Tortoise-shell, called *Cambe*,[4] is much valued in the Indies.

[1] *Mestif*, or *métif*, is the Fr. corruption of the Port. *mestiço*, a half-caste; though Pyrard elsewhere, and also Mocquet, write *métice*. Cotgrave has *mestif*, a mongrel. The now obsolete Anglo-Indian form was *mustees* or *mustice* (see Yule, *Glossary*, s. v.)

[2] See *supra*, p. 78.

[3] From *coquet*, the syn. of which are "caque", "baril", and "tonnelet" (see earlier editions of Ducange, s. v. *Cochetus*).

[4] M. *kahabu*; Sin. *kæsubu* or *kæsumbu*. The tortoise-shell of commerce is, according to Mr. Bell, supplied by the "hawksbill" variety (*Caretta imbricata*). Pyrard describes it more fully hereafter in his Treatise (vol. ii). The natives take it both on land and as it floats on the water (*T. Bom. Geo. Soc.*, i, 79). The price of this article, as we shall see later, was 1 larin the *gau* (=¼ lb.). Maldive tortoise-shell is of first-rate quality, and always finds a ready sale in Ceylon and

It is found at the Maldives, and is largely traded in. It is a tortoise of an uncommon kind, found only there and at the Philippines. It is pretty and highly polished, and quite black, with much natural marking. It is in greatest demand at Cambaye, where it is made into women's bracelets, and into pretty boxes and caskets set in silver.

The people of the Maldives likewise make a good traffic in rush mats[1] of perfect smoothness, which they make very prettily of divers colours, adorning them with patterns and figures so neatly that nothing can be nicer. The Portuguese and Indians alike prize them, so that there is much trade in them. So also with cloth of cotton and silk, which is brought to them raw, and by them worked up. They do not make white cloth, but only patterned and figured, and in small pieces of an arm's length and a half in width for their dress, and other kinds for the women, and for turbans, all exceedingly beautiful and fine.[2] So the Maldives are frequented

Bengal. What is purchased at Málé at Rs. 16 to Rs. 25 per cwt., is sold in Ceylon at Rs. 5 to Rs. 10 per lb. The average value of the annual imports into Ceylon since 1856 is £1,296; in one year, 1875, they amounted to £2,184 (Bell, *Rep.*, pp. 85, 105).

[1] "The well-known Maldive mats (M. *tuḍu kuna*) are made only in Suvádiva atoll, from a rush (M. *hău*) which thrives best there. In delicacy of pattern, in happy combination of the only three colours adopted,—black, yellow-brown, and white,—and in permanency of dye, these fine mats surpass anything in the same line the world over, and have justly obtained unqualified commendation. The best quality are worked up on Gaddú island, the ordinary mats at Havara-Tinadú, and a small kind on Gemaná-furhi" (Bell, *Rep.*, 88). The large fine mats are valued at Rs. 5 to Rs. 6 even at Málé, and can rarely be procured in Ceylon under Rs. 8 to 10 (*ib.*, 106).

[2] "Two or three qualities of cotton cloth are woven, chiefly in Málosmadulu (Eda-furhi island), Aḍḍú, and Suvádiva atolls, though occasionally made elsewhere for private use. A peculiarity in this article consists in the uniform tasteful colouring of the waist and head-cloths, sometimes plain red, or blue edged with red an inch wide, but more commonly of a rich chocolate colour, relieved by a black stripe between two of white on either side, and finished at the ends by a narrow yellow silk border and a neat fringe. The dyes employed are excellent, particularly the

from all quarters for their commodities, inasmuch as they possess so many things that foreigners prize and require. In exchange, everything that the islanders are in need of is imported from elsewhere, such as rice, white cotton cloth, raw silk and cotton, oil of a certain odoriferous grain, used only to rub the body after bathing; areca for chewing with betel, iron, steel, spices, porcelain—in short, everything they have not; and all these at favourable prices, by reason of the number of ships touching there, and the easy access. Gold and silver are also imported, and, once entered, never allowed to leave the country. They would not give the least bit of it to any foreigner, but keep it as treasure, or make it into trinkets for the women.

CHAPTER XVIII.

Curiosity of the Maldive king.—His genealogy.—Political changes at the islands.—The king's wives, and other matters.

Having said enough of the island, I come now to tell more particularly of the king of the Maldives, his genealogy, wives, conduct, and divers events that happened in his time. This king often asked me about the king of France, his age, manner of life, wars, armaments, ships, cannon, and other matters, and if the two ships we came in belonged to him. I answered him in some detail on these points, and said that if

red and chocolate, which are extracted from a root, M. *ahi* (*Morinda citrifolia*). The black dye is obtained by boiling gall-nuts and rusty iron together in coco-nut water. The price of cloths of native manufacture is much higher than that of the various coloured ones imported from India, in consequence of the demand induced by all persons being expected on public occasions to wear the former. The natives also spin a large quantity of foreign cotton. The spinning-machine (*tatun*) is simply a large and small wheel of light framework" (Bell, *Rep.*, 88; and see *T. Bom. Geo. Soc.*, i, 81).

our king were to send ships to the Indies, it would not be two or three only, but two or three hundred, which surprised him much. He also inquired if the French were the *Franki* or *Franqui* who were spoken of in the Indies. This question I could not well resolve at the time, but since then I have learnt that this name Franki signifies all the Western peoples: to wit, the French, Italians, Spaniards, and other Europeans, but principally the French, who in former days, by their great conquest in the holy wars of the East, wherein they took the leading part, have left their name in the Indies, since then applied in common to the rest.

The king of the Maldives asked me many other questions, among others, of the court of our king, which I described to him at length as best I could. Then I enlarged upon the greatness of the king and his state, with all which he was highly pleased. On their part, the queens, princesses, and other ladies inquired much of the queens and princesses here, and how many wives the king had, and were greatly astonished to hear that, though so great and powerful, he had but one. But chiefly they desired to know how the ladies here conducted affairs of love—for they cared to talk and hear of nothing but love. They were vastly amazed when I told them that the ladies of these parts had no male intimates but their husbands. They also thought it a strange custom to salute wives with a kiss before all the world, and wondered at the great liberty I told them our wives had; yet they praised and commended it highly in contrast to themselves, who are always shut up. They put many more questions to me on the subject of love and women, and their conversation with men.

Thus was I ever a welcome guest at the palace, and went frequently to entertain them with various stories in answer to their questions. The king, among other things, liked to hear in detail all about the building and management of our ships. He was much astonished when I told him that the dye of red scarlet[1] was made with the urine of men who drank wine only, in so much that he flung away a scarlet bonnet he wore, and on that account would no longer use it. They had found in our vessel some brushes of pigs' bristles and scrapers of the same; but when he knew what they were, he had them burned outside his palace, and was much annoyed at having used or even touched them. He also wanted to burn some boxes and chests covered with sea-wolf[2] skin, thinking that it, too, was pig's skin. He wanted to know about everything, and to what uses each was put. He much admired the art of making parchment and paper, and above all was curious to learn our science of navigation, and often made me bring the charts and marine instruments, the knowledge of which I imparted to his pilots. He could hardly believe all I told him of our France and its king, whereof he had never heard tell before.

But to come to the genealogy of this king of the Maldives. I shall tell what I heard there, how he and his family came to the throne. His father had been Catibe of an island. About fifty years before this time the king of these islands, who was of noble and ancient lineage, seeing that he was but

[1] "Scarlet" was a woollen cloth, generally of that peculiar shade of red to which it has given the name. Here Pyrard speaks of "red scarlet"; in vol. ii he mentions "violet scarlet". Froissart, in the fifteenth century, speaks of white scarlet; and Marot, in the sixteenth, of green. The derivation of the word, which appears in French of the twelfth century as *escarlate*, must still be considered uncertain. Littré favours *Galaticus*, *i.e.*, of Galatia, but admits the want of any intermediate form. In English, Piers Plowman and Chaucer use the form *ciclatoun*, which seems identical with the Pers. *saqalát* or *saqlatún*, and which Mr. Skeat thinks may be the original of the word scarlet. The Pers. terms are now applied to European broadcloth, but there is evidence of their application in the middle ages to some kind of silk and gold brocade. See Yule's *Marco Polo*, Bk. i, ch. 58, *note*, and especially his *Discursive Glossary*, s. v. "Suclât", where will be found the best history of the word.

[2] *I.e.*, some kind of seal. In the *Hawkins' Voy.* (Hak. Soc., p. 196), we read of "sea-wolves or seals".

ill-obeyed, and was unable to withstand a formidable rival who wished to depose him, was inspired of God with a resolve to quit all. He departed secretly with his wife and some of his family, without saying a word of his destination to anyone. He went straight to Cochin, where he became a Christian, along with his wife and some of his followers, sending back such as would not be baptized. For this cause his rival, who was his near relative, was at once accepted as king. The name of the latter was *Haly*, of the former *Assan*. The ordinary title is *Rascan*, which signifies "King"; but when they sign, they always put "Sultan", as do all the Mahometan kings. They say there are but five kings of their religion who have a right to use the title Sultan, which means Sovereign—that is to say, the Turk, the Persian, the Mogor, he of the Maldives, and the king of Achen or Sumatra.

This former king, then, when he became a Christian at Cochin, wrote word to all his subjects that they should become Christians, and pay him their wonted tribute, otherwise he would come and see to it with a large army of Portuguese, who had promised him their aid. The new king and the Maldive people made answer that they would no longer acknowledge him; that if aught was due to him he might come and get it; and that if he preferred to be a Christian he should remain where he was; as for them, they would sooner die than change their faith. Hearing this, he asked the aid of the Viceroy of the Indies at Goa, who promised it, but on terms that he should not go in person, as it was feared that he would not agree with his people, or might bring the Portuguese into difficulties. The Portuguese army then set out, but were not able to effect anything, and lost a galley with three ships, and a goodly number of men, and so were constrained to retire. The following year they returned with a stronger force and better pilots, and the new king went out bravely to meet them, though he knew himself lost; he might perhaps have escaped, but he preferred to die in battle rather than to retreat with shame. He was vanquished and put to death, and the Portuguese made themselves masters of Malé, where they built a fortress,[1] and thence sallied forth to compel the submission of the other islands, and put many of the inhabitants to the sword. Then they assembled all the chiefs of the islands, and told them

Old Fort Wall at Málé

they desired to leave them at peace, and not to constrain them in any way, nor to change their religion, if only they

[1] "The fort, being at present (1835) filled up with earth, is a solid mass, in height about twenty feet, faced with stone, and on it are mounted ten guns, which, though very old and almost useless, are taken care of by being covered in. As no native inscription is to be found on this fort, similar to those on the bastion built at the angles of the wall that partly surrounds the island, and as it exhibits signs of more skill than has been evinced in the other defences which appear to have been constructed by the natives, having a round front and gentle slope upwards from the inner line of the base, it seems probable that it is an erection of the Portuguese" (Christopher, in *T. Bom. Geo. Soc.*, i, 57). Mr. Bell says that it has been partially excavated since Christopher's time: he also noticed some twenty or thirty iron guns lying about in the rank vegetation, and two brass guns with Arabic inscriptions.

would pay the king his dues. These terms being accepted, they left one of the island chiefs to govern, and to remain always at Malé with the Portuguese commandant, on terms that he should take no political measures but after consulting the Portuguese and the island chiefs, and that all the trade should be in the hands of the Portuguese alone.

I have heard it said by the islanders that the trade and prosperity of the islands were never so great as when the Portuguese governed there. The governor appointed by the Portuguese to rule under them as viceroy was a lord, a native of the island, and of their religion; but he did everything in the name of the Christian king who lived in the Portuguese territory. This lord was grandfather to the wife of him that was king in my time. The Portuguese in this way ruled the islands in peace for the space of ten years, during which time the father of this king and his brother were Catibes, each of his own island, but, with the pride of their race, would never submit to the Portuguese yoke, nor obey the governor whom they had left in power. On the contrary, they rebelled and levied a force of men and galleys for war, and retired to the atollon *Ouadou,* otherwise *Souadou,* at the southern extremity of the islands, while the Portuguese dared not follow them, nor cross the *Candou* or channel of the said atollon; so that this atollon, and the islands belonging thereto, were never subject to the Portuguese, nor any of the other islands and atollons to the south of that channel.

These two brothers then built a strong fort, and being distant about eighty leagues from Malé, where the Portuguese were, they became in time so strong in men, arms, and ammunition, that they, as it were, held Malé and the Portuguese in check, so that they durst not come out without daily experiencing a harassing war. This lasted for eight years, at the end of which arrived four galleys of Malabar corsairs for the purpose of war and pillage, as was their wont. The two brothers accosted them, and agreed with them to make war upon the Portuguese on terms of half the booty; so one day, getting word that the captain of the fortress and island of Malé was gone to Cochin with a goodly number of Portuguese soldiers, they could not miss the opportunity, and resolved to attack the fortress: which project they carried out so well, that one night they surprised it by escalade, and made themselves masters of the place, putting to death upwards of 300 men that were within, and taking prisoner the native governor who was set there by the Portuguese. The place being taken and sacked, the Malabars, having got their agreed share of the spoil, were going home, leaving the two brothers masters of the town; but they, jealous to see so much of the riches of the islands being carried off, resolved to attack the Malabars. This they did, and, after a long engagement, at length were left victorious, and got both the booty and the galleys, sending the men back to the Malabar coast, and thus repaid with treachery the good service they had of them.[1]

[1] Tradition still keeps alive in the Maldives the story of those stirring times, and of the national heroes who threw off the Portuguese yoke. The following is from the mouth of Mr. Bell's Maldive pandit, a native of Nolivaran-faru, in Tiladummati atoll:—"When Sultan Hassan, who was the son of Sultan Yusub, left the islands, Ali, his rival, reigned in his stead. Incited by Hassan, who had become a Christian, the Portuguese made an attempt to take Málé, but failed for want of ammunition. They returned two or three times, and after four years' war took Málé, and slew the Sultan Ali. His death was on this wise,—being faint and parched with thirst during the final attack, he was seen by a toddy drawer from the neighbouring island of Viligili, who, crossing on a coconut-shell raft (*sic*), offered the wearied Sultan some sweet toddy. As he drank, a shot put an end to his life. His body was washed ashore on an islet westward of Malé (only dry at low tide), called to this day *Ali Rasgefánu Ziare*.

"The Portuguese left as their governor at Málé a half-caste named Andiri Andiri (? Andrea), whose father was the sole survivor of a wreck at Huvadu atoll, and married a Maldive woman, leaving two sons, Andiri and another. During the Portuguese rule there was also a Viyadou (? Port. *Veador*) living at Bára, in Tiladummati atoll, as

In this manner the two brothers became kings of the islands, and equally shared the throne without any quarrel between them. They were both men of great valour, and were acknowledged as such by the people. All the lords and chiefs of the islands submitted to them, and such as would not, had permission to retire to their own private islands without taking part in any way in affairs of state. There were many who would not obey, esteeming themselves of better lineage than the two brothers, who nevertheless knew how to make themselves feared; and when one would not obey them, they sent a force at once to sack and pillage his island. They married wives of the best houses of the country, and were acknowledged throughout all the islands and atolls as absolute kings. As for the Portuguese, they were indignant at the rebuff they had received at the Maldives, and

Atoluveri [*cf.* the 'thief of Baura', referred to in the letters patent of the Christian king, Dom Manoel, *i.e.*, Hassan, dated October 2nd, 1561; see post, App. B]. At Utimu, in Tiladummati atoll, lived Husain Katibu Takuru-fânu, father of the noble brothers, Muhammad Bodu-Takuru-fânu and Hassan Kilage-fânu. On the death of their father, the brothers, with a lad named Ali Dadahelu, went to Málé to obtain for one of the brothers the title and office of *Katibu*, held by their late father. They asked, 'In which of our two names?' 'In that of the elder,' replied Andiri. Henceforth the elder was always styled *Bodu Takuru-fánu*.

"This elder brother induced the *Viyadou* at Bára to build a *gundara*, which he stole, and therewith yearly visited the Malabar coast, and at length surprised and killed the Viyadou. The brothers and the lad then removed their families to Minicoy, and carried on for years a desultory war throughout the atolls. They gradually regained them from the Portuguese, and finally captured Málé and slew Andiri, the governor. The elder brother then occupied the throne till his death. He was succeeded by his son, Kalá-fanu [Sultan Ibrahim of Pyrard's time], who came to his death by the hands of some strangers, and was buried at Kanimidu, in Kolumadulu atoll."

It will be seen that the tradition differs from Pyrard's narrative only in minor points, such as that the Portuguese governor was a half-caste. As to the Sultan Hassan, who became a Christian under the name of Dom Manoel, and the Portuguese accounts of their invasions of the Maldives, see App. B.

were resolved to avenge it; so the next year they sent an army to the islands, and carried on the war for a long time; but the two kings defeated all their forces. This war lasted three years. These kings were very powerful, and possessed two fortresses, that of Malé, and the other at the atoll of *Souadou*, or *Ouadou*, in an island called *Game*.[1] At length both parties considered that it would be for the good of the country and of trade to come to some sort of understanding, rather than to continue this war to a doubtful issue; accordingly, they made a treaty, with these conditions: that the Maldive kings and their people should be left in peace to possess the islands in like manner as their predecessors, save that they should give a certain pension to their Christian king, his successors and heirs, to be rendered at Cochin, but without acknowledging him in any other way; on the other hand, that the Mahometan kings at the islands should not be allowed to take the title and name of king, though they were to be absolute in all things, but only that of prince, duke, or the like. Also, that those two only should be entitled to this name, in their language *Quilague*, and that they should be responsible for the payment of the pension of the Christian king, who on his part was allowed to have a factor there. Furthermore, all natives of the Maldives desiring to traffic with other countries, were bound to take a passport from the Portuguese, as were all the other Indians that were at peace with them. Such were the terms of this peace, which has endured to the present day.

As for the Christian king, he gave a third part of his revenue to the king of Portugal: this revenue consists of these *bollis* and *cairo*,[2] which is rope made of the coco-tree.

[1] *Gaṅ*, in Huvadu atoll, lat. 0° 17′ N., spelt *Ghang* in the Adm. Charts. It is doubtless the same word as the Sin. *gama*, "village". There are said to be traces of an old fort still visible.

[2] So called by the Portuguese, from Malayálam *kayár*, Tam. *kayiru*, hence our form "coir". See Yule, *Gloss.*, s. v. The M. is *rónu*.

They (the Maldive kings) send every year at their own expense four ships, of 150 tons burthen each, laden with it, and that is at the risk of the Maldivians until the ships get beyond the banks at the [northern] end of the islands: beyond that point, the risk is with the Christian king. Notwithstanding this peace,[1] the Maldivians bear a deadly hatred to the Portuguese.

The two brothers reigned together in peace for twenty-five years. The personal name of the elder was *Mahomet;* he was also called *Bode ta Courou*,[2] signifying "great lord"; he married the wife of the king who was slain at Malé by the Portuguese. The younger was called *Assan Quilague*, and married the daughter of the same king, so that the two brothers had for their wives a mother and daughter. That deceased king had a son, who, on seeing these brothers become kings, never came to court, and was allowed to live in peace. I have seen him many a time, and his sister too. These two kings had great difficulty in maintaining their position, for they had risen from low estate, and there were some always on the point of revolt; but the kings never gave them time to do anything, for as soon as they got the slightest word or suspicion of their intentions, they took the proper measures. As it happened, the elder brother only had a son, while the younger had a daughter, who was of

[1] The terms of the treaty as between the Portuguese and the Maldive princes *de facto*, do not appear in the Portuguese records. The tribute payable by the ex-king to the Portuguese treasury is frequently alluded to. From the King of Spain's despatch of the 10th January 1587, it appears that Dom Manoel (Hassan) engaged to pay, and did pay, to the Portuguese 500 bahars of coir (*Arch. Port. Or.*, Fasc. 3, No. 23). If Pyrard is right in saying that his tribute was one-third of what he received, the Maldive tribute would be 1,500 bahars of coir. In 1606 the ex-king Dom Filippe complained to the King of Spain that his revenue, which formerly amounted to 18,000 xerafins, had dwindled to 5,000 (*Liv. das Monç.*, i, 147).

[2] *Bodu takuru;* the title shows that he was not of royal or even of high birth.

noble birth on her mother's side,—for in that land nobility passes by the mother as well as by the father. The son of the elder was the king we found there, who was not of lineage so good as the daughter (of the younger), for his mother was taken by the king for her beauty alone. And there they have many wives, but there is always one who is the chief, though all are lawful wives.

Subsequently, the younger of the two kings being fallen into a grievous sickness, it befell that his wife's brother, who was the greatest noble in the land, revolted against them. He bore the name of his island and fortress, to wit, *Misdoue Quilague*.[1] This island, which I have visited, is 30 leagues distant from Malé towards the south, in the atollon *Nilandoue*. Thither the elder brother proceeded in force with secrecy and despatch, bidding them say nothing to his brother, who was sick unto death. At length this lord was taken and put to death, and all his island pillaged. But when the news reached Malé, his sister, the younger's wife, had such sorrow that she wished for death, and they had some pains to prevent her laying hands on herself in her despair; whereupon her husband, all sick though he was, swore that if God should give him health again, his brother should rue it. For all that he died of that sickness, and men said that he was more valiant than his brother.

The reason why this elder brother despatched these great lords was, that he knew that his son would be king, and he misliked that such rivals should exist; for the son was still young, and was never like to be as valiant as his father. And so his humour turned out, as I to some extent saw, for he was in nowise inclined to war, but solely to letters, sciences, and manufactures, and he was also much given to women, as, indeed, was nothing remarkable in that land. It

[1] *Mídú*, the island of the *Mí* tree. It is omitted in the Adm. Chart, but lies on the N.E. of South Nilandu atoll, in lat. 3° N. It is inhabited. The revolt of this lord, *Midu kilaye-fánu*, is still known in tradition.

is highly necessary to be valiant there, for the stronger wins the day, and they that would rule must slay the kings that be. Three were once slain in a year, the memory whereof keeps the kings in perpetual fear and apprehension. This elder brother lived three years after the death of the younger, and had his son acknowledged for king before his death, causing all his servants and subjects to swear allegiance to him.

During the lifetime of these two kings a great ship was wrecked on their island, in which were a great number of men, as well Indians as Portuguese, and among others a young boy, seven years of age, of Portuguese and Indian birth. For him the two brothers conceived an affection as great as though he were their own son, and had him brought up in like manner at the house of the elder; there he kept the king's son company, both being of the same age, and was made to adopt their faith. He was one of the finest boys one could see, of such high spirit, that, as I heard from all the natives, he attained in perfection to all their sciences and accomplishments.

The elder king caused him to be instructed in all kinds of exercises, in like manner and with like respect as his own son; while he, finding himself in this condition, believed himself to be brother to the young prince, going everywhere as his peer. But when he grew to years of discretion the kings bade tell him who he was, and advised him to be ever a good and faithful servant of the prince and future king. Moreover, after the death of the younger brother, the other made him marry his brother's daughter, the noblest and richest match in the kingdom; her he would like to have given in marriage to his own son, did not their law forbid the marriage of cousins-german; wherefore, for fear lest some other great lord of the realm should get her and make war upon his son, he preferred to give her to this young man, in whom he had perfect trust and confidence, as being his own creature; also he considered that, as a stranger, he could have no pretension to the throne.

After the death of his father the young prince peaceably succeeded; the young Mestif lord became daily more brave and gallant, more beloved and honoured of the people and all the foreigners. He was admiral, or *Vellanas*, and one of the six elders or *Mouscoulis*, and captain of a company, or, as they call it, a *Sardare*.[1] So then, seeing that the king was no warrior nor addicted to arms, while he himself was greatly esteemed for his valour, he became presumptuous, and began to despise the king and to pay him but little regard; wherefore the king entertained some jealousy, and feared lest the youth, enjoying all that favour and goodwill with the world, should take it into his head to dispossess him; so he took counsel with his friends, and resolved to put him to death rather than run the risk of greater troubles. Yet he could hardly bring his mind to do it, as well for the friendship he bore him as for the special trust regarding him wherewith his father on his death-bed had charged him, and further, that he was married to his cousin. Notwithstanding these considerations he continued his designs, being prompted by information brought to him daily, that this man was secretly treating with the Portuguese to make them masters of the kingdom and get himself made king under them. On his part he lacked not warning of the king's ill-will towards him, and could full well have saved himself had he been so minded; but he heeded not, saying that he was innocent of the charges against him. So one day, the king sending for him at an unwonted hour, though he doubted it would go ill with him, yet on that account he omitted not to go, nor indeed had he time to refuse. On his arrival in the great hall of the palace, where the king sat awaiting him with all his lords and guards, he made a profound reverence to the king, who saluted him in return, and bade him be seated in his proper

[1] M. *sarudáru*, Pers. *sardár*.

place. This he did, and forthwith issued from behind the tapestry, men with ropes and arms, who seized and bound him, and then dragging him along the ground, carried him to a place on the seashore, about a thousand paces off, where they put him into a boat and slew him, and then cast his body into the sea. When his wife heard of it she fell into such grief and sorrow that it was more than two years ere she would see the king or the queens, or even go to the palace. He left a son, who was fifteen years old when I left the Maldives, and was not at all like the Indians, being as fair as men of these parts. Such was the end of this unfortunate lord—an example to all foreigners who would rise above their condition in these lands and elsewhere.

Some time after this king lost his father, he began to ill-treat the wife that survived him, who was his own step-mother, and was called *Manaye Quilague*,[1] and whom his dying father had especially commended to his care; whereupon, in her indignation, she was resolved to be avenged. She had a brother who was one of the captains of the realm, very rich and valiant, named *Pammedery Calogue*,[2] whose son, a man of high breeding, was afterwards one of my greatest friends. This woman, then, and her brother conspired against the king's life, with design to make this boy king and his father lieutenant-general, and to divide all the offices of state among those of their faction. But their enterprise was discovered, and the king had them seized and forthwith given over to justice, swearing an oath that whatever justice should ordain should be carried out without hope of pardon. They had their hands cut off, this brother being the first to suffer, and were then exiled to *Souadou*. As for the step-mother, she was bereft of all she had, as also was her brother, and she was even tortured to make her dis-

[1] Perhaps a misprint for *Manike*, the fem. of *Maniku*.

[2] *Fámudéri kaloge-fánu.* Probably this *calogue* is a mistake for *quilague:* the former being an inferior title.

cover her treasure. So little security was there in the political estate of the Maldive king; treasons and attempts were practised upon him day by day, and the spoil remained to the stronger.

There was afterwards another revolt, which lasted a long time, during which this king was forced to quit the island of Malé, and retire to another called *Gouradou*,[1] ten leagues off. This revolt was raised by a great lord of the country, named *Parenae tacourou*,[2] who had a number of galleys and big ships, with which he pillaged and ravaged all the islands whereat he cast anchor. The king withdrew to this island of Gouradou because the access to it was narrow and exceeding difficult, and a very expert pilot was required to find the passage. This lord, then, became so strong and puissant that wheresoever he landed he caused to be borne over his head a white parasol, called *ou du ad*,[3] which is a mark of royalty; and in all other respects he made himself served and obeyed as king, distributing and granting to his followers the revenues and offices of the state. But after the king had sent against him many ships and men at arms, at length he was caught: for I shall say, in passing, this king never went to war himself, he only despatched forces; nor was he valiant like his father, who always went in person, and as soon as he heard of anyone bestirring himself, he gave him no time, but took measures at once.

As for this rebellious lord, the cause of his capture was that while his galleys were in the south of the islands, the currents then running east bore the greater part of them to Achen, in Sumatra, and the remnant of the force, thus weakened, were all taken. Most of the men were put to

[1] *Gurádú*, in S. Málé atoll, lat. 3° 53′ N. In this island, according to Pyrard, the Sultan afterwards found his grave.

[2] *I.e.*, the *Fáruná*, the minister next in rank to the *Quilague*.

[3] Now *hudu hai*; *i.e.*, *hudu* or *sudu*, "white" (as in Sin.), and *hai* = Sin. *sat*, "umbrella".

death with their leader, and the remainder only had a hand cut of, and were then sent into exile: for thus it is enacted by their law that those who conspire against their prince, or make attempts on his person, have their right hand cut off. Of those who were carried to Achen, some returned after a time, the king extending to them his grace and pardon.

With regard to these currents, of which I have just spoken, they run for six whole months (each way), so that if a vessel happens to be at the northern extremity of the islands it is no great matter, for then it is only carried to Cochin, on the coast of India, or thereabouts, about 150 leagues distance, or to some of the islands along that coast. But if they cannot make the island of Ceylon, they are carried to Sumatra, a distance of about 500 leagues; and if ill-luck has it that these currents carry them away at the close of the *Monsons*[1] or Seasons (when the current carries them, they call that *behigue*[2]), and before they make land anywhere, they are caught in the other current; as often happens, they are infallibly lost, as I have seen in a number of cases, when they were expecting to make land every night, and were without water and other provisions. If the current carries them to the west, they are borne straight to the Arabian coast, which is much further off than that of Sumatra; but most often they are dead before they get there. One day I saw a boat which had been carried off by these currents, and while it was a long way out, suddenly the currents changed and brought it back to these islands; but most of those on board were dead, and the rest only skin and bone, to such straits had they been reduced.

I have made mention above of Gouradou. I was at that

[1] *Monsoons.* As to the history of this word, see Dozy and Engelmann, *Gloss.*, and Yule, *Gloss.* Pyrard writes also *monssons*, *muesons*, and *muessons*.

[2] Correctly *behigeṇ gos*, "sailing with the wind and current"; *cf.* Sin. *bæhigana gos*. The old English phrase was "spooming along before the sea", as used by Drake.

island one day, and saw the mast and rudder of the ship that was lost there, wherein was the foreign queen who died in child-bed while I was about the king. I was told that it was the richest ship conceivable. It had on board some 500 persons, men, women, and children, for the Indians take the greater part of their household to sea with them. These 500 persons were nigh all drowned, and there remained but a hundred saved. This queen's father and mother, to whom the ship belonged, were among those that perished, and she, at that time but a child, was saved by chance. This ship came from Sunda, laden with all kinds of spices and other merchandize of China and Sunda. Judging merely from the mast of this vessel, I thought it the largest I had ever seen, for the mast was taller and thicker than those of Portuguese carracks; and the king of the Maldives built a shed of the length of the mast to keep it as a curiosity. I saw also another mast and a top much larger than those of Portugal. Thus was I led to believe that in the Indies they build vessels larger and of better material than in Portugal or anywhere else in the world. The greatest ships come from the coast of Arabia, Persia, and Mogor,[1] and some have as many as 2,000 persons on board. They build not their ships with as many decks as we, for they have but one, the main deck, and below they have none, not even a 'tween deck; as for their water, they keep it not in pipes and jars as we do; but on each side of the main-mast, which goes down to the ship's bottom, they fix two wooden cisterns, well joined and secured, so that the water is well preserved, and there are merely holes for drawing the water as from a well. These are of greater capacity than our pipes,

[1] *I.e.*, the coasts of the present Scinde and Guzerat, and such ports, including Surat, as were not in possession of the Portuguese. The application of the word *Mogor* to the territories of the Great Mogul is adopted by the author from Portuguese use. See Yule's *Glossary*, s. v. "Mogul".

and take up less room. But I observe that our system of pipes is better, for one reason, namely, that if any accident happens to these cisterns they lose all their water at once. It is not so with us, for in case of a cannon-shot, all that can happen is the loss of one or two pipes; or if any one goes bad, all the water is not spoiled. Throughout the whole of India they nowhere use our system of pipes. They use only certain handsome jars, of finer shape and lacquer than I have seen elsewhere. Some of these will hold as much as one pipe, or even more. They are made in the kingdom of *Martabane*,[1] whence they are exported, and take their name throughout all India. The water never goes bad in them, and the jars are kept shut by a key.

But to return to this ship of the queen, which was lost at the island of Gouradou, I would tell what, during the time I was there, befell an honorable, rich, and discreet merchant of Bengal, called *Mouhamede Oaca*, and his wife, also a foreigner, and very beautiful and fair-complexioned for those parts. She was called *Canboé Boubou*, *Canboé* being her personal name in the language of Bengal, and *Boubou*[2] signifying Mademoiselle. Both were wrecked with the queen; they were her slaves, and were about thirty years of age, and had no children. The queen had such an affection toward them that she made them

[1] Mr. Bell saw some large earthenware jars at Málé, some about two feet high, called *rumbá*, and others larger and barrel-shaped, called *mátabán*. The name seems to survive also on the Madras coast; *e.g.*, we find in Mr. P. Brown's *Zillah Dictionary* (1852), "Martaban—name of a place in Pegu: a black jar in which rice is imported from thence." Linschoten (i, 101) writes: "In this towne (Martaban) many of the great earthen pots are made, which in India are called *Martauanas*, and many of them carryed throughout all India of all sorts, both small and great: some are so great that they hold full two pipes of water." See also *op. cit.*, p. 268; and Yule's *Glossary*, s. v. "Martaban", where the quotation from Ibn Batuta shows that the term was current in the fourteenth century.

[2] *Búbú* is a Hind. term for lady, used in the same way as *bíbí*, though perhaps of different origin.

stewards of her household, and placed all her confidence in them, seeing that they had been about her in their youth; thus they rose to extraordinary wealth, to credit and favour with her majesty: but no sooner was their kind mistress dead, in manner already described, than every kind of misfortune and disaster overtook them. Theirs was the happiest home in the world, the fullest of concord and love; but, as misfortune would have it, their house adjoined the warehouse or lodging of the factor of the Christian king at Goa, who always has one such at these islands. This factor was a man of Cochin, of the race of Gentile Canarins, but baptised and naturalised as a Portuguese in dress and manners. He had been baptised as a child, and had a wife and children at Cochin; he was called Simon Rodrigue, and was at this time about twenty-seven years of age. It is customary not to leave these clerks or factors there, when they are Christians, for more than a year or two, so as they may come and render their duty to the Church, for in these islands there is no exercise of the Christian religion; but this fellow would not return so soon, and remained there four years. He learned exceedingly well the language and customs of the country, and made himself so agreeable to the king, and to all the inhabitants, that although he was recalled, and three other clerks one after another were sent to succeed him, yet he managed so cleverly, by making presents to the king, that he had not to budge. The king also, being written to, answered that he would not detain him, but could not and would not force him to go against his will. So this clerk and the merchant's wife being neighbours, fell into an intrigue of the closest kind, and indulged their amours at their ease, the merchant being often absent at his trading.

This continued for the space of two years without discovery; but at length the husband became aware of it, and getting certain information by means of spies, resolved to have his satisfaction. The more easily to attain his end, he made as though he were going abroad for a fortnight, according to his wont. He equipped a barque in the usual way, took leave of his wife, commending all his affairs to her keeping, and departed; but after nightfall he put back to land, and about eleven o'clock at night went straight to his wife's bedchamber, and finding her not in her bed, he presently went to the palace to find the king, who used never to retire till after midnight. The first person he met was the master of the galleys and all the king's ships, who was to all appearance an intimate friend of the factor; yet, as an instance of the faithlessness of these people, he was the first to apprise the king, and to assist the merchant in obtaining justice, as we shall see hereafter. The husband, on being introduced to the king's presence, made his complaint that his wife was abed with a Christian, whom they call *Caparou*,[1] and that he and his wife were Mahometans, whom they call *Mousseliman*,[2] that is, the faithful, and that his majesty should be pleased to have justice done. On hearing this, the king ordered the master of the galleys to take twelve soldiers of the guard, and to put the factor to death, and cast his body in the sea. These men forthwith surrounded his house, and knocked at his door to gain admittance. The poor factor was so astonished he knew not what to do, yet trusting to the king's friendship for him, and to the master, who cried out to him to open the door, with assurance of safety, he was so ill-advised as to open it, then throwing himself at his feet, prayed him to save his life; but he was slain on the spot, the other being the first to strike him. At this result those who had owed him money were well enough pleased, as also was the king, who wanted to be possessed of his great wealth, the which he seized incontinently. The Portuguese, too, were not annoyed; and thenceforth it was arranged that the

[1] Ar. *kafir*, "infidel".

[2] *I.e.*, *Muslimân*, the Persian plural of *Muslim*, but widely adopted as a singular, as in our form *Mussulman*.

factors should no longer be men of Cochin, but of the islands. The unfortunate man being thus slain, the husband went straight to his wife to do the like to her; but he was with difficulty restrained, and she was cast into prison, to come up for judgment thereafter. At first it was proposed to drown her, but seeing that the man was dead, and his goods seized, they were content to punish her in the usual manner, as all others are who are taken in adultery or lewd practices, but somewhat more rigorously. Her husband refused even to see her, and got married again, this time to a young girl of the country, as I shall tell hereafter,[1] with what came of that marriage.

To return to the king of the Maldives. Some years after the death of his father he became enamoured of a married woman, the fairest in complexion and beauty in all the land, and abandoned his first wife, whom his father had made him espouse, in order to get this woman, who had three daughters as fair as herself, all married to princes and great lords. I have often seen her arm, as she showed it to us out of coquetry, and it was as white as that of the fairest in our country here. Her husband was a pilot, the cleverest in the country in his profession and in trade, and a man of large means. The king and this woman loved each other much, and he was minded to marry her, while she daily strove to persuade her husband to consent to leave her, but he would do nothing; wherefore in her anger she advised the king to put him to death. This the king for the love of her resolved to do; and having sent for him one day to give him some information about navigation on the country chart, when the man came, and was making his obeisance, the king gave him a blow with a dagger, intending to plant it in his abdomen, but the man raised his hand to parry the stroke, and turned the dagger straight into his eye, which it put out. He was not otherwise hurt, for I saw him often afterwards. He

[1] P. 265.

was an agreeable companion, and he it was who gave me the news of our mate and comrades who escaped from the island of *Pouladou,* having himself seen them chained by the feet. So, to return to this woman, she got the king to marry her, but, after living together for a while, he fell in love with her who was the chief queen while we were there, and so got tired of the other,—who, in truth, was the lewdest woman in the world, abandoning herself indifferently to all sorts of men, slaves, as well as others. Yet that was not the sole cause why the king left her.

Now the king had two nephews, brothers, of whom the elder was married to the richest young lady in all the islands, the grand-daughter of the governor of the country under the Portuguese rule. She was also sister to the prince, who came to our ship, and with whom the king was so annoyed that he boxed his ears, as I have related above.[1] This lady was of noble birth, young and beautiful, and so the king became enamoured of her; but the mischief was that her husband would not leave her, nor she him: for she had no ambition to be queen, preferring her first condition and liberty. The husband and wife, then, aware of the king's intentions, resolved to escape in a barque along with a younger brother, who afterwards died with the king, as I shall tell hereafter; but while carrying out their plan they were unluckily surprised at their setting out: the king's galleys caught them and brought them back to Malé, where the poor husband was constrained to quit his wife, for sorrow whereof he was for a whole year without going beyond his house, and so died. It was also much against the will of the young lady,—as, indeed, she afterwards showed, for she never bore the king any goodwill, and always had other male friends.

Before marrying her, the king was constrained to leave his other wife, who would not by any means consent to quit

[1] P. 69.

him, for a separation must needs be by the free will and consent of both parties, otherwise the man restores her dowry to the woman, and then quits her whether she will or no; but it is dishonourable and scandalous for a woman to take it. This the king did in the case of this first queen, for he gave her her dowry and rank, and left her, and then married the other. The former remained unmarried ever after, for the king did not permit her to marry again, and without that none would dare to espouse her. Her first husband would not speak to her again, although they had had three daughters of their marriage. The king liked this man much, and did him many benefits. This lady was very gay in her dress, pearls, and jewels, and the king gave her a fine house in the island, where she resided at her ease in all respects, but without marrying again. She spent her time in pleasure, and was much visited, and had a large retinue of servants and slaves. As for the other, the king never afterwards abandoned her; and when he was killed she was still with him, with two foreign women; but she always maintained her regret for her first husband, who was, as it were, first prince of the blood, and lieutenant-general of the forces. The king being now well on in years, and having reared no children while he was young, saw that those he might now have would be still young when he came to die, and would be liable to be set aside and bereft of their inheritance; he therefore resolved to have no more: and accordingly, while I was there I heard that for four or five years he had no intercourse with this chief queen, because she was very prolific, and had already by him a son and a daughter, both of whom died at six or seven years of age. And yet these people have no scruples in killing the child in its mother's womb, deeming it better for them so to die than come into the world. But the queens had no great concern that the king went not to see them, for they were never in want of male friends, who used to visit them when they pleased.

But to return to the merchant of Bengal, that would not take back his wife, as related above. He married another woman, who was thought to be the most lovely in all the islands: and in truth she was no whit inferior to the fairest in these parts, save that her skin was not quite so white. She was eighteen or twenty years of age, and was chosen by him for her beauty alone, being neither noble nor rich: he, however, had plenty of means for both. Now a second misfortune befell him, for as he lived near the royal palace, no sooner did the king set eyes on this wife, than he became violently enamoured of her, and having attained his desire, even compelled her to separate from her husband, whom he threatened to cast into the sea, should he refuse to consent, insomuch that the unfortunate man was constrained to quit her with all possible regret; and, three months before the great Maldive disaster, the king took her to wife, because the Pandiare told him that, to free his conscience, it were better for him to marry her than to continue in the sin wherein he was. Such were the misfortunes that befell this poor merchant one upon another, which had never occurred but for the death of his kind mistress.

CHAPTER XIX.

The Maldives, when peopled.—Of many other memorable events which occurred at these islands and in the neighbourhood, during the sojourn of the author there.—Of a vessel of Tananor, and the story of a Malabar captain's dealing with the Maldive king, and his hapless fate; and the adventures of the king's nephew and brother-in-law.

Having described the Maldive polity, and the more remarkable events that happened before fortune cast us there, I now come to speak of the most singular and memorable occurrences during the space of five years I resided there. But first I must not forget to tell what I learned of the islanders concerning the first peopling of the Maldives, and how the inhabitants changed their religion.

They hold that the Maldives began to be inhabited only four hundred years ago, and that the first who came and peopled them were (as I have already said, in passing) the Cingalles[1] of the island of Ceylan,[2] which is not far distant, and were idolaters, but afterwards changed their religion, it being about one hundred and fifty or two hundred years at most since they received Mahometism, through the Moorish and Arabian navigators, who, while trading over all the continent and islands of the East Indies, brought there also their law, which has since remained in most of those parts. It also appears that it was then that the Tartars, who extended their dominion throughout the East, and even to these islands,[3] became infected with this accursed and false doctrine of Mahomet, which has wasted three-fourths of the world. The Maldive people have ever since retained this law, as I have fully described in my treatment of their religion and ceremonies.

I come now to what happened at the islands in my time, and to these facts my testimony will be good and sufficient, for I either witnessed or was personally acquainted with the greater part of them.

I will begin with what happened to a vessel of Tananor,[4] which came to trade there a year after our arrival at the

[1] From the Port. form *Chingalas*. The native adjectival form is *Sinhala*.

[2] All the earlier writers spell Ceylon with an *a*, as the French do still; the native name is *Lankáva*. For the evolution of the name Ceylon, see Yule's *Glossary*.

[3] This, of course, is a mistake. The Maldives were never in subjection to the Tartars, by whom he means the Moguls, nor indeed to any Indian power except, perhaps, to the Raja of Cananor.

[4] *Tanur*.

islands. This vessel was about five hundred tons burthen, and belonged to the king of Tananor, a kingdom situate between Calicut and Cochin. This king was a Gentile, and of the race of Nairs. There may have been aboard some five or six hundred men, well armed, good Malabar soldiers, and they came there to trade. Their principal cargo was rice, but they had much other merchandise, such as pepper, areca (which is eaten with betel), cotton, butter, oils for rubbing the body after washing, a quantity of white cotton cloths, pottery, iron and copper utensils: so that it was very rich, and their purpose was to barter all these for the merchandise of the country. But the Maldive king would not let them tarry in the roadstead of Malé more than three days, and then sent them to cast anchor at an island called *Bandos*, where I had been sick, distant about two leagues north from Malé. The reason of this was that he was afraid they meditated some treasonable surprise. He caused all their fighting men to disembark, all well armed and equipped, in good health and ready for action. But they had not been there more than two months ere they were all dying of the fever, although the air and water of that island Bandos is better than at Malé. Most of the men remained at Malé, all their goods being placed in cellars and *banquesalles*, constructed for the purpose. They were there six months and more, bargaining and selling and loading their ship; but during that time the island fever wasted them so cruelly, that there remained no more than a hundred of them alive, and those enfeebled in such wise that they were constrained to engage another crew of the islanders to work the ship back to Tananor. It was a most experienced pilot of these islands who brought them there, wherefore they bore him much ill-will, saying that he had brought them there on purpose to make his king heir to all their riches. At the islands they lost the chief of their captains, whom they regretted much. The rule is, when the captain or master of a vessel dies there, the vessel and cargo go to the king, who seizes them; but this was not so in this case, because it belonged to the king of Tananor.

As for the private property of the deceased captain, it was not taken by the king, although it appertained to him; but this was for the reason following. That captain had brought with him his son, a young man of twenty-five, called *Houssains Caca*,[1] the bravest soldier, the most noble gentleman in address and figure, and the most skilful gunner in all the coast of Malabar. Desiring that he should stay with him, the king worked him with the fairest promises, wherewith the young man was satisfied, as well in order to save the goods which the king gave over to him in their entirety for so consenting, as by reason of a difference he had with the second captain, who was then in command of the vessel. Moreover, the king caused to be delivered to him all his goods that were on board, which he had never otherwise got out; besides which, by remaining there, he became heir to all his father's goods, which he must have shared with his other brothers had he returned to his own country, and would have had to pay for most of what his father had got on credit. He was thus welcomed and esteemed by the king, who moreover granted to him a high dignity, viz., that of master of arms, called by them *Esdru*,[2] one of the most honourable offices in the land, requiring great capacity and experience. The king had only one such in his islands, and he was a great lord, as, indeed, the like officers are considered among the nobles and soldiers, as well in these

[1] Persian *kâkâ*, an uncle; used also among the Mâppiḻḻar of Malabar as a term of respect, and sometimes by other classes when addressing respectable Mâppiḻḻar.

[2] M. *eduru*, or, according to the fuller title, *eduru maniku*. Though the office has no doubt lost its importance since the Maldives came within the *pax Britannica*, and the profession of arms became a mere pastime, there are still four of these fencing-masters at Málé, who are held in some respect (Bell).

islands as on the continent. But this appointment caused the death of the young man, by reason of the jealousy which ensued between him and the former master, who was a native of the country, and the son of a previous master, and was much respected by all the lords and soldiers.

With these people there is no greater mark of dishonour and disgrace than the loss of respect between their masters and them. And since arms are held in such high honour, they respect masters in arms more than all others, and exalt them to the rank of princes and lords, for they give instruction to the king and the chief prince. Aforetime there was but one academy, so, when this new master came, there were two, and many of all ranks quitted the old master for the new, seeing that he knew the use of arms according to the system of the Nairs and Malabars, which is esteemed the best in the Indies.[1] And the king, in order that he should be recognised as a master, presented to him, in the presence of all the court, a bracelet, which he placed on his arm with his own hands, that being the badge of this office. This bracelet was a link of gold with buttons of the same, round, and hollow within, containing the royal sign and cipher written on paper.

These two masters, then, being jealous of one another, it came to pass on the day of a great festival, such as Easter is with us, that after dinner, according to custom, all the princes, lords, gentlemen, and soldiers went to the king's palace for an assault of arms, and to challenge one another, whereby it is seen who are most adroit in the use of arms. This lasts for three days. These two masters stood on opposite sides with their scholars beside them, and these went forth to fence one with another. The elder master had more scholars, and was more popular than the other, against whom he got up an idle brawl, setting one of his

[1] The *panikan*, or fencing-master, was held in great respect on the Malabar coast. See Yule's *Glossary*, s. v.

scholars against one of the other,—for there, to lay the blame on a scholar, is to attack the master. So arose a great *mêlée* between the two parties, and some soldiers were wounded. When the king heard of it, he wanted to know who was to blame, and being informed that it was the elder, he reprimanded him severely, and said aloud that the first of them that should cause any mischief should have his hand cut off: this he often caused to be done, even for trifles, when he was in anger; and both masters he ordered to live peaceably, themselves and their scholars. Nevertheless, the friendship which the king bore to the new master was ever increasing, in such wise that he gave him all the titles of honour he could confer on the greatest in the realm, among others, that of *Darade Tacourou*,[1] as who should say "Count" or "Duke". Further, he made him change his former Malabar name, by proclamation throughout the island, as the custom is, and made him captain of a company, and caused him to walk with the highest grandees as their equal. These latter conceived such envy towards him, that they resolved, in concert with the elder master, to work his death any way they could. In truth, the man did not know how to steer in his course of prosperity, for he abused it, and often started a quarrel with the chief men, and even with the highest grandees of the islands; but the king supported him in everything. He took in marriage such women as he pleased, and they thought themselves highly honoured in being married to him, as much for his personal merit as for his dignity and favour with the king. And what was a further advantage to him, he had for his comrade and scholar the king's brother-in-

[1] M. *Dáharā Takuru* (*fanu*). As above indicated, this was a mere title in Pyrard's time, and so it remained down to Christopher's time, by whom it is assigned to the sixth vizier, without special duties (*T. Bom. Geo. Soc.*, i, 71). In Ibn Batuta's day the *deherd*, as he calls him, was commander-in-chief. The title seems to have fallen into abeyance now.

law, the brother of the chief queen, of whom I have frequently spoken; these two held each other in such friendship, that this was at length the cause of his downfall: for, at the end of two years, during which this favour lasted, they resolved to go away together, and he (the master), the better to conceal his enterprise, took in marriage a widow of the grand Pandiare, who resided at the southern end of the islands, in the atollon called *Souadou*. For this purpose he took occasion to depart from Malé; but he was no sooner gone, than his enemies, feeling that the game was now won, went and told the king, giving him to understand the nature of his enterprise with the prince. The king forthwith took counsel with his principal advisers, the six Mouscoulis, and sent a captain with forty soldiers in a barque to bring him back, at the same time ordering them to do him no harm. But all the chiefs then about the king, and among others the former master, gave secret instructions that they should put him to death, and then say that he had opposed his arrest by force of arms, so should they make their peace with the king. All which they carried out, for they found him at the first halting-place, without arms, and there they slew him, and brought back word to the king that they were forced to do it, seeing he would not render himself up at the king's command. The king was grievously vexed, but took no further steps in the matter.

Having spoken of the fortunes of this stranger, I shall now tell of what I saw befall some of the princes of the country. At the time of our arrival there, the king had no children, but only a nephew, aged twenty-two, and called, like himself, *Ibraim Callam*.[1] This prince ought to have succeeded him. At that time he was in disgrace, and absent from the court, because he had gone to Arabia without taking

[1] *Callam* is probably the Pers. *Kalân*, "great": this is the only place in the text where the title is applied to an individual. The word, however, appears in the Vocabulary for "prince"; and see above, p. 209.

or getting leave of the king, and before going had pillaged some of the islands. Three years after our coming he returned, but dared not come to Malé at the first for fear of the king, who was presently apprised of his arrival at some islands in the north, which belonged to him, and at which he was married. The king received the news with joy, for he loved him and treated him as his son. But false news was brought to his ears daily, that his nephew had designs against him; and this was done by those who wished him ill, and by flatterers, of whom this court was full. Notwithstanding this, the king delayed not to send an armed galley to fetch him, while he, being innocent, made no scruples about coming to the king with only ten or a dozen of a body-guard, and some servants and slaves. But as soon as he arrived at the court, all his soldiers were cast into prison, with their feet passed through two pieces of wood in which holes were cut, which is their mode of securing prisoners. They also use chains and irons for this purpose. As for the prince, he suffered nothing, but that he was two months without seeing the king, though he came day by day to the palace, and sat in the place assigned to the public in general. One of the queens, the first of them, sent him a single leaf of betel, and that was a great honour, and the highest he could hope for: for that is done to the royal children alone, and this distinction of itself showed him to be sole heir to the throne, and chief prince. It is the custom of the country, when one is in disgrace, to go every day to the palace and to wait in the court there until the king speaks to him, and takes him again into favour. The nephew was at length received into favour by means of the grand Pandiare, who was of the Cherife[1] race, that is, of the race of Mahomet. For, being sent for by the king to preach before him as usual, before beginning his sermon, he made a

[1] Sherif, a descendant of Hassan through either of his sons, Zaid and Hassan el-Musanna.

humble request and petition to the king that he would be pleased to permit his nephew to come and hear the sermon, the which the king granted, for the friendship and respect he had for the Pandiare: nor would any but he have dared to make the request. The nephew came, and from a distance catching sight of the king, made a most profound reverence, like the lowest subject of the realm; whereupon the king said but two words, *Ana poute iringua*,[1] which is to say, "My son, be seated." This he did, everyone rising to yield him the highest place. While the sermon lasted, which was more than an hour, the young prince lifted not his eyes nor his head; and the same day all his attendants were set free, and he was forthwith received into favour, and treated with the honour and dignity proper to the heir to the crown. The king made him his lieutenant-general, and commander of all his men-at-arms, or as they call it, *Dorimesnas*.[2]

After he was restored to the king's good graces, there was always great jealousy between him and the king's brother-in-law, the chief queen's brother, who had been well enough pleased at the absence and disgrace of this prince, seeing that thereby he was nearest to the king's favour, and held the highest offices, which were now taken from him on the return of the prince. The king always called him his son, to the end that all the world should honour him as his true and legitimate heir. This prince, once, being enamoured of a certain lord's wife, who was of extreme beauty, he carried her off with her own consent, and kept her a long while, whereof the husband made complaint to the king, but got not any satisfaction; indeed, the young prince had

[1] Mr. Bell thinks this should be *Anádé futá irindé*, "Come, son, be seated". *Futá*, "son" (Sin. *puta*), is now used only in the southern atolls; in the north and at Málé, the word is *darifulá*.

[2] At present the *Doriméná kilage-fanu* and the *Doriméná maniku-fanu* have nothing to do with the soldiers; and, indeed, no such appointment has been made during the present reign.

him beaten in such wise that he was fain to give his wife up altogether. Such is the way of them in that country.

As for the king's brother-in-law, the rival of this prince, he was a young lord, aged about twenty-five years, one of the handsomest men in figure and accomplishments in the islands, resembling more those of Europe, as he was fair, though slightly olive in complexion. He was learned in all the sciences, as mathematics, astrology, navigation, etc., and in the exercise of arms. I taught him to cipher and write in French; and in truth I never found any difference between those people and ourselves, whether in mind or body, save that they are slightly olive, yet withal there are many fair persons, both men and women. His sister and he were of the best family in the country, being of nobler birth than the king himself. So this lord, in chagrin for the loss of his offices at the nephew's return, began to take counsel with his sister, the queen, as to the means of avenging himself; and her anger against the prince was greater than his. The first means they took was by charms and sorceries, which are very frequently employed, to work both good and evil. In this business they employed many to work sorceries, which they call *Quenuery*,[1] against both the king and his nephew, who were made very sick thereby, and had to get other sorcerers to cure them. The king ever after this was exceeding wroth with the queen and her brother. But she hated the king to the death, and had long wished to put an end to him, if she had had the opportunity, for she was tired of being kept by force as a captive, and she was never satisfied; and being so rich and noble in her own right, she cared nothing for the honour of being queen, and would have liked a husband of her own choice. So her brother and she, seeing that their first measures had not succeeded, resolved to try another, viz., to escape secretly by night in a barque, with all her trinkets, jewels, and wealth,—for all the rest of her property was in

[1] M. *kanveri-kan*.

another island belonging to her, called *Maspillaspoury*,[1] forty leagues to the north of Malé, where her mother, a widow, resided.

The prince, having framed his project, communicated the enterprise to the foreign master of arms of whom I have spoken above, and to another lord, whose father the king's father had in former days put to death, for fear lest he should rise against him, being as he was one of the most valiant lords in the kingdom: he was called *Cassin Tacourou*. So, too, this young lord his son was very brave, and very ill content that he was but a simple soldier, and had not the rank of his ancestors, wherefore he gave ear to the prince, who was in other respects his great friend, and promised him the queen in marriage; while to the foreign master he promised another sister that he had. Their design was that the prince and the young lord should remain in the island to carry off the queen, while the master should go on before, as he did. Now it is a custom of the islands that the soldiers carry no arms when they go forth from Malé to the other islands; all must be left in the magazine of the king, to whom they belong. They carry, indeed, daggers and other small-arms, but not fire-arms; but when they go anywhither by command of the king, they may carry all sorts of arms. This is to prevent revolt; also, a certain number of soldiers only are allowed to go at the same time, and the return of these is awaited ere others are allowed to go; and this leave is given only during the westerly winds, which is their winter, and they have to return before the easterly winds, which is their summer time.

In the conduct of this enterprise they won over to their party thirteen of the best soldiers in the country, but one of the thirteen discovered them, and gave warning to the

[1] *Máfiláfurhi*, in Fadiffolu atoll (*Marfile-foori* in the Adm. Ch.), in lat. 5° 20′ N., apparently not inhabited now. The name would seem to mean, the island of the *Mâpillar*.

king, who bade keep all secret: for he was hardly able to believe it, and wished to see what it really was. So he commissioned that lord who had brought me from the island where we were lost, and in whom he had most confidence, to take a certain number of soldiers and to find out the truth. This being done, the barque was seized, with the prince and his soldiers, who were all punished in the usual manner. As for him, he got no more than a severe reprimand from the king, and was kept in disgrace more than six months. It is to be noted that during their disgrace they have no care to dress themselves, or to deport themselves in the proper style, and they take no more part in affairs than if they were dead to the world. As for the queen, though the king was very angry with her, she said but four words to him, and he was at once appeased. What befell the master of arms I have already related. After this, on the day of the feast of the dead, when the king with his three wives went to visit the sepulchres of his ancestors, the queen caused her brother to be at a place where they had to pass, and there he came, plainly attired and without arms, as the custom was, and saluted the king, who returned his salutation and took him back into favour, and conferred upon him again all his offices and dignities. He was one of the six chief *Mouscoulis*. All the soldiers that were in this affair were at once set free, and restored to their former position. Albeit, this prince, being a man of spirit, as he afterwards showed himself, finding that he was not restored to all his offices, nor held in the same consideration as before the return of the king's nephew, continued in displeasure and discontent, and being no longer able to bear it, he resolved to betake him to Arabia, along with the husband of his other sister, who was at the time the grand Pandiare. They went off in secret, without taking leave of the king, who was exceeding wroth with them and with the queen, who had given them as much gold and silver as they wanted. The king was especially astonished at the Pandiare, who had quitted so worthy an office; but the latter chose rather to obey the queen and the brother-in-law than him. They went to Mecca, in Arabia, where the Pandiare died, and the prince, after a voyage of eighteen months, came back in a Cananor ship to Cananor, where he was well received of the king, who was very desirous to have him stay there, promising him armed support in case he wished to make war against the Maldive king.[1] But the king of the Maldives, on hearing of this, wrote to him at once, and made the queen write too, to beg him to return, with promises of new dignities. The letter of his sister was of more avail than that of the king. So he returned, and had all that was promised to him, and the country remained in peace until the death of the king and his nephew, the manner whereof I shall relate hereafter.

CHAPTER XX.

Accidents and casualties to ships at the Maldives.—Arrival of Hollanders.—A wandering Jew.—A captain of Mogor and his adventures; and of some ships wrecked there.

When I was at the Maldives, the king of Mangalore, an idolater, once upon a time sent to the king of the Maldives a galley fully laden with rice as a present, and to renew and confirm their ancient friendship through an ambassador who

[1] Âli Raja of Cananor turned the visit of Ranabandery Tacourou to good account, for, on the death of Sultan Ibrahim in 1607, this prince succeeded to the throne as his vassal. That Âli Raja already had designs upon the Maldives, if not possession of some of them, appears from the journals of Steven van der Hagen's voyage. That Dutch captain was at Cananor in 1604, but could not get the Raja to take the Dutch side against the Portuguese. He warned the Dutch not to make any attempt upon "his Maldive islands" (*Rec. des Voy.*, iii, 17).

accompanied the gift. The Maldive king received him well, and sent in return a present of the rarest and choicest things to be found in his kingdom.

About the same time the Hollanders[1] were guarding Point de Galle, in the island of Ceylon (of which I shall speak more fully hereafter in its proper place), with two or three ships only, it happened that two large vessels passed there on a voyage from Achen in Sumatra, and other places in Sunda, laden with the produce of China and other countries, and were on their way to Arabia. The Hollanders soon made them lower their sails, but seeing they were not friends of the Portuguese, they received them kindly, and they were for two or three days enjoying good cheer together. The larger of the two ships was going, as they said, to Mogor, Surrate, and Cambaye, the other was going to the opposite coast. The captain of the large vessel was quite young, and a native of the Mogor country. The king of Achen had killed his father in order to acquire his wealth, for he was the richest man in all the Indies, and was called *Chamy*.[2] He had much property in Sumatra, and that was the cause of his death. His only son, who was of the same name, and resided in his youth with his mother at Surrate, was very handsome, fair, and well to do, and may have been then about seventeen or eighteen years of age. The other captain was a Turk, aged twenty-five years. He was the strongest

[1] As will be seen, the Dutchmen on board the native vessels mentioned in the following passage, told Pyrard of the death of Queen Elizabeth. It is, therefore, probable that the *rencontre* off the coast of Ceylon took place sometime in 1604. I do not find it mentioned in the Dutch Collection. The Zeelanders had, in 1602, sent a factor to Cambay on board a Turkish vessel from Achin (*Rec. des Voy.*, ii, 525). And in January 1604, some Turks came to the Dutch at Bantam, and thanked them for the kindly treatment of their countrymen and their goods by the Dutch cruisers off Ceylon (*ib.*, p. 673). See further in the following chapter as to the determined efforts of the Dutch to open trade with Cambay.

[2] Perhaps *Shámi*, a Syrian or Western.

man I ever saw, and was renowned throughout all India for his great valour.

So, when the general of the Hollanders heard all this, and that the young captain was going to Cambaye or Surrate, between which places there is only an intervening river, he called together this captain and all the merchants, numbering about thirty or forty men of wealth and position, along with the ship's officers, and bade them tell the truth and say without fear where they were going; to which they replied as before. But this was out of fear, for their intention was to go to Arabia; but they durst not say so, for the Grand Mogor and the Hollanders were good friends, and the Hollanders also had factors at Cambaye and Surrate, which are in the country of the Mogor. At length the general bade bring him the book of the law and a piece of biscuit, upon which he made them swear, according to their custom, that they were speaking the truth. This they did, whereupon the Hollanders requested them to take two of their factors, with a quantity of goods, to Cambaye, with some presents for the Grand Mogor, and for the lords of Cambaye and Surrate. This they promised to do, and the general gave handsome presents to the captain and to the merchants, together with a stock of victuals.

So, taking the two Hollanders and the goods, they departed in great friendship, and the two vessels made straight for the Maldives, which was their course to take, either by the north end of the islands or through them. This is the cause of the prosperity of that country; for the islands are situate halfway between Sunda and the coast of Arabia and Persia, and there are no other islands between whereat provisions can be had. Every year upwards of five-and-twenty or thirty ships pass there, of which not two go there of deliberate purpose, on account of the dangers there; and but for the necessity of passing through them, they would not go there at all, and the islanders would be constrained to go elsewhere to purchase their necessary supplies. The passage is feared as well on account of the currents and reefs as of the fever which is peculiar to the islands, the Malé fevers being known everywhere. Most of the vessels are brought there by the currents, so that they are obliged to sojourn and do some traffic there, by reason of the *Monssons*, which change from one quarter to the other.

These *Monssons*, or *Muessons*, are winds which change for the summer and winter, every six months. They most frequently cheat the sailors who start too late, for the wind comes on to blow contrarily while they are out; they also cheat them by sometimes blowing for a shorter or a longer period one way than the other; and a favourable wind will sometimes cease too soon, and a contrary wind will continue too long, sometimes a month or six weeks, and even two months, beyond expectation. This obliges them to stay seven or eight weeks longer than they like, as I have frequently seen happen. I have also known them put to sea at the close of these Monssons, believing that they would last long enough for the voyage, and when they have got within fifty leagues of Arabia, they have been obliged by the contrary wind to return and make the Maldives again, or even the coasts of Sunda. In these return journeys some of them get lost. On some occasions, when they have passed the northern end of the islands, sailing on the current from the east, and are thinking they have escaped the reefs, one morning the current changes, and the western current carries them away to the islands of the south, where they are wrecked among the reefs. This is what happened to the large vessel in which the queen was, which, as I have related, was lost in the south.

But to return to the two ships voyaging to Arabia: when they arrived at the islands they were not minded to stay there, yet they were forced to await the other Monssons, which did not come for seven or eight months,—for the

Monsson which was then blowing was not yet over. They did not come to land at Malé, so not much was seen of them, because of the sickness which prevailed there; but, as was usual, they chose another island, thirty or forty leagues to the north, called Maspillaspoury, belonging to the chief queen, because it is the most healthy of all. The two ships cast anchor and remained there. The custom in such cases was that on their arrival they came to salute the king with presents. The king liked these casual arrivals much, and received the unfortunate men with the kindest face in the world; but his smile was a deceit, and was worth nothing in the long run.

For his usual plan was to endeavour to get the vessels to come to his island, which they never would; and when he found them to be too strong, he ceased to importune them, fearing to lose their goods and traffic; but when he saw that they were weak, he made them come, under one pretext or another, pretending to be angry with them, so that at length they fell into his power, if perchance the captain of the vessel came to die; in short, nothing passed through his hands without a part sticking to them. When a vessel or merchant happened to arrive at his island, he caused a *banquesalle*, or storehouse, to be assigned to it or him for depositing the goods, and the admiral took an account of everything in writing, and had the sails hauled down and took them and the rudder into his possession. The king was heir to such as died there, whether they left ship or goods behind them, wherefore most ships would not go there, or, as soon as their captain died, they sailed off as soon as possible.

While these two vessels were awaiting the other Monssons all the chiefs and principal men went to salute the king with fine presents. All were rich men, some of them Mahometans, and the rest Banians of Cambaye. The king received them in great state, and for their entertainment had a large bullock killed, and also gave each a cow or bullock, that being a mark of great goodwill. He treated the young captain with exceptional honour, saying that he had known his father well, and on that account was glad to see him. The captain replied that this was the first voyage he and his ship were making, and that he had been to the king of Achen, who had killed his father, to see if he could get from him some recompense; that he had been well received by that king, who had given him many slaves, a ship, and merchandise, and he had promised to return to him. After the Maldive king had thus given him a cordial reception, surrounded by all his court, in the usual fashion, he bade give them lodging, wherewith they were all well pleased. I went to see them in the evening, and they gave me good cheer, and told me they had on board their ship two Hollanders on their way to Surrate, at which news I was overjoyed, and had hopes of hearing some news from France; but they told me that the Hollanders did not want to come to Malé, as much from fear of sickness as that they had nothing to do there; besides that, they had heard tell of the king's humour, concerning which I sent them in writing a few words of advice in French.

Nevertheless, the king was informed that they were there, and what merchandise they were carrying, principally woollen cloth, which they had taken from the Portuguese, elephants' teeth and other things, and some silver. The king sent word that he had great desire to have a fine bit of cloth, and the captain said that he would have to send one of his own people to choose it, which he did; but the chief factor sent his companion to the king to settle the price, and to show him different sorts, so that was a good occasion for me to see him. He brought me the compliments of his companion, who sent me a fine piece of white cotton cloth, there being no white cloth in these islands, but all coloured. He brought to the king as a present an exceedingly beautiful matchlock, with its furniture, and a handsome sword, with which the king was well pleased. In exchange, the king gave some mats, and I did the same, for these are the rarest things manufactured at the island.[1] This factor was eight days at Malé, and the king took two pieces of his cloth, one red and the other violet, for which he paid in silver.[2] The factor then took his departure, and I saw him no more. He could speak French, and I acted as interpreter. The king would never give me leave to go where they were, and they frequently sent us letters, accompanied with some little presents.

As I am on the subject of the two Hollanders, I will tell what happened to them. The captain and merchants who had promised to take them to Cambaye told them frankly that they were going to Arabia, and that what they had told the general was said through fear of being thwarted in their design. The two factors therefore began to unload all their goods; whereupon the captain of the other vessel, who was a Turk, told them that if they wished he would carry them to Cambaye or Surrate in all safety. They accepted the offer, and went with him. Since then I have heard that before they got there one of them died. It was good luck for them to have had the opportunity of proceeding, for otherwise they had been forced to remain at the islands, and been lost, both themselves and their goods: for the king would never have let them go, so as at the last he should get possession of their merchandise.

About the same time came to Malé a man who was a Jew in faith and race, and knew a large number of languages; among others, he spoke Arabic and the Indian tongues well. He was a man of Barbary, and the greatest scoundrel in the world. The English had taken him to England, where he

[1] See above, p. 241.

[2] Above (at p. 242), he says that the Maldivians never allowed gold or silver to go out of the country. Probably the Dutchmen here would take nothing else; and, as will be seen, the king had designs upon the whole ship.

had learnt English well. About the same time that we left France four ships also left England, and the general took this fellow as his body-servant; and he was with him in the Indies.[1] He was already at Achen when our general arrived there, and he it was who informed me that the general had been poisoned by the Portuguese.[2] As for the English general, when he saw that he could not load with pepper at Achen, he went to Bantan in Java, where this Jew robbed him of twelve or fifteen hundred pieces of forty sols Spanish, and made his escape. With the English he was of their religion; with the Mahometans, of theirs; whereas he was all the while a Jew. He married a wife wherever he happened to be, and thus had four or five wives in India. He

[1] The English general here alluded to is Captain James Lancaster, who left Tor Bay on the 20th April 1601, with four ships—the *Dragon*, *Hector*, *Ascension*, and the *Susan*. The journal of the voyage is printed in *Lancaster's Voyages*, Hak. Soc., pp. 57-107. Lancaster arrived at Achin on the 5th June 1602, and at Bantam on the 16th December 1602. This Jew is mentioned as having been with Lancaster at Achin. The conferences with the Sultan's ministers were carried on in Arabic, and the chronicler notes, "Now the general (before his going out of England) intertained a Jew who spake that language perfectly, which stood him in good steed at that time" (p. 81). There is no mention of his having robbed him at Bantam. The character, as drawn by Pyrard, is of a not uncommon type, found a little later at Mocha, where, on the 8th May 1609, some of Captain Sharpeigh's men were lodged in the house of "a talkative lyenge Jewe w'ch spake Spanishe" (*ib.*, p. 123). A hundred years before this we find Jews playing the same *rôle*. In 1510, two Castilian Jews were taken by Simão Martinsz in a vessel going from Mecca to Calicut. "These Jews turned Christians: to the one was given the name of Francisco Dalboquerque, and to the other Alexandre Dataide. And Afonso Dalboquerque, as long as he lived, employed them as interpreters especially Alexandre Dataide, because he knew many languages, and had a great aptitude for business. And after the death of Afonso Dalboquerque they went to Portugal, in the time of King D. Manoel, and from that country returned to India, and from India they proceeded to Cairo, where they again became Jews" (*Comm. of Af. Dalboquerque*, Hak. Soc., ii, 230).

[2] Below, the author says that he had this information from the two Hollanders.

embarked at Achen in a ship of Surrate, which had lately passed by the head of the Maldives, and was so ill-advised as to land with all his goods. He had still left about one hundred and fifty crowns, for he had spent all the rest. After stealing the money he had gone to Surrate, where he married. At length, on this last voyage, being arrived at Malé, he came to make offer of his services to the king, under the pretext that he was a good gunner; but he knew nothing about it. He was well received at first, but when it was seen that he was a liar, no further notice was taken of him. Soon after he fell sick, and begged me to get his leave of the king; and I, making the request through the lord with whom I resided obtained it with great difficulty. He said that he was married in Guzeratte, and had a child there, which was partly the cause why his leave was granted; though after he got it he remained three or four months longer, and spent the remainder of his money, and then embarked with the richest merchant of Cananor, a Malabar Mahometan, and the greatest man of that place next to the king, Ali Radia. This merchant had a wife at the Maldives, and did a large business there, there not being an atollon whereat he had not factors and merchandise. Some of his ships and barques were always at the island: his name was *Poecaca*. So the Jew went with him to Cananor.

As for the young captain of whom I have spoken, I will now tell of the adversity which befell him and his crew. He sojourned at the islands some six months, doing much traffic the while. Though this was contrary to their purpose, they were obliged to do it for the need they had of the island commodities: thus, they took in exchange coco-cord, called *Cairo*,[1] and cocos themselves. But the merchandise they most eagerly desired was *Cambe*,[2] or tortoise-shell, which comes from these islands. The best are the largest and

[1] Tam. *kayiru*.

[2] M. *kahabu*, or *kahambu*. See above, p. 252, *note*.

thickest, a *Gaut*,[1] or quarter of a pound, being worth a larin at least. But as the commodity is in great request elsewhere, they will only take gold or silver in exchange, whereas for other things they will take merchandise. They sold me pepper at no more than two sols the pound, and four pounds of silk for a crown, while the natives bought it (of me) at a higher price; for the strangers used to like me much, and gave me many presents, in order that I should assist them in selling their goods. Our intercourse was in the Portuguese language, and I acted as their factor there. Many a time they have entrusted me with more than two hundred crowns' worth of merchandise on credit; in all cases giving me a quarter of the profit on the sales, so that I made considerable gain through them. It was the young captain who liked me best, and put the greatest confidence in me, wherefore I the more deeply regretted the misfortune which overtook him; for many of his chief men and richest merchants of his ship died, and the custom there is, as I said, that the king inherits the property of foreigners that die there. The king had prevented the captain and his merchants from proceeding to the island where their ship was, and had taken a quantity of their merchandise on credit, for he never used to pay until ships were on the point of sailing, thus thwarting them in their departure at their own time, and preventing any designs against his government. So they were bereft of all means of getting away; for as soon as a vessel arrives, the *Miruaire*, or admiral's sergeant, presently has the rudder carried off to the king's palace, whence it cannot be regained without the admiral's permission.

One day the king sent for this captain to get from him by soft speeches and flattery an account of his vessel's cargo, the amount of it, and the names of the owners: all which the other told him in good faith, for he was the best man for a Mahometan I have ever met, and showed his whole manifest.

[1] See above, p. 189, where it is spelt *gaux*.

When the king had looked over this, he told him that he was heir of all that had died, and that the captain had no interest therein, but should have his freight paid for all of it. This was agreed to, as also that the king should send his own people to get out this merchandise, which was of great bulk. The person sent for this purpose was the lord with whom I had resided so long,[1] seeing that in him the king placed most confidence. He took with him forty or fifty soldiers and mariners in barques; but the party was not as had been intended, for all the merchants of the ships went with this lord; and there remained with the king as hostages only the captain, two of the chief merchants, and the pilot, who was a brave fellow. When they were all arrived at the island where the ship lay at anchor, it being then late, the natives went ashore, while the merchants went on board to await the morrow; but at night they took counsel together that they would sooner die, every man of them, than let this merchandise be taken; and they resolved that, in order to get back their hostages, they would have to seize this great lord, whom the king loved so well that he would not have lost him for all the world's goods. So in the morning, when this lord was walking along the strand with two followers, suspecting nothing, the ship's folk of a sudden seized and carried him by force into their boat, wherein they had plenty fire-arms, and so held him prisoner; then they send word to the king that as soon as he shall send back their hostages, his people will be delivered up. When the news reached Malé, it was the most pitiful case in the world to hear every man crying aloud with his neighbour; nor was there any man but did so, and thus displayed, at least in appearance, his sorrow for the king's sake: the which I felt in real earnest, for this lord was the best friend I had in all that land. It was about midnight when the news came, and at once everybody arose in as great hurry and trouble as if the king himself had been seized. On

[1] *I.e.*, the lord named *Assant Caounas calogue.*

the other hand, the sad consequence was that the captain and his people were forthwith bound and laid by the feet in irons. This caused me many a heartache, for he was so warm a friend to me that I knew not for which of the two I mourned the most. Everyone pitied this captain, but none durst open his mouth on his behalf, for the king was in the greatest passion that ever was, and was terrified lest they should carry off that lord, insomuch that of a sudden he had three galleys armed and launched for the pursuit; but if he had had twenty, they could have done nothing, for the vessel set sail as if to go. Seeing this, the king's nephew, who commanded the galleys, with all speed sent a boat to parley and to arrange for delivering up the men on each side. This was accordingly effected, and war was thus avoided. Meanwhile, these poor Hollanders who had been witnesses of this disturbance were in great difficulty what they should do; and when the folk of the vessel asked them if they would re-embark in that ship with their merchandise, they replied they would not, nor would have aught more to do with men of such treachery, and preferred to go with the Turk captain, which they did; albeit one of them died on the way. As for the large vessel, when it came near the Arabian coast it sank to the bottom, and was lost with all on board, as we heard a year after. Many of the islanders made a large profit out of this quarrel, and I most of all, for I owed more than thirty crowns to the captain and the merchants, and I refused to pay that over to the soldiers, as it would have been for their own advantage, and not for that of the king, because the greatest men in the island owed as much, and they durst not ask it of them. Several times more than two hundred soldiers came to get it, for they had an account of all such as were indebted to the people of the ship; but I held out firmly that I owed nothing, and had paid for all I had taken. At length they sent word to the king (for they never dare speak to him themselves, unless he so orders or himself raises the question), but he replied that there was good security for what I owed, and he would answer for it, but not for all that such and such men owed, naming some of the chief men, as I said just now; that they should themselves pay their debts, if they could, and that I should pay anon. This stopped them short, for they would not have dared to open their mouths against these other lords that owed anything; and I heard nothing more of it.

The lord who had been seized by that vessel died a year after his deliverance, and I never saw the king weep as he did then: for three days he attended him and never left his bedside. He had him buried with the like ceremonies as if he had been his own brother or son, and ever after showed affection to his three sons who survived him, taking them to himself and giving them offices in his household. It is a rule in that country that when such men as he, that have acted as stewards, come to die, the king calls for a statement of his affairs; he then takes all their property, giving to the wife and children as much as he thinks fit. So, two days after the death of this lord, his widow and his four children, three sons and a daughter, came to the palace with all their accounts and papers, and a great array of servants, carrying gold, silver, and other valuables, according to the practice of those that have had the management of the king's affairs; but the king took the accounts and destroyed them without looking at them or taking any of the property, and said aloud and clearly that he gave it all to them, bidding them serve him as faithfully as their father had. One of the sons, as soon as his father died, brought and hid in my house property of more than five hundred crowns' worth, of which no one knew anything but he and I; and all his secrets he confided to me. The chief queen loved him dearly, wherefore the king prohibited him from coming to the palace; but he ceased not to go in such secrecy that none was aware of it.

By the way, the two Hollanders who came in the large vessel told me some news of France, and what had happened during the five years since my departure; among other things, the happy birth of Monseigneur the Dauphin, the king that now is,[1] whereat my companions and I were greatly rejoiced; next, of the death of the queen of England,[2] and of the Mareschal de Biron.[3] They told me also what had become of our admiral[4] the Croissant, and how our general, Monsieur de la Bardelière, being at Achen in Sumatra, was poisoned by the Portuguese, and feeling himself mortally struck, embarked forthwith and set sail, for fear lest the king of Achen, according to the custom of all Oriental countries, should seize his ship in case he died there. But he died ere he rounded the Cape of Good Hope.[5]

[1] Louis XIII, born at Fontainebleau, 27th September 1601; succeeded to the throne on the murder of his father, Henri IV, 14th May 1610; his mother, Marie de Medicis, being regent.

[2] Elizabeth died 24th March 1603.

[3] Charles de Gontaut, Duc de Biron, born 1561, celebrated for his valour at the battles of Arques and Ivry, and at the sieges of Paris and Rouen; and for his friendship with Henri IV, whom he afterwards sought to betray by treasonable correspondence with Spain and Savoy. He was beheaded at the Bastille, 31st July 1602.

[4] Here used, as by numerous French and English writers of the period, for the chief ship of a fleet. See *Hawkins' Voy.*, passim; *Linschoten* (Hak. Soc., i, 9), and *New Eng. Dict.*, s. v. Milton alone, in his well-known lines, "the mast of some great ammiral", affects the Italian form. At this time it was the common word, and the commander was almost invariably, as here, designated "general".

[5] The *Croissant* arrived at Achin, 24th July 1602, and left 20th November of the same year, "apres avoir sejourné", says Martin, "aux Indes l'espace de 5 mois ou environ, où avions eu le trafic libre, de plusieurs sortes d'epiceries et de quelques autres singularitez naissantes au pays" (Martin, *Voy.*, 90). It was there again met by Spilberg, whose chronicler says that the French had not done much business (*Rec. des Voy.*, ii, 516, 526). The Sieur de la Bardelière died as they passed the line, on the 1st December, after an illness of four months, attributed by the French chronicler to the climate and country, and not in any way to his having been poisoned by the Portuguese. Following his last wishes, the Sieur de la Villeschar was elected to fill his place (*ib.*, p. 91). See also Cunat, *St. Malo illustré par ses Marins*, 78; and an article on Bardelière by Cunat, in Lovet, *Biographie Bretonne*.

His ship, which was not half laden, got as far as athwart the Cape Finisterre, when the sailors were nearly all dead, and the remainder so ill that they could hardly walk, while the ship was so full of leaks that she was making water on all sides, and was sinking. Then by good fortune they fell in with two Hollanders' ships, who salved the merchandise and took the remaining men to England, and had the third part of all they salved for their pains. The men of the Croissant had taken ten Indians at Achen, at wages, to assist them in the return voyage, but most of them died going or returning Those who escaped were paid and sent back by the Hollanders. There was also an Indian who came to Holland and remained there three years, where he learned to speak Flemish and a little French, for that the mate with whom he lived in Holland was a Frenchman; and on his return to the Indies he recounted to all the Indian kings the marvellous grandeur and magnificence of Holland; but he spoke also of the great esteem and regard the Hollanders had for the kingdom of France.[1]

[1] The *Croissant*, after a terrible storm, rounded the Cape in January 1603, and reached St. Helena 3rd March. Leaving that island on the 19th, she reached Ascension on the 25th. On the 15th May the wearied remnant of the crew, who were suffering the extremities of hunger, and eating dogs and rats, sighted Terceira (Azores), and on the 21st fell in with three Flemish ships coming from Venice. The end of their sad story had better be told in Martin's own words:—"Nous les priasmes de nous recevoir en leurs vaisseaux et que nous leurs ferions part de nos marchandises selon la coustume de la mer, surquoy ils nous firent quelques offres generalles, nous promettant nous venir trouver le lendemain, ce qu'ils firent demandant quelques uns de nostres. pour traicter particulierement sur ce subject; à la fin nous fusmes contrains transporter en leurs vaisseaux, ce que chacun avoit de particulier, et leur donner le pillage de nostre navire: lequel, peu de temps apres, s'emplissant d'eau, coula de luy mesme a fond à nostre veue. Demeurasmes sur lesdits navires Flamens, du 23 jour du mois de May, jusques au 11 jour de Juin, qu'eusmes la cognoissance de l'isle d'Angleterre, et le 13 posasmes l'ancre en la radde de Plemurs [Plymouth] (Martin, *Voy.*, pp. 100, 101). Estancelin says that eight Indians brought home by the *Croissant* were still at St. Malo in 1604 (*Voy., etc., des Norm.*, 54).

CHAPTER XXI.

Of a captured Portuguese vessel that was wrecked.—An ambassador from the king of the Maldive Islands.—A vessel of Achen.—A Malay native.—A Maldive confession.—The discovery of a strange island; and other events.

While I was at the Maldives the Hollanders had captured from the Portuguese a fine and good ship, and brought it, with all its cargo, to Achen, where they had discharged it into their magazine for sale there. They then found by chance a ship-captain and sixty sailors, who had lost their ship on the coast of Sumatra, and were men of Guzerate and Cambaye. The Hollanders asked them if they would serve them faithfully, and on their so promising, and giving such and such security at Achen, the Hollanders gave them this Portuguese vessel, victualled and equipped in all necessary respects, on a contract to carry one of their factors with merchandise to Cambaye, after which the master should dispose of the ship as he liked. The master and his crew, well enough pleased with this windfall, accepted the offer gladly. The Hollanders loaded the ship with more than 60,000 crowns' worth of goods, consisting of cloth, ivory, lead, iron, steel, sulphur, silver, precious stones, and other valuables. This ship made sail straight to Cambaye, but they were unable to pass the Maldives without paying forfeit like ourselves: for one fine night she went upon the reefs of the island and was wrecked. They saved their cargo in like manner as we did. I saw the Dutch clerk and factor, named Martin Dombe, a native of Zeeland, and a man of fine presence and education. He and the master and mariners remained about two months at Malé, after which the king gave them a barque to take them off. The master, who was a Mahometan, and well known at the islands, begged the king to treat the factor kindly, which he did. I saw this Martin Dombe afterwards at Cochin, as I shall relate in the proper place.[1]

It is impossible to describe the cruelty and tyranny exercised by the king towards the mate of this ship, a man of about thirty-five, and his son, a boy of twelve or thirteen, and two of their men, who were accused of having concealed some of the ship's treasure,—to wit, gold, silver, and precious stones; for he kept them upwards of a month in prison, beaten and whipped every day, and bound with their faces to the ground, without anything to eat, save such as was given them in small quantities in secret. But I may say also that I never saw such constancy and courage as was theirs, for they could never be got to avow anything, until at length they had to be liberated, when it was evident that they would not die. I was never astonished at anything so much as at that, that they did not die a thousand times over, with all the ills they endured. They were nothing but skin and bone when they came out of prison; but what I admired most of all was the resolution of the little boy, to undergo all that suffering with patience so great. When, then, the king saw that he could draw nothing from them, he had them doctored and nursed, and gave them some money to get home withal. Yet true it is that they had hidden this money whereof they were suspected.

About a year before we left the Maldives, there came to the king an ambassador from the Christian king of these islands, who lived at Goa, of whom I have already spoken. This ambassador was a Portuguese, and told me he had been at Rochelle in France. He was about fifty years of age, and was named Dom Adrien de Gouia.[2] He came in considerable state, accompanied by some other Portuguese and Christian Indians. The subject of his visit was a certain dispute

[1] His name was Martin Domburgh. For his subsequent history, see below, ch. xxviii, and vol. II, ch. vi.

[2] Adrian de Gouveia.

which existed between that young Christian king and his uncle, Dom Paulo,[1] who resided at Cochin, the latter wanting to take part of the tribute coming to the said king. A suit was pending about it in the Parliament at Goa for a long time, during which this Dom Paulo enjoyed the receipt of it, —for, under the treaty of peace, the Maldivians were not obliged to pay the tribute elsewhere than at Cochin, where the uncle was. At length, the Parliament of Goa having ordained that the Christian king, Dom Philippe, should have of the Maldive king and all the chiefs of the country a certificate to the effect that they recognised him as the king, he therefore sent this embassy with a quantity of presents. But the Maldive king took but little notice of it, and the ambassador waited there for two months without getting an audience, such was the pride and haughtiness of this king in a matter wherein he perceived no gain for himself; and when he was got to do business with them, his demeanour was exceeding proud. In fine, it was four months ere the ambassador got his despatch, which was granted, when he asked it, with offerings of the rarest gifts, as well from his master as from himself.

About the same time was wrecked there a ship belonging to the king of Achen. It had not intended to come there, but to Masulipatan or to Bengal, yet the calms and currents brought it there perforce. The king got all this merchandise, which accrued to him by law. The captain saved much gold, silver, and precious stones, and was well treated by the king, who gave him a barque well furnished with provisions to go away in. But I will tell what happened to one of these Malays (for so they call all the people of Sunda and the parts about Malaca). Having saved a large amount of property,

[1] This seems to be a slip: the name should be Dom Pedro. See vol. II, ch. ix, where the lawsuit is again referred to, and the name of the uncle given as Pedro. In the royal despatches, too, where frequent mention is made of the Maldive princes, only one brother of Dom João is mentioned, and he under this name (see App. B).

the captain and some of the chief men wanted to dole it to the others according to their own notions; but three of the men resolved to have their share or die in the attempt. So one day, espying the captain as he was taking a walk by himself, they attacked him in such wise that but for the succour of the inhabitants he must have been killed, or forced to surrender his booty; but he was saved for the nonce. Being a brave and courageous man, and knowing the natural temper of the Malays,—to wit that they are irreconcilable in their enmities, and never swerve when once resolved upon anything, and make no more ado about the life of a man than of a chicken,—he bethought him to be beforehand with them. So, with the assistance of some of his own party, he lay in wait, arms in hand, for the three men as they came out of their temple or mesquite, and attacked them with such vigour, that the most valiant of them, and the author of the quarrel, was laid low, and the two others were wounded, and only saved by the people of the island. They defended themselves bravely, and he that was killed received many wounds; for they are a cruel and vindictive race. The king was very angry, and ordered the Pandiare to do justice in the matter, which he did in this wise. He summoned the captain and the two survivors before him, and after inquiring all that had passed, he found that the dead man had come by his death justly, for having tried to kill his captain. But he could hardly make the others come to any agreement, for the captain was by no means willing to pardon the two others, and would do nothing but at the express command of the king. Finally an agreement was come to, the Pandiare ordering the two men to kiss the feet of the captain, and to ask his pardon, which they willingly did. He also made them recite aloud a confession in Arabic—as, according to their law, all have to do who have committed any fault: for criminals and convicts are not allowed to have speech of or intercourse with the rest until they have first made confession of their fault before the Pandiare, or others deputed by him to receive it (these being the Naibes, and no others), and are thus absolved. The Pandiare made the captain do the like, because he had slain a man, and all were afterwards good friends. Yet the two men would not embark with the captain when he went, saying that he would throw them overboard: for that race put no confidence in one another, whatever reconciliation they may have come to; so that they preferred to wait until the next Maldive ship should be sailing for Achen. When the captain went, the king of the islands wrote to the king of Achen, and sent him some presents; for they were good friends, and often sent letters and presents to each other. As for the wrecked ship, it is the general custom that all belongs to the lord of the country where the wreck is; and another lord would take it for an insult if the merchandise of a ship of his that was wrecked were restored to him.

Some time afterwards, the king sent on two occasions a very expert pilot to discover a certain island named *Pollouoys*,[1]

[1] M. *Fólávahi*; the first part of the word is, perhaps, the Malay *pulo*, "island". There can be little doubt that this island, around which so much fable had circled, was one of the Chagos archipelago. A very small island of the Peros Banhos group is still called *Poule*; but as most of the names of these islands are French, the identification is doubtful. The northernmost of that archipelago is in 4° 44′ S., and the southernmost of the Maldives (Addu) in 0° 44′ S. It is not surprising that the Maldivians knew little or nothing of islands so comparatively near, when we bear in mind that they were at the mercy of monsoons and currents, whose direction is east and west alternately, and that the Chagos Islands lie almost due south. More of them seems to have been known to the Maldivians than Pyrard was aware; for in the letters patent of 1560, issued by the ex-king Dom Manoel from Cochin, he describes himself as king not only of the Maldives, but also of the "seven islands of *Pullobay*" (see App. B). As for the devils, all we need say is that an island inhabited by them was a commodity which any respectable Mahomedan community of those days could hardly do without. See Lane's *Arabian Nights* (1877), i, 323; iii, 84, as to the demons called *Sealáh* and *Dahlán*, and the island *Bartáil*. The island of *Pollouoys* seems to have been famed beyond the Maldives. Vincent

which is still almost unknown to them, except that they say that long ago one of their barques landed there by chance (so they find it stated in their histories), but were forced to leave

le Blanc, while in Pegu, picked up the following story, where the legend is obviously mixed up with references to the cannibalism of the Battas of Sumatra or of some of the wild tribes of Arakan (see *Cathay*, pp. 100-1), and the mention of the kings of Achen and Bengal would seem to identify the island with *Pulowé*, to the north of Sumatra, rather than with the far-off Chagos. Geographical difficulties, however, did not trouble the great traveller of Marseilles :—"South-west of the isle of Seilan are the Maldives, many in number and very dangerous for their shelves of sand and rocks; but I will say no more of them, because my knowledge is but small; besides, they have amply and exactly been described by others; but I will say something of a wonderful island beyond the Maldives towards the south, some 12 degrees from the Line, and called *Polouis* or *Polouois*, now desert, though formerly inhabited and flourishing, which (as I since learnt at Pegu) was governed by a prince called *Argiac*, a potent king of many islands and kingdoms; he having many children by several wives, gave this island to one of the gallantest of them, named *Abdenac*, for his portion, with several treasures. This *Abdenac* was possest of it peaceably for five years space: his elder brother, called *Argiac* after his father, the king of Achen in Sumatra, refused him the share of treasure his father had left him, whereupon the other, enraged, craved the assistance of the king of Bengale, who furnished him with ships, wherewith he invaded his brother, burnt his towns, and put to death most of his followers, but received a mortal wound himself. Returning to his island of *Polouis* with the treasures he had regained of his brother, and finding himself near death, he distributed all his wealth among his own people, and bequeathed his island to his *Dume* or evil spirit, as his heir, intreating him to preserve it to the Day of Judgment, when he hoped to return to the world.

"This will made, he died, and had no other sepulchre than the bowels of his kinsmen and friends, according to the custom of that region, where in many places they eat the dead flesh of their kindred and near relations, persuading themselves the soul to be sooner at rest than if they permitted the corpses to putrify in the earth, and that no sepulchre is so honourable as the bowels of a dear friend.

"This island falling to the evil spirit's share, he became so turbulent that, from the time he took possession, the island was no longer habitable nor approachable; and all the inhabitants forced to retire into the adjacent isles. Ever since, this place remained desert; yet there are great store of birds and beasts. Sometimes the Maldivians have landed there by chance, but have been forced immediately to retreat, the evil

by reason of the great miseries wrought by the devils who, as it is said, possess the island, and cause the great, horrible, and perpetual storms, which rage with such fury in the seas there that ships cannot remain at anchor. They said also that the devil visibly tormented them. As for the island, it is said to be very fertile in all sorts of fruits; and the large medicinal coconuts which are so dear at the Maldives are believed to come from thence; others, however, think that they come from the bottom of the sea. I did not hear whether there was any betel or not. The island is under the tenth degree beyond the line, and about 120 leagues from the Maldives. The Maldive kings have many a time sent vessels to discover it, but they have never known where to find it; and such as have landed there have done so by chance. Had this pilot who was sent discovered it, it was intended to try and people it. They took with them some sorcerers and magicians to treat with the devil and come to terms with him, for they know not how to conjure him: they only pray him to do something, and promise him their vows, and offer gifts and banquets. But this pilot could not find the island, and was unable to return straight to the Maldives; in such case all that can be done

spirits do so perplex them, raising great tempests on that sea. Being at Pegu, I heard a famous magician had promised the king to bring him some animals from his island, and also the treasures of *Abdenac;* but the demons did so perturb him, he could not effect his purpose; for as he was taking footing in the island, and beginning his conjurations he had writ upon a leaf and put into the hands of one of his boldest disciples, they were, by the illusions of Satan, so suddenly terrified, that the miserable disciple fell dead upon the place, and the master magician was so horribly beaten and dragged by the devils to the ship side, that his companions had time only to re-embark him and hoist sail for Pegu. All the rest were strangely tormented and beaten, except the master's mate and the seamen, who were wiser, for, knowing the condition of the place, they would not put foot on land, which afterwards they were glad of. Thus was the magician served, and 'twas almost past his skill to recover himself" (*V. le Blanc*, i, 106-7).

Pyrard's story of the island will be found summarised in the *Quarterly Review* of 1814, p. 57.

is to make Achen, or, better, Ceylan, or the Cape of Comory. Both times that the pilot went he lost the greater part of his men by death. He used to say that he would pursue the discovery or die in the attempt. The reason why they always met with storms was that they every time went in the winter, while the winds and currents from the west prevail; and that was for the cause that had they gone during the east winds, and had not fetched the island,—as, indeed, was a matter of great uncertainty,—they had been borne towards the Ethiopian coast, and had perished there. This pilot was vastly keen to take me with him on this voyage, and I was as anxious to go; but the king would not permit it, knowing that if ever I reached the coast I would never return to the island. But while I remained there I witnessed the arrival of a tall ship of Bengal, laden with the merchandise of that country. It came to the islands solely to load the *bolits* or shells of which I have spoken so much. The captain of that ship died, and the king inherited all; and but a little thereafter another captain from Guzerate died also, and the king succeeded to his property too: wherein may be seen the great profits and revenues of the king arising from these casualties.

There was also a king of Ceylan, who, out of desire to make a present to the king of Cochin, equipped a galley and loaded her with cinnamon of the finest, and with areca, but after her setting out the calms and currents brought her to the Maldives, into a channel where the current was not strong enough to carry her beyond the islands. Yet those on board were unable to fetch land, till the islanders went out with their barques, and with plenty of ropes, anchors, and oars, and so salved the ship and brought her to anchor. Those on board, thinking to coast along and to make land every day, had not taken much provision, wherefore, after being a long while at sea ere they reached the island, they were so feeble and worn with hunger and thirst, that they could do nothing, having nought to eat but cinnamon and areca. If, indeed, they had not made land at these islands, they had made none nearer than the coasts of Arabia or Melinde, upwards of 900 leagues off, and so full soon had died. The island where they anchored is called *Itadou*,[1] to the south of Malé, from which it is distant about 50 leagues, in the atoll *Adoumatie*. The merchandise carried by them was in great request at the islands, and more the areca than the cinnamon: for they can no more want this areca than we bread and wine. They were constrained to sell their goods for the wherewithal to live. But the custom of these islands is, that none dare do business with strangers without permission of the king; yet they omit not to trade in secret, only when that is known they pay a fine, and all the merchandise is forfeited: it is allowed, however, to give some fruits, and to give food and drink. The strangers, too, must give their merchandise in barter without fixing the price, for it is the province of the king and the elders to fix the prices of foreign merchandise, that is, of all that comes not in the usual way of trade; for they use not so with what comes in the ordinary way, and is brought by the Malabars that come there frequently with their wives, children, and servants. These are permitted to traffic everywhere, like the folk of the country, and are subject to the same police and regulations.

This Cingala captain of the vessel of Ceylan had not brought any money, expecting to find at Cochin all commodities and credit. So, having no money to buy food, he made an offer to the king of all his merchandise for a supply of victuals, that so he should get away. But the king, well knowing that all the merchandise would fall into his hands, paid no attention, and only caused provisions to be supplied from day to day. Then arose the question of discharging the goods and getting the galley on dry land in order to refit her. But the islanders, who are a mischievous race, and seek only

[1] *Hitadú*, in Haddumati atoll, lat. 1° 46′ N., wrongly named Henadu-Adu in the Admiralty charts.

the ruin of the poor strangers, while they were assembled from all the neighbouring parts, and were receiving good pay for hauling the galley on shore, out of malice drove her on a sand-bank, where she broke up; and the poor captain and his men, thus left without a ship, were obliged to remain there for some time. Then they fell sick, and nearly all died, and among these the captain, whereby the king became heir to all the cinnamon, which they call *Poniembous Thory*,[1] and the areca, called *Poua*.[2] If the Cochin king had written for it, he would have sent it all to him. He afterwards thought to send it to Arabia, and at the time when he was killed there was a large vessel all laden to convey it thither; but that was taken, with everything else, as I shall relate hereafter.[3]

Shortly after this, arrived another vessel from Massulipatan, laden with rice, white cloths, oils, and other goods suitable to the island market. The captain was sixty years of age, and had hair as white as cotton and as long as that of women. His ship came to anchor 30 leagues south of Malé, and had come there to load fish for Achen. This captain took a great fancy for me, but he died at Malé, so the king forthwith sent to fetch the ship; but as they were bringing it by night it struck a reef, and all was lost. There was also a tall vessel of Cambaye, which cheated him cleverly; for the captain, casting anchor at an island 40 leagues to the north from Malé, sent four of his chief men to salute the king with presents. Their object was not to remain there, but only to get some ropes, victuals, and other commodities. So, when they feigned a desire to traffic, the king was well enough pleased, and waited to get his share; to this end he desired not that the four men should return, and told them to write word to their

[1] In the Vocab. Pyrard writes *ponianboutory*. Chr., more correctly, *fonitori*, and Bell, *fonitorhi*. *Foni* = Sin. *pæni*, "sweet", as in *pænidodan*, "sweet orange"; and *torhi*, "bark" or "skin". Pyrard introduces *anbu*, "mango", and makes it the "bark of the sweet mango".

[2] Sin. *puwa*.

[3] *Post*, ch. xxiii.

captain to come to Malé with his vessel. But they, knowing that their captain desired to be off, and fearing that he would leave them there, and so save their wages, got the king to permit them to return, under promise to bring the vessel, for which purpose he gave them a body of soldiers. But when once they set foot upon their own ship, they full soon sent back the soldiers with rounds of shot from their cannon and arquebuses, and flights of arrows. The king was much annoyed, and threatened punishment to some strangers who were residing in the said island, and likewise to the inhabitants of it, as being the parties who had caused the ship's people to abandon the notion of coming to Malé for traffic. He would have liked nothing better than to see them come and anchor at his own island, seeing that when they were so far off he could not make such dispositions as suited his purpose. But it would be impossible to describe in detail all the vessels that came to these islands while I was there. I have only made mention of those to which some misfortune or other notable accident happened. All the aim and object of the king and his subjects was but to bring about some mischief, for he used to give some portion of the wrecked ships to his ministers, and among others to the soldiers. But he gave nothing out of the ships whose captains died there: of these none but he drew any advantage.

CHAPTER XXII.

Divers judgments passed for adultery, lewdness, and other crimes. —Amorous humour of the Indian women.—Of the Grand Pandiare; and the strange resolution of a Mulatto.

I shall now relate divers occurrences that happened during my time to particular inhabitants of the island; among others, to a Gentile Canarin of Cochin, a man of great means and position. For eight whole years he had come and gone about the islands, having everywhere houses, factors, and domestics, speaking the language quite well, and being, in fact, naturalised. One day this man was surprised lying with a woman of the islands. He had kept her for six months, and she was but a poor servant-girl. He was presently haled with her before the Grand Pandiare, to whom he protested that he had done her no manner of harm; that he desired to become of their faith, and would marry the woman. This was done, and he became a Mahometan; and it appeared that he had for a long time desired this end, for that he owed much money at Cochin, as to which he became bankrupt. He espoused this woman and made a great lady of her: for there, strangers, both men and women, can wear whatever they please. When he made the promise he was set free, but upon her judgment was passed according to the law: all her hair was shaved, then she was bathed in old and stinking oil, her head put in an old sack of sail-cloth, and then she was beaten at all the cross-roads and round the island. This is their manner of punishing all men and women taken in adultery or fornication. But there, as here, money does everything and saves from everything. As for the conversion of the man, he was borne in triumph through the streets and round the island, accompanied by the greatest lords, and by the people of all sorts and conditions; he was presented with much money and raiment and a new name: for there, names are given at pleasure and by whomsoever, be it father, mother, kindred, or even the first comer; and also at any time, and not only at birth or circumcision, insomuch that it seemed to me they give names as we do here to dogs and horses: for the name first given by whomsoever is the one that sticks to a man.

The king likewise granted dignities to the new convert, making him purveyor and distributor of all the rice and other provisions and merchandise wherein the king trafficked.

It is a highly honourable office, and he had other men under him.

The Pandiare that passed the said judgment was a Cherife of Arabia, that is, one of a family the most respected and noble among these people, as being of the race of Mahomet. He was a very good man, and was greatly beloved of the king. He had great goodwill toward strangers, and blamed the king for, among other things, his evil treatment of us, seeing that we were their friends, and enemies of the Portuguese, and that the kings of Achen, Java, and other countries gave a cordial reception to all Europeans, such as the French, English, and Hollanders, as he had observed in those countries which he had visited. To which the king replied that he was much displeased with him; that such counsel came not well from him, but from the lords and elders of the island. This Pandiare was returning to Arabia from Achen, where he had been well received, and, loaded with much wealth, was returning with it; but on passing through the islands the king heard of it, and so besought him to remain, that he at length consented,[1] and became so familiar with the king as to be permitted to eat with him, an honour never done to any other person.

While this Pandiare was in office I saw him one day do examplary justice on a large number of women. They were about twenty-five or thirty in number, some of the greatest ladies in the land, who were accused of a crime whereof I never heard tell before; it is practised only at the Maldives, and is called *Pouy tallan.*[2] In truth, the women of all India are naturally much addicted to every kind of ordinary lewdness;

[1] Very much Ibn Batuta's case. See App. A.

[2] M. *fú* vel *fui*, "pudenda", et *talaŋ*, Sin. *talaŋda*, "percutere". Pyrard addit hæc, "scilicet pomo quodam utuntur ibi crescente, apud illos *Quela* apud nos *Banana* vocato, quod tam longum quam palma plerumque est, tam crassum quam brachium pueri decem annos nati. Quem vero ad modum hoc abutuntur tam fœdus tam turpis tam immanis est ut plura de illo pudeat me referre."

but those of the Maldives in particular are so tainted with this vice that they have no other talk or occupation, and hold it a boast and a virtue one with another to have some bravo or gallant, upon whom they lavish all such favours and tokens of love as a man could wish of a woman. Among other things, they never let them want for betel, prepared and served in some elaborate and extraordinary style, with some cloves put inside, or else a little black seed, the most tasty, odoriferous, and pleasant to the mouth that can be conceived. As for the men, they cull flowers and arrange them neatly in the manner of bouquets, and send them to the ladies out of gallantry. There are certain white flowers[1] of a full scent on which they can write and grave what they will with the point of a knife, and thereon they write three or four verses on the subject of their passion. Money and other valuable things they give not much to one another; and when these are given, it is more on the part of the women than of the men. To the women the men are exceedingly courteous and obliging.

Many reasons may be assigned for the fact that the women are of a disposition so hot and amorous; but the principal seem to me to be that they are exceedingly lazy, and do nothing but ever lie rocked in daintiness. Next, that they are continually eating betel, a very heating herb; and in their ordinary fare use so many spices that sometimes I could hardly put the food to my mouth; also garlic, onions, and other such heating things. Add to this, that the climate is directly under the line, a condition which renders the men more sluggish and less capable; yet for all that, most have two or three wives apiece,—I mean such as can afford to keep them. They are also lazy, idle fellows, more like women, their chiefest exercise being to lie abed with them, and then more often with desire than effect.

[1] Probably the *champaka* (*Michelia Champaka*), or "temple flower", as it is called in Ceylon.

But to return to the justice done upon those women: two at first were taken in the act, one of whom was married to one of the king's chief officers, and he loved her dearly. Now, their law and custom obtains that when a king's officer or any of his family is a delinquent, before proceeding to justice the Grand Pandiare sends word to the king, asking if it be his pleasure that the process be according to the ordinary forms. This the king never refuses. So the Grand Pandiare, having informed the king of the conduct of the two women, the king replied that he willed justice to be done, not only upon these two, but upon many others, who, as he had heard, had for a long while been engaged in this business, and that a strict inquisition should be made. Forthwith, too, he sent the husband of one of the women, with two of his most intimate advisers, to assist at the inquiry and trial, and bade them expressly tell the Pandiare to omit no part of his orders, for that if any remained unpunished, he would take the law into his own hands; insomuch that all the people incontinently assembled from all parts of the island, and even the highest grandees came, many of whom to prosecute their own wives. During this procedure the king had all the doors of his palace closed, so that none should enter to beg the royal favour towards his wife: thus was equal justice done. The poor wretches all accused one another, and even the men who had personal or hearsay knowledge of it, brought them forward, and named aloud whose wives they were. About thirty of these women were publicly punished; first they had their hair cut,—a mark of great infamy with them; then they were beaten with thick thonged whips of leather, in such wise that two or three died. Thereafter all were absolved, with a warning that if they returned to these practices they should be drowned. Subsequently, however, I saw certain of the same party who were again arrested, and were not drowned, but only beaten with those whips which are called *gleau*.[1] The sin of man and man is very common, and though the book of their law prescribes the penalty of death, yet they heed not that; and nowhere in the world are these enormities more common and less punished; wherein may be seen the curse and wrath of God upon these wretches, who are led by the falsity and unrighteousness of their law to fall into the abyss of these horrible vices.

About the same time I saw justice done upon a youth of seventeen years of age. He was the son of an Ethiopian Cafre and of a woman of the islands, such a one being called Mulastre.[2] He had the greatest resolution and courage that I was ever witness of, for alone he had the assurance to attack six or seven other men. He became so mischievous, that with a single companion he went about the islands in a boat, thieving and harrying whatever he could, and assaulting the poor folk in cruel fashion. But at length he was caught, and had his right-hand cut off. While he was being punished, I saw no change upon his countenance, nor did he utter the slightest cry, no more than if he was feeling nothing. This punishment in no way changed his humour, for he was no sooner healed than he returned to his former courses, insomuch than when he was caught again they were constrained to cut off his left-foot, whereof he made no more account than of his fist: for his resolution was such that he himself taught the man that was cutting him how he ought to do it, without ever showing any trace of pain. He had by him a vessel full of boiling coco-nut oil, into which he himself thrust his leg, all as though it had been cold water. I think that such determined courage has never been seen in a boy. Withal, his evil nature so led him to larceny that no sooner was his leg healed than he took to

[1] Mr. Bell has not traced this word; the ordinary term for whip is *durrá*.

[2] Mulatto, properly applied, as here, only when one parent is a negro.

crawling out at night to commit robberies. He was also horribly addicted to sodomy; so at length the king was forced to send him into exile, and to put him to death.

But to return to the Grand Pandiare who carried out so many executions. After remaining a short time longer at the island, he got leave to go to Arabia, with a ship laden with great riches; but his departure was not without much sorrow on the part of the king and all the people, who regretted him extremely, for he was there regarded as a saint. He made fair promises of returning, but for all that had no mind thereto. His successor in the office was one who had espoused the sister of the chief queen, and was a great noble and of good family: he died in Arabia, as I have said.[1]

Such is what I have been able to note and remember of the most memorable events which took place at the Maldive islands during the time I was there; and before finishing this chapter I shall further say that during the five or six years I was at that king's court I saw nearly his whole government changed, and the greater part of the officers of his household and court come by their deaths in various ways. This ofttimes gave me a foreboding that the end and period of his government was drawing nigh.

Also I must not forget to mention that I saw happen there a great eclipse of the sun at high noon (this was in the year 1605), which lasted three hours.[2] All the people were greatly astonished, and cried and howled in strange fashion, saying that it was an evil omen, and signified that they should lose the greatest of them. And, indeed, in the same year, one of the king's wives died in childbed, and soon after the king himself was vanquished and slain, and all his estate was overthrown, as I shall relate in the chapter following.

[1] *Ante*, p. 277.

[2] This eclipse took place on the 12th October 1605; total at 1 P.M., Paris time; visible in Europe, Asia, and Africa (*L'Art de Vérifier des Dates, etc.*; Paris, 1770).

They all carefully observed the day, hour, and minute of the eclipse, and it was recorded in the public archives.[1]

CHAPTER XXIII.

Of the expedition of the king of Bengal to the Maldives.—The taking of Malé island.—Death of the Maldive king, and voyage of the author to Bengal, with a description of the islands of Malicut and Divandurou.

Having then resided at these islands for the space of five years, or thereabouts, but sorely against my will, this long sojourn gave me a knowledge of the country, and an acquaintance with the language, manners, and customs of the inhabitants, greater, perhaps, and I may say it without vanity, than any other European has ever had. Wherefore I have been led to enlarge with so much particularity and exactness my description of the islands, well knowing that none before me has written to the same effect: and perhaps it will be long ere another will make so long a sojourn; for, indeed, men go there but rarely, and then against their will, by reason of the great hazard and peril attending the voyage, which induce them to avoid the islands as much as they can. In the next place, they have been little known up to now; and if misfortune should carry any other person there as it carried me, it is unlikely he should meet with the same favourable treatment and liberty that I experienced. This will gain me an excuse with my readers if I have been somewhat lengthy and tedious in this description of the Maldives; but I have

[1] "In the Sultan's palace at Málé is said to be preserved a national record styled *Tárikhu* (Ar. *Tárikh*, "history"), or *Muskuli foi*, in which all important events and matters of State have been faithfully noted for centuries, in the old Maldive character (*dives akuru*), in Arabic, and in the modern native character (*gabali tána*)" (Bell, *Rep.*, 41). We may in time hear more of these archives.

thought that since God had granted me grace through the means of my misfortunes to learn so many particular things, I was obliged to share my knowledge with the public and my country, to whom my good intentions at least will be acceptable, showing that I am not ungrateful for the favours of God in that He hath granted me to know all these things, and at the last hath been pleased to deliver me miraculously, in such wise as I shall now relate.

But first I must not omit a dream I had while asleep at night at the islands two days before my deliverance, for it is worthy to be known. I dreamed that I was gone forth of that country, and was in full liberty in a Christian land. I was infinitely overjoyed, but at my awakening I was full sorely astonished to find my dream false. Nevertheless, though I was exceeding sad, I arose, and falling on my knees prayed God with all my heart and soul that He would be pleased of His grace to deliver me out of this Mahometan servitude, and to set me again on Christian soil, where I could resume the free exercise of my religion, which I had been constrained to discontinue for so long a time. Then I made a vow to make a voyage to St. James in Galicia,[1] there to render thanks to God. Two nights after that (it was in the month of February, in the year 1607) the king had warning of the coming of an armada of sixteen galleys or galleots, which were already preparing to enter the islands. The news greatly astonished both the king and his people, for they had no word of it before, and the suddenness of it surprised them. He commanded at once to put in the sea such galleys as he had, to the number of seven, let alone other vessels, barques, and boats, which were there in great number: and everyone set to this work with all his might; but they could not get it done speedily enough ere the enemy's sails came in sight.

[1] Santiago Compostella, the famous shrine in Galicia of the patron saint of Spain. As will be seen hereafter, Pyrard was enabled to perform his vow.

His consternation was then the greater, wherefore he commanded his people forthwith to ship all the most valuable riches he was possessed of, and so to save himself and his wives in the more distant islands of the south, where the enemy could not land because of the difficulties of the passages.

At first sight of the galleys all the people were greatly taken up, some with attending to the galleys and vessels of the king, others to their own barques and boats, so as to ship themselves and their goods and seek safety in the other islands. As for me, as soon as I saw the alarm was real, I called to mind my dream and the prayer I had made to God but a while before, and began to take some hope: and chiefly, when I perceived at a great distance the enemy's sails, I resolved, with my three companions, to seek an opportunity of safety and a deliverance from captivity, as we had so far found grace with God. But I leave you to imagine in what apprehension we were lest they should seek to prevent us from embarking, the which we had to manage or die in the attempt. But our good luck would have it that the alarm was so hot and sudden that they had no time to recover themselves, far less to think of us. So we had to save ourselves that day or never, and what happened was a true miracle for us. Meanwhile, during the great tumult which ensued at the sight and approach of the enemy, we made as though we were as greatly distressed and distracted as the rest, and made the same hurry; insomuch that the country folk, seeing us to be of like action and countenance with themselves, entertained no distrust of us. But I certainly believe that if the enemy's galleys had not appeared before the king had embarked (as I shall relate presently), and had we remained in the island without embarking with them, the king would not have failed on his return to have put us to death, all four,—that is, if the enemy had not cared to land, or the alarm had proved false. But God, having pity upon us, permitted the enemy to appear before the king and his people were ready, and this was the sole cause of our liberty. Meanwhile the enemy was ever approaching, and the king perceiving this, came forth of his palace and took to flight with the three queens, his wives, who were borne in the arms of some gentlemen, as a nurse carries her infant. They were covered each with veils and taffetas of divers colours, figured in the Chinese style, and as large as shrouds. They did not come forth from the palace till the king did, and he embarked with them. I was at the moment burdened with arms and other goods, which I was carrying to put on board the galleys, and being all soaked and in mean attire, the king met me and told me I was an honest man, and should take courage, using a word to me which is common throughout all India, namely, *Sabatz*,[1] that is to say, "Grammercy"; it is used also to praise a man for something he has done well. When he said this word to me tears of pity came into my eyes, for he wept and made the greatest lamentation to see himself obliged to quit all, and to see them thus bear away his wives, who on their part were bathed in tears, while all the people were in the saddest plight throughout the streets, and one heard naught but groans, cries, and howling of women and children. The king, having embarked for his safety in his royal galley, called by them *Ogate Gourabe*[2] (*gourabe* means "galley", and *ogate*, "royal"), along with his wives and his nephew, was constrained to leave behind the greatest part of his wealth, and all his arms and cannon, of which he had a great store in the island, for he had no time to arm himself or to ship them; and then, at the same moment when all the rest were on board, he gave the word to use sail and oars, and to take the route for the south and the atollons of Souadou. When all the galleys were gone saving the smallest, which

[1] Pers. *Shābāsh!* "Bravo! well done!" (Yule, *Gloss.*).

[2] M. *gurábu*, Ar. *ghurâb* (Yule, *Gloss.* s. v. *Grab*). Mr. Bell has not been able to trace the word *ogate* in the modern language.

was tarrying to load some goods, then said I to my companions that it was time to seek safety in the wood, fearing lest they should compel us to embark with them. Nevertheless, I made another journey to the king's palace with the islanders, and let them all take their loads first and go ahead towards the galley, while I, in place of following them, took a path aside and gained the wood, as did two of my companions from another quarter,—the third was got on board I know not how, though he had the same designs as we; but the galley was soon taken. Afterwards I learnt from him that he had been impressed on board by the islanders. So on that day we all four were borne on the same course of fortune, without knowing anything of one another. We were for more than four hours in the island along with some poor folk, all the rest having gone. I wandered about the king's palace, where there were all sorts of things, gold, silver, and jewellery, lying about; but I never dreamed of touching any, nor even of hiding the silver that I had, the which I gave to a friend, along with the trees, a boat, and a house I had purchased: that was to the son of the lord who had brought me out of the island Peindoüé, whereof I have spoken; to him I gave all I had. My companions saved some stuff they had hidden.

As soon as the captain of the enemy's armada discovered that the king was fled, he ordered eight galleys to the pursuit, while the other eight anchored at the island whereon I was. I gave myself up to the first that landed, and implored them to save me. At the first, not recognising me as a Frenchman, and believing me to be a Portuguese, they were about to kill me, and, stripping me naked, took from me all I had. But when they found that in truth I was not a Portuguese, they treated me more humanely, and conducted me to their captain, who took me under his protection, assuring me that I should suffer no evil; then he had me clad in other garments, and bade me remain in his galleys for my safety, at least for that day and night. Afterwards I was allowed to go where I liked throughout the island, without anyone saying a word.

The eight galleys that were bidden to go after the king came up with him and to close quarters, whereupon the king, attempting to defend himself, was slain by a pike-thrust, followed by sword-cuts; his wives were taken prisoners, and his nephew was drowned. No harm, however, was done to the wives, save that they lost all their trinkets, which were seized by the soldiers and mariners, these being the most dangerous fellows at pillage: these mariners are called *Moucois.*[1]

The cause of the taking and death of the king was that there was no wind, but the greatest calm possible, and that the enemy's galleys were better for rowing than those of the king, which were only good for sailing, and of no use for oars. Had there been but a little wind they could not have caught him; but his ill-fortune cast him into this fate, which he fully merited for the great cruelties he had used. Not one of the island vessels was taken in this chase; and had the king and his wives embarked in them, they would have had a chance of escape; but his hour was come, and for my part I hold that it was by the mercy of God he was thus slain at the first shock, so that he saw not the sad and piteous spectacle, which met my eyes, of the condition of his wives and state. There was, however, no great massacre, for except the king and two or three others slain with him, and as many wounded—among others, a young soldier, the son of a Portuguese *metiz*, who had aforetime been wrecked in his

[1] The *Mukkavar* are a fisher caste of Malabar, as Pyrard himself describes them later. But there is no doubt that the present expedition came from Bengal, as there were rejoicings when they returned home to Chittagong. Possibly there may have been some Mukkavar on board, but more likely the author thought he was justified in giving the Malabar name to people of the same class in Bengal.

ship at these islands[1]—there was no one harmed, except, also, his nephew, who, thinking to save himself by swimming, was drowned by reason of weakness, sickness, and of the melancholy and sorrow that he had for his wife, who had died in child-bed but a while before. He had abducted this woman from her husband, as I have related above.[2]

The enemy having thus seized and pillaged all the king's galleys, they collected them together, except two that were lost upon the shallows and reefs. They brought back, too, the three queens in a miserable plight, and lodged them in the house of the king's nephew, adjoining the royal palace. This house was also called palace, being enclosed by walls, and of the same form as the king's, only smaller: all the other houses of princes and princesses are called *Gandhouere*,[3] that is, "palace", while other houses are called *Gué*.[4]

The queens were put in that palace, for all day and night the men were ransacking the king's palace and carrying off everything that was of value. In his nephew's there was nothing to take, because all his property had been shipped off in good time; besides, this nephew had not much goods, no more indeed than what the king gave him, in addition to a small patrimony. Had he been richer, the king would have been afraid lest he should wage war against himself. Soldiers were placed on guard over these poor queens, who were kept in the semblance of prisoners, that so they might be led to discover the king's treasures; but this they could not do, for they knew nothing about any such; and I well know that the king let none know of these, except a certain secretary who had escaped among the first. Each of the queens was allowed a female servant to wait upon her, also three gentlemen of the king's household; but neither these nor the women durst go without the house, and the three gentlemen entered not

[1] See above, p. 255. [2] See above, p. 273.

[3] M. *gaḍuvaru*; see above, p. 219, *note*.

[4] M. and Sin. *gé*.

the queens' apartments, nor even saw them, but tarried with the soldiers to see what good or ill-fortune should befall their mistresses. All this was done according to the General's command. As for me, I went to see them often, the natives not being allowed to enter. I used to go in as often as I liked, and gave them what advice and consolation I could, for I heard all that was said about them. With tears in their eyes they asked me again and again if I sorrowed greatly for the death of the king, who had such affection for me. I answered I did, and now that he was dead I was minded to go away and remain no more at the islands, having no longer a master there. Had he not been slain I should never have gone away. All this was very far from my desire and thoughts. Nevertheless, I assured them that I would not withdraw without taking their advice and leave: this they highly approved, and promised they would never desert me. As they asked me what was being said of them, I told them they were held prisoners to point out the king's treasures (as they had already been informed), but that they should do nothing, for all threats of carrying them off were but to terrify them. I had myself heard from the chief men that they would not carry them off, with which news they were greatly pleased, and they besought me not to leave them.

They begged me also to go to and fro among the enemy, to bring word of all that was said and done, the which I did willingly enough, and discovered to them all I could glean from every quarter. The queens also told me in private a great deal about each other,—viz., the chief queen, the foreigner from Bengal, who was as fair and white as the women of this country; and the young one, whom the king had but recently taken, in manner already described.[1] She told me with sorrow that she brought misfortune wherever she was (this they call *sompas*[2]), and that since the king had taken her, every

[1] See *supra*, p. 265.

[2] Mr. Bell has not been able to explain this word.

disaster had befallen them. I was deeply grieved to see them in the state they were, having aforetime seen them so richly and luxuriously apparelled; they were indeed but poorly dressed, and had hardly anything but their own gowns left them, and everything was searched. But saving that, there was no harm or violence done to their persons, nor to their honour; not even a lewd word was passed; and all the girls and women of the island were treated in like manner. Their food was brought from the house of the Pandiare, who remained in the island along with the other clergy and many beside; but these did not for all that escape the general sack. The Pandiare did indeed save somewhat, for his house was the refuge of all, men and women alike, for personal security only, their goods being pillaged there as elsewhere. Yet he managed to appease in some degree the fury of the enemy, being held by them in some respect. I, too, though in the hands of the General and his army, was treated with much favour and courtesy, the reason whereof was our cannons, which indeed were the object of their enterprise and coming to the islands. They had not been used to see such pieces, and were in great straits how to mount and get them on board, not knowing by which end to take them. Therefore they took me with them to show them all the tackle and the way to use it; and they were well pleased with all I told them, for I gave them information as well in that respect as concerning the other equipment of our ships, and also the affairs of the islands, whereof I had good understanding. For all this they valued me much, and were exceeding kindly towards me. Another thing was that the pilot who had brought them thither was a native of the islands, though a resident of the continent, and I had often seen him at Malé. He well knew what regard the king and the lords of the country had for me, and this, rumoured among them, won for me the more respect. Yet did this vile fellow for gold betray his king and country, for all that the king had a great affection toward him, and gave him no cause of complaint; for the landing on these coasts is so difficult and dangerous, that the rest of the party had never dared come without him to guide them, and so was he the cause of the whole disaster. At this juncture I often went to the Pandiare's house to visit a number of my friends that were there, not daring to venture abroad; amongst others, the three sons of the lord with whom I resided so long. They counselled me to be gone, saying that the king their master was dead, nor were they nor I under any protection now; but all the others advised contrarywise, that if they had but one coco-nut, they would give me half; yet I took the advice of the three, one of whom had a gunshot wound. They were severely put to the torture, and all had to pay a ransom.

Three or four days after the arrival of this army there came to Malé a barque sent by the dead king's people, to ask leave of the General to convey some rice and other commodities for the funeral ceremonies of the late king, who was buried at the island *Gouradou*,[1] where that great master was of whom I have already spoken. It had been his fixed intention and desire to be buried at Malé, as I shall now tell; but they never keep their corpses, and have no custom of embalming them, or of conveying them from island to island. At length the General gave permission to take all that was required for the purpose, and so they did, and would even have taken me along with them, as they strongly suspected that I was minded to escape.

Had the king been slain by others than of his own faith, they say he had been blessed and sanctified (such a one

[1] The tradition is that Sultan Ibrahim was buried, not at *Guradú*, but at *Kanimídú*. When he escaped from Málé he took a course towards Huvadu, and the island Guradú in S. Málé atoll would lie directly in that course.

they call *Chayde*[1]); then had they made no ceremony, but buried him as he died, without washing the body or performing any other customary act; but though he did not die in defence of the faith, they did not perform the ceremony wont to be observed at the obsequies of a king, but buried him as any ordinary countryman of the islands, albeit this was to their great sorrow. They were even at much pains to get a white cloth for a winding-sheet, and a coffin to put him in—him who in his lifetime had so lavishly given to all the poor of his kingdom when they were in need. He had always by him more than thirty coffins ready made, for himself, his queens, and court, for use when occasion was. He had also caused to be built a magnificent shrine, and a burial-ground entirely enclosed, in Malé, with a view to being buried there. It was the best constructed of all, but God willed not that he should be laid there. Such are the common results of war, and so was it here, where all the wealth that he had collected was involved in havoc and useless waste; for whatsoever the soldiers could not carry off they utterly destroyed.

It was most pitiful to see the ravages committed in the island, and especially at the king's palace; for all the private citizens had secured their goods in their boats, and lost nothing: the boats being small, escaped in all directions, and sailed faster than the galleys. All that belonged to the king and queens, however, was pillaged, and nothing was saved either of what was in the galleys or on shore. Moreover, as the misfortune of these poor islanders would have it, there was a large ship belonging to the king all laden and ready to sail eight days before, but their magicians and astrologers had put it off to this very day, as being a lucky day for weighing,—so had they made it out by their reckoning and

[1] M. *Sáhidu*, Ar. *Shahid*, "martyr".

ephemerides; but they had made a sad mistake. The voyage was to be to Arabia, and she could not get away from the islands by reason of the great calm which befell, whereby she was seized, like everything else. The cargo of this vessel consisted, among other things, of the cinnamon that the king had of the ship of Ceylon, which a while before had been wrecked at the islands, as I have said[1]; the rest was merchandise of the islands, the greater part being coco produce. The enemy, in sacking the ship, took only the island stuff; for as for the cinnamon, they left it to its fate, with the vessel, which never made another voyage, as I afterwards learnt at Goa, and as I shall relate in the proper place.

At length, when the enemy had tarried in the island for the space of ten days, gathering their booty and loading their ships with all the valuables they found, and five or six pieces of cannon, large and small, that were there, they withdrew, and set the queens and all the rest of the people at liberty. They took no prisoners with them, except the chief queen's brother, brother-in-law to the late king. At first I believed they took him in order to get a ransom; but afterwards I learnt, on the contrary, that it was with his own consent, as he wished to go to visit *Ali Rhadia*, the king of Cananor, for a purpose I shall explain hereafter. On my part, I went and took farewell of the queens and my friends, not without tears, indeed—theirs of sorrow and chagrin, but mine of joy. When it came to embarking, all the captains got a-quarrelling which should have my companions and me in his galley. At length I embarked in one, and my three companions severally in three others, and we did not see each other for a long time.

As for what followed at the Maldives, I heard afterwards, while at Goa, that the natives fell into a bitter civil war. The king had died without children or nephews, and the kingdom there never goes to females, no more than in

[1] See above, pp. 299-301.

France.[1] Four of the greatest lords in the country banded themselves one against another who should be king; and this war continuing a long time, the king of Cananor, *Ali Rhadia*, had despatched a goodly armament of galleys, under the guidance of *Rana Banduy Tacourou*, the chief queen's brother, whom the Bengal galleys had taken prisoner, as has been said. By means of this army he had at length established that prince upon the throne,—who was, indeed, as next of kin, the lawful heir,—but on condition that he should hold it of him, and regard him as his suzerain. He scattered all who were causing trouble, and so restored peace to the islands.[2] Such is what I heard at Goa. But to return to what befell us: we embarked, as already said, at the Maldives, intending to make our course up the Gulf of Bengal. The

[1] Pyrard has fallen into an error exactly the converse to that of Masudi, who, visiting Ceylon (and ? the Maldives) in A.D. 916, records that the islands were governed by a queen, "for from the most ancient times the inhabitants have a rule never to let themselves be governed by a man" (*Masudi*, by Sprenger, i, 335). We have little knowledge of the rule of succession in pre-Mahommedan times, though we are informed by Ibn Batuta, corroborated by tradition, that at the time of the conversion a king was on the throne. Since the Mahomedan conversion female sovereigns have been exceptional. Thus, in Ibn Batuta's time at the island, a queen was on the throne, in default of male heirs. And later, the islands were ruled, for two or three years prior to 1759, by or in the name of a queen Aminá (Bell, *Rep.*, 33).

[2] As will be remembered, this chief, on his return from Arabia, paid a visit to Âli Raja at Cananor, and was with difficulty induced to return to the Maldives. At that time a treaty seems to have been negotiated, whereby the aid of Âli Raja was secured, to obtain for Rana Banda the possession, and for Âli Raja the suzerainty, of the islands. As will be seen hereafter, the Bengal fleet, which took away this prince as well as Pyrard, touched at Minicoy and at the Laccadives, but proceeded to Chittagong without touching land on the Malabar coast. When Pyrard afterwards leaves Chittagong for the Malabar coast, he makes no mention of the Maldive prince; it may be conjectured that he was left at the Laccadives to make his own way across to Cananor. According to tradition gleaned by Mr. Bell, he was afterwards known as *Máfilafurhi Rasgefánu*, from the name of his family island.

passage between the islands is very dangerous, by reason of the reefs and banks, which are exceeding numerous; and no one would dare to steer through them without having native pilots, as we then had. The island from which the dead king came, by name *Oustisme*,[1] being at the head of the others, and quite the last, they cast anchor there, and set themselves to slay, sack, and pillage, carrying off everything they could find. We saw by day a wonderful number of barques and boats sailing away in all directions. Having refreshed themselves with a half-day's sojourn at this island, they passed orders as to their course, in case they should happen to separate,—as, indeed, they did, by reason of the great calm. At length we got out of the islands, by God's grace. The calm was such that we were about three days in reaching a little island named *Malicut*,[2] which is only thirty-five leagues to the north of the Maldives.

[1] M. *Utímu:* Tiladummati atoll, in lat. 6° 52′ N. It is noteworthy that our two great authorities on the Maldive islands, Ibn Batuta and Pyrard, both landed here, the one on his coming to, the other on his departure from, the islands. The fact of landing at it seems to have led the former to give its name to the atoll, of which it was but a unit, *Teeim*, according to this traveller, being one of the provinces or climates. It is not quite at the head of the others, as Pyrard states here: indeed, he says, but a few lines below, that after leaving it "at length we got out of the islands". The northernmost island of the Maldives proper is *Turacun*, in Heawandú atoll, in lat. 7° 7′ N.

[2] Minicoy, called *Maliku* by the natives, lies in lat. 8° 14′ N., being separated from the Maldives by the Eight-Degree Channel, the distance being about 68 miles. This channel is the course generally adopted by steamers proceeding to Ceylon during the S.W. monsoon. The island is about 7 miles by half a mile broad; it still belongs to Cananor. Pyrard is right in his statement that the people of Minicoy are of Maldive race and language. The population, according to the last census (1881), is 3,915. The majority follow a seafaring life, the island possessing six large vessels fit for the Bengal trade, four coasting vessels, and eight fishing-boats. Their trade is with the Maldives, the Malabar coast, Ceylon, and Calcutta. Minicoy has thriven to a great extent, owing to being free of the restrictions which require the Laccadive natives to carry all their produce to particular Malabar ports. Recently a lighthouse

This island is surrounded with very dangerous banks, which have to be carefully watched. Three of our galiots that had kept together cast anchor there; the others had separated. This island of Malicut is only four leagues in circumference; it is wonderfully fertile in coco-trees, bananas, millet, and other products of the Maldives; all sorts of fruit are abundant. The fishery is very good; the climate more healthy and temperate than at the Maldives; the people have the same customs, manners, and language as those of the Maldives. This island was at one time part of the Maldive realm; but a king gave it to his brother as a portion. It is now governed by a lady, who holds it of the king of Cananor, for the sake of greater security. This queen gave me a very good reception, for she had often seen me at the court of the king of the Maldives, her near relative. When she saw me she began to weep, as did most of the inhabitants, with sorrow for the death of the king, the story of which I have told.

After tarrying about two days at this island we set sail and made for the islands of *Divandurou*,[1] thirty leagues from

has been erected on the island by the British Government. One of the staff employed in its erection has written an interesting though short account of the island and its inhabitants (*Minicoy, etc.*, by Bartholomeusz; London, 1885). For further information, see Report by E. G. Thomas, in *Mad. Journ. of Lit. and Sci.*; Hunter, *Imp. Gaz. of India*, art. "Laccadives"; and *Encyc. Brit.* (9th edition), art. "Laccadives"; Bell, *Rep.*, 41.

[1] *I.e.*, the *Anduru* islands, from the chief of them, generally called *Androt*, which contains the tomb of the apostle of local Mahommedanism. The name *Laccadives* (*Laksha Dwípa*, "the Hundred Thousand Isles"), by which they are generally known, is that applied by the people of India, and was evidently meant to include the Maldives. Albirúni speaks of the Maldives and Laccadives as *Divah Kuzah* and *Divah Kanbar*, the "cowrie" and the "coir" islands. By the natives they are called *Amendivi*, from the island *Amini*, or simply *divi*. Barbosa says they are four in number, and were called *Malandiva* (*Barbosa*, Hak. Soc., p. 164). The Portuguese generally called these the *Mammale* islands, from the great Cananor merchant who controlled their trade; and the same name survives in Lancaster (*Voy.*, Hak. Soc., p. 10). The Lacca-

Malicut to the north; they are five in number, and vary from six to seven leagues in circumference; they are eighty leagues distant from the Malabar coast, right opposite Cananor. They are under the rule of the king of Cananor, who also possesses thirty of the Maldive islands, that were ceded to him about fifty years before by a king of the Maldives, to whom he had given succour against a revolt of his own people.[1]

These islands of *Divandurou* are inhabited by Mahometan Malabars, most of them rich merchants, who drive a great trade throughout India, and especially at the Maldives, whence they export much merchandise, and where they keep resident factors. They have the same customs and languages as the people of Cananor, Calecut, Cochin, and the rest of Malabar: their soil is very fertile, and the climate good. The Malabar corsairs, when on their voyages, often come there to refresh, and in most cases, being quite like natives, marry there. Albeit they fail not betimes to pillage them too, for all the friendship that is between them: for they do hold gain above all the friendship in the world, and when they cannot reap any booty from their enemies,

dives consist of ten islands,—Amini, Chetlat, Kadamat, and Kiltan (with Bitra, which is uninhabited) are British; Agathi, Kawrati, Androt, and Kalpéni (with Suheli, uninhabited) are the property of the Cananor Raja, but since 1877 have been sequestrated for non-payment of tribute, and are at present also under British administration. Another classification obtains:—Amini, Kalpéni, Androt, and Kawrati are *tarwat* islands, in which alone the high-caste natives reside; the rest are *melacheri*, or low-caste islands. The total population in 1881 (excluding Minicoy, which is the personal property of the Raja) was 11,287. See further the authorities cited in the preceding note, and also the valuable account, from a naturalist's point of view, by Mr. Allan Hume, in *Stray Feathers*, vol. iv; Calcutta, 1876.

[1] It must remain uncertain which were the thirty Maldive islands ceded by the Maldive king, and who was the king who ceded them. They could only have been ceded during a very serious revolt, such as that which ended in the abdication of Sultan Hassan (Dom Manoel), A.D. 1552, so that we may believe that the islands were given up by that Sultan, rather than by his rival Ali, who succeeded him.

being anxious not to return empty-handed, they fall upon their friends. These islands are, as it were, a half-way house for merchandise between the mainland and the Maldives and Malicut.

Having refreshed ourselves four or five days at these islands, we again set sail, now towards the south, in order to double Point de Galle, which is a cape at the end of the island of Ceylon. On our way we fell in with a great number of whales, which thought to upset our galiots; but those on board, with drums, pans, and kettles, set up such a din as caused them to make off.

We also fell in with some galleys or *padoes*[1] of the Malabars, on one occasion just at daybreak when the sky was cloudy and thick, so that we did not perceive them till they were close upon us. I was never more astonished than to see the perfect order of their sailors, all armed and ready to charge. We were taken unawares, while they had been the first to sight us; but being friendly, they only passed by. They numbered three galiots, and we the same. For the rest, before closing this chapter, I would say, for the better understanding of what has been described above, that this army, which thus attacked and sacked the Maldives, was sent on behalf of the king of Bengal, a kingdom lying beyond these islands, on the mainland, under the tropic of Cancer. The principal motive which had induced him to make the enterprise was to seize the cannon that the king of the Maldives had gotten out of our wrecked ship, and the many others he had obtained in like manner. The cannon in question was the most beautiful example to be seen anywhere, and had great renown in the Indies, many kings and princes having been continually on the point of coming to see it.

[1] Malayâlam *paṭak*, a country craft not now in use, frequently mentioned by the Portuguese writers.

CHAPTER XXIV.

The kingdom of Bengal, and some observations thereon.

After a month's voyage we arrived at Chartican,[1] a port of the kingdom of Bengal, where we were received by the inhabitants with much rejoicing. On landing, they took me with them to salute the king, who is not, however, the great king of Bengal, but a petty king of this province, or rather a governor, with the title of king,[2] as is generally the case in those parts. The great king of Bengal lives higher up the country, thirty or forty leagues off. On being presented to this petty king, he received me with great kindness, and gave me my full liberty, saying that if I would remain with him he would do great things for me: and, indeed, he bade bring me raiment and food day by day in great abundance. But after a month's sojourn there I found a ship of Calecut, whose master asked if I would go with him, saying that the Hollanders' ships often came to Calecut, and there might be some in which I could get a passage to France, since I was minded to return thither; whereto I gladly agreed, seeing I had no other aim but that, and on that score I declined all other favours. I therefore took my leave of the king, which was granted me without difficulty.

I was so short a time in Bengal, that I cannot record many of its characteristics; however, here is what I picked up.

[1] Chittagong, properly *Chatigam;* in the Portuguese books, *Chatigão* and *Porto Grande;* to be distinguished from *Sātgāuw*, or *Porto Pequeno*, the two ports being regarded as the eastern and western limits of the Ganges' mouth. See *Linschoten*, Hak. Soc.; Correa, *Lendas*, iii, 649; and Yule, *Glossary*, s. v. *Chittagong*, *Porto Pequeno*, and (in Supplt.) *Satigam*.

[2] This petty Raja was probably the "Mugg" (*Magh*), or king of Arakan (Yule, *Gloss.*, s. v.); the Portuguese called him *o mogo*, and the people *os mogos* (*Livro das Monç.*, i, 348, 350, 353; ii, 226, 392.)

The kingdom of Bengal is of great extent; it lies in the middle country of the Indies, and is said to be 400 leagues in length, so the king is the most puissant prince in India, after the grand Mogor. About the time I left, the Mogor had declared war against him, and the king was preparing to receive him with more than 200,000 men and 10,000 elephants.[1] He has many tributary kings: for instance, the kings of Aracan, of Chaul,[2] and other great lords, as well Mahometan as Gentile, who are bound to furnish him, when he goes out to war, with a certain number of men, elephants, and horses. They also pay him tribute for such harbours as they have in their territories; and at all of these a great trade is carried on in all sorts of merchandise, the merchants exporting large quantities of goods, by reason whereof they dare not risk the loss of this king's goodwill.

The country is healthy and temperate, and so wondrous fertile that one lives there for almost nothing; and there is such a quantity of rice, that, besides supplying the whole country, it is exported to all parts of India, as well to Goa and Malabar, as to Sumatra, the Moluccas, and all the islands of Sunda, to all of which lands Bengal is a very nursing mother, who supplies them with their entire subsistence and food. Thus, one sees arrive there every day an infinite number of vessels from all parts of India for these provisions; and I believe it would be still greater, were not the navigation so perilous by reason of the banks and shallows wherewith all this Gulf of Bengal is full. So it happens that when the Bengal ships are behind their time, or are lost, rice is fabulously dear, and there is a cry, as it were, of the extremity

[1] The preparations for, and the progress of this invasion, and the policy of the Portuguese, are given at some length in the King of Spain's despatches of the 19th March 1612, and 15th March 1613 (*Liv. das Monç.*, ii, 226, 391-4).

[2] As pointed out by Mr. Rivara, this is a palpable error, Chaul being on the other side of India.

of famine. On the contrary, when the navigation is good, the rice is as cheap as if it grew in the country, and fetches no more than four deniers the pound. The country is well supplied with animals, such as oxen, cows, and sheep; flesh is accordingly very cheap, let alone milk-foods and butter, whereof they have such an abundance that they supply the rest of India; and pile carpets of various kinds, which they weave with great skill. There are many good fruits,—not, however, cocos or bananas; plenty of citrons, limes, oranges, pomegranates, cajus, pineapples, etc., ginger, long pepper,[1] of which, in the green state they make a great variety of preserves, as also of lemons and oranges. The country abounds with sugar-cane, which they eat green; or else make into excellent sugar, for a cargo to their ships, the like not being made in any part of India except in Cambaye and the other countries of the Mogor adjacent to Bengal, these countries being of the same climate, language, and fertility. There is likewise exported from Bengal much scented oils, got from a certain grain, and divers flowers: these are used by all the Indians after bathing to rub their bodies withal. Cotton is so plentiful, that, after providing for the uses and clothing of the natives, and besides exporting the raw material, they make such a quantity of cotton cloths, and so excellently woven, that these articles are exported, and thence only, to all India, but chiefly to the parts about Sunda. Likewise is there plenty of silk, as well that of the silkworm as of the (silk) herb,[2] which is of the brightest yellow colour,

[1] Long-pepper is derived from two shrubby plants, *Piper officinarum* and *Piper longum*, and is to be distinguished from black and white pepper, both of which are obtained from *Piper nigrum*. Calcutta is still one of the chief ports for the export of long-pepper, the other regions being Malabar and the Archipelago. See Yule, *Glossary*, s. v. "Pepper".

[2] This grass-silk is referred to by Linschoten as a kind of linen: "It is yealowish, and is called the hearbe of Bengalen, wherewith they do most cunningly stitch their coverlits, pavilions, pillowes, carpets and

and brighter than silk itself: of this they make many stuffs of divers colours, and export them to all parts. The inhabitants, both men and women, are wondrously adroit in all manufactures, such as of cotton cloth and silks, and in needlework, such as embroideries, which are worked so skilfully, down to the smallest stitches, that nothing prettier is to be seen anywhere. Some of these cottons and silks are so fine that it is difficult to say whether a person so attired be clothed or nude. Many other kinds of work, such as furniture and vessels, are constructed with extraordinary delicacy, which, if brought here, would be said to come from China.

In this country is made a large quantity of small black and red pottery, like the finest and most delicate *terre sigillée;* in this they do a great trade, chiefly in *gargoulettes*[1] and drinking-vessels, and other utensils. There is a great quantity, too, of huge reeds or canes, as big as a man's thigh, and six or seven fathoms high, hollow inside, and knotted like those here. They are harder to break than any wood in the world; of these, levers and rods are made to carry over the heaviest weights, and are used throughout India, even at Goa and elsewhere: so much so, that the Portuguese and the Indians use no other poles for their palanquins and litters: these are

mantles, ... likewise they make whole peeces or webbes of this hearbe, sometimes mixed and woven with silke, although those of the hearbe it selfe are dearer and more esteemed, and is much fairer than the silke. These webbes are named Sarrijn, and it is much used and worne in India" (*Hak. Soc.*, i, 96).

[1] Port. *gargoleta.* For a fuller description, see vol. ii. It was an earthenware vessel with a spout, whereby the liquid was poured into the mouth from a distance, to avoid contact. The manner of so drinking is shown in a cut in Knox (*Ceylon*, opposite p. 87). The word is used and the practice described by several travellers in Portuguese India, this mode of drinking being adopted by the Portuguese themselves. To be clumsy in the use of a *gargoleta* at once proclaimed a person to be a *reinol*, or "griffin", fresh from Europe (*Linschoten*, Hak. Soc., i, 207; *Mandelslo*, Eng. trans., p. 105; *Fryer*, "gurgulets", p. 47). The word remains current both in India and Ceylon as "goglet", a water-bottle. See Yule, *Glossary*, s. v. The Sinhalese, I believe, call it *gurulota.*

everywhere called *Bambou.*[1] When one of these is bent into any required curve and heated, it remains so always, and will sooner break than lose its curve. Of these, too, are made their measures for measuring all their goods, such as rice, grain, oil, butter, and the like. Measures of all sizes are made of them. These reeds grow in quantity elsewhere in India; but this is their original home, and here they are found in greatest plenty. These canes will not bend double; and they are mottled black and white. There is another kind,[2] of a different shape and thickness, the largest of this sort being no more than four thumbs' girth, and very tall. It is porous, hard, and very pliant, so that you can bring the two ends together without its breaking, and yet it is very strong: of this are made walking-sticks and canes for chastisement; they raise the skin

[1] There is some doubt whether the word *bambu* is Malay or Canarese. The question is discussed by Col. Yule (*Glossary*, s. v.), who remarks that, while Marsden gives it as good Malay, Crawfurd, on the other hand, says that it is only used on the west coast of Sumatra. Col. Yule believes the true origin to be the Canarese *baṇwu*. In the Portuguese writers of the latter half of the sixteenth century, it generally appears as *mambu* (*e.g.*, De Orta and Acosta). I do not find it mentioned in the statistical works of 1525 contained in the *Subsidios, etc.* The author seems here to refer to the giant bambu, of which it is believed Bengal is the true habitat. It has been planted at the Botanic Gardens at Peradeniya, Ceylon; and there, Dr. Haeckel says, it attains a thickness of two feet. Col. Yule would seem to require corroboration of this statement. I have seen, though not actually measured, these magnificent specimens, and have been assured that in Ceylon the plant attains greater dimensions than in its native regions.

[2] This would seem to be the Malacca cane. Linschoten, in his account of Bengal, describes its appearance and use in much the same terms:—"There groweth likewise marble-coloured reedes, whereof you may see many sortes in the custodie of Paludanus, which the Portingalles call Canas de Bengala, that is, Reedes of Bengala. Within they are full of pith, and are about the thickness of Spanish reedes, but somewhat thinner, and when they are greene they bowe and bend like willow twigges. They are outwardly of divers colours, and speckled as if they were painted. They use them in Portingall for olde women to beare in their handes when they goe abroad or uppon the stones" (*Linschoten*, Hak. Soc., i, 97).

wherever they fall, but never break it, however tender it may be. They are neatly shaped, and are naturally of a mottled colour, white, yellow, and black: there is great trade in them to all parts of India, for they are found nowhere else. By rubbing hard two sticks of this cane together, fire is produced as from a match: and they are used for this purpose. There is yet another sort of cane, which never grows thicker than the little finger, of the same form and growth as the other; it is as pliant as an osier, and is called *Rotan*.[1] Ships' cables are made of it, and many kinds of neatly plaited baskets, and other wicker things. In short, it is used as cord, and can be split into any number of strips. It is a fathom and a half in length. It is trafficked in everywhere, and is in great demand for its use in manufacture; it is white, and not mottled.

This country abounds with elephants, which are exported hence to all parts of India. There are rhinoceros[2] also, and some say unicorns, too, which are said to be found in this land only. They say other animals will not drink at a well until a female unicorn has steeped her horn in the water, so they all wait on the bank till she comes and does so.[3]

[1] Malay, *Rotan;* Correa, De Orta, and Linschoten all write *rota.* The English form *rattan* appears in Fryer (1673).

[2] I use the word as a plural, as in orig. and in the English version of *Linschoten.*

[3] The unicorn localised in those parts was no doubt the rhinoceros itself: see *Marco Polo*, bk. III, ch. ix, and *note* by Col. Yule, and the following passage from Linschoten:—"Some thinke it (the rhinoceros) is the right unicorne, because that as yet there hath no other bin found, but only by hearsay, and by the pictures of them. The Portingales and those of Bengala affirme, that by the river Ganges, in the kingdome of Bengala, are many of these rhinoceros, which when they will drinke, the other beasts stand and waite upon them, till the rhinoceros hath drunke, and thrust his horn into the water, for he cannot drink but his horne must be under the water, because it standeth so close unto his nose and muzzle; and then after him all the other beastes doe drinke" (*Linsch.*, ii, 9). As to the right of first drinking, Pyrard's myth pictures

In short, I find no country in all the East Indies more abundantly supplied with all things needful for food, with the riches of nature and art; and were not the navigation so dangerous, it would be the fairest, most pleasant, fertile, and profitable in the whole world. They usually keep an ambassador at Goa; but when I was preparing to leave Goa to come home, there arrived an ambassador extraordinary at the court of the viceroy, and it was said that he had come to ask some assistance.[1]

One of the greatest trades in Bengal is in slaves; for there is a certain land subject to this king where fathers sell their children, and give them to the king as tribute; so most of the slaves in India are got from hence. Many of the merchants castrate them, cutting them when they are young, and not only the testicles, but also the entire organ.[2] I have seen many of this kind, who appeared to have but a little hole for the passage of water. This is in order to put them in charge of the women, and of the keys of the house; they trust them in all things, and never their wives. Such is the custom among Mahometans, for they quit their wives very frequently. Nowhere in India are slaves of so little value, for they are all old and knavish villains, both men and women.

The people are well formed in body, the women are pretty, but more shameless than elsewhere in India. The men are much given to trafficking in merchandise, and not to war or arms,—a soft, courteous, clever people, but having the repute of great cheats, thieves, and liars. They trade in

as a polite gallantry on the part of the other animals (*place aux dames!*) what in Linschoten appears as subservience to a male tyrant. I have no space here to discuss the unicorn generally; those who are disposed to entertain his existence may consult the note of Mr. Badger (*Varthema*, Hak. Soc., pp. 46-8).

[1] This embassy is not mentioned in the royal despatches, and perhaps was not reported by the viceroy.

[2] See *Barbosa* (Hak. Soc., p. 180); *Varthema* (Hak. Soc., p. 258); Beckmann (*Litt. der Alt. Besch.*, ii, 132).

many places, making long voyages; so do many strangers frequent their country: for example, Persians, Arabs, and the Portuguese merchants of Goa and Cochin. Under the government of this king are men of many religions, viz., Jews, Mahometans, and Gentiles, or pagans, these latter showing as great a diversity of ceremonies as of countries and provinces. The great king is a pagan; he of Chartican, whom I saw, was a Mahometan.

The Gentile people of this Bengal country have for their pagoda,[1] or idol, a white elephant; it is but rarely met with, and is deemed sacred. The kings worship it, and even go to war to get it from their neighbours, not having one themselves, and sometimes grand battles are fought on this score.[2]

As for dress, the men attire themselves bravely with very

[1] For a dissertation upon this perplexing word, see Yule's *Glossary*, s. v. There can be little doubt that it comes from *bhagavat*, "the holy" or "blessed", *i.e.*, god. Col. Yule gives a series of quotations in which the word is used, as here, of an idol; the application to a temple is of course more common.

[2] As need hardly be said nowadays, the white elephant is merely an albino, and with blotches of pink, which rarely extend over the whole body. I do not know an earlier mention of it than that by Horace (*Ep. II*, i, 196): "Sive elephas albus volgi converteret ora." The king of Ceylon had one at Anuradhapura in the fifth century A.D. (*Mahavanso*, c. xxxviii, p. 254). In the fifteenth century, Abd-er-Razzak saw one at Bisnagar. "The king possesses one white elephant of an extremely great size, on whose body are scattered here and there grey spots like freckles" (*India in Fifteenth Cent.*, i, 27). The references to white elephants in the books of the Portuguese and Dutch period are too frequent to be mentioned. Such animals were prized as rarities in all the countries of India, but received special veneration in Buddhist lands. As to Ceylon, see Tennent (*Ceylon*, ii, 285), and Knox (*Hist. Relation*, p. 21). The white elephant cult attained its greatest proportions in Burma, Pegu, and Siam, and the reference in the text to wars for the possession of the white elephant is probably to the great struggle in 1568 between the kings of Pegu and Siam, as to which see *Linschoten*, (Hak. Soc., i, 98, 102); *Mandelslo* (Eng. trans., p. 127); Pallegoix (*Siam*, i, 152; ii, 2, 85).

large cotton shirts, which fall to the ground; over it is worn a silk mantle, and on the head a turban of very fine linen. The women wear little chemisettes of cotton or silk, reaching to the waist; round the rest of the body is thrown a cloth or taffetas; when they go abroad, they wear about that a large piece of silk, with one end brought over the head.

They are disorderly and very barbarous in their eating and drinking; they have many servants, and have each three or four wives, very richly adorned with gold chains and pearls.

They make wines of sugar and other materials, and get drunk therewith.

A large number of Portuguese dwell in freedom at the ports on this coast of Bengal; they are also very free in their lives, being like exiles. They do only traffic, without any fort, order, or police, and live like natives of the country; they durst not return to India,[1] for certain misdeeds they have committed, and they have no clergy among them. There is one of them named Jean Garie,[2] who is greatly obeyed by the rest; he commands more than ten thousand men for the king of Bengal, yet he makes not war against the Portuguese, seeing they are friends.[3]

[1] Here used in the Portuguese sense, meaning the western coast of the peninsula dominated by the Portuguese fortresses. Linschoten, in the same way, describes India as extending from Daman to Cape Comorin inclusive (i, 62-65); and in another place says that the rhinoceros is not found "in India, but only in Bengala and Patane" (ii, 8).

[2] Perhaps a misprint for *Garcie*, i.e., *Garcia*. I do not find this renegade mentioned in the Portuguese despatches.

[3] The Portuguese at this time settled in Bengal were chiefly men exiled for crime (*homisiados por delitos*), who occupied themselves partly with piracy, and partly in leading armies of rival Rajas (Hunter, *Stat. Acct. of Bengal*, vii, 110-1; *Livro das Monç.*, ii, 393). One of these, Nicote, had shortly before this time practically usurped the throne of Pegu. Another, Sebastian Gonzales Tibão, a man of low birth, rose to eminence in the invasion of Bengal and Arracan by the Mogul, to which allusion is made above. After engaging to support the king of Arracan, he turned traitor, and with his fleet harried the whole coast of that state (*Faria y Souza*, III, ch. viii). The king of Spain was con-

In this land is the great river *Ganga*, otherwise called the Ganges, the most renowned in the world. The natives hold that it comes from the Earthly Paradise; their kings have been curious to have its source discovered, but they have never discovered it, for all their journeys and expense. Its mouth is at twenty-three degrees from the equinoctial, towards our pole; but whether this is the famous Ganges of the ancients, or that of Canton in China, as some will have it nowadays, I leave to the discussion and decision of the learned in such things; any how, the common opinion of the Portuguese and many others is that this is the true Ganges; if its situation does not correspond, at least its name does.[1] From this river comes that excellent wood called *Calamba*,[2] which is believed to come from the Earthly Paradise. It is very dear throughout India, and more esteemed than any other, being more rare and odoriferous; very little of it is found, and then it comes floating to the seashore, or the banks of the river; it is also found on the shores of the Maldives, and I have met with it there many a time.

tinually urging the viceroys to reduce Portuguese affairs in Bengal to a more settled and satisfactory condition; but, owing to the greater urgency of matters in Ceylon and elsewhere, this region was left a prey to lawless ruffians (*Livro das Monç.*, i, 350).

[1] This passage would seem to be an insertion by, or at the dictation of some of Pyrard's learned friends who had read the current literature (see *Linsch.*, i, 92). Mr. Rivara thinks it not impossible that Pyrard may have seen the first Decade of Barros at Goa, where there is a similar passage (liv. ix, cap. i); but he admits against this theory that De Couto, in his dedicatory epistle to his fourth Decade, states that at that time there was but a single copy of Barros in India. Some of Pyrard's patrons in Paris may have read either Barros himself, or Ulloa's Italian version of the first two Decades (published at Venice, 1562). But it is more likely that he or they had read Linschoten, whose work had appeared in French in 1610, this passage and those immediately following being a mere transcript of *Linsch.*, Hak. Soc., i, pp. 92 and 93.

[2] The finest kind of *lignum aloes*. See *Linschoten*, i, 120, 125, 150; *G. de Orta*, f. 122; Yule, *Gloss.*, s. v. "Calambac".

This river breeds also a large number of crocodiles, and is marvellously rich in fish; in short, it is the wealthiest in all produce in the East Indies, and after it comes the Indus, the river of Surate and Cambaye.

The Indians regard the Ganges as holy, and believe that when they have washed therein they are absolved of all their sins; and Mahometans as well as Gentiles deem the water to be blessed, and to wash away all offences, just as we regard confession. They, however, believe that, after bathing there, they are altogether sanctified, even saints.[1] And they come from afar to wash them there, as do the Mahometans at the sepulchre of Mahomet at Mecca.[2] This is all I was able to observe of this kingdom during the short time I was there.

CHAPTER XXV.

Voyage to Calecut by way of Moutingué, Badara, and Marquaire; also concerning the famous captain Cogni-aly.

As I have said, my companions and I embarked in a ship of Calecut: we were at sea for three weeks, and at length made land at the port of *Moutingué*,[3] which is situate between

[1] Dr. Burnell (*Linsch.*, i, 93, *note*) points out that the Ganges is not mentioned in Vedic literature as a sacred river, but assumes that character only in the much later Puranic books. As regards the superstitions about the Ganges, he refers to Goldstücker's article in Chambers's *Encyclopædia*, reprinted in his *Lit. Rem.*, i, 63, *et seq.*

[2] *I.e.*, in the water of the Zem-Zem well. See Burton's *Pilgrimage*, vol. iii.

[3] *Muttungal*, now Port No. 12 of the Malabar district. It lies almost midway between Chombaye on the north and Vadakkara on the south, all three being situate a short distance to the north of the Kōṭṭa river. This port, at which Pyrard landed, has not found its way into the maps of the coast, nor into any catalogue of the Malabar ports, except that of De Couto (*Dec. XII*, cap. xviii), who mentions it as *Motangue*.

Cananor and Calecut: it is one of the harbours of refuge for the Malabar corsairs and pirates. The country is under the king of Moutingué, who is a Nair king.

I was never more astonished than on my arrival there to see so many men-at-arms: every one there carries arms, as well Mahometans as idolaters, from the age of ten or twelve, —that is, all the Nairs or Malabars, for the villain folk carry none at all. I was received with great courtesy by the Malabars while I sojourned there. I was conducted to the house of a great lord, a Mahometan Malabar. The Malabars have no nobility among them, either in distinction of names or orders, so far as I could discover.[1] I tarried at Moutingué for the space of three days with this lord, my companions being with another, and we were well entreated. The king himself came to see the lord with whom I was, and I was much surprised to see him thus. He was one of the handsomest men, and of the best figure I ever saw, save only that he was of a slightly olive and ruddy colour, as are all the Nairs; but his figure was of excellent proportions, and somewhat resembled that of his majesty of Calecut, beside whom this personage was but a petty kinglet; and when he spoke of him, it was with great respect and in terms of honour. When I entered his house, one of his attendants brought a stool a foot and a half square, and less than half a foot high, which he placed in the middle of the hall: upon this the king sat, while all the lords stood round about. They touched the furniture and walls of this house no more than they wished others to do to theirs, when they came to see them. The king questioned me much about France, when I told him I was of that country, and asked me the difference between the English, the Hollanders, and us. Next he inquired of the estate and greatness of the king (of France), and asked me to come and see him, and even begged

[1] Meaning probably the Mahomedans. There are at least eighteen different classes of Nâyars.

the lords to bring me there, which they did. His residence is more than a quarter of a league from the sea-shore, where my companions and I were lodged. The building is on a height, with drawbridges, which are used at all their castles and palaces[1]: these are fortified with good terraces and walls, and a careful watch is always kept. This king has a single elephant only, which is very tame.

Besides this port of Moutingué, there are two others of the corsairs close by, just two short leagues from one another: one is called *Chombais*,[2] on the Cananor side, and the other *Badara*,[3] towards Calecut: Moutingué is in the middle. All are on the coast, and well fortified with great entrenchments to protect them from the descents of the Portuguese, with whom they wage war to the death. Each of these ports hath its own king, but all are in some way under the Samory.[4]

[1] This description of a fort with drawbridges tallies with that of the existing fort at Vadakkara, which Pyrard describes below, p. 346.

[2] *Chombâye* or *Chombál*, Port No. 11 of the Malabar district, about two miles north of Muṭṭungal, and five miles north of Vadakkara. This is a very old port: it is mentioned by Barbosa under the name *Chemobai* (Lisbon edition), or *Chemonbay* (Barcelona edition), as a town of the Moors, possessing shipping (Stanley's *Barbosa*, Hak. Soc., p. 152). It appears as *Camboa* in the *Sommario* of Ramusio; as *Chomba* in De Barros; as *Somba* in P. Vincenzo; and as *Chomamba* in De Couto (*Dec. XII*, cap. xviii). It is not, however, given in the tolerably full list of Malabar ports by Andrade.

[3] *Vadakkara*, Port No. 13 of the Malabar district. It appears in Keith Johnston's atlas as *Waddakurray*. De Couto mentions it as *Baregare*, along with another town, *Coriare* (not given by other authorities). P. Vincenzo calls it *Bergare* (lib. v, c. i). Alex. Hamilton (i, 301) visited the place, which he calls *Burgara*, and says it produced pepper and the best cardamoms. Dr. F. Buchanan (*Journey, etc.*, ii, 514), who also visited it, names it *Vadacurray*, "which by Europeans is commonly called *Barragurry*."

[4] The Samorin of Calicut, who derived most of his influence from the Mahomedans who flocked to his ports. At this time the corsairs of these northern ports carried on the war against the Portuguese with his secret favour: it therefore served his purpose with the Portuguese not to claim any direct control over them.

This king of Moutingué would have had us stay with him, and gratified us in all things; he even allowed the Mahometan lords to kill a cow to give us a banquet, a thing they are not wont to do. The captain in whose house I was was called *Moussey Caca*,[1] and he with whom my companions were had for his name *Mestar Cogni-aly*.[2] These two were the chief men of Moutingué.

We remained there four or five days. The king and the Malabar captains expected that we would remain altogether, and begged us hard to do so. For my part, I said I wanted to go to see the great king *Samory*; to this they made no answer, not daring to say me nay: they even counselled me to go thither. I then took leave of the king and of my companions who wished to remain there,—for one was going with a Malabar captain in another direction, four leagues off in the Calecut territory. I set out with another captain, the most valiant and brave on all that coast, who has the most galleys of his own: he is called *Cousty Hamede*. He took with him some *Jangay*,[3] who are Nair guides: they tarry

[1] *Mûssa Kâkka*; as to the latter appellative, see above, p. 268.

[2] *Kunhâli*, from *Kunhi*, a youth, a term of endearment, a title, as here; and *âli*. The title of a great Mâppilla family of corsairs, as to whom we hear more presently.

[3] These Nâyar guides or guards are mentioned by most of the travellers who have visited the Malabar coast. "Those who desire to proceed thither" (says Fah Hian of the Deccan) "should first pay a certain sum of money to the king of the country, who will then appoint people to accompany them and show them the way." The guards of the king of Bidjanagar are called *djandar* by Abd-er-Razzak (*Ind. in XV Cent.*, p. 34). Barbosa, after stating their general employment as mercenary troops, proceeds:—"And if anyone is in apprehension of another man, he takes some of these nairs, as many as he pleases, into his pay: and they accompany and guard him: and on their account he goes securely, since no one dares to molest him: because if he were molested they and all their lineage would take vengeance on him who should cause this molestation. These guards are called *Janguada*" (Stanley's *Barbosa*, p. 129). De Couto gives a full account of them, calling them *jangadas* (*Dec. IV*, liv. VII, cap. xiv). So does P. Vincenzo, under the name

about the gates of towns to escort for payment such as have need of them. All the great lords keep some of them on fixed wages, which the king gives them. Every one takes some, the weak for safety and protection; while great folks, who go with retinues of followers well armed, take them only to bear witness that they have not attacked the Nairs, in case it should happen some dispute arises between the Nairs and them, and this often befalls them: for the Nairs are much addicted to drunkenness, whereas the Malabars drink no wine, and are not at all quarrelsome or treacherous without cause: thus they have often some contention between them, but the king deals them indifferent justice. These Nairs are very thieves on land, and would for a petty consideration kill a man. They do rob the towns and markets privily, and none dare say anything against them. It is true that all are not of this sort, but only some discontented soldiers. 'Tis on the coast these do most prevail, one party of them robbing by land, the others by sea. So there be none that dare go anywhere without these soldier guides.

The Malabars do no robbery by land. When they have a quarrel among themselves, the king allots to each a Nair or Archer as a surety, and forbids them to attack one another. These Nairs are kept at the expense of the Malabars; and

Giancadas (*Viaggio*, liv. I, cap. xl). Among the items of revenue of the old Malabar princes, Burton mentions *Chungathum*, or "protection": "Whenever a person wished to place himself under the safeguard of a man of consequence, he paid from four to sixty-four *fanams* annually for the privilege. He might also make an assignment on particular lands for the payment. The sum was devoted to the maintenance of a kind of sentinel, similar to the belted peon of the Anglo-Indian settlements, furnished by the protector to his dependent. In cases of necessity, however, the former was bound to aid and assist the other with a stronger force" (*Goa and the Blue Mountains*, p. 198; see also pp. 224, 244). See also, as to travelling in India generally, *Tavernier*, pt. II, bk. i, cap. 8. The word is *changngâtam* "convoy, guard, income of Rajas from granting such guards, grants of land to persons liable to such service, companion".

while they are there, the Malabars durst not fight, otherwise the aggressor would be held guilty of high treason, and would have to answer for it before the king himself. It is said the Malabars maintain a feud for seven years.[1] These Nairs are so dreaded, that were a Malabar to wound one of them, and had no Nair witnesses to prove that he was not the aggressor, it would be ruin to all the Malabars in the town. All these Malabar towns along the coast are full of Nairs, armed in all fashions, so much so, that as I journeyed I seemed to be in a camp of 20,000 men. Sometimes one cannot walk in the streets; but in the evening all the world goes abroad, save only the Mahometans and Moucois, who have a separate quarter on the sea-shore, in front of the Malabar towns; and also the Gentile artisans, whose houses are usually near the town of the Malabars for whom they work.

So, although the country belongs to the Malabars, yet, in speaking of the Malabars, the Mahometans are more properly intended; they are but seldom artisans, almost all being merchants, robbers, or sea warriors. There is no class of nobles among them; their distinction is solely in valour and wealth, and all sorts of men are welcomed among them. They but seldom keep slaves, and none[2] are constrained to go to the wars with them. They are trustful towards all men, and care not to compel others to go where they go. They provide a free table for all comers, and each has his own dish: that is, all soldiers. All their people are employed, for such as are not brave enough for soldiers, they make mariners, or press them into service for hire, or use them for selling the produce of their robberies. Their galiots they

[1] Referring to the *Kuḍippaka* or *Kuḍuppu*, "house or family feud", about which much curious information exists. When a man was slain it was customary to burn his body in the house of the slayer, who was of course also burnt.

[2] That is, none of the Gentiles; a few lines lower he says they do press their own people to go to the wars.

call *Pados*.[1] All the merchants of the coast, when they hear that the galiots of the pirates are about to come in, hold themselves in readiness to buy their goods cheap, and then they have the assurance to go and sell them in the markets of the very merchants of whom they were taken. These latter frequently buy them back a second time; and though they recognise their own goods, that matters not, so long as they have the Portuguese passport. The priests of their religion, too, and the poor are on the look-out, and come distances of thirty leagues to get their share; for they well know that these Malabars have made vows, in case they make a good prize, to give so much to the poor, and never fail to acquit themselves therein. Likewise they have their holy places, or *Ziares*,[2] places and temples especially kept for the purpose, where they pay their vows as at the Maldives. These priests are employed only at marriages and at the temples. They have no hand in administering justice; and all are habited in the Arab fashion, that is, entirely in white. In their company are a sort of men called *Abedalles*,[3] who have taken a vow of poverty, and so go about the world. Sometimes there will be thirty or forty of them in one place, yet they travel not more than two or three together, most often alone. They have alms given them, and, indeed, are passing urgent in demanding the same. They all sleep in the temples. They are the best company in the world, for they know all languages, and it is a great pleasure to entertain them; they have traversed all parts of the East, carrying their bit of baggage upon them. Money, cotton cloth, and silk are what they mostly get, and as much to eat as they will have. Some of

[1] Portuguese form of the Malayâlam *paṭak*, a country craft not now in use. Mr. Logan says it was intermediate in size between a *manji* and a *pattimâr* (as to both which, see Yule, *Gloss.*, s. vv. *manchua* and *pattamar*). In vol. II, ch. ii, Pyrard calls the *manjis* of Goa also galiots.

[2] Ar. *Ziyârat*, a place of visitation; see above, p. 176.

[3] *Abd-Allah*, "Slave of God", a Mahomedan ascetic.

them live in great austerity, according to their faith. These tarry near the temples, and ask for nothing; they would sooner die of hunger. They are very solitary, and all hold the faith of Mahomet. The Gentiles have also their *Abcdalles*, which are like to our hermits, and are called *Joguies*.[1] They, too, do go about the country, but only among the Nairs and other Gentiles. They eat nothing that has had life. The king of Calecut has one by him, whom he treats with great respect: he is regarded as a saint. All the Joguies that pass that way go and lodge with him, as it were at a monastery or hospital set apart for the purpose. It is two musket-shots from the king's palace, and is exceeding well constructed; it was built and endowed by the king. The other Nair kings, who merely give these folks passing cheer, receive them at their palaces, where they may tarry as long as they please. They cover their bodies with some kind of powdered ash, made with water into a white paste. They commonly wear large sea-chestnuts[2] as pendants in their ears, which have holes large enough to admit the thumb; others, the greater among them, wear gold and silver gilt in the form of these. Their diet is like that of the Bramenis and Banians of Cambaye and other places, who taste not anything that has had life. There is another sort of folk that wander about, just as here: that is, the charlatans, who exhibit beasts, taking their wives and children about with them, and dance and tumble in all manner of ways. I never saw any such good mountebanks, nor any that did such juggling and tricks of legerdemain.

But to return to my departure from Moutingué. I took the road for Calecut by land, a distance of twelve leagues, taking for my escort and guidance a body of Nairs from town to town. These are very numerous, being only two leagues

[1] *Jogi*, a Hindu ascetic: see Yule, *Gloss.*

[2] *Chastiganes de mer;* Anglicè, "sea-urchins"; Italicè, *frutta di mare.*

or so apart. Each man receives four *tarents*,[1] which are small silver coins, each of the value of one-sixteenth of a larin.

So I arrived at *Badara*, two leagues from Moutingué, on the Calecut road. The lord[2] there gave me even a better reception than the other had. He had two palaces, one of which was for his wives, for he had several, according to the law of Mahomet. I sojourned there about fifteen days. These three ports, Chombaye, Moutingué, and Badara are within the ambit of a single bay. Cangelotte,[3] another harbour of the corsairs, who rule a great extent of countries and peoples, is at some eighteen leagues to the north, near Barcelor, and between those places no succour can be afforded by land. But as between these three they succour one another in this fashion: they have certain lofty buildings erected upon piles on the sea-shore; there they keep sentinels to scan the

[1] Malayâlam *tâṛan*, an obsolete silver coin of Malabar and the Deccan. In 1443, six *taras* went to the *fanam* at Bijayanagar (Abd-er-Razzak, *India in XV Cent.*, i, 26); while in 1504 a fanam was worth fifteen taras (*Varthema*, Hak. Soc., p. 130). By this time, a century after Varthema, the depreciation had not gone far, as Pyrard assigns the value of a larin and also of a fanam at sixteen *tarents*. The fanam, be it remembered, was at this time always a gold coin. The târam was not adopted by the Portuguese. Elsewhere Pyrard gives the European value of the coin, viz., three deniers, or a quarter sou. P. Vincenzo says it was worth a *bajocco*. The name is probably from *târa*, a star.

[2] Formerly known as the *Vâḷunnavar* of Vadakkara, now as the *Kadattanâd Raja*. A. Hamilton gives an interesting account of his visits to this local potentate, who claimed to be the king of the corsairs: he calls him *Balanore Burgarie* (i, 301). He was also visited by Dr. Buchanan (ii, 514). The ruins of his castle still remain (Sewell, *List of Ant. of Madras*, p. 245).

[3] *Kâṇyirôṭu*, short for *Kâṇyiram Kôṭu*, the place of the *Strychnos nux vomica* trees, the modern Cassergode in S. Canara; one of the earliest Mahomedan settlements on the coast. It is called *Canharoto* by the Portuguese writers, and is mentioned in the royal despatch of 1st March 1613, as a place of robbers, under the control of the Samorin, where it was proposed to erect a fortress (*Liv. das Monç.*, ii, 352).

horizon. They know within a little when the Portuguese fleet may be expected, and have intrenchments ready on land to obstruct their landing.

While I was at Badara there passed by sixty sail, all galiots, and two galleys, on their way from Cochin to Goa. There was such a calm that all the Malabars there treated the matter lightly. Those of the other ports, however, set out to assemble themselves at that port, off which the fleet lay, and so give succour to their friends. The Portuguese call their own galiots *Navires*,[1] and those of the Malabars, *Pairaus*.[2] Most of these vessels were *Chetils*,[3] that is to say, merchantmen. Immediately on arrival the Malabars draw up their *Pados*, or galiots, on the beach. I was witness to the most gallant behaviour on the part of one of these Pados, which was returning from war. All the Portuguese fleet was lying at the entrance of this great bay; the Pados, not perceiving them, found itself of a sudden engaged with sixty sail. Retreat being impossible, she took the bold resolution to run through the midst of the fleet, and so to make her own port, which was *Chombaye*. The crew capsized her, and though hard pressed by the Portuguese, saved themselves by swimming. The Portuguese got nothing for their pains, and after the fleet had retired, the owners brought their Pados safely to shore.

These robbers and pirates must take great booty, for be-

[1] Port. *navios*.

[2] Port. *parāos*, borrowed, as Col. Yule suggests, either from the Malayâlam *páṛu*, a boat, or from the *práhú* of the Eastern Archipelago. The early use of the word *parāo* by Varthema, as a Malabar word, would seem to indicate the former as the correct source.

[3] Malayâlam *chetti*, a trader, used all over South India and Ceylon, similarly to "Banyan", further north. The Portuguese wrote *Chetins* and *Chatis* (see Yule, *Gloss.*, s. v. *Chetty*). I do not know any other authority for the use of the word for merchant-ships, though it is analogous to our "merchantmen".

sides the cost and expenses of their *Pados* and galiots, they have to pay customs and passport duties to the Nair king of the land; then they are subjected to the giving of all sorts of gratifications and presents,—as, for instance, to the king of Calecut and to their own king. They were wont thus to make gifts to the late king *Cognialy;* they have to give to their allies; and finally, to their priests and the poor, and in fulfilment of vows made at their *Ziares*.

The lords there do the same, and they own their *pados* like the rest. For there is no privilege of nobility among them, and no respect of persons, saving the aged, the wealthy, and the brave. When they set out for war, and for a round of expeditions, they appoint a general of the whole fleet, whom they obey during that voyage only; when it is over he returns to his former position. If any prize is taken, they give him a present, as they may be minded, though he has no right thereto; the rest is equally divided.

During my sojourn at Badara I often made excursions on foot up the country, which I found to be of fair prospect, very productive, well timbered, and pleasant. The soil is red and sandy, and the country open. The Nairs near the ports gather themselves to the coasts and to the king's palace when the alarm is given that the Portuguese or others are coming to attack the Malabars.

As for the king's palace, it is unapproachable from the sea side: it is situated on the top of a hill, about three musket-shots distance from the sea, the Malabar town being between; the hill has been cut down like a four-square wall. The king hath another castle, a league and a half up the country, where he keeps his wife and all his family, and also his Pagoda, which he took me to see. He is about sixty years of age, not so handsome as the rest of his race, but of a fine figure. I went often to Moutingué to see my companions. One of them went thence to another town two leagues from Badara, towards Calecut, and in the Calecut country, ten leagues from that city. This town is called *Marcaire Costé*[1]; the Portuguese call it Cognialy's country.[2]

This lord with whom I was at Badara loved me as a brother. He had a wife residing at Marcaire Costé (which is a fortress), and took me there many times. I saw my companion there, and stayed with him awhile. This district of Marcaire belongs to the king of Calecut, and, like the rest of the Calecut realm, is at peace with the Portuguese. The pirates and corsairs dare not land and equip their *pados* there,[3] but all the men of the place go a-robbing like the rest. The rich have their *pados*, which they keep at places under the king of Badara, and at the other pirate ports, and bring their booty, the proceeds of their robberies, home by land. The Malabar Indians make no distinction, until it be explained to them, between the English, Hollanders, and French. This is what made them like us so much, viz., that they saw we were hostile to the Portuguese. They asked me if I was of the same religion as the Portuguese; and when I answered yes,—why, then, said they, do you make war upon them? When I replied that they did the same upon other Mahometans, they remarked that that should not be deemed strange as to them, who were all robbers and pirates, a trade that was no dishonour to them, seeing they practised it from father to son. A man who would be welcomed among them must be always talking of warring against the Portuguese, and always speaking ill of them,—for, in truth, I never heard a good word said for them.

The real cause why this lord liked me so much and

[1] That is, the *kôtta*, or fort, of the *Mârakkâr*. Although Pyrard is aware that the latter is only a personal title, he presently calls the place by the names *Marcaire* and *Costé* successively.

[2] Throughout the eleventh and twelfth *Decades* of De Couto, the fort and town, as well as its ruler, are called *Cunhale*.

[3] That is, since the destruction of the place in 1600 (see App. C), and because of the stringent treaty made between the Samorin and the Portuguese after that event.

caressed me so greatly beyond the others, was that he had a mind to go to the Maldives the next year with a fleet, and seeing that I had acquaintance of the language and the country, and being informed by many merchants and Malabar pilots who had seen me there, how I had been entertained by the late king, he held me to no other talk but of the Maldives, inquiring closely which were the best islands, the richest individuals, and if I knew where the king and his queens kept their treasure, insomuch that he was like to have detained me by main force. The other lords were of the same mind, and made me the most flattering offers, so that I had had much pains to escape, but for the use I made of the name of the great *Samory*, whom I told them I was minded to visit. That alone restrained and silenced them, and by this means I got out of the mess, to their great chagrin. So with this purpose I bade them farewell, and took the road straight for *Marcaire Costé*.

Going from Badara to the Calecut country one has to pass a river, and there is a king also between, called *Auriole*.[1] He has no port, so he bides ashore. He is a friend to the Portuguese, and an enemy to the Malabars in his heart; but he makes no concealment of this: for though they do business together, they do not themselves pass or repass the border. Through his land flows a river that hath its mouth at Mar-

[1] De Couto, in his description of the attack on Kunhâli's fort, mentions a territory up the river, exactly as here placed by Pyrard, but calls the people *Arioles*, and the territory *Ariole* (*Dec. XII*, liv. I, cap. xviii, and liv. II, cap. v). On the other hand, the king, in a despatch dated 12th January 1591, speaks of the *Arioles* as "lords of powerful vassals, neighbours of Cunhale, who could give him aid or prevent him being assisted" (*Arch. Port. Or.*, Fasc. 3). The word is probably a title, namely, *Âyirôn*, *i.e.*, lord of one thousand Nâyars (*âyiram* = 1000); the "king" was probably a Nâyar chief, who at the time had made himself independent (of the Kôlattiri), for Pyrard, further down (p. 375), says his territory lay across the river from *Kôṭṭakkal*. It would seem therefore that this *Âyirôn* was at this time in possession of the *Putu paṭṭanam* country of *Kôlattanâd*.

caire, and carries boats afloat for more than five-and-twe leagues of its course.

It is impossible to describe in detail the welcome and good friendship extended to us by the Malabar Mahometans and Nairs. They counted themselves lucky when they got us under their roofs, saying that God had greatly blessed them; and most of them put in writing the day and hour of our coming in, and told their children to remember the day they saw us. All ran out upon the road to see us, when they heard tell of our name, and how that we were enemies to the Portuguese.

Having spent fifteen days or more at Badara, I went to Marcaire to find my companion, and we made up our minds to go together to the Samory, with the king's leave and that of Cousty Hamede, who was loth to give it, like the rest: for I used to go at my pleasure to *Costé*, to his wife's house, for meat and drink and sleep. Receivers, clerks, and other officers of the king of Calecut are always stationed at the town of Costé: they have a customs-house there, and examine all vessels and goods arriving at the port; in the evening they return to their lodging, half a league out of the town. The Portuguese have done all they know to conquer these four towns and ports, but always without effect, and to their own loss and discredit, chiefly so at Badara, where they have lost many of their men; for it is an exceeding strong port, all surrounded with water. They got soundly beaten there only a month before my arrival.[1]

I tarried ten or twelve days at Marcaire before going on to Calecut, and while I was there the lord *Cousty Hamede* came many a time, saying it was to see me, though the truth was he had his wife there. He would not let me quit him, or take another lodging than his, whether for sleeping, eating, or drinking. On the other hand, the king's receivers, who are

[1] Mr. Rivara notes that, owing to the want of historical documents relating to this period, he has not been able to trace the details of this expedition.

held in high honour there, gave us an allowance, saying it was a great indignity, as well for the king as for us, if we were fed by any but him, seeing we were in his country, and minded to go and visit him. Besides this allowance, they gave great entertainments in our honour, as did all the other lords, as well Nair as Mahometan, and were desirous to accompany us toward the king. They gave us every day a *Panan* each, which is a piece of gold money of the king, in value about four sous and a half. It was more than double what we could spend. All this Marcaire country, which I went far up, is very good soil; for about four[1] [forty] years it has been the principal retreat of all the pirates, and their king resided there.

Here dwell most of the Malabars, owing to the strength of the place; and here the king of Calecut sets a governor to rule all the Malabars of his realm, including those of the other towns and ports of the pirates and corsairs; which governor they acknowledge as their king, but subject to the Samory, for they must needs be ruled by one of their own faith and race. One such he gave them named *Cognialy*,[2] with the title of lieutenant-general: he was called Cognialy Marcaire, for Marcaire means lieutenant or viceroy.[3] This Cognialy was chosen for the post on account of his valour, and retained it for thirty or forty years; and by his robberies in all directions he became very powerful. He was the grandest corsair ever seen in those parts, and his district being large, men came from all sides to reside there. The fortress is small; past it flows a fine river, navigable for boats for

[1] I agree with Mr. Rivara that the *quatre* here is a misprint for *quarante*. De Couto dates the rise of the elder Kunhâli from 1572, and the place had been destroyed as a fortress seven years before the time of which Pyrard is writing. See further, App. C.

[2] *Kunhâli*, a family title borne both by the founder of the fortress and the corsair whose fortunes are here told, whom Pyrard confuses.

[3] It is really *Mârakkâr*, for *Mârggakâran*, from *mârggan*, "a way or law", and *kâran*, "a doer". There were Marakkars at all the pirate ports. It is still a common honorific title among the Moormen of Ceylon.

more than twenty leagues, down which are borne all kinds of goods. At the mouth of this river he erected, by leave of the king, a large fortress, in the fashion of ours, of strong walls, built with lime and sand, and having a supply of fresh water within. Beyond this, he constructed two large forts to guard the mouth of the river, so that all vessels came in to safe moorings under the fortress, and abode there out of all danger and trouble. The fortress protected the town, which was also fortified as well on the sea as on the land side; it was almost surrounded by the sea and the river. It is a large town, well peopled, with great buildings, streets, and shops, all well planned, as at Calecut and elsewhere on the Malabar coast: even among these towns it is one of the most beautiful, wealthy, and strong. It is built on an eminence, and the fortress towers above; while down below, on either side of the river, next the sea, are the two forts which protect the whole haven and the river's mouth. This town is reduced to half its importance in all respects since the death of *Cognialy Marcaire*, the manner whereof I shall now relate.[1]

This Cognialy was obedient in all things to his king, under whose favour and goodwill he had made himself so strong: and the king, who up to that time had warred against the Portuguese, was well content to have so redoubted a champion. The port and the town were worth as much to the king as those of Calecut itself. Down the river are borne much pepper and other produce, enhancing the wealth of the town and port. In a hall of the mansion of a great Malabar lord of this place, I saw all the adventures and victories of Cognialy, as well by land as by sea, very well painted and

[1] The Portuguese expeditions against Kunhâli in 1599 and 1600, which are here narrated at some length, though eclipsed in importance by the Ceylon wars, vie in tragic interest with any conducted by the Portuguese in India. Although they form the central subject of the eleventh and twelfth *Decades* of De Couto, they have been little regarded in modern historical notices of the period. The site of the fortress is shown, with the main outlines of the story, in App. C.

coloured, with all the galliots, galleys, and other vessels that he had taken or sunk, very skilfully represented. His fame and terror were spread abroad from the Cape of Good Hope even to China; and I was assured that he had at a single blow cut a galley oar in two, and likewise had cut down a man with a sword by his side, hewing man and sword with a single cut. He had a brother as valiant as himself, named *Cousty Moussey.*[1] Their power was greater than that attained by any others in those parts: they took innumerable ships and galleys of China, Goa, and other places, as I observed in these paintings. This Cognialy was likewise one of the cruellest men in the world, and his great strength and power led him to despise his neighbours, even the king of Cananor,[2] who had formerly been his protector and suzerain, and had aided him in all his projects. He harried in all directions, and all men's goods. None could number the cruel barbarities practised by him and his against all sorts and conditions of men, without distinction: among others, against his own neighbour, the Nair king Auriole, already mentioned, whom he robbed and pillaged and drove from his kingdom: he cut off the nose and breasts of that prince's queen, and had himself acknowledged as king. At length, puffed up with prosperity, he would no longer recognise the Samory, and rebelled against him, refusing to deliver up some vessels of his subjects that he had taken; and when commanded so to do, he set all such commands at nought.

The Portuguese were well enough pleased with this revolt of Cognialy,—which, indeed, they had fomented, believing that his speedy ruin was certain, as well on account of the exces-

[1] De Couto mentions *Cutimuça* as the nephew and great general of Kunhâli, meaning nephew of the elder and, perhaps, brother of the younger Kunhâli: Pyrard knows only of the younger pirate chief (*Dec. XI*, cap. viii; and see App. C).

[2] *Âli Raja*, Sea King, or King of the Deep, who was the naval commodore of the Kôlattiris, and whose ancestor was the great Mammâli, known in connection with Maldive history (see App. A).

sive barbarity of his cruelties and robberies that he had practised, as for his presumption and revolt: insomuch that, without delay, they sought for peace with the king of Calecut, who, out of desire to chastise his faithless vassal, too gladly hearkened thereto. The next year, which was 1599, the viceroy of Goa equipped a powerful fleet, under the command of his own nephew, by name *Louys de Gusman*,[1] who, with a view to surprise the fortress by a *coup de main*, entered the country of king Auriole, a bitter enemy of Cognialy, for the reasons already stated. This territory lay across the river, over which the Portuguese threw a bridge of thirty or forty boats, lashed one to another. A captain, named *Louys de Sylva*, with 300 of the bravest men of the fleet, was appointed to effect a landing on the other side, upon the signal being given. That was to be done by night, and the Samory was to despatch at the same time a land force, aided by Portuguese. Cognialy and his brother, being well warned of all this, got themselves ready at all points, without any display of doing anything. The result was that the 300 men who had crossed were repulsed, and their captain, Louys de Sylva, killed with a musket-shot. Seeing this, the soldiers turned about, and thinking to find their boats where they had left them, discovered that they had been removed. Meantime, the garrison of the fortress sallied out, and cut them all down: the most of them were drowned, and only about twenty or thirty saved themselves by swimming, the rest being unable to swim on account of their armour. As for the Nairs and Portuguese, who were to make the land attack, Cognialy had prepared entrenchments on the road they had to traverse, held by a force of arquebusiers.

The bulk of the Portuguese army, on attempting to land, were completely repulsed, and for their folly sustained a loss of 500 men, and re-embarked in disorder. The king

[1] Dom Luiz da Gama was brother, not nephew, of the viceroy, Dom Francisco da Gama.

of Calecut afterwards told the Portuguese it ought not to have been done in this fashion, but with deliberation. So the general returned to Goa crestfallen, and with the loss of the best part of his army. The Portuguese that were with the Samory took great umbrage at this, saying that he had betrayed them, and had led them to the slaughter; for that the men he ought to have sent, as he had arranged with them, were not on the spot at the proper time to give the agreed signal. But the cause of the miscarriage, in fact, was the intrigues of Cognialy and his people, who had received good information, and had at once sent a force of armed men to bar the passage; and to such effect, that the others could not be at the agreed place at the agreed time.

The Portuguese, afterwards informed of the truth of the whole business, were little disheartened at having been beaten once, and resolved to make the attempt a second time, so as to make themselves masters of Cognialy and his territory, according to the assurance they had given to the king his master. So the following year, which was 1600, *André Furtado de Mendoce*,[1] an old and brave captain, and the most dreaded Portuguese soldier in India (he died coming from Goa to Lisbon, on the same voyage as that on which I returned, as I shall relate below), took measures with the Samory to entrap Cognialy, and arranged together that the king of Calecut should come in person by land, while the Portuguese army, under the command of the said André, should arrive by sea: this they did, and Cognialy was besieged. Some grand sorties were made, with great losses on both sides. There are said to have been 60,000 Nairs present. I afterwards heard the whole story, both from the Portuguese, and from the Malabars and Nairs of the fortress;

[1] André Furtado de Mendoça, the greatest Portuguese captain of the time. He succeeded to the government of India on the 27th May 1609, and ruled till the 5th September of the same year. See further, App. C, and vol. ii.

but these said that the cause of the taking of Cognialy was the lack of provisions; for that Cognialy, having so soundly beaten them on the first occasion, little thought they would return so soon, and so was taken by surprise. He had despatched two large ships under *Metar Cognialy*, a great captain of Moutingué, to get provisions; but they could not re-enter the harbour; and so, after a long siege, seeing himself reduced to extremities, and after proving his mettle on many occasions, at length somewhat basely surrendered. It was said that he did so owing to some charmed betel the king had sent him, whereby his courage failed him. Others said it was out of pity at seeing his men in such great straits, that he would sooner die himself than see so many men suffer on his behalf. Another reason was that his brother, Cousty Moussey, was dead, who would never have permitted a surrender in this sort. Yet the thing which most led him to it was his despair of succour; for he had insulted the kings and princes of whom he might have expected it. So it was that he asked a parley, saying he would surrender to the mercy of his king, of whom he asked pardon. But the king could no longer save him: for it had been agreed between him and André Furtado that the fortress should be rased to the ground, and the booty halved, and that all the people should go to the king and Cognialy to the Portuguese, or Cognialy to the king and the people to the Portuguese. The king demanded the people. The compact being concluded, all the Nairs were drawn up on one side, and the Portuguese on the other. Cognialy then came forth, and proceeded to salute the king and ask his pardon. The king called upon him to deliver up his sword, and taking it, struck him two or three light strokes on the shoulder, as if in jest, and then addressed him in these words: "Cognialy, you have given me much trouble and grief"; at the same time turned to the Seigneur André, saying, "Take Cognialy: he is yours." He was forthwith seized and placed in a galley; the fortress and the forts were entirely demolished, while the town was left in its former condition, albeit it was sacked, and the people sustained no further loss. The two armies then retired.

When the news of the capture reached Goa, bonfires were lighted, the bells were rung, and the *Te Deum* was sung, and two days[1] after the return of the army Cognialy was beheaded. He was first asked if he would become a Christian, to which he replied that he was willing, provided his life was spared; but if he was to die, he preferred to die in the faith of Mahomet. Such were the fortunes and the miserable end of king Cognialy. Yet did the Portuguese afterwards pay dearly for his head: for the Malabars, in revenge, put to death all the Portuguese they could lay hands on: and the king of Calecut had great regret for having delivered up so valiant a man (he had done so out of anger and revenge), for Cognialy and his brother were esteemed the bravest captains in all the East Indies.

As for Cognialy's fortress, I have seen it many a time: the walls were still standing, to the height of two men's stature, so that it were easy to fortify it, and it could soon be refitted in case the king went to war with the Portuguese. When we left Goa, the news had arrived that the king intended to break the peace, to build sixty galleys or pados, and to reconstruct the fortress; and when the Hollanders went to him, he promised to put the place in their hands. Wherefore the factor or agent of the Portuguese who was there went and complained to him that he had received these Hollanders, and other enemies of the king of Spain, and that he was therefore resolved to return to Goa. The king made no further reply, than that he might go at his pleasure, for that he would detain no one by force.

There is no king in India who can damage the Portuguese

[1] We know from De Couto that the interval was longer than this, but not the exact time; also that De Couto himself interviewed Kunhâli in prison (see App. C).

by sea so much as he: for the coasts of his realm can furnish an immense number of Malabars, and it is very rich in supplies. He has some very wealthy men in his kingdom, and all are courageous and loyal: he has also plenty Moucois to man his pados. These Moucois are in the position of slaves to the king and the Nairs (as I shall explain below): they call the king in their language *Tambiraine*,[1] meaning "God". I know for certain that the Samory has an understanding with all the Malabar pirates, that they give him money and pay a tribute underhand. I am aware of this, from having often accompanied the captain, *Cousty Hamede*, when he went to treat secretly with the king's officers, which he did only by night, for fear of being seen. All the other lords and captains of the Malabars do the same, as I have observed many a time, and as the king's own officers assured me: and there is good reason for it, for he assists them in all things, and provides them with money when they have none, which they repay in full, and with interest. Every year many thousand men leave the Samory's territory to do their robberies on the sea along with the rest. On land these corsairs are the most gallant and honourable gentlemen in the world, and they are daily endeavouring by presents and flattery to get the Samory to break the peace with the Portuguese, and to give them this fortress of Cognialy. This Cognialy has left a son, also called *Marcaire*, or Viceroy: I have often seen him, and have eaten and drunk in his house. He resides mostly at Costé and Chombaye, with one or other of his two wives; and although since the death of his father the king has appointed no one in his stead, and has not recognised this son as his successor, yet he is treated with greater respect than anyone else, and the title is preserved to him for his father's sake only. Many have aspired

[1] *Tamburân*, title of grown-up member of Malayâli Rajan families; it means "lord" or "master", also "god". The title of a junior member is *Tambân*.

to the post, for which very reason the king appoints none to it, and thus keeps the land in peace. All affairs go directly before the king, or the Nair lords commissioned for the purpose, and justice is done throughout the country in all matters by them alone.

My companion and I, having stayed more than twelve days in this Marcaire or Cognialy's country, took leave of our friends. The king's officers, whose permission we asked for our departure, told us that, if we were minded to go to the king, they would give us letters and money; but we had no need of money except for crossing the river and paying the Nair guides. Had we not been liable to find our Nairs drunk with *arac*[1] (which is a kind of *eau de vie* made with the wine of the coco-tree), we should, in fact, have had no need of it at all, by reason of our letter of commendation, which ran in the name of the king: but that must not always be trusted to. We made only four short leagues a day at the most, sometimes only two. They made us lodge in their houses, although others were provided for us. Indeed, I cannot describe all the hospitality and honour we received on the road. The question always was who should have us; but they did not dare to press us to stay against our will, however much they desired it, seeing we were going to the king; and our passport insured us a good reception on all hands. We were about eight days on our journey from *Costé* to Calecut, although we might well have done it in two. It was our halting at this place and that, and the hospitality and welcome accorded to us everywhere, which caused us to take all that time; and in truth it would be impossible to describe the universal welcome given us, so full of honour, courtesy, and affection was

[1] The Ar. *araḳ*, "perspiration, exudation, distilled spirit", has spread over all Asia. Throughout the tropics arrack is made from the coco-tree; arrack punch used to be a favourite beverage both in India and England, and then frequently shortened to "rack-punch"; but since the days of Jos. Sedley both the name and the drink have gone out of fashion.

it: for even the greatest folks disputed among themselves which should entertain us. But I must remark that these were the Malabar Mahometans, and not the Nairs; for the latter, though liberal with their money, fruits, and all else, like not that strangers should eat and sleep in their houses, if they can help it, except in case of great necessity: and those of them that are of the Brameny race are the most particular in this respect. Though the others make the same difficulty, they are not so scrupulous as the Bramenys.

For the rest, if it were not for the excessive heat of the sun in those parts, it would be impossible to tell the pleasure and satisfaction of travel in that land, which is the fairest and most agreeable ever seen or even imagined: for the country is all open and sandy, but the sand is hard and firm as sandstone; and by the road-side are houses and buildings always in sight, and towns every league or half league, the most distant being two short leagues apart. The whole country is well peopled, and covered with fruits, which are common property and free to passers-by; and these fruits are the finest in the world, there being none of the same kinds or so good in these parts. Moreover, all along the roads one meets with great numbers of people, Nairs and Malabars, men and women: for everyone goes about there in perfect safety, so long as he has a Nair or *Jangaye* in his company. For a party of twenty or thirty persons, one Nair suffices; and if a man goes alone he wants no less, though it costs him more; but the greater the party the greater is the Nair's profit. There are many marshes and salt-pits to cross between *Costé* and Calecut, and two rivers to cross by boat,[1] about a league from one of which is a very fine

[1] Pyrard must have struck somewhat inland on his way to Calicut, as there are certainly not two rivers to cross between Kôṭṭakal and Calicut, when the route lies along the sea-shore. He probably crossed the *Agalapuḷa* river or backwater, and afterwards the Ellattûr river, by some inland road.

town, where we passed a night, named *Coluotte*,[1] where the Portuguese once had a fortress and a residency, as at Calecut; but they have lost the one as the other. I saw it as I passed, for it is not altogether demolished; it was even stronger than that at Calecut. This is all that I remarked on the journey.

[1] This is the northern *Kollam*, inflected, it is *Kollaṭṭu*, written *Coulete* by Barros and Andrada. It is a very ancient seat of trade, about 1½ mile north of Koilandi, and locally called *Pantalâyini* Kollam; but foreign writers have generally omitted the *Kollam* (see Yule, *Gloss.*, s. v. "Pandarāni"). Mr. Logan has kindly supplied us with the following note, showing that it was here that Vasco da Gama first landed in India. "Following Correa, I think it is clear that da Gama's fleet first anchored at *Kâppaṭṭ*" [the *Capogatto* of the Portuguese writers; see Yule, *Gloss.*, s. v. "Capucat".—Ed.], "the position of which is well known, about ten or eleven miles north of Calicut. Correa does not say that the fleet was moved after thus casting anchor at Kappaṭṭ, but the fact is mentioned by other writers, who, moreover, give the name of the place to which it was moved, viz., *Pandarane*. Now *Pandarane* is undoubtedly *Pantalâyini*, one of the *Desams* (small hamlets) of the *Amsam* (parish) in which Kollam is situate. It is the *Fandarina* of Edrisi, the *Fandaraina* of Ibn Batuta and Rashíduddín, the *Fundaraina* of the Tohfat, the *Flandrina* of Friar Odoric, etc." [see Yule, *Gloss.*, s. v. "Pandarāni"]; "and to go further back, it is probably the *Patale* of Pliny. The place has long been known because of its trade facilities. Off it, is one of those curious mud-banks, as at Calicut, Narakal, and Alpey, which protect shipping under shelter. Even at the present day, ships from the Red Sea and the Gulf almost invariably make for it when running over to India at the close of the south-west monsoon. The tradition, that da Gama's ships spent the monsoon season of 1498 at this place, has been current on the coast from the very commencement of the British administration. Da Gama sighted Mount Deli on the 26th August, and even at that time of year a country vessel would nowadays make for North Kollam for protection against occasional squalls. In 1793 the cruiser *Morning Star*, used by the settlement commissioners, took shelter here during the monsoon, they reporting, among their reasons for so doing, that da Gama's fleet had sheltered there. The tradition had probably come from the Portuguese themselves, and as it is consistent with all the accounts, I have little hesitation in accepting it."

CHAPTER XXVI.

Arrival of the author at Calecut, and a description of that kingdom.—The king and people: their manners, religion, and ways of life.

Having at length arrived at the town of Calecut, the first officers of the king whom we met with were the receivers of the king's dues, who have a house on the seashore, erected on piles, where they remain by day only: for the town and harbour are more than a league in length, and there are three of these buildings, for the watching of all the goods that are landed, for the taking of the number and quantities in writing, and for the conveyance of them thence to the *Alfandigue.*[1] This is a great square building of stone, with galleries above and below, and vaulted with stone arcades like those of our Place Royale,[2] but not so grand or so elegant, with a large number of rooms and warehouses for keeping all the different sorts of goods separate. Over the door is written the name of the goods kept in each warehouse; an officer of the king has one key, while the owner of the goods has another, and neither can enter without the other. The goods remain there till they have paid the dues and the customs, and the exports have to pay as well as the imports. This *Alfandigue* is two or three hundred paces from the sea, between the town and the port: it is strong and well guarded, all the the doors being well locked, and none may enter but on business, for the guards are always stationed there. Mistakes

[1] Port. *alfandega*, from *fondoc*, the Arabic form of the Greek πανδοχεῖον, a magazine; *cf.* Sp. *fundago*, Ital. *fondaco*, Fr. *fondeque* or *fondique*. See Littré (s. v. *fondique*), Ducange (s. v. *funda*), Dozy and Engelmann (s. v. *alfandega*); and Yule, *Cathay*, p. 355.

[2] The Place Royale, now Place des Vosges, remarkable for its arcaded galleries, was begun by Henri IV in 1604, and completed in 1612. It was the great new feature of Paris when Pyrard was preparing his second edition.

cannot well be made in the charging and discharging of goods, and in levying the king's dues, by reason of the number of clerks and officers who have to pass them, and these are all Nairs or Bramenis. And there is no port in all the kingdom so small but has its clerks, who, when the goods belong to merchants of the country, merely take a note of them; and at the end of six months or a year the merchants come and pay the gross amount. These officers are all men of quality, and highly respected. They have their offices and Alfandigues at the ports, where they pass the day; in the evening they return from the towns, and pass the night at their homes, which are usually not far from the town, half a league or so: they do not forgather with the crowd.[1]

When these officers saw us, and had heard whence we came, they were greatly joyed to have the presenting of us to the king; yet, by reason of the heat, they made us accept a lodging in the town, where we spent the hot hours of the day.

This town is not like the others of the Malabar coast, for it has its inns and drinking-shops, where food and lodging have their price. In the evening the officers gave us over to the soldiers of the guard, who conducted us to the king, whose palace is a half league from the town of Calecut. The

[1] The excellent management of the customs department at Calicut has been remarked by many travellers. In strong contrast to that of the Portuguese alfandega, it was characterised by a high degree of commercial honesty, which must account, in great measure, for the greatness of the port in the palmy days of the pre-Portuguese period. Thus, Abder-Razzak (*India in XV Cent.*, i, 14), says: "Security and justice are so firmly established in this city, that the most wealthy merchants bring thither from maritime countries considerable cargoes, which they unload, and unhesitatingly send into the markets and bazaars, without thinking in the meantime of any necessity of checking the account, or of keeping watch over the goods. The officers of the custom-house take upon themselves the charge of looking after the merchandize, over which they keep watch day and night. When a sale is effected, they levy a duty on the goods of one-fortieth part; if they are not sold, they make no charge on them whatsoever." See, too, *Barbosa*, Hak. Soc., pp. 110-111.

soldiers escorted us thither with all honour and respect. The king, aware of our coming, came down to the lower hall of his palace, because it was night. He was accompanied by ten or twelve Nair pages, all gentlemen, with large gold or silver gilt lamps, full of oil, for they use not candles or torches. Each lamp had six wicks, with snuffers as large as the finger, also of gold or silver gilt, and a large vessel of the same full of oil, so that the lamps should always be supplied. These lamps are hung from a great silver gilt rod, the end of which is fixed in the ground, while above it is curved outwards, so that the lamp does not inconvenience or soil the person who holds it, neither does it run over. The seats in the hall were of wood, well polished and handsome. They use also large black polished stones, like marble, for sitting upon. The king never sits in public, but remains standing.

The king held in his arms his little nephew, the prettiest and best bred child that could be, aged about three years, whom he greatly caressed as the heir to his throne: for there, the children never succeed, but only the nephews, the sons of sisters. He made a show of us to the little nephew, and asked him who we were, and made him approach and touch us to see if he was afraid of us, but he was not at all. After having questioned my companion and me for more than three hours he bade his interpreter in Portuguese ask us, amongst other things, what was the difference between the Hollanders and us (knowing, as he did, that we were not Hollanders), and which was the more puissant prince, Count Maurice, or the king of France. I told him that without comparison it was the king of France; but he replied that the Hollanders said the same of their Count Maurice, and the Portuguese of their king, and that he knew not what he ought to believe; whereto I answered according to the truth. At length, having asked how I had come to Calecut, and with what mind, and I having recounted all my adventures, and telling him that my only intention in coming there was to find the Hollanders (who were the more welcome strangers, as I had been told), he informed me that in truth, some three weeks or a month before, thirteen ships had come there and remained for nine or ten days; that he had given them permission to trade, and promised his friendship; and that the Hollanders had made him a present of two large cast-metal cannon (which had been taken from some Portuguese ships, and with which he was on that account less well pleased when he came to know it), and some other things that Count Maurice had sent him: that in return he had given them divers presents, such as jewels and gold chains, and had also given them leave to build a fortress; and that they had forthwith departed, promising to come again the following year.[1] He added that we were most welcome, and that we should want nothing while we were his guests.

The interpreter who interrogated us was a *Banian*,[2] and

[1] It is somewhat difficult to identify the Dutch fleet here spoken of. Van der Hagen arrived at Calicut with thirteen ships on the 27th October 1604, and had an interview with the Samorin, at which a treaty was concluded, and remained till after the 8th November (*Rec. des Voy.*, iii, 17). The Dutch chronicler does not say that he presented any guns. The next Dutch visit was that of Verhœven, who arrived, also with thirteen ships, on the 8th October 1608, and remained till the 16th. He, also, had an interview with the Samorin, at which the Van der Hagen treaty was confirmed; and at this meeting Verhœven presented to the Samorin two guns, which the Dutch had taken in a Portuguese ship, the *Bom Jesus*, at Mozambique (*Rec. des Voy.*, iv, 47-59). This incident is illustrated in *De Bry*, pt. IX, icon iv. Now Pyrard himself arrived at Calicut about the end of June 1607, some fifteen months before Verhœven. The conclusion is that the Samorin spoke to him of the visit of Van der Hagen, and that in writing his book some years after, the author inserted the details about the guns from what he had heard, probably at Goa, of the visit of Verhœven.

[2] Banyan, from *vaṇiya*, a Gujaráti trader. The name came to be applied to all Hindu merchants and brokers. The author, when he says, "and Brahman", does not mean that the Banyans were Brahmans by caste, nor, probably, that this individual was of Brahman caste, but merely that a Banyan was a Hindu. For illustrations of the use of the word, see Yule's *Gloss.* s. v.

Brameny, by race and religion, and spoke good Portuguese. He called himself broker (*courratier*) of the Flemings, or Hollanders,—that is, one who buys and sells merchandise, and acts as interpreter also, and is paid both by the vendor and purchaser. The king bade him to lodge us, and to take all care of us: he was called *Maniassa*.[1] He gave us a lodging at the house of a great Pandiare[2] and Mahometan Cherife, one of the greatest nobles of Calecut: it was at some distance from the town and the palace, and was one of the finest houses at Calecut. We had hardly established ourselves there ere we were told by him and other friends that the Portuguese were minded to do us a bad turn, and had conspired against us,—as, indeed, was the fact, and as we came to know afterwards. Whereupon the interpreter, fearing that we should come to harm, took us from that house after a stay of two or three days, and prepared us a lodging in the *Alfandegue*. This man was a kind of factor and agent to the king, in regard to the vessels despatched by the king to different parts. The Moucois commonly called him Marcaire,[3] or king's lieutenant; but that was merely to flatter him, as indeed they do to all the king's officers: albeit, he has the superintendence of all vessels used by the king in trade. We had also a servant given us, and each of us received daily two *panants*,[4] which are pieces of gold, in value four sols apiece, and also cloths for raiment, and all else

[1] Malayâlam *Maṇiâṇi*, an agent or manager.

[2] Probably used in the Maldive sense, of a cadi or judge.

[3] See above, p. 350.

[4] The value here given to the *fanam*, *i.e.*, 4 sous, leads me to believe that the *larin* of Malabar was of inferior value to that of the Maldives. In Malabar, the larin and the fanam were, according to the author, of the same value, 16 taras; therefore the *larin* of Malabar = 4 sous. The Maldive larin, Pyrard more than once says, was equal to 7 or 8 sous, *i.e.*, nearly twice the value of the Malabar *larin* and *fanam*.

The Old Virây fanam = 4 to a rupee.
„ New „ „ = 3½ „ „

that was necessary: for this man was so careful of us that he never quitted us, for fear we should complain of him to the king. Moreover, he was greatly desirous of being in the good graces of the Hollanders, who had given him such fair promises; and I know that the Portuguese bore him a deadly grudge on that score. When we had been there some fortnight or three weeks our companions who had remained at Moutingué arrived thence. They were treated as we were, and we all lodged together. In this way we resided at Calecut for about eight months, and I thus had the means to learn and observe both the country itself and the manners and character of the inhabitants.

Between the town and the king's palace there is nothing but houses, and there is no place in all India where contentment is more universal than at Calecut, both on account of the beauty and fertility of the country, and of the intercourse with men of all races, who live there in free exercise of their own religions. It is indeed a marvellous sight to see the great multitudes that are there, principally around the king's palace, where you will see a vast crowd of men, all in arms. All the greatest lords go every day to salute the king, who is greatly esteemed as a man of high spirit, albeit of a changeable humour: for he will greatly love, and then as greatly hate the same person, and afterwards of a sudden receive him again into his friendship. Wherefore no one puts his trust in him: he will take from any hand that gives, and himself confessed that he was a friend to those who gave him the best presents. He is very affable and pleasant, as well to strangers as to his own people, yet is he very choleric also, and is greatly feared by all his Nairs, who are ever apprehensive of his anger.

On one day, amongst others, I saw a female acrobat, one of the best dancers and tumblers that could be seen: for I have in my time seen many such, both men and women, but none to compare with her in the strange things she did, so that I could not but believe she employed some kind of diabolical art. This woman having come to do her perilous feats, the king and his wife were in a gallery to witness them, together with one other princess. There were some Nairs who obstructed the queen's view, and the king cried out to them once to keep back; but I believe that, owing to the great crush and noise of the crowd, they did not hear him; whereupon he, out of anger, himself stepped down with the fan-screen which his page was holding, and began to lay about him without respect of persons. It was the most pitiful sight in the world to see all the lords, soldiers, and others there fleeing hither and thither, and putting their hands to their heads in token of obedience: all of them would have quitted the scene of the exhibition, had he not himself commanded them to remain.

While I was at Calecut, all the lords used to bid us eat and drink with them, and to make us presents of gold pieces, silk and cotton cloths, and fruits. Among these was one of greater authority than all others,[1] for in the absence of the king he used to govern the city of Calecut. His house was about a league from the royal palace, situate upon a lake, and built of stone, of about a half-league in circumference, as all their other tanks are.

On a certain holiday (though it is far from easy to know when the Nairs' holidays are, for they never work) this lord had asked us to dine with him, my companion and myself, —a thing rarely done; but he was not very scrupulous. He was not of the Brameny race, and except the flesh of the ox and cow, he ate anything. So he went to bathe, for it is a custom with them when they come from among the crowd, considering themselves polluted, to bathe in these tanks.

[1] The Talachchennôr, or Nâyar of Calicut, is here alluded to. To the present day he signs for the Samorin during an interregnum. The house referred to is probably that which used to stand on a tank lying to the east of the public road to Beypore, beyond Mînchanda.

Now, two other great lords came to bathe at the same time in this large tank, one of whom was a relative of the king—I believe his nephew—for the king has a large number of them; the other was a man of high authority, having the command of a large body of Nairs, and was deemed a very valiant fellow. The king's nephew bearing the other a grudge, sent word to ask how it was he dared bathe at the same time with him, and threatening to drive him off. The lord, not wanting in courage, made no other reply, save that he boxed the ears of him who brought the message from the prince, bidding him to take that to his master. The prince, informed of this affront, forthwith assembles all his men, as also does the other on his side, so that there arose a great hubbub and affray between the two parties. The lord who had asked us to dine made haste to see what was afoot, and was never so astonished as to see such hosts of men assembled in arms in so short a time, and sought to put the matter straight. The king, on being informed of all that had passed, straightway ordered his nephew—who was his brother's son, and not his sister's—to be seized and put to death. The bell was rung at the royal palace, which at once became full of people waiting his commands. There were a number of people wounded in this affray, and the nephew of the king, fearing his wrath, took to flight, and with great expedition crossed the river which separates the Calecut kingdom from that of a king named *Chaly*.[1] This nephew was a great friend and protector to the Portuguese. It was five or six weeks ere he was allowed to return to favour. I saw him when he came back on his way to salute the king, along with a hundred of his followers, who had been in the same disgrace.

[1] Châliyam, which stood where the Beypore railway station now is (see plate in *Correa*, and *Linschoten*, Hak. Soc., i, 73, *note*). It was one of the earliest Mahomedan settlements, and probably gave its name to the piece-goods called *Shaleeats* (see citation from Ibn Bat. in Yule's *Gloss.*). The Portuguese form was *Chale*, which our author follows.

This example shows what the sudden anger of the king means, and how he was slow to pardon even his next of kin; yet was his wrath always with some measure of justice.

The whole coast from Barcelor to the Cape Comorin is called *Malabar*[1]; and though there be many provinces and divers countries there, yet are they all of one language, law, and religion, of like government, classes, and ranks of men, according to their respective races, and above all of the same manners. There be many kings, such as those of *Cananor*, *Moutingué*, *Badara*, *Calecut*, *Tananor*,[2] *Cochin*, *Coilan*,[3] and many other kinglets too numerous to mention. But the greatest and most puissant king is he of Calecut, who is called *Samory*.[4] This is the distinguishing mark of his grandeur above all the rest, this word having the same meaning as Emperor with us. The king of Cochin is the greatest next to him, and assumes to be his peer, and this

[1] The limits usually assigned to Malabar are Mount Dely on the north, and Cape Comorin on the south (Yule, *Cathay*, 450; *Barbosa*, Hak. Soc., 101; *Fra Bart.*, Eng. trans., 103). Barros (*Dec. I*, liv. IV, cap. vii) puts the northern boundary at Carnate, near Dely; De Couto (*Dec. XII*, liv. I, cap. xviii) puts it at Cananor; others, erroneously, as high as Goa. Linschoten (i, 65) and Mandelslo (p. 87) agree with Pyrard in assigning Barcelor (*Bârkûr*), in S. Canara, as the northern limit; and if we go by language, as Pyrard does, they are right, as this is the northern boundary of Malayâḷam.

[2] Tanur.

[3] Quilon (*Kollam*). For references to the mediæval history of this place, see Yule, *Cathay*, 455; and *Gloss.*, s. v. "Quilon".

[4] One of the titles of the king of Calicut is *Kunnalakôn*, *i.e.*, King of the Hills (*kunnu*) and Waves (*ala*). The Sanskrit equivalent is *Samudragiri raja*, or shortly, *Samudri raja*, whence the Samorin, or Zamorin, of the Portuguese and other European writers. "This king became greater and more powerful than all the others; he took the name of *Zomodri*, which is a point of honour above all other kings" (*Barbosa*, Hak. Soc., p. 103). "The town of Calicut he (Cheramân Perumâl) gave to one of his best beloved servants, together with the title of Samoriin, which is as much to say as Emperour and chief of all the rest" (*Linschoten*, i, 72). As to the last quotation, the probability is that the first Samorin was a Home Ruler, and rebelled against the last of the Perumâls.

is why they are so frequently at war.[1] The others are petty kings of petty territories, who, though they be all kings with sovereign power in their own lands, yet revere and respect the greatness of Samory, speaking of him as their lord, and daring not to disobey him. This I say with assurance, for I have heard it from the mouths of many of these kings themselves. The king of *Coilan*[2] being so remote, at the very point of Cape Comorin, maintains more of his sovereignty than the rest; when I left India he was holding the Portuguese in siege on land.[3]

The kingdom of Calecut is of very great extent, and of a temperate sky. It is situate between Cochin and Cananor, at nine and a half degrees from the equinoctial, towards the Arctic Pole. The principal town, which is on the sea-coast, bears the name of the kingdom. The country is flat and without mountains, fertile in all the necessaries of life, such as fruits, grain, beasts, and pasture, save that for the bulk of the inhabitants rice has to be procured elsewhere, that grown in the country not being sufficient[4]: they take no other

[1] Before the Portuguese time the greatest Malabar prince was undoubtedly the Samorin. The Raja of Cochin, supported by the Portuguese, throve so much in trade, that Linschoten, only a few years before this time, considered him the greatest king of the coast. But Linschoten did not know much of Calicut, and in Pyrard's time the Samorin had the scale again turned in his favour by the waning of the Portuguese power and the organised system of piracy of which he was patron. The Samorins, however, never regained their earlier supremacy; and, a few years later, the Padre Vincenzo Maria accounts the Raja of Cananor the first, the Raja of Travancore the second, and the Samorin only the third in importance, of the Malabar princes.

[2] So called from the Portuguese *Coulão*: we call it *Quilon*. Its native name is *Kollam*. This very ancient port of Travancore was known to the Arabs as *Kaulam*; it is the *Columbum* of which Friar Jordanus was appointed bishop. It is mentioned in the Chinese annals as *Kiu-lan*.

[3] This expedition of the Portuguese is referred to in the king's letter of 17th February 1611 (see *Liv. das Monç.*, ii, 36), where it seems Quilon was then under a queen. Pyrard did not visit the place.

[4] This is true of the present day. Malabar pays for its rice by exporting coffee, ginger, coco-nuts, areca-nuts, and other palm-produce.

merchandise from their neighbours. There is abundance of pepper, which is the principal source of the country's wealth; of gems, which are very plentiful there; and of cotton, whereof they make a very fine white cloth,[1] and divers kinds of painted and patterned tapestry.

CHAPTER XXVII.

More of Calecut.—Classes of the people: Bramenis, Nairs, Moucois, and others, and characteristics of the country.

The kingdom of Calecut, like all the rest of the Malabar country, is inhabited by two sorts of people, foreigners and natives. The foreigners are those properly called *Mahometan Malabars*, who long ago came from elsewhere to inhabit this country, but only the sea-coasts. The natives are Gentiles and pagans, of the same religion as those of the greater part of Southern India.

They are divided into three ranks of life, Bramenis,[2] Nairs, and the common people. Among the Malabar Nairs, as among the Canarins of Goa, there are some Bramenis, but all are fundamentally of but one and the same faith,—that is, they are idolaters.

The Bramenis are of the most noble race, honoured and respected of all others; they have their peculiar habits of life, and practise a more religious and austere observance of their faith; for besides living scrupulously according to their religion, they have this peculiarity, that they never eat

[1] Whence our word *calico*, as to which, see Yule, *Gloss.*, s. v.

[2] Pyrard writes the sing. *Brameny* and the plur. *Bramenis*. The Port. wrote *Bramenes*, and the earlier English, *Brachmanes*. All the European forms seem to have come through the Greek Βραχμᾶνες, from the Sansk. *Brahmana*. The Brahmans of Malabar are called *Nambûtiris*, *i.e.*, trusted persons.

flesh or fish, or anything that has had life, or drink aught but water, and they preserve this austerity from father to son for all generations, never mingling or allying themselves with other people. They preserve an inviolable rule that the daughters of Bramenis never marry but with Bramenis, and the same with the men, who also may never marry a second time. Their habit is a frock of cotton cloth, with a white turban on the head, and red slippers on the feet. This frock or cassock, which they call *Libasse*[1] or *Cabaye*,[2] is of very white cotton, reaching to the heels; under it is a large white cloth hanging down to the mid thigh, which they fold twice or thrice, and pass between the legs in front and then fasten behind at the waist. Round the waist they wear a pretty scarf of fine white cloth, like that of the turban. Over the shoulders they are wont to carry a piece of white or coloured cloth, of silk or cotton, in the style we wear our mantles. All wear their hair long, and all the Bramenis, Banians, and Canarins wear pendants in their ears.

The only mark distinguishing them from other people is a cord of three strands of cotton, which they wear next the skin. It is a kind of order given to them at their temples, with great display and solemnity; and one could not do a Brameny a greater injury than to break his cord: in that

[1] The Ar. *libās* means a garment in general. Lane (*Mod. Egypt.*) uses the same word for "drawers". The author probably brought the term from the Maldives, where, as Mr. Bell now informs us, the word is applied to the loose-fitting over-chemise worn by the women there, and described above, pp. 166-7.

[2] French form of the Port. *cabáya*, itself taken from the Ar. *ḳabá*, a vesture. Col. Yule suggests that the word was taken to India by the Portuguese. But the following passages from Correa and the Albuquerque *Comm.* rather point to its prior existence in Eastern parlance, and to its being previously unknown to the Portuguese. "Cabaya is a garment such as a pelote is with us" (Correa, in Stanley's *Three Voyages*, p. 132); "Cabayas, or native dresses of silk" (Alb., *Comm.*, iv, 95). *Kabáya* is still a common word in Ceylon for a coat or jacket, worn by a European or native.

case he would have to get another with like ceremony, otherwise he would no longer be a Brameny. So also if one is punished, he is first degraded and his cord removed; likewise, if he intermits any of his ceremonies he is deprived of it, and is then no longer of this order. They are of divers professions, according as they are inclined: some serve in arms with the Nairs, performing the same duties and wearing the same dress as the latter, except that they maintain always their rules of living and abstinence from flesh, and are always distinguished by the said cord. The rest are either priests and sacrificers to their idols (for it is from this race alone these may be taken), or else they live as they will, as merchants, of which class there is a great and very wealthy body, both in this kingdom and in the rest of India. They are an industrious people, learned in astrology and other sciences, of great experience in all matters, and exceedingly adroit, besides being soft and pacific in temper, and men who keep inviolate their faith and word.

In short, they are held in the same honour and repute as here the clergy, philosophers, and doctors. Some of them in Goa practise medicine and the apothecary's art, after the mode of the Portuguese and of Europe. They are of all other vocations too, and the highest honour that a gentleman could desire would be to be of this race. They excel both in learning and wit, and are very judicious in all things. The king of Calecut himself is a Brameny, and wears the cord. When they go about the town with their *Cabaye*, or white cotton garment, and meet some stranger, they at once tell who they are and their race, in order to be acknowledged for what they are (for their cord, being worn next the skin, is not seen). Among all the Christian Indians[1] they rank next after the Portuguese and the Indian Metifs. Moreover, Metifs whose mothers are of a lower caste are not

[1] *Sic.* He probably means the Indians who inhabit the Portuguese territories.

esteemed equal to those born of a Brameny mother, for these latter hold their heads as high as the Portuguese themselves. When a Brameny would swear, he puts his hand on his cord, and then he must be believed. However poor they may be they maintain their rank and rules of life, and other folk in passing salute them by bowing the head as a mark of respect. Kings put their entire trust in them, and always keep some of the chiefest of them about their persons, both for religious purposes and as counsellors, and follow their advice in all things. They are not all equal, but there is one greater than all the rest.[1]

I have heard it said that the cause of the expelling of the Portuguese and the ruin of their towns and fortresses was this, that they had spoken slander of the Bramenis and their law, and that the Bramenis had complained to the king, and had demanded vengeance for it, exclaiming that if he drove not out that race, he and his house would come to a miserable end. Whereupon the king bade sound the bell and assemble his council, whereat it was resolved to drive them forth; and the king gave out that for as many stones as were brought to him from their fortress, he would give so many pieces of gold. So in but a short time this fortress was razed, and the garrison pillaged of most of their property. The Portuguese have had two fortresses[2] there, one after the other; both are in ruins and the garrisons expelled, and now they have none.

[1] This account of the Brahmans is coloured by the author's knowledge of Brahmans elsewhere. The *Nambûtiris* of Malabar do not engage in trade, nor do they carry arms.

[2] The fortresses at Calicut and Châliyam are probably meant. The former was built in 1513 (Barros, *Dec. II*, liv. VIII, cap. vi), and destroyed by order of D. Henrique de Menezes in 1525 (*ib.*, liv. IX, cap. x). The latter was built in 1531 (*Dec. IV*, liv. IV, cap. xviii), and taken by the Samorin, 4th November 1571 (Couto, *Dec. IX*, cap. ii). This was the first fortress lost by the Portuguese in India. As Châliyam was not in Calicut proper, the author may have had in his mind the fortress begun to be built at Ponani, 21st December 1585 (*Dec. X*, liv. VII, cap. v), but never finished; or that at Kollam, *v. s.*, p. 360.

It would seem that the king of Calecut has done well to drive them out, for they would have done to him even as they have done at Cochin and other places. They come in under colour of friendship and suavity towards the kings, and then by their encroachments endeavour to subdue them. He of Calecut had given them free admittance, but when he saw that they took more than he gave, he took prompt measures ere they made their position stronger. The king of Cochin, not having been so well advised, now has to receive at their hands a thousand insults, in such wise that when the viceroy of Goa went to the succour of Malaca, as I shall relate hereafter, and passed by Goa, the king sent him a number of almadies, or boats, laden with provisions, fruits, and other refreshments; but the viceroy, by name *Don Martin Alphonse*,[1] would not so much as look at or receive them, and had them all cast into the sea, bidding tell the king with proud words that on his return from Sunda he would visit him to his cost. This was because the king had been unwilling to deliver up something that he had demanded; but he was happily prevented from seeing him again on his return, for the viceroy died at Malaca.

Another time, when the Hollanders were before the harbour of Cochin, the Portuguese would not allow the king to enter their town. This shows the pride of these fellows, and with what insolence they scold any that give them the smallest occasion. But the king of Calecut, having been more prudent, now laughs at the other kings, who thus find themselves under the curb of the Portuguese.

But to return to the Bramenis, who were the cause of the expelling of the Portuguese: those who reside among the Banians and Canarins are all the same. As for the Canarins,[2]

[1] Dom Martim Affonso de Castro, eighteenth viceroy, assumed office January 1605, and died at Malacca, 3rd June 1607.

[2] The Portuguese form, so written by Garcia de Orta, though Barros writes *Canarijs*. The name was applied to the natives of the coast and

they differ not at all in their dress, but the Banians wear red slippers, much pointed in front, the point being raised somewhat high, with a knob of the same leather. The Canarins of Goa and the neighbourhood wear *Alparcas*,[1] which are a kind of sandals with several leather soles, and a number of little leather straps above, which pass between the toes and over the foot, and so hold it. These straps are of gilt leather, with little gilded buckles and fastenings.

These white dresses worn by the Indians of Goa are not at all convenient, because the soil of Goa is red, like bolarmeny,[2] insomuch that, whether in summer or winter, the dust or mud stains and soils all their garments. They change them, however, every day, and sometimes oftener. The greatest of these Bramenis and other Gentiles have always many men with them; one carries the parasol, another a silver box full of betel, a third, a silver flagon of water for washing. After obeying the calls of nature they wash the private parts; they also carry some water in their palan-

interior north of Malabar, as far as and including Goa district, *i.e.*, all that is now comprised in the Konkan (Bom. Pres.) and South Kanara (Madras Pres.). But, as Dr. Hunter says, the very name is a misnomer, for but a small part of the population of this region are Kanarese. If applied to the Kanarese people and language, it should be used of Mysore and other districts above the western ghâts. The other form of the name, *Karnatic*, has, "by one of the strange processes of history", come to be applied to the Tamil country on the other side of the peninsula, below the eastern ghâts (*Imp. Gaz. of India;* and see Yule, *Gloss.*, s. vv. *Canara* and *Carnatic*, and in Supplement, *Canarin*).

[1] *Alparca*, "hempen shoe", contraction of *alpargata*, from Ar. *pargat*, "sandals"; Vieira, *Dict.*, s. v. Ces. Federici calls them *alperche* (Hak., ii, pt. II, 222). Linschoten (Hak. Soc., i, 257) says that the Canaras and Decanins differ from the Guzeratis and Banians in their shoes, "which they wear like antiques with cut toes, and fastned above upon their naked feete, which they call *alparcas*." Mandelslo (p. 93) says that the Deccanis dress like the other Banians, "save that their shoes, which they call *alparcas*, are of wood, tyed up over the instep with straps of leather."

[2] *I.e.*, "Armenian bole", or *terra sigillata* (Cotgrave). Vincent le Blanc describes it in like terms (i, 77).

quins—that is, the rich. None of them eat ere they have washed and bathed: and then they use simply a cloth to cover their private parts, leaving off the rest of their clothes while they eat. Their food must be prepared by those of their own race, or even by themselves, no matter how great folks they be: for after food is touched, whether cooked or during the cooking, none durst touch the man who has or carries it; if they had to die, they would not eat anything that had been touched by a man or woman who was not of their race and faith. But the other Gentiles may well eat that which has been touched and prepared by the Bramenis, yet in no case do superiors prepare food for those who are beneath them.

All their women have the nose pierced, and wear therein trinkets of gold, silver, and jewels. They also wear rings of gold and silver on their toes, and in their ears large round plates of the same, as large as little saucers, with many gems set round the edge and in the middle. All these are worn by the wives of Bramenis, Banians, and Canarins, not by those of the Nairs, nor of the Moucois or other Malabars. They wear also bracelets, called *Manile,*[1] from the hand up to the elbow: of these, some are of gold and silver, others of glass or of tortoise-shell, which is much prized, and is worked up with all colours and in all patterns. All the fingers are also covered with trinkets and rings.

All these Gentiles abstain from the flesh of the cow, just as the Mahometans from pork; and they are so bound to this superstition, that most of them, when they become Christians, enter into a bargain that they shall not be compelled to eat it. Nor do they ever eat the flesh of oxen, bulls, or buffaloes. They dislike also to quit their own style of dress, and this

[1] *I.e.*, Port. *manilhas*, "bracelets". Pyrard seems to have taken it to be a native word. It occurs in Sir Thos. Herbert (edit. 1677, p. 114), "manilios and armolets of silver", and in Alex. Hamilton (*New Acc.*, i, 303) as "*manila*, or wrist jewel".

they are allowed to keep, along with many other superstitions; which leads to the belief that they are not by any means good Christians—and the fact is, most of them become Christians of necessity. The Mahometans of Cambaye, Surratte, and Guzerate, countries of the great Mogor, and the Banian Gentiles, have amongst them no superior or inferior race, though they have classes of various qualities and means, according to which they win respect and honour: and except the Nairs, all these Gentiles are artizans and merchants, and not men of war. The first thing they meet when they go out of their houses, whether birds or quadrupeds, they honour and worship the whole day, and ask of their priests and sorcerers, in whom they put their trust, what they have to tell of these things.[1]

The *Joguies* are hermits that wander about the country, and are treated much as the religious orders in these parts. One sees also a large number of charlatans and sorcerers, who charm serpents, so that they can do no harm: some of these one sees of 22 or 23 feet in length. These Gentiles drink only out of copper pots, except the great, who use gold and silver gilt; and it is to be remarked that they never touch the vessel with their mouths while they drink, but only pour the water into their mouths from above. The Portuguese themselves have adopted this custom, as also that of never eating with spoons, and numberless other fashions, from the Indians, who never change theirs.

They marry very young, most often at seven and eight years of age, both men and women. The Gentile women, who burn themselves after the death of their husbands, first take off all their trinkets, and give them to whom they will. As for widowers, they make no other sort of mourning for

[1] This is a notion commonly entertained at this period of the Hindu religions; see *Linschoten*, i, 248. It arose from the practice of the natives drawing their omens from what they first saw in the morning or on commencing a journey, etc.

the death of their wives, except that they cannot marry again.

When they fast, which is but seldom, they go for a day, or at most two, without eating or drinking more than they are obliged. They believe that after death their souls pass into the bodies of cows, buffaloes, or bulls, and that when the cow or bull dies, they take to other bodies; and I believe that to be the reason why they will not eat the flesh of these, viz., on account of their notion of the passage of souls from one body to another. They have received this from the ancient tradition of the Brachmanes and Indian Gymnosophists, who were instructed in the doctrine of Pythagoras, for he was the first author of this Metempsychosis.[1] They have places of retreat for wandering beasts, and are mindful to give food and drink to birds and all other animals. They would not for anything in the world willingly permit the slaughter of any animal, and would sooner redeem it with money. But the Nairs eat of everything, except of the cow, bull, and buffalo, and use swine's flesh freely. All these Gentiles are badly off when they go a sea voyage, or get into gaol, or among a crowd of strangers: then most of them put up with dried and preserved fruits, or with a kind of rice, half cooked and then dried, which keeps two or three years. It is greatly used for provisioning all the Indian vessels, and serves them as biscuit does us; they eat it in handfuls, as the Brazilians do the *Mandoc*[2] flour, though it has a better taste than that. They eat it usually with sugar, dates, and other native fruits: they call it *Aualu*.[3]

The wives of these Bramenis, Banians, and Canarins of

[1] This is evidently not Pyrard. One cannot think that he of his own learning knew much of Pythagoras and metempsychosis; the spelling *Brachmanes*, too, differs from his usual *Bramenis*.

[2] See vol. ii.

[3] Mal. *avil*, Tam. *aval*, "unhusked rice steeped in water and then dried and bruised" (Winslow, *Tam. Dict.*). De Couto (*Dec. VII*, liv. x, cap. xi) writes *avēla*. Rivara says it is now vulgarly known as *fōvo*.

Goa and Guzerate are very pretty and of good figure, and some are as fair as the Portuguese. The men commonly wear the beard broad, rounded and thick, and shave it under the chin; others use another style,—that is, the Turkish. All the Indian ladies—that is, the rich—wear a massive collar of gold, set with precious stones, of two or three fingers' width. All the men, Gentiles as well as Mahometans, anoint the body and smear it with sandal and other odoriferous drugs; while the Gentiles, at the entrances to their pagodes, in lieu of holy water, present to those who enter pounded ashes of burned corpses, among them considered a very sacred thing.

As for the Nairs, they are all nobles,[1] and meddle with neither handicraft nor trade, nor any other exercise but that of arms, which they always carry: and in these they do exercise themselves continually from the time they can wield them, and when out of their houses are never without them. They are all lords of the country, and live upon their revenues, and upon the pensions which the king gives them. They are the most handsome men, of the best figure and proportion I have ever seen. In complexion they are tawny, in height slim and tall; the best soldiers in the world; hardy and courageous, exceedingly adroit in the use of arms, with such dexterous suppleness of limb that they can bend in all possible postures, and can parry and avoid with subtlety all blows aimed at them, and at the same time make lunges at their antagonists. Yet they never go to sea, and are of competency only on land. The greatest lords amongst them, and the most honoured, are those who keep schools for teach-

[1] They are of the *Sudra* caste, but are on the footing of the *Kshatriya*. Their functions in the State organisation are pithily described in the Kêraḷalpatti as *kaṇ*, *kei*, *kalpana*, "the eye" (they were the overseers, or supervisors), "the hand" (emblem of power), and "the order" (the givers and carriers of orders)—"so as to prevent the rights" of all classes "from being curtailed or suffered to fall into disuse."

ing the use of arms[1]: for they do greatly honour and revere their masters in arms; and none durst undertake this mastership without the express permission of the king,—as, in fact, is the case throughout all the East Indies, as well among the Mahometans as among the Gentiles. These masters are distinguished from the rest by wearing on the right-arm a thick gold ring[2]; the great lords, too, wear the same, but of a different pattern; the rest, who are soldiers of the middle class, wear one of buffalo or bull horn. The Nairs go quite naked, and march abroad so, covered only from the waist down with a large cloth of fine silk or cotton, very white, which reaches to the knees, and is then passed between the thighs; the feet are bare, and so is the head, only they let their hair grow without ever cutting it, and this distinguishes them from the vulgar herd. They wear the hair long without cutting it, and tie it neatly on the head, carefully arranged in a bunch, and they are careful to dress and wash the head every day. Those of the Brameny race are habited the same, only they wear their cord, which serves to distinguish them. They carry always a shield on one hand and a sword in the other, or else a javelin, or muskets, matchlocks, or pikes. Their women are dressed in the same style, without other accessories, saving the arms: insomuch that it is impossible to distinguish a boy from a girl, unless she is of age, and the breasts are seen.

When the girls are grown, there is another thing by which you discern them from the boys, and that is the rich ornaments they wear of gold and precious stones: for their necks

[1] These masters were on the Malabar coast called *Paṇikar* (see Yule, *Gloss.*, s. v.).

[2] "The principallest or chiefest of those Nayros, which are leaders or Captaines of certaine numbers of Nayros, weare a Gold or Silver bracelet, or ring about their armes, above their elbowes: as also their Governours, Ambassadours, and Kings, whereby they are knowne from other men, for otherwise they goe all naked" (*Linsch.*, Hak. Soc., i, 283). As to the use of these official rings at the Maldives, see above, p. 189.

are laden with necklets, carkanets, and chains of gold, pearls, and stones: their large ears are the same, a fourth part of the ear drooping on each side. Then they have bracelets and heavy rings up to the elbow, and on the fingers, both hands and feet being all covered with jewels, and thick rings on the legs, everything being of gold or silver gilt. Be it noticed that I have never seen plain silver used for ornament by the Nairs or their women, so it is a wondrous sight to see the ladies of quality so richly adorned and dressed, each according to her means.

The ordinary residence of these Nairs is not in the towns but in the country, except that by day they assemble in large numbers to attend upon the king, wherever he may be, even in the towns of the Mahometan Malabars, as I have already said. They employ themselves in the hunting of tigers, which are exceeding savage beasts, very plentiful in that country. I have seen some that without aid did attack and kill tigers, and among others, one which dragged the body of a tiger before the presence of the king, his own face and ears being sorely torn. Very frequently, and upon any pretext, they will draw upon each other with naked swords and shields. Many of them, besides the exercise and ordinary profession of arms, are given to the sciences. I have known many of them very learned in mathematics, but chiefly in astrology.

Although all are educated to arms, and are exceedingly valiant and resolute, and take no thought for their lives, yet are they most gentle and humane in their conversation, most courteous and cultivated, according to their notions. Such was my experience while I was among them, and mixed with them familiarly, and had most of them for my friends. Yet there are in the country districts some soldiers that are highwaymen and robbers, who attack passers-by and kill them without mercy, if they be not on their guard. But all strangers, and even the Mahometan Malabars who live among them, are wont to take a Nair escort, as I have said, when they journey even to the next town, giving him a piece of money, and changing their guard at every town. By this means one can travel securely throughout the whole Malabar country without coming to any harm, passing amid thousands of Nairs; and this may be done by the most feeble old man or the youngest boy among them.

They have similar ceremonies and superstitions to those of the Bramenis (and even among these are the Bramenis the most respected), save that their manner of life is less austere. They are allowed to eat anything; but they must use frequent ablutions, and must not associate, eat, or drink with any but of their race. To the same intent, they never marry or eat with such as are not of their faith, nor use anything that belongs to them, or that they have touched: it must first be washed, if it is a thing that can be washed, otherwise they go and wash themselves after using it; if they did not, they would consider themselves polluted. Only with the Bramenis do they live without difference or ceremony, as the Bramenis with them; yet do these not ally themselves in marriage, but a Nair with a Nair. Should it happen that a Nair woman kept company with any but a Nair man, they would kill her soon enough: so, if Nair men were to go with other women, they would be punished with death. This rule is observed inviolably, in order to preserve their race from pollution with strangers or the villain stock, towards whom they bear themselves in such sort that these will not dare to approach them: and, in fact, when the Nairs go about the town and come across the villains, they cry, *Popo*,[1]

[1] Malayâlam *Po! Po!* "Go! Go!" "For as the Nayros go on the streetes, and they (the common people) heare them call, they step aside, bowing their armes and stooping with their heades down to the ground, not daring so much as once looke up before the Nayros be past" (*Linsch.*, Hak. Soc., i, 284). So Mandelslo, later:—"They (Nairs) always go with sword and buckler, wherewith they make a noise in the streets as they go, and perpetually cry out *Po*, *Po*, that people should make way

—that is, that they should get out of the way; otherwise, if they should chance to touch them, they would resent it, and would strike them.

All the Nairs like to have their ears large, which they acquire by an artifice; for they pierce the lobes of their children's ears, as well males as females, and stuff the hole with little rolls of palm-leaves: this causes them to dilate, and from time to time they insert larger rolls to make them dilate the more, until they will extend no further. They esteem it a great beauty to have their ears thus large, and then they load them with gold and precious stones for ornament, and to bear them down. Amông others, I have seen the queen of Calecut, and many other ladies and lords, who had them so extended as to reach to the breast and further.

The Nairs may have but one wife at the time; but it is not so with the women: for every woman may have as many as three husbands at once if she likes (but a Nair woman of the Brameny race may have one only), and all contribute to support and maintain the wife and children, without any quarrel or jealousy on this score. And when one of the men is in the house with the wife, which is allowed only for a day and a night at a time, when she has other husbands, he leaves his arms or some other signal at the door, and the others will not dare to enter until he be gone forth.[1] The advantage they derive from this custom is, that one who hath not means himself to maintain a wife, may have a third part

for them" (p. 109). Varthema's account is the converse; he says that the common folk "always go crying out with a loud voice, and this they do in order that they may not meet the Naeri or the Brahmins"; for if a Nair should, for want of this precaution, come across a low-caste man, he might instantly kill him (*Varthema*, Hak. Soc., p. 142; and so *Barbosa*, Hak. Soc., p. 143; *Thevenot*, Eng. trans., iii, 89).

[1] The signal at the door is deposed to by most of the witnesses (*Linsch.*, Hak. Soc., i, 280; Conti, in *India in XV Cent.*, ii, 20; cf. Abd-er-Razzak, *ib.*, i, 17; *Barbosa*, Hak. Soc., p. 126).

of one, and the cost of her maintenance is only in this proportion. Nevertheless, for this cause is there an uncertainty of blood, and whose the children are cannot be truly known; wherefore fathers are not succeeded by their children, but by their nephews, the sons of their sisters, this being a more certain line. Their uprightness of conversation between men and women is most admirable; for although girls and boys live together, these as naked as those, yet there will never escape them a lascivious word or glance, nor any indecent act. They hardly ever laugh, regarding laughter as a great incivility and indiscretion, never to be indulged in without good reason, and then they observe in whose presence they are.[1] For the rest, they are by no means depraved; sodomy and incest are never heard of.

The true and original Malabars may be considered to be the Nairs, for, as I have said, they are the lords of the country, and the nobles are they who keep schools of arms, whither all the other Malabars go to be taught: and [? but] when one speaks of the Malabars without saying more, one means the Mahometans of this coast. The Malabars keep up great state in their towns, and consider themselves all nobles and men of honour, none of whom would do any toilsome or vile thing: all such work they make the *Moucois* and other villains do for them for hire. All their time is taken up with soldiering, and they all know the use of arms, as well merchants as pirates and the rest; for after going through this training they become merchants or corsairs, esteeming the one profession as good as the other, without any distinction. As for the artizans, they are all Gentiles, either native born or strangers. A Malabar, of whatever quality, never goes abroad through the streets without carrying arms like the Nairs. Their

[1] When simple natives are in the presence of a European official, and cannot restrain their laughter, they hide the face with their hands. Mr. Hartshorne goes so far as to say that the Veddas of Ceylon *never laugh* (*Fort. Rev.*, vol. xix, p. 410); but I am aware that this is doubted.

name and quality are according to their estate and profession, besides which they have honours peculiar to their race. They only marry with the poorer women of their own calling. Of the Nairs, those who stand about the town gates to escort travellers are the poorest of them, and they love to do this rather than any handicraft or other unworthy work. This condition is in no wise disgraceful to them. They would not be permitted to do aught in derogation of their nobility, and, indeed, would rather suffer every kind of hardship. The attire of the Nairs is fair white cloth, over which they wear round the waist a large scarf of red tafetas, with a fringe half a foot wide, half gold and half silk, of the same colour.

The third class of the inhabitants of Calecut and Malabar are the common people, who throughout all these countries are much despised, vile and abject beings, just like slaves. They are called *Moucois* or *Poulia*.[1] They have a quarter to themselves without the towns, next to the sea, and in other remoter places. They are of divers conditions; some live on the sea coast, and durst not venture to reside inland; these are properly called *Moucois.* They are all fishers or makers of salt, and on all the Malabar coast none others are employed as oarsmen and seamen, for which service they are hired. Their wives and daughters do all kinds of service on land, taking all sorts of work, and even carrying burdens, like the porters here. They scruple not to yield themselves for hire to any men whatever, no matter of what birth, race, or religion, having nothing to fear from their husbands, who durst not say a word, and meekly suffer it. And there are none other concubines or public girls but the wives and daughters of these *Moucois* and *Tiua*,[2] or artizan class; for the other

[1] These are by no means identical, as Pyrard (*infra*) seems to be aware. *The Mukkuvar* are the fisher caste, and are higher than the *Pulayar*, who are predial slaves (*pula* = pollution). See *Varthema*, Hak. Soc., p. 142; *Linsch.*, Hak. Soc., i, 279, and Dr. Burnell's note there.

[2] *Tiyar* or *Tivar.* These are, properly speaking, and as Pyrard pre-

women abandon themselves only to those of their own caste. The Moucois women lack not beauty, and some are fairer than the other women; their mothers prostitute them for money at the earliest age they can. The fairest and youngest of them may be enjoyed for seven or eight *tarans*,—that is, equal to two sols; and the mothers are not bashful in coming and offering them. This is a commoner practice there than anywhere in the world. All the Moucois, as well men as women, have much trouble in going about the streets when they meet the Nairs in any narrow passage, for they are constrained sometimes to wait a long while till they have passed, even when they are carrying a load.

In the country there are others of like condition, but of different offices and professions. One class they call *Tiua*, who gather the produce of the coco-tree; others are artizans; others, who till the soil, are called *Coulombin*,[1] and yet these are all of the same caste, who marry one with another, albeit there are certain grades and distinctions among them. Thus, the tillers of the soil are the most honourable, next the artizans, then the *Tiua*, and the last, the most vile and abject, are the *Moucois* fishers.[2] All these common people are attired in the same fashion; that is, they are naked, except for a little cord girdle, whereto is hung a bit of cloth, or a leaf, or a

sently indicates, toddy drawers, and are said to have come from Ceylon, hence their name *Tivar* = islanders (*Linsch.*, Hak. Soc., i, 279, *note*).

[1] Probably the *Kurumbar*, an extensive low-caste tribe of the ghâts, though Mr. Logan thinks he cannot have seen any of these so near the coast, and that he may mean the *Kollanmâr* (blacksmiths or artizans). The *Kurumbar* are referred to by P. Vincenzo as *corombini*, a middle form, which leaves little doubt as to the identity of Pyrard's *coulombin*.

[2] The castes below the Nâyars are thus classified by Dr. Burnell: (i) *Tîvar;* (ii) *Mukkuvar;* (iii) *Pulayar*, or, as in Malabar proper, *Cherumar*, who are "the ruling tribe of the fourteen castes of jungle-dwellers" (Gundert, *s. v.*). But, as Mr. Logan points out, there are other well-distinguished castes; *e.g.*, between the Nâyars and Tîvar come the professional schoolmasters and astrologers, and below the Tîvar, the basket-makers, etc.

piece of bark, to cover their shame; the women use a cloth round the waist, reaching to the knees, and wear the hair long. The men durst not wear long hair, like the Nairs, so they cut it all round the head, except that they leave on the crown a thick bunch of a hand's length; they durst not shave it altogether, for that is their mark of distinction.

Also they may not have their ears long, like the Nairs, but only three fingers' length at most. Both men and women have them bored and opened, but the pendants they wear are only of silver or copper or other material, and not of gold, like the Nairs. The king appoints certain of their chiefs and headmen to rule over them, and these, with their wives and children, have permission to wear gold and jewels; but there is always a difference in the weight and size between theirs and those of the Bramenis and Nairs. Thus are they distinguished from the Nairs: in form and colour they are less comely, being blacker and of lower stature, and ill-proportioned; they would not dare approach or touch the others,[1] nor enter their houses, as already mentioned; they have even their own separate temples. For the Nairs employ them solely to do their hard work; while in their houses they employ only Nairs and gentlemen of their own class who happen to be very poor.

These Moucois fishers catch a large quantity of a sort of little fish which is no longer than the hand, and as broad as a little bream; the Portuguese call it *pesche cauallo*,[2] and it

[1] That is, the Brahmans and Nâyars.

[2] The *cavalla*, or *cavala*, a name given by the Portuguese to perhaps more than one species of fish of the size of sardines. Bluteau describes it "peixe do mar: he quasi sarda grande assim como sarda parece Cavalla pequena." It is mentioned by several travellers on the Malabar coast. P. Vincenzo says: "A kind of sardines, which they salt and dry in the sun; the largest are thrown away as noxious, wherefore all the beach of Malabar is often strewn with them. In some places they are so plentiful that waggons are laden with them. They serve for food to the dogs and crows. Frequently, too, they extract from them a thick black oil, called *sciffu*, for oiling their ships" (lib. I, cap. xxxiii). Phil. à S. Trin.,

is the most common fish on all that coast, wherefore there is very great traffic in it, the method being to cut it in half, salt it, and dry it in the sun. They fish also for another kind, which is not eaten fresh; they use only nets and lines, and most of their boats are of a single piece of wood, and are called by them *Tonny*,[1] and by the Portuguese *Almedies*.[2] The largest are made of many timbers: these they call *Thaury*. They are all of the same build, flat-bottomed, and speed well to the oars. Order was given by the king to catch a certain number of fish every day, which the chief of the Moucois was charged to supply to us free of cost.

There is one religion only, common to all the natives of Malabar, as well Bramenis and Nairs as the Poulia or Moucois. They are all Gentiles,[3] and worship the rising sun. In

writing of Goa, says, "There is another very small fish vulgarly called *cavalle*, which is good enough to the taste, but not very wholesome" (Fr. trans., p. 383). Fra Bart. writes of "the *ayla*, called in Portuguese *cavala*" (Eng. trans., p. 240). Sir T. Herbert writes *cavalloes* (p. 28). The fish above described may, perhaps, belong to the genus *Equula*, two species of which are named *E. caballa*, by different zoologists (see Yule, *Gloss.*, and *Suppt.*, s. v. *Cavally*; Day, *Fishes of India*). Pyrard, when he reaches St. Helena on his way home, mentions a little fish there under the same name. This fish, still called *cavalley*, is identified by Mr. Melliss with the *Caranx denter* (Bl. Schn.) (*St. Helena*, p. 106).

[1] Malayâlam and Tamil *tōṇi*, from Sansk *drōṇi*, "a trough", hence a boat, or, as the Canadians would say, a "dug-out". In Anglo-Indian it becomes *doney*; *vide* Yule, *Gloss*.

[2] Port. *almadia*, from Ar. *Al ma'diyah*, properly a raft. "*Almadias*, whereof some are hewen out of a peece of wood, and so narrow that a man can hardly sit in them, etc." (*Linsch.*, Hak. Soc., i, 262). They would seem, however, to have been of considerable size, as Pietro della Valle says that they were similar in all respects to the *manchuas* of Goa, having as many as twenty to twenty-four oars, except that the latter had "a large covered room in the poop" (Della Valle, Eng. ed., p. 102).

[3] At this time, no doubt, the Mukkuvar were all or nearly all Hindus; but the social advantages of the Moslem religion, proceeding from its non-acknowledgment of caste, have tended to convert large bodies of the lower castes; and now the Mukkuvar are mostly Mahomedans (Burton, *Goa and the Blue Mountains*, p. 241). Such is one explanation; Mr. Logan gives another: "To keep up a supply of sailors for

their temples is an image of a cow or other figure, which they worship; they have the like respect to the same animal alive, insomuch that they would not think of killing it or eating the flesh. This rule is observed with great strictness, not only by the Bramenis, but also by the Nairs, who eat everything but that, and by the Moucois.

When by chance a Gentile becomes Christian, as happens frequently, if his wife will not become of the same faith, she must act in all respects as if her husband were dead, except that she does not burn herself alive: she only cuts her hair, separates herself from all society, and lives the rest of her days in solitude. These Gentile kings put not any restraint on liberty of conscience in their territories; for every day one sees at Calecut and other places a mixing of Christians and Moors or Mahometans, and these Mahometans rival each other in assisting those who are converted to their faith. If a Mahometan becomes Christian, and his wife cares not to do so, she is not obliged to perform the same ceremonies as the others: she can marry again three months afterwards, which is the prescribed interval.

They recognise that there is a God, but say that as he is good there is no need to pray to him or worship him, since he does no evil. The Bramenis, as I have said, observe more peculiar ceremonies than the Nairs; and the Nairs, like the Bramenis, have some customs of their own which they most religiously maintain (which is not the case with the Moucois or common folk), for they hold intercourse only with the Bramenis, and consider themselves polluted by intercourse with others. They take their food seated on the ground, and eat off Banana leaves, which serve them for plates, even though they have or could have others, and these are used but once. They never eat without first washing the whole

the pirate crafts, the Zamorin established a rule that a certain proportion of children born to Mukkuvar should become Muhammadans." The custom is still kept up.

body. They are so superstitious, as I have said, that when their servants bring them their food or drink, should it happen that one not of their faith did but touch the servant as he passed, he must cast all the food upon the ground, and so the dinner is lost. So, if such a one entered their house and touched their furniture, the walls, or the door, they would not eat in that house ere they had washed it and performed certain ceremonies. In short, they touch no one of another religion without being polluted; and they observe this rule in such wise, that if some of them were sitting together upon a bench or other seat, and a man of another religion came to sit by them, they would incontinently rise; and if he had seated himself before they were aware, they would go and wash the whole body: this I have often seen happen in my own case, when I have sat by them without thinking of it. Thus have I seen, if they would hand something—as, for instance, a stick or a sword—to one of another religion, they toss it into the hand of the other, so as not to touch him when he would put out his hand to receive it. I have observed, too, that the soldiers of the king's body-guard, who lie upon mats and *esteres*,[1] warned me in good time to take care not to step upon or touch with my feet these mats and *esteres*. If they give such a one to drink, they allow him not to touch the vessel, but make him open his mouth, and pour therein from a distance; they often treated me in this fashion. For all that, I took note that the Nairs make not so much ado, save that on being polluted they must take the trouble to go and wash themselves entirely, and so all the Nairs that live among the Mahometan Malabars, who associated with me, made no scruple to touch me, or to let me touch them, after they were once polluted and before they went to wash. They were wont to advise us, when they had just bathed, that we should not touch them, so as not to give them the trouble to go and

[1] Port. *esteira*, "rush-mat".

bathe again; but, after being polluted by the merest contact, they would make no more ado or ceremony about the matter.

Among the Nairs are some men and women that have the feet and legs as thick as the body of an ordinary man. There is nothing hurtful in this: it is born with them. Some have only one thus large, while others have both, and you see plenty of them with this infirmity; I have seen even the greatest lords have it. The thickness is more or less in different cases, and the leg is hard and coarse like a wart; nevertheless, they suffer no pain from it, and are ready for everything, and are good soldiers. It is inherited with their blood. I have seen others in the Indies besides the Nairs who had these thick legs, but nowhere so many.[1]

At their marriages they make much ceremony, with feasting and rejoicings. At the commencement, when matters are arranged, they proceed to the temple or pagode, where they go through some ceremonies before their parents, who are Bramenis; but what they are I cannot describe, as I was not allowed to enter. Next, for a space of fifteen days, the kindred and friends of the parties, both men and women, conduct the bride daily to the house of the bridegroom; there they pass the day in rejoicings. The women, in gay attire, sing and play upon divers instruments, such as little drums like tambourines, flutes and hautboys, and to this

[1] Elephantiasis, in India commonly called "Cochin leg", or "St. Thomas's leg", from its prevalence in the south of the peninsula, mediæval travellers seeing in it the hereditary punishment of the apostle's murderers. "Here are also those elephant-legged St. Thomeans", writes quaint old Dr. Fryer, who had heard the disease attributed to snake-bite, and also (more reasonably) to "drinking bad water (to which, as we to the air, they attribute all diseases), when they travel over the sands, and then lying down when they are hot till the earth at night is in a cold sweat, which penetrating the rarified cuticle, fixes the humours by intercepting their free concourse on that side, not to be remedied by any *panacea* of their *Esculapian Sectators*" (*New Account of East India*, p. 53). The ailment is common also in Ceylon (see Cordiner's *Ceylon*, i, 182; Davy's *Ceylon*, p. 485; Pridham's *Ceylon*, p. 690).

music they dance, while the men spend the time in looking on. To all present, even to strangers, are presented a portion of betel, and very sweet-smelling scents dissolved in water, to rub the body withal, and so to perfume it. The betrothed are always present there, seated on a higher place, and very richly attired and adorned. I have seen some so loaded with gold trinkets and precious stones that they could hardly carry them; and I believe that they had borrowed them, for I have seen many wearing as much as the value of 200,000 crowns—indeed, the worth was not to be estimated. The hall where these festivals are held is nicely hung and adorned with tapestries of silver and gold. There the table is spread twice a day for the whole assembly, and that at the expense of the bridegroom; in the evening the women conduct the bride back to her own house. At length, at the close of the fifteen days, the betrothed are magnificently dressed and mounted upon an elephant richly adorned with trappings, each upon a seat facing the other, and joining hands. With which ceremony the kinsmen and friends, surrounding them with great pomp, conduct them in procession through the whole town, to the sound of music, tarrying awhile only before the houses of the kinsfolk and friends. Then do some come out to receive them, presenting betel, fruits, flowers, and comfits in the native style, rubbing and sprinkling the elephant on which they are mounted with scents, such as sandal and other perfumed woods, and drugs dissolved in scented water, wherewith they bathe his head and trunk; nor durst they omit this, for otherwise the elephant would resent it. Then they proceed forward and do the same at the next halt. The kinsmen and friends consider it an insult if they be not visited in this fashion. So at length they descend at the Pagode, where they remain for awhile; thence to the house of the bride, where the marriage ceremony is concluded. There every one presents a coco-nut, which the Nair in charge of the elephants takes for himself, and everyone residing in every house where the elephant stops must give a coco-nut, besides all those who assist at the nuptials. For the rest, on all this coast they do commonly marry very young,—that is, about the age of nine or ten years.

As for funeral ceremonies, in the first place, all the Gentiles, the Bramenis, Nairs, and Moucois burn the body; and to this end assiduously collect during their lives scented woods and other materials, and expensive odorous drugs, to burn their own bodies after death. The ashes are divided among the kinsfolk, who preserve them in great honour, and mix some with water on their feast days, and smear their faces withal, as already said. On the death of a Brameny, his wife is bound to show in what affection she holds him, by burning herself alive, leaping into the fire which consumes the corpse of the deceased: this is done with great solemnity in presence of the relatives, and to the sound of music. I have seen the burning of five or six in this sort while I was at Calecut.[1] If they like not to be burned, they may avoid it, but then they are infamous; they have their hair cut, they no longer hold up their heads, and are driven from the society of ladies of honour, without being able to marry again. Yet do most of them prefer to undergo this infamy rather than to be burned. The wives of the Nairs are not required to do this, although 'tis said that one will sometimes cast herself upon the fire out of affection, and of her own free will. But they are not bound to do it, and are even free to marry again without dishonour, provided they are not of the Brameny caste. This rule does not obtain among the common people. I have never seen them to wear mourning for their relations, albeit, when the king dies, all the men of the kingdom shave their beards and hair entirely.

[1] As to the rite of suttee, or *satí*, which is here referred to, see Dr. Burnell's note to Linschoten, i, 247, and Yule, *Gloss.*, s. v. But Mr. Logan informs me that Pyrard is in error, if he means that those whom he saw at Calicut were *Nambûtiris* or Malayâli Brahmans. The custom does not obtain among these. The women must therefore have been from the Konkan, or elsewhere.

As for their sicknesses, they have no medicines or cures but sorcerers,[1] which are equipped like very devils, and come only by night to see the sick, with fire in their mouths, at the ears, feet, and hands, and are all covered with a false skin, and having upon them an endless number of bells that make a strange and horrible din. They also perform divers gestures, grimaces, and superstitious tricks, and make offers and promises to the devil, and all this in the presence of the sick person, who deems himself much relieved thereby. Likewise, when they desire to know the issue of anything, they have recourse to these sorcerers and soothsayers, who are in the pay of the king, the princes, and the lords, as well Gentile as Mahometan. While I was there, the king, having a great affair against the king of Cochin, as I afterwards came to know, wanted to consult one of his sorcerers about it, and made him appear before all the people. I saw a most hideous man appear, all covered with a false skin, the hair of his head so long as to touch the ground, tall man as he was: he had also bells at his neck, on his arms and legs, and round his waist, which did make a wondrous jingling din. He ran five or six paces forward, then as many back, and kept roaring unceasingly all the time he was before the king, who did not descend from his gallery to the place where the sorcerer and all the people were gathered. He spoke some words to the king, and I believed that he was a sorcerer, but everyone told me he was a devil. It was said that this sorcerer had come more than sixty leagues during the night without a halt; afterwards, when he was ready to depart, he was seen to run like lightning, and to enter their Pagode or

[1] The practices here described are those of the *shamans*, or devil-dancers, which reappear with curious identity in the most various regions (see Tylor, *Prim. Cult.*). The local reference is to the *Velichchapâdo*, "enlighteners", the oracles of the various temples, who fall into trances, and whose frenzied utterances are still to the present day accepted as divine commands.

temple, whither the people followed him: he was there a long time, making a great noise as with bells and kettles. This sorcerer made the most fearful cry I ever heard; he did many magic tricks, and had two swords in his hands which he brandished continually. These were of a different fashion from the ordinary swords, being more edged; with these he struck himself on the bare head, and fell on his belly upon the points of them, without injuring himself.

They all complain of the apparitions of demons, and the harm they suffer from them, as at the Maldives, and in all those parts where are the Gentiles and Mahometans, which things, I believe, happen to them for their not believing in the Christian faith, and so being still under the power of the demons. As for me (thanks be to God!), I experienced nothing of the kind, except that on the night of my arrival at Badara, having no place to retire to, I went and lay me down in a Mosque for the sake of company, and because these places are more commodious and fresh for sleep and repose, as well by day as by night; they are all well matted and carpeted, instead of being paved. While there, my spirit was so burdened with illusions, and I heard so many noises, that I could not rest. I also felt myself to be so oppressed that I could neither speak nor breathe. The noise which I heard all the night was as if one were rolling a number of balls all over the ceiling and wainscotting of the Mosque, and I thought every minute that it would give way and fall upon me. During the evening there had been a goodly number of strangers, travellers, and wayfarers resting there; but having some distance yet to travel, they took to the road at midnight in the cool, while the moon was shining bright. Thus had I been left alone, and it was then that fear seized me in good earnest. All I could do was to pray to God, and so remain for the night; for there was no visible way to escape, this temple being outside the town, and distant from the houses: it is one of the largest temples they have there. At length, at break of day, when I began to recover myself a little, behold, two or three *Moucois*, who set a crying and yelling like very devils, with voices that were frightful and fearsome indeed. They were at the summit of the Mosque, where I could not see them before, nor tell what was the cause. It is their custom to call the people, as I have already said in speaking of the Maldives; but day being now come, I went forth without saying a word to them. This is all I saw and heard in that country of their apparitions and devilries. For the rest, these Mosques, wherein wayfarers repose and obtain a common refuge, are those of the Mahometans only, and not of the Nairs. In these great temples they cook every day, at the king's expense, a great quantity of rice, and distribute it to the poor and to all comers, who receive it with great solemnity. They give this rice a violet colour, and the ceremony is part of the service of the pagode, and there is as much ado about taking this rice as about the consecrated bread with us. When they are in their Pagodes, which are very dark and obscure, there are numerous lamps burning, and a terrible din of tinkling prevails from the sound of the bells wherewith the sorcerers there are covered. These fellows make frequent leaps and grimaces, crying and yelling at the entrance of the door. Within the court is a great well for bathing, and within the Pagode at the door are some ashes of the dead, whereof they take a little and rub it upon their forehead and breasts, as we do the holy water. The Moucois have their Pagodes apart, which are of a horrible darkness; they enter them more rarely than the Nairs; in fact, they never go but once a month at the new moon (save also when they celebrate a marriage, which is done in their Pagode, with the festivities pertaining to it); they are always occupied at their work. As for the Nairs, besides their solemn festivals, which are very frequent, they never pass a day without going to the Pagode, each by himself, to say his prayers, short though they be. They have some of these Pagodes in certain places which they visit on certain days of the year, and they will come thither for their devotions from a distance of thirty or forty leagues. There are two or three annual festivals, principally that of New Year's Day, which is in the month of April, when all the Nairs, the courtiers, and their attendants come to visit and salute the king, while he from the window of a high gallery receives their salutations, and tosses to each a packet of betel, which he gives by way of largess, and some pieces of gold, to some more, to others less; and this is a present which they value extravagantly, as coming from the king's hand. He gives these presents not only to the Nairs, but also to all sorts and conditions, for he gave to us as well, and also to some Christian Indians, who were habited in the Portuguese fashion.[1]

For the rest, the kingdom of Calecut is a very powerful state, and of great extent: it is the state which has given the greatest trouble and caused most of their reverses to the Portuguese, ay, and does so daily still; that is by reason of the authority and puissance of the king, who is held in wondrous affection, being feared and obeyed by all his subjects and dreaded by all his neighbours. His country is thickly peopled; it has great and beautiful cities, whereof the chief is Calecut, which gives its name to the whole realm. The second is *Panany*,[2] which is inland; it is a great city, and a

[1] For a description of one of these festivals which the Samorin left the siege of Kunhâli to attend, see De Couto, *Dec. XII*, liv. IV, cap. iv. The feast in April is called *Vishu*. It is called the vernal equinox. The Malayâli year is too long, and the equinox has shifted in consequence.

[2] *Panane*, or *Ponani*, twenty-eight miles south of Calicut, and forty-eight miles north of Cochin. Barbosa says it was in his time "a city of the Moors amongst whom a few Gentiles live". "The Moors are very rich merchants, and own much shipping. The King of Calicut collects much revenue from this city" (*Barbosa*, Hak. Soc., p. 153). Although Pyrard says the river at Ponani was only navigable for boats, it would seem to have been fit to carry sea-going ships at an earlier period. Varthema talks of a fleet issuing from it (Hak. Soc., p. 275);

fortress on the frontier of the kingdom of Cochin, and has always an ample garrison. The king resides most part of his time at these two towns, and chiefly at *Panany*, because of the perpetual war that he wages with the king of Cochin, as also because it is the pleasantest residence in his country. But it is not a seaport; it has only a river navigable for boats, which falls into the sea twenty-five or thirty leagues off, and forms the boundary of the two kingdoms. Besides these there are a great number of other towns and villages throughout the country, whither the king betakes himself frequently when he goes to visit his domains, all of which are everywhere so peopled that they could not be more so, and the houses and closes are very near together, viz., about a gunshot apart. What causes the country to be so thickly peopled is its most excellent and temperate climate: the seasons are the same as at the Maldives. They have their crops—that is, they sow and reap—twice in the year; and all the year long there are fruits in great abundance, and of the most excellent quality in the world. Moreover, the country is very pleasant and agreeable, being watered by many fine rivers and streams, and everywhere by springs of the most excellent water. No country in all the Indies is better furnished with all commodities. The whole country is covered with fruit-trees, cocos, jack, mangos, bananas, pineapples, cajus, lemons, oranges, pomegranates, mirabolans, Indian pears (which do not resemble ours), and cotton-trees; plenty of melons and water-melons (*patèques*), which are a kind of pumpkins of prodigious size, eaten raw, like melons; ginger, peas, beans, and other good fruits, which anyone passing by

and in November 1506 the place was stormed by the Portuguese fleet under the Viceroy F. de Almeida (*Varthema*, p. 286; Stevens' *Faria y Souza*, i, 124-5). Under a treaty made with the Samorin in 1584, a Portuguese fort was begun to be built at Ponani in December 1585, but soon after abandoned (De Couto, *Dec. IX*, cap. ii; *Dec. X*, liv. VII, cap. v; *Linschoten*, Hak. Soc., ii, 169). It is a seaport, and not "inland", as Pyrard erroneously describes it.

may pluck and eat without any preventing him: all neighbours, too, use their fruits in common. But the greatest wealth of the country, and that which alone is exported, is pepper, which abounds marvellously there. A tax is paid on it to the king, besides which he buys it all, and despatches it in his own ships to the Straits of Mecca or the Arabian Gulf, the port of the Arabs, whence he receives in return many commodities, and principally gold: in a word, it is the principal wealth of the country. So, too, there is great store of precious stones of all sorts, excepting diamonds; but plenty of emeralds, rubies, sapphires, cat's-eyes, etc.; the remaining source of wealth is cotton cloth.

Among animals native to the country are elephants, which they domesticate when young, and employ in war, and in carrying and drawing burdens. All belong to the king, and no private person may possess one. If anyone hath need of one for any purpose, even to ride, he addresses the king's officer that hath the care of them, and on payment of a piece of money he receives one without difficulty, either for one day or for more, the hire being according to the time he is kept. There are a great number of tigers, which are very savage, and the most common occupation of the Nairs is to chase and slay them. You see, also, wild pigs, like our wild boars, roebucks, cows, buffaloes, goats, dogs like ours, and monkeys innumerable. There are quantities of parrakeets, wild pea-fowl, poultry, and very large pigeons. The serpents are of great size and very dangerous, but for all that none is so bold as to kill one, for that the king, the Bramenis, and the Nairs worship them with great superstition, believing them to be spirits of God, created to afflict man and to chastise him for his sins: some there are of 22 feet in length and more. All the country is also full of foxes,[1] that come by night even into the towns and enclosures of the houses, and course about like the dogs here, and all night one hears

[1] *I.e.*, jackals.

nothing but the noise of them in the gardens and ways. There are also quantities of monkeys, which do much harm, and are very big, insomuch that all the inhabitants, as well of the towns as of the country, are constrained to put trellises to all their windows to keep these creatures out; for they are exceedingly importunate and cunning, and the reason why they are so numerous is that it is not lawful to kill them: the king forbids it. The skin is of a greyish colour: it is a pastime to see them leap from tree to tree. One day, among others, while one of my companions and I were on our way from the town to the king's palace (except at some places there are houses and shops all the way between), we were met by three of these monkeys, the largest and most fearsome I ever saw. They stood on their hind feet, at ten or twelve paces from us, grinding their teeth as though they would do us some injury. We had neither rod nor stick, and there were no stones about, so that, owing to our ignorance at that time of the nature of these animals, we were in great straits; however, we showed no sign of fear, and pretended to take up stones to cast at them, whereupon they at once took to flight and leapt into the trees.

The town of Calecut is the court, and, as it were, a summary of the whole kingdom. I resided there much, and I can say that it is a very fair and great city, situate on the sea-shore, in extent from one end to the other more than a league and a half of beach, and along the whole of that distance between the town and the sea are only the houses of the Moucois, the fishermen, and other poor folks, who also have there their Pagode and temples. All the beach or strand is covered with *almedies*, or little fishing barques, and other vessels. The circuit of the town is more than five leagues, but what is called Calecut is, in fact, a large district covered with handsome, large, and magnificent buildings and spacious enclosures, in such wise that a single house requires a very large space for all its gardens, orchards, fish-ponds, and plantations. And all around are mansions of this sort only, full of people, as well Nairs, Malabars, and Mahometans, as all manner of foreigners, who are welcomed there. For it is not as in the other towns of the Malabars, which are only occupied by the Malabars: here you see all sorts of temples and Pagodes, large and well built, for all the several religions, of which I shall speak anon.

There are many public tanks, which are very large, well paved, and furnished with balustrades of stone work, and are well cleaned and maintained. Each religion has its own; and there is one such that is a quarter of a league in ambit of the square. These are very necessary, owing to the excessive heat of the climate. The walls of this town are not very strong: it is only enclosed with earth-works and low walls. The houses are not built in order or arranged in streets as in Europe, but are scattered about in confusion: but in one part of the town, that next to the sea, and near to the great magazine of the king called *Alfandeque*, there is a quarter of about a half league in circuit, which is built and arranged in streets, as in these parts. In that part of the town are only shops, of all manner of trades, artizans and merchants, which are necessary for the public weal. All this quarter has a barrier round about, although it is within the enclosure of the whole city. In these houses they keep only such furniture and utensils as are necessary.

Their markets, which they call *Bazar*, or little towns, are so full of people all the day long that it is difficult to pass them. These people are of all races, from the Cape of Good Hope to Japan. At nightfall everyone shuts his warehouse and shop securely with bars and heavy iron padlocks, and goes home with his family to his dwelling-house, which is as I have described, with its gardens and enclosures. The buildings of this *Bazar* are very large and well constructed of stone and wood, and supplied with shops, warehouses, and yards, all securely enclosed: these serve only to keep their merchandise and goods, or for the purposes of their crafts, and there they spend the day only. There are three large spaces in these enclosures, where the market is held every day of the week. This market is surrounded with gates and walls, and the gatekeepers let none pass the night in these warehouses containing the merchandise; and yet nothing is ever lost, so excellent is their judicature and police. In these enclosures remain only officers and gatekeepers, whose duty it is to keep watch and ward throughout the night. There is not a single temple there. The vessels which enter and anchor at Calecut, bringing all that merchandise, ride there with no great security, for there is no proper port or harbour, but only a roadstead, so that when the wind is from the sea they are in great peril. The land is low, and there is a little cape or promontory jutting out into the sea.

As for the fashion and form of the buildings of the country, it is to be noted that the common people build with earth, and thatch their houses with coco-leaves, but not with such care and skill as the Maldive people. Taking some earth, they mix it with water, and mould it into large squares, which they dry in the sun, and then use for their walls; but the rich and well-to-do build with good stone, and roof with tiles. All their buildings are square, like four arcaded pavilions with a court in the middle. Their carpentry and joinery is the handsomest and prettiest it is possible to see: it is worked of divers agreeable designs, as we do our finest side-boards and tables, and all painted. Their houses have stories, but not so many as ours. Some have two or three buildings of this style in the midst of others; that in the midst has a smaller court and arcade; the others are round about it in a square. They construct their houses and courts in this fashion, to avoid spilling or casting a drop of water or any dirt upon their floors, which are as clean as a table of highly polished wood.

All the houses of the Malabars are of this sort. They have large porches at the entrance to their houses, as well poor as rich, within the enclosure: for all their houses are enclosed with walls,—that is, those of the rich; the rest have ditches and good strong palisades of wood, and note that these are so high that when one wants to go from one house to another one must ascend a ladder of five or six steps, and so descend, while on both sides are wooden barriers which close with locks. You never see there any house but has its garden and orchard, small or large. These porches or *Auiards* in front of the houses are for receiving passing strangers, both for giving them meat and drink, and also a place to rest and sleep; they take them not inside their houses, so that they may depart during the night when they will, and whenever their boats, or if they be wayfarers, their fellow-travellers, are ready to depart.

But to return to what concerns this town of Calecut in general: it is the busiest and most full of all traffic and commerce in the whole of India; it has merchants from all parts of the world, and of all nations and religions, by reason of the liberty and security accorded to them there[1]: for the king permits the exercise of every kind of religion, and yet it is strictly forbidden to talk, dispute, or quarrel on that subject; so there never arises any contention on that score, every one living in great liberty of conscience under the favour and authority of the king, who holds that to be a cardinal maxim of government, with a view to making his

[1] One particular feature of the freedom enjoyed by the merchants at Calicut may be noticed. The law of wreck of the sea, by which a wrecked vessel and its cargo went to the king as a casualty, prevailed all over India, and at the Maldives, as Pyrard has frequently said. Similar law applied to vessels whose captains died at the islands. And in other parts of Malabar, in the old days, a vessel taking refuge in a port to which she was not bound, was liable to be plundered by the inhabitants. But according to Ibn Batuta (iv, 97) and Abd-er-Razzak (*India in XV Cent.*, i, 14), these barbarous prerogatives had no place in the law of Calicut.

kingdom very rich and of great intercourse. If by chance there should arise any difference or disturbance on that subject, he who began it would receive corporal punishment, as being guilty of treason, without hope of pardon or remission of sentence. This is why everyone lives there in great peace and concord, notwithstanding the great diversity of races and religions of the inhabitants, and of strangers and sojourners: for besides the native Gentiles and Mahometans, there are many Christians. In former times the Portuguese lived there, and had two towns and fortresses, which they had permission of the king to build near the sea, yet was there never friendship or any good understanding between the two; in so much that these towns and fortresses were captured and razed by the native kings and the Portuguese driven out, and at the present day they have neither town nor fortress there, as I have remarked already. At present, however, they are at peace, and the Portuguese by divers presents cultivate as best they can the friendship of this king, whom they fear more than any other. For the purposes of trade, there is at Calecut a factor on behalf of the Viceroy of Goa, assisted by a clerk, along with their wives and families. This factor is a kind of agent or ambassador, having also the power of issuing passports to the Indian merchants; for at all the harbours and ports of India, which are at peace with the Portuguese, the latter have these factors for this purpose, otherwise the merchants would have much trouble in going for passports to the Portuguese towns.

There reside also two Jesuit fathers, the one an Italian, the other a Portuguese,[1] who are well received of the king, and get from him a pension of a hundred crowns a year, worth more than five hundred in Spain, besides what they have from

[1] The Italian was Padre Jacomo Fenicio (Guerreiro, *Relaçam Annual*, Lisboa, 1607, f. 118*a*). The Portuguese, Pyrard says below, was Father Hilaire.

the king of Portugal for their living and maintenance. They have builded a very handsome and large church,[1] with an enclosure and cemetery attached, near the sea-shore, on ground presented by the king; and they have the king's leave and licence to convert the people to Christianity, so long as they use no constraint. Their labours had borne good fruit at the time of my departure, for there were already a good number of new Christians.[2] They preached publicly in their church, and not elsewhere. They are very well housed, and have very fine gardens, and before their church is a large cross. The Christians all have their houses in the same quarter near to one another, which they have themselves built. There are, however, some among them that are not Christians, and even in the same house will sometimes be found inmates of different religions. Among these new Christians none, I believe, will be found to eat the flesh of cows, bulls, or buffaloes, as I have already said. These Jesuit fathers had the ear of the king, who liked them much, and they took great care to do nothing displeasing to him. They used to go often to the palace of the king to treat of affairs, assisted by Portuguese, Indian Christians, and Mestifs. We enjoyed their society sometimes, and they gave us a good reception. But the king and all the men of Calecut frequently gave us warning not to eat or drink with them, for fear lest they should poison us; also not to go abroad at night, lest they should do us some injury,—that is, the Portuguese in general; for they were extremely jealous and concerned at

[1] This was probably the church of which the Samorin himself laid the foundation stone in 1591, under the provisional treaty made with the Jesuit, Francisco da Costa. The Samorin's endowment of the church was continued by Hyder Ali, and is still paid by the British Government at Rs. 50 per month.

[2] The term "new Christians", properly, as here, applied to all converts, had at this time, as will be seen in other parts of this book, come to be used in Spain, Portugal, and their colonies as a synonym for Jews, who were required to observe an outward conformity with Christianity.

our presence there, and at the king's favour towards us. This jealousy they did afterwards openly discover, as I shall tell anon. Having spoken of the Christians resident at Calecut, I shall proceed with what concerns the other religions that are practised there. Among others, the Jews have their own quarter and synagogue, which none enter but they. The Mahometans, although they be of divers races and countries, yet have no difference of religion (except the Persians), and frequent the temple of the Mahometan Malabars. There is also another race of Gentiles besides the natives, who, albeit of the same religion, make no alliances with them, nor go to their temples, but have their own Pagode, using none other: of such are the *Banians* of Cambaye and Diu, who have their own Bramenis, and hold them in the greatest honour. Yet the Bramenis of Malabar may freely enter their Pagode, as having common rights with them. This leads me to say that they are the one race in India who are throughout all the countries held in the highest esteem, for there are some of them among all the Gentile Indians. These Banians observe the same austerities as the Bramenis, and all the same rules, but are inferior to them, and do not intermarry with them. In all other respects they agree, in dress, manners, and customs.

As for justice, it proceeds from the king alone, and throughout all his kingdom there is no other judge but he. For all that, justice is well administered and awarded to all gratuitously; for if anyone commits a crime, or will not pay his creditors, complaint is made to the king, who, after inquiry into the truth of the matter, accords such judgment and satisfaction as the case requires. In his absence the chief officers of state administer it. If it is some foreigner or Moucois who has a suit against another, he addresses his plaint to the first Nair he meets, and the Nair gives judgment and execution on the spot, without being paid anything for it, unless the complainant gives of his mere motion and liberality. That is the procedure only in cases of lesser consequence; as for great crimes, no step is taken without the knowledge and pleasure of the king, to whom must be addressed every claim of right. The punishments are imprisonment for a term, mutilation of members, or death, if the crime be of that gravity. In such case the criminal is delivered over to elephants or tigers, who incontinently tear him in pieces at the word of command: they have no other form of execution. The prisons are all at the king's palace; and the Malabars and all manner of foreigners are subject to the jurisdiction of the Nair kings, albeit one hears of but few lawsuits among them.

With regard to the language[1] of the whole Malabar country, it is peculiar to these people; the character and letters also are peculiar. They write with iron bodkins upon palm-leaves, which are yellow in colour, and very thick. Such is all I was able to observe in the kingdom, town, and people of Calecut. I now come to what concerns the grandeur and power, the manners and life of the king, the queen his wife, and of their court and palace.

The greatness of the king will be recognised from what has already been said of his state and kingdom. He is called *Samory* by all the Indians, a word of great weight in their language, and equivalent to Emperor, for he is one of the greatest and richest princes of India. He can put under arms 150,000 Nairs, without counting the Malabars and Mahometans of his own kingdom, and the innumerable pirates and corsairs of the coast, whose services he can command.

All the Nair kings of this coast are his vassals, obeying him and yielding to his majesty, except the king of Cochin, with whom, although a prince of the same faith, manners, and customs, he is almost always at war: that, however, is only since the Portuguese have been at Cochin, for it is

[1] *I.e.*, Malayâlam.

they who foster and maintain this hostility. In former days the king of Cochin recognised him as others do, but now makes himself out to be equal with him, not yielding on any point, the cause being that he trusts to the support of the Portuguese, without which he would not long survive.[1]

This prince, when I was there, was about fifty years of age, and had reigned about thirty-five.[2] He is handsome, tall, and erect; nimble, slim, and well proportioned in limb. He loves his people, and is beloved and obeyed by them, feared and dreaded by his neighbours and enemies. He has but one wife, like the other *Brameny Nairs*,[3] and at this time had no children. He resides, as I have said, sometimes at *Panany*, sometimes at Calecut; but often makes a tour of his kingdom. When he travels he does so with a very great company, having always about 3,000 men in his following. He rides upon an elephant, of which animals he hath a great number. Wherever he passes all assemble in arms to accompany him, insomuch that sometimes he hath more than 10,000 persons. His principal seat is at Calecut, where he hath a very handsome and well-built palace, all enclosed with good walls and moats, with drawbridge to the gates, and water all around in the moats. A large number of soldiers day and night guard the gates, which are four in number. They admit no one unless he is well known, nor such a one without questioning him, and conducting him or having him conducted to the part of the interior whither he desires to pro-

[1] As to the former subjection of Cochin to Calicut, see *Barbosa*, Hak. Soc., p. 156, where it is said that every new Samorin made entry into Cochin and exacted a tribute of elephants; also that Cochin had no right of coinage.

[2] His age is probably overstated here. In 1600, only seven years before, Couto says he was a little over thirty. "This king was a tall man, well proportioned, a little over thirty years of age, and among his followers was well seen to be a king" (*Dec. XII*, liv. IV, cap. i).

[3] The Samorin is of *Sâmanta* caste, as are some other Malayâli rajas. The ladies of his family have Brahman or Kshatriya husbands.

ceed. If he wishes to speak with the king, he is passed from one guard to another until he arrives at the door of the apartments where is stationed what you might call the body-guard, and these gain him speech of the king. I have said there are four gates at the four great entrances; but before reaching the apartments of the king you have to pass three gates on each avenue, and at all points soldiers are on guard, without counting those at the doors of the king's apartments. Besides all these guards, there is a strong body in the middle of the palace, in a covered place built expressly for the purpose, and all the other guards take their orders from this one. Overhead is a great bell, which only sounds for the assembling of men-at-arms at the palace, and about the king when he hath need of them. At all the gates of the palace there are spaces with closed barriers and palisades round about, for fear lest the crowd should approach the gates. Outside these barriers, and near the gates, are men whose only duty it is to give fresh water to all the thirsty that ask it; and when anyone wants a drink, whatever his quality or religion, they give it him in the manner described.

These men deputed by the king to give drink in this way are mounted upon benches or tables, of the height of four feet, under the shade of the trees, which is very pleasant and agreeable.

They have large vessels in the form of pitchers, with a tube or pipe a span and a half long, and made of gilded copper. Those who are athirst approach these men without entering the enclosure, and offer their mouths without touching the vessel in any way; the water is then poured into their mouths from above, and all the while the pipe or vessel must be more than a span from contact with them. But before they give them to drink, they give them one or two pieces of coco to eat, instead of bread. This mode has been ordained by the king, by reason of the fierce and excessive heat of that country, and the great multitude of people that throng to the palace every day. The Portuguese in India have adopted this manner of drinking. There are plenty of wells in the country districts, and even at the king's palace; but it is not permitted to drink at them, for they are guarded, and only certain priests may draw water there for their superstitious observances.

All the avenues of the palace are marvellously beautiful and delightful. All the roads are straight, like pall-mall alleys, and relieved on both sides by high terraces and palisades covered with trees of all sorts, among others, many of the trees they call *tristes*,[1] of which they make saffron. Throughout all the country their roads are of this fashion, or nearly so.

Between the town and the palace is about a quarter of a league, the road being as described, with fine mansions on either side; in front of the gate of the palace is a great square, where the market is held every day in the morning of all kinds of merchandise of the country, but not foreign. It is opened at seven o'clock, and one of the king's officers has the duty of sounding a bell to warn the king's servants

[1] *Nyctanthes arbor tristis*, thus called "the sorrowful tree", as Linschoten says, "because it never beareth blossoms but in the night time, and so it doeth and continueth all the yeare long: it is a thing to be wondred at; for that so soon as the sun setteth, there is not one blossome seene upon the tree, but presently within halfe an houre after, there are as many blossomes uppon it, as the Tree can beare . . . the flowre being white and in the bottome somewhat yellow and reddish, which in India they use for saffron" (*Linsch.*, Hak. Soc., ii, 58-62). According to De Orta, who had not found it anywhere in India except at Goa, this shrub had been brought from Malacca (f. 17*b*), but it is now known to be indigenous in sub-Himalayan forests (see Brande's *Forest Flora*, 314). A fine but transient buff or orange dye is made from the flowers. For a picture and another account of it, see Acosta, *Tractado*, p. 224; also P. Vincenzo, lib. IV, cap. ix. Dr. Fryer (p. 143) speaks of "the *arbor tristis* at St. Thomas his Mount", but this would seem to be a kind of passion flower, distinguished by P. Vincenzo as "il fiore di S. Tomaso" (cap. X). Mandelslo describes the *arbor tristis* as belonging to Sumatra (p. 137).

and purveyors to go buy what is necessary for his house, for none would dare buy anything ere the king's household was supplied. That done, the bell is sounded a second time to call the merchants; but before the merchants enter, the tax-farmers take their dues off even the smallest of the goods. Before the king's officers have taken what is due to them, no one would dare to go near or touch any goods, least of all anything eatable. Even after that, unless they be Bramenis or Nairs, they would not dare so much as touch any goods that are for sale ere a price has been made, and then they are obliged to take them. Care has to be taken also in going through the market, where all those that sell are seated, not to touch either their persons or their goods, unless they be of the same caste and religion. This market lasts only about three hours or more, and they come from all parts of the town and elsewhere to buy, in order afterwards to sell at the great market or *Bajar*, which is held every day and all day. After ten o'clock you see no one in the market near the palace, and everyone goes about freely. At that place, too, besides the shops and warehouses of particular trades, there are three or four large spaces for the people, wherein to bargain and sell their goods. All these houses and shops are used solely to hold the merchandise, yet throughout all the rest of the town there are great and rich merchants, who never come to this Bajar, having their own warehouses full of goods, which they sell not by retail, but wholesale.

Near this large square where the market is held is a large building where the king's money is struck, which is current on all the Malabar coast. This consists of gold pieces with his effigy on one side and a pagoda or idol on the other. These pieces are of the value of about four sols, and are called *Phanans*. Another sort of small silver coin is made of the same form and design, worth three deniers each, and called *Tarens*, of which sixteen go to a Phanan.[1]

[1] As to the *fanam* and *tara*, *v. s.*, p. 344.

Foreign money, too, is used, provided it be gold or silver. Amongst others, there are quantities of silver larins, which come from abroad, and of which I have already spoken in my discourse of the Maldives. This kind of money is current throughout all the Indies, and is made in many places, but the best is coined at Ormuz.

But to return to the king's palace: it is a very large enclosure, and contains many blocks of houses, all detached and well built, of many stories and galleries, with flower-beds, and orchards, tanks, fish-ponds, and canals, all fitted and paved with stone, and constructed on all sides of stone steps leading to the bottom. Add to these many springs and fountains, whose water is cold and excellent to drink. In the palace, too, is a magazine or arsenal, full of arms, cannon, powder, and munitions of war. But the great and chief arsenal of the king is at *Panany*, for that is his chief war town.

Hard by there is a block of buildings allotted to the secretary and clerk to the king, for keeping all the registers. The order and system is most admirable herein, and I have ofttimes wondered to see the great number of men with no other duty or work all day but writing and registering. These posts are of much honour; the clerks all reside in the palace, but in different apartments, and they have different duties. Some make entry of all goods arriving for the king; others, the dues and taxes paid day by day; others, the expenditure of the king's household; others, the most notable incidents of each day, both what happens at court and in the rest of the kingdom; in short, all news, for he has everything registered; and each clerk has his separate room. They keep also a register of all strangers who come there, taking their names and nationalities, the time of their arrival, and the business that has brought them, and so they did with us. It is a wondrous thing to observe their number and the perfect order that exists among them, and how fast they write on their palm-leaves, as described: these are of the length and breadth of the leaves of coco-trees, but thicker and stiffer. They make of them a kind of book, by means of holes in the thicker ends of the leaves, through which they pass a fillet, and thus bind together as many as are required.

The king hath the like writers in all towns, ports, harbours, and frontier passages of his kingdom, who render account to those of the palace, all being well organised and in obedience one to another, each having his proper superior. Throughout the whole Malabar coast there is the same manner of writing and the same ordering thereof.

About five hundred paces from the palace and the enclosure of the king's residence is the great *Pagode* or temple of the king (though he hath also a small one in his palace): that is the principal of all the many temples in the country. Inside is the figure of the idol which they worship, and also call *Pagode*. This figure, which is placed in the inmost part of the temple, has the head of a man, but exceeding hideous and frightful, of the same fashion as we are wont to figure devils. I have observed this temple and *Pagode* of the king at leisure. It is all covered in, the walls lined on the inside with bright and polished copper, and with doors of the same. Before the entrance there is a large porch and a close, like a churchyard, well secluded and near the gate of the temple; next there is a little pond or bathing-place, where they bathe, and at the door on the inside are some burnt ashes of the dead, as at the other pagodes. Proceeding further, one meets a copper figure in the form of a cow, and that is only seen through a grill; further on is another figure, of which I have spoken, which is of gold, enriched with precious stones. The whole temple is of itself very dark, but there are a great number of lamps burning within, which makes it quite clear. The Gentile Nairs on their way to the king fail not all to go in and worship this idol; albeit they tarry not long over their prayers. This idol, too, I could only see through bars, for none is allowed to enter there unless he be of their religion, caste, and quality.

With regard to the person of the king, I may say in the first place that in accoutrements and dress he differs in no way from the other Nairs, being no more clothed than they, except that he wears not so many ornaments, valuables, or precious stones as the other lords. But on a day of festival or solemnity it is not possible to see (anywhere) more gold or gems than he carries; but this happens rarely, and at the great ceremonies only[1]; for ordinarily he wears only a little gold chain round his waist, having a jewelled clasp in front. When he takes a walk he is always accompanied by Nairs, as well within as without his palace: he never employs others. The great lords go before and behind, but none by his side, while his guards line the way on both sides as he passes. When they salute him, it is their fashion, both gentle and simple, to put their shields or bucklers under one armpit, and their swords under the other, joining both hands over their heads, thrice separating and closing them, and thrice saying *Tabiran*,[2] and once *Samory*, meaning thereby that after God, whom they call *Tabiran*, the Samory comes next.

When the king rises in the morning, as soon as he sees the sun he prostrates himself before it with a fixed regard, as also

[1] According to De Couto, this description is not overdrawn. That historian thus pictures him as he came to meet Furtado de Mendoça at the siege of Kunhâli's fort:—"He wore so many ornaments, and on his arms such a quantity of jewelled bracelets, that they extended from the bend of his elbows down to his thumbs, wherewith he was so weighted that he was obliged to have two pages each sustaining one arm. From his neck hung a collar of inestimable value. In his ears, earrings of the same assay, set with beautiful rubies and diamonds, whose weight extended the ears down to the shoulders, so that the value of what he carried upon him was indeed great. He was naked from the waist to the head, while round the head was bound a cloth of gold and silk in many folds, the ends reaching half-way down the leg, and round the head a jewelled coronet of four fingers' width, very richly set and of great value" (*Dec. XII*, liv. IV, cap. i).

[2] *Tamburān*, "lord".

do all the Nairs, and addresses his prayers to it, holding his hands over his head and opening and shutting them three times. After that he straightway rubs his body all over with odoriferous oil; this lasts about an hour, and then he goes to bathe in one of the ponds within the palace close. To get there he passes along a lengthy covered way leading to it. Standing in the water, is a closet or pavilion of trellis-work to which he betakes himself; at the brink is another, with a covered passage between. While he is in the water the lords and officers rub him and tend him, and everyone there does what he can to assist; but it must be taken for granted that none of those present gets into the water, however great a lord he be. After being well bathed and rubbed he enters the other closet on the brink, where he gets well dried; after this he has his whole body slightly rubbed with a more precious and sweet-smelling oil than before, this being done with the hands until all the oil has been rubbed in, and none appears on the skin. This done, his valet takes some colours and powdered wood, with other odorous drugs mixed with scented water, and applies the same to his forehead and to his body above the waist, together with some leaves and flowers of different sorts, which they paste on wherever they have put these scented stuffs, and particularly on the forehead and breast.[1] It is only the king and great lords who may deck themselves out with such show and curiosity, and so preserve themselves more carefully than the rest from pollution: the reason being that it would take much time and trouble to be always washing and dressing again and again. After all this they moisten a little of the ashes of their ancestors, and smear that on the forehead and breast: the rest of the people do this too, but all that other dressing is indulged in only by the king and grandees, and by the king more than all: it is his chief manner of adornment.

While the king is at his bath, every morning, without

[1] Similarly to the Maldive custom, see above, p. 165.

fail, some dozen or fifteen of the prettiest girls in the country, of whom the eldest is not twenty years of age, all beautifully adorned with gold and jewels, and dressed in white in the native style, some bearing large basins, others vessels of gold or silver gilt full of water, take some fresh dung of cow or bull and mix it with water in these vessels, while others dash some water upon the walls and pavements of the palace; they then with both hands rub the dung thus mixed upon the pavements and walls. All the Gentiles in general do the same in their own houses, deeming it both a very good and a very righteous practice. This washing is done twice a day in the king's apartments; all the pavements and walls of the halls and courts and passages used by the king when he goes to the pagode, or to his other apartments for dinner, are thus cleaned; and notice is previously given whither he intends to proceed, in order that there be no omission of what is proper.

When he comes forth of his bath he most often goes to the temple, and thence to his food in another palace within the same enclosure, which is a part of the grand palace, devoted entirely to that purpose. While he takes his repast he sits upon a piece of well-polished wood, and eats off balsam leaves, like the other Bramenis. He never eats either flesh, fish, or anything that has had life, for he is of the Brameny caste, and wears the cord like the rest. He eats nothing but rice, cooked with milk, butter, and sugar, and divers kinds of broths made of vegetables, herbs, melons, cucumbers, and other fruits, such as water-melons (*Pasteques*), etc. What remains of his meal is cast to the crows and other birds, as I have seen done in the case of the other Nair kings, who are all of the same law.

This prince is magnificently served by his officers, of whom he has a vast number. He takes his food at noon, and eats but once a day, and is three hours at table. He goes to bed very late, and after a collation of some fruit or preserves of the native sort. After his dinner he despatches his business, and then changes his apartment, going to another prepared for him to receive all comers; and it is not that wherein he sleeps, takes his leisure, or eats. Here he is, as it were, exposed to public view, and if any would speak with him he may; if no affairs present themselves, he passes the time with his lords, and is much amused with buffoons and mountebanks, whereof he has always a goodly number. The Nair kings and lords often play a game of chance, which is a kind of chess, played with dice. He takes pleasure also in seeing the Nairs fence with one another with sword and buckler, whereat they sometimes get wounded; others, again, use pikes.

When a lord or Nair has been a-hunting, he delights in being able to present his game in public to the king, who is much pleased thereby. About the king are always a number of the children of the great Nair lords, who serve him as pages, one carrying his sword and buckler, another his parasol, another his gold box filled with betel—which he chews continually, according to the custom of all the Indians of the East—another his fan, wherewith he is fanned unceasingly, while another bears a gold basin into which he spits, for never in any place wherever he may be does he spit upon the ground: and no one would dare to spit upon the pavement of the halls, chambers, or galleries, but only in the courts and places where it is allowed.

As for the queen, she lives in a separate palace, yet within the same enclosure as the great palace. She never eats with the king, and is seen but rarely, and then only at the windows and galleries of her palace or of the king's, whither she frequently proceeds by a gallery which communicates between the two, and there they see each other in private. She bathes in the same manner and with the same ceremony as the king, and in the same pond; but they cannot see each other, for they each have their own end of the pond with a space covered in. She has ordinarily her ladies about her, who pass the time for her. The pond where they bathe is well enclosed and locked, and none but the king and queen do bathe there; there is a gallery whereby the queen descends on her side, and another for the king on his side. The ladies who are present to wash the queen do not enter the water, but remain in the closets and pavilions that are upon the pond, where the oiling, drying, and perfuming is done; and these ladies use all the same artifice and ceremony towards her as the lords use towards the king. The queen is of the Brameny race as well as he. She has her own Pagode, where she betakes herself with her ladies, then to her own apartments to take her food, and so on, as with the king. Only great ladies are about her person, and she has the pavements or boards, and the walls and passages where she goes, cleaned with this cow-dung of which I have spoken. I must not forget to mention, in passing, and as the opportunity arises, the great honour rendered by these people to cows, however low-bred, filthy, and all covered with dirt and dung they may be. They are allowed to enter the king's palace, and whithersoever their way leads, without anyone disputing their passage; even the king himself, and all the greatest lords, give place to them with the utmost respect and reverence, and the same with bulls and oxen.

But to return to the queen: in her dress and attire she differs in no respect from the other Nair wives and ladies, or even from the princesses and great ladies, except that their ornaments are a little more charged with pearls and jewels. The mark of the greatest honour and grandeur with them is to have their ears large, as already described, and this queen had them so large that they reached the nipples. She is nude from the waist upwards, like all the other women, but covered all over with divers trinkets, pearls, and jewels, as are all other women of every rank, as I have frequently remarked in speaking of them. These ladies had as much curiosity in seeing and speaking with me as I with them. For during all the time I resided in this state of Calecut, I always lived at the court, where I was much beloved and caressed by the king, and by all the lords and other Gentiles about the court. They had been very glad if I had remained always with them; not only the lords, but the king himself was anxious by all expedients to get me to *Panany* or Cognialy's *Costé*, in case I should get tired of Calecut, telling me that he would come there in a few days if I would go and await him there, or that he would take me there himself, that so I should not leave him. But I could never bring myself to accept his offers, for the great desire I had to return to a Christian land, and also because the two Jesuit fathers there were at me every day, persuading me to go thence to Cochin or any other territory of theirs. One of these fathers behaved very roughly and cruelly toward us; he was an Italian, but I forget his name.[1] The other, a Portuguese, named Father Hilaire, was very pleasant and agreeable, and consoled us unceasingly, assuring us always that we should be exceedingly welcome among his people.

So, after sojourning there all that time, we took resolution to depart, in manner and with the fortune to be described in the following chapter.

CHAPTER XXVIII.

Of the kingdoms of Chaly, Tananor, and Cochin.—Imprisonment of the author, and other occurrences.

We had remained about eight months at Calecut, my companions and I, waiting always for some Hollander ship to take us back to France. Seeing at length that none arrived, the Jesuit fathers of whom I have spoken counselled us to go to Cochin, and put ourselves in the hands of the Portuguese, as being the best means of returning home. To this end they gave us letters of introduction and recommendation, that so we should come to no harm. We believed them

[1] See above, p. 405.

at the time, accepting their offers and trusting their words, insomuch that we took the letters, with their instructions as to the conduct we should observe when we reached their [*i.e.*, the Portuguese] territory. We then settled our little affairs and took leave of the king, and the lords our friends. All were grieved at our departure, and chiefly the king, who made us even fairer offers than ever before. He told us we were free to go or to stay; if we were resolved to go, he would not prevent us,[1] but above all we should take especial heed not to trust ourselves too much to the Portuguese. He bade give us money, and a passport containing orders that wheresoever we passed throughout his territory his officers and receivers were to furnish us with everything we needed. Only three of us desired to go, for our other companion was a Hollander and a Protestant, and said he would not budge from Calecut, or ever put himself at the mercy of the Portuguese, who had treated him ill on a former occasion.[2]

Having, then, completed our preparations, which lasted some days, we took the final step of departing and taking to the road, to the great regret of all the people, Gentiles, Mahometans, and the rest; all but the Portuguese, who desired nothing better. The man who had attended us on behalf of the king, named *Manjassa*, a bitter enemy to the Portuguese, well forewarned us that we should suffer for it; but that he had nothing to gain by keeping us. We bargained with some sailors to take us in their *Almedie* or barque as far

[1] The immemorial parting speech of a noble host to his honoured guest: so Alcinous to Odysseus:—

οἶκον δέ τ' ἐγὼ καὶ κτήματα δοίην,
εἴ κ' ἐθέλων γε μένοις· ἀέκοντα δέ σ' οὔ τις ἐρύξει
Φαιήκων. (*Od.*, vii, 314-5.)

[2] Pyrard and his two companions, whose fortunes are henceforward followed, were French Catholics; the fourth, who escaped from the Maldives, is here described as a Hollander, but above (p. 91) as a Fleming, who was a clever worker in wood. Below, it seems he was a gunner.

as Cochin, which is but twenty leagues from Calecut. It was now towards the end of February 1608; but we were betrayed by our boatmen, who were Mahometans and Moucois, for they told us they would set out at night when the tide was high, that then they would come and fetch us, and that we should hold ourselves in readiness with our goods. We believed their word; but they came about midnight and called us; they told us that they were going forward to the *Almedie* or boat, which was at a distance about half a league from where we were. The day before they had showed us where we had to embark, right in front of the Portuguese quarters, or rather a little further off; we were then lodged at the king's *Alfandigue*. We took the road with our bundles all along the sea-shore to find the boat, and the moon was shining brightly. When we got near the place where we believed them to be, we were accosted by twenty or thirty Portuguese, Metifs and Indian Christians, all well armed. They were in ambush under the shadow of the Almedies of the Moucois, which are all on dry land (for when they return from the fishing they haul them ashore with their cargo, in such wise that the whole beach is covered with them). These Portuguese fell upon us, crying "*Matar, matar*"; that is to say, "Kill, kill", and gave us some blows to frighten us the more. They seized us and bound our hands tightly behind our backs, threatening that if we spoke a word we were dead men. They held swords to our throats in this fashion for more than an hour without stirring from the spot, while some of them went to their quarter to speak with the fathers and their factor, and to take counsel what should be done with us. We begged them on our knees not to put us to death without confession, for that we were Catholics; but they mocked at all that, and called us *Luteranos*.[1] He who had

[1] Boullaye-le-Gouz says that before the Spanish domination many French resided amongst the Portuguese in India, but since then the Inquisition had been very severe, and the French were frequently arrested as *Louteranos* (p. 200).

carried out this manœuvre was not the factor, but a captain of Cochin, who had been at Calecut for some time, to get back a ship that had been captured by the Malabar corsairs, which the king caused to be restored to him on payment of money at a good bargain. This captain was a metif named *Joan Furtado*,[1] a cruel and wicked man, and we could not well make out whether the fathers and the factor were in the plot or not.

While they were taking counsel with the fathers and their factor or agent, we were under guard of some soldiers, still crying for mercy. They then returned, and threw us, bound and throttled, into an Almedie, from which we thought we were to be cast overboard and drowned. When the Almedie put out to sea she half filled with water, in the which we lay, believing we were going to the bottom, so many people had she aboard. They had stripped us quite naked, and taken from us everything we had. When on board they freed our arms a whit, and presently the captain asked us what counsel and advice had been given to us by *Manjassa*, the man who had charge of us, and said he would kill him, but upon his word and honour we should take no harm. So we went coasting along till we had passed the territory of the king of Calecut, and were athwart that of the king of *Chaly*,[2] a friend of the Portuguese. He it was who harboured

[1] Not identified.

[2] Châliyam; see notes above, pp. 368, 374. The town is mentioned by Ibn Batuta (*Châliyât*), by Barbosa (Lisbon MS., *Chiliate;* Barceloni MS., *Chaliani*), "where there are numerous Moors, natives of the country, and much shipping"; in the *Sommario* of Ramusio (*Chalia* and *Calia*); by Barros and Linschoten (*Chale*); by Andrada (*Charé*). The Portuguese fort (see above, p. 374) perhaps gave it the name *Cinacotta* (*qu.* "little fort"). "We passed *Cinacotta*", says P. Vincenzo, "at the mouth of the river *Ciali*, where the Portuguese formerly had a fortress" (liv. I, cap. xxxiii). The same writer speaks of "the kingdom of *Sale*, so called from its situation among the lagoons" (liv. III, cap. iii). G. de Orta thought *Chinacota* (as he writes it) meant "fort of the Chinese" (ff. 58*b*, 188). Camoens, perhaps with poetic licence, speaks of the "lofty towers of *Chale*", built by Nuno da Cunha (*Lusiadas*, x, 61).

the nephew of the king of Calecut when he was in disgrace with his uncle, as related above. There they landed, taking us with them. No houses were to be seen. After taking counsel afresh among themselves, they bound us still more strongly, and sent some of their fellows to Calecut to hear what was said about us. What annoyed them most was that our other comrade, the Hollander, was not with us, as they thought he must be; the fact being that he would have accompanied us as far as the boat, had he not by good fortune been taken sick. They regretted the loss of him much, as he was a gunner by craft. I know not how it happened, but the king and all the people of Calecut knew all about it the same day: for, as I afterwards learned, our comrade who remained, when he heard the news, went straightway to the king, exclaiming that he would remain no longer, and, in fact, returned to Moutingué, to the Malabar corsairs there, who received him gladly, because, as I said, he was a good gunner. But as soon as the king of Calecut was advised of this, he sent for the Jesuit fathers, the factor, the writer, and all the other Portuguese there, and was hot in his anger against them, telling them he would have them answer for us, for it was currently believed we were killed. The fathers and the rest made their excuses, as to which the king made them swear upon the Jesuit fathers' book; they put all the blame upon him that had seized us. Forthwith the king sent and burned that ship of his that was there, and the fellow has never dared return there since, as I was informed some time afterwards at Goa.

Having thus landed in the Chaly country, they consulted together for about half an hour. This we thought meant judgment of death for us; but presently the captain returned and told us we were in perfect safety in his hands, swearing to us by the Holy Gospels that nothing should harm us, and bidding us be of good cheer. We, however, put no trust in his word, and remained praying on our knees, so that they were at the greatest pains to reassure us. We could not make him believe that we were Catholics, for he always called us *Lutheranos*, although we went so far as to ask for even their beads and books to pray to God withal, and said the service along with them; but they kept saying that all this was but a make-believe. They led us about a league and a half across country, and then concealed us so well that none of the neighbouring village discovered us. They gave us good enough cheer, but that did not raise our spirits, for we deemed ourselves adjudged to death, and as men who await only the appointed hour. The shed in which we were was always well closed and barred, for fear lest any should perceive us. They remained there for a whole day, awaiting the return of the messengers to Calecut. They brought us Portuguese clothes, which they made us put on, in order that none might recognise us. We had till now carefully preserved the passport of the king of Calecut; so, when his messenger had returned, the captain came and asked if we had not a passport from the Samory. We answered yes, and gave it to him. We never saw it again, and all this was done of design, and they made us march by night and not by day. So at nightfall they took the road to Tananor,[1] and we marched all night by the light of the moon, and came to a halt at daybreak at the town of *Chaly*, which is four or five leagues from Tananor: there we spent another day. In the evening they took from us also the letter the Jesuit fathers had given us, and during that night we arrived at Tananor,

[1] *Tânûr.* I don't know where Pyrard gets the extra syllable. The king was the Raja of *Vettatt Putiyangâdi*, known to Malayâlis as the *Vettatt Raja*. The family became extinct in 1793, after the British occupation. Tânûr is a very ancient place. Barbosa (ed. Hak. Soc., p. 153) says it belonged to a lord who dwelt inland, and had "much shipping and trade, for these Moors are great merchants". It appears in the *Sommario*, in Barros, Andrada, etc., as *Tanor*. P. Vincenzo says it was in his time incorporated with the kingdom of Cochin (liv. III, cap. iii); but this is probably erroneous.

the king of which place was the same who had delivered over the two Hollander merchants or factors to the Portuguese of Cochin, as I have told above. The Portuguese have a church there, also a Jesuit father, a factor, and some other Christians, as at Calecut. Before entering the town, the captain sent word to the priest and the factor to give them notice of our coming. It so happened that one of the Jesuit fathers of Calecut had already arrived there, and while we were waiting in a little wood, the boy who had been sent returned with a letter which made them all very sad and anxious, and to all appearance they were hampered with us, and regretted they had ever captured us; for neither the Jesuit father of Calecut, the one named Father Hilaire, nor he of Tananor, nor even the factor, wished to be mixed up in the affair, —at least they so pretended. They required that we should be taken to some place remote from the town, for fear of being discovered by anyone. The Calecut father went back forthwith, lest it should be said that he was a consenting party. After two days there they resolved to have done with us, and to send us to Cochin, twelve leagues off, and put us on board a large Almedie manned by Moucois, and two soldiers and their servants. But before despatching us they took from us the Portuguese clothes they had given us, and left us each with nothing but a cotton cloth of the size of a shroud, wherewithal to clothe us, and cover us by night as well as day. They assured us we should be well received at Cochin, and should come to no harm, and that they had written a letter to the captain of Cochin, and to the Jesuit fathers, and had also sent on the letters we had of the Calecut fathers, which would be of use to us. But, in fact, they acted quite otherwise, for they sent word that they had taken us at sea, and had slain all the Malabar corsairs and the Moucois of the ship; and further, that we were coming with a design to rebuild the fortress of Cognialy, which the king of Calecut had promised to the Hollanders, as, in fact, the rumour went at Calecut; indeed, they told us to say that we had been taken prisoners at sea. All that was said with two intentions, the one to make an open avowal of our capture, the other, the hope of reward for having achieved so good an enterprise.

These Moucois who escorted us make no fires in their Almedie, wherefore they cook beforehand large pots of rice, and keep it steeped in cold water, so that it does not go bad. Moreover, they fry a large quantity of salt fish of the small kind the Portuguese call *Caualle*[1]; they also carry a quantity of fruit and cocos: upon this fare they supported themselves, as we did, too. We sailed nearly all day and all night, and about ten o'clock in the morning arrived at Cochin. We were left for a considerable time before being put on shore, because the soldiers of our guard went to seek the governor with their letter. It was astonishing the great crowd of people who came to look at us.

It was about an hour and a half ere we landed; everyone was telling us we were to be hung, at the same time pointing out to us a large square on the right hand as you enter the town from the river. This square is called by the name of St. John, and has a fine church. They showed us a gallows-tree, whereon two or three Hollanders had been hung. On the other side of the river was the very handsome residence of the bishop. All this gave us but a poor hope for our future. We were then landed, and a miserable sight we were, all naked, save only for the covering of a mere rag of cotton. We were forthwith taken in charge by a Portuguese sergeant, whom they call a *Merigne*,[2] who was accompanied by seven or eight slaves, Christian Caffres of Mozambique, each with his halbert or partisan. These are bumbailiffs,

[1] *V. s.*, p. 388. Mr. Logan says this fish must be the sardine-like fish, common on the coast, and called *matti* by the Malayâlis; it is perhaps the same as that called by Day *chupea longiceps*, which he says is called *mutthi* in Canara and North Malabar (*Fishes of India*, p. 637).

[2] Port. *meirinho*, a tipstaff or usher.

and are called *Pions*[1]; all the Portuguese sergeants have a great many always with them. These sergeants and all other officers of justice never go about without a stick (their mark of office), which is as thick as a musket-stock, and of the length of an arm and a half: this they call *Vara de Justicia.* They carry no arms except a sword, but at night they are well armed with a cuirass, and a morion on their heads. They go on their watch at eight or nine o'clock till a very late hour, and beat all the streets, and so cause all persons to retire.

This Merigne then took us to the captain of Cochin, that is, the governor; for at all the Portuguese places in India they call their governors captains.[2]

This captain was a great noble, and questioned us of divers things. His daughters and wife had a curiosity to see us as a rarity, for in those parts wives and daughters are never in the society of men. He accordingly sent us to their chamber, where they eyed us all over, and were amazed at our condition, and mocked the Portuguese, that let themselves be so often beaten by the Hollanders, English, and French; for they make no distinction between these three nations. The daughters were very pretty, and regarded us with some pity; I believe they would have done us a good turn if they could or durst, but they had no means of so doing. They were Mestifves, and as pretty and fair as girls here. After they had asked us questions of one sort and another, the captain ordered the Merigne to take us to the *Oydor de Cidade*,[3] as being robbers and his proper game. As we were marched through the streets, it was a marvel to see the immense

[1] Port. *peão*, Sp. *peon*, from *pé*, "foot"; orig. a foot soldier, then an orderly, and now used all over India for a messenger on the staff of an official (see Yule, *Gloss.*, s. v.). The badge of office of the Anglo-Indian peon is a brass plate, fixed on a shoulder-belt of cloth.

[2] The governor of a Portuguese town is called *capitão de cidade*.

[3] *Ouvidor de cidade*, *i.e.*, "town's magistrate".

crowd that followed us, some taking pity upon us and telling us to have no fear, but to put our trust in God; others calling us *Lutherano* robbers, that should be hung. This Oydor, or criminal judge, after interrogating us and getting our answers, sent us back to the captain, saying that he was our proper judge, for that we were prisoners of war, and came under his cognizance. Whereupon the captain, seeing that the Oydor would not take charge of us, and himself having no desire for the job, commanded the Merigne (who also was much bothered, as he had nothing to gain in the business) to take us to the prison, to await an opportunity of being sent on to Goa, to be there judged by the viceroy, for that he would not take any cognizance of us. Indeed, we were no more questioned thenceforward, but were at once cast into prison; and there was none who offered us even a glass of water or a morsel to eat during all this time, that is to say, for more than four days.

This prison is the only one in all the town of Cochin, and is called the *Tronco*.[1] It is built in the form of a large and lofty square tower, and high above, in the middle of the floor, is a large square hole, like a very trap or the hatches of a ship, which is closed and locked; there they let down the prisoners in a scale or wooden table, which they lower with a rope, and draw up again by a pulley. It is six or seven fathoms in depth, like a well, and below there is no door, but only a large square window in the wall, of an arm and a half's length in thickness, to admit some light. This hole or window is trellised with thick, square-cut bars of iron, through which you can pass a two-pound loaf of bread, and through which the gaoler does pass whatever he gives to the prisoners, just as one would put bread into an oven with a long-hafted shovel. This grill is triple, for there is one within, one without, and one betwixt. This prison is verily the most frightful

[1] The name of the chief prison at Lisbon, and thence applied to similar prisons at Goa, Cochin, and elsewhere.

and cruel, I think, that exists in any part of the world, and yet some have been in it for five or six years. While we were on the upper floor, they wrote down the names of all three of us on paper. That upper prison is set apart for such as give a good sum of money to the gaoler, who notwithstanding puts their feet in irons, however great folks they be. Up there they keep also such as are sick, by leave of the judges and magistrates. The first man we met there was a Hollander, named *Martin Dombé*, who lost his ship on the Maldives, as I have related.[1] The sight of him assured us a little, but when we saw they were going to put us below, we began to be greatly saddened. This Hollander told us he had been there a very long time, and that it was only recently he had been brought above, and that the Jesuit fathers were the cause of his being badly treated. I will tell hereafter what happened to him. We found there also a gentleman who had been at Marseilles, and spoke French well. He asked me for news of Monsieur de Guise,[2] having seen much of him at Marseilles, and also been in his service. He also inquired if we had anything to live upon, and learning we had not, he gave us a gold piece of the value of a croisade. At length they lowered us down into the prison with the

[1] Martin Domburgh; see above, pp. 292-3, and in vol. ii.

[2] Charles de Lorraine, fourth Duc de Guise, born 20th August 1571. After the assassination of his father, Henry, the third duke, in 1587, he was kept a prisoner in the castle of Tours, until he made his escape in 1591. He took a prominent part on the side of the League during the next three years, but at length submitted to Henry IV, under treaty arrangements effected by Sully. The allusion in the text is to his capture of Marseilles in 1596, when it was on the point of being handed over to the king of Spain, an enterprise which he conducted with admirable skill and courage. In 1617 he led the royal army of Champagne against the leagued princes, and it 1622 achieved a naval victory over the insurgents of Rochelle. In the disputes between Louis XIII and Marie de Medicis he adopted the side of the queen-mother, and in 1631 was constrained by Richelieu to leave the kingdom. He chose Florence as his place of exile, and died at Cuna, in the Siennese district, in 1640 (*Nouv. Biog. Gén.*; Michaud, *Biog. Univ.*).

rest. There were there about six or seven score prisoners —Portuguese, Metifs, and Indians, Christians, Mahometans, and Gentiles, of all sorts and conditions. Among these we were treated with some courtesy.

Among the prisoners there was an elderly person that was a kind of judge over the rest, who obeyed him.[1] Everyone gives him an entrance fee, for his goodwill, half of which he gives to the gaoler. He is a Portuguese or Metif, and it is his duty to maintain the lamp before the image of Our Lady. Mass is said on all festivals and on Sundays at the outside near the grill, where it can be heard within. This prison is the most filthy, stinking, and noisome place imaginable, for the prisoners perform all their necessities one after another in vessels, which are voided only in the evening. This engenders such an infection, and an atmosphere so stinking and stifling, that one can hardly breathe. For at night the grill is shut with a trap-door from above, so that the heat of the climate, added to that of the place where so many people are huddled up pell-mell, engenders a close and stifling atmosphere, wherein it is impossible to survive long without becoming sick. A lamp is allowed to hang there alight all night, yet even that full often for want of air goes out. Gaolers are always on the watch to guard against any enterprises, and every night they search the goods and clothes of every inmate: and there is a great iron chain reaching from one end of the prison to the other, to which is fastened the foot of everyone imprisoned for crime: they did not, however, subject us to this treatment. Everyone is constrained to remain naked, both day and night, by reason of the heat; and one has even to lie sideways for want of room, and because of the great number of persons there; yet for all that one must perforce touch one's neighbour, in such wise

[1] Such a *doyen* of the inmates of a prison was a well-recognised personage in England,—*e.g.*, Mr. Melopoyn at the Marshalsea (*Roderick Random*, ch. lxi).

that the sweat exudes in large drops. Some slaves and paupers were employed in refreshing the company with a large fan, both day and night, for which service the elder or judge of the prison gives them something: without that it were impossible to live through it. We were the most pitiful sight in the world to witness after we had been there four or five days.

It was a great consolation that every day there was given out of pity a *demy tengue*,[1] equal to five sols here [*i.e.*, in France], to every Portuguese or Metif; and to the rest, once a day, some cooked rice and badly prepared fish, about as much as would serve one for a single meal, with some water to drink: this was given every morning, to last till the next day at the same hour. Water was also given for washing and bathing, and everyone washed all naked with the rest. One thing I remarked throughout all India, that the Gentiles and Mahometans, at their washing and bathing, never discovered their private parts, but always kept them covered with a cloth. It was only the Christians that had no shame in the matter, and even took pleasure in exposing them in a vile and disgusting manner. While we were in this miserable plight no one without was minded to aid us, because of our betrayer who had captured us, and of the false letter he had written against us: that was the cause of our being so cruelly entreated. There we remained nine or ten days, and I believe if we had remained there longer we had been all dead men: for the heat and infection were insupportable, and caused our whole bodies to be covered with large boils and eruptions, which gave us very grievous pain.

[1] Port. *meia tanga*. Mr. Da Cunha (*Indo-Port. Num.*) states that half tangas were coined a few years later than this, under the viceroy, J. Azavedo. The author seems to indicate the existence of the coin here. It is no doubt overstated in value, as in vol. ii he gives the value of the silver tanga of Goa as 7½ sous in India, and 5 sous in France. The current Portuguese value was 60 to 62 reis (see Yule, *Gloss.*, s. v. "tangha", and in Supplt., "pardao").

At length, by the advice of certain of the Portuguese prisoners, we wrote a letter to the Jesuit fathers of the Cochin college. The superior presently came to visit us, and recognising us to be Frenchmen and Catholics, went to request the governor to order our release. The governor replied that he could not do so absolutely, but that he would send us to Goa, to the Viceroy, and that meantime we should be enlarged in the town, on condition that he would answer for us at all times, and especially when called upon to produce us. This was effected, and during all that time, about six weeks, we were fairly treated, being well received by some and badly by others. We had but little time and opportunity to learn all the particulars of this kingdom and town of Cochin, which is one of the finest districts and most healthy towns of the Portuguese in India; yet I will shortly describe what I was able to note during my sojourn.

The kingdom of Cochin is situate under the altitude of eight degrees from the equinoctial, towards the latitude of the Arctic pole. It is one of the kingdoms of Malabar. The country has the same climate as Calecut, and is equally fertile in the same trees, herbs, and fruits; indeed, the two states are contiguous. Living is cheap, except that bread is dearer than at Goa, because the wheat comes from Cambaye to Goa, and is carried thence throughout all India. The orders and distinctions of the people—that is, of the Nairs and Moucois—are the same; the manners and customs are similar to those of Calecut, wherefore it would be wearisome and superfluous to repeat a description of their manners, customs, and police, seeing it would be all the same as is set forth above. The country, in like manner, abounds with pepper and with precious stones; but all the pepper is taken by the Portuguese, to whom the king of Cochin sells it: he collects it from all parts of his realm, stores it in his granaries, and sells it when he thinks fit, and not otherwise.

This king is not so puissant as he of Calecut. The Portuguese have always assisted him, and even now assist and succour him, albeit in a secret and underhand fashion: but for that the king of Calecut had long ere this subdued him. Indeed, it is said that in former days the kingdom of Cochin was subject and tributary to him of Calecut.[1] At the present day, however, he is no longer so, and that is owing to the Portuguese, as I have said. He is sovereign over his own territory, and holds himself equal with the king of Calecut; and on this account they are always at war and on bad terms. Wherefore, according as the Portuguese support the king of chin, so does the Samory support the Malabars and the other enemies of the Portuguese. The latter have never had so good a friend in the Indies as the king of Cochin, nor has anyone given them so much trouble as the Samory: ay, and he does so still every day.

There are two towns of Cochin, the one being the old town, distant from the sea about a league and a half, where the king resides; the other only a league from the sea, at the mouth of a large river, upon which also the old town is. The new town belongs to the Portuguese, and is fortified with good walls and a citadel.[2] The kings of Cochin have given them this place, and some land round about, over which they exercise full dominion. The bay and mouth of the river is large; in it appear three great rocks in a line, lying, like the coast toward the north, between a quarter N.W. and a quarter S.S.E.

[1] Pyrard is quite correct. The Samorins, with Mahomedan assistance, had made all the Malabar chiefs their dependents, except perhaps the Kôlattiris in the extreme north, and their cousins, the Travancore family, in the extreme south. To the disaffected the coming of the Portuguese was a godsend (as to Cochin, see *Barbosa*, Hak. Soc., p. 156). Hence the favourable reception of the Portuguese at Cannanore, Cochin, and Quilon.

[2] Excellent plans of Cochin will be found in Baldæus, and in Ressende (*Sloane MS*. No. 197).

After Goa, the Portuguese have no town so fine and large as Cochin. It is built of very handsome houses, churches, and monasteries; and the Portuguese and Christians there have the same order of government as at Goa, whereof I shall speak at large hereafter. They have a bishop, many churches and convents, a Jesuits' college, and a royal hospital for the Portuguese, as in their other towns. The river is a fair broad stream, and affords good harbourage. At the entrance from the north—that is, on the left side—is a little island, containing the handsome and splendid mansion of the bishop, which they call *Vaypin*.[1] The town is very populous, as well with Portuguese as Indians, both Christian (of whom there are a large number) and infidel, who, however, are not permitted to exercise their paganism in the town, but have to go without, to places depending upon the king of Cochin. There is great traffic and shipping there, and vessels come and enter this river from all parts: in short, for traffic and affluence of all the necessaries of life, it is a second Goa. This great shipping has rendered the country of the Cochin king busy, rich, and opulent; the king himself has become more wealthy and powerful, because he sells promptly all the produce of his country, and receives in return all that his country has need of, besides the tribute and presents that he gets daily from the Christian, Moor, and Gentile merchants. The king and the inhabitants, as well Nairs as Moucois and other Malabars, Gentiles and Mahometans, agree well with the Portuguese, and live in peace. There is a vast number of Jews there that are very rich, and all the other different nations live in perfect liberty as to religion, each having its own temple,

[1] *I.e.*, Vypeen island point. The formation of this island between the backwater and the sea (and it is still an island, as Mr. Logan informs me, contrary to Dr. Burnell's note in *Linschoten*, i, 69) is said to have taken place in A.D. 1341. Its name, *Putu Veppu* (*i.e.*, new deposit), is given to an era still in limited use among the people about Cochin.

except in the Portuguese town, which is reserved to that nation. The town where the king resides is called by the Portuguese *Cochin de riba*, or *Dacyma*,[1] that is, the upper, because it is higher up on the river than that of the Portuguese. The Cochin country is flat, very fertile, and well wooded, like the rest of the Malabar coast. Between the two Cochins are continuous houses, like suburbs, and it is the same all round. The country is well peopled and rich; and in the old Cochin is a market, where there is great traffic, and the king takes his dues there, as he does upon all merchandise coming from abroad. Certain tribute is levied on behalf of the king of Cochin in the Portuguese town, while the Portuguese levy dues on all goods for the king of Spain. There is also at Cochin a vast number of elephants and horses. The Nairs in the Portuguese town give place to the Portuguese, and let them pass when they meet them; in the old Cochin the Portuguese do the same to the Nairs: so the king has ordained, in order to avoid all disputes; but this is done only there. When the Nairs and Malabars walk in the streets, they clang their shields against their sides without ceasing, so loud as to be heard afar off, and so the rest of the people retire to their dwellings.[2] This clanging is also a kind of brag, and he who makes the most noise is the most esteemed. These shields and arms are made by the Gentile artizans, and are very beautiful, being worked in designs of all colours, gold, silver, and azure, varnish and lacquer. They are studded, too, with large gilt nails. The beautiful workmanship of these idolater Indians is indeed wonderful. Their children are taught to work from the age of five or six, and they have the keenest aptitude possible, understanding in but a short time all they see done. It may be remarked, however, that they follow their crafts from father to son, and marry their children to others of the same condition.

[1] Port. *da riba*, "of the river"; or *da cima*, "upper".
[2] *V. s.*, p. 383.

Justice is administered between them [*i.e.*, the Portuguese] and the traders or inhabitants, of whatever nation or religion, according to the laws and regulations of Portugal, and the king of Cochin has no jurisdiction except over his own subjects and criminals who take refuge with him. So also in like case the Portuguese cannot follow their criminals into the territory of the king of Cochin, or any further than the limits of the assigned territory.

For the space of six months from the month of May or April, sometimes earlier, sometimes later, until the month of November or thereabouts, no ships or barques enter the Cochin river. The reason is that the west wind comes from the sea, and the heavy and continual rains throw up from the land side such a quantity of sand at the mouth of the river, that banks are formed of such a height that it is impossible for either ships or barques to pass them. But when the rains cease there comes a contrary wind from the east, which drives the sand into the sea, and renders the river navigable for all manner of large craft.[1] This happens not only at Cochin, but all over India, at the mouths of rivers, which the Portuguese call *barre*[2]—that is, entrance.

The principal trade of Cochin is in pepper, and only the kings of Calecut and Cochin exercise it. The king of Cochin

[1] Mr. Logan informs me that this theory is not correct. The sand-banks are formed, not in the monsoon, but in the fair season (Sept.-May). The bar is cleared by the tidal scour during the monsoon, and the river is then closed for navigation, owing not so much to the state of the banks as to the heavy surf on the bar. Our engineers use every effort to promote the tidal scour, which, with the river current, clears the bar. A year or two ago the river forced a new passage for itself through the Vypeen island; and this, the *Cruz Milagre* gap, had to be closed at considerable expense.

[2] Port. *barra;* Bluteau defines the term as "the entrance of a port by which alone ships can enter or leave it; or, the entrance of a port where between the two shores the tide ebbs and flows; the bar of Goa is one of the best ports (*sic*) in the world, but you cannot enter or leave it without the tide."

stores it, buys it, and collects it; he has some of his own, and also takes tribute of others who have it, and the rest he buys through his factors, and has magazines for storing it. He keeps it sometimes two or three years before he sells it. Nowhere in all the Malabar Indies is there so much pepper as there and at Calecut, for the Portuguese, who trade everywhere, cause it all to be brought there. The next greatest trade is carried on with Bengal, and the merchandise carried there most frequently is the little shells of the Maldives, wherewith every year many vessels are laden. The Maldive people call them *Boly*, but the other Indians call them *Caury*[1]: in these they make a marvellous profit all over India. Where the Portuguese are well received, they associate with the natives and join in their voyages; yet all the mariners and pilots are Indians, either Gentiles or Mahometans. All these seamen are called *Lascar*, and the soldiers *Lascarits*.[2] All this trade between Cambaye and the Cape of Comorin is subject to much peril, because of the Malabar corsairs. When the fleet leaves Goa a large number of private galiots go with it for safety. These galiots are called *Navis de Chetie*, and the men-of-war *Navis d'Armade*[3]; in such wise that sometimes you see a hundred and fifty sail together, both at their setting out and return.[4] Nor is it only Goa which supplies these galiots: they come also from all the other Portuguese towns in India. All the ships of the Armadas are equipped at the expense of the king of Portugal, for they never speak there

[1] Hind. *kauri*, hence our "cowry" (see Yule's *Glossary*).

[2] For the history of these words see Yule's *Glossary*. The distinction made here (and here alone, in books of this period) is preserved in modern times. Throughout the East, *lascar* is applied to a native seaman; in Ceylon *lascoreen* means a native gunner, or a trooper of the Governor's native body-guard.

[3] Port. *Navios de Chatins*, and *navios da armada*.

[4] Such a fleet of merchant vessels under convoy was called a *Cafila* (see vol. ii, and Yule, *Gloss.*, s. v.).

of Spain or the Spaniards, but of Portugal, Goa, and the Indies only.[1] The arms of the Indian Government are a sphere; they put that on one side of their money, and the arms of Portugal on the other.[2]

CHAPTER XXIX.

Voyage from Cochin to Goa.—Of the kingdom of Cananor and the estate of the Malabars.—An accident which happened to the author.

We remained at Cochin, imprisoned and at liberty, about two months. In the meantime there arrived a fleet of fifty Portuguese galiots, under the command of a Portuguese lord. He was on his way from the coast of Cape Comorin and from Point de Galle in the island of Ceylon, and came to Cochin for refreshment in passing. This is their ordinary practice; for the Portuguese and the viceroy of Goa are wont every year at the beginning of summer, which is in the month of September, to equip two fleets[3] of a hundred

[1] It will be remembered here, as elsewhere, that Pyrard's sojourn in India was during the "captivity" or subjection to Spain (1580-1640). During this period India was governed entirely through the *Casa da India* at Lisbon, and altogether in the interests of Portugal and the Portuguese officials, who, as will be seen in vol. ii, jealously excluded Spanish interference.

[2] I have not observed any of the Portuguese Indian coins to have both the sphere and the arms: some have one and some the other. Some, such as the *roda* and the *vintem*, have the wheel of St. Catherine, which perhaps Pyrard mistakes for the sphere.

[3] These armadas, which are the subjects of frequent description and reference in the histories and despatches, were called respectively *Armada do Norte* and *Armada do Sud*, or *do Malavar*. The chief captain of the latter was called *Capitão Mór da Costa do Malavar*: and his vice-admiral sometimes bore the patent of *Capitão Mór do Cabo de Comorim* (De Couto, *Dec. XII*, liv. I, cap. viii).

galiots, along with three or four large galleys. Half of this fleet they send to the north, as far as Diu or Cambaye, and thereabouts, to guard the coast, and hold their power over the sea, and prevent any from sailing there without their passport. The other half they send to the south, as far as Cape Comorin, for the same purpose, but principally to purge the sea of the Malabar corsairs, who wage war with them and with all traders. So it is, that in those parts of India none dare navigate the seas without a passport from the Portuguese, unless they feel themselves sufficiently strong to resist, as do the Arabs and the men of Sumatra and others, who are always at war with them.

So while this fleet was refreshed for the space of five days, being about to return to Goa, which is distant from Cochin 100 leagues to the north, we employed the Jesuit fathers to get us a passage to Goa; this they did, using their offices with the governor of Cochin, who delivered me to the general of the fleet, to be put into the hands of the viceroy.

The governor, by name *Don Francisco de Meneiso*,[1] a near relative of the general, who bore the same name, put us back into prison two days before, with irons on our feet of more than thirty or forty pounds weight; thus were we escorted to the galley by two Merignes, assisted by their pions or tipstaffs. We were so loaded that we could hardly walk; these irons were only a foot in length, but, being very thick, they wounded our feet and legs sorely. The general of the fleet having received us, incontinently placed us in a galiot,

[1] Don Francisco de Menezes. In the royal despatch of 5th March 1612, the king says he is informed that this captain, while governor of Cochin, took some goods from the citizens and did not restore them, also that he prevented a neighbouring raja from paying a visit to the bishop of Cochin; and gives order for an inquiry to be made, and in case the charges be found proved, he is to be deprived of his office (*Liv. das Monç.*, i, 198).

with the irons on our feet, and thus set out from Cochin at the beginning of May 1608.

As ill-luck would have it, I fell into the hands of the cruellest fellow in the world, the captain of the galiot wherein I was placed, by name *Pedro de Poderoso*,[1] for neither he nor his men had any more pity for me than for a dog. Having these irons on my feet, I could not move from one place, so that everyone in going to and fro stepped upon me. This galiot was a very small one, and yet had such a number on board, that there was hardly room to lie down at full length. The crew insulted us in a thousand ways, exclaiming that as soon as we got to Goa we should be hung all three. The only consolation I got was from a religious of the order of St. Dominic, who, with a comrade, was with us. In these galiots they have a number of drinking vessels like glass water-bottles, but made of *cally*,[2] a white metal like tin, but much harder. As I have said, they never touch the vessel with the mouth while drinking. One day, when I was not taking care, I happened to touch it when I was taking a drink. A soldier observing me, forthwith came and gave me a violent cuff, which I bore without saying a word. The reason why the captain was so cruel towards me was that he had been taken prisoner and badly treated by the Hollanders, and thought we were of that nation. During our voyage we had contrary winds and rain all the way to Goa, for it was already the beginning of winter, so we were twenty days in going from Cochin to Goa, a voyage which with a good wind we could have done in two or three days. Moreover, on the evening of the first day after we set sail, we had the misfortune to meet a large merchant vessel of Malabar. Our galiot was anxious to board her (they are always anxious to be the first on board, as well for the profit

[1] Probably *Pedroso*: several officers of this name were serving in India about this time, but I do not trace a *Pedro*.

[2] Malay tin, elsewhere spelt *calin* and *callin*; *v. s.* p. 235.

as for the honour), and we ran into her with such violence with our prow, that the *dasoure*,[1] one end of which extends beyond the prow, struck the ship with that end of it, the other end being lashed to the galiot's mast. The shock of the two vessels was so great that the cable which held this *dasoure* (and which was so heavy that it required ten or a dozen men to lift it) snapped asunder. I was then on the deck, with my feet in the irons; it fell upon my back, and so remained for some time, and it was with great difficulty that ten men got me out. I was like dead, and could not speak, while they threw water upon me to bring me round. There was no surgeon on board, save some miserable barber, whose only skill was to bleed or to dress a slight wound. I was promptly bled, and had some kind of plaster clapped upon my back, which caused a high inflammation. I received the greatest assistance from this good Dominican monk, and I cannot tell you all his good treatment of me, for he supplied me with a clean shirt, stockings, clothes, a mattress, a pillow, a sheet, and other necessaries; and as for food, with his own hands he brought me in secret everything he could lay hands on, and left his own meal untouched to give it to me. He begged the captain to take off my irons, which he allowed, but from one foot only. In fine, this good monk brought me everything he could for my cure, and I believe that, without God's grace and his, I had been dead a hundred

[1] ? Spritsail boom. I cannot trace the word; it is not in the Port. Dictionaries of Vieyra, D. Vieira, or Roquete. Rivara, in his edition of Pyrard, translates it *verga*, "yard"; but this is not in accordance with the text, which speaks of the other *end* being lashed to the mast. The nearest approach to the word I can find is *ceuadera vela*, "voile ceuadere ou civadière, qui est la voile plus petite du navire, le beaupré du navire" (Oudin, *Tresor*, 1645, s. v.); *cevadere*, "the spritsail of a ship" (Cotgrave). Pyrard may have heard this word used with the genitive *da* before it. In the first edition (1611) he does not describe the accident in detail, but in recording his arrival at Goa, says: "j'estois lors fort malade à cause que le mast de la galliote étoit tombé sur mon dos, et m'avoit tellement blessé, que je fus en danger de mort."

times over. In fact, all who saw me get the blow and survive it, said it was a miracle, as it was the severest blow a man could receive without being killed; yet had I been cured at once, the wonder would not have been so manifest. The captain, seeing me thus wounded, put me in the forecastle, which is the most uncomfortable place in the ship; for it is there that everyone does his necessities, and the waves come in the most; where, too, if they wanted to cast or heave the anchor, I was always in the way. Add to this, I was always in either sun or rain, and was all the while suffering the greatest pain, believing that the spine of my back was broken; and I was more than a month ere I could do more than drag one leg after the other. I ate well, but without power of digestion, and became so wizen, thin, and pale, that on arrival at Goa I was a very mummy, or like a corpse dried in the sun. The captain had been content if I had died, so as to have me thrown overboard forthwith. If I was turned on one side I could not turn to the other. I even ate and drank lying, with the greatest discomfort and incredible pain; and if I so much as raised my head, I felt the most extreme thirst, while every hour the ship's water was failing. Throughout all this I got no aid but from the good monk and from the cook, who was a Canarin of Goa, and a Christian; for the place where I lay was where they did the cooking, in such wise that the heat and smoke tormented me sorely; and, to complete the picture of my condition, they kept threatening me that I was to be hung at Goa.

As for our voyage, we coasted along the Malabar country, passed in sight of Calecut, and cast anchor at Cananor, which is forty leagues distant from Cochin. There we sojourned three or four days.

Cananor[1] is a handsome town, situate on the sea-shore, and

[1] Properly *Kannanûr*, *i.e.*, the village (*ûr*) of *Kannan* (a common Malayâli name). It was the chief seaport of the kingdom of the Kôlattiri family, cousins of the Travancore rajas. Before Pyrard's time the

has a good harbour: it is one of the Malabar kingdoms. Of its condition it will not be out of place here to note what I observed (although I have already touched the subject, but not in detail), both on this occasion when I was at Cananor, and formerly when I arrived from Moutingué and Badara, and departed thence for Calecut, as well as on other occasions. The Malabar coast is inhabited, as I have said, by two sorts of peoples, natives and foreigners. The natives are Gentiles—that is, the Nairs, who alone inhabit the inner country; the foreigners, those of whom I am now speaking, are properly called the Malabars, as being the inhabitants of the seacoast of Malabar. It is quite certain they came from elsewhere, some say from Arabia; but that is a long time ago. They speak the same language and none other; they obey the Nair kings, and pay them tribute for the land they occupy; they are extended over the whole length of the coast, and their towns are for the most part densely peopled. Their religion is the law of Mahomet. They are kindly people, and are also rich merchants, and well skilled in trade, and the best soldiers in India, both on land and sea, and make as much profession of arms as do the Nairs. In their hands is the whole shipping and trade of the country. In their ships and galleys, and in all their business and work by land, they make use of the Moucois and Tiua, and other villein folk, paying them wages. They agree well, and are very good friends with the Nairs, but in their presence they do not sit down, nor even touch the walls or furniture: this comes from the ceremony and superstition of the Nairs, for the Malabars have no scruples of the kind. The king of Cananor is a Malabar, and one of the kings of Malabar: in his territory the Malabars are not subject to the Nairs, although there is a Nair king in the Cananor country. The latter, however, has no authority nowadays, and the Mala-

Mahomedan chieftain of Cannanor (Ali Raja) had become independent of the Kôlattiri.

bars of the whole coast, both merchants and corsairs, respect and honour this king. The people of the country have told me that it is not long since the Malabars of Cananor were in like condition with the rest of their race, and obeyed that Nair king, but that they became so strong that they made a king for themselves, and no longer recognised the Nair king nor paid him any tribute: he resides far in the interior, and is often at war with the king of Cananor. This king of Cananor is very rich and powerful, for he has plenty of men subject to him, besides the other Malabars of the whole coast, whom he calls upon in time of need. He is called *Aly Ragea*,[1] and is a Mahometan, like the other Malabars. He is powerful on the sea, has a large number of ships, trades all over India, and for this purpose has a number of factors at different places. The islands of Diuandurou belong to him, and the Maldives are at present held of him.[2] He is very courteous, humane, and affable, and, more than any of the other kings, is fond of the society of foreigners. The Portuguese are at peace with him, and by his permission hold a small fort[3] in Cananor, containing a church and a Jesuits' college. Nevertheless, the other Indian kings call

[1] *Âli Raja* ("Sea King"). The family of this chieftain was originally Nâyar, and dependent on the Kôlattiri rajas. One of the family embraced Islam, and was made captain of the Kôlattiri fleet, with the title of *Mammâli Kitavu* ("Muhammad, Chieftain of the Sea"). As captain of the fleet he was admitted to all the important counsels of the Kôlattiri, and ultimately became independent about the year 1525. The Âli Rajas were regarded as the heads of the Mâppilla community on the coast down to the end of last century. They played an important part in history after the establishment of the English factory at Tellicherry.

[2] See App. A.

[3] The Portuguese got this fort originally from the Kôlattiri, not from Âli Raja. It was named Fort Angelo. Falling into the hands of the Dutch in 1662, it so remained till 1771, when the Dutch sold it to Âli Raja. During the wars with Tippu it was twice taken by the British, and at the present time is garrisoned by our troops. Linschoten (i, 67) says it was "the best fortresse that the Portingalles have in all Malabar". A plan will be found in Ressende's *Livro do Estado* (Sloane MS. No. 197).

not this king of Cananor a king, saying that he is not so of right, but only by force.

Of these Malabars, too, some are corsairs and pirates, who for the six summer months, when the navigation is good, sweep the seas for more than two hundred leagues of coast, so to harry all the ships they find, as well Portuguese as Indian, and even those of their own brethren, the Malabars (who carry their merchandise at that season alone); this often happens. While at sea they are no respecters of persons further than this: they choose a chief when they set sail; when they return the chief is so no longer, and has no more power; they usually have as many as eighty or one hundred galiots well equipped. Moreover, they make the best soldiers in the world, being exceedingly brave and courageous. They are always at war with the Portuguese, to whom they give great trouble. The Portuguese have not seen their way to put an end to them from the time when they first came to the Indies to the present, and they have been oftener defeated by the Malabars than victorious over them. The war between them is very cruel and merciless, for the Malabars are so courageous that they never surrender, and prefer death. I have seen them, when in battle with the Portuguese, on perceiving that they were the weaker side, and could not avoid being taken, all come to one side of their galiot, and go down with their booty, galiot and all, and even sometimes to wait till some Portuguese had boarded their vessel, so as they should perish with them. When taken prisoners by the Portuguese, they remain at forced labour in the king's galleys all their lives, none being able to ransom them. When they take any of the Portuguese, they usually put them to death, or keep them for some time, to see if any will come and redeem them; if not redeemed they are put to death.

To him that takes one of them prisoner the king of Portugal gives ten *pardos*[1] in reward, and the prisoner is his slave all his

[1] As to the *pardão*, see vol. ii, and Col. Yule's valuable article in the Supplement to his *Glossary*.

life. To the Indians, of whatever race they may be, the pirates do no harm beyond pillaging them, for they let them go with their vessels and more bulky goods. What is passing strange is, that at sea they let not off even their own fathers, saying that it is their trade and custom to be sea-rovers, and they must seize every opportunity when it presents itself. For all that, they are by land the best folks in the world, the most humane and tractable. They have four harbours of refuge in the realms of the Nair kings, where they build their galleys, whence they sally forth, and whither they return with their booty. These harbours are well fortified on the sea side only, for with the Nair kings who have given them these refuges they have a good understanding, being subject to their judicature and paying them tribute. This understanding is highly profitable to these petty Nair kings, who are inaccessible by land. These ports are Moutingué, Badara, Chombaye, and Cangelotte, which these kings have given them permission to build. When in the winter time they return from sea they become good merchants, going hither and thither among the neighbouring places to sell their goods, both by land and by sea, using then merchant ships that also belong to them. They often go to Goa and Cochin to sell their merchandise and trade with the Portuguese, obtaining Portuguese passports, though in the previous summer they may have been at war. It is not only the Malabars of these ports who lead this kind of life, but also all others of the whole coast, when they are minded thereto, as indeed they usually are; but inasmuch as they durst not embark at other places, they come overland to these ports and there take ship; they afterwards return home to resume their ordinary life, and then only when they think fit. It is a thing worthy of admiration how these people, whether at sea or in their towns, although they have no masters, nevertheless agree so well together that no dispute, quarrel, or discord arises among them. In these towns they have indeed some very rich and great Malabar lords, who build and equip these galiots, pay the soldiers and pressed hands, and send them to sea without budging from home themselves, except to be chiefs of a large expedition, on which occasion the booty belongs to them. These lords have a most commendable custom, observed among all the Malabars, which is that every wayfarer, of whatsoever religion, and whether rich or poor, coming for a lodging to their houses, gets good cheer at no cost to himself.

When the Hollanders with their fleet passed by Cananor they fired some cannon-shots, and the king sent them a quantity of presents; they made as though they would blockade the place, but he begged them off, promising that when he took some other place he would give it to them.[1] Thus is this king friendly to all, and a lover of peace. In the town of Cananor is a fine market every day, called *Basar.* The country is fertile in all kinds of produce: there is great quantity of pepper, and much trade done therein: the Portuguese have not the upper hand there, as elsewhere. They (the Cananor people) send many vessels laden with pepper to Arabia. The corsairs nowadays respect this king; but while they had their *Coginay Marquaire*[2] they took but little account of him. The town of Cananor is situate under the eleventh and a half degree towards the north.[3]

All the Malabars of Cananor and the neighbourhood have but two professions, those of merchant and corsair; the merchants buy the goods filched by the others to sell at a higher price, even though they have been taken from their own

[1] The reference is probably to the fleet of Steven Van der Hagen, which arrived at Cannanor on the 26th October 1604. There was some firing, but it was at some Portuguese, who attacked the Dutch boat at its landing from an ambuscade. The Cannanor people took no part in this; and soon after the raja sent a deputation on board with a letter, in which he gave the Dutch to understand that he intended to maintain a strict neutrality as between them and the Portuguese (*Rec. des Voy.*, iii, 16).

[2] *Kunhâli Marakkâr.*

[3] More precisely, 12° N.

relatives and friends. They have no nobility but that of valour and riches. The Malabar merchants are recognised by their dress, and not otherwise; for while both merchants and corsairs usually carry arms, the merchants do not wear their hair long; they have a bonnet of red scarlet, in the form of a skull-cap, and most frequently a kerchief wound round it in the fashion of a turban, and called *Mondou*[1]; these kerchiefs are of gold embroidery and coloured silk. They wear the beard half shaved, but without moustaches. Also they have a little skirt of silk or cotton reaching three finger-lengths below the waist, and below that a cloth down to the knees. Then they have other pretty kerchiefs wherein they tie up and conceal their money. It is the habit of these merchants, as well as those of the Maldives and other places, to carry everything with them when they go to sea, both their petty baggage and their beds for sleeping on, for they will never sleep on other folk's beds if they can help it. The corsairs wear their hair long like women, and never cut it; they tie it in a bunch, like all the other Indians, and cover it with one of these pretty kerchiefs; they go quite naked, except that they are covered with a silk cloth as far as the knees, and have another handkerchief round the waist. All the Malabars, as well corsairs as merchants, carry knives with hafts and sheaths of silver—that is, such as can afford it; these are all beautifully fitted with little pendants, such as tooth-picks, earpicks, and other instruments. The corsairs wear the beard shaved, but never shave over the mouth nor the moustaches: these they wear like the Turks, in such wise that some have moustaches so long that they tie them behind the head. All the Malabars are covered with thick hair over the stomach and elsewhere; they wear no slippers. Their women are dressed like the other natives, and wear nothing upon their hair; they carry a quantity of gold earrings and rings and trinkets on their fingers and toes. They have a

[1] Malayâlam *mundu*, which means simply a cloth.

little light jacket of cotton down to the waist, and another silk or cotton cloth which reaches from the waist down to the feet. They go barefooted, and are very fair in complexion, and most of them are short of stature: the men are of middle height. The women are pretty, and addicted to licentious practices like the other Indian women, but not to the same extent as in other places.

When they find a stranger at one of these Malabar corsairs' ports, who is willing to go to the wars with them, they feed and maintain him all the winter, him and his wife, for they marry as soon as they settle awhile in any place. They engage in good time some soldiers and Moucois at high wages, which they advance to them to bind the bargain. When they are ready for the fray they take some betel, and some *Amfian*[1] or poppy juice, which most of the Indians use. They take this betel and *amfian*, or *afeon*, and swear fidelity thereupon. After making a prize, and before coming ashore, they search every man on board and the whole ship. The captain and chief men lay hands on everything, and account conscientiously to the owner of the galiot or pados. It is incredible the fatigues these fellows will undergo at sea, and how they endure hunger and thirst. They have plenty of cannon and other arms; but of money and other valuables they carry with them not so much as five sols' worth: all that they leave on shore. As soon as they have taken a prize they come in to discharge, and return to sea at once, if there seems a likelihood of other booty; if not, they remain at home for that year and consume the produce of their theft and rapine for the next six months. This is all I was able to observe of the Malabar coast and polity.

[1] Opium. The form *amfian* is the Port. *amfião*; *afeon* is the Ar. *afyun*. This Port. form is a corruption of the Arabic, and only came into use after the Portuguese went to India: this is seen from the passage in De Orta, where his interlocutor says: "Queria saber a certeza do *amfião*, que é o que a gente desta terra uza, se é o que chamamos *opio*" (f. 153*b*). The Ar. form came from the Greek ὄπιον.

But to return to Cananor: we sojourned there three or four days waiting for a favourable wind, but seeing it did not come, and there was no hope of it, owing to the commencement of winter, as I have said, we set sail and resumed our course for Goa, I being ill all the while. Meanwhile, that good father the monk was doing all he could with the general of the fleet and the captain of our galiot to get me left at the hospital of Cananor; but he (the captain) would not permit it, giving all sorts of reasons, and saying that if I died he would have me thrown overboard for a *Luterano* dog as I was. Whereupon the monk comforted me, and bade me to be of good courage, and even brought me from the town some drugs and sweetmeats, and all else he considered needful or useful to me. In this way we made our way to Goa, where we arrived in the month of June following. I was then very ill with my wound and the hardships I had endured on board, by reason of the inhumanity of the captain, who treated me, as I have said, with the utmost indignity and barbarity, and would have done worse but for the succour and charity of the monk, who comforted me on every occasion and resisted his harsh conduct. I must not omit to mention here the name of this good monk of whom I received so much favour; he was called *frere Manuel de Christ.*[1] As soon as the galiots were anchored at Goa, I was carried to the hospital, where I was well treated and cured of my sickness. It is verily a royal hospital, excellent and magnificent in all respects, where the sick, both rich and poor, are served with the utmost care, propriety, and kindliness. I will describe it more particularly hereafter, as also the town of Goa, the surrounding country, the police arrangements, and all else that is noticeable, as well as what happened to me while I sojourned there. But the size of this volume constrains me to conclude here the story of the first part of my voyage, and

[1] I have not found this good Dominican mentioned elsewhere; it may be hoped that the rest of his life was as praiseworthy as is this episode.

to leave the rest for a second, where, with God's help, I shall relate in detail my voyage to Sunda and the Moluccas; the navigation of the Portuguese, with whom I afterwards sailed, and their arrival in Brazil; and finally my return to France.

END OF VOL. I.

THE VOYAGE
OF
FRANCOIS PYRARD

INTERIOR OF CHURCH OF S. FRANCIS OF ASSISI AT GOA.

THE VOYAGE
OF
FRANCOIS PYRARD
OF LAVAL

TO THE EAST INDIES, THE MALDIVES THE MOLUCCAS AND BRAZIL

TRANSLATED INTO ENGLISH FROM THE THIRD FRENCH EDITION OF 1619, AND EDITED, WITH NOTES,

BY ALBERT GRAY,

FORMERLY OF THE CEYLON CIVIL SERVICE

ASSISTED

BY H. C. P. BELL

OF THE CYLON CIVIL SERVICE

IN TWO VOLUMES—VOL II, PART I.

GYAN

Published by

Gyan Publishing House
5, Ansari Road
Daryaganj, New Delhi-110002
Phone: 011-47034999, 9811692060
E-mail: books@gyanbooks.com

Distribution Network
gyanbooks.com
India, USA, Canada, UK, Australia, France

ISBN : 978-81-212-4199-1 (Set)
ISBN : 978-81-212-4772-6 (PB)

2nd Impression 2020

Printed at: Gyan Press, Delhi.

The Voyage of Francois Pyrard
Author: Albert Gray

THE VOYAGE

OF

FRANÇOIS PYRARD

OF LAVAL

TO THE EAST INDIES, THE MALDIVES, THE MOLUCCAS AND BRAZIL.

TRANSLATED INTO ENGLISH FROM THE THIRD FRENCH EDITION OF 1619,
AND EDITED, WITH NOTES,

BY ALBERT GRAY,

FORMERLY OF THE CEYLON CIVIL SERVICE.

ASSISTED

BY H. C. P. BELL,

OF THE CEYLON CIVIL SERVICE.

IN TWO VOLUMES.—VOL. II, PART I.

BURT FRANKLIN, PUBLISHER
NEW YORK, NEW YORK

CONTENTS OF THE SECOND VOLUME.

(PART I.)

LIST OF ILLUSTRATIONS.

"Por terra jaz o Emporio do Oriente,
Que do rigido Affonso o ferro, o raio
Ao grão Filho ganhou do grão Sabio,
Enverganhando o Deos armipotente.

Cahio Goa, terror antigamente
Do Naire vão, do pérfido Malaio,
De barbaras Nações . . . ah! que desmaio
Apaga o Marcio ardor da Lusá Gente.

Oh Seculos de Heróes! Dias de Gloria!
Varões excelsos, que, a pezar da Morte,
Viveis na tradição, viveis na Historia!

Albuquerque terrivel, Castro forte,
Menezes, e outros mil, vossa memoria
Vinga as injúrias, que nos faz a Sorte."

M. M. de Barbosa du Bocage.

"Surely, at this day, with us of Europe, the vantage of strength at sea (which is one of the principal dowries of this Kingdom of Great Britain), is great; both because most of the Kingdoms of Europe are not merely inland, but girt with the sea most part of their compass; and because the wealth of both Indies seems, in great part, but an accessory to the command of the seas."

Fr. Bacon, *Of the true Greatness of Kingdoms and Estates.*

INTRODUCTION.

THE author has chosen to make his arrival at Goa the dividing point of his two volumes. He might have closed the first with his escape from the Maldives, and thus comprised in the second the whole of his description of Portuguese India. While he was on the Malabar coast, at the pirate ports and at Calicut, he was within the sphere of Portuguese action and diplomacy, while at Cochin he was a Portuguese prisoner. But the scheme of division is nevertheless a reasonable one. At Chittagong and on the Malabar coast he was still at a distance from the centre of action, and not till he arrived at Goa was he able to take a comprehensive view of the first great European dominion in the East. Moreover, it was not till he arrived at the Portuguese capital, at which regular communication was maintained with Europe, that he began to take hope of once more returning to his native country.

The two volumes are composed on the same method. In the first the narrative proceeds down to the arrival of the author at the court of the Maldive king. It is then suspended while he gives a detailed view of the island kingdom in all its departments, and is not resumed until the arrival of the hostile fleet which conveyed him to India. The story of four-and-a-half years' residence is only to be gleaned from occasional personal references. In the second volume the personal narrative breaks off at his liberation from prison, a few weeks after his arrival at Goa. At that point, when he was first enabled to make his observations of Goa and Portuguese India, he discards dates and the sequence of events, and bids his reader receive his impressions of the Portuguese dominion, classified and arranged under a series of chapters. When he has completed this general view he gradually resumes the thread of his narrative, relates various occurrences at Goa immediately prior to his departure, and so proceeds with his homeward voyage. Of his twenty months' residence with the Portuguese (May 1608—February 1610) the events of the first and last few weeks only are narrated with dates. As respects the interval, personal details are introduced more as illustration and in warranty of truth than as subject-matter. He informs us, indeed, that he made two voyages in Portuguese ships, the one to Malacca and the Eastern Archipelago, and the other to Diu and Cambaye, but he vouchsafes neither dates nor names of the ships or commanders; and while he states that on these expeditions he fought under the Portuguese flag, he gives us neither time, nor place, nor enemy. The personal narrative may, however, be pieced together.

Pyrard arrived at Goa, wounded by his accident and ill from his bad treatment during the voyage from Cochin, about the end of May 1608. Of his two companions, one was afflicted with a serious ulcer; the other, though suffering from fatigue, was otherwise sound. By the kindness of the officers of the fleet all three were admitted to the Royal Hospital. After three weeks' careful treatment in this splendid institution, Pyrard and his healthy companion, ignorant that they were still prisoners, pressed the Jesuit father (*pae dos Christãos*), to whom the Government assigned the superintendence of native and foreign Christians, to be allowed to go out and see the city of which they had heard so much. After a few days they were discharged from the hospital, but, to their surprise, in charge of *meirinhos* (sergeants) and their peons, who escorted them to the *Sala das bragas*, one of the Goa prisons.

On a later occasion Pyrard was again a patient in the hospital. His description of it is one of his most attractive chapters. The institution, originally instituted by Albuquerque for the treatment of Portuguese soldiers, and into which no native was received as a patient, was at this time under the management of the Jesuits. The nursing arrangements seem to have been excellent, strict regularity being accompanied by cleanliness and good feeding. It is a relief to find no charge of peculation laid against this department of administration. The medical service, unfortunately, seems to have been lamentably bad even for that age, and the mortality excessive (see pp. 11, 14, *note*). No doubt a large percentage of the cases were those of cholera, scurvy, and enteric fevers, with which the science of the time was unable to deal. But, on the other hand, the best available skill was not employed—that of the physicians who had experience in India. Every viceroy as he came out was in the habit of appointing his private physician, who had accompanied him, to the charge of the hospital. At the end of three years, when he was beginning to understand his work, he was superseded on the arrival of the next viceroy.

Pyrard was held a prisoner in the *Sala das Bragas* for about two months, and was then released by the intervention and good offices of a French Jesuit, Father La Croix. It was now about the end of August. He and his companion were forthwith placed on the roll of soldiers for service. He made two expeditions with the Portuguese armadas, one to the north as far as Diu and Cambaye, the other to Ceylon, Malacca, and the Archipelago. It seems probable that the shorter voyage was performed first, and that he embarked some time in October in the armada of the south, which was wont to leave Goa annually in that month, for the protection of commerce, and for supplying the eastern fortresses and factories with reinforcements (p. 117). In any case he must have been absent from Goa during the latter half of September, because on the 17th the Dutch admiral Verhoeven appeared at the river bar, and blockaded Goa for ten days. As we know from other sources, this event caused great consternation in the city; but Pyrard's only reference to Dutch blockades does not imply that he was a spectator of any of them.

His short sojourn in Ceylon only gave him time to gather a quantity of hearsay information about the island. At this time the Portuguese had their fortresses at Colombo and Galle, besides smaller forts at other places on the western coast. They had not then occupied Jaffna, nor any point on the eastern coast. The Dutch under Spilberg, following their usual policy of seizing points unoccupied by their rivals, made their first entrance in 1602 by Batticaloa on the east. The diplomatic relations with the Kandyan king, successfully commenced by that captain, had been abruptly stopped by the murder in 1603 of Sibalt de Weer, the only captain of Oliver de Noort's fleet who survived the terrible sufferings of the first Dutch voyage of circumnavigation.

This event delayed the progress of the Dutch in Ceylon for some years, and it was not till 1609, the year after Pyrard's visit, that an offensive and defensive alliance was formed with the Kandyan queen, Donna Catherina. The Portuguese had committed in Ceylon their great error of attempting to enlarge their dominion from the possession of a few forts and the command of the sea, to a conquest of the whole island. They considered that the fortress policy, proper as regards the continent of India, did not apply to an island like Ceylon; but they took no account of the difficulties of guerilla warfare in a mountainous country covered with dense jungle, and they over-estimated their own strength. The whole period of their undisputed supremacy in India had been employed in fomenting an internecine war in Ceylon, and in the end they were masters of hardly a mile of territory outside their forts. In 1597, the same year in which the Dutch made their first appearance in Indian waters, the Portuguese obtained from the Kandyan king, Dharmapála, a legacy of the throne which he had ceased to occupy, and were thus further committed to their fatal policy of conquest. The Dutch gave but an intermittent support to their native allies; the war which ensued was signalised by every species of atrocity and treachery, and the long miseries of the Portuguese occupation ended for Ceylon in the capitulation of Colombo in 1656.

From Ceylon Pyrard passed to Malacca. His chapter on that great fortress and emporium, in which the Portuguese up to this time had succeeded in focussing the whole trade of the far East, is mainly devoted to an account of the siege of 1606, and the destruction of the viceroy's relieving fleet. His account of these events is valuable, though in some details inaccurate; it represents the unofficial story as related to him by the Portuguese officers or soldiers, some of whom, perhaps, had been present.

From the occasional personal references in the general description of the Eastern Archipelago, which is comprised in chapters xii and xiii, we gather that the places actually visited by the traveller were Bantam and Tuban in Java, the islands of Madura and Báli, Ternaté, one of the Moluccas, and Banda. At this time no foreign power had an established position in Java, though both Dutch and English agents were admitted at Bantam. The great object of the European rivals was the possession of the Moluccas, or Spice Islands. In 1599 Van Nek had expelled the Portuguese factors from Amboyna, and established relations with the Moluccas, though the Portuguese had a fort at Tidoré. In 1601 the Portuguese sent an armada under André Furtado to expel the "rebel Hollanders", and re-establish the Portuguese supremacy. He succeeded in retaking Amboyna, but arrived before Ternaté in 1603 with an equipment exhausted by nearly two years' continuous service at sea. Despairing of proper reinforcement from Goa, he had applied to the Governor of the Philippines. That officer deemed it prudent to send the succour, though he himself had designs on the islands on behalf of Spain. Even with this reinforcement Furtado failed to take Ternaté.[1]

In 1605, before anything further was done on behalf of the king by either division of his subjects, the Dutch again swooped upon the islands. Under Van der Hagen they drove the Portuguese from Tidoré and Amboyna, and were supreme for the moment. That captain, however, left the islands insufficiently garrisoned, and in 1606 the Spanish governor of the Philippines, Pedro de Acuña, carried out his long

[1] De Morga's *Philippine Islands*, pp. 216, 226.

meditated expedition and expelled the Dutch from all their positions, except Amboyna.

In 1607 Matelief, fresh from his naval victories off Malacca, succeeded in dislodging the Spaniards from Tidoré. Thus Pyrard found Tidoré and Amboyna in the hands of the Dutch, and Ternaté in those of the Spaniards. The miseries of the wretched Moluccans, cursed with the endowment of the coveted clove, were not yet at an end. In 1611 the Spaniards conquered Banda and retook Tidoré, and not long afterwards the Dutch retook Ternaté.

When the news of Van der Hagen's successes at the Moluccas reached Goa, it was accompanied by information that a combination was on foot between the Dutch, and the Rajas of Achin and Johore, for a general attack upon Malacca. The Portuguese promptly equipped a powerful armada, the largest which had ever left Goa, and it was ordered by the king himself that the viceroy, Martin Affonso de Castro should proceed in command. Ignorant that a new Dutch fleet under Matelief was already on its way to Malacca, the viceroy was minded to break up the confederacy by a descent upon Achin. A landing was effected, but the assault was repulsed, and the force was re-embarked with the loss of some men and much credit. Thence turning to Malacca he found himself face to face with Matelief, who was well-informed of his movements, and had raised the siege. De Castro was no match for Matelief. The sea-fights off Malacca, though obstinately fought, resulted in the complete destruction of the Portuguese fleet, and De Castro remained at Malacca only to die, as some said, of chagrin.

Besides describing the places actually visited, our traveller adds short accounts of the rest of the Archipelago, such as Sumatra, including Achin, Borneo, and the Philippines. The more interesting passages of this part of his narrative are those in which he describes the course of trade as between the Eastern islands, China and Japan, Spanish America and the Philippines, and Portuguese Goa and Malacca.

Pyrard has nothing to say as to the doings of the English in those seas. Our chief factory in the East, and that but a small one, was then at Bantam, cargoes being picked up wherever we were free from the molestation of Spaniards and Dutch. In 1606 Middleton had been warned off the Moluccas by the Spaniards, and off Banda by our old allies the Dutch.

On his return from the Malacca voyage Pyrard states that he remained another six months at Goa to pass the winter (the S.W. monsoon), before his departure from India.[1] It is probable therefore that he reached Goa about the end of May 1609; he does not state clearly that he was at Goa when André Furtado assumed office as Governor, that is on the 21st, and he misdescribes that proceeding.

This last period of six months was a busy and interesting time. Furtado, on his assumption of office, at once commenced great doings in the arsenal.

[1] See pp. 179, 261.

Armadas were equipped to be despatched as usual to the north and the south, and in addition a great expedition was on foot for the discovery of the Zambesi and the gold mines of Monomotapa. Besides these, the regular fleet from Portugal was expected in September, and the homeward fleet would have to be loaded and despatched by the end of the year. Pyrard does not tell us in what he was employed; he was still on the roll of soldiers, and as a *soldado* got his provisions at the house of one of the great lords.[1] He was within an ace of being taken for service either with the armada of the north, or that for Africa.

There does not seem to have been any notion of compulsion in this matter. He was invited to go with the northern armada by the lord who gave him his provisions, and he was "greatly importuned" to join the Mozambique expedition.[2] He was, however, saved by events. In September arrived the fleet from Lisbon, bringing a new viceroy, Ruy Lourenço de Tavora, to whom Furtado yielded up the government. By this time the Portuguese had an unusual number of foreigners on their hands. They had Pyrard and his two French companions; they had Richard Wickham, who had been kidnapped from the *Union* on the coast of Zanzibar; they had the survivors of the seventeen Englishmen captured in one of the boats of the *Hector* at Surat; and, lastly, they had the survivors of fifteen of the crew of Captain Shar-

[1] See p. 269. [2] See p. 235.

peigh's ship *Ascension*, which had been wrecked off Chaul. The King of Spain's orders were that no foreigners should be permitted in the Portuguese territories, especially those who came in their own ships. So large a number of spying foreigners naturally alarmed the new viceroy, and he at once put the whole of them into prison. He might have put them to death, but at this time the Portuguese hatred of their Spanish masters induced them to be lenient towards others. De Tavora, therefore, was glad enough to get rid of the intruders by providing them with passages in the homeward-bound fleet.

It is chiefly in the course of his narrative of these last six months at Goa that Pyrard makes mention of some interesting characters. The foremost figure is that of André Furtado de Mendoça, the greatest Portuguese captain of his time, who had begun his service at the side of King Sebastian on the disastrous field of Alcazar-quivir in Morocco. Then we have that interesting personage, Archbishop Menezes, whose forcible conversion of the Nestorians to the Roman communion had no doubt won for him the patent of succession to the governorship of India. Then we have a pleasing picture of the Jesuit, Father Stephen, the first Englishman in India, the learned Father La Croiz, and the more famous Father Trigaut, who, with humanity and tact, performed the part of English and French ambassadors. Next we have our friend Richard Wickham, whom Pyrard describes as "a man of proud and noble bearing, like a captain", and who was afterwards to show his pride to Richard Cocks in Japan. At Goa, too, Pyrard met the well-known French traveller, Jean Mocquet, the keeper of Henry IV's museum at the Tuileries, and surgeon to the viceroy, Conde de Feira, and to the governor Furtado. He heard of, but did not see that more mysterious Frenchman, Henri de Feynes, otherwise the Count de Monfart, whose sketch of his wanderings, published in French under the one name and in English under the other, is so jejune as to have been deemed mendacious. Feynes' companion on the homeward voyage was the Portuguese captain, Bras Correa, the principal actor in, and survivor of the desperate engagement off Fayal in 1593, between the *Chagas* and three ships of the Earl of Cumberland, whose prisoner he was for a year afterwards in England. The history of that fight, of one ship against three, though far from agreeable to our national vanity, and incompatible with the notion that in the days of Elizabeth all the heroism and chivalry were on one side, will, we may hope, be some day unearthed from Purchas and De Couto and retold. The story of the *Chagas* has as worthy a place in Portuguese annals as has that of the *Revenge* in ours.

The general description of the city of Goa, then in the crisis of its fate, though enjoying its greatest commercial prosperity, needs no recommendation. The topographical passages are frequently interspersed with some picturesque incident or grave reflection; and written as they were from memory, are wonderfully accurate and minute. The government and social life of the Portuguese are described in terms which might be considered harsh if they were not true, and the absence of all malevolence in the description is seen in numerous kindly observations.

Following the description of Goa and of the far East, come chapters on the Portuguese settlements on the east coast of Africa, a description of Ormus, and lastly the cities on the coast of India north of Goa. With the exception of Diu and Cambaye, Pyrard does not seem to have visited any of these parts. They will not, however, be found wanting in interest. On the East African coast he deals successively with Mozambique, Sofala, and Mombasa. His references to the Zambesi and the gold mines of Monomotapa are of considerable interest, now that it is seen that the waterway of the Zambesi must become the principal means of access to the great lakes of Nyassa and Tanganyäka. To him, however, the more important subject was that of the two severe sieges which Mozambique had lately sustained from the Dutch. As he relates, the second, that in 1608 by Verhoeven, would in all probability have succeeded but for the desertion of three men from the Dutch ranks. One of these men, a Swiss, Pyrard met on the carrack in which he returned.[1]

[1] It is characteristic of the strange wanderings men had in in those days, that in 1601 this Swiss and a friend were serving under the Duke de Mercœur against the Turks in Hungary. His friend was taken prisoner by the Turks, and no doubt after perilous adventures found his way to Goa. The Swiss was with Mercœur when he died at Nuremberg in 1602, afterwards he took service

The description of Ormus contains a notice of the Prince Turun Shah, who had been executed a short time before at Goa, and some details as to the enormous profits gained by the Portuguese governors of that island-fortress, at which was centred the whole trade of Persia with India. Next follows a chapter on Diu, Cambaye, and Surat, including all that the traveller was able to learn of the Great Mogul. The trade of Cambaye which the Portuguese, by means of their fort at Diu, compelled to pass through their hands at Goa must have then been enormous in bulk. The *cafilas*, or merchant fleets under convoy, were in the habit of coming south to Goa twice or thrice a year, numbering in the aggregate 300 or 400 vessels, bringing chiefly indigo, as also wheat, vegetables, etc., in fact, the provisions of Portuguese Goa. At times some of these ships got astray, and were captured by the Malabar pirates, who were in the habit of running north at the proper seasons for the purpose, and Pyrard says that they but seldom failed to capture some of them.[1] "I have seen them while I was there (at Diu), seize at one swoop forty or fifty of them, and that was no uncommon occurrence."[2] A short account of Chaul and Bassein, at the latter of which the Portuguese got their timber and building stone, and constructed such ships as were built

with the Dutch, deserted to the Portuguese at Mozambique, and was taken to Goa, where he met his friend from whom he had been parted seven or eight years before in Hungary.

[1] See p. 246. [2] See p. 255.

in India, concludes the description of the Portuguese possessions.

As to the state of the Portuguese Government of India at this time, Pyrard's narrative, though not written in historical form, is a valuable instalment of history, and especially so because it almost exactly synchronizes with the hiatus in the Portuguese official chronicles. The *Decadas* of Barros, as continued by De Couto, extend only to the year 1600, that is, to the fourth year of the twelfth decade.[1] The so-called 13th Decade of Bocarro, which ought to have begun with the year 1607, does not take up the history till the viceroyalty of Azevedo in 1612. The gap of twelve years is to some extent bridged over by the recent publication of official documents by Mr. Rivara at Goa, and by the Royal Academy at Lisbon. In Fasciculo 1° of the *Archivo Portuguez Oriental*, Mr. Rivara publishes, among others, the letters from the King of Spain to the municipality of Goa in 1610 and 1611, and thirteen letters from the municipality to the king, ranging in date between 1600 and 1609. Fasciculo 6° of the same collection contains a collection of despatches and orders of the king, and proclamations of the viceroys, throughout the seventeenth century, and comprises much matter illustrative of the first ten years of the century. On the other hand, the Lisbon Academy, in their *Documentos Remettidos da India*, or *Livros das Monçoes*,

[1] The eleventh decade is lost, but in the Lisbon edition of 1788 the principal events are supplied from official sources by the editor.

three volumes of which have been issued (4to., 1880-5), publishes the despatches of the king to the viceroys, commencing with the year 1605.[1] These volumes, which are admirably edited, would prove a mine of interest to any historical student who may hereafter devote himself to the not uninteresting history of Portuguese India.

For the proper understanding of this volume, this introduction should comprise, first, a historical sketch of the rise and progress of the Portuguese dominion in India; secondly, an examination of the methods of Portuguese government and finance, of the connection between the king at Madrid or Valladolid and the *Casa da India*, or India Office, at Lisbon—between these authorities in Europe and the viceroy, and between the viceroy and the chief officers at Goa and the captains of forts; and, lastly, a *résumé* of the politics of Western Europe at the beginning of the seventeenth century. These neither my space nor my knowledge enables me to supply. Some general remarks may, however, serve to explain the remarkable events of those few years, when the dominion and prestige of the Portuguese in the East, after a hundred years' growth, fell irretrievably and suddenly as a house of cards.

The first fifty years of Portuguese India was, as "every schoolboy" knows, the age of heroes; they produced not only Da Gama, but the great Affonso

[1] The manuscripts of these despatches, ranging from 1605 to 1651, were returned from India by order of the king in 1777; the third volume, recently published, extends only to 1616.

d'Albuquerque, Francisco d'Almeida, and João de Castro. The deeds of these heroes are recorded as well by Correa and Barros, as by their individual biographers, and are still more widely famed by Camoens. By the time De Castro died in 1547, the main positions had all been won. Another fifty years brings us to 1597, fifty more years of monopoly undisputed by any European nation. This period we might suppose the Portuguese would have employed in consolidation, that so they might without fear have met their enemy in the gate. But the truth is, that their dominion could not be consolidated. It consisted only of a string of fortresses stretching round the vast coast line from the Cape of Good Hope to China. Throughout all these seas no merchantmen could safely pass without the Portuguese passport, and without paying the Portuguese dues. But the races who in their cities and villages were not actually under the Portuguese rule, had not forgotten the brighter days of the fifteenth century when the ocean trade was free, and the cosmopolitan Arab carried the chief part of the produce of both worlds. These people resented and ever continued to resent this novel dominion of the sea. Thus we find that so late as 1570, not only was there no consolidation, but that the empire was nearly extinguished by a great combination of native princes. In India, Chaul and Goa, and in the East, Malacca, were simultaneously besieged; while the Malabar corsairs, whose piracy was largely a national resistance, were never in fact put down or propitiated. At the end of the century as at the beginning they had enemies ever at their doors.

The conquests, such as they were, were made in the first half of the sixteenth century; during the second the Portuguese were hardly able to hold them against their native enemies. The modern Portuguese, with pardonable patriotism, are wont to attribute the loss of their eastern empire to the sixty years' subjection to Spain, which began in 1580.[1] But in truth that event only precipitated other causes of ruin. The prevailing characteristic of the first fifty years was ferocity[2]; that of the second

[1] I should, however, here refer, as an exception, to an excellent little book by G. de Magalhães Teixeira Pinto, chief judge of the court of Goa in 1823, published by Mr. Rivara in 1859, under the title *Memorias sobre as Possessões Portuguezes na Asia*, etc. The judge attributes the Portuguese misfortunes to the following causes:—(1) The great extent of the line of forts, the reinforcements for which, amounting to 3,000 men a year, drained Portugal and prevented any effective resistance being made to Spain in 1580; (2) the destruction of native commerce by the Portuguese monopoly; (3) religious fanaticism in war and in the Inquisition, wherein Christians proved themselves more cruel than Mahomedans; (4) bad policy of Albuquerque in selecting Goa as his capital, and in extending the Portuguese conquests to Malacca, whereas the dominion ought not to have been carried beyond Cape Comorin; (5) the bad government, one of the chief causes of which was the shortness of the viceroy's term of office. The Judge admits that the Spanish domination was only the finishing stroke, and that if another was wanted, it was found in the imbecility of the government of Philip III.

[2] The conduct of the great De Castro and his captains at the siege of Diu, towards the close of this period, may serve for an example:—"The first that entered the city was D. John, then D. Alvaro and D. Emanuel de Lima, and the Governor, all several

was dishonesty. Throughout the whole period the religion of Christ was invoked for the sanction of acts of cruelty and oppression, hardly surpassed even in the annals of the East. Nor was it alone in the later years of the century that the fidalgos led notoriously evil lives in India. What manner of men they were before 1550, when measured by a high standard of morality, appears in the pathetic letters

ways, making the streets and houses run with blood. The women escaped not the fate of the men, and children were slain at their mothers' breasts, one stroke taking away two lives" (*Faria y Sousa*, iii, 113). Diu they meant to keep, and resisting cities have always suffered hardly; let us see, therefore, how they dealt with territories they had no intention of keeping. Immediately after the siege D. Emanuel de Lima, by De Castro's order, "scoured the coast of Cambaya with 30 ships, extirpating all the towns on that shore. The city of Goga, one of the chief of that kingdom, was taken without resistance, the inhabitants flying to the mountains. It was plundered and burnt: then pursuing the inhabitants they were found at night about a league off, asleep, and all put to the sword. All the cattle in the fields were either killed or hamstrung. This was done in several other towns, and with many ships along the coast of Broach" (*Ibid.*, p. 114). De Castro then enjoyed his Roman triumph at Goa. Subsequently Broach was entered by one Menezes, "who entered it by night, killing many asleep and others as they awaked. The city could not be maintained, and therefore was plundered and burnt" (*Ibid.*, p. 119). Soon after, Castro himself marched to the coast, where he left neither town, wood, nor flock or herd of cattle that could be seen but what he destroyed with fire and sword" (*Ibid.*, p. 121). The next year Castro "began in January at the river Charope, two leagues from Goa. He spared neither living creature, vegetable, nor the very stones, but burnt and slaughtered all as far as the city Dabul", etc. (*Ibid.*, p. 125). This took place two leagues from Goa more than thirty years after the Conquest. Fifty years later the inhumanity of Azevedo in Ceylon was rewarded with the viceroyalty.

of Francis Xavier, and may be seen even in the eulogies of their historians. Still it is true that from 1580 onwards corruption spread rapidly throughout the whole of the Portuguese service in the East. No moral obligation was felt by the Portuguese in India to aid in filling the coffers of a Spanish king. Offices not in the gift of the king, and probably those too, were privately bought and sold; heinous offences were condoned,[1] trials indefinitely postponed, and judgments left unsatisfied by bribery of the judges and the governors. Gross misappropriation of the public money went unpunished, and left the treasury unable to pay the legal claims of the soldiers and minor officials, who had not access to the public chest. The law was widely different both in its provisions and in the manner of its execution, as between Europeans and natives.

As regards slavery, Goa was like a colony of Sir John Lubbock's ants; not only did the Portuguese do no manual labour himself, he subsisted upon the labour of his slaves. According to Pyrard, Portu-

[1] "I am also informed", writes the king in 1591, "that the Viceroys and Governors of India with much laxity grant pardons in cases of the penalty of death and perpetual exile, contrary to the form of my ordinances and of the regulations sent by me to the High Court of Goa, and because one of the principal obligations incumbent upon you in that Government is the care and concern with which you ought to proceed in all matters of justice, and because from this large exercise of the pardoning power no amendment can be looked for in the numerous cases of atrocities committed in those parts, I enjoin and charge you again most earnestly to act in this matter, as I hope and feel sure you will." (*Arch. Port. Or.*, Fasc. 3, No. 83.)

guese ladies seem not to have been ashamed to share in the more disgraceful earnings of their female slaves.[1] It is needless to say that all slaves were treated worse than dogs. An *alvará* of the king dated 1599, begins in this wise: "To all to whom this my order shall come, I the king give you to understand that I am informed that in the city of Goa, and in other cities, fortresses, and places in the parts of India, the captive slaves are chastised by their masters with much rigour, being put to severe and painful torture by cruel and exquisite means, whereby many die in the said torture, or afterwards die thereof, and that to conceal the evil so done the masters bury them in their houses and gardens, whereby great scandal results," etc.[2] In justice to the king, it must be added that the *alvará* goes on to order that murder of slaves is to be punished in the same manner as that of free men. Their general treatment, however, continued to be so bad that Pyrard assigns it as one of the chief causes of the Portuguese misfortunes.[3]

Should the Hakluyt Society publish its promised edition of the *Soldado Pratico* of De Couto, corroborated as it can be, and as we hope it will be, by references to historical facts and official documents, it will be seen that the charges brought against the Portuguese in regard to the government of their dependencies do not err on the side of overstatement.

In the meantime I will present, as an epitome of

[1] See p. 67.

[2] *Arch. Port. Or.*, Fasc. 3, No. 372.

[3] See p. 210.

the Portuguese system, a document which is in its way quite a curiosity, and may be given here as being dated only four short years after Pyrard's departure from India. The exigencies of the poor Spanish king were then even greater than in the days with which we are now concerned, while the public morality was at a still lower ebb. Affairs were in a desperate condition when a happy thought seems to have struck some administrative genius, that it would be as well if the money paid for offices in India were paid into the royal treasury instead of into the purses of the governors and their satellites. However that may be, on the 2nd May 1614, King Philip III, or rather we may assume the Duke of Lerma, sent out to India an *alvará* (order in council) in the following terms[1]:—

> "To all to whom this my order shall come, I the King make known that, for just and great considerations of my service, and for the preservation and defence of my estate of India, and for the common good of the vassals and inhabitants thereof, all which move me hereto, and for a remedy of the public necessities which cannot at present be speedily repaired from my treasury, however important they be, I do order that for this time only, and for the term of three years, all the fortresses,[2] offices, and voyages[3] of that estate be sold, with liberty to such persons as shall buy the same to enter thereupon, in pre-

---

[1] It is No. 353 in Fasc. 6° of *Archivo Portuguez Oriental*, Goa, 1875.

[2] *I.e.*, the captaincies of the fortresses.

[3] The right of making a voyage to a particular place or region, or merely taking the profits of such voyage, untrammelled by dues. See pp. 173, 174.

cedence of all others already appointed thereto,[1] but after the same are vacated by the persons in possession at the date of the sale; and by this my order I do give power, commission, and all such sufficient authority as he may require, to Dom Jeronimo d'Azevedo, my councillor and viceroy of the said estate of India, so that he shall have power in my name to make, and that he do make such sales to the persons who shall bid highest at public auction, which shall be conducted in the presence of him and of the officers of my treasury, in manner accustomed at the auction of the royal rents, and subject to the regulations now ordered by me to be sent to the said viceroy, which will enable him upon the said sales to make the necessary contracts and writings, and to pass the patents and appointments in respect of the fortresses, offices, and voyages, so to be sold, to the persons who shall purchase them, and to sign the same in my name so that they have effect in the form aforesaid, and to cause the purchasers to be put in possession without dispute or any prohibition, such as otherwise might be alleged by those already appointed by reason of their being about to enter, or of the long subsistence of their letters patent, which, granted in satisfaction of services or for other cause, may have been signed by me and passed by my Chancery; inasmuch as for this time only, and for the term of three years, and for the causes and reasons herein stated, I abrogate them and hold

[1] Every French soldier is said to carry a field-marshal's bâton in his knapsack. It is more matter of fact that numbers of Portuguese carried appointments to offices for years in their pockets. While A was in office, B, C, D, etc., all had their patents of succession in turn as vacancies should occur. Nor were these grants strictly confined to the male sex. In many cases the captaincies of forts and offices of financial trust were granted in effect to widows and orphan girls, in reward of the services of their husbands or fathers. Such appointments were made in favour of "whomsoever she may marry."

> them so abrogated, preserving, however, their force and vigour for the future, and directing that on the expiration of that time they shall have their effect according to the priority of each in date, and I direct, and my will is that this shall have force and vigour, and that my orders in this respect be executed in their entirety, in like manner as if this were a letter (*Carta*) commenced in my name and sealed with my seal depending, notwithstanding the ordinance of Book II, tit. 40, which says," etc., etc.

The King of Spain, in whose name this strange edict was issued, was the same of whom Pyrard speaks throughout his book in terms of distant awe. So, too, unless we knew more of Philip III than poor Pyrard did, might we look back with some respect upon the original of the fine equestrian statue in the Plaza Mayor of Madrid, in the production of which artistic falsehood the talents of Pantoja and John of Bologna are said to have been combined, or the equally noble equestrian portrait of him by Velasquez, in the museum of the Prado. Fortunately, however, for the verification of history, we have a truer portrait of this great king from the hand of the Venetian ambassador at his court, and we now know that Philip III was a very little man, with pink cheeks, flaxen hair, and yellow beard, with a melancholy expression of eye, and the protruding under lip and jaw of his Austrian race. Not only of less than mediocre size, he was beneath mediocrity in mind, and had scarcely any education. His evenings were spent in his favourite pursuits of dancing and gambling; his days in moodily wandering among his woods and in shooting rabbits. His chief ailments were the result of gluttonous over-eating. The affairs of Mexico and Peru, of the East Indies and his European dominions he left to his master, and their real ruler, the Duke of Lerma. He is believed not to have known the purport of any state document to which his signature or seal was attached.[1]

In another respect than that of the state of their government, namely, in seamanship, the Portuguese were severely handicapped in the struggle with the Dutch and English. The experience of a whole century of annual voyages had not taught them the virtues of small and handy ships, such as were at that time used by the Dutch and English discoverers. They continued long after the severe lessons taught them by Drake and Cumberland to build and overload huge carracks of 1,500 and 2,000 tons burthen, which were unwieldy alike in storm and in fight. Crowded with passengers they were kept in the filthiest possible condition[2]; scurvy and dysentery frequently reduced the crew and passengers by one half in a voyage, while most of the remainder had to be sent to hospital. Such tales of this terrible ordeal would be told by the survivors who lived to return to Portugal, that it is no wonder that few volunteered, and that the outward bound ships had to be filled with

[1] For references to the Venetian documents see Motley, *United Netherlands*, vol. iii.

[2] See Mocquet's account of his voyage out to India in 1608, also *infra*, p. 196.

kidnapped boys,[1] and the armies of India recruited with malefactors.[2] During the first few years of the Dutch irruption the Portuguese made a show of resistance, but by Pyrard's time they had come to think only of their lives, and as the Dutch always gave quarter they sought it when they could not escape. "Now", says our author, "they fight no more."

The aim of the Dutch, who appeared in the Eastern seas for the first time in 1597, was to tap the markets which the Portuguese did not control, or at any rate to attack the Portuguese chain of monopoly at its weakest point. They chose their ground in the Eastern Archipelago, and chiefly in the Molucca group. After 1600 they were joined in that region by the English, whose motives were the same, and all went well for the trading companies of the two nations—so long as Elizabeth lived. It was an evil day for England, and especially for the rising East India Company, when James deserted the Dutch cause and made his treaty of 1604 with Spain. Hence flowed the malignant churlishness of the Dutch towards the English of Middleton's expedition of 1606, which contrasts so strangely with the friendliness shown to Lancaster in 1602. Hence, too, in after days ensued the terrible massacre of Amboyna, which wrung the heart of England for half a century, and was never avenged. England had as yet put little of her strength into the work, and that little was insufficient to cope with the superior energy of

[1] See p. 193. [2] See p. 143.

the Dutch. But the success of the latter in the Archipelago, where their profits were enormous from the first, to some extent diverted their attention from India proper, upon which they made only occasional enterprises, and those chiefly on the coasts of Coromandel, Bengal, and Pegu. So it was that in 1608, when the Dutch had in fact almost broken down the Portuguese monopoly, the English, shirking greater endeavours in the far east, essayed to start a factory at Surat, and to send an embassy to the Great Mogul.

The policy of the two races who were in turn the successors of the Portuguese, at this time presents a marked contrast, attributable to the state of affairs in Europe. The United Provinces were approaching the end of their long struggle for independence, which as yet had not been formally admitted. During the last years of the struggle, while Maurice played a slow chess game with Spinola in the Low Countries, the Dutch policy was to strike hard at sea and in the Indies. Their achievements during the last three or four years were indeed brilliant. Van der Hagen took the Moluccas in 1605; Matelief besieged Malacca and destroyed the Portuguese fleet in 1606; in the following year Heemskerk destroyed the Spanish fleet in the Bay of Gibraltar, and Van Caerden demolished the town, and nearly took the fortress, of Mozambique. The fear of losing the Indies was the strongest argument which weighed with Spain when she yielded to the terms of the truce of 1609.

England, on the other hand, had no such desperate

game to play. The affairs of the East India Company were not yet a national question, and the merchants of the first voyages were instructed to find cargoes where they could, and establish factories as far as was possible in unoccupied places. This policy was continued throughout the seventeenth century; and while the Dutch were occupied in the warlike enterprises which were signalised by the capture of Malacca in 1640, of Calicut and Colombo in 1656, and of Cochin and the other Malabar forts in 1660-4, the English had unobtrusively established factories round both coasts of India, and prepared the way for the great events of the succeeding century. It is a curious fact that the capture of Ormus in 1622, in which a small body of English assisted the Persians, was the only occasion on which our countrymen fought the Portuguese by land. Nor since the death of Elizabeth had there been any serious combats with the Portuguese in the eastern seas; and it is probably due to the Elizabethan prestige, which the misgovernment and incapacity of James had not yet wholly destroyed, that Englishmen were, as Pyrard states, acknowledged to be "kings of the sea".

The history of Portuguese India subsequent to the departure of our traveller does not concern us here. The empire of the sea had already vanished; the Portuguese restrictions and passport regulations were soon disregarded, and could not be enforced, and trade found new channels and new marts. As regards territory, some of the most notable losses have already been stated. Their fortresses and factories in

Malabar, in Ceylon, and in the Eastern Archipelago were forcibly wrested from them by the Dutch; the few still remaining to them on the western coast of India have been left to them by the English as undesirable or unnecessary acquisitions. Chaul and Bassein, it is true, are now British, but they were taken, not from the Portuguese, but from their intermediate conquerors, the Mahrattas. Diu and Goa still remain in Portuguese occupation, but their possession is rather as custodians of some ancient monument than as administrators of an integral part of modern India.

Of the remains of great Goa I have been enabled to give some illustrations to this volume from a collection of photographs obtained for me by my friend Mr. W. Lee Warner, Secretary to Government at Bombay. The interior of the Franciscan church is given as a sample of the fine proportions and elaborate decoration of the Goa churches. This edifice, 190 feet in length and 60 feet in breadth, is described by Careri as "one of the best churches in Goa, with a roof curiously adorned with fretwork, and it is like one entire mass of gold, there being so much of this metal on its altars." "It recalls to memory", says Fonseca, "the numerous triumphs which were commemorated within its walls amid pomp and pageantry, the solemnity with which crowds of proselytes were baptised, the *autos da fé* celebrated in the presence of the viceroy and his court, and the funeral obsequies of many illustrious persons."

The magnificent shrine of St. Francis Xavier, the gift of the Grand Duke of Tuscany, of which an illustration is given opposite page 62, is likely to remain the most enduring memorial of Portuguese India. On the last exposition of the body of the Apostle, in 1859, it is computed that no less than 200,000 persons collected from all parts to do homage at this shrine.

The Arch of the Viceroys, which is presented opposite p. 47, was built in 1597-9 by the viceroy Francisco da Gama, principally to commemorate his grandfather, the great discoverer, whose statue appears in the lower niche. Above is seen the image in bronze of St. Catherine, the patroness of Goa. Between the niches runs the following legend:

"REINĀDO EL R. D. PIELIPE I° POS A CIDADE AQUI DOM VASCO DA GAMA I° CO|NDE ALMIRANTE DESCOBRIDOR E CONQUISTADOR DA INDIA SENDO VI|ZOREI O CONDE DOM FRANCISÇO DA GAMA SEU BISNETO. O ANNO D. 97. JULIUS SIMON. ING. MA. INV."[1]

Soon after the erection of this arch, which Francisco da Gama had compelled the municipality to build against their will, the count's enemies (who were many) suborned a French engineer to remove and cast down the statue of Vasco, which was done secretly by night; the discoverer was quartered in contempt of his unpopular grandson, and the broken pieces were exposed in different parts of the town. The statue now seen in the niche was substituted a year or two later.

[1] F. N. Xavier, *Ser. Chron.*, pp. 7, 8.

The portraits of the two governors of India of this period, the Archbishop Menezes (opp. p. 89) and André Furtado de Mendoça (opp. p. 267), have been obtained from the Resende MS. at the British Museum through the courtesy of Mr. W. de Gray Birch and the Trustees.

The number of illustrations thus selected as of especial value in connection with the narrative, has prevented me from utilising some interesting photographs of Portuguese Malacca which were sent to me by my friend, Sir Frederick Dickson, K.C.M.G., whose kindness I desire here to acknowledge.

Finally, I would record my obligations (which I omitted by an oversight to express in the introduction to vol. i) to Mr. W. Logan, of the Madras Civil Service, for his assistance in the elucidation of some topographical and other details in the author's description of the Malabar coast.

It has been found necessary, owing to the unusual proportions of these volumes, to divide the second, for purposes of publication, into two Parts. The author's departure from Goa seems a fitting point at which to close the first; in the second will be found the description of the homeward voyage, the residence in Brazil, and the supplementary chapters.

A. G.

CHRONOLOGY OF PYRARD'S VOYAGE.

(VOL. II.)

INCLUDING PRINCIPAL EVENTS MENTIONED OR REFERRED TO.

	1598.	Philip II assigns the sovereignty of the Netherlands to the Archduke Charles and the Infanta Isabella; death of Philip II, and accession of Philip III.
13 Feb.	1600.	First Voyage of English East India Company, under Lancaster (returned Sept. 1603).
16 March	,,	Capture of Kunhali's fort by Furtado de Mendoça.
25 Dec.	,,	Ayres de Saldanha assumes office as 17th Viceroy of India.
18 May	1601.	The *Croisant* and *Corbin* leave S. Malo.
July	1602.	Wreck of the *Corbin* at the Maldives.
	1603.	Death of Queen Elizabeth; accession of James I.
23 March	1604.	Second Voyage of English East India Company, under H. Middleton (returned 1606).
17 April	,,	Van der Hagen before Mozambique.
	1605.	Capture of Amboyna and the Moluccas by the Dutch under Van der Hagen.
Jan.	,,	Martim Affonso de Castro assumes office as 18th Viceroy of India.
	1606.	Expedition of the Spaniards to the Moluccas; capture of Ternaté and Tidoré.
May	,,	De Castro with powerful fleet leaves Goa for Malacca; Archbishop Menezes, Governor of India.
30 May	,,	Siege of Malacca by the Dutch, under Matelief.
June	,,	Matelief destroys the Portuguese fleet.
	,,	Third Voyage of English East India Company, under Keeling and Hawkins.
Feb.	1607.	Pyrard leaves the Maldives for Chittagong.
,,	,,	Commencement of peace negotiations in the Netherlands.
29 March	,,	First siege of Mozambique, by Van Caerden (raised, 29th June).

25 April	1607.	Destruction of the Spanish fleet in Gibraltar Bay, by Heemskerk; death of Heemskerk.
4 May	,,	Armistice between Spain and the United Provinces.
May-June	,,	Residence of Pyrard with the Malabar pirates.
3 June	,,	Death of the Viceroy de Castro at Malacca.
June	,,	Arrival of Pyrard at Calicut.
17 Oct.	,,	Arrival of P. van Caerden with Dutch fleet before Goa.
Feb.	1608.	Pyrard leaves Calicut; taken prisoner to Cochin.
29 March	,,	Conde de Feira leaves Lisbon as 19th Viceroy.
15 May	,,	Conde de Feira dies off coast of Guinea.
June	,,	Pyrard arrives at Goa.
28 July	,,	Second siege of Mozambique, by Verhoeven (raised, 24th August).
24 Aug.	,,	Arrival of W. Hawkins at Surat; he proceeds to Agra.
(?) Sept.	,,	Pyrard visits Diu and Cambaye.
17-27 Sept.	,,	Verhoeven with Dutch fleet blockades Goa.
(?) Oct.	,,	Pyrard leaves Goa with the Portuguese fleet for Ceylon and Malacca.
Feb.	1609.	Departure of the traveller H. de Feynes (Count de Monfart) from Goa.
8 April	,,	Truce of twelve years between Spain and the United Provinces, signed at the Hague.
26 May	,,	Arrival of the traveller Mocquet at Goa.
27 May	,,	D. André Furtado de Mendoça assumes office as Governor of India.
5 Sept.	,,	D. Ruy Lourenço de Tavora assumes office as 20th Viceroy of India.
21 Sept.	,,	Edict for the expulsion of the Moors from Spain.
26 Dec.	,,	Departure of Furtado and Mocquet from Goa.
3 Feb.	1610.	Departure of Pyrard from Goa in the *N. S. de Jesus*.
14 May	,,	Assassination of Henry IV of France.
31 May	,,	The *N. S. de Jesus* doubles the Cape.
25 June	,,	Arrival at St. Helena.
10 Aug.	,,	Arrival at Bahia; discharge and abandonment of the carrack.
7 Oct.	,,	Pyrard embarks in a Flemish hulk for Europe.
3 Nov.	,,	Pernambuco sighted.
5 Jan.	1611.	The Azores sighted.
15 Jan.	,,	Pyrard lands at the Bayonne islands, and proceeds to Santiago Compostella.
3 Feb.	,,	Pyrard embarks at Corunna for La Rochelle.
5 Feb.	,,	Arrival at La Rochelle.
16 Feb.	,,	Returns to Laval.

ADDENDA ET CORRIGENDA.

Page 4, line 6 from bottom, for "hours", read "days".

Page 12, line 4 from top, for "then", read "there".

Page 18, line 9 from top, for "this one", read "the large one".

Page 21, line 15 from top, omit "had".

Page 22, line 17 from top, omit "that", and insert "Gaspard Aleman by name, who".

Page 32, line 10 from bottom, for "miles", read "leagues".

Page 32, last line, for "each has its parish church and others", read "the island has its parishes, as well as other churches".

Page 33, line 2 from top, for "Daugin", read "d'Augin".

Page 33, line 4 from bottom, for "ticket or token", read "stamp or mark"; and for "They carry this ticket wet with ink", read "The stamp is steeped in ink and applied".

Page 33, line 3 from bottom, omit "clapping it on there".

Page 35, line 8 from top, for "three", read "very".

Page 46, line 16 from bottom, for "less", read "more".

Page 47, line 8 from top, after "seen", insert "The gate of this esplanade is near the great gate of the town, which is beneath the viceroy's palace".

Page 52, line 5 from top, for "*ruo*", read "street".

Page 62, line 5 from top, for "1553", read "1552".

Page 83, line 2 from bottom, for "to officers", read "in offices".

Page 89, line 17 from top, for "a dish", read "dishes".

Page 95, line 11 from top, after "him", insert "for I came away at the time".

Page 105, line 18 from top, for "crossings", read "crossways".

Page 106, note 2, for "January", read "February".

Page 114, line 1, add note, "Probably miswritten for *Moe tol*, the first part of the word being the Maldive *moya*, 'foolish'."

Page 116, line 7 from bottom, *dele* "and".

Page 120, note 2, for "envooloit", read "enrooloit".

Page 121, note 2; so, too, De Couto makes his *Soldado* say, "Just as the poets relate that those who passed the river Lethe lost all memory, so do most of the viceroys on rounding the Cape of Good Hope lose everything, including fear of God and of the King" (*Soldado Pratico*, Sc. 6).

Page 124, line 5 from bottom, for "Ten", read "Twelve".

Page 131, line 2 from end of chapter, for "six sols", read "five sols".

Page 145, line 2, The king whom André Furtado conquered was not Don Juan, but the Tamil King of Jaffna.

Page 203, note, for "Portuguese merchants", read "Portuguese Jews".

DEDICATORY EPISTLE.

TO

MESSIRE

CHARLES DURET,

Sieur de Chevry, Councillor of the King in his Council of State and Privy Council, President of his Chamber of Accounts in Paris, and Intendant of his Finances.

MONSEIGNEUR,

I remember, when I had the honour to present to you the first edition of my book, that you not only deigned to receive it with a favourable eye, but also made me so sensible of the effects of your courtesy and liberality, that I have felt myself under great obligation to you from that time on. I have also become aware how your generous courage hath ever led you to all noble and virtuous actions, and how the great offices whereto your merit hath enabled you to attain were alike suitable to your capacity and justly your due. I must frankly avow that all this hath made so deep an impression upon my mind, that for a recognition, according to the littleness of my power, of the benefits and honour which I have received of you, I have deemed it my duty, in acknowledgment of your many praiseworthy qualities, to dedicate to you this second part of my book; wherein you will find, far more amply than in preceding impressions, the continuation of my voyages, and the story of misfortunes and adventures no less various than strange and even wondrous. This, MONSEIGNEUR, *I humbly beseech you to accept as favourably as I freely offer it, and at the same time to collect as it were the last planks of my shipwreck, and to take into your particular protection my miserable fortunes, which for the future I shall esteem happy, if so be that they receive that strong aid which I have ever expected of your natural bounty and humanity; these your qualities I am constrained to publish abroad, as one who is resolved to remain for the rest of his days,*

MONSEIGNEUR,

Your very humble and obedient servant,

FRANÇOIS PYRARD.

CONTENTS OF THE SECOND VOLUME.

(PART I.)

CHAPTER XX.

CHAPTER XXI.

CHAPTER XXII.

SECOND PART

OF THE

VOYAGE OF FRANÇOIS PYRARD,

FROM HIS ARRIVAL AT GOA TO HIS RETURN TO FRANCE.

I THINK I have been not ill-advised in dividing my voyage into two parts, and thus making a separation; for this good reason, that after so many years of travail, perils, and misery, there must be some point at which the attentive reader —who, I am assured, has had his share of the fatigue— may conveniently pause for refreshment. Nor, perhaps, could I have divided the story of my voyage at a more fitting juncture. For although the greater part of it remains to be told,—viz., not only the return home, diversified as that was by perils and accidents, but also the sojourn at Goa, and the voyage to Sunda and the Moluccas,—yet was all that mere child's-play in comparison of the tribulation and misfortunes of the first part. Such was my despair of ever again seeing my native land, that the arrival at Goa is like a revival of hope, and the commencement of a happier fortune. Add that thenceforward I have always lived among Christians, and no longer, as before, under subjection to infidels, deprived of the exercise of our Holy Religion.

CHAPTER I.

Arrival at Goa, and description of the hospitals and prisons there.

On our arrival at Goa—the principal seat of Portuguese Government in India, the residence of the Viceroy and the Archbishop, situate under the altitude of 16 degrees towards the Arctic Pole,[1]—the general of the fleet that had brought us from Cochin, by name *Don Francisque de Meneiso,*[2] a near relative of the Archbishop[3] (who was then holding the place of the Viceroy, the latter[4] having died at Malaca, as I shall relate hereafter), sent orders to the captain of the galiot wherein I was to remove the irons from my feet and send me to him. The captain replied that I was so ill that I could not stir, or that I must be carried to the Royal Hospital rather than elsewhere, seeing I was in such a sick and wounded condition. This was done, and the irons were removed from my other foot; and I verily believe that the Holy Spirit had then touched the heart of this captain, who had theretofore been so barbarous and cruel towards me, for none could be more kindly and merciful than he then became. The good monk, *Frère Manuel de Christo,*[5] gave me his benediction, and bade me adieu, both of us shedding tears, saying that he could not hope to see me again for a long while, as his sojourn at Goa was but short, seeing that full soon he was departing for *Chaoul*[6] in the north. So we parted, to my great sorrow, and to his also.

[1] More precisely, 15° 31′ N.

[2] This Francisco de Menezes does not seem to be mentioned elsewhere. The captain of Cochin at this time was of the same name (see vol. i, 441); as also was the governor of Brazil (see below, ch. xxvi).

[3] Fr. Aleixo de Menezes.

[4] Martin Affonso de Castro (see ch. xi).

[5] *Supra*, vol. i, 441, 451.

[6] Chaul (see further, ch. xix).

The captain having received the general's command to have me carried to the hospital, had me landed by means of the seamen or *Lascares*,[1] who laid me on the beach along with one of my companions, who was also sick of an ulcer, the result of a wound in the foot, where gangrene had set in for want of proper treatment, and so grievously that he was like to die.

We were borne to the hospital by Caffres, who do the work of porters and carriers, no carriages being used there. They put us down upon seats at the gate and in the shade. There we remained a full hour, the officers of the hospital being at dinner, for it was about mid-day. Viewing it from the outside we could hardly believe it was a hospital; it seemed to us a grand palace, saving the inscription above the gate, *Hospitale del Rey nostro Seignoro.* On one side of the gate are the arms of Castille and of Portugal[2]; on the other those of the Portuguese Indies, viz., a sphere. At length we were admitted within a large gateway, where were a number of chairs and seats, upon which they lay the sick as they come in from time to time. Nothing is done until the physician, surgeon, or apothecary has seen them and certifies that they are sick, and of what ailment, that so they be placed in the proper part of the building. We were examined with many others that were there, including some people of quality that were brought in *palanquins*,[3] or litters. We were then carried

[1] See vol. i, p. 438.

[2] Mr. Rivara doubts whether the arms of Castille were here at all, for the two crowns of Spain and Portugal were never in fact united, and throughout the Spanish domination India was governed from Lisbon as a dependency of Portugal. The hospital is now in ruins, and the arms in question have disappeared. However, the arms of the two crowns are never elsewhere found in conjunction. I may remark, too, that letters of this period from the King of Spain to native princes invariably run—"I, Philip King of Portugal" (without mention of Spain); and that Philip II of Spain became Philip I of Portugal, and so on.

[3] Hind. *pālkī*, Pāli *pallanko*, Skt. *palyaṅka* (see further Yule's *Gloss.*, *s. v.* "Palankeen"). The form in use at Goa is seen by Linschoten's illustration of it.

up a lofty and magnificent stone staircase, all the sick being kept in the upper story, and none below, except when the number is very great,—as, for instance, on the arrival of the carracks from Portugal. As soon as we had our place assigned to us, the Jesuit doctor and superintendent of the house ordered that we should be properly attended to; so it was that two beds were brought for us. As soon as a sick person is cured and gone forth, his bed (called *esquif*[1]) is removed with all its apparel. Thus there are no beds made except there be sick to occupy them. These beds were speedily prepared. They are beautifully shaped, and lacquered with red varnish; some are chequered and some gilded; the sacking is of cotton, and the pillows of white calico filled with cotton; the mattresses and coverlets are of silk or cotton, adorned with different patterns and colours. These are called *Gouldrins.*[2] The sheets, etc., are of very fine white cotton. Then came a barber, who shaved all our hair off; then an attendant brought water and washed us all over, and gave us drawers, a white shirt, a cap, and slippers, and also placed beside us a fan and an earthenware bottle of water for drinking, and a chamber-pot, besides a towel and a handkerchief, which were changed every three hours. We had nothing to eat at that time, for we had to await the ordinary. Be it noted that the superiors and officers of this hospital are Portuguese; the servants are Bramenis, or Christian Canarins of Goa, who have to feed and attend upon the sick with great care, and to be always at hand, and who dare not disobey any

[1] Port. *esquife*, "a narrow bedstead used in hospitals or for the siesta" (D. Vieira); "petit canot, cercueil, petit lit d'hôpital" (Roquette). In French it was, formerly at least, used both for a bier and a small boat; our "skiff" has only the latter meaning.

[2] Hindustānī *gūdrī*, a quilt. Below (ch. xix) he mentions them by their Portuguese name, *colcha*. Linschoten (i, 62) combines the two: "They make also faire coverlits which they call Godoriins Colchas, which are very fair and pleasant, stitched with silke, and also of cotton of all colours and stitchings."

sick person when he asks anything in reason. These are salaried servants; and the Portuguese officers every hour visit all the sick to see if they want anything, and whether they be doing anything prejudicial to their health, or contrary to the doctor's orders.

In the evening they brought us supper at the appointed hour, to each a large fowl roasted, with some dessert, so we were astonished at the good cheer we received. Next morning we were surprised to see our other companion, who came not only to see us, as we supposed, but by command of the general, who gave him an order to be brought there, and a recommendation to the Father superintendent, although he was only suffering from fatigue. We did not know the reason of this at the time, but afterwards learned that he was anxious not to be treated as a prisoner any sooner than we were; but more of this anon.

This hospital[1] is, as I believe, the finest in the world, whether for the beauty of the building and its appurtenances, the accommodation being in all respects excellent, or for the perfect order, regulation, and cleanliness observed, the great care taken of the sick, and the supply of all comforts that can be wished for, whether in regard to doctors, drugs, and appliances for restoring health, the food that is given to eat, or the spiritual consolation that is obtainable at any hour.

[1] The Royal Hospital of Goa was certainly a splendid institution, and this account of it is the best extant. Linschoten mentions it without detail (i, 237); V. le Blanc says it excelled that of the Holy Ghost at Rome, or the Infirmary of Malta. It was founded by Albuquerque, on the capture of the city, and was the care and pride of successive kings and viceroys (see numerous references to it in the *Liv. das Monç.* and the *Arch. Port. Or.*). No doubt the order and regularity, the cleanliness and good living, readily won the admiration of a traveller who had gone through so much as Pyrard: these were provided under an elaborate code of rules (given in the *Arch. Port. Or.*, Fasc. 5, No. 838). There was, however, something radically wrong in its management, and our author curiously mentions below the frightful death-rate at this time, without casting any reflections on the authorities.

It is of very great extent, situated on the banks of the river, and endowed by the Kings of Portugal with 25,000 *perdos*[1] (each worth 25 sols of our money, and in that country 32½ sols), let alone the endowments and presents which it receives from the lords. This is a large revenue for the purpose in those parts, seeing food is so cheap, and the management so good; for the Jesuits who carry it on send as far as Cambaye and elsewhere for wheat, provisions, stuffs, and all other necessaries. It is managed and governed by the Jesuits,[2] who appoint a Father to the post of governor.. The other officers are Portuguese, all men of quality and gentility; as for the servants and slaves, they are Christian Indians. The Jesuit Father is superior over all the rest, who are like the inmates of a large monastery, each having his own office; even the porter at the gate is one of them. These officers chide the sick much, and rate them when they see them do anything they ought not to do; but the servants durst not say a word. The slaves do all the vile and dirty work, going every day through all the chambers of the sick with large pitchers, whereinto they void all the vessels, scrubbing and cleaning everything. There are private places with large earthenware basins for the necessities of the sick; these are emptied out by the slaves, who also bleach, wash, and dry all the linen, and perform other services within the hospital walls. There are physicians, surgeons, and apothecaries, barbers and bleeders, who do nothing else, and are bound to visit each of the sick twice a day. The apothecary is one of the household, and lives in the hospital, and has his shop well

[1] See Col. Yule's long article on the *pardão* (*Gloss.*, Supplt.). It was the same as the *xeraphin*, five tangas. At this time, by Col. Yule's reasoning, which seems conclusive, it was worth from 4*s.* 2*d.* to 4*s.* 6*d.*, which would make the endowment considerably over £5,000.

[2] It was managed by the *Santa Casa de Misericordia* till 1591, in which year the Jesuits took it over at the king's request. In 1596 they gave it up, but resumed the management again in 1597 (*Fonseca*, pp. 229, 230).

stocked at the hospital's expense; but the physicians and surgeons are not of the household, having their residences in the town.

The sick are sometimes very numerous, and while I was there there were as many as 1,500,[1] all of them either Portuguese soldiers or men of other Christian races of Europe, of every profession and quality, who are all received; for the Indians are not taken in there, having a hospital apart, endowed by the townspeople, wherein are received only Christian Indians. There is still another hospital for the women of the Christian Indians, also endowed by the town, to which women only may go.

All the water which is drunk on the premises comes from *Banguenin*.[2] Twice a day the servants fetch large pitchers of this water, wherewith they fill the vessels of the sick, who may drink as much as they like. Each sick person has a little table by his side for keeping his conveniences upon.

The physicians, apothecaries, and surgeons visit the sick twice a day, at 8 o'clock in the morning and at 4 in the evening; when they enter a bell is rung for an advertisement, as also is done at the hours of meals. The masters, surgeons, and lords are assisted by many others in the applying of unguents and medicines. During these visits to the sick some servants of the hospital accompany them, bearing large lighted braziers, casting forth much incense and other aromatic odours.

Some Jesuit novices are employed in searching for and collecting old linen throughout the town for the use of the

[1] Linschoten (i, 237) says that 500 at least in the year entered it, "and never come forth till they are dead". Mandelslo, who visited it in 1639, says it was "able to lodge above a thousand sick persons" (p. 101).

[2] A small village in the parish of St. Peter, to the west of the city. The fountain of Banguenim was the most cherished possession of old Goa, being its sole good well (cf. *Linsch.*, i, 183; *V. le Blanc*, i, 77). It is almost superfluous, however, to quote the latter, as most of his facts and names as to Goa seem to be taken from Pyrard.

hospital, for new would not be proper. Servants follow the surgeons with large baskets of lint and prepared linen.

The Jesuit Fathers have taken this hospital in charge, and most worthily acquit themselves therein; were it in the hands of others it could hardly be maintained upon twice the present revenue. In this hospital are apartments for each ailment. No one is allowed to enter the precincts without being searched, to see if he be bringing to any sick person any article of food or drink injurious to his health. No arms are carried within : they must be left at the gate.

People are allowed to enter the hospital to visit their friends only between 8 o'clock and 11 in the morning, and after dinner between 3 and 6. The sick are allowed to eat with them; and when the servants see a friend come to visit a patient, they bring a larger portion than the ordinary. As much bread is given as is asked for. The loaves are small; sometimes three or four are brought for a single sick person, and very often they cannot eat one. Much would be lost if the loaves were larger, for a loaf once broken is never served a second time. The bread is very delicate, and is made by the bakers of the town by contract. There is no word of wine for the sick inmates, although they have a stock of wines of Spain, Portugal, and the Indies; but it is not allowed to be given without the doctor's order, and this is granted but rarely. They give them no less than a whole chicken, roast or boiled, or a half chicken, for they have no capons. If one desires or requires more he gets it. The sick are tended and treated there with all possible propriety and delicacy. Every three days they have an entire change of linen, which is of very fine cotton.

At 7 o'clock in the morning they bring the sick their breakfast of white wheaten bread, and rice cooked with milk and sugar; the rice is brought from Cambaye and Surrate. Water is drunk, wine not being allowed. At 10 o'clock dinner is brought, conformably to the doctor's orders, most frequently consisting of boiled or roast fowls, with preserves for dessert. At 5 o'clock supper is served; they get excellent soups, made of divers meats cooked with *Boues*,[1] which is a cooling fruit, as large as our cucumbers. These meats are mutton, fowl, and chicken, well served with rice. Meat is eaten every day, except by those who prefer eggs and fish on fast days: for they get anything they ask for, unless it is forbidden by the doctor. When the doctor makes his visits he is accompanied by a number of writers. In the first place the apothecary takes the names of such as have to receive anything in his line, and then what each has to get. The same is done by the surgeons, bleeders, and clerk of the kitchen. For a clerk of the kitchen goes twice a day to see all the sick, and writes down their names and what they like to eat, and that is brought to them; nor has anyone a fault to find for not getting his ordinary at the accustomed hour.

All the plates, bowls, and dishes are of China porcelain. After the dinner the Portuguese officers go and visit all the sick, asking aloud through all the rooms whether everyone has had his ordinary, and so they do after supper. All the sick are lodged separately, according to their ailments, and all the utensils even have their own rooms apart. All the cots are in one large place, with their bands to form the bed rolled up; in another all the pillows; in another all the mattresses, coverlets, and so with the sheets, shirts, and other linen for the use of the hospital. They have a large stock of drawers, without which no Portuguese in India ever sleeps: these reach down to the feet, because all their shirts are very short, coming down no lower than the mid-thigh. In the same way there are separate places for slippers,

[1] This would seem to be a kind of pumpkin, but I cannot trace the word. Mr. F. N. Xavier gives the word *Bus*, meaning cereals in general, in the *Novas Conquistas*. Rivara translates it *Bendés*, that is, the Bendy or bandicoy (*Abelmoschus esculentus*), as to which see Yule, *Gloss.*, *s. v.*

vessels, and pots of various use. As for shirts and drawers, hats, boots, stockings, nightcaps, and jackets, which they give the patients on their recovery, all these are kept separate. Of each of these articles there is so great a number that it would be impossible to keep them in order unless they were thus kept apart. So, too, with the food and provisions, each room has its own officer, who keeps the key, and puts into writing the account of the contents, whereof he gives a memorandum to the principal writer, who keeps an inventory of everything, even of the sick, their names, and the days of their arrival and departure. There is also a treasurer for the money. All these account to the Jesuit Father, who accounts to none.

The clerk keeps an account of all the gold, silver, clothes, goods, and other property of the sick, which he registers in presence of the Father and the other officers; the whole is made into a bundle, with a ticket bearing the name of the owner stitched upon the bundle, and put away in a separate room. Their soiled linen is washed for them. The sick, if they have the means, and are so minded, give something to the servants, and a general account is stated upon their departure,—for none of their own things are used in the hospital; and if a sick person dies all his property is carried off to the *Misericorde*.[1] If the deceased has made a will, the fraternity, called the *Hermanos de la Misericorde*, become his executors; if there is no will, they preserve the property and await news of the heirs: if these be found, all is delivered to them; but they always give a portion to the *Misericorde*. If no heir is found, then upon the return of the next post from Portugal, where the matter is advertised, the *Misericorde*

[1] The *Santa Casa de Misericordia* at Goa was an offshoot of the great charitable fraternity of Portugal, the *Irmandade de Misericordia*, which in 1498 superseded the *Irmandade de Piedade*. There were similar fraternities at Cochin, Chaul, Ormuz, etc. Mr. J. G. da Cunha says that the ruins of the Misericordia at Chaul are still known by the natives by the name *Misri*.

disposes of all the gold, silver, goods, and clothes, the proceeds being given to the poor. The sick are washed twice a day, and the whole hospital cleaned. Two Jesuits, and more if need be, are in attendance, who do nothing else but go round confessing and comforting the sick, administering the sacrament, and giving them beads for saying their prayers. Mass is celebrated every day: in short, they are supplied with everything they require.

The sick are laid in large beds at two feet distance one from another, and upon several mattresses of cotton or tafetas, piled one upon another. The cots are low, painted of all colours, and supplied with curtains.

The most common ailments of the country are burning fevers and dysenteries, besides the venereal diseases, which are very prevalent, but only where the Portuguese are, and not elsewhere in India. If the sick die and have entrusted any property, even their accoutrements, to the Jesuit Father, all such is delivered into the hands of the officers of the Misericorde, which fraternity are obliged to bury the corpse honourably, though the deceased may not have had or left any sufficient means for the purpose.

If, however, the patient recovers his health, the Jesuit Father restores to him all his property, besides giving to every person that goes forth of the hospital a complete suit of clothing, if he has need of it, and a perdo, equal to 32½ sols. However rich a man may be, there is none but will gladly have himself taken to this hospital, to get better treatment than at his own house, as indeed he will.

In every year more than 1,500 corpses are removed from this hospital, while the number of sick admitted is infinite.[1]

[1] There may be a confusion here, the number 1,500 being already given as the number of inmates when he was there (cf. Linschoten's statement cited above, p. 7, *note*). The king, in his despatch of 17th Feb. 1607, writes that he is informed that every year from 300 to 400 Portuguese, between the ages of 18 and 30, die in the hospital, and in some years many more.

Inasmuch as the arrival of the fleet from Portugal sometimes brings more than 300, the least number of inmates is from 300 to 400. Only Portuguese and old Christians are admitted for treatment then. Yet true it is that some Jews among the companies arriving from Portugal pass for Portuguese, though they be only new Christians. All men that come with the Portuguese from these parts, all such being called *Homo Branco, i.e.*, white men, or old Christians, are welcomed there. No women are allowed to enter, sick or sound. Nor are any householders received, neither men, women, nor children, nor any Portuguese servants: there are others established for them, if they be poor. This hospital is only for the *Soldades*, that is, for such as are not married or domiciled, but are soldiers of fortune. In short, only those that are not married, nor belong to a household, nor are servants, are taken in; and among those that go there are often gentlemen of good family, there being no dishonour in the matter,—for, indeed, it is for these gentlemen and soldiers of fortune that these hospitals have been established in the cities of the Indies. Sometimes they are visited by the archbishop, the viceroy, and many lords, who make gifts to them of large sums of money: and everyone takes pleasure in seeing so splendid a place, where all the rooms are clean and white as paper. The galleries, too, are finely painted with stories from the Holy Scriptures.

There are two churches in the hospital, both enriched with the finest decoration possible. The one is upstairs, at the end of the great hall, for the worst patients, who hear mass there: it is dedicated to Our Lady. The other is below, dedicated to St. Martin, for those in better case, who hear service there when they please, along with the officers and domestics of the house. The greatest festival of the hospital is that of St. Martin, which is the day of the dedication of that church, —for that was the same day on which the Bastion, whereon this church has been built, was captured from the idolaters by the Portuguese.[1] On that day they make a general procession.[2] All the Portuguese and Metifs, of whatever quality and condition, who have any ailment, secret or other, if they desire to be treated and tended at that place at daybreak when the surgeons are there, are permitted to go without any cost to themselves. As soon as a man is better they dismiss him. If, however, one wishes to stay a while longer, he has no scruples to say that he has become worse. Continuing fevers they cure promptly by bleeding, which they resort to continually, and so long as the slightest fever is present. The idolater Indians use not bleeding at all. As for the pox, it is no mark of shame there, nor any disgrace to have had it several times: they even make a boast of it. They cure it without sweating, with China root. This malady prevails only among the Christians, and they prefer it to fever or dysentery. Another ailment is prevalent which attacks them suddenly, called *Mordesin*,[3] and is accompanied

[1] This is an error. As he will tell us himself, Goa was taken on St. Catherine's Day (25th Nov.), and there was no previous assault, certainly none on St. Martin's Day, the 11th. Besides, the origin of this chapel is well known. It celebrated the victory of João de Castro at Diu in 1546, won on St. Martin's Day. When the victor entered Goa in triumph, part of the city wall adjacent to the hospital was broken down to give passage to the procession, and at the breach first a niche, and afterwards a chapel, was dedicated to St. Martin. A slab in the wall at the niche commemorating the event was, on the downfall of the hospital building in last century, transferred to the chapel of St. Catherine, where it now is. It has a figure of St. Martin on horseback, and bears the inscription, "Por esta porta entrou D. João de Castro, Defensor da India, quando triumphou de Cambaya e todo este muro lhe foi derrubado. Era de 1547 A." (*Correa*, iv, 637; Couto, *Dec. VI*, liv. iv, c. 6; Sousa, *Or. Conq.*, Pt. I, *Conq.* i, Div. i, 37; Rivara, *ad loc.*; *Fonseca*, p. 227).

[2] This procession continued to 1830, the home government then refusing to sanction the charge of the expenses to the public treasury.

[3] *I.e.*, cholera. According to Col. Yule, the word is the Konk. or Mah. *modachī*, or *modshī* (see the interesting article in his *Glossary*, *s. v.* "Mort-de-chien", to which form the French missionaries seem to have the credit of reducing the word).

with grievous headache and vomiting, and much crying, and most often they die of it. They are very subject to poisoning and bewitchments, whereof they die in a decay. When the carracks arrive from Portugal the greater number of the sick are ill of the scurvy, and with ulcers on the feet and legs. When one has taken medicine, or is weak, he has servants charged to look after him, to raise him, and carry him. These are Christian Indians; they are neatly dressed and clean, and very soft and agreeable in their manner: for if one of them were rude to the sick, he would be expelled at once. Medicine is practised there as in Spain. It is of great honour and profit to be physician of this hospital; he is usually physician to the viceroy, and brought out of Portugal.[1] The Jesuit Father who has the superintendence remains in office as long as the Company please, and as he is thought fit for the work: two or three years, more or less. The Jesuit Fathers frequently send out a change of spiritual Fathers; the Father Superior, however, has the combined administration of spiritual and temporal affairs in the hospital, and gives his orders to all.

As for the building, it is very large and ample; it has many galleries, porticoes, ponds, and gardens with pretty walks, where the patients that are beginning to recover go to

[1] As he says above, p. 7, the physician and surgeon did not reside in the hospital. In 1605, the municipality, calling the king's attention to the frightful mortality (*supra*, p. 11, *note*), attributed it largely to the inexperience of the physicians who came out with each viceroy, and were forthwith appointed to the charge of the hospital. In three years, and often less, when they were beginning to understand their work, they were superseded on the arrival of a fresh viceroy. This complaint was repeated in 1606, and in Jan. 1607 the king directs that the physician and surgeon of the viceroy be not appointed, but that these offices be given to the men of the greatest experience and skill (see *Arch. Port. Or.*, Fasc. i, 2nd ed., 2nd part, 186; *Liv. das Monç.*, i, 85). This order is repeated 23rd Jan. 1610 (*Liv. das Monç.*, i, 303), but withdrawn by the despatch of 30th Jan. 1613 (*op. cit.*, ii, 300). Probably while in force it was not obeyed.

take the air and a bath: for they get a change of air as soon as they begin to get better, and are placed with such of the rest as are not more sick than themselves.

Throughout the whole hospital there are lamps, lanterns, and candles at night-time, but more lamps are used, as the candles are of wax. The lanterns are made of oyster-shells, as is all the glazing in the churches and houses of Goa.[1] In the midst of this hospital there is a handsome, large, paved court, in which is a large well where the sick bathe themselves betimes, as has been said. The Portuguese and the Metif householders who are sick and in need are treated at their houses by the Misericordia and by the wealthy, who let them want for nothing. There are other hospitals for the natives of the country that are in the town: these are for Christian Indians only.[2] The town possesses two hospitals, one for women, the other for men; but these are in fact one only, being merely separated for the sexes.

The poor Portuguese and Metifs never go a-begging, but they send petitions to the rich; and their women have themselves borne in a palanquin to the residence of the viceroy, the archbishop, and the great lords, and present their requests and petitions in person. In short, it would be impossible to describe all the other peculiar customs of the place, and the perfect order and regularity preserved in this admirable hospital. Thus, if a person is wont to have himself purged or bled every year, though he be not otherwise ailing, if he goes there he will be admitted for the period of his purgation.

But to return to my companion and myself. After we had been carried into the hospital and admitted, on the following day the general of the fleet that had brought us sent

[1] "Large windows (in the houses at Bassein), two stories high, with panes of oyster-shell, which is their usual glazing among them in India" (*Fryer*, 74). Mr. Fonseca (p. 158) says that this is still the fashion at Goa.

[2] Noted also by Linschoten (i, 237).

thither our other companion also, as I have said. We were all then given in charge of the Jesuit Father, under an order that we were not to be let go without previous notice given to the general, who is called the *Capitan Mayor*.[1] The Father would not tell us that we were prisoners in his hands, for fear of saddening us, and he consoled us in every way in his power, and gave us as good treatment as the greatest of the Portuguese: though, forsooth, it would have been difficult to treat us any better than the rest, all being so well and indifferently treated, both as respects food, medicine, and other treatment, and each being served in his turn and according to written prescription, without any difference between gentle and simple. Seeing ourselves to be thus well treated, we believed we were already at liberty, insomuch that at the end of twenty days, when I began to feel better, I spoke with the Father, and told him, thanks to God, I was well, and wished to depart with the one of my companions. But the Father asked what haste we were in, and that we should wait till our other companion was cured. That, however, was a long business, for it was more than three months ere he was brought round. But we did not learn the reason of his answer, for he wished first to have a word with those who had put us in his hands, knowing well as he did that when we went forth we should not be so well dealt with. Wherefore he was ever putting off our departure, though we pressed him with our desire that we had to see that fine town whereof we had heard such an account. He having at length given notice to the general, five or six days thereafter came two *Merignes*[2] with their *Pions*,[3] and demanded us of the Father, waiting at the gate while the Jesuit Father came to us and said: "My friends (*Irmanos*), arise; since you are so desirous to go, permission is now given; follow me"; whereat we followed him joyfully, and he gave

[1] *Capitão Mór.*

[2] *Meirinhos.*

[3] See vol. i, p. 428.

each of us two (for the other was still sick) hose, a doublet, a cassock, shoes, and a hat; two shirts, two pair of drawers, quite new (they do not wear stockings, the breeches reaching down over the feet); also a piece of money, viz., a *pardo*, worth 32½ sols, or about 25 sols in France. Then we had breakfast, though we little required it for the haste we were in to be off. He gave us his benediction, and we took our leave, thanking him for all the kindness he had shown us. I understood shortly after what pity this Father had felt for us, for he gave us all the consolation he could. On descending the grand staircase we met the two sergeants with their writs, and with halberds and partisans: they seized us forthwith, and bore us off in rough sort. When a prisoner is led off, the sergeant walks in front with the *vare*,[1] or stick, while the Pions march behind the prisoner, who is bound with cords, the two ends of which are held by them. I leave you to imagine our astonishment after joy so short, to find ourselves in the hands of these devils of Caffres,[2] fellows more black than coals.

In such wise did I come out of this hospital. I was there again on another occasion afterwards, when I was ill for fifteen days. Many other times, too, have I gone there to visit my companion and other friends, wherefore I have desired to describe in detail all I have seen and learnt about it, esteeming that there is none other such in all the world. If in the other towns of the Portuguese there are not others of the same kind in proportion to their size, the poor Portuguese are very greatly to be pitied, seeing the great number of them in that land, their poverty of means, and the grievous maladies and infirmities to which they are subject.

Thus were we taken to the prison, which is called the

[1] Port. *vara*.

[2] Used in the modern sense for natives of the Mozambique coast, large numbers of whom were imported as slaves. At times they gave great trouble by their brawls and robberies (*Liv. das Monç.*, i, 200).

Salle, and not without reason; for it is the most foul and filthy place in the world, as I believe.[1] There are four general prisons at Goa, besides other private ones: the first is that of the Holy Inquisition[2]; the second is that of the archbishop,[3] close to his residence; the third, the *Tronquo*,[4] at the viceroy's palace, the chief and largest of all; and there is a large wing of the building containing other prisoners of all sorts, the one whither we were taken being in aid of the former. In this one is held once a month a general audience, at which the viceroy is usually present. It is like the Conciergerie here. These prisons at Goa are not so bad as those of Cochin. The Inquisition and the Ecclesiastical Court have two; the archbishop has one of these, and he has power over all the clergy. The Jesuits and he this long while have had a suit at the Court of Rome, they not wishing to have any superior over them but the Pope and their own general.[5] The judges and officers of the Inquisition are irresponsible judges. Nevertheless, the archbishop still has much power, but he does not use it, for the others hold their offices of the king; but if any of them was guilty of any misfeasance, he would have cognisance of it.

The prison to which we were conducted is in the town,

[1] In orig.: "car c'est le lieu le plus ord et sale qui soit au monde comme ie croy". The play upon the words *salle* and *sale* cannot well be given in English. This was the prison of the Strand (*Ribeira*), where the prisoners condemned to the galleys were kept. It was commonly called *Sala das bragas*, from the *braga* or iron ring which held the prisoner's ankle. (*Rivara.*)

[2] The prisons of the Inquisition (being more than one) were called *Carceres*. (*Rivara.*)

[3] Called *Aljabe*, from the Ar. *al-jabr*, "prison". Dellon writes it *aljouvar*.

[4] Tronco, the principal civil prison, as at Cochin (see i, p. 429).

[5] The Jesuits, by their power at Lisbon and Rome, held their own against all their opponents, who comprised not only the archbishop and the Franciscans, but also the municipality. Those who care to follow the disputes may consult the index to the *Arch. Port. Or.*, and the *Liv. das Monçoes*.

near the river, and called the prison of the *Viador de fasienda*, who has his house outside the town, but near the river. The *Merigne* made a charge against us on his paper on behalf of the criminal *Oydor*.[1] The gaoler and his wife were Metifs. The gaoler having asked who we were, and learning that we were Frenchmen and Catholics, advised us not to lose heart, and that he would not put us in the Salle with the rest. This Salle is a place where all the galley slaves and other sorts of vile people are cast pell-mell in a stinking air, sometimes two or three hundred and more. No criminals are placed there, except in order to take them afterwards to the Tronquo. It is at the discretion of the gaoler, who is called Merigne de Salle, to put everyone indiscriminately in this Salle. Men of quality give him money to get themselves put into private rooms, of which there are two, one for the Gentiles and Mahometans, the other for the Christians. He never grants this favour but for money, save to foreigners like ourselves, who received much kindness and were allowed much liberty, and were not obliged to sleep with a gang of slaves and galley prisoners with irons on their feet. There were lamps lighted, and at one end of the room was the lodging of the Merigne or sergeant; at the other, towards the outer gate, was his son, with his servants and slaves keeping guard, because the prison is by no means strong. At the two ends were two bells for finding whether either party slept; for when the father rang his bell, the son replied with the same number of strokes. From the whole body of convicts are taken two squads or watches for keeping guard themselves, and all night long there is nothing but shouts and answers from one squad to the other. The first cries as loud as he can, "*Vigia, vigia!*" *i.e.*, "Wake, wake!" Those who are on the watch for that hour, ten or more, answer one

[1] Port. *Ouvidor*, "one who hears", *i.e.*, a magistrate. Our own judges' commissions used to run,—"*oyer et terminer*", and now "hear and determine"; and we speak of the magistrate *hearing* a case.

after the other. If they are behindhand ever so little, the slaves of the household would come and beat them forthwith. So there is the greatest din possible all night, the which, along with the great heat, prevents the least repose.[1] At nine o'clock in the evening they chant their service and prayers in Portuguese, in a loud voice. The wife and daughters of the gaoler treated us with much kindness, bringing or sending us things to eat and drink without his knowing anything of it. The prisoners are assisted with alms from the well-to-do, and the officers or *Confrères* of the *Miséricorde*, called *Irmanos*, come to visit all the prisoners once a month, as well as all the poor of the town that are on their list. In the same way the poor widows and orphan girls are fed at the expense of this fraternity. Much is given to the old Christians, and a little to the new Indian Christians. The Father for the Christians, who is a Jesuit, comes also and gives to the prisoners; but that does not happen every day. The ordinance of the King of Portugal is, that all prisoners of war and strangers are to be maintained; but the officers embezzle the money that is devoted to the purpose. They should receive six pardos a month each, the same as the pay of soldiers. This is equal to 9 livres 15 sols of our money, and provides better cheer than ten crowns here. We advanced a petition to receive that which the king was pleased to grant us. This was presented by the *Merigne de Salle* to the

[1] Such was a night in Old Goa; and here is one at modern Rio de Janeiro:—"Above the cry of Cicada, and the moaning of sea, and the rustling of palm-leaves, all through the long night, . . . you can hear a strange and melancholy song rising in wild bursts on the night air: a barbaric, monotonous, and sad chorus, such as Israelite bondsmen might have sung long ago in Egypt. And this too is a chorus of bondsmen, of African slaves. For there are limeworks on Paqueta Island; and by night and day, unceasingly the naked blacks toil on in batches. The night watchers are obliged to sing this chorus at intervals, so that their master in his bed, if he chance to awake, may know that they are toiling and watching, and not falling to sleep with weariness" (Knight, E. F., *Cruise of the Falcon* (1884), i, 81).

Viador de Fasienda,[1] by name *Garsias de Mella*, who replied to it; but that was after a very long time, by reason of the great number of hands it had to pass. So we could not get our money till six days before we left the place; and for fear lest any should take it from us, we gave it to the gaoler's wife to keep for us, my companion and I contracting with her to be fed for one *tangue* a day each. This tangue is worth seven sous and a half there, or five sous here. She treated us very well for that; but we were set at liberty five or six days afterwards, and this gave rise to a dispute with our good hostess: for when we asked for the remainder of our money she would not give it, saying that she had spent it, and that we might go on eating and drinking in the prison there every day at the agreed price; save on that understanding we should have had nothing. But as we were obliged to provide ourselves with some necessaries, we were much annoyed at this refusal, besides that we had no great wish to return to that gloomy place; and afterwards we were maintained in the town for nothing, as I shall relate anon. Whereupon we went to complain of her (for her husband took no part in the affair) to the *Viador de Fasienda*, who at once ordered our demands to be complied with, though we lost a good part of our money on the account stated. What vexed us most of all in the business was losing in this way the good graces of her, her daughters, and family. When our money was returned to us in the presence of the *Viador* and a number of captains, there was amongst the rest a Castilian captain—the only one I saw there—who, seeing that they

[1] *Vedor da fazenda*, as Linschoten says, "that is, the upper surveyor of the king's goods" (ii, 226). The office of chief vedor da fazenda was the most important next to the viceroy at Goa, and to the *capitão de cidade* elsewhere. As there was no efficient audit of his accounts, and it was no crime for a Portuguese at this period to cheat the King of Spain, his embezzlements were on a vast scale. There were several vedors da fazenda—*e.g.*, "dos contos", "da carga das naus de Cochim" —as this Garcia de Mello was (*Liv. das Monç.*, i, 104).

did not give us all our money, and that we were dissatisfied, took pity upon us for the trick that had been played upon us, and told us he would recompense us, and would give us the rest of our money at his house, which in fact he did. He told us he was a Spaniard, and not a Portuguese, and was named *Dom Pedro Rodriguez.* He afterwards returned to Portugal with us. A month afterwards the slave of one with whom he had a quarrel gave him a heavy blow on the head from behind with a *bambou* (he was a *Caffre*); but he, not a whit taken aback nor losing time, drew his sword and slew the fellow, and forthwith fled to the church. He had his grace at the end of two hours. But inasmuch as the Spaniards are not very well received there, he was constrained to return to Spain.

The manner of our getting out of this prison was in this wise. After we had been there about a month, that Jesuit Father that is over the Christians came to the prison. He it is who is charged by the Society of the Jesuits to solicit the deliverance and liberty of Christian prisoners. To this end he is bound to visit the prisoners continually, to see if there be any Christians among them, or any that are minded to become Christians, and to be ever soliciting the viceroy or the judges or other parties to obtain their deliverance. So when he came to the prison aforesaid, and on inquiry found that I was a Christian and a Frenchman, he told me to have patience, and that I should full soon be set at liberty, informing me that there was a French Jesuit of Rouen, named *Etienne de la Croix,*[1] who was at the college of *Sainct Paul*

[1] Etienne de la Croix, born 1579 at St. Pierre-de-Bogerat (Eure); entered the Society of Jesus 1599; sailed for India 1602. At Goa he was appointed to teach philosophy and theology at the Society's college at Salsette, was master of the novices, and afterwards rector of the college. He was distinguished both for learning and zeal, and enjoyed great influence by reason of his tact and charitable works. Acquiring a knowledge of Canarese and Mahratti, he wrote several works and pieces in those languages; among others, a poem on the Passion, which

de Goa. To him I wrote a letter, and next day he came to me. He was overjoyed to see me, and consoled me, assisting me with some money, and told me he would busy himself on my behalf as if I were his own brother, to get his superior to speak with the viceroy and obtain my liberty.

That Father presented a request to the viceroy,[1] with which, however, the latter refused to comply, at first using great threats, and saying that I ought to be put to death, seeing I had come to that country contrary to the ordinance of the king, and to the treaty of peace between the Kings of France and Spain; that he could not set me free, but would send me prisoner to the King of Spain to do with me as he was pleased. At length this good French Jesuit Father employed such importunity for the space of a month, that I was set at liberty. All the while he failed not to come to see me every day, and aided me by all means in his power, and my companion also.

When we got out of prison we went to eat and drink with the soldiers at divers houses of the lords, so that it cost us nothing to live, for we were enrolled as soldiers. I remained at Goa with the Portuguese for the space of two years, receiving the pay of a soldier, going hither and thither in their expeditions, as well along the coast to the north as far as *Diu* and *Cambaye*, where I remained for a while, as to Cape *Commorin*, and even to the Island of *Ceylan*.

was sung in the college on Sundays during Lent. He died at Goa, 24th Sept. 1643. His only extant work (the copy at the National Library at Lisbon being the only one known) is a discourse in Mahratti verse on the life of St. Peter,—*Discursos sobre la vida do apostolo Sam Pedro . . . compostos em versos lingoa bramana marasta. Empressos em Goa, na Casa professa de Jesus*, etc., 1634, tom. 2, fol. (Pinto do Matos, *Biblio. Port.*; Da Silva, *Dicc. Biblio. Port.*; Backer, *Bibl. des Ecr. Jes.*; Crét. Joly, *Hist. de la Comp. de J.*; *Lettres Edifiantes*).

[1] Pyrard uses the term viceroy somewhat indiscriminately. At the time of which he is writing (1608) there was no viceroy, but only a governor, viz., the Archbishop Menezes, who held office till May 1609.

But before coming to the description of Goa, I have this further to say of the prisons, viz., that all the others are subsidiary to the *Tronco*, which is the great prison. Also, that while we were still in prison certain Arab prisoners were brought there, all brave men, well behaved and of fine figure. These were the chief men of a vessel, in which all the rest had been left, the soldiers and seamen, as slaves of the King of Portugal. But it happened that the captain, who had captured their ship, and who, on his way from Lisbon to Goa in a galion, had fallen in with them on their way to *Sumatra* in a vessel richly laden with gold and other goods, was so ill-advised that, in the place of these Arabs, he put on board that vessel some Portuguese, and expected her to follow him to Goa. But the Arabs that were left in the vessel rose against the Portuguese, and took the ship and the Portuguese prisoners. They afterwards wrote word to Goa to get the Arabs in exchange for the Portuguese, which was done. This shows that when you take a prize you must put on board men of valour and judgment to man her.

CHAPTER II.

Description of the Island of Goa, the chief inhabitants, and lords.

Goa is an island which was formerly a dependency of the kingdom of *Dealcan*, or *Decan.*[1] It is about eight leagues in circumference, and has seven fortresses guarding the passage. It is surrounded by a river,[2] which flows from the said king-

[1] He confuses *Hidalcão*, the Port. form of the name of the Bijapur kings, with *Deccan*, the south country (of the Peninsula), generally applied throughout the Port. period to the Bijapur kingdom. *Dealcan* for *Hidalcão* occurs also in Linschoten (i, 176), and in Mocquet (p. 319).

[2] The *Mandovi*, which rises in the Parvor Ghât, in the province of Sâtari, 38½ miles in length (*Fonseca*).

dom of Dealcan and falls into the sea two leagues from the town, whose foundations it washes. At the mouth of this river are two forts, one on each side, to prevent the entrance of hostile ships. A league up this river is the fort and passage[1] of *Pangin*,[2] which is in the island. It contains a captain and governor on behalf of the viceroy, who has the absolute command there. All ships and vessels whatsoever must speak there, and receive a passport and quittance, whether inward or outward bound. The vessel is examined and certain dues are paid. In short, it is impossible to pass either by night or by day without his knowledge, inasmuch as the passage is narrow and close to the fort, where a good look-out is kept. On this island the Portuguese have built a fine town, called after the name of the island,[3] Goa. It is about a league and a half in circuit, not including the suburbs. It contains a number of forts, churches, and houses

[1] *Passage*, in translation of the Port. *passo*, which Linschoten uses. *Passos* were ferries or gates from the island to the mainland or other islands, each guarded by a fort or guardhouse. Ressende (Sloane MS. 197), in his description of Goa, proceeds by taking these in order, thus *Passo de Ribandar*, *Passo de Daugim*, etc.

[2] Pangim was the chief fort protecting Old Goa at the time of Albuquerque's assault (*Albuq. Comm.*, ii, 88), and during the whole of the sixteenth century it was so used by the Portuguese (see plan and description in Ressende MS., fol. 248). De Orta (fol. 37) calls it "fortaleza pequena". During the few years before Pyrard's arrival the government constructed a strong fort a little to the west, on the point immediately opposite the fort of *Reis Magos*. This new fort (which Pyrard does not mention) was called that of *Gaspar Dias*, from the previous owner of the site. Fonseca says it was built in 1598, but the despatches in the *Liv. das Monç.* show that it was not complete even in 1607. Pangim is now the capital, and so alternatively called *Nova Goa*. The first step was the removal of the viceregal residence from Goa to Pangim in 1759. The custom-house was removed in 1811, the other public departments followed, and in 1843 Pangim was declared the capital of Port. India by royal decree (*Fonseca*, 99).

[3] Not so: the name of the island was *Tissuary*, but commonly called Goa, from the name of the city.

built in the style of Europe, of very fine stone, and roofed with tiles.

It is now about 110[1] years since the Portuguese made themselves masters of this island of Goa, and I have been often astonished how in so few years the Portuguese have managed to construct so many superb buildings, churches, monasteries, palaces, forts, and other edifices built in the European style; also at the good order, regulation, and police they have established, and the power they have acquired, everything being as well maintained and observed as at Lisbon itself.[2] This town is the metropolis of the Portuguese state in India, which circumstance has acquired for it its power, riches, and celebrity. So, too, the viceroy makes it his residence, and has about him a court like the king himself. Then there is the archbishop, who is over the spiritual affairs,[3] the court of parliament,[4] and the inquisition. Besides the archbishop there is another special bishop for the place, so that it is the headquarters of religion and justice for the whole of India; and all the religious orders have their superiors there. All departures of ships of war, as well as of merchantmen sailing for the King of Spain, are made from this place. For the spiritual affairs of the Indies there are four bishops and an archbishop. The Bishop of Goa has juris-

[1] *I.e.*, from 1618, the year in which this edition was written, as appears towards the end of this chapter. Goa was taken 25th Nov. 1510.

[2] The current proverb was: "Quem vio Goa excusa de vêr Lisboa" ("If you have seen Goa you needn't go to Lisbon").

[3] This archbishop was the first primate of the whole East. Goa had been an archbishop's see since 1559, and a bishop's since 1537. Now that the Port. possessions have dwindled, and all the East has vast numbers of Catholics of other races, the *padroado* of the Goa see is a real grievance. But how to get rid of it? It is a question of pride and prestige, and is at present occupying the best brains of Rome and Lisbon.

[4] Used in the French sense, and meaning the *Relação*, or Royal Court of Justice.

diction as far as *Mozambique*. He of *Cochin* reaches as far north as Barcelor, and to Malaca. Then there is a Bishop of *Malaca*, and another of *Macao* in China, all of whom are subject to the Archbishop of Goa.

It is a marvel to see the great multitude of people that come and go every day by sea and by land, on all manner of affairs. The kings of the Indies that are at peace and friendship with the Portuguese have almost all of them ordinary, and often extraordinary ambassadors there, coming and going in the course of the settlement of treaties, while the Portuguese do the same on their part. As for merchants, who are continually going to and fro the East, there seems to be every day a fair for all the different articles of trade in which they deal.[1] For although there are some kings who are not at peace with the Portuguese, nevertheless their merchandise and produce fail not to come to Goa, brought thither by friendly merchants who go and buy of them. And whatsoever hostility there may be betwixt them, if the Indian enemies would be willing to take a passport and assurance, they might come in all security; but they have too much pride, and prefer to go elsewhere.

All the island of Goa is mountainous and sandy, the soil is red like *Bolarmeny*,[2] and very pretty pottery and vases of fine quality and design are made of it, as of *terre sigilée*.[3] There is found there also another kind of earth even finer in grain and quality, which is blackish or somewhat grey: of this also they make numbers of vessels that are as fine as

[1] Linschoten likens the daily assembly of citizens and merchants at Goa to the "meeting upon the burse in Andwarpe" (i, 184).

[2] "An astringent earth brought from Armenia, and formerly used as an antidote and styptic" (Murray's *New Eng. Dict.*, *s. v.* "Bole"); "the astringent and medicinable red earth or mineral called *bolearmenie*" (*Cotgrave*).

[3] *Terra sigillata*, "a medicinable earth" (*Cotgrave*); also known by the names *terre Guerinienne*, *t. de Lemnos*, *t. Blesienne* (from being found near Blois).

glass. The island is not very fertile,—not that the soil is bad, but by reason of the mountains. For (only) in the more humid hollows and valleys rice and millet are sown which bear twice a year. The country there is always green, as in all the other islands and lands between the two tropics, for the trees and herbs are always green there. There is also a great number of *Palmero* or *orta*,[1] like our orchards here, full of *cocos* trees planted close together; but these grow only in well-watered and low ground. They produce the largest revenues to the Portuguese at Goa. They are enclosed with walls, and, along with a house and pretty garden, are called *orta*, wherein they take their recreation with their families. Water is led thither by canals among the trees, and those who have not this appliance are at great pains to carry water for the trees by hand. They let these gardens to the *Canarins* of Goa, who make a profit and take the produce. This is worth a good deal at Goa, because of the wine, which is in great request. The Portuguese retain some only of these gardens for their own pleasure, and make very pretty alleys and tunnels amid these gardens or orchards, set off with fountains and grottoes. The soil of the island would of itself be good enough, but being full of high mountains, and also of people, and without being very confined, it is found to be unproductive. The inhabitants prefer to work and traffic by sea and land, rather than to amuse themselves with rearing cattle; besides, too, the island is too full of houses and people for that. So it is that the island of Goa produces little of itself, and yet everything is cheap.

This island is formed by the fair broad river which surrounds it, and also forms other islands, which are inhabited by natives and Portuguese. The river is of some depth, but large vessels, such as the carracks and galions of Portugal, on their arrival are stopped at the mouth, which is called the

[1] The Port. *orta*, a garden, came into Anglo-Indian use on the Bombay side as *Oart* (see Yule, *Gloss.*, s. v.)

Bare. They are constrained to halt outside this *bare,* although it is not closed. After being discharged they are taken up before the town, two leagues off. At the entrance to this bar, where the ships lie at anchor both on arrival and departure, there are, as I have said, two fortresses[1] built against the Hollanders and other foreigners, to prevent them from entering and casting anchor in the river, as has been sometimes done by the Hollanders. They forced an entrance, and burnt and sunk a large number of ships that were there, and even held the bar for the space of ten or twelve days, in such wise that not a single boat even could enter to Goa,[2] while they themselves obtained water and provisions from the land. It is a great misfortune alike for the Portuguese and the Indians, when they arrive a little late at these rivers and bars, to find them choked, as happens there and at Cochin, and at most other places in the Indies during the winter. In that case they must wait and lie at the mercy of the weather and of their enemies, who most often come and destroy them there: for when the bar is thus closed and choked with sand, not a single boat can go in or out, but must wait. Wherefore, before leaving a port, they have to make their calculations to winter wherever they may happen to be. Thus, then, the Portuguese have built these two

[1] At the fortress of *Agoada* on the north, and *Cabo* on the south. These were without the bar, which is that part of the estuary between Bardes and Pangim. The big ships were discharged at Bardes (*Linsch.*, i, 178). As to the position of these forts, see the Chart of Goa from Ressende's MS. in *Albuq. Comm.*, Hak. Soc., vol. ii, at p. 88.

[2] In chap. xv he refers again to this blockade, but there says it lasted nearly three weeks, and gives the number of Dutch ships as six. The reference (founded on hearsay) is partly to the blockade of Van der Hagen, who with ten (of the thirteen) ships under his command arrived before Goa on the 21st Sept. 1604, and did not leave till the arrival of eleven Portuguese ships of war, on the 14th Oct.; and partly to that of P. van Cardaen, who arrived before Goa on the 17th Oct. 1607, and left on the 20th of the same month. On the first occasion the Dutch did not burn any Portuguese shipping; on the second they burnt the carrack of the admiral of the fleet in which the viceroy, Conde de Fera, had sailed. Pyrard refers several times to this ill-fated fleet.

fortresses to guard their bar and to keep their vessels in security, and to prevent their enemies from approaching and getting water.

At the entering in of this river, on the left hand, is the land of the *Bardez*, belonging to the Portuguese. Here is a very fine spring, whereat departing ships supply themselves with water. It is on the low ground, and from a distance appears to be of white sand. The Portuguese call such places *Agoadas*.[1] At this place is one of these fortresses, a very strong one, and well equipped with cannon.[2] The land of the Bardez is lofty and mountainous. It is opposite to the city of Goa, covering all its northern quarter, opposite to which that fortress is. The other fortress is on a height upon a cape of the island,[3] a high rocky promontory opposite the

[1] *Agoada*, a watering-place.

[2] This fortress was begun some years before, to protect the bar from the Dutch. Its construction was hurried on, the municipality taking for the purpose a duty of one per cent. on all shipping. Although described as above by the author, it was not at this time completed (see *Liv. das Monç.*, i, 334, despatch under date 17th Feb. 1610). An inscription on its main gate records that it was finished in 1612 (Fonseca's *Goa*, p. 40). The fort stands on a high and rocky headland, the citadel being 260 feet above sea level. In the seventeenth century its summit was lighted with a beacon, and is now supplied with a lighthouse. The rock had many springs, one of which has an inscription on the rock dated 1624 (*ib.*). During the British occupation of Goa at the beginning of this century, this fort was described as follows: "The fort of Agoada seems to have consisted originally of nothing but a large battery, nearly on a level with the water. Subsequently a wall was run up the side and along the top of the rock, to secure the rear of the battery, and still more recently a small but strongly built citadel, surrounded by a deep ditch, has been made on the top of the height, and the communications between it and the battery strengthened" (Brit. Mus., Add. MS. 14,384, f. 29).

[3] A description of the *Cabo* fortress, so called, as it was in 1634, is given by Ressende (Sloane MS. 197, f. 249; see *Dalb. Comm.*, iii, 278). Its equipment consisted of four bronze guns. Barracks had been begun for a guard of a dozen men, but were never finished; and Ressende has to record that at the time of his report "no captain or Portuguese soldier serves here, but only one negro!" The British report on Goa

first-mentioned fort. On the summit is a handsome monastery of the Capucines, called *Nuestra Señora del Capbo*, that is to say, Our Lady of the Cape.[1] It is well built, and the archbishop often goes there for five or six days at a time for his recreation. All ships, whether galleys or other vessels, entering or departing, and whether for the wars or for traffic, whether Christian or other, salute this monastery in passing with their guns. These forts are very necessary for guarding the entrance of the river and the Agoada spring; yet sometimes they cannot prevent enemies from casting anchor at the bar, and so cutting off the Portuguese vessels. This causes them much trouble; but it is not so easily done now as before these forts were built. The river entrance is very wide, and so continues up as far as the town. There are a large number of heavy wooden piles driven in at divers places in this river, and at certain passages only is the depth sufficient for ships to enter; for there are many shallows in all the river-bed between the bar and the town, so that with all these piles it is a difficult matter to sail inwards and outwards, without passing under the fortress of *Pangin*, where the water is very deep. The fortress is midway between the bar and the town; its position is therefore of great importance, and the captain of it sends at once to examine vessels, and to see their receipts and quittances. They must get his discharge, and pay him certain dues. All

at the beginning of this century thus describes the fortifications :—"A wall is carried across a narrow part near the extreme point of the rock so as entirely to cut it off, and a battery runs along the foot of the rock. The battery is now dismantled and in ruins, and the wall falling to decay" (Brit. Mus., Add. MS. 14,384, f. 29).

[1] He confuses the chapel so named, which was built about fifty years before this time, and the Franciscan monastery, built at the side of the chapel in 1594. The latter was a favourite resort of Archbishop Menezes and succeeding prelates. In modern times it has been converted into a summer palace for the governor (*Fonseca*, p. 44). Note that the author occasionally gives names, etc., in Spanish form. The Port. name here is "Nossa Señora do Cabo".

other discharges granted at Goa are useless without that one, so the place is worth much to the captain and the writer.

There is very good lodging in this fort. The viceroys on their arrival from Portugal always land and tarry there, till they make their entry and take possession. The palace within it is a handsome and comfortable residence, and the retiring viceroy goes and stays there till he takes his departure: for there are never two viceroys in the city at the same time; but as soon as the one has delivered over the government to the other, he retires to some place without the town, and there is no more ceremony nor visits paid betwixt them, except such as are formal, even though aforetime they were good friends: such is their pride. This Pangin residence is one of the most beautiful and agreeable in the whole island. The river, as I have said, is a very fine one, and comes from afar, from the countries of the *Dealcan* or *Decan*; it abounds with fish. It can be navigated in boats for more than thirty miles of the country, and contains a large number of islands peopled with natives, both Christian and Gentile.

Goa is furnished all round its circuit with seven passably good fortresses; no need, indeed, for them to be very strong, because the river protects them. Among these seven are included the two first named, but not that of the town itself, which contains the viceroy's palace, and is situated on the banks of the river; adding that, there are eight in all, besides that of Bardes, which protects the spring.[1] They extend entirely round the island, and each has its parish church and

[1] As he is enumerating the forts of Goa Island, he need not have mentioned Bardes; having mentioned it, he ought to have said "those", viz., Reis Magos and Agoada. By the "two first-named" he must mean *Cabo* and *Pangim*, including with the latter the recently erected but hardly complete fortress of *Gaspar Dias*. The eight, then, are—1, Cabo; 2, Pangim; 3, Madre de Deos; 4, S. Braz; 5, Santiago; 6, S. João Baptista; 7, N. S. de Guadalupe; 8, The Viceroy's Palace.

others.[1] After the viceroy's comes that of *Madre de Deos, i.e.*, Mother of God, otherwise called *Daugin;* there, too, is the parish church of *St. Joseph,* and a Capucine monastery possessing a very fine garden, which is often visited by the viceroys for recreation. This monastery has the same name as the fort. The others are *St. Bracs; St. Iago,* which is more than a league and a half from *Madre de Deos,* but is connected with it by a wall, because in the summer the river is very low, and this wall prevents an entrance being made from the mainland; next is the fortress of *St. Jean Baptiste,* and then that of *Nuestra Señora de Guadalupes.* All are of the same construction, and governed by like rule; each has its prison for keeping suspected persons, as regards whom the captain of the town also is kept well informed. If a slave endeavouring to escape is retaken, he is put in there and kept till reclaimed by his master, who is obliged to pay the expenses of his keeping. The same prevails in all the other lands held by the Portuguese. Each fort has a captain, a writer, and a guard of soldiers; also a bell for making signals. All who leave the island for the mainland, for the purposes of trade or to get provisions—that is, the Indians and Canarins of Goa, as well men as women and children—must go to the captain of the *Cidada* (that is, the city) and get each his ticket or token. They carry this ticket wet with ink upon their arms, which are naked, clapping it on there; then the officers at the gate see it, and after effacing it let them pass,[2] and each of the two places costs them a *Bouseruque.*[3] On

[1] If he means that the forts and parishes were coterminous, he is in error. Old Goa was divided into four parishes in 1545, viz., 1, Cathedral; 2, Rosary; 3, Luz; 4, St. Lucia. In 1594 Archbishop Menezes added four more, viz., 5, St. Alexius; 6, St. Thomas; 7, Trinity; 8, St. Thomas at Pannelim (*C. de Kloguen*).

[2] Wm. Barret (*Hak.*, i, 217) and Linschoten (i, 180) give practically the same account of this toll; but they both say that the mark was stamped upon the naked arm. Pyrard is probably right.

[3] Port. *basaruco,* a base coin of copper, lead, tin, or tutenague, worth

their return they take the same token from the captain of the fort. By this means they ascertain the number of people coming and going: for there are writers at every point who make up the register. This is done also to discover whether any of them that pass be not accused of larceny or murder, or escaped from prison, or guilty of other misdeed. No difficulty is made of the entrance of all comers—that is, of all natives of the mainland; but if any be foreigners, they are arrested. The Portuguese are on no pretext allowed to go on to the mainland, unless they have families at Goa, for fear lest they should join themselves to the Indian kings. It is a wondrous thing to see the great crowd of people coming or going in procession along the highways. None but Christians carry arms there. All the forts are well equipped with cannon. By night no boats are left on the other side of the water: all are brought close up under the forts. None of the infidels, whether natives or strangers, carry any arms, except they be of the following of the ambassadors. All the passages bring in large revenues, both from the merchandise and from the large numbers of people passing them. The boatmen pay tribute to the Portuguese, and each of the passages has its office. So at the other islands too, inhabited by Christians and infidels, there are passages. In all these said forts and passages there are many dwelling-houses, parish and other churches, monasteries, hermitages, and chapels here and there.

In all this island of Goa, as well as in the surrounding country, and I may say throughout the rest of India, it rains continually for a space of six months, which is their winter,[1] and at Goa more heavily than elsewhere. So during all this

two reis, or, as Linschoten says, a Hollander's doit (see Yule, *Gloss.*, *s. v.* "Budgrook"; and Da Cunha, *Indo-Port. Num.*).

[1] Here, as elsewhere in the book, and by all the old writers of all nations, used for the rainy season, *i.e.*, in Western India ("India" in Portuguese usage), the period of the S.W. monsoon, May—September (see Yule, *Gloss.*, *s. v.* "Winter").

period there is much mud and dirt, which soils the clothing, and especially that of the Moors and Gentiles, which is of white cotton, and trails at their heels. They are obliged to have the Fête-Dieu in February or March, because in the season we celebrate it there is too much rain.[1] In the island over against the city there is a very fine pond called *La Goada*,[2] of more than a league in circuit, and natural. On its banks are three fine mansions of great lords, who have built them there for their pleasure, with spacious orchards and gardens, fruit trees, and cocos. The soil is good for fruits, but only in the marshy places.

As for the people who inhabit this island of Goa, they are of two sorts, natives and strangers. The natives are the *Bramenis*, *Canarins*,[3] and *Coulombins*,[4] all Gentiles; the Bramenis are everywhere and always masters and superiors among the idolaters. The Canarins are of two sorts, for such as are engaged in trade and other honourable callings are held in much greater respect than those who engage in fishing, or practise mechanical crafts, as for instance oarsmen, gatherers of coco produce, called *Sura*,[5] and followers of other mean occupations. Yet there are other inferior castes beneath all these, who occupy themselves with viler work, and live in

[1] Corpus Christi is celebrated by the Catholic Church on the eleventh day after Whit-Sunday, that is, always towards the end of May, or in June. Della Valle notes the change made in India, and says that it was kept there on the Thursday next after Dominica in Albis (first Sunday after Easter).

[2] A mistake for *Lagoa*, "lagoon", the name by which, as appears from Linschoten's map, this pond went. He evidently confuses it with *aguada*, "well, watering-place".

[3] Rivara says that nowadays the term *Canarin* at Goa has a somewhat offensive sense, and is applied exclusively to native Christians.

[4] The lowest caste of the Goanese, Konk. *Kunambī*, Mahr. *Kunbī* = agriculturist: see note to Linschoten (i, 260), who writes *Corumbijn*.

[5] Malayālam *sura*, "toddy", from Skt. *surā*, "spirituous liquor" (see Linschoten, ii, 48, *note*, and Yule, *Gloss.*, s. v.). Pyrard, like Linschoten, seems to apply it to the unfermented sap.

great poverty and squalor, and like savages: these they call Coulombins. Among the strangers are the resident proprietors of the island, who are the Portuguese. They are the lords of it, but allow the former inhabitants to remain there in all security and enjoyment of their goods. By the ordinance of the King of Spain, they may not make slaves of them as of the rest, this privilege having been obtained of the king. As for the other inhabitants, they are all Indian strangers residing there by permission of the Portuguese, to whom such of them as are not Christians pay a poll tax. Of old Christians, besides Portuguese, there are a very few Castilians, but a number of Venetians and other Italians, who are the best received: there are also some Germans and Flemings, a good number of Armenians, and some English; but of Frenchmen not one, save the Jesuit Father already mentioned, and a Lorrainer from Nancy, called Jean de Seine, and another Walloon, whom I saw there, named Father Nicolas Trigaut,[1] a native of Douay, who afterwards, while I was still there, was sent to Cochin, and subsequently to Malaca, and thence to China, where he remained some years, visiting six of the provinces of that great kingdom, as well as all the houses and residences of the Society. He was afterwards sent to Europe on business of his Order, on which occasion he re-traversed the whole of the East Indies, and,

[1] Born at Douay, 1577. At age of 17 entered the Society of Jesus, and studied at Ghent. In 1606 proceeded to Lisbon and embarked for India, arriving at Goa 10th Oct. 1607. Here he was detained by bad health till 1610, when he embarked for Macao. The reason for his return to Europe was to obtain more missionaries to work the vast field which he saw lay open in China: and with this aim he published at Rome the work referred to below. It met with speedy success, and he was enabled to return to the East in 1618 with no less than forty-four coadjutors, many of whom, however, died on the way. He himself fell ill at Goa, and was long in danger. In 1620 he again proceeded to China, where he administered the whole work of the Society, employing his leisure in studying the history of China. He died at Nankin, 14th Nov. 1628.

coming by way of Persia, Arabia Deserta, Egypt, Cyprus, Candia, Zanthe, at length landed at Otranto, thence to Rome, Spain, France, and the Low Countries. Thence finally he has in this year, 1618, departed to return to the same Indies with a goodly number of companions, all adepts in some profession, and with a large supply of divers kinds of pretty conceits and varieties of these parts to take to those,—as, for instance, some excellent pictures, maps of the world, geographical charts, globes, astrolabes, clocks, and other instruments, mathematical and musical, which are greatly esteemed in those countries. This Father Trigaut, being at Rome, had printed there a very ample and exact history of China, drawn as well from the memoirs of Father Matthieu Ricci,[1] who had lived there full thirty years, as from the information he had himself acquired on the spot: this history, composed by him in Latin, has since been translated into several languages.[2] I neither could, nor should have passed over in silence what I have just paused to say of this good Father, both because of my having seen and known him at Goa, and because of his personal worth and merit as shown by the goodness of his life, his knowledge and experience, his extensive travels and intimate acquaintance with all the countries of the Indies, and, not least, his understanding of

[1] The celebrated Jesuit missionary, born 1552, founded the Jesuit College at Nankin, and was in great favour with the Chinese Court, chiefly by reason of his scientific knowledge, which, by his ample acquaintance with the Chinese language, he was enabled to impart to the natives. He died at Pekin, 1610.

[2] Its title is *De Christianâ expeditione apud Sinas susceptâ ab Soc. Jes. Ex P. Matthæi Ricii ejusdem Societatis Commentariis*, libri v, se auctore P. Nicolao Trigautio Belg. ex eâdem Societate, 4to., Romæ, 1615. Trigaut's first published work seems to be a letter addressed from Goa (Christmas Eve, 1607) to the Jesuits of Flanders, and published under the title *Lettre écrite*, etc., Bordeaux, 1608, 8vo. A second edition of the Ricci Commentaries was published at Augsburg in 1615. His other works are *De Christianis apud Japonicos triumphis* (1623), and *Regni Sinensis descriptio*, and a Chinese Dictionary (1639).

many different languages, both of this part of the world and of that.

But to return to my relation of Goa: the Indian people that are not Christians are very numerous; they are the *Banianes* of Cambaye and Surate, and the *Bramenis*. I have heard it often said among the Bramenis of Calecut that the island of Goa belonged to them, and that on that account they were bitter enemies of the Portuguese. So it is that such of them as are men of honour and spirit will never reside in any place under the rule of the Portuguese, who are too overbearing and proud towards them; for which reason the most part of them have gone to reside at Calecut, where they enjoy complete security and liberty. The Moors and Mahometans come from all the coasts of India, as from Guzerate, Persia, and elsewhere. There are there also a goodly number of Chinese and Japanese. Among the Portuguese there are great differences in regard to their estimation: for the most esteemed are those who have come from Portugal, and are called "Portuguese of Portugal"; next are those born in India of Portuguese father and mother, and called *Castiri*,[1] that is, of their caste and blood; the least esteemed are the offspring of a Portuguese and an Indian parent, called *Metices*, that is, Metifs, or mixed. Those born of a Portuguese father and a Caffre, or African negro mother, are called *Mulastres*,[2] and are held in like consideration with

[1] Misprint for *castici*, which should be *castiços*, "of good birth". Mr. Teixeira Pinto, judge of Goa, in his *Memorias sobre as Poss. Port.* (Goa, 1859, 16mo.), points the distinctions of these terms thus:—"The Portuguese, whether of Europe or Brazil, are at Goa called indifferently *Frangues* or *Fringuins* or *Reiñoes*; those born in India of pure Portuguese blood, *Castiços*, corresponding to the *Creoles* of America; half-castes are *Mestiços*; children of native Christians are *Canarins*; those of 'Gentile' or heathen parentage are *Conkanos*." (*Mem.*, p. 168.) The term *castiços* was adopted in Anglo-Indian use as *castees* (see Yule, *Gloss.*, s. v.), but without any acknowledgment of purity of blood.

[2] Mulattos.

the Metifs. These Metices plume themselves much when their father or mother is of Brameny race. In Bresil the offspring of the two races are called *Mameluques*.[1]

As for the slaves of Goa, their number is infinite; they are of all the Indian nations, and a very great traffic is done in them. They are exported to Portugal, and to all places under the Portuguese dominion. The Portuguese carry off the children, seducing them by fair speeches, and leading them away and hiding them, both little and big, and as many as they can, yea, even though they be the children of friendly races, and though there be a treaty of peace whereby they are prohibited from taking them for slaves; for all that, they cease not to kidnap them secretly and to sell them.

CHAPTER III.

Of the City of Goa, its squares, streets, churches, palaces, and other buildings.

Having spoken of the island of Goa, I now come to the city, of which I shall in the first place say that it is not over-strong; and whosoever should make himself master of the island would be master of the town also, which has no staunch fortress, but is strong in men alone: for though it is enclosed with walls, yet are these walls low, like those wherewith we enclose our gardens here. It is strong on the riverside only. The old walls of the town were higher and

[1] Ar. *Mamlúk*, "one bought", *i.e.*, a slave. The name has travelled west from Egypt, as Capt. Burton shows (Hans Stade, *Hak. Soc.*, p. 45, *note*). Sultan Saladin chose for his *mamelukes* those of a mixed Turk and Circassian breed. The term thus became the equivalent of the Port. *mestiço*. The Mamelukes of S. Paulo acquired a terrible name in the eighteenth century; but in that district of Brazil the term has given way to *Caboclo*. Mr. Bates, however, states that it is still used in the Amazons (*Nat. on the Amazons*, vol. i, ch. i).

stronger, and had good gates, which no longer exist; for the town having increased more than two-thirds in size, all those ancient buildings are now useless. The Portuguese take no thought to protect it on the land side of the island, because of the good passages, to which they trust entirely.

The north side of the city is built on the river, and is half a league in length, having many gates, each guarded by a warder. These are crippled fellows, who get the place by way of compensation, and for life. Between the town and the river are three large esplanades along the water-side, separated and enclosed with good walls, which are connected with those of the town, and run out into the river, in such wise that none may enter or depart but by the gates (whereat these gatekeepers search everyone), or else by water in boats. The first of these esplanades one meets in arriving at the town from the west is the largest and finest, and is called *La Riviera grande*[1] (for they call these esplanades *Rivières*). It has two gates entering to the town. It is very well laid out, having some terraces and ramparts, with cannon to defend the river. The commander there is the *Viador de Fasienda*, who has a good and strong residence within it, having a gate on the town side, and another on the riverside; and he alone has the privilege of closing these gates every night for fear, not of enemies, but of the robbers of the town.

This Viador is overseer of all finances, and also of everything that goes on in Goa, as well affairs of war and shipping as all other affairs, he being the second personage next after the viceroy in all that pertains to the affairs of the king. Over against his lodging in the said esplanade is a fine church

[1] Port. *Ribeira grande*, in early days called simply Ribeira, or *R. das naus*, or *R. das armadas*. This was the great arsenal of Goa, and included the docks and the mint. It was a royal precinct under the Vedor da Fazenda, and exempt from the jurisdiction of the municipality.

called *Cinq Achagua*,[1] that is to say, "the Five Wounds", richly adorned and garnished, at which there are two priests only. In the porch of this church is a space well enclosed with barricades, where every day this Viador and the other officers of the king assemble, seated round a table to transact all business that presents itself; for all the other officers, and chiefly those who have to do with embarkations, reside there too. All these lodgings and the esplanades in that part belong to the king, so that these officers are lodged there all their time at his expense.

It is on this *rivière*, or esplanade, that they mint the money, cast the cannon, and do other ironwork necessary for the ships of war or trading vessels. It is a marvel to see the number of artizans working there in all materials, without observing either festivals or Sundays, saying they are about the service of their king. Each of these craftsmen has a grand master, called *Mayor*, who is a Portuguese, having command over those only of his own art; as, for instance, carpenters, masons, blacksmiths, master mariners, caulkers, gunners, founders, etc., who are all or mostly Indians. They are all paid on Sunday mornings, and work not on that day after noon. It is the finest sight in the world to see the vast number of ships that are there, as well in the harbour as on the beach. There, too, are lodged the elephants, when there are any in Goa; but while I was there, there were none. But be it noted that all the officers, *mayors*, have their own offices and places for keeping and locking up all the material and utensils proper to their craft; the workmen, too, have their own places. All these offices are vaulted with stone, and strongly built, for fear of fire. The Viador, from his gallery, sees from one end to the other all that goes on, as well on the esplanade as on the water; and every night there are

[1] Port. *Cinco Chagas*. An extra-parochial chapel for the arsenal (*C. de Kloguen*).

Dead-payes[1] on guard, and the sentinels cry aloud and respond to one another. All this is out of fear lest their ships should be set on fire, of which there is a vast number, both Portuguese and Indian. These men are hired, whether Indians or Christians, and are called *Naicles.*[2] There are a great number of them, and are relieved at daybreak. Their duty is to carry out the orders of the Viador, to go messages for him, and do other service like petty sergeants or beadles. All the artizans are called over twice a day. There is the *Contador,*[3] who pays them, and the *Puntador,*[4] who pricks them off and measures their work in such wise that if their work be short they have to suffer a like abatement of their time. But this leads to much abuse, for if the Contador and Puntador are so minded, they count as they please. The money is distributed and paid there in public, except large sums, which are paid separately. In this same place is the prison of the Salle, wherein I was placed; thither the Viador sends all sorts of men that are under his charge and belong to him. This Viador has two *Merignes,* or sergeants, and one writer. All these officers well understand how to steal and to fleece the public. There is a little galiot, called *Manchoué,*[5] well

[1] In orig. mortepayes. "Dead-payes: soldiers in ordinary pay, for the guard of a fortress, or frontier town, during their lives. In France they be exempted from the Taille" (*Cotgrave*).

[2] Hind. *nayak*, a leader or chief, but in Portuguese and British India applied to native officers of the rank of corporal (see Yule, *Gloss.*, *s. v.* "Naik").

[3] Accountant, "the officer who presides in the tribunal of the *Casa dos Contos*" (*Bluteau*).

[4] A mistake for *Apontador*, an overseer; from the pricking off, the author would seem to connect it with *punctuar.*

[5] Port. *manchua*, from Malayāl. *manji*. Col. Yule describes it only as a large cargo boat, but at Goa it meant a large gondola (Mandelslo, p. 98, indeed, mentions it as a gondola), rowed, however, and not pushed. P. della Valle calls it *manciva* "going with 20 to 24 oars, only differing from the *Almedies*, in that the *Mancive* have a large covered room in the poop" (Letter VIII). It was probably the same which Fryer (p. 70) calls a "baloon".

covered in, which the king provides him with for going to and from the ships, and hither and thither by water: it takes only eight or nine hands to man it. The viceroy has one also, so have the great officers, and even the archbishop, and many other private persons. It is very comfortable, being built in the form of a carriage, saving that it has no opening at the sides.

But to return to the Viador. There is no one at Goa, after the viceroy, who can look after himself and play the thief as he can; for whatever is over of all shipments, from Portugal and all other parts, whether provisions, utensils, or other goods,—all that goes to him, and he does what he likes with it. And when the ship starts again he has to furnish her with all her provisions, equipments, and utensils, on which he makes a further robbery; for against every sol of cost he charges two, and the viceroy and he understand each other full well.[1] The viceroy makes the order for all payments and gifts in writing, and the Viador pays nothing unless he sees a certain mark on his signature, or unless he is told by word of mouth, and the treasurer does the same. For the payment of cash the intervention of others is required, but the expenses and outgoings for ships, and the balances remaining in respect thereof, all these are in the hands of the Viador de Fasienda alone.

At the two gates of this esplanade, or *rivière*, are porters and guards stationed, who let none go out or come in without searching them, for fear lest they should have stolen something. In that place no shipments are made, except on behalf of the king or of the said officers. The place is of great length and breadth, but four times as long as it is broad.

[1] Fully borne out by De Couto in his *Soldado Pratico*; indeed, the historian goes further: for example, he states that when the *vedor* bought Ormuz horses for the king's service, and paid 200 cruzados apiece for them, he would charge 600 cruzados in his accounts; and in many cases he shows that out of two sous charged, the king frequently got no value at all.

In breadth it is two hundred paces, and it is all full of valuable property belonging to the king.

Turning to the east from this place you come out near the Royal Hospital inside the town, and you enter another large square, also enclosed, which is between the said hospital and the *Rivière.* It is only a landing-place for fishermen, and a place for all other classes of people to take boat or land. This place is called *Caye de Sancta Catherina,* or *Bazar de Pesche,*[1] meaning "fishmarket", the fish being landed and sold there.

This quay is very convenient when the fleet arrives from Portugal, for as soon as the sick are landed they are close to the gate of the hospital, whose walls enclose the town on that side. All the merchandise is landed at pleasure, for that of the fleet mentioned pays no dues at Goa. This place is, as it were, the middle of the whole town; it has terraces, and gates which are shut only when required. All the bank of the river, along the whole length of the town, is slime and mud. But when the vessels of Portugal arrive it is a marvel to see the crowd of people on the quay of all sorts, slaves and other Christians, Canarins, Cafres, and other Gentiles, who are like porters or carriers, there called *Boye,*[2] that is,

[1] *Caes de Santa Catherina*, or *Bazar do peixe.*

[2] Tel. and Malayâlam *bōyi*; Konk. *bhūi*, the caste from which carriers were taken, and used in Portuguese India for carriers and porters; *e.g.* (in 1554), "hum bóy do sombreiro", an umbrella boy; "bóys d'aguoa", water-carriers (S. Botelho, *Tombo*, 57); (in 1591) "the *bois* or mouços who carry such palanquins", etc. (*Arch. Port. Or.*, Fasc. 3, 324). The above is from Yule's *Gloss.*, *s. v.* "boy". Pyrard's fanciful interpretation "ox", Port. *boi*, may be due either to himself or to some Portuguese friend who would have his joke. It is repeated by Boullaye le Gouz (p. 211), who finds a parallel indignity in the use of the term *mulets* by the French gentry towards their chair-men. As is well known, the term "boy" is in common use in West and South India, and in Ceylon and China, for the native personal servant of a European. Col. Yule, rightly, I think, recognises in this more modern use the English "boy" employed as the Latin "puer". It is noteworthy that the Portuguese (see

"ox", and carry whatever heavy fardels there may be; for they use no carts, but carry everything on their shoulders with *bambous*, which are reeds as thick as the leg. This wood is the hardest to break or snap I have ever seen. To carry a cask of Portugal wine, containing three hogsheads or thereabouts, takes four, six, or eight of these fellows, according to the weight, with two of these *bambous*, each carrying an end on his shoulder, and so with other goods. But in building they use carts, though without iron tires, for fear of wearing the pavements; they are drawn by buffaloes and oxen, and serve to carry stone and timber. These *Boye* when laden continually chant their songs, which consist of some cock-and-bull stories strung together in question and answer, and they keep incessantly running. All the streets are full of these fellows at all sorts of jobs, either carrying *Sombreros* or *Parasoles* and *Palanquins*, or aught else that may be required, and they are always to be found at certain cross-roads. This esplanade is thus quite a public place.

But the other *rivière* or esplanade, which is next to it, is well enclosed all round, even far out into the water: it is called *la Ribere dos Gallees*,[1] for in this place lie the galleys of Goa, which are of the same build as those of Spain and Italy; but there are only some three or four of them at most. This esplanade is well built and provided with every requirement, as well for the masters of the workshops, the equipment of the galleys, as for the convicts, who are all there, save a certain number that are in the prison of the Salle for the purpose of work there. These galleys never go to sea except in case of great necessity.

Among these galley convicts I saw one that was a Malabar,

above) used their own equivalent for "puer", viz., *mouço*, as the equivalent for the Indian *bóy*; and further, it is curious that the Anglo-Indian "boy" is in vogue chiefly in those parts of the coast which were formerly Portuguese.

[1] *Ribeira das galés.*

and brother of the great Malabar lord and captain named Cousty Hamede,[1] of the town and fort of Badara, whereof I have already spoken. This convict had turned Christian; he was about thirty years of age, and was called Don Pedro Rodrigo, and was a good-looking fellow. I believe that if he had been at liberty he would not long have remained a Christian. He did not work like the rest, but had command of a squad of convicts, being, however, in chains, as were the rest, even when they went to work in the town, which was often enough. I accosted him several times, and spoke to him for the sake of his brother, who took a liking to me, and gave me a good reception when I passed by Badara and *Marquaire Costé*.

But in regard to these convicts and captives, I will say in passing that the King of Spain never allows an exchange of prisoners, and this is a maxim of policy in those parts: for if that were allowed they would not be greatly concerned about letting themselves be taken. The Portuguese, however, believe their Government to be less damaged and weakened by one man losing his hand or his life, than if they had to pay 10,000 crowns of ransom, and it is well known that their fellow-countrymen will not fail to ransom such as are taken prisoners. There is, too, another reason, which is this, that this procedure gives more courage to the Spaniards and Portuguese, who on other accounts are under a greater obligation to fight well and to avoid being taken, for it is not the King of Spain who ransoms the prisoners, but themselves or their relatives; and if they have not the wherewithal, it is provided by the *Misericorde*, or by people of means and wealth. As for the Indian prisoners taken by the Portuguese, they all belong to the king, who gives a reward to the soldiers that took them, that, is ten *Pardos* for each prisoner; and though the prisoner were to offer all the gold in the world as ransom, he cannot recover his liberty,

[1] See vol. i, pp. 339, 349, 357.

PRINCIPAL GATE OF THE CITY OF GOA,
COMMONLY CALLED THE ARCH OF THE VICEROYS.

but remains ever a galley-slave ; so that when the Portuguese happen to be themselves taken, every endeavour is made to get them back by money, and not in exchange.

But to return to these river passages whereof we have spoken ; the gates are guarded by keepers, and no person may enter except on business. The place is very handsome and spacious, and the viceroy descends by a little gate from his palace, and takes boat without being seen. All the merchandise forming the cargoes of the carracks and large vessels going to Portugal must be shipped there, and the Viador de Fasienda has a little house on the water-side, and goes to and from the vessels to inspect them and to keep accounts, and to register everything that is shipped. Three per centum is paid on exports from Goa ; but if an agreement be come to with him, you pay very little. All the quays are very well walled, and most of them have stone steps. Entering the town on the right from this place are the magazines and arsenals of war material and guns, with large, well-built, and strong warehouses. The town gate on this side is the most handsome and magnificent ; it adjoins the viceroy's palace. This gateway underneath is all painted with the wars of the Portuguese in India, while above the entrance is a fine image, a bust of Sancta Catherina, all gilded. This saint is the patroness of Goa, for it was upon her feast-day[1] that the Portuguese made themselves masters of the island.

Besides these places there are others on the river that are neither enclosed nor guarded like the preceding. There is one such between the river and the palace of the viceroy, *La Fortaleza del vice Rey.*[2] It is some seven hundred paces in length, two hundred in breadth, very straight and com-

[1] Nov. 25.

[2] The viceroy's palace stood on the site, and seems to have retained much of the masonry, or at least design, of the palace of the Sabaio (*Dalb. Comm.*, iii, 17 ; Fonseca's *Goa*, 194).

pact, and built up on the river-side with a fine wall with steps of stone. On one side it is enclosed by the walls of the viceroy's palace and of the town, and on the other by those of the other esplanades. This esplanade or quay, called *terrero grande*, is generally employed for mooring all the vessels of the Indian merchants that come to land there, both on account of the *Fortaleza* of the viceroy, which covers it, and because the viceroy from a window or gallery can see all that goes on. This place is always crowded with ships and vast numbers of people.[1] It contains a very handsome building, resembling the Place Royale at Paris in style, but not otherwise: it is called *l'Alfandequa*,[2] and there they store and sell in gross all kinds of grain, which may not be sold or taken elsewhere. The customs dues are paid there. There is another large building, called *Banquesalle*,[3] where are stored goods that are not for food; the dues are paid for them there, and thence they are conveyed to the houses. There is still another house there, where the weights are kept, called by them *el pezo*.[4] Next are the houses of the officers and renters. As soon as the ships are discharged they pass further up the river, and remove from in front of the fortress of the viceroy, giving place to fresh arrivals.

At the end of this quay there is a very large circular esplanade, where is held one of the markets, and the greatest in all Goa, so far as regards provisions. They call it *Bazar Grande*, that is to say, grand market. Every day market is held there, for they never keep provisions from one day to another; they even go twice a day, for dinner and supper. Even on Sundays and holidays provisions are sold there.

[1] "On landing we find ourselves within the quay of the viceroy's fortress. A luxuriant but lonely grove of palm-trees stands now on the site of this once busy pier" (*Fonseca*, 191).

[2] *Alfandega;* see i, 361, where he likens the custom-house at Calicut also to the Place Royale.

[3] See i, 85.

[4] Port. *Peso.*

There are several other squares and markets or bazaars, but none such as this. Over against it is a very fine square, containing the church of the Jacobins or Dominicans,[1] exceedingly well built and decorated, with some pretty water. There are many other parish and other churches, most of them dedicated to Our Lady.

As for the fortress, or palace of the viceroy, it is a most sumptuous construction; and all in front is a very large square on the town side, called *Campo del passo*,[2] where the nobles and courtiers assemble on horseback, on foot, and in their palanquins. For the viceroy never goes abroad without the previous day causing drums to be beat through the town, that so the *noblesse* may be advertised to assemble on horseback at early morn; and they remain there till he comes forth, all in their best array and order. Opposite the viceroy's gate is a large building, wherein the parliament is held, called *Cambra Presidialo*.[3] The first president is called *Desembarguador Mayor*.[4] It is the principal court of justice in India for the Portuguese; there is another subject to it. This palace of the viceroy is not strong in cannon on the town side; but it is a good and commodious residence. On entering you find on your right the prison, called *Tronco*, which is a wing of the palace; on the left are the magazines and the

[1] The Dominicans first arrived at Goa in 1548. This church was begun in 1550, and finished in 1564, and was thereafter the headquarters of the order, though they afterwards built two colleges in other parts of the city and suburbs (*Fonseca*, 250). Fryer says it was a huge fabric, with a magnificent front ascended by many steps, and surpassing the cathedral. The pillars were gilded, and the sacristy contained many vessels of great value (p. 149). It was seen and admired by Careri in 1695 (Churchill, *Voy.*, iv, 205), and by De Kloguen in this century (p. 118), and later by Dr. John Wilson (*Or. Chr. Spect.*, v, Ser. I, p. 123). This magnificent building was demolished in 1841, its treasures dispersed, and its stone used chiefly for barracks (*Fonseca*, 254).

[2] *Campo* or *terreiro do Paço*, the "Court-square".

[3] *Camara presidial;* the High Court was, however, generally called the *Relação*.

[4] *Desambargador Mõr*, "chief justice".

royal arsenal. The palace is supplied with all necessaries, such as a church, a clock, and water. Even the royal treasury is partly there; the other part is in the Franciscan convent. There are two large and handsome courts, with an entrance from one to the other. In the first court, on the left-hand, is a grand staircase, very broad, and built of stone, which leads to a great hall, containing paintings of all the fleets and vessels which have gone to the Indies, with their numbers, dates, and names of the captains. Even the ships of war that have been wrecked are portrayed there. It is a fearful sight to see so many lost ships. In short, there is not a small vessel that has gone from Portugal but is there portrayed, with her name inscribed, along with her history and achievements.[1] Further on is another and larger hall, which is that of the viceroy himself, and of the *noblesse*, where the council is held. In it are life-size paintings of all the viceroys who have been in the Indies.[2] All comers are not permitted to enter; and guards are placed there. The palace is on high ground, and is very strong on the river-side, supported by very lofty walls; it has the finest prospect in the whole town. The stables are not within, but adjoining on

[1] Fonseca (p. 195, citing *Boletim e Ann. do Cons. Ultramarino*, No. 155, p. 41) remarks that down to 1612 the number of ships which had left Portugal for India was 806. Linschoten (i, 219) adds that the names of all the captains were given.

[2] This interesting gallery of portraits, previously mentioned by Linschoten (*ubi supra*), and afterwards by Mandelslo, who seems to have taken them to be of European princes, is happily preserved in the Governor's palace at Pangim (*Burton*, 42; *Fonseca*, 100), though it seems the "restorer" has been let loose among the pictures. There can be little doubt that the beautifully coloured portraits of the viceroys in the Resende MS. at the British Museum (Sloane MS. 197), were copied on the spot from these pictures, though Mr. Birch (*Dalb. Comm.*, i, Intro., p. ix) finds in the MS. no acknowledgment of their source. I have compared the photograph of the Governor Nuno da Cunha, in J. G. da Cunha's *Chaul and Bassein*, which is "copied from an ancient oil painting in Goa", with the portrait of the same governor in the MS., and find them to be obviously from the same original.

the right-hand of the entrance. There is an exit on the river-side, but that door is not open except when the viceroy is pleased to go to the water. His guard is a company of a hundred men, all habited in blue, which is their ordinary livery. They are always close to his person, and are in waiting at the door of the palace or of any house wherein he may be; and when he walks abroad the drums and fifes are played. These archers carry halberts, and are all Portuguese, but they are not held in the same honour and repute as those who go with the armies, the latter being volunteers. In addition to these there are porters at the gates of the fortress.

Proceeding from this palace to the town, you enter the most handsome street of Goa, called *la Ruo drecho*,[1] or "straight". It is more than 1,500 paces in length, and on both sides has many rich lapidaries, goldsmiths, and bankers, and also the richest and best merchants and artisans in Goa, all Portuguese, Italians, or Germans, as well as other Europeans. This street ends with a church, the most beautiful, rich, and highly decorated in Goa. It is all gilded within. This is the church *de la Sancta Misericordia*, dedicated to *Nuestra Senora Dasera*.[2] Over the portal, in the most conspicuous place, is a bust in stone, gilded, of *Don Alfonce Albuquerque*, who took the island of Goa.[3] Near this church is a monastery for orphan girls of good family to

[1] *Rua Direita*, so called because nearly all the others were curvilinear. It was in this street that Fitch and Newberry took a shop in 1583 (*Hak. Voy.*, i, 211).

[2] This is a mistake. The church of *N. S. da Serra* adjoined the Misericordia, but the latter had its own chapel. The former church was built by Albuquerque in 1514, in fulfilment of a vow made in the Red Sea, when his ship the *N. S. da Serra* was in danger. It is still standing, but roofless, and used as a cemetery (*Fonseca*, 245). The *Santa Casa*, with its chapel, was built in 1520, the chapel being, after the time of Pyrard, rebuilt as a large church, "the ruins of which still excite admiration" (*Fonseca*, *ib.*).

[3] The statue was removed to the Artillery Barracks at Pangim some years ago, and was being re-erected, "with a new nose and other requisites", at the time of Burton's visit (*Goa*, p. 41).

reside at until they get married. The married Portuguese also, when they go a voyage, put their wives in there, against their return. Widows also, who wish to retire from the world, are placed there, and even repentant girls are allowed to enter; no visitors are permitted.[1] This grand *ruo drecho* is otherwise called *Laylon*,[2] because of the auctions and sales of clothes, and all other kinds of merchandise, even slaves and horses, that are conducted there; in such wise that on every day except Sundays and holidays, from six in the morning until noon, it is as full of people as it will hold.

Half-way down this street is one of the oldest and largest buildings of the town, called *Casa da Santa Inquisitione*,[3] where all the officers of the said Inquisition are lodged. The same order is observed as in Portugal, albeit the justice administered there is more severe in the case of the richer classes. In front of this house is a large square or market, and on the other is the town-hall, a moderately good

[1] Rivara points out that the author confuses two institutions,—(1) the Retreat of S. Mary Magdalen for repentant women, and (2) the Retreat of the Serra for orphan girls. Both were established by Archbishop Menezes in 1606, and perhaps at this time the two classes were to some extent mixed. On the 12th March 1611, the king writes that, according to his information, the first-named Retreat was becoming a resort for the soldiers, and orders its suppression. On the 12th March 1612, he again calls for a report (*Liv. das Monç.*, ii, 94, 210).

[2] Port. *leilão*, from the Ar. *i'lām*, "proclamation". The Port. word has been adopted in Hindustani as *nīlām*, and in Chinese as *yélang*, and at Amoy as *lélang* (Yule, *Gloss.*, s. v. "Neelām"). As to the street and auction, cf. *Linschoten*, i, 184-5, and see his picture of the scene in the English edition of 1598.

[3] The Holy Office was established in Goa in 1560, and installed in this palace, which had been the viceroy's down to 1554. It was a stately edifice of three stories. The evil celebrity of the Inquisition of Goa has made this building a chief object of attraction to all travellers (for references, see *Fonseca*, 210). The tribunal of the Inquisition was abolished in 1774, and the Marquis de Pombal directed that the building should be used again as the viceroy's palace; but this was not carried out, and the edifice was finally razed to the ground, 1828-30. As to the tribunal, see further below (ch. vi).

building, called by them *Cambre de Cidade*. The Palace of the Inquisition is a very magnificent building, with a very fine large hall, and grand and lofty staircases, all built of the finest stone: no king's palace has so fine a hall.

Close by is the great church called *Assee*,[1] as we should say here "cathedral": it is dedicated, with its churchyard, to Our Lady. It is a grand and superb design, but it is a difficult task to finish, it being now fifty years since it was begun. Adjoining thereto is the *Casa do Arcebispo*, or house of the archbishop.[2] That of the bishop is hard by, where is also the prison of the church. Right opposite the churchyard of the great church is the convent of the Franciscans,[3] the handsomest and richest in the world: in the cloister there is painted the whole life of St. Francis, in gold, azure, and colours. This church is much frequented; it is erected upon very high ground: the great square in front is all paved with large stones, and there are

[1] Port. *a sé*, or *Sé Primacial*. It was dedicated not to Our Lady, but to S. Catherine. The first church was built by Albuquerque in 1511, and became the cathedral in 1534. In 1562 the viceroy, D. Franc. Coutinho, commenced to rebuild it on a magnificent scale; but as the work was done principally at the expense of the royal treasury, it was not half finished in 1623 (*Della Valle*), nor quite finished till 1631. It is 250 feet in length and 115 feet high. Dr. Fryer says it was hardly surpassed in grandeur by any church in England; and Dr. W. H. Russell speaks of its "vast and noble proportions" (*Prince of Wales's Tour*, p. 232). A view of it is given in Burton's *Goa*. There is a daily service still.

[2] The archbishop's palace is to the north-west of the cathedral. It does not appear in what year it was built. It was abandoned in the plague year (1695), since which time the prelates have lived at Pangim and elsewhere. This palace, however, still stands complete, 230 feet in length by 108 feet broad, and is now tenanted only by the *curé* (*Fonseca*, 209).

[3] The convent was begun in 1517, and the church in 1520. The Franciscans were expelled in 1835, and their property, then exceeding £13,000, confiscated by Government. Both the convent and the church were splendid edifices: the latter is still in fair preservation; the former is a fine ruin (*Fonseca*, 220-225; Xavier, *Res. Hist.*, p. 25).

broad steps for ascending to it. At the end is a great cross of stone, very lofty and highly wrought; thence you go down a street which leads straight to the Royal Hospital. On the left is the Chapel of *Sancta Catherina:* by this entry the town was taken, for there was here a gate and a rampart. This chapel is never open but on the day of the festival. Over the door is engraved in letters of gold the day and year of the capture,[1] and one of the finest ceremonies and solemnities of Goa is the general procession made on that day,[2] all the clergy and other townspeople assembling in their best array and magnificence, and bearing many effigies and mysteries, accompanied by music, mummeries, and other ridiculous things, as is done here at carousals and interludes; and so they use at all their popular processions.

Ascending thence you come straight upon a space called *Basar piquaine*, that is to say, "little market", in the midst of which is a portion raised six feet or thereabouts, all surrounded by a wall, and called *Terrero dos gallos;* that is, "the place of cocks", because fowls and other live stock are sold there.[3] Thence you come, near the middle of the town, to the Church of the Good Jesus, which is the church and house of the professed Jesuits. Next you enter the Hatters'

[1] The inscription was placed over the door in 1550, on the rebuilding of the chapel. It runs thus: "*Aqui neste lugar estava a porta por que entrou o Governador Affonso d'Alboquerque e tomou esta cidade aos Mouros em dia de Santa Catirina anno de* 1510 *em cujo louvor e memoria o Governador Jorge Cabral mandou fazer esta casa anno de* 1550 *á custa de S. A.*" The slab, with the inscription, is still to be seen in the wall near, but not over, the door (*Fonsèca*, 226; Rivara's *Pyrard*).

[2] The procession is still kept up, but proceeds from and returns to the cathedral (*Rivara*).

[3] A mistake; the *terreiro dos gallos* was the open space where cock-fighting went on. The sport was prohibited by Viceroy M. de Albuquerque in 1594 (*Arch. Port. Or.*, Fasc. 3, No. 157). From Pyrard's ignorance of the origin of the name, we may argue that the prohibition was effectual.

street,[1] very handsome, broad, and long, ending in a space called the *Pillorillo vieyo*,[2] that is to say, "the old pillory"; this also is a market, with a raised place surrounded with a stone wall. Opposite to it, in a large building, is the ordinary court of justice of Goa; and another for the police, with a handsome slaughter-house. Six or seven streets meet at this point, among them the largest of all, called *Ruo Grando*, which is one of the finest to be seen anywhere: it brings you straight to the principal church of the Jesuits, which is their college, dedicated to the Conversion of St. Paul.[3] Further on, passing under the cloisters and buttresses of the church, you come upon the outskirts of the town: and between the College and Church of St. Paul and the town gate is the Church of St. Thomas,[4] a large parish church; thence forth of the town you arrive at a large open space called *el campo St. Lazaro*, or *S. Iago*, because it is on the way to the village and fort of St. James. In this same campo is the *Hospital de S. Ladre*,[5] where the lepers are

[1] *Rua dos chapelleiros.*

[2] *Pelourinho velho.*

[3] The college was originally built by the fraternity of *Santa Fé* in 1541, and taken over by Francis Xavier in 1543 on behalf of the Jesuits. The inaugural ceremony is described by Correa (*Lendas*, iv, 289). It thereafter became the centre of the Society's propagandism in India, the Jesuits being thence known in India as *Paulistas*, or Paulistins. The church was built in 1560. "Some years afterwards a crack was noticed in one of its walls, and it was therefore supported from the outside by three arches. These arches were so wide and lofty that a high road passed beneath them, and so handsome that the building was called after them the Church of St. Paul of the Arches" (*Fonseca*, 263). C. de Kloguen (1827) found both college and church in the last stages of ruin, and a few years later both were demolished by Government.

[4] Built about 1560 to contain a bone of St. Thomas, which was as much of the Apostle's remains as the people of Meliapur would part with. It was in ruins in 1827, when C. de Kloguen was at Goa, and there are hardly any traces of it now (*Fonseca*, 271).

[5] The hospital of S. Lazaro was founded about 1530 (see royal despatch, *Arch. Port. Or.*, Fasc. i, No. 2), and was placed under the

kept: the building is handsome and well-constructed. The church has a pretty chapel dedicated to St. Louis, King of France. This hospital contained some sick; it was founded and is maintained by the town. On the other side, and right opposite, is a very fine tank or lake with many river-birds. In this *campo* all the cavaliers and gentlemen have their tournaments,[1] with their canes and oranges, on the days of St. John and St. James, the patron saints of the Portuguese and the Spaniards, and of St. Catherine the patroness of Goa: there, too, the inhabitants hold their shows.

On the other side, out of the town, is a place enclosed with walls, called *Mata Vaca*,[2] where animals are slaughtered. On the same side is the Court of Justice, and there is there a gallows-tree erected on four posts. Executions take place a quarter of a league from the town. They are constrained by reason of the heat to slaughter animals outside the town,

management of the municipality and the Misericordia. It was the scene of Xavier's earliest labours on his arrival at Goa in 1542. De Kloguen found it still in use in 1827, but it was finally closed in 1840; and the buildings are now in utter ruin (*Fonseca*, 268-70).

[1] As to these tournaments, etc., see further, ch. vii. Della Valle, in 1623, was present at the festa of St. John the Baptist. He says that the viceroy and all gentlemen of quality first rode through the city "in habits of masquert, but without vizards", and having heard mass in St. John's, proceeded to the street of St. Paul, called *La Carriera de' Cavalli*, which he describes as the finest open space in Goa. "Here, after many companies of Canarine Christians of the country had marched by with their ensigns, drums, and arms, leaping and playing along the streets, with their naked swords in their hands, for they are all Foot: at length all the Cavaliers run two *carriers* (careers) on horseback, one downwards from the Ch. of St. Paul towards the city, and the other upwards, running matches of two to two, or three to three, according to their attire agreed, with their Morisco cymiters, and at last they came all down marching together in order, and so went to the Piazza of the viceroy's palace, and so the solemnity ended" (P. Della Valle, *Eng. trans.*, 88).

[2] The place of cow-killing: so Linschoten, ii, 71 (*matavaquas*); though the common Portuguese for a slaughter-house is *matadeiro*, or *matadouro*.

and all the entrails and blood are buried on the spot. It is forbidden to all persons to slaughter elsewhere than there. Near the convent of St. Augustine is a large square or field, used only for exercising horses.

But it were an endless task to tell in detail the names of all the streets, squares, churches, monasteries, palaces, and other sights of Goa. Suffice it to say that it is all well laid out, that the *Banianes* and *Canarins* have their own streets, as also have all the divers merchants and craftsmen; for example, the goldsmiths have their own street, the lapidaries theirs, and so on[1]: in such wise that there is great public convenience, and when one has business to do in anything, one has only to know the street. And what caused me to tarry thus long in my description of this town is this, that whosoever knows it well, knows the whole estate of the Portuguese in the East Indies.

The number of churches there is a marvel: there is no square, street, or cross-roads without one; for example, those of *St. Augustine* and *Nostra Segnora de Gracia*, which are churches of the same Order, and dependent upon each other.[2] Behind this convent, outside the town, is their Novice-house, a handsome and well-constructed building. One goes from one to the other under cover by a fine lofty

[1] Fonseca (p. 157) gives the names of twenty three of the principal streets, among them the *Rua de Surradores* (curriers), *R. dos Ferreiros* (blacksmiths), *R. dos Ourives* (goldsmiths), *R. dos Judeus* (Jews), *R. dos Banianes*. Compare Linschoten, i, 228.

[2] The Augustinian monastery, first built in 1572, was rebuilt in 1597, and dedicated to *N. S. de Graça*. The church was dedicated to St. Augustine. These, with the Novice-house and a College, all standing on a splendid site on the hill of the Rozary, formed perhaps the finest group of buildings in Goa. Mandelslo says that one viewing it from a short distance "would take it for one of the noblest palaces in the world" (*Eng. trans.*, p. 101). It had fine galleries, halls, and cloisters, a vast number of dormitories, and a good library; all travellers have testified to its splendour; *e.g.*, Careri, Dr. Claudius Buchanan, Capt. Franklin, Dr. Wilson, and C. de Kloguen. The monastery was closed in 1835, and all the buildings are in ruin.

gallery on pillars and arches, and of considerable length: building goes on continually at this convent, the archbishop being of this Order. The convent is situate on the highest point of the whole town, on a mountain: over against it are the Churches of *St. Anthoine*[1] and *St. Roch*,[2] belonging to the Jesuits. In another place is the Monastery of the Nuns of *Saincte Monique*,[3] then the Church of *Nuestra Senora del Rozero*,[4] the Convent of *St. Thomas*,[5] and others. So that as

[1] The royal chapel of St. Antony, the national saint, on the Rosary hill, did not belong to the Jesuits. It was under the priests of the cathedral till 1606, when Archbishop Menezes handed it over to his own order, the Augustinians (*Fonseca*, 304).

[2] The chapel of St. Roch was adjacent to the great new Jesuit college of St. Paul. The college, which Dr. Fryer says was the largest religious building in Goa, had recently been constructed, and a year or two after Pyrard's time the students were transferred to it from the old college of St. Paul (see above). St. Roch remained the popular name for both chapel and college (*Fonseca*, 315).

[3] The great convent of Sta. Monica was begun by Archbishop Menezes in 1606, and completed in 1627; it was used, however, as the building went on. There was room for 100 nuns, with much additional accommodation for novices, lay sisters, servants, slaves, etc. In 1630 the viceroy describes it as larger than any convent in Portugal except Odivellas. In 1683 it attained great vogue by reason of an aged Sister, who, on dying, was discovered to be marked with the Stigmata, and narrowly escaped canonisation. During the gradual abandonment of old Goa in the last century, this convent suffered with the rest; in 1804 there were sixty-one, and in 1827 thirty, nuns; and in 1835 novices were refused. When Fonseca wrote (1878) there was but one aged nun left, and she is probably gone now. The above is by no means the only miracle manifested at this nunnery: let the unsatisfied reader consult the *Historia da Fundaçáo do R. Convento de Sta. Monica da Cidade de Goa*, by Fr. Agostinho, Lisboa, 1699; and Careri, in *Churchill's Voy. IV*. A good account of the convent appears in the *Chronista de Tissuary*, i, 215, by Rivara.

[4] *Nossa Senhora do Rozario*, on the Rosary Hill, made a parochial church in 1543. The feast of the Rosary was celebrated here with much pomp and circumstance (see P. della Valle). It is still occasionally used.

[5] The college of St. Thomas Aquinas at Banguenim, built 1596-7. It belonged to the Dominicans. In 1695, described as "large and beauti-

well in the town as in the suburbs, and throughout the island, there are about fifty churches and monasteries.

Of these churches four belong to the Jesuits. The first and principal is founded in honour of the Conversion of St. Paul. The college is the principal one in all the East Indies, wherein I have seen as many as 2,000 children and more at their studies, as well Portuguese as Indians. The Jesuits take nothing from the scholars for their instruction.

Adjoining this college is another fine house of the same Fathers, called the Seminary, where the children are boarded.

The second church or college held by the Jesuits is in the middle of the town, as handsome or even more so than the first-named: the church is founded in honour of the name of JESUS[1]: as I have said, it was richly built and all gilded within; it is not yet complete, but the work is proceeding day by day. I have seen there a cross of solid gold, which the company of Jesuit Fathers have had made for a present to the Pope: it was three feet in length, four fingers in width, and two in thickness, and embellished with all manner of precious stones, richly set: it was priced there at more than 100,000 crowns, and was sent to his Holiness by the vessel on which I embarked on my return.[2] This second house, which is that of the monks,[3] is entirely

ful, inhabited by twenty-five fathers" (*Careri*), visited by De Kloguen in 1827; closed in 1835. The roof fell in in 1844, and no trace of it remains (*Fonseca*, p. 322).

[1] The church of *Bom Jesus* is the most notable in Goa, partly for its architecture and decoration, and chiefly as now containing the tomb of St. Francis Xavier, on which account the whole church is well maintained. It was begun 1594 and consecrated 1605; but, as Pyrard says, was not finished even in his day. The church contains several memorial chapels besides Xavier's, and also some inscriptions, and many pictures of scenes from the life of the Apostle of the Indies.

[2] Col. Yule kindly made inquiry for me at Rome as to this cross, but no news could be obtained of it.

[3] The Professed House of *Bom Jesus* was begun in 1586, and completed about 1589. Mandelslo, who dined there and got the best Canary

dedicated to public service, viz., to confessions and administering of the sacraments, and for receiving into the Church and baptising infidels. It is in that the Father that is over the Christians resides; he is bound to go every day to the prisons to visit the Christians and others who would be converted to Christianity, to solicit their enlargement and to assist them with alms, as he did me many a time.

There is another house of these same Fathers adjoining this second church; it is called *Cathecuminos,* and is for catechising and teaching the new Christians: they are fed and supplied with clothing there, until such time as they are instructed and baptised: over these the Father of the Christians has charge, as over the whole house.

From this place, one day of the Feast of the Conversion of St. Paul, I saw come forth about 1,500 Indian persons, men, women, and children, habited in Christian fashion, to make their procession through the streets of the town, marching two and two, each having a bough or branch of palm in his hand, to distinguish them from the others, as being still unbaptised. Thence they went to the first church and college of St. Paul of the Jesuits, where they were all baptised.

Before they were baptised one of the Jesuit Fathers, as I saw, gave them an appropriate sermon upon the excellence of the Christian religion, that none should come there by constraint, that if any one of them had any regrets, he was free to withdraw and go forth of the church. Then all answered with one voice that they were well satisfied, and that they were willing to die in the Christian faith. Being baptised, everyone retired to his own house: if any of these were poor, to him the Jesuit Father gave some money by way of alms. This is repeated every year with the like

he ever drank, describes it in glowing terms. Anquetil du Perron calls it "a superb building, which would have been regarded in Europe as one of the most beautiful religious buildings" (*Disc. Prél. au Zend Avesta*, p. ccxiv).

pomp and solemnity as above, besides that many are baptised every day in private. I have also seen many a time great numbers baptised in the church of the Franciscans, on the morrow of Christmas, even as many as eight hundred.

The day of the Conversion of St. Paul, in this College of St. Paul, is held a great festival and ceremony. The viceroy, accompanied by all the nobility, to the number of 200 or 300 gentlemen on horseback, well mounted and caparisoned, proceeds to this church, and after the service dines with the Jesuit Fathers: this he never does but on this day only.

All the scholars of the Jesuits, richly dressed in all manner of silk liveries, come before him in line of battle, half mounted and half on foot, but all armed, and are paraded before the viceroy; the rest of the day is spent in different games and rejoicings.

The third house and church is founded in honour of St. Roch, and is called the Novitiate, where are the Portuguese novices who aspire to be Jesuits, to prove themselves whether they can persist in the observance of the rules. None are received as Jesuits, except such as are the offspring of Portuguese fathers and mothers; but the Indians can become priests. The other religious orders receive Metifs, but not pure Indians.

The fourth house of the Jesuits is situate half a league without the town: it is a handsome pleasure-house, with pretty fountains, and serves to cheer them up and to restore to health such as are sick, of their own Order only. These Jesuit Fathers are in great numbers there, and throughout India where the Portuguese are established, and about some of the infidel kings, where they have attained great results in the conversion of Indians to the Christian religion. The monks of the Orders of St. Dominic and St. Francis do the same.

All the churches and monasteries of Goa are superbly built, and most richly equipped and adorned with numerous reliquaries of chased gold and silver, with pearls and precious stones: as, for example, that containing the body of the ever-blessed Francis Xavier,[1] which is in the Church of St. Paul. This good Father was the first who, in the year 1553, essayed the voyage to China to preach the faith, surmounting all sorts of difficulties and obstacles which beset his path, and happily arrived at his destination ere death cut short the course of his holy and religious enterprise, the fruit whereof God reserved to those who have afterwards so nobly and with so great success laboured there. He died of sickness in an island near to China; his body was

[1] Even a sketch of the life of Xavier cannot be attempted here. The literature is already bulky: reference may be made to Padre Lucena, *Vida de F. X.*, etc.; Bouhours, *Vie de St. F. X.*, Paris, 1682, 4to; Bartoli, *Asia;* F. da Sousa, *Oriente Conquistado*, 1708; *Life of St. Francis Xavier*, by Father Coleridge, London, 1872; *Resumo Historico da Maravilhosa Vida, etc.*, by F. N. Xavier, Goa, 1861, etc. Suffice it here to say that he died at Sancian, off China, in Dec. 1552; his body was brought first to Malacca, and thence to Goa (1554), and deposited in St. Paul's, in a crystal coffin enclosed in another of silver. He was canonised in 1622, and in 1624 the body was removed to Bom Jesus (see Della Valle): that is, what was left of it, for in 1614 the Pope got the right arm, which, on being supplied with pen-and-ink, wrote the name "Xavier" (*Hamilton*, i, p. 257); and in 1554 a pious Portuguese lady, determined to possess a relic, had bitten off one of the toes (*Fonseca*, p. 297). Note as to this, that in 1556 a physician certified the body to be still free from corruption and to yield blood. For many years he was frequently exposed to view, but latterly these occasions have been more rare; once in 1782, and not again till 1859. Of the last exposition a very full account, with all minutest details, is given in F. N. Xavier's work, above mentioned, which also contains (as does Fonseca's *Goa*) a drawing of the saint as he then appeared. About the end of the seventeenth century arrived from Italy the magnificent tomb (the gift of the Grand Duke of Tuscany) in which the saint now reposes. It had not come when Careri saw the church in 1695. From Fonseca's drawing, this tomb must be a very beautiful sample of Florentine workmanship. It stands about twelve feet high, and is constructed of jasper and the finest marbles. A series of bas-reliefs are carved with scenes from the life of the saint. The silver coffin, with its jewels, is said to be a treasure in itself, and it also has the life portrayed in relief in thirty-two panels.

SHRINE CONTAINING THE BODY OF S. FRANCIS XAVIER,
APOSTLE OF THE INDIES,
IN THE CHURCH OF THE BOM JESUS, GOA.

afterwards brought to Goa, and laid in this church in a shrine of silver gilt, whereto great honour is paid, the body being to this day exhibited entire with great ceremony on the day of the Conversion of St. Paul.

The buildings of these churches and palaces, both public and private, are exceeding sumptuous and magnificent: the work is done for the most part by the Canarins, both Gentiles and Christians. The houses are built of lime and sand. The lime is made of the shells of oysters and sea-snails. The sand used is that from land, and not that of the river. The houses are covered with tiles, for window-glass is not employed; but in lieu thereof very thin polished oyster-shells, of a lozenge shape, and set in wooden frames. These give as much light as paper windows or horn lanterns, but are not so transparent as glass. Building stone is got in the island: but that used for columns and other grander work is brought from *Bassain*, and is there obtained in very long blocks of very great strength. It is like grained stone, but of better appearance. I have never seen in this country single columns of stone so thick and long as those there. The extent of their buildings is considerable, but they are of but few stories: they are coloured red and white, both without and within. The staircases are very wide, made partly of stone and partly of red earth, like *bol*, or *terre sigillée*, which serves for plaster. Nearly all have gardens and orchards, though not large, with wells within their enclosures.

As for the suburbs of the town, there are seven or eight of them, and they are very large: and all the buildings of them, as of the rest of the island, are in the same style as those of the town: albeit the shops are not so magnificent and gay. Carts drawn by buffaloes or bulls are used to convey the materials for building. These carts are not made with iron wheels. The pavement of the streets of the town is of fine, broad stone, and clean enough: that is to say, such of it as is on the slope, for the rest is very muddy. When it rains one sees streams all over the town, and the water runs in large, deep, vaulted, and paved canals: in winter this keeps the town very clean in some parts, but the streams in the streets are so broad, that at times one has some difficulty in crossing from one side of a street to the other, save that in some places there are little bridges and arches, but for which it would be impossible to cross.

CHAPTER IV.

Of the markets, slaves, money, water, and other remarkable things at Goa.

Having spoken in the preceding chapter of the squares of the town, I shall proceed to say something of the markets. These markets, as far as regards provisions, are held every working day, and even on the lesser festivals, from six or seven in the morning until noon; so, too, the great market, which is held all along the great straight street, the one end whereof touches the Misericordia, and the other the palace of the viceroy. This street is very handsome and broad, full of shops of jewellers, goldsmiths, lapidaries, carpet weavers, silk mercers, and other artizans. While this market is afoot, there is so great a crowd in the street that one can hardly pass. They fear neither rain in winter nor heat in summer, by reason of the large *sombreros* or parasols which everyone carries; these are six or seven feet in diameter at the least, in such wise that when a crowd is assembled they all touch one another, and the whole seems but one covering.

About three months before I left Goa it was ordered that the large square between the town-hall and the Inquisition should be taken as an addition to the market, which was too small. This market is called *Laylon*, as I have already said, because of the auctions that are held there. There are to be found there all sorts of persons, nobles and humble, of all nations and religions, buying and selling, or meeting for the purpose of business, for the place serves as an exchange. The auctions are not conducted by sergeants, but by others who do the business on their own account, paying a rent to the king; for there is no office, position, or craft so petty, but is farmed out on behalf of the king, who gets something from it. Sales of property, as well under orders of court as voluntary, are held there. Many, too, sell goods there as is usual in shops, without crying them at auction. The persons who conduct the auction-sales are called *Pregonneurs*,[1] or criers; they have to give ample security, for frequently large and valuable trinkets are put in their hands.

In this place are to be seen all kinds of merchandise, among others, numbers of slaves, whom they drive there as we do horses here[2]; and you see the sellers come with great troops following. Then in order to sell them they praise them and put them up, telling all they can do, their craft, strength, and health, while the buyers examine them, question them, and scan them all over with curiosity, both males and females. The slaves themselves, hoping better treatment with a change of masters, show their disposition and praise themselves to take the fancy of the buyers. In buying, however, a certain day is agreed upon beforehand for repudiating or closing the bargain, so that they have time to learn the truth.

You see there very pretty and elegant girls and women from all countries of India, most of whom can play upon

[1] Port. *pregoeiro*, a crier.

[2] Linschoten says they were sold daily "as beasts are sold with us" (i, 85). Dr. Burnell (p. 270, *note*) shows that the Portuguese did not begin, but merely continued an immemorial trade in African slaves. The British in India followed suit (see quotations in Yule's *Gloss.*, s. v. "Caffir").

instruments, embroider, sew very finely, and do all kinds of work, such as the making of sweetmeats, preserves, etc. All these slaves are very cheap, the dearest not being worth more than 20 or 30 perdos, of 32½ sols each. Girls that are virgins are sold as such, and are examined by women, so that none dare use any trickery. They deem it no sin to have intercourse with their slaves whom they have bought, so long as they are not married: for a girl's master being the man who marries her, she may not be so used after a man has plighted his troth to her. Some of these girls are very pretty, fair, and comely, others are olive-coloured, brown, and of all colours. But those to whom they are usually most attracted are the Caffre girls of Mozambique and other places in Africa, who are as wondrously black, with curly hair; they call these *Negra de Guinea.* It is a remarkable fact which I have observed among all the Indian peoples, as well males as females, that their bodies and perspiration have no smell, whereas the negroes of Africa, from both sides of the Cape of Good Hope, stink in such wise that when they are heated it is impossible to approach them: their savour is as bad as that of green leeks.

In the Indies, if a man has a male child by his slave, it is legitimate, and the slave becomes free, although she cannot leave her master without his consent; after his death, however, she is enfranchised, and she can be no more sold. The largest revenues and wealth of those at Goa are from the labour of their slaves, who, every evening, or at the week's end, bring what they are required to produce; others, again, are retained at their houses to wait upon them.

In this market are also to be seen a great number of other slaves that are not for sale, but themselves bring the work they have done, such as tapestry, embroideries, and needlework; as also preserves, fruits, and other things. Others earn money by fetching and carrying anything required. The girls deck themselves out in fine style for this purpose, so as to be more attractive, and to sell their goods the better. Sometimes the men call them into their houses to see them, and there talk to them of love, whereto they, being nothing loth, yield at once, the men giving them something.[1] Often, too, they manage love affairs for their mistresses in whose service they are, and never play a contrary game, or violate their confidence, being very faithful. All the money they can make in this way they must give to their master and mistress, who allow them to earn it so, giving them such share as seems good to them, but they do not always return a complete account. All these Indian women, as well Christian as others, and the Metisses also, prefer the company of a man of Europe or old Christian to that of an Indian. They get more money from them, and deem themselves more honoured by their society; for they love white men from these parts, and though some Indians are quite fair, yet they love them not so much.

In this market also are sold great numbers of horses, splendidly caparisoned for the most part. They come from Persia and Arabia, and are like those of Barbary; they are worth 500 pardos in their skins.[2]

In short, one sees there the wealth of the Indies in all kinds, and jewels the finest that can be seen. There also are the money changers, called *Cherafes*,[3] of whom there are several at other points. Their shops are at the ends of streets and at the cross-roads, all covered with money, whereof they pay a tribute to the king. Their gains are

[1] See *Linschoten*, i, 186.

[2] Taking the *pardão* at 4*s*. 2*d*. to 4*s*. 6d. (Yule, *Gloss.*, Supp.) this would be about £104 to £112 apiece. Linschoten corroborates the statement: he says good horses fetched 400 to 500 pardãos, and the best as much as 1,000 (=£224)! No doubt large numbers perished on the voyage, and in order to keep down the price they were imported into Goa free of duty (Cesar Frederick, Lond., 1588, p. 4; Wm. Barret in *Hak. Voy.*, i, 215).

[3] The "Shroffs" of Anglo-Indian use, *i.e.*, bankers, money changers, or cashiers. The word is Ar. *ṣarrāf* or *ṣairafi*.

very great, for it is necessary at Goa to have money to go to the market, where everything is of the very cheapest, and one only buys what is required for the hour, and not even for the whole day. So that one is half-burdened with this money, which is bulky and heavy, and of small value withal. There are several kinds of it. The first is that called *Bousuruques*,[1] of which 75 go to a *tangue*. There are other old *bousuruques*, of which 105 go to the *tangue*. Then there are little bits of copper without any mark, called *arco*,[2] 240 of which are worth a *tangue*, which is equal to 5 sols of our money, and 7½ sols there. Some of this money is of iron, the rest of *callin*,[3] a metal of China. When they have amassed a large quantity of all sorts of money they change it with the partisans[4] or farmers, giving them the silver and gold money, which is struck at Goa, for the receivers take no other in payment. As for the *Larins*,[5] which is the silver money referred to, and whereof I have spoken elsewhere, it comes from Persia and Ormuz, and is in request all over India, because it is of very good silver, and useful and handy for all occasions. These money changers must be at their shops on all Feast days, and even on Sundays,

[1] Port. *basaruco*, perhaps connected with "bazār"; but see Yule, *Gloss.*, s. v. "Budgrook". This coin was minted all through the Portuguese time, generally of copper, sometimes of tin and tutenay; it varied greatly in value. De Couto says that the Moors of the mainland made large numbers of counterfeit *basarucos* and smuggled them into Goa (*Soldado Pratico*, 128). Linschoten gives the same value to this coin (75 to the *tanga*). A great deal of information as to these coins will be found in Mr. G. da Cunha's *Indo-Port. Numismatics;* but most of his statements as to intrinsic values must be corrected by a perusal of Yule's *Gloss.*, art. "Pardão".

[2] Port. *arco*, a hoop. Rivara says the coin is still in use under the name *roda*, "wheel"; but the roda is a stamped coin, taking its name from St. Catherine's wheel, which it used to bear, and it is, in fact, the *basaruco*. I suspect that the *arco* consisted of bits of thick copper wire bent down in the fashion of the silver larin.

[3] See vol. i, p. 235.

[4] "Farmers of the king's revenues" (*Boyer*). [5] See vol. i, p. 232.

and they durst not decline to change a piece at the ordained rate. They weigh the gold and silver.

The silver money of Goa is *Perdos*, half *perdos*, *larins*, *tangues*, the last named worth 7 sols 6 deniers apiece, besides what comes from Spain, which is worth more at Goa, for there silver is one-third dearer than in Spain. The copper and iron money, which they call Bousuruques, is of little value, like our farthings. The gold pieces are *Cherufins*[1] of 25 sols the piece, and the *Venisiens*[2] and *S. Thomé*[3] of 50 sols: other kinds of Spanish gold money are not to be seen, for gold is worth much less there than in Spain.

Over against the square of *Lailon*, of which we have spoken, is another called, as I have said, *Pilory viejo*, or "old pillory", where there is held in the daytime a market of all sorts of fruits and eatables. But when the night comes on and the sun sets, and the *Merignes* or sergeants have withdrawn, there is held another market, called *baratilla*,[4] that is to say, "at cheap prices", of all sorts of stolen goods, such as clothes, arms, and other things which are sold in fear at very cheap rates. The whole square is full, large though it is; and though it be night the sergeants sometimes pass by, and when they are sighted everyone speedily gets out of the way; afterwards, however, when they have passed, all these vendors return to sell their merchandise: there are at times from four to five hundred of them.

[1] Port. *Xerafim*, from the Ar. *ashrafi*, in early days the gold dînâr = 11*s*. 6*d*. according to Col. Yule, but at this time less than half that value. Wm. Barret says: "5 tangas make a seraphine of gold." In Portuguese times, however, the term is generally applied to a silver coin called the *pardão xerafim*.

[2] Venetian sequins were worth a little more than *S. Thomes*. M. Barbosa puts them at 11½ to 12 tangas.

[3] So called from the figure of St. Thomas on the reverse (see cut in G. da Cunha, *Indo-Port. Num.*, pl. 2). It was first coined by Garcia de Sá, 1548-9. According to Manoel Barbosa (*Rem. Doct.*) it was worth 10 tangas, or 600 reis, in 1618 (*i.e.*, about 9*s*.).

[4] Port. *baratilha*, a cheap or petty auction.

In this square of the old pillory are to be found the bleeders, called *Sangueradores*,[1] and all who require them to bleed the sick go fetch them thence. They are all Christian Indians, as are all the surgeons and apothecaries.[2] As for the barbers, most of them are not Christians; they go about the streets shaving all comers: for the common folk have no scruples about being shaved in the open street; men of quality go within their shops for the purpose. These barbers are very handy fellows, and work for very little. Most of the Portuguese have their beards and heads shaved.

As for the fresh water used in the island of Goa, it must be remembered that the river surrounds the whole island, although the tide comes up as far as the town, rising and ebbing. But there are here and there a number of springs of water, good and excellent for drinking, which come from the rocks and mountains, and becoming streams, water the island in divers parts; and this is the reason there is so great a number of coco and other fruit trees. As for wells, there are few houses that have none, but they are not for drinking, the water not being good except at some. These wells serve only for bathing, and for washing the body, for cooking, for laundry purposes, and other needs. For there, both men and women of the half-castes bathe their private parts, after they have done the offices of nature, as do the Indians. There are also some fish-ponds and reservoirs, very pretty and built of stone.

But of the ordinary water that is drunk, as well in the city as in the suburbs, the best, healthiest, and lightest, to my mind, is that which is fetched a quarter of a league from the town, where there is a large, beautiful, and clear spring,

[1] Port. *Sangradores*.

[2] Linschoten (i, 230) says that the native physicians gave themselves great airs, having *sombreiros* carried over them, and that the Portuguese, from the viceroy downwards, put more trust in them than in their own doctors.

called *Banguenin*, coming out of the rocks. The Portuguese have had it enclosed with walls, and well supplied with good channels; while lower down are large reservoirs, where most of the men and women come to bleach the linen: these folks are called *Menates*[1]: and there are other reservoirs for bathing and washing the body. So that the way there is well trodden and much frequented, although it is difficult of access, because you have to ascend and descend three or four great hills. All the people there are going to and fro for this water alone, and even at ten o'clock at night there are some will assemble, armed, and will go in their shirts and drawers to bathe there. This water is sold in the town. The slaves distribute it everywhere, and carry it in large earthenware jars, holding about two buckets, and sell it at five *bousuruques* the jar, that is, about six deniers. They take their stand with their jars at certain cross-roads, and go not crying it about the town. They make bargains with their masters how much they are to account for the day, and they have to feed themselves upon their work, except on Feast days and Sundays, whereon their masters find them food; also when they are ill. The same is done in all other trades. The Portuguese might have had this spring led into the town by aqueducts and conduits, but they say that it enriches them, and occupies their slaves, and that strangers would get the enjoyment of this good water without any cost: for there are more strangers there than native inhabitants; for which reason they have not thought fit to conduct this water into the town.[2]

There is another very good fountain over against *S. Domi-*

[1] Malayālam *maināttu*, a washerman, used in Indo-Portuguese as *mainato*.

[2] A short-sighted policy indeed; the want of good water in Goa was one of the chief causes of the frightful epidemics which led to its present desolation. The Conde de Linhares in 1630 endeavoured to remedy the defect by bringing the Banguenim water to the city by an aqueduct (*Fonseca*, p. 150).

nique, that comes from a mountain on which is a fine church called *Nuestra Senora del Monte.*[1] It is very convenient, having reservoirs for washing linen. It is conveyed into the town for sale, and being nearer at hand, is sold at three bousuruques only. It is nothing like so good as that of *Banguenin.* Besides this, there are other waters round about the town, which are often passed off for *Banguenin* water. In the washing of linen they show a marvellous delicacy, and withal it costs but little. All their linen is of very fine cotton, and very durable; it is also very good for the health, as I found after experience of it for ten years. The *Menates* will bring you your shirt and a pair of drawers, very white and cleaned with soap, for two bousuruques; moreover, they return it all crisped and folded in a pretty fashion; for they soak it so, and then leave it to dry, so that this crisping lasts a long while, and the linen seems damasked and made in that way. They use this linen as well at table as for their beds, for shirts, bands, handkerchiefs, etc. Most of them change their linen every day. A very fine shirt costs but one tangue, or seven and a half sols. Of these cotton clothes a marvellous quantity are brought to Goa.

But to return to the waters: that of *Banguenin* is esteemed the best and the lightest, also none other is drunk at the hospital.

The Gentiles drink no other water but that of their house-wells, unless they go and fetch it elsewhere themselves, for they are afraid lest others should put something into their drinking-water. They drink from copper goblets made in the form of little pots, which they never touch with their mouths in drinking, as I have already said,—a custom observed by

[1] The hill is close to the Dominicans' convent. On the summit, which commands a view of the whole city, a chapel of Our Lady was built soon after the conquest. It had evidently been reconstructed as a "fine church". The present building, probably the same seen by Pyrard, is well preserved, but disused except on the annual festival (*Fonseca*, 256).

the Portuguese and Christian Indians also. All drink water only, men and women, girls and boys; it is great shame to them to drink wine, and to reproach them therewith is highly offensive. The women drink it not at all, but the men of quality drink a cup or two at most at their dinner and supper, but a little only, and without water. This wine comes from Portugal, and such as cannot afford that drink only *vin de passe*.[1] That of Portugal is worth forty sols the *canade*,[2] which is our pint; whereas the best *passe* is worth only twenty-five bousuruques, or six blanks,[3] and is good and strong. The Portuguese wine is a trifle sour when it reaches Goa. The other wine is white, called *arac*, and is worth only ten bousuruques; it is for folks of low condition and slaves, and they often get drunk of it; it is like *eau-de-vie*. They drink water from vessels made of the prettiest and finest earthenware possible, and the water from them is extremely good and cold. These vessels are enamelled and figured with a thousand different designs, animals and flowers; the enamel is of three colours only, black, white, and red; it is as fine

[1] Port. *vinho de passas*, "raisin wine". Pyrard distinguishes it from arrack, but it was merely arrack with an infusion of Muscat raisins. They are steeped for three or four days in a proportionate amount of arrack, and then taken out; the infusion is strained and poured into an arrack-barrel, and kept for six or eight months. To this infusion was sometimes added another of dates, to give it sweetness. This *vinho de passas* is not in use nowadays, but another concoction is, called *vinho de borra*. About 3 or 3½ xerafins' worth of arrack is put into a barrel that has contained wine from Europe, and kept for six or eight months, the dregs (*borras*) of other barrels are added, and after six or eight months it clarifies, and burnt sugar is added to give colour. This wine, when old, is confounded with white wine, but when rubbed in the palm of the hand it is seen to be a make up, and not the real white wine of the grape. Nowadays, too, a wine is made of weak arrack, with juice of caju, jambolão, and other fruits, the disagreeable odour being removed by means of vegetable charcoal (*Rivara*). "The Portuguese prepare it (arrack) so well with raisins and other ingredients that it is as good as any of their Portugal wines" (Houtman's *Voyage*).

[2] Port. *canada*.

[3] "Half of a sol, a piece of money which we call also a blanke" (*Cotgrave*).

and delicate as glass, and every vessel has a cover. Those in ordinary use are in the form of glass jars, save that the mouth is wider, and the lower part of the neck is less thick. There is a piece of the same ware which is very thin, and all pierced with little holes in pattern, having inside little pebbles which cannot come out: this is for cleaning the vessel. They call these *Gargoulete.*[1] The water comes out only a little at a time, and is let flow from above into the mouth, without a drop being spilled; they deride those who cannot drink in this fashion, as they did us. But I find that this method is in other respects not a good one, for it engenders windiness, for which reason many Portuguese do not adopt it. They have no glasses, except what are brought from these parts or from Persia, and that is but little, and moreover not much esteemed, as they get the *pourcelaines* of China at small cost.

But to return to the island and town of Goa: it is, as it were, the landing-place and halting-place for the whole of the Indies. It is wondrously peopled (not to speak of the strangers who are continually landing there), as well with Portuguese who are masters there, as with Metifs, Indian Christians, and a great quantity of Indian infidels, Mahometans or Gentiles, Banians of Cambaye, Canarins of Goa, Bramenis, and others of like condition who live there, carrying on a great trade and business, many of the richest of them possessing 80,000 to 100,000 crowns and even more. These are the men who farm the revenue, and hold all the great monopolies, as well from the king as from private persons, and both in merchandise and in other things; and nothing can be sold without the consent of these farmers. These classes of the people have streets to themselves, where they keep shops for each article of trade. For the Portuguese out there engage in no mechanical arts, in whatever necessity they may be, but call themselves all gentlemen, and live

[1] See vol. i, 329, *note.*

like noblemen, save that they traffic when it seems good to them, in gross but not retail. They, too, have the sole right to carry or possess arms, a right which is not conceded to the Indians, unless they be Christians.

The Portuguese men of quality never travel except on horseback; they have a large number of horses which come from Persia and Arabia; they are beautiful and good horses, like those of Spain, save that they are smaller; they are broken by the grooms, who are men of the Dealcan country, and very adroit.

The harness of these horses comes from Bengal, from China, and Persia; it is all of silk embroidery, and enriched with gold and silver and fine pearls. The stirrups are of silver gilt, the bridle is adorned with precious stones and silver, with silver bells. When they do not ride, they have themselves borne in a litter or *Palanquin*.

When they proceed about the streets they are followed by pages on foot, lacqueys, and slaves, in great number, bearing arms and dressed in their liveries. They never go forth but they cause to be carried over their heads by one of their slaves a parasol or sunshade, which they call *sombrero*, and those who cannot afford to possess slaves carry these themselves over their heads.

The women of quality, too, go not forth except seated and borne in a *Palanquin*, which is a kind of litter carried by four slaves, covered with a silk or leather hood, and followed by pages and a number of female slaves, all gaily dressed in silk; for silk is so common in those parts that even the valets are all clothed with it, and the ladies and gentlemen of quality prefer to wear serge stuffs from Europe.

Only the Portuguese may hold offices and benefices; and the soldiers of the garrison are Portuguese. The merchants and artisans are all Indians, as I have said, and they keep shops, paying a tribute to the king as well for their merchandise as for their shops.

CHAPTER V.

Of the government of Goa.—Of the viceroy, his court, and magnificence.

The city of Goa is governed by the viceroy, whose power extends over the whole of the East Indies. Every three years the King of Spain sends one out, who never makes his entry until his predecessor has made his exit, the latter retiring to a house appointed for the purpose. As soon as he has withdrawn, the other makes his entry with great magnificence and triumph.

He is escorted by the whole city, which goes forth to meet him at his castle of *Pangin*, with a fleet of galiots, *Manchouas*, and other vesssels. These gentry of the town represent the clergy, the noblesse, and the third estate, who accompany him, and give banquets in his honour, and keep open house the whole day. The viceroy then lands near the town, and thence proceeds with all this company to the *Asseo*, or cathedral church, where a *Te Deum* is sung; all the bells of the town are rung the day long. Thence he takes his way to the palace in the same order, where he has a display of all the wealth and curiosities of the town. All the day thousands of salvos of cannon are fired, and all night there is a blaze of fireworks. He is accompanied continually by instruments of music, trumpets and clarions, from the time he sets foot on land till he reaches his palace, which is a good quarter of a league's distance. Along his way are prepared many triumphal arches, each estate and guild of merchants making theirs in rivalry of the rest: these are in great numbers and of great beauty.[1]

If it happens that the viceroy dies within the three years,

[1] Barros and Couto likewise describe the ceremonies observed at the change of viceroys; perhaps the fullest account is that in Barros, *Dec III*, liv. IX, c. iii. (See also F. N. Xavier, *Scr. Chron.*, pp. 5-14.)

another is sent out by the King of Spain; and in the meantime the city is ready for the emergency, and one of the governors named in the letter of the King of Spain is taken; for usually these letters contain a power of substitution[1] of one person for another; that is to say, failing one, that such another should be the person: in this way many are named. These letters are not opened except in case of need, and the Jesuit Fathers are the keepers of them. They are opened in the town-house, in presence of all the principal Portuguese. When no one is named in the letter, then all the clergy, noblesse, and chief burghers assemble, and choose one of themselves, subject to the king's approval, as happened while I was there[2]; in such case the person elected is called Governor of India, and not Viceroy.

While I was at Goa I saw four that had been appointed one after the other.[3] He who was viceroy when I left was called *Dom Louys Laurence d'Estable.*

The viceroy there is obeyed like the King of Spain, and

[1] *Via de successão,* "method or course of succession". The ceremony is described by Linschoten (ii, 204), and by Philippus à S. Trin (Lat. edit., p. 228; Fr. edit., p. 282). These commissions were numbered and dated, and the most recent was opened first. Philippus describes the ceremony as taking place in the church during the funeral of the deceased viceroy. The body was brought within the church in the midst of the assembled grandees. Then the casket containing the *vias* was produced and opened by means of three keys kept by the secretary, chancellor, and treasurer respectively. If the person named in any *via* was abroad or dead, the next was opened, and in this way no less than six had to be opened on the occasion at which Philippus assisted.

[2] This is a mistake, as Mr. Rivara shows. The only governor who succeeded by substitution in Pyrard's time was André Furtado de Mendoça, and he was found to be nominated on the opening of the *vias*.

[3] He refers to (1) the Archbishop (Aleixo de Menezes) by nomination in the *vias*, in succession to the viceroy M. Affonso de Castro, who had died at Malacca; (2) the Conde de Feira, sent out as viceroy in 1608, who died on the voyage; (3) A. Furtado de Mendoça, who succeeded as governor by *via*, 27th May 1609; and (4) the viceroy Ruy Lourenço de Tavora, who arrived from Portugal 5th Sept. 1609.

has the same authority, having power to grant pardons, or to condemn to death without appeal, save in the case of gentlemen, called by them *Fidalgos*. For these, when they appeal, whether in criminal or civil matters, are sent prisoners, chained at the feet, to Portugal.[1] I saw at Goa a soldier who, being condemned to death for having slain a man, was being taken to the place of execution, a quarter of a league from the town. It happened by his good fortune that he was met by the viceroy's son, recently appointed to the government of Ormuz, being then from ten to twelve years of age.[2] He inquired who he was, and the convict threw himself at his feet and sued for mercy. The boy asked his tutor if he might claim this of his father without incurring his anger, and being answered that he might, he went forthwith to the palace and made humble suit to his father for the pardon. The viceroy granted his prayer, provided the crime was not one which touched the state or the king's service; and being informed that it was not, he was well enough pleased to see this kindly nature in his son. All the soldiers were exceedingly grateful to him, and so the poor criminal was delivered.

The viceroy treats none with familiarity, nor ever goes to assemblies or banquets. He goes abroad but rarely, except on the great festivals and on days when he is so minded. On the evening preceding the day when he intends to go forth, drums and trumpets are sounded throughout the whole town as a warning to the nobility, as I have already said,

[1] Surely, chained only if criminals. See Linschoten, i, 218.

[2] A manuscript note in Mr. Rivara's copy gives the name of this boy as Christorão de Tavora. As will be seen below, the child had not left to take up his government when Pyrard left India. The captain of Ormuz at this time was Henrique da Noronha. He was being frequently reprimanded in the royal despatches, and was dismissed, it seems, in 1610. It is likely that the viceroy's son was appointed to succeed to a casual vacancy of the office, which the viceroy, perhaps, brought about by traducing the holder. It does not appear whether the boy ever in fact took up the command.

who assemble in the early morning before the palace, all on horseback and in grand array. I have on occasions seen some three and four hundred or more of them. These gentlemen are superbly apparelled; their horses are barbed and covered with gold, silver, brocades, pearls, and precious stones. When each of them arrives there and dismounts, they have their master-grooms in waiting, who are all Moors, that is, Mahometans of Balagate or Decan, whose charge is to mind and groom the horses. These fellows are very expert with horses, and are not a whit afraid of any animal, however wild or vicious. They will mount him without saddle, spur him and urge him to his full speed, without ever falling off. Their horses are as sleek as can be. To tame and break them they use drums covered with bells, like our basque tambourines; and to make them amble they attach little balls to the joints of their legs. I have never seen horses so swift as those there. Most of them come from Persia; some from Arabia, and these are esteemed the best. They eat but little; they get hay, but most often green grass. They give them also a certain grain like lentils.[1] They are so careful of their horses that they cover them, when in stable, entirely, and even lay kinds of mats for them to lie upon. They water them always in the stable, and picket them by the heels for fear lest they hurt themselves.

But to return to the Portuguese lords and gentlemen: when they dismount, these master-grooms hold their horses, of which they take great care, carrying always themselves horse-tail switches, fitted in a handle, for brushing away the flies; also a towel and a soaked sponge, and a curry-comb in a sac, to wipe away the foam and sweat from the horse, and to rub him down and polish him when he requires it. They carry fine horsecloths of red velvet for the most part, fringed with gold

[1] Meaning, no doubt, chickpea (*Cicer arietinum*, L.), which is now known all over India as "gram" (Port. *grão*, "grain"). See Yule, *Gloss.*

and embroidery. The most costly and valued of these are those of red scarlet. These are for covering the horses when their masters are dismounted, for when they are mounted they use neither horsecloths, nor riding-boots, nor spurs, for riding in the town. The stirrup-straps are of silk, the buckles and other mountings of silver, as also are the stirrups. The horse's tail is tied up and enclosed in a truss, with clasps and buckles of gold and silver, set with pearls or stones. Besides these horses, they often have carried behind them also their litter or *Palanquin*, and always, whether on foot or on horseback, their sombrero or parasol, for the heat as well as the rain. Even when they go a-foot they have their horse led and palanquin borne behind; also a number of pages, as many as ten or a dozen.

These pages are not nobles, but little boys brought out of Portugal, not grown enough to bear arms. They are habited all in silk, in the liveries and colours of their masters, and wear mantles. Their service only is to attend their masters and to carry messages, which they call *Racates*.[1] They mingle not with the other serving-men. Besides these pages, they have six or seven huge *Cafres* of Mozambique carrying swords, with mantles like men-at-arms, and habited otherwise than the pages, but in the masters' colours. They take these men with them for security, for these Cafres would die sooner than see their masters come by the smallest hurt, so courageous are they; and if it be night they carry other arms, such as pikes and halberts. They are called *Pions* or *Cafres*. For the Portuguese never follow after their master,

[1] Port. *recado*, a message or errand: the plural, *recados*, is used as our "compliments". The expression seems to have been taken up by the English of Bombay and Surat, as in 1675 we find Dr. Fryer (p. 71) stating that a Jesuit near the former place sent "his *Recarders* (a term of congratulation, as we say, *our service*) with the presents of the best fruit and wines, and whatever we wanted." Unless Dr. Murray and his coadjutors can give earlier authority, I venture to think we have here the original of our modern phrase, "kind regards".

however great he be, or when they do so it is on horseback as do the gentlemen here after the princes and lords.

When the viceroy, who was at Goa while I was there, went forth, his son was wont to go, not by his side, but about two or three hundred paces behind, along with his gentlemen, and serving men; and ordinarily such of the latter, even the chiefest of them, as wished to please the viceroys, tarry with their sons; the rest go with the viceroy.

In church and at processions the viceroy takes the right side and the archbishop the left. Next after comes the son, who holds the government of Ormus, for he is the first governor after the viceroy. For the rest, the viceroy in his person is not observant of so much magnificence as are the lords. All who have horses, though they be not nobles by birth, fail not to accompany the viceroy; for they call themselves all nobles.

When the viceroy or the lords return to Portugal, they sell all their horses to the new comers.

When a viceroy arrives in the Indies he lands at *Pangin*, as I have said, and then sends to give notice of the fact with his letters of appointment, which are opened in the Town-house before the other viceroy, who prepares to quit office, and the officers of the new-comer set about furnishing and preparing the palace.[1] For the next seven or eight days preparations are made to receive him like a king, and in this view great expenditure is made. The retiring viceroy comes to meet the other, and makes a speech to him; how that he leaves everything in his hands, in what fashion he ought to conduct himself, as well towards the Indians as the Portuguese, with whom, on account of their arrogance, he ought to

[1] Linschoten says that the departing viceroy made a clean sweep; "there stayeth not a stool or bench within the house, nor one pennie in the treasure, but they leave the house so bare and naked as possible, so that the viceroy must make provision for to furnish it, and gather new treasure" (i, 221).

use the curb. That done he withdraws, and some state visits are paid. As soon as the viceroy quits office he receives no longer the title of *Seigneurie*,[1] for in the Indies only the viceroy and the archbishop get this title. To the others they say *Vostre merce*,[2] and to ecclesiastics *Reverence* and *Paternité*. The new viceroy takes out almost all the officers of his household, and appoints no others, unless some have died on the way. The king pays and maintains all his servants.

As soon as he has arrived all the ambassadors of the Indian Kings come to salute him, while he despatches couriers to all the friendly kings to confirm the alliance, and they send to him extraordinary ambassadors with presents,[3] forming as it were a new alliance with him. Next, all the Christians, that is the Indian Christians (not the Portuguese, who wish not that their number be known), show themselves before him under their Portuguese or Metice captains, for all are obliged to appear in arms. They do not all appear in one day, but each parish has its own feast-day. This takes place in the presence of the viceroy, in the field of *S. Lazaro*, or else they march past in order before the fortress, the viceroy sitting in his gallery. The captain makes a harangue, and all take the oath to him. The infidels are not paraded, and are not allowed to have arms in their houses.

The viceroy never goes out to dine anywhere, except on the day of the Conversion of S. Paul, at the College of the Jesuits, or, on the day of the Circumcision, at the church[4] of the Good Jesus. He is served with his meat and drink in royal style, and eats alone, except sometimes when the archbishop goes to the palace to dine with him. On these feast-days the greatest lords eat at his table, but not opposite to

[1] Port. *vossa senhoria*.

[2] Port. *vossa mercê*.

[3] The Jesuits formerly had these as perquisites by royal licence, but Luiz de Ataide (1568-1571) and subsequent governors took them to themselves (*Linschoten*, i, 221).

[4] Read "the Professed House".

him, nor of the same dishes. Many delicate and excellent dishes are sent to him from the great houses, but he never tastes them, for he is too much afraid of being poisoned. He trusts only the Jesuits; and even has Jesuit apothecaries, who frequently give him medicines. So it is that these fathers do greatly enjoy his credit and confidence.

As for the salary and fixed pay of the viceroy, it is but a small matter compared with the great profits which he can make during the three years of his office; these amount sometimes to a million of gold.[1] His fixed pay is 30,000 croisados,[2] each worth two perdos or thereabout. This however, would not be sufficient for his maintenance, were it not for the presents, profits, and other perquisites which amount to a large sum. As soon as he arrives, all the captains, governors, and king's officers come promptly to meet him, and to obtain some favour of him, either an expedition, a dignity, or other such thing; and with this view they give him grand presents, and even without such intent, according to the value and revenue of their fortresses, whereof the least is worth from twelve to fifteen thousand croisades, for they cannot well plunder and make their fortunes without his favour. All of them have their offices for three years only, during which they must amass enough for the rest of their lives.

The viceroy makes large gifts and rewards to officers, revenues and money to such as have served the king well,

[1] "These viceroys have great revenewes, they may spend, give and keepe the king's treasure, which is verie much, and doe with it what pleaseth them, for it is in their choyse, having full and absolute power from the king, in such sort that they gather and horde up a mightie quantitie of treasure, for that besides their great allowance from the king they have great presents and gifts bestowed upon them" (*Linschoten*, i, 220). Milburn (*Or. Comm.*, p. 306) states that some of the viceroys returned to Portugal with £300,000, and some of the governors and generals with £100,000.

[2] Equal to about £14,000 a year at present rates. The Governor-General now receives only £1,250 salary.

as well as to cripples, widows, and children: all this at the expense of the king. He has many offices in his gift. Those who have been in the king's service must have their certificate from him, and then only is it valued; it must also be signed by the captains who are present at the embarcations. But the mischief is that the viceroy takes money of all those gifts and offices, and makes out to the king that he has given them in full. In this way he answers numbers of petitions for gifts and presents, and the *Viador de Facienda* and the Treasurers are in league with him, none of whom like parting with money. For all that, they charge the king in account, and so they do with the pay of the soldiers, officers, and mariners.

With regard to the ordinary alms-giving of the viceroy, it is twice a week, and on the feast days and Sundays when he goes forth. This alms is only given to the poor Christian Indians: his almoner gives them some money in the great square in front of the palace. Should there be some woman who is a widow of a Portuguese, she is put aside, and she receives more than the Indian women. The poor soldiers, mariners, and other Portuguese, come into the great painted hall of which I have spoken. The women and children are in another, and the viceroy sends his master of the household with his almoner to give them money. On such a day he will give two or three hundred perdos. All the Portuguese women and girls come in covered Palanquins, and present their applications which they call *Peticions*,[1] wherein is contained their request, and the ground of it; the next day they come to see if there be any answer to it. Those who are sick may send for their answers. This alms is given conformably to the quality of the individual. The viceroy receives all these *Peticions* himself and replies on the following day. Out of all these he makes for himself a double profit. Besides that, he often sends alms to the

[1] Port. *petições*.

prisons, churches, hospitals, and other sacred places, and procures marriages for many girls and widows.

So it is that for the three years the viceroy and the other captains and governors are in the Indies, they take more pains to enrich themselves than to protect and preserve the State; and in so short a time they are unable to effect great results in war. For in the first year, it is all they can do to learn the details and forms of Government, know the various peoples, and despatch fleets and armies. The second year, they fill their purses. For they give nothing of their own, and if aught has to be given to kings, lords, ambassadors, etc., it is at the expense of the king. The Portuguese captains and lords receive no other presents than licences to make voyages and to trade, or privileges and office. Such as have no places, hope to become generals, captains, lieutenants, and to have command of the armies, or of the war and merchant fleets, which the king despatches. The third year the viceroy in some cases employs in visiting all the fortresses of the Indian coast, with a large force, that is between Coilan and Ormus.[1] But he draws large profits from this voyage, as well from the captains and governors, as from the other officers, and from the countries visited, although the king is debited with the whole expense. So it is no wonder these viceroys enrich themselves so much, nor that their servants and officers, who to the number of fifty or sixty live at the palace sumptuously, do the same. Also when any disaster befalls the viceroy on his way from Portugal, as happens often enough, the news brings little grief to him that is in office. This, indeed, happened the year before I came away, for the viceroy who was coming, called *Comte de Fera*,[2] died

[1] Linschoten states the tasks to which the viceroys addressed themselves during each of their three years in almost identical terms (i, 222) and intimates that this division of their time had become systematic and proverbial.

[2] D. João Pereira Frojas, Conde de Feira, appointed as nineteenth viceroy to succeed D. Martim Aff. de Castro, who died at Malacca in June

on the coast of Guinea, and his body was taken back to Portugal. He was coming out with fourteen ships, whereof only five arrived safe at Goa; the rest were lost or taken by the Hollanders.[1] It is to be noted that, of all that die in the Indies, the bodies of viceroys only are taken back to Portugal.

When the viceroy takes his departure, he chooses what vessels he will, and causes them to be victualled for himself and his suite; this is called *Matelotage*[2]: and some time is taken in its preparation. When the Portuguese learn that a viceroy, archbishop, or great lord, or captain is going, they try to get a passage, and leave to go with him: for every one in the ship gets his victuals, except the crew and officers who have their wages: all the gentlemen and soldiers, however, are maintained gratuitously; for when those great lords prepare to embark for Portugal, they cause to be shipped victuals for so many persons, besides their ordinary suite. It is greatly a matter of favour to get enrolled for a passage in the viceroy's list: it costs fully two or three hundred perdos to get well fed.

For the rest, it is great misfortune for the Portuguese in the Indies, when they get a troublesome and choleric, or

1607. F. y Sousa writes of him: "He raised in all men great expectation, as well for his personal merit as the greatness of his quality, and the preparations for his voyage were suitable, being the greatest that till then had been. His squadron consisted of six ships and eight galleons." He set out on the 29th March 1608, and died off the Guinea coast on the 15th May. His body was sent back and arrived at Lisbon 24th July (Stevens' *Faria y Sousa*, iii, 153).

[1] The fortunes of this ill-fated squadron are described in detail by Mocquet, who set out with the viceroy as his medical attendant. Mocquet himself arrived at Goa: of the lost ships he mentions particularly the carrack *Saluaçion*, wrecked on the coast of Arabia; the *Oliveira*, which when hotly pursued by the Dutch was run ashore, burnt, and abandoned by its crew on the *Ilhas Quemadas*, near Goa; and the galleon *Bom Jesus*, captured by the Dutch near Mozambique (Mocquet, *Voyage*).

[2] The victuals put on board ship, from *matalote*, a sailor.

vicious viceroy (as indeed is often the case), as well on account of their debauching women and girls, as of other vices. For they have so much privilege, power, and authority, that when they take a fancy to a pretty girl or woman, it will go hard but they have their way, whether by money, friendship, or force. But there is hardly need of force, for the women are nothing loth, deeming themselves in luck and boasting thereof; as for their husbands, they are sent on expeditions hither and thither.

But it happens often enough that, as all this wealth of the viceroys accrues to them from pillage and robbery, so the sea inherits it, and all is miserably lost. This frequent change of viceroys is displeasing to the Portuguese and to the Indians, as is no less that of the governors of the various forts and other officers. To illustrate which they tell a parable, how that one day there lay a poor man at the door of a church, his legs full of ulcers, and so covered with flies as was pitiful to behold; up came a neighbour who, thinking to do him a kindness, drove away the flies: whereat the poor patient was much vexed, saying that the flies he drove away already had their bellies full, and would not bite him more, whereas those that would come would be hungry and would sting him worse. So it is, they say, with the viceroys, for the gorged depart and the hungry arrive.[1] Nevertheless the King of Spain maintains these changes for two reasons. First, for fear of revolt, for they do not all enter upon their

[1] Æsop's fable of the Fox and the Hedgehog, in which the latter proposed to drive away the flies. Aristotle (*Rhet.* ii, 20) says that Æsop told this fable to the Samians to teach them that they were better off under the rich than under demagogues. La Fontaine used it (*Liv.* xii, *Fab.* xiii), with this moral:

> "Nous ne trouvons que trop de mangeurs ici-bas :
> Ceux-ci sont courtisans, ceux-là sont magistrats.
> Aristote appliquoit cet apologue aux hommes.
> Les exemples en sont communs,
> Sur-tout au pays où nous sommes.
> Plus telles gens sont pleins, moins ils sont importuns."

offices at the same time; but now one, and again one. The second is, to enrich and satisfy his subjects. As for himself, he gets no profit from it. The viceroys, being there so short a while, cannot take resolution to revolt; for as I have said, all the governors and captains of the forts do not assume and retire from office at the same but at different times. Furthermore, almost all have their wives, children, and property in Portugal. And when they could do it, they would require to be avowed by some powerful king in Europe, who would act as do the Spanish kings in Portugal. For if they had not a market for their merchandise and goods in Europe, all their Indies would avail them naught. They would need also supplies of men, money, munitions of war, ships, and merchandise from Europe. For the maintenance of this Empire is so great a business as would require a puissant king to undertake it, one who would have to bide his time by sinking more than he would draw from it. But in another aspect there is a recompense. In the first place, the general merit of the increase of Christianity; secondly, the alliance with all the most powerful kings of India; and lastly, the enrichment of all his people and realms, who but for the Indies would frequently be dying of hunger. Also there would die by the law in Portugal more men than now, were it not for these foreign lands, whither they are sent in exile to fight against Infidels, and to serve their king for the rest of their lives.

CHAPTER VI.

Of the Archbishop of Goa, the Inquisition, ecclesiastics, and ceremonies observed there, with other occurrences.

Having spoken of the viceroy and his state, it will be not out of place to say something of the archbishop, the first prelate in the Indies. He who held office while I was at

DOM FR. ALEIXO DE MENEZES

3d Archbishop of Goa and 1st Primate of the East Indies 1595—1610:
36th Governor of India 1606—1609.
(From the LIVRO DO ESTADO DA INDIA of P. Barretto de Resende.
Sloane Collection No. 197.)

Goa, was of the order of S. Augustin, whose habit he wore; he was aged about fifty years, and had been fifteen or sixteen years in this charge. For charity and alms-giving he had a great reputation. He had built and endowed a large number of monasteries and convents. He gives alms in public to all sorts of needy folk, in like manner as the viceroy; but he gives it oftener, inasmuch as he goes abroad oftener. He is served at table in the same way. For a long while he held both offices of viceroy and archbishop together.[1] He gets the title of lordship like the viceroy; he has power over the clergy in the Indies, and there represents the Pope. He is served with covered dishes, and eats in public. They have a custom to cause a dozen poor folk to eat at their table of the same viands, but seated lower than themselves; but this archbishop causes them to sit at another table opposite his own. That is at dinner and supper. He is served with a dish of silver gilt, and the poor with porcelain. These poor are not Indians, but Portuguese soldiers and mariners, that are reduced to need, whether by play or by not receiving their pay. When he is at table the door of his dining-room is opened, and his attendants choose and pass in such twelve as they think fit. It is amusing to see them striving for the first place, and he that once gets a seat does not give it up. I have often eaten there when I had no money. When there are more than twelve, the remainder wait in the great hall until the archbishop has eaten, and then something is sent to some of them of what is over from his table.

The revenue of this prelate is marvellously great; this one had a steward worth 60,000 crusadoes, and all his other servants and officers were proportionately rich. These servants are called *Criados;* most of them were from Portugal. The

[1] From the departure of M. Aff. de Castro for Achin in 1606, until the 27th May, 1609, when he was succeeded by A. Furtado de Mendoça.

others are slaves, called *Captivos*.[1] His almsgiving is not always of his own purse, but every year he receives large sums in pence for this purpose. He draws large profits and presents from all the other prelates and ecclesiastics in the Indies. He holds his own court and has his own prisons at Goa; also he has the superintendence of the Inquisition, and gets his share of the goods of such as are haled thither. This man takes great thought about building churches and monasteries, and chiefly one of his own order, which he enlarges and enriches greatly;[2] also he has reserved for himself a lodging there, whereto he retires for two or three days at a time. Sometimes he goes for eight whole days to stay at another called *Nuestra Senora del Capbo*, which is a convent of the Capuchins or Recluses, at the entrance of the river. He goes thither by water in his *Manchoue* or little covered galiot.

When the viceroy or the archbishop goes anywhither by water, they are accompanied by an infinite number of *manchoues* of lords. On board of these is excellent music of cornets-à-bouquin, hautbois, and other instruments; all the great lords have the same. When the archbishop goes through the streets it is in his palanquin, accompanied by many gentlemen on horse, and prelates, each in his own palanquin. Then follow numbers of pages and armed retainers on foot. His Portuguese servants or *Creados* ride on horseback. At the grand solemnities and public processions he walks in his pontifical robes, and has a cross like that I saw in the church of the Jesuits, whereof I spoke above.[3]

[1] Implying capture in war; those kidnapped or bought in market overt were simply *escravos*.

[2] Menezes caused several churches to be built, among the chief S. Alexius and the Holy Trinity. He enlarged and enriched the monastery of the Augustinians, his own order, and also founded the nunnery of Santa Monica, and the Retreats of the Serra and Mary Magdalen.

[3] See p. 59.

This he has carried before him by a chaplain or an almoner. In the court of his house and in front of it are always a large number of horses and palanquins of lords and others, who have come to see him on business, or to pay him a visit. He never leaves Goa,[1] and never makes any visits, leaving that to his Bishop of Goa.[2]

This prelate had a great desire to return to Portugal, but he durst not go, for the king must first send out another to relieve him. Nevertheless he had obtained his leave, and had made all his preparations as to provisions, and *matelotage* for more than a hundred persons, besides his own suite, who far exceeded that number; and it costs at least 300 perdos to maintain a man from the Indies to Portugal. My two companions and I presented our petition to him, that he would be pleased to allow us to embark in his carrack, to which request he acceded, as he did to numberless others. But about a month before the ships were ready to depart, he took it into his head to remain another year, and in fact I have since heard that he returned safely to Lisbon a year afterwards.[3] While I was yet in the Indies I heard tell that the King of Spain was greatly incensed against him for the matter of the death of the King of Ormus, whom he caused to be burned at Goa, as I shall relate hereafter.[4] For all the Portuguese said that he alone was of this counsel, the viceroy[5]

[1] A mistake: the author seems not to have heard of his famous visit to Malabar in 1599, and the synod of Diamper, when Menezes reduced the Nestorians to subjection to the Roman see. He also visited the churches of the north. Other archbishops did the like.

[2] He was a bishop *in partibus*, not titular Bishop of Goa (*Rivara*).

[3] He left Goa in Dec. 1610, and arrived at Lisbon 22nd June 1611. His return is noted in an English letter from Lisbon, 26th June 1611, three Englishmen from the *Hector* and the *Ascension* having come in the same carrack (*Cal. St. Pap.* E. I., No. 575).

[4] See ch. xviii, where he is described as the brother of the King of Ormuz.

[5] A mistake; there was no viceroy at the time, Menezes himself being governor (see ch. xviii).

and all the noblesse, and even the Inquisition, being willing to save him; but the archbishop had his will by a lavish use of pistoles, wherewith he was well furnished. For my part, I found him a good-natured man, and free-handed in almsgiving. He supplied us with the means of buying clothes and shirts when the time came for our embarking. He often spoke to us and did us many a good turn. He was principally astonished that the French had been able to round the Cape of Good Hope, seeing that the Kings of France and Spain were in alliance, and had a friendly understanding. Wherefore he deemed those that did it all to be pirates and robbers, which was the opinion all there had of us; and that it did not seem so strange in the English and Hollanders, who were enemies of their country and religion. For all that, this archbishop did not say, like the rest, that we ought to be hanged, with the charter and passports of our king round our necks.

For a long time the Jesuits and he have been at law, for they decline to recognise him in aught, but only the Pope and their General; this lawsuit is pending at Rome. When he goes abroad a large *sombrero* or parasol is borne over his head; and be it noted that his, and that of the viceroy and the other great lords, are very magnificent, and covered with velvet or other silk stuff, and in winter with some fine waxcloth, the stick prettily worked and painted with gold and blue.

As for the other prelates, they hold their sees under the same regulations as in Spain. The Inquisition[1] consists of two fathers, who are held in great dignity and respect; but the one is much greater man than the other, and is called *Inquisidor Major*. Their procedure is much more severe

[1] The Inquisition was first established in Goa in 1560, abolished in 1774, re-established in 1779, and finally closed in 1812. Its great celebrity is due to the account by Dellon (*Relation de l'Inquisition de Goa*, Paris, 1688, Eng. Trans., Hull, 1812). To us it is chiefly known

than in Portugal; they often burn Jews, whom the Portuguese call *Christianos noeuos,* that is to say, "New Christians". The first time they are taken before the holy Inquisition, all their goods are seized at the same time; they are seldom arrested unless they are rich. The king supplies the cost of this process to everyone who has not wherewithal. But ordinarily they attack them not except they learn that they have amassed much property. Nothing in the world is more cruel and pitiless than this process. For the least suspicion, the slightest word, whether of a child or of a slave who wishes to do his master a bad turn, is enough to hang a man; and they give credence to a child, however young, so only he can speak. Sometimes they are accused of putting their crucifixes in the cushions whereon they sit and kneel; sometimes of striking the images, or of refraining from eating bacon; in short that they are still secretly observing their ancient law, though they conduct themselves in public as good Christians. I verily believe that whatever is desired is assumed of them. Only the rich are put to death, while the poor get off with some penance. And, what is most cruel and wicked, a man who would do evil to another will, in revenge, go and accuse him of this crime. When the other is arrested, there is no friend will dare say a word for him, or

by the dramatic picture of the *auto-da-fé* in Marryat's *Phantom Ship.* It is said that the chief merit in its final closure is due to Dr. Claudius Buchanan, who visited Goa in 1808, and whose *Christian Researches in Asia* appeared at a time when England was able to exercise a strong influence upon Portugal. The reader should consult also the account of it by the Carmelite Philippus à Sanctâ Trinitate, who relates that the *samarras* of the condemned were, in his time, painted with their own effigies amid flames and demons, and that these were taken off before the final scene, and afterwards hung up in the Dominican church for a memorial. Philippus and Dellon also state, what Pyrard omits or did not see, that the inquisitors frequently tried and condemned dead men —a grim pastime! The heretical bones were dug up and carried to execution in a box, their former possessor being represented by an effigy, carried aloft on a pole. See the procession depicted in Dellon's cut.

will visit him, or lift a hand in his behalf, no more than for a person charged with high treason. The people durst not speak in public of this Inquisition but with very great honour and respect; and if a chance word should escape a man, having but the smallest reference to it, he must forthwith go accuse and denounce himself, if he suspect that anyone has heard him. Otherwise, if another denounce you, you will be at once arrested. It is a terrible and fearful thing to be there even once, for you have no proctor or advocate to speak for you, while they are judges and parties at once. The form of the procedure is all the same as in Spain, Italy and Portugal. Sometimes men are kept prisoners two or three years without knowing the cause,—visited by none but officers of the Inquisition, and in a place where they never see a fellow-creature. If they have no means of livelihood, the king gives it them. The Indian Gentiles and Moors, of whatsoever religion, are not subject to this Inquisition unless they have become Christians, and even then are not so rigorously dealt with as the Portuguese or new Christians from Portugal, or other Christians from Europe. But if peradventure an Indian, Moor, or Gentile inhabitant of Goa, had dissuaded or hindered another that was minded to become Christian, and that was proved against him, he would be punished by the Inquisition, as would be he who has caused another to quit Christianity; such cases often happen. The reason why they treat these Indians thus rigorously is that they suppose that they cannot be so steadfast in the faith as the old Christians; also that it will prevent the rest from being led astray. For the same reason, too, they permit them to retain some of their petty Gentile and Mahometan superstitions, such as not eating pork or beef, not drinking wine, and keeping to their former dress and ornaments, that is among men as well as women that are become Christians.

It would be impossible to calculate the number of all

those put to death by this Inquisition in ordinary course at Goa. I shall content myself with the single example of a Hollander jeweller or lapidary, that had resided there five-and-twenty years and more, and was married to a Portuguese Metice, by whom he had an exceeding pretty daughter of marriageable age, and had amassed goods to the amount of about thirty or forty thousand crusadoes. Being at that time on bad terms with his wife, he was accused of having the books of the pretended[1] religion, whereupon he was arrested and his goods seized. One half was left to his wife, the other to the Inquisition. I know not what befel him, but I am inclined to believe that he was put to death, or at the least lost all his property; he was a Hollander. They did not treat in like sort a Portuguese soldier, who had married both in Portugal and in the Indies; but he was poor. They sent him in our carrack to Portugal as a prisoner to Lisbon; had he been rich, they had never taken the pains to send him. For the rest, all the other Inquisitions of the Indies depend upon that of Goa.[2] It is upon all the greater feast-days that they carry out their judgments. Then they cause all these poor culprits to march together in shirts steeped in sulphur and painted with flames of fire; the difference between those that have to die and the rest being that their flames are turned upwards and the others downwards. They are led straight to the great church or *A See* which is hard by the prison, and are there during the mass and the sermon, wherein they receive the most strenuous remonstrances. Thereafter they are conducted to the *Campo Sancto Lazaro*, where the condemned are burned in the presence of the rest, who look on.

But to speak of the ecclesiastics of the Indies, there are of them a vast number of all the religious orders, all maintained by the King of Spain, besides those that come to beg, to

[1] *I.e.* Protestant.

[2] In other parts of India there were only commissaries.

whom is given much in charity, the king himself giving some provision. The parish priests are all paid equally, and the king takes all the tithes, the Pope having permitted him to do so[1]; the profits and offertories of the Church go to the priests and vicars. All the ecclesiastics are habited in cotton serge, wool being there too scarce and dear, and having to come from Portugal, while cotton is very agreeable on account of the heat. There it is not as here, for all the religious orders baptise, confess, and hold cures, and also administer all the sacraments, just like the secular priests, whom they call *Clerigos.* Native Indians, and men of all manner of religions are ordained as priests, but not as Jesuits, whom they require to be Christians born of both father and mother of Europe. All the ecclesiastics are passing rich and make their private gains. The Jesuits have everything in common, and when they go upon a journey anywhither, they carry nothing save their breviary. They only preach the doctrine and manage the colleges in those lands, teaching all manner of sciences, and instructing the children of both Christian Indians and Portuguese.

Their principal and chief college in all India is *S. Paul de Goa,* which they have caused to be built over against their house and church: and all the classes therein are well distinguished and ordered. The scholars enter not into the house of the fathers; while the masters go not forth of their house to come to their classes, nor pass through the street to get there. They often have representations of plays and comedies, with wars and battles, as well on foot as on horse, and all in exceeding good order and array. I estimate there are more than 3,000 scholars in this college. When they go to their studies, before entering the class, they go and hear mass at the church of S. Paul; and on leaving the class, all those of the same class-room put themselves in order, and with loud voice chant through the street some

[1] So too in Brazil, and in Spanish America.

prayers and orisons with their creed. Only the children of under fifteen years chant thus on their way; those of fifteen years and over do not so. This they practice so as daily to be attracting the heathen to the faith.

On every feast-day, and Sunday after mid-day, the masters and other appointed Jesuits, go in procession through the town with crosses and banners, chanting with all their scholars, who march in order according to their classes, all singing, young and old. Followed by a great number of the inhabitants, they proceed to the Church *du Bon Jesus*, the house of their Order, where a Jesuit father catechises them; and the whole church is filled with benches for this purpose. The women go thither also to hear the catechising, nor fail they a single festival or Sunday. These Jesuit fathers take no money from the scholars.

All persons of Goa on going to be confessed, are required to get from the priest that has confessed them, a certificate for the communion, the which they must deliver up ere they will be received at the table. The ticket is marked with the name of Jesus. This has been ordained against the new Christians, who often enough used to go to the table without confessing.[1]

On All Souls' Day, all the Portuguese of the Indies are wont to send, according to their means, bread, wine, and other viands, to the tombs of their deceased relatives and friends. During the service you see all these tombs covered with the victuals, but afterwards, when everyone is withdrawn, the priests or monks come and collect them, and they are obliged to pray God for the souls of the departed.

They fast on Christmas eve as here, and dine at noon; but before going to midnight mass, which begins at eleven o'clock at night, they have a very choice collation, fully equal to a supper, except that they partake neither of flesh

[1] This may be so; the custom is, however, still in use in Portugal, and seems to be the same as that of giving bronze "tokens" in the Scotch church.

nor fish; but of everything else they eat and drink without stint. And chiefly the women, mistresses as well as serving-maids, look forward to this night, because when they all go to the mass they turn the devotional occasion to account for the enjoyment of their amours. All the streets are then hung with lanterns. On Christmas Day in all the churches are represented the mysteries of the Nativity, with divers characters and animals introduced speaking, as we have them here; also marionettes and large rocks, and men within who make these figures act and speak as they will; everyone goes to see it. Even in most of the houses and at the cross-streets they do the same; it is a prettier sight at that season there, than at St. John's here. All along the streets, throughout the squares and wards, are tables laid with fine white napery, and covered with all manner of sugar-plums, dry comfits, marchpanes,[1] which they call *Rousquillos*[2], fashioned in a thousand ways; whereof every one buys to give away in presents. It is like a fair, and lasts till after Twelfth Night. By night they go and affix large bills (*escriteaux*) inscribed with an *anobon*, that is to say "good new year", accompanying the same with instruments of music.

When Easter comes round, all Holy Thursday and Friday there are general processions, as in all countries of the King

[1] Fr. *massepain*. "Marcnpanes are made of verie little flower, but with addition of greater quantitie of filberds, pinenuts, pistaces, almonds, and rosed sugar" (Markham's *Countrey Farme*, 1616, p. 585). See also a full recipe in that rare volume *Le Patissier François*, Amsterdam, Elzevir, 1655; also in *Delightes for Ladies*, 1608. They were made sometimes in the form of macaroons (which are still called massepains in France), and sometimes in large fantastical designs (as still common in Germany). At the marriage-feast of the Prince of Mantua, in 1581, were three large statues of marchpane, each four palms high, "l'une figurait le cheval du capitole, au naturel; l'autre un Hercule avec le lion; et l'autre une licorne plongeant sa corne dans la bouche du dragon" (V. Cervio, *Il Trinciante*, 1593, p. 48).

[2] Port. *Rosquilhos*, dim. of *rosca*. Linschoten gives the word for "bread baked like cracklings" (i, 198).

of Spain. Then, too, crowds of penitents of all qualities beat themselves, and go on their knees with their arms crossed. It were impossible to describe all the strange and superstitious ceremonies and forms observed of them. Some places then are, in the manner of hospitals, furnished with great store of vinegar, comfits, bread, wine, and other sorts of refreshments, with plenty white linen. The vinegar serves them to foment their bodies, the other things to refresh them with eating and drinking, and the linen to wipe and rub themselves withal.

All the churches have exceeding fine monuments. The interiors are richly ornamented and curtained: the pavement is scattered with herbs and flowers, with large branches with fair broad leaves on all sides. Most part of these are palm. The same is observed outside; and all around the churches, and even in the streets, which are exceeding clean, they erect quantities of herbs, and flowers, and branches. In the approaches to the said churches are great rows of palms set on either side. All this is done on the days of the great festivals of each church. They have also for the service of the church goodly companies of hautbois, cornets-à-bouquin, drums, violins, and other instruments. At the doors are sold all manner of cates, and quantities of trinkets and baubles. All their festivals begin at noon of the eve thereof and end at noon of the festival days; thereafter is more solemnity. All the streets and frequented places, and the churches where the festivals are held, are posted with pardons and indulgences.

All the new Christians, as well men as women, wear necklaces of wooden beads at the neck. The Portuguese and Metifs carry theirs in the hand, and in their conversation, business, and other actions, never fail to finger these paternoster beads. I know not what they say, but I have often seen them do the like while playing at dice. They have a custom, when the Holy Sacrament is elevated at the mass, that every one raises his hand as though he would point to it, and cries with loud voice, twice or thrice, *Deos de Misericordia*, and strikes his breast. They use no consecrated bread as we do here. When their slaves, as well men as women, go to the mass they wear iron fetters at their feet, at least such as are suspected of a desire to escape.

In the matter of their marriages, a man never sees his mistress but at the church which she frequents, and he never speaks to her. She is gaily attired in the Portuguese mode, and covered with pearls and jewels. If she pleases him, he goes to her house on the morrow with a priest and the *fiance*.[1] After that, he may go and see her, but not so as they be left together alone. Weddings are usually in the afternoon, and they go in grand solemnity to the church. The bridegroom is sometimes escorted by eighty or a hundred well caparisoned horses; and all the kindred and friends on both sides assist. The bride is accompanied in like manner with Palanquins, wherein are all her female relatives and friends. She is conducted by two of her nearest female relatives, and the bridegroom by two of his male relatives, up to the church, and the presence of the priest. These four are called *Comperes* and *Commeres*.[1] After espousal, they are reconducted home in like manner with a band of trumpets, cornets, and other instruments, playing from the church to the house, while the passers-by throw over the company much flowers, scented water, sugarplums, and comfits, these things being the perquisite of the servants who collect them. When they are arrived before the house the bridegroom and bride, along with the nearest male and female relatives and elders enter within, while the young

[1] *I.e.*, pledge; hence the verb *fiancer;* the noun is now rare and antiquated (see Sainte Palaye, *Dict. Hist. de l'Anc. Lang. Fr.*).

[2] In relation to the parents of the spouses, they are called *compadres* and *comadres;* to the spouses themselves they are *padrinhos* and *madrinhas* (Rivara).

men friends are bidden to remain without. These meanwhile amuse themselves with causing their horses to caracole, run and leap before the house, and throwing oranges, and darting canes and reeds at one another. The bridegroom, bride, and all the rest that have gone within appear at the window balconies, whence they look on at these pastimes. This done, they come down and enter a lower room, where are presented to them all manner of fruits and comfits, along with *Banguenin* water. The bridegroom then dismisses them with all politeness. Afterwards a banquet is served to all the relatives: this lasts not long, and all retire.

In their baptisms they use the like ceremony and solemnity as in their marriages. The priest plunges the child three times in the consecrated water. They have also a large silver-gilt dish full of *rosquilos*, or marchpanes, biscuits, macaroons, and other sweets, with a wax-taper stuck in the midst, and a gold piece attached.[1] All this is for the priest, except the dish.

When the feast-day of a monastery or convent comes round, they give a great banquet to a large party of their friends. The priests and vicars do the like on the feast-days of their churches.

All the Christians at Goa, as well Portuguese and Metifs, as rich Indians, when they go to church do so with vast pomp and ostentation, followed by their servants, pages, and armed retainers in array. They are borne in their Palanquins, but for all that omit not to have their horses led after them, while their pages carry sombreros, chairs or embroidered stools, and two velvet pillows, this is, when they are people of quality. They all wear swords at the side, and behind march all their servants and slaves, whereof the richest have as many as twenty or five and twenty. But they never go without their great beads in the hand:

[1] The coin, now a sixpence, has with us got inside the cake, and this perquisite is lost to the clergy.

and they have a cushion carried with them to kneel upon. In a word they proceed with the greatest pride in the world, and are so haughty that one of their servants must needs take the holy water in his hand to give thereof to his master or mistress; but this servant must be a man or a boy; for neither women nor girls approach or touch the holy-water vessel.

The rich ladies of quality go but seldom to church, save on the great feast-days, and then superbly attired in the Portuguese mode. Their gowns for the most part are of gold, silk, and silver brocade, enriched with pearls, gems, and jewels at the head, arms, hands, and waist. Over all they wear a veil of the finest crape in the world, reaching from the head to the feet. The gown and veil of girls are of all varieties of colour: those of the married women, black. They never wear stockings. Their gowns and petticoats trail upon the ground: their pattens, or *chapins*,[1] are open above, and cover only the soles of the feet; but they are all broidered with gold and silver, hammered in thin plates which reach over the lower surface of the *chapin*, the upper part being covered with pearls and gems, and the soles half a foot thick with cork. When they go to church they are borne in palanquins which are fitted up with the greatest possible richness; the interior contains a large Persian carpet, called by them *Alcatif*,[2] some of which would here cost five hundred crowns. Then they have two or three

[1] Ital. *cioppino*. These pattens were of Turkish or Eastern origin, and much used in Venice and Spain about this time. Also in England, but the affectation was much ridiculed:—"By'r Lady, your ladyship is nearer heaven than when I saw you last by the altitude of a chopine" (*Hamlet*, Act ii, sc. 2). Tom Coryate gives a description of these *chapineys* (similar to that above) as he saw them at Venice in 1611, and Evelyn found them still fashionable there in 1646. The Venetians also called them *calcagnetti*; see Molmenti, *Vie Privée à Venise*, 1882, p. 306; Fairholt, *Costume in England*, 3rd ed., ii, 72. Examples are to be seen in the British Museum.

[2] Sp. and Port. *alcatifa*, from the Ar. *al-qatifah*, a carpet (Dozy et Engelmann, *Glossaire*).

large pillows of velvet, or brocade of gold silver and silk, the one for the head, the other for the feet. They are followed, each according to her quality, by other palanquins conveying their children, and maids, or *Criadas*,[1] who are either Portuguese girls or Metices. Each palanquin usually holds but one person, and that is specially so in the case of a master or mistress, save when betimes they take in one of their children; but in the case of the others, they hold two persons. As for the female servants, and slaves, they go behind afoot, and sometimes there be fifteen or twenty of them richly attired in silk of all colours, with a large veil of fine crape over all, which they call *Mantes*;[2] but these are not habited in the Portuguese fashion, having large skirts of silk to serve them for petticoats. They also have smocks of exceeding fine silk, called by them *Bajus*.[3] Amongst them you see some very pretty girls, of all the nations of India. Be it noted that the husbands send thither also their pages, with a well dressed man or two, Portuguese or Metifs, to escort them, and to hold their hands after they be got down from their palanquins: most often these ladies enter the church in their palanquins, such fear have they of being seen without. They wear no masks, but all are painted to an extent that is shameful. However, it is not the ladies that fear to be seen; it is the husbands that are in the highest degree jealous of them. One of these maid servants, or slaves, carries one of these rich carpets or *Alcatifs*, another carries two costly pillows, others a finely gilt chair of China wood, a velvet bag containing the book, handkerchief and other things whereof they have need, a pretty *estere*,[4] or mat of fine fabric to put over the carpet, and a fan, together

[1] Port. *criada*, a woman, maidservant.

[2] Port. *manta*, a mantle.

[3] Hind. *bāzū*, "a kind of short shirt reaching down to the hips, with very short (if any) sleeves; sometimes open at the upper part of the chest in front" (*Qanoon-e-Islam*, p. xv).

[4] Port. *esteira*, a mat.

with other requisites. When these ladies enter the church, they are assisted by a man or two, who take their hands, for they cannot walk alone owing to the height of their pattens, which are frequently half a foot off the ground,[1] and are not made fast over the foot. One of these men takes in his hand some holy water, whereof she partakes, then she proceeds to her place forty or fifty paces off, taking at least a good quarter of an hour in getting there, so gravely and deliberately does she step: she carries in her hand beads of gold, pearls, and precious stones. Thus is their mode of progression according to their means, and not according to their quality. When they take their children with them, they make them walk in front. The maid servants and slaves are well enough pleased when their mistresses go not to mass, for then they go alone, and can at the same time meet their own gallants; and so they do full often, and never betray or accuse each other.

Such are the most singular and remarkable things observed by me at Goa: but I should never have finished, had I desired to particularise and tell in detail all I learnt in the two years or so during which I resided there. I content myself with having touched some subjects generally, leaving my readers to judge all the rest on that footing.

Concerning the divers descriptions of goods that are landed at the Goa, from all parts of the Indies, we shall speak in their own place, when we deal with the several countries whence they come.

[1] "There are many of these *chapineys* of a great height, even half a yard high; and by how much the nobler a woman is, by so much the higher are her *chapineys*. All their gentlewomen [at Venice] and most of their wives and widows that are of any wealth, are assisted and supported either by men or women when they walk abroad, to the end they may not fall" (T. Coryate, *Crudities*). "Elles sont si hautes, qu'en les portant, quelques-unes paraissaient des géantes; et même il y en a qui ne sont sûres de ne pas tomber, à moins de bien s'appuyer sur leurs esclaves" (Casola, *Voyage*).

So it is that a man who has been at Goa, can assure himself of having seen the greatest curiosities of the Indies, that town being the most famous and renowned for the traffic of all the Indian nations. For they carry thither all that their own country can produce, as well manufactures as produce, and other commodities, all which are to be found there in plenteous store. You will see arriving there more than a thousand vessels laden of all goods; wherefore are provisions exceeding cheap, more so, indeed, than any where else; what would cost fifty sols here, is worth no more than five there. Most of the provisions, fruits, and other delicacies, and commodities come from Dealcan. Sea fish is so abundant there that there is more than is wanted, although they eat more of it than of flesh. It forms nearly all their nourishment, and (be this also noted), cannot be kept more than four and twenty hours, on account of the heat of the climate, which incontinently spoils all their viands. All along the streets, and at the crossings, you see numbers of men and women frying and boiling fish for sale, which they serve with their sauces and seasonings.

However, I repeat that, having resided about two years and more at Goa among the Portuguese, I cannot tell or express all the affronts, insults, and ill-usage, that I suffered there. And in truth I may say without vanity that if during the time of my voyage I had any, even the smallest hope of returning to France, I should have been more curious to learn and remark all the fairest and strangest things in that country. But from the day of our wreck down to that whereon I landed at Rochelle, I never had one moment's hope of return: this was the reason that I took no trouble to acquire so much gear as I might have done. For there needs there but a small store to maintain a man, all things being at low prices. I have not, however, omitted to remark a good many things respecting their wealth and trade, inasmuch as I was in most parts of India, as well with the

Indians themselves as with the Portuguese, with whom I served both in the North and in the South in scouring and defending their coast, and in convoying their merchant vessels in their voyages to and fro. But I will say with confidence that if the Portuguese had believed that I had so much as a thought of recording anything about them, either of the navigation to the Indies, or other particulars of their government and trade, they would never have allowed me to return; but would either have put me to death, or sent me to exile, as they do their own malefactors and other foreigners. But I guarded myself well from giving them the slightest suspicion.

I was well forewarned by the example of others, as of an English ship's boat on the coast of Melinde, near the Zanzibar islands, which they took (as I shall describe hereafter)[1] finding a man on board with the lead in his hand, sounding and reconnoitering the coast: him they put cruelly to death in manner they are not wont to use to other foreigners; and though I confess that I have but little of a high spirit, yet did I lead them to believe I had much less, for fear of giving them a bad opinion of me. I even made them believe I could neither read nor write, and that I understood not their language; and in order to live among them, I had to obey them in all things. So if any of them wished me ill or did me a wrong, I strove by all means to make my peace with him, and to make friends with all. In such wise I passed about two years and a half[2] with them, not counting the time we occupied in returning from Goa to Portugal.

I may also say that the English that were at Goa, who were taken prisoners in the river and *bara* of *Surrate*, as I shall relate in the proper place,[3] told us that the ship called

[1] See below, ch. xx. The English ship was the *Union*.

[2] In fact, only one year and a half, from his arrival at Goa in June 1608 to January 1610, or twenty months, dating from his capture outside Calicut.

[3] See ch. xx.

the *Croissant*, our Admiral, on her return from Achen in Sumatra, had cast anchor at the island of St. Helena, and that then an English vessel,[1] coming from the Indies, arrived there laden with goods, but weak in men; and that those on board the *Croissant* had formed a design to surprise her, the English ship being in better condition, and not making so much water as the other, which was all open, and in such a state that she could not get as far as France, as I have heard. But their design having been discovered by a young gunner of the *Croissant*, that was an Englishman, the ship forthwith weighed her anchors during the night, and sailed with the gunner who gave them warning. This caused the English not to be friends with us, and to speak contemptuously of our nation: they are all exceeding proud, and not like the Hollanders.

I was also curious to inquire after our mate and our eleven other comrades, who escaped from the Maldive Islands in a boat during our shipwreck there, as has been said above; but I could not discover aught, save that they were arrived at *Coylan*, a territory of the Portuguese, and that the mate was dead in the hospital of *Coylan*, along with some others, and the rest were taken prisoners to Goa, whereof some were shipped off on a return voyage to Portugal, and the others were gone here and there with the Portuguese armies, and no one knew what had become of them. When I was at Goa, arrived some men sent on behalf of the king of Calecut, to get back certain Mahometans, whom the Portuguese held prisoners, having taken them in some Arabian ships; on being claimed by the Samory, they were forthwith delivered into the hands of his envoys. As these men of Calecut were of my acquaintance, they told me with full particu-

[1] This was probably the *Susan*, of Lancaster's fleet, under command of Henry Middleton, who returned to England, June 1603, two months before Lancaster. The *Croissant*, as Martin tells us, was at St. Helena in March 1603.

larity, all that had passed at Calecut since our seizure, and how the king was at once informed of it, and his great wrath on that score against the Portuguese, who made every kind of excuse, casting all the blame on the captain that had seized us, who afterwards came to no good, as I have related at length already.

I saw also arrive there a barque of the Islands of *Divandurou*,[1] fully laden with cordage of the coco-tree; they call these cords *Cayro:* the mate of the barque spoke the language of the Maldives, and I had seen him at Malé island, so that we knew each other well, and were vastly pleased both of us to meet again. I had often seen him at the house of a great captain of the Malabars named *Cousty Hamede*, his relative, at the town of *Badara*.

He it was who then told me all the news that had passed at the Maldives since my departure, after the great disaster, and the death of the king at the same time, and how a new king had been established, and the country was very peaceful, all of which I have related above in its own place.

But before I finish this chapter, I do not wish to omit what I learnt at Goa of the Hollander named *Martin d' Ombes*,[2] who was wrecked at the Maldives while I was there, and whom we met in the prison of Cochin, as has been told above; for he then told us with some particularity all that befel him; namely, that when the king of the Maldives gave him this barque, whereof I have spoken, he saved property worth more than nine or ten thousand crowns in gold, silver, pearls, precious stones, and other costly and precious goods, wherewith he betook himself to *Caelle*,[3] a place near Cape Comorin, where is held the greatest fishery of pearls on all

[1] The Laccadives, *v. s.* vol. i, p. 323.

[2] Martin Domburgh, see vol. i, pp. 392-3, 430.

[3] Kayal, six miles south of Tuticorin; "a great and noble city" (*Cail*), says Marco Polo, Bk. iii, ch. 21, see Yule, *Gloss.*, *s. v.* "Cael". Barbosa (*Hak. Soc.* ed., p. 173) says it was the headquarters of the pearl fishery, but subject to the King of Kollam (*Quilon*).

that coast. There he sought a Jesuit Father, that had his ordinary quarters there, who by fine words and promises of safety, persuaded him to go direct to Cochin, and gave him a letter of recommendation, that so no trouble should befall him: but as his ill-luck would have it, no sooner was he arrived there than he was lodged in that great prison where we were cast, and there he had remained two whole years in dire misery: that during this time there, the Jesuit Fathers had converted him and made him a Catholic, with promises of delivering him incontinently after his conversion: that being advised of the wealth that he still had in his possession, they gave him to understand that he might entrust that to them in all security, to keep for him, giving him thereout as often and as much as he would, and that meanwhile they would give him interest and a handsome income for his maintenance, in such wise that they contrived to get out of his hands all that he had managed to save: they supplied him every day with the means of living, but not of living so well as he would have wished. Meanwhile he insisted upon his demand, that since he had become Catholic, they should set him free, as they had promised; this, however, they had not done. So much we learnt from his own mouth. But after we were separated, I learnt of some Christian and Gentile Indians of Goa, that they had at length taken this poor man from prison, and had shipped him for Goa with irons on his feet, and that as he had demanded of the Jesuit Fathers the restitution of all he had placed in their hands, they had replied thereto that that was reasonable enough; but for greater safety they would charge themselves to pay the whole at Goa, by means of a letter of exchange which they gave him addressed to the Father Superior of their order; but as the worst ill-fortune would have it for this poor wretch, as soon as he left for Goa, he became suddenly swollen as large as a cask, and at length died between Cochin and Goa. It was not known what had befallen him;

but the Indians who told me the story, held it for a certainty that he was poisoned. However that may be, such was the unfortunate end of this poor Hollander, which shows how few escape these long voyages, and amid how many divers and contrary accidents they fare, and that it is a special grace of God when they return safe and sound, as I have. But I will now come to more singular and remarkable matters, concerning as well the country of Goa, and its surroundings, as the Portuguese and other inhabitants there, which I shall relate in the following chapters.

CHAPTER VII.

Of the Exercises and Games of the Portuguese, Metifs, and other Christians at Goa, their dress and manner of living, and of their wives.

The exercises of the Portuguese, as well at Goa as at other places in the Indies, consist in the first place in the use of arms and riding, and in making, on Sundays and holidays, a thousand passades and careers on their horses, during which they throw oranges, canes, and reeds, all being equipped and arrayed in their best. No feast day passes, but they have some amusement to which all the people go, ranging themselves in procession. All the ceremonies and solemnities of the feast become there like fairs, with banquets and music of all sorts of instruments; thus do they mingle their pleasures with their devotions. They delight much in going on the river in their Manchoües, built in the form of Galiots, where they are under cover with music, in these they go from the town to places belonging to them or their friends; these places are pleasure houses with gardens and orchards, which they call *hortas*, containing groves of coco-trees, called by them *Palmeiro*, there also are many reservoirs and streams of clear and fresh water, wherein they bathe, and taking their collations and other refreshment in the shade.

As for cards, dice, and other games of chance, they are allowed there, and certain houses are set apart for the purpose, the keepers of which pay a rent to the king, and none durst play elsewhere under pain of a heavy fine. The keepers of these gaming academies and offices make very great profits: for the number of players ordinarily assembled there is quite wonderful, and most of them drink, eat, and sleep there, taking no other exercise. The accommodation is excellent in all respects, the saloons and rooms are very handsome, well lighted and gaily hung, and servants are always at hand to serve them with what they require. I have never seen elsewhere gamesters more freehanded and magnanimous: for the winners give of their money freely to the onlookers, that is, those who act as umpires, and who are willing to take it. This act of gentility is called *Barbo*.[1] Nor is it any shame to receive it, for it is considered more in the light of an honourable present than as alms. They sometimes give large gold pieces; and full often when I had no money, I used to go and see them play, and they were more careful to give to me than even to their Portuguese fellows or Metifs. Most of the soldiers that have no money go there frequently. They give much also to the servants of the house who wait upon them; but the servants' masters exact a certain tribute thereout.

During the play some girls, the servants and slaves of the master and mistress of the house, play instruments, and sing airs to give pleasure to the company, and mark you, these are the prettiest girls they can find. The play is fair and

[1] A misprint for *barato*, which is thus explained by D. Vieira; "a fourth part of his winnings, paid by a player to the keeper of a gambling house, also a portion given by players to onlookers who decide questions in their favour" (*Dict. Port.*).

without quarrelling, by reason of the regulations and order that are maintained there; and though one were the greatest lord in the world, he can only play in these public places: yet there are separate rooms there according to the quality of persons. At this gaming is a vast amount of money spent. Among other games they play much at chess and draughts, and at all sorts of games on the chess-board. They have no tennis, but play only at hand-ball; also they indulge much in skittles and bowls. They have also companies of conjurers, mountebanks, and buffoons for their pastime; and shows of snakes and other rare animals. Every one there, as well men as women, learns to sing and play upon instruments, but they do not engage in dancing.

As regards their manner of life at home, all, whether men or women, girls or boys, on arriving at their homes, forthwith cast off their nether garments. The men go about in their shirts and drawers,[1] which reach down to the heels, and are extremely white and fine: then they take off their hats, and don a *montaire* or *galetaire*,[2] as they call it, which is of velvet or taffetas, and in the form of a hat, but with a brim on one side only. The women take their ease in their smocks or *Bajus*, which are more transparent and fine than the most delicate crape of these parts; so that their skin shows beneath as clearly as if they had nothing on; more than that, they expose the bosom to such an extent that one can see quite down to the waist.

They wear nothing on the head but the hair plaited and tied up. From the waist downwards they wear a very handsome cotton or silk cloth; but not so transparent or so fine

[1] *I.e.*, pyjamas, or "long drawers", as the English sometimes called them (see Yule, *Gloss.*, under both words).

[2] Port. *monteira*, *gualteira*, caps of velvet or other soft stuff, the generic being *carapuça*, under which name Mocquet describes the thing. He says they were made more or less in the form of morions, with a vizor, and were thus used for nocturnal brawls and robberies at Goa (p. 309).

as the smock; for one can see nothing through it, it is like our taffetas. Most of the men, when minded to marry, are not content with seeing the girls, that are proposed to be given to them, in their holiday or parade dress, that having too much artifice. They prefer to see them going to market, or at home in their private attire, such as I have described, in order to form an opinion of them in their natural simplicity, and to see whether they be well proportioned or mis-shapen. Also at that juncture they do not wish to see them painted, as they are when they go abroad in their finery.

The diversion of the women is to sing and play instruments all the day long; sometimes they visit each other, but seldom enough; day and night they also use betel like the Indians.[1] Their husbands are very jealous, but they are so amorous and so addicted to fleshly pleasures, that when they find the smallest opportunity, they fail not to use it. Nor lack they both opportunities and gallants, being not only fair but rich, and of their abundance they give to the soldiers their gallants. And what gives them the greater assurance is that maid servants and slaves are well enough pleased to serve their mistress, and to win for them some pretty fellow, as I have mentioned elsewhere. But the husbands keep a careful watch over them, and when their wives go a visiting, they send with them some page or other trusted person to observe their actions. For all that, the women are so cunning and full of artifice, that they almost always succeed in their intrigues.

All the women of the Indies make much use of a certain fruit, like a large medlar, that grows not upon a tree, but upon a shrub, and is all green, round and prickly on the outside, and full of little seeds within. It is found nearly everywhere in the Indies, and among other places in large

[1] Rivara says the Portuguese ladies of Goa no longer chew betel, but are fond of smoking.

quantities at the Maldives, where it is called *Moet ol*, that is to say, "Madman's herb." In other parts of the Indies it is called *Dutroa*.[1] When the women wish to enjoy their amours in all security, they make a drink for their husbands of this fruit infused in their beverages or in soup. An hour afterwards they become giddy and insensible, singing, laughing, and performing a thousand antics, for then they have lost all consciousness and judgment, and know neither what they are doing, nor what is being done in their presence. Then do the wives make use of their time, admitting whom they will, and taking their pleasure in the presence of their husbands, who are aware of nothing. The effect lasts five or six hours, more or less, according to the quantity of the dose. Then they fall asleep, and at their waking believe they have been asleep all the while, without remembering aught of what they have done, heard, or seen.

Also when the men want to enjoy a girl or woman, and cannot attain their end, they get them to take some of the same stuff, and when they are in this folly, they do unto them as they will, without the women being aware of it afterwards. While I was in that country, many were found to have become pregnant without knowing whence this had happened to them. But were one to take a large dose of this fruit, he would infallibly die of it. When the soldiers and others cannot obtain possession of a woman, they tamper with their maid-servants, who sell and betray their mistresses for money in this manner, by giving them to drink of this

[1] *Datura Stramonium*, Skt. *dhattūra.* The uses to which this intoxicant was put at Goa are described in much the same way by Linschoten (i, 210; ii, 68-72); by Mocquet (p. 312); by Sir T. Herbert (p. 337), etc. De Orta gives an anecdote of its use for thieving purposes (f. 83), and Fryer (p. 33) says it was given to widows when they were about to perform suttee. Pyrard's and Linschoten's form, *dutroa*, came into English as *dutry* (*Fryer*), and Col. Yule (*Gloss.*) quotes "Make lechers and their puñks with dewtry Commit fantastical advowtry" (*Hudibras*, pt. iii, c. 1).

herb. True it is that the slaves are so maltreated by their masters and mistresses, who lord it over them cruelly, that it is nothing strange that they should have their revenge. One day at Goa, I saw one aged eighteen or nineteen years, that cast himself into a well and was killed, to escape the fury of his master, who was running after him to chastise him.

But though the women at Goa are exceeding lewd, and though the climate and the diet of the country inclines them thereto, nevertheless neither there, nor in the other towns of the Portuguese, is there any public brothel, nor is any allowed to be kept, as in Italy. They conceal their sin as much as they can, though there is no more lack of it there than in many other places.

The Portuguese, Metices, and Indian women and girls bathe and wash the private parts daily, as also do the other Indian women that are not Christians.

One of the recreations of the Portuguese at Goa, is to assemble at their doors with five or six neighbours, and there to sit in the shade chatting, all in their shirts and drawers, with a number of slaves about them, some fanning and keeping off the flies, others scratching their feet and other parts of the body, and removing parasites. Thus do most of them pass their time, courteously saluting the passers-by, and glad enough when they will tarry to have a chat with them, and accept the proffered seat.

When they take their food, and at their lying down and rising up, they have all their slaves, as well girls as boys, to play music for their pleasure; also while they eat they have some slaves to fan them, and to keep off the flies from the victuals, otherwise it would be difficult to avoid swallowing some of these flies, whereof there is great abundance throughout all the Indies.

The most ordinary pastime of the women is to remain all day long at the windows, which they call *Ventanes*:[1]

[1] Port. *ventana*, a window.

these are exceedingly handsome, lofty, and spacious, in the form of galleries and balconies, with jalousies and trellises gaily painted; so that they can see without being seen.

CHAPTER VIII.

Of the Portuguese Soldiers at Goa, their manner of life and taking Ship. Divers Expeditions, and the order observed by them in War.

Regarding their manner of war and soldiers, you must know that from the beginning, the Portuguese have had continual war with the Malabars, who are the pirates of the Indian seas, also with other Indian kings and peoples, for example those of Arabia, the kings of Sumatra, Java, Jor, which is on the terra-firma of Malacca, and other islands of Sunda, and of the coasts and continent of all the Indies. And now that the English, Hollanders, and other foreigners have taken the course of Indian navigation, this has brought a new war upon their hands, a war that has reduced them sadly, and is like to ruin them, insomuch that they have been constrained to reinforce their naval armies. For all their war is on sea and not on land, whereof they hold none. Sometimes, however, they have a war with some individual kings of the continent, who have broken the peace and the treaties mutually agreed upon. In such case they put armies in the field, and calling out their levies from the towns and fortresses. But for their armies on sea they have perpetual employment, two being armed and equipped every year, as I have said.

For the protection of all the coast of India, from Goa to Cambaye, and sometimes as far as Ormus on the one side, and Cape Comorin on the other, to prevent the raids of the

Malabar pirates, they equip two armadas[1] at Goa, one of which, called *Armada del Nort*, goes as far as Ormus; the other, *Armada del Sud*, goes as far as Comorin. Each is composed of fifty or sixty war galiots, without counting those of *Chetie*, or merchantmen, and including one or two grand galleys like those of Spain. These armadas depart in the month of October, at the beginning of their summer, which lasts six months more or less, and that is the time when the Malabar corsairs are afloat. These galleys are rowed by prisoners and convicts, and the same order is observed as here. The galiots[2] have fifteen to twenty benches on each side, and there is but one man to each oar, these, however, are not convicts or prisoners, but Canarins, natives of Goa, Bardes, and Salsetes, or else Colombins, who are the most vile drudges of people, engaged at an agreed hire. They call these *Lascary*, and their captain *Moncadon*,[3] the galiot *Navie*,[4] and those of the Malabars, *Pairaux*.[5]

Besides these two regular armadas, others go to Malaca, to Sunda, to Mozambique, and other places where they are required, or some project is afoot; but these armadas are composed of round vessels like the galions, hulks, and ships of India, with some one large galiot. These go with succours and reinforcement to their several possessions, such as the Island of Ceilan, Malaca, Mozambique, and other places where they are making a war or are attacked.

All these armadas are at the expense of the king of Spain.

[1] See vol. i, pp. 438-9, where he has already said all this.

[2] The galiot was a smaller galley with but one mast. In Europe it had ordinarily three men to each oar (Fournier, *Hydrographie*; Pantera, *Arm. Nav.*, p. 48). Probably convicts and prisoners were used exclusively for the galleys, owing to the intolerable and incessant labour involved.

[3] Port. *mocadão*, from the Ar. *mukaddam*, a head man, ganger, or boatswain (see Yule, *Gloss.*, s. v., "mocuddum"). According to Linschoten (i, 267), he was a contractor for native hands, and received their wages in a lump.

[4] Probably represents the Mahr. and Hind. *nāo* or *nāv*, "a boat".

[5] See vol. i, p. 345.

Other galiots, too, and ships come forth from the several Portuguese ports and havens, and join themselves to the fleet. The vessels are well armed, for in sweeping the coast, they go in to anchor at all the ports of their friends and allies, both for the purpose of taking along with them such as care to follow them, and such as are ordered to do so, and also for the refreshment of the fleet and for trade. With these armies go also a great number of trading ships and galiots, called *Navies de Chatie*, to distinguish them from the others, which are called *Navies d'Armade.* For their trafficking and commerce, these merchantmen await the convoy of the Armadas, for fear of the pirates, who render it impossible for them to sail alone. Most of the soldiers even, such as have the wherewithal, omit not the trade on their own account, while making voyages in the king's service. This is permitted to them, nay it is even necessary on account of the scantiness of their booty and pay. The ships of war are equipped at the expense of the king, but the Chaties are at the expense of their owners who freight them; nevertheless they must be subject and obedient in all things to the General of the Armadas, who is called *Capitaine Major.*

In the great galleys there may be two or three hundred men-at-arms, and in the other great galiots, which are called *Fregates*, about one hundred; in the smaller, which are the *navires*,[1] about forty or fifty. There are some still smaller, called *Manchoües*, containing perhaps fifteen or twenty men. As for the round ships,[2] their number of men is according to their size.

Concerning the order and manner of their embarkments: when they would make a shipment of men at Lisbon for the Indies, they make a levy of soldiers from all Portugal,

[1] Probably a misprint for *navies*, as above.

[2] That is, sailing ships proper, such as carracks, galions, and caravels. Long ships were for oars principally, with auxiliary sails, such as galleys, galiots, fustas, brigantines, etc. (see Jal, *Gloss. Naut.*, under these heads).

by towns and parishes, as is done here of pioneers, and all sorts of people are taken, of whatever quality and condition they be, provided they have attained the age of nine to ten years.[1] Then they are enrolled, and are paid and rated for soldiers. If they cannot find any that will go of their own accord, they take them by force, and of any age, and enroll them in the *Caza da India Orientale*, which is the India Office ordinarily held in Lisbon; they have to give security up to the time of their embarking. The whole of their pay for the voyage is advanced to them, because most of them are children of poor peasants, and have need of habiliments and arms: their pay is according to their quality. Their manner of counting is by *Raiso*, as in Castille by *Maravedis*, which is a certain coin worth a farthing and a half of our money; and they say so many thousand *Raiso*.[2]

Among the soldiers enrolled there are some dignities and qualities more honourable than others, some of birth and extraction, others of service and valour, or granted by favour. And they are paid accordingly, some more, some less. They are paid at Lisbon for the whole passage to the Indies, and not by the month, and they have not to provide any provisions for their private use, the king furnishing all whereof they have need in the way of victuals, refreshment, and munition of war. These titles and qualities are acquired by them in Portugal, yet does the viceroy fail not to grant the like

[1] "Five carracks sailed on the $\frac{4}{14}$ instant for the E. I., laden with merchandise, and carrying, in place of soldiers, children and youths from the age of ten upwards, to the number of 1500; in a few years they say these children will be able to do good service, their bodies being well acquainted with the climate of those countries; think it were an evil course to follow in England for planting inhabitants in Virginia; it is forced by necessity in Lisbon. If the peace with Holland take not effect, the Portugals may lose their Indies before the children are able to do any service."—Letter from Lisbon dated March $\frac{18}{28}$, 1609, in *Cal. S. Pap.*, E. I., No. 432.

[2] *I.e.*, milreis. The *ree* or *rea* was retained in Bombay accounts as $\frac{1}{400}$ of a rupee down to 1834 (see also Yule, *Gloss.* s. v.).

to a certain number that merit it or that he desires to favour in the Indies. A noble by birth is called *Fidalguo* simply. Others are called *Fidalguo de la Casa del Rey nosso Señor*, or "gentlemen of the king's household": these are the most esteemed of them, and most of the appointments are honourable. Others are *Mosso Fidalguo*, that is to say, ennobled by the king or great lords by favour; others, *Cavalleyro Fidalguo*, or "Chevalier nobles": others, *Mosso da Camera* and *do Servicio*, or "gentlemen in waiting": others, *Escuderi Fidalguo*, or "gentlemen esquires".[1] Those that have no title or dignity are called solely and simply *Soldado*. They take these dignities rather than others, because these entitle them to have their expenses charged and orders obeyed, and also to be rated higher. Besides these titles they have another, that of *Honrado*, or "honourable", which they all like to have among themselves. The most that a soldier can have, even the chiefest of them, for the passage from Lisbon to Goa, is fifty or sixty crusados.

When these soldiers are embarked in the carracks they are divided up into squads or companies to keep the watch or guard, which is changed at night and not at daybreak.

And although these enrolled soldiers have no titles or dignities, yet do they not omit to assume honour among themselves, calling themselves all "gentlemen", though they be of low condition:[2] nor have the nobles any jealousy of this, seeing that this is understood among themselves but not by the Indians, nor does it a whit diminish the nobility of the others, lists of whom are every year sent out from

[1] This description of the titles of Portuguese soldiers is almost identical with Linschoten's (i, 188-9).

[2] They assumed titles in order to deceive the secretaries at Goa :—"Des qu'ils sont là, pour vils et abjets qu'ils soient, ils s'estiment tous fidalques et nobles, changeans leurs noms obscurs à des noms plus illustres ; comme je sceus là d'un certain qui s'envooloit pour la guerre, et avoit changé de nom trois ou quatre fois, comme il fut recogneu par les secretaires et écrivains de Goa" (Mocquet, *Voy.*, 305).

Lisbon to the Viceroy of Goa. These titles which are used among themselves, are only to make the Indians believe that they are all of goodly and illustrious parentage, having no race of vile churls among them. Wherefore they will not that any Portuguese or other (European) should do any vile or dishonourable work, nor should beg his livelihood, they will rather maintain him to the best of their power. Insomuch that the greatest of them treat the lowliest with honour, and they infinitely prize the title, "Portuguese of Portugal," calling such an one *homo blanco*, or "white man." All the poor Indians they despise, as though they would trample them under their feet. So these Indians were all amazed when we told them that these fellows were sons of porters, cobblers, drawers of water, and other vile craftsmen.[1]

According to their titles, qualities, and merit, they have their rewards after having served seven years. Those honours and titles, given by the soldiers to each other, are not used until they have passed the Cape of Good Hope, for then they abandon almost all their former manners and customs, and throw their spoons into the sea.[2]

When they are arrived in the Indies at any place belonging to the Portuguese, they are free to go wheresoever they

[1] Mocquet gives an amusing account of a swineherd, Fernando, who having dubbed himself Don, and riding through the streets of Goa on a fine horse and in sumptuous attire (at the expense of some half-caste woman), was suddenly met by the son of his old master in Portugal, who cried, "Good heavens, Fernando, how are you?" The Don at first denied, and then confessed his identity, begging the other not to divulge his secret.

[2] For the Portuguese to round the Cape was to drink of Lethe. Sir W. Scott furnishes a parallel passage:—"If you want rogues, as they are so much in fashion with you, you have that gallant cast of adventurers who laid down their consciences at the Cape of Good Hope, and forgot to take them up again when they returned" (Preface to *The Surgeon's Daughter*). The throwing overboard of the spoons is in reference to the fact that they used no spoons in India: "There they eate nothing with spoons, and if they should see any man doe so, they would laugh at him" (*Linschoten*, i, 207; see also *Della Valle*, iv, 301).

will, without being obliged to any one, and they are not even constrained to go to war, save on extraordinary occasions, on the other hand they are not paid nor rated.[1] Only they go to eat and drink at the houses of those four great lords who give food to all soldiers in the winter, they can also go for meat and drink to all the monasteries at all seasons; for at the houses of the said lords, food is given only in winter, when the soldiers are on shore, and the armadas are returned home. They like better to be fed than to receive money; for being addicted to play, they would gamble all incontinently. As for the money that is advanced to them for their voyage, they durst not fail to buy out of that whatever is necessary for the voyage, under pain of punishment. The two armadas of the North and the South get an advance of two quarters' pay, which amounts in all to thirty-six perdos.[2] The other armadas that go further off get an advance of three-quarters. If they are more time on the voyage, they are paid for it, and on their return get another quarter's pay. The viceroy also betimes gives them something extra, when he wishes to gratify the soldiers. The number of the soldiers is never published, although it is known by the rolls: for they will not that the Indians should know their numbers, as I have already said. The other inhabitants, and the native Indian soldiers, who are Christians, are numbered, but not the Metifs, who are as the Portuguese.

Although the great majority of these soldiers are sent out, some impressed, and others volunteers, yet when they are in the Indies all are free to remain or to return to Portugal.

[1] So great were the disorders at Goa, owing to the presence of an idle soldiery, that the government were constrained to induce them to take up their quarters at the other towns, Chaul, Daman, Diu, etc., by allowances of ten pardãos and their victuals during the monsoon months (Boullaye-le-Gouz, *Voy.*, p. 198).

[2] Some thirty years later the pay of a soldier for a six months' voyage had fallen to ten pardãos (*Boullaye-le-Gouz*).

They must, however, have their leave and passport of the viceroy, which indeed they obtain with some difficulty except they have some interest, or can show a legitimate cause. But the real cause why so few came back is that on the return voyage the king provides them with water only, while it costs one at least three hundred perdos to get back to Portugal.[1]

When they are newly arrived in the Indies, they are called *Raignolles*,[2] that is to say, "men of the kingdom," and the older hands mock them until they have made one or two voyages with them, and have learned the manners and customs of the Indies: this name sticks to them until the fleet arrives the year following. When they are met in the street, and are recognised for *Raignolles*, the little children and shop boys cry after them. The Indian merchants are glad enough to see them, for they are easier to take in.

If the soldiers from Portugal look forward to get a reward or benefaction from the king, they must serve him there for seven years, without counting the year of their going out; the *Metifs*, or Indian-born, serve for eight years. Nor is it enough for them only to remain there: they must embark in all the warlike expeditions that present themselves; for which they receive good certificates, called *Certidous*,[3] from the

[1] So Linschoten (ii, 229), who adds that they were not allowed a passage home until they had served three years in India.

[2] Port. *reinol*, pl. *reinoes*, "of the kingdom" (*i.e.*, Portugal). At this time the word had exactly the same meaning as our Anglo-Indian "griffin", and our colonial "new-chum" (see *Linschoten*, i, 208; *Mocquet*, 304). Pyrard says above (p. 121) that the Portuguese called themselves "Portuguese of Portugal", probably owing to the derogatory meaning of *reinol*. Later, however, as Portuguese blood became more and more mixed, this word became a term of pride. A century later we find A. Hamilton speaking of the pride of "the *Reynolds* (*sic*) or European fidalgos" (*New Acct.*, i, 251). So in the present century (see above, p. 38, *note*). The author's remark, that it took a year for a *reinol* to wipe out the stain, reminds one that it takes the same time at an English public school for a "new fellow" to work out the penalties of his condition.

[3] Port. *certidão*.

viceroy and the captains, who forget not to enter in their certificates all their good service rendered, that so they get their recompense accordingly. If they cannot show that, they receive nothing. If they wish to be recompensed, they must return to Portugal, at the end of the said period, otherwise their service is lost: and sometimes for want of means many cannot go and so lose all, for they must be there in person. But if they die on the way or in the Indies, their wives and children, or other next heirs, can present these certificates, just as they themselves might. Those who return before the fixed time get no reward, no more than those who, being in India, do no service there.

A vast number of the soldiers are sent to the Indies in exile for their misdeeds: these durst not return before their time has expired. They are sent to Ceilan, Mozambique, Malaca, and other places to garrison them: these get only their pay without hope of other reward; most of them marry and remain there all their lives.[1]

Concerning the little boys, that are shipped and paid as soldiers at Lisbon, when these arrive in the Indies they are not rated as soldiers, unless they are sufficiently strong to bear all sorts of arms; but they fail not to find places: for the lords, captains and gentlemen, take them for pages, although they are of low birth. They do no menial service for their master and mistress, except attending them abroad, they are most sumptuously habited in their master's livery. Ten or fifteen of them may be seen following one of these lords, and they mingle not, nor associate with the slaves. When they are grown and able to bear arms, their master gives them some money to buy arms and clothes, and then they join the expeditions with the others, and their seven

[1] The use of India as a Botany Bay is above referred to as one of its chief advantages to Portugal (p. 88). In times of peril a free pardon was given to these exiles on condition of service with the armies, as on the occasion of the Siege of Kunhâli (*Arch. Port. Or. Fasc.*, vi, No. 899).

years commence from the time when they cease to be pages; so they follow the profession of arms.

These soldiers are all free, and there is none can command them but the viceroy, except when they are enrolled, shipped, and are receiving their pay for going to a war. For then the captains and generals of the armadas command them during that voyage only. All the unmarried, who have made profession of arms, can call themselves soldiers; saving of course the clergy, who wear not the sword. This word—soldier—then, includes all the unmarried: they are prohibited from wearing mantles, to distinguish them from the married men who wear them. The married men cannot be compelled to go to the wars, and when they desire to go, it is a great dishonour to them on account of their wives they leave behind. For great respect is there paid to a married man, whom they call *Casado.* The soldiers like not to see married men shipped along with them, being apprehensive, lest they should inadvertently, and without intending any offence, address to them some indecent language, such as they use among themselves. A married man would be gravely insulted by such words. Nevertheless necessity sometimes requires them to go; but they must wear their mantles, so as to be recognised.

As to the number of these soldiers, Portuguese and Metifs, I have seen in Goa alone more than four or five thousand, besides the Indian soldiers who are innumerable. These cannot hold themselves on a par with the Portuguese, nor eat with them, although they be Christians, and although their men and women can intermarry with theirs. So that the soldiers, to keep their estates, offices, and honours, both in the town of Goa, and in other possessions of the Portuguese, must be married, or enrolled as soldiers, and in the pay of the king.

The order of their embarking for the wars is as follows. Over every fleet, whether ordinary and extraordinary, the viceroy and his council appoint a general and also captains, fixing the number of vessels, and causing to be delivered to the said general and captains money for all the expenses. Next, drums are beat and criers go through the town to warn all that will to enroll themselves at such and such a place. The captains are curious to choose the honest men and best soldiers, and give them gratifications and honours to induce them to come with them. For there soldiers, being bound to none, go and ship themselves with whom they will, and are under obedience to them only for the voyage: they are paid by the quarter, and in advance. All those in command are appointed by the viceroy and most often by favour, and they are the best rewarded, receiving more pay and more booty. For instance, those in charge of the victualling, the munitions, and other expenditure, all get their profit, each in his office which he wins according to the strength of his interest. It is a great honour and favour to be general, even to be captain of a vessel, for he commands a large body of honourable soldiers who on land are as good or better than themselves. The *Viador de Facienda*, or Superintendent of the Finances, pays the soldiers. The generals and captains have the duty of engaging and paying the expenses of the crew, the mariners, etc., and providing for their advances in money.

For the rest the money advanced to the soldiers against their embarkation is only to provide them with clothes, arms and other commodities. As for provisions, they have to take no thought on that score, being well fed at the expense of the king on board ship, and according to the produce of the places visited. When they are at sea they take the ordinary ship's victual, that is to say, rice with butter, sugar, lentils, and *mangas*.[1] This is a fruit of the form of an olive, but much larger, they have other sorts of them which they

[1] The mango: from the Tam. mān-kāy (see Yule, *Gloss.*). In North India and Ceylon it is called *ām* and *āmba*, from the Skt. *amra*.

salt. Frequently, too, they have biscuit, and the drink is water only. They eat also a salted fish named *pesche cavalo*,[1] along with rice. But when they are at anchor in some port, as they frequently are, they get all kinds of victuals that are procurable at the several places, at the expense of the king. Those who go on shore and care to live there, do so at their own expense. On board, each soldier has his own dish and eats by himself. The captain holds all his soldiers in great respect and honour: they are treated vastly different from our soldiers here. For there, the title of soldier is the most honourable that one can have, and none is so rich or of such quality, as to be disgraced in giving his daughter in marriage to a soldier.

When a soldier has once received his pay, and the quarter for embarking, and afterwards tries to hide so as not to go, if he is apprehended, he is corporally punished and sent to prison. In these vessels there are two kitchens, namely, one for the captain and soldiers, and one for the mariners and sailors. In every vessel there are three or four Portuguese pages, rated and fed like the soldiers: they serve only the captain, lieutenant, and soldiers, and such clergy as are with them, whether Jesuits or of other orders: for there is no vessel without these clergy on board. Most nevertheless have their private slaves and valets; and these pages only attend them when they take their meals in the ship. Some of the soldiers are of fine appearance and quality, yet are much the same as the soldiers of our regiments, all being infantry armed with arquebuse, pike, spear, little China bucklers, bows and arrows. They use corselets but little, while they value highly those collars of buffalo hide, and laced jerkins, which are solely for sword cuts, and for arrows shot from afar. They make use also of burgonets and iron helmets. On land they wear sailor's breeches, which require ten ells of stuff, and are exceeding ample and wide below,

[1] See vol. i, pp. 388, 427.

and reach to the ground; with these they wear no stockings, and it is impossible that they could run in such breeches. But when they are on board, they wear them of another style, which they call *à la Française*, as about thirty years ago such like were worn in France. These are very short and tight, and with them they wear no stockings or shoes, for they say that shoes would deprive them of a firm footing on the vessel, whether in the rigging or on the deck. At night they have tents of palm leaves made expressly for the purpose of protecting them from the rain. They have also mats and mattresses for sleeping upon, and carpets of Persia, or of Cambaye, which are smaller. In the morning they fold and wrap these up and lay them aside. On board ship there is so little room that when you lie down you can hardly stretch yourself at full length.

Having spoken of their embarkations and manner of living at sea, I will now say a word of their conduct when they are in the towns, and principally at Goa. On returning from their voyages they reside in what towns they please, as also may those who have not taken part in the voyage. Some take a notion to live in one sort, others in another; but most of them keep company with girls and women, whom they call *solteras*,[1] that is licentious and unmarried women, living with them quite openly, as if they were married. These girls or widows deem themselves highly honoured when a white man, meaning one from Europe, courts their society. They will entertain and feed him as best they can, and wash his linen when need be. On the other hand the soldiers, or *amigos*, as they are called, maintain and support these women in all things, and are as jealous of them as if they were their proper wives, and will readily attack and slay one another in duels on their account. But it is a great misfortune for a soldier or other Portuguese or foreigner to have intercourse with

[1] *Solteira*, a spinster; then, as he says (but not now), used in the above derogatory sense.

these immodest Metices, or Indian girls, for one sees but few men come out of it without peril. For if they know that a man is paying his addresses to other women or girls, or is meaning to marry, or to quit them on any other ground whatever, infallibly they will poison him with a certain drug, which can keep him alive for six months, but at length will kill him,[1] wherefore a man must use great cunning and dissimulation in quitting them. For the rest, the children of these unions are not held for bastards, but inherit both from the father and the mother, if neither the one nor the other is married.

Fifteen days before we left Goa, a master's mate of one of the three carracks which left before us, named Manuel Fernando, went to visit the mistress of a soldier. The latter arriving at the same time gave him a swordcut in the neck, and leaving him for dead, took refuge in a church. But the woman and her maid-servant budged not, whereupon the magistrate coming up, in no wise punished the women nor him that had fled. The wounded man was carried to the hospital, and on his recovery seeing that his vessel, wherein all his goods were already shipped, had gone, he was constrained to come in ours. He bought a passage accordingly, without a word said. In short, those women are exceeding fond of the men of these parts. As for the soldiers who cohabit with them, they fail not to embark when called on, like the rest.

The others who do not ordinarily live with such-like women, club together nine or ten of them, more or less, and take a lodging: this is very cheap there, for a lodging that would cost twelve crowns a month here, would not fetch one there. They furnish it with beds, tables, and other utensils,

1 The drug on which this story is founded is not specified. Linschoten (i, 211) describes its potency as being still more marvellous: "It will lye six yeres in a man's body, and never doe him hurt, and then kil him, without missing halfe an houres time. They make it also for one, two, or three yeares, monthes, or dayes, as it pleaseth them best."

and have a slave or two in common. They ordinarily reside in the lower rooms on account of the great heat. There are also other lodgings, with no separate rooms, for letting only to soldiers or other foreigners of little means. Others again of more commodious sort are to be let as here. These soldiers live a knavish life, for the most part, at least such as have no cleverness. Some carry on intrigues with married women or widows, who support them; others gain the favour of lords and gentlemen, who do not allow them to want; others engage in trade, or gamble. And these four lords, of whom I have spoken, keep open table for all. Although they thus live in common, they never eat two together, but each has his portion, as I have said, and then has more wine, bread, flesh, and fish than two could eat. Such, too, as care not to go and eat at the lord's house, send their servant to bring their dish and portion to their own home.

All day long you see them in their parlours, or at their doors, seated in chairs in the cool shade, all in their shirts and white cotton drawers. There they sing and play the guitar or other instrument. The place is all overspread with foliage, and water is thrown about to keep it fresh. They are vastly polite towards the passers-by, freely bidding them enter, sit, make themselves at home, and have a chat. They never go about the town all at one time, but at most two or three, sometimes not having more than three or four dress suits to serve ten or twelve of them. For all that, when you see them walk through the town, you would say they were lords with an income of 10,000 livres, such is their bravery, with their slaves behind them, and a man carrying over them a big sombrero or parasol. There are places where these slaves are to be hired, and one can be got for half a day for a vintain,[1] which is worth six blanks. They walk in their suits of silk with the greatest pride imaginable. But as

[1] Port. *vintem*, a base copper coin. Wm. Barret says that fifteen basarucos "make a vinton of naughty mony".

soon as they are arrived at their lodging they doff these promptly, and others take them who may want to go to town in their turn.

These soldiers roam abroad at nights, and make it somewhat dangerous to walk about the town after eight or nine o'clock, for although the archers and sergeants are on their rounds, the soldiers go in stronger bodies. They have a bad custom, which is that they never make their assaults singly man upon man, but most often four or five of them fall upon one alone, and slay him whether it be night or day. By night they murder and rob, and make no scruple about killing a man for money.

Thus do the soldiers conduct themselves in the Indies, on shore and at sea; some well, the rest ill, according as their fortune is good or evil. But most of them in the end marry and go into trade: for some care not to return to Portugal, having a sufficiency out there: others cannot return for want of means. It costs them but little to live there, for they drink only Banguenin water, and a man is well lodged for a tangue, or six sols a month; insomuch that with six blanks or three sols a day, a man can get along and have good cheer enough.

CHAPTER IX.

Of the kingdom of Dealcan, Decan, or Ballagate, and the neighbourhood of Goa.

But because the island of Goa, and the surrounding country, now under the power and influence of the Portuguese, were anciently an appanage of the kingdom of Dealcan or Decan, whereof we have often spoken, it will not be out of place to tell something of what I have heard at Goa of that kingdom.

It is now a hundred and ten years and more the Portuguese have held the Island of Goa, for the recovery whereof out of their hands the kings of Dealcan have done all they could by force of war; they have even laid siege to it twice,[1] with two very powerful armies composed each of 200,000 men, and each siege lasted nine entire months. And the King of Dealcan used to say blusteringly, that to fill up the river, and make a passage for his army to the said island, he needed nothing but the *alpargues*,[2] or shoes, of his own people. And indeed, he did nearly fill it up with earth and stones in one place, and thereby got the means of carrying over a certain force of men; but they met with a handsome reception and repulse from the Portuguese. But what astonished the king most was the cannon of the Portuguese, which was of considerable weight, whilst he had none. He at length recognised that he could not take the place by force, but that on the contrary he would gain more benefit and wealth from traffic and intercourse with the Portuguese, than if Goa belonged to himself: on the other hand, the Portuguese saw that they could not remain there for any length of time without the friendship of this

[1] In 1570-1, and (?) in 1583. The first siege was in pursuance of the great confederacy of the Kings of Bijapur and Ahmednuggur and the Turks led by Ali Adil Shah of Bijapur, and of the Kings of Achin and Johore in the far East, to drive the Portuguese out of India. Chaul was besieged at the same time. The siege of Goa was raised chiefly by the terrible ravages of disease in the investing army. The Venetian Cesar Frederick was in the city at the time (*Hak.*, ii, pt. II, p. 219). For a fuller account see Decadas; Faria y Souza, *As. Port.*; and Antonio de Castilho, *Comentario do cerco de Goa e Chaul no anno de* 1570, Lisbon, 1573, 8vo., and 1736, 4to. The second siege, in which the Turks are said to have lost 20,000 men, chiefly by disease, is interesting to us from the fact that our countryman, Edward Webbe, fought as master-gunner in the Turkish army (E. Webbe, *His Trauailes*, 1590, 4to; reprint by Arber, 1868, 8vo.).

[2] Port. *alparca*, from the Ar. *pargat*, sandals (Vieira, *Dict. Port.*). At the siege of Famagosta, in 1571, the Turkish leader made a like boast:—"By means of country people who went to Famagosta to ransom prisoners, Mustafa caused it to be reported in the place that his force was so overwhelming that if each man would but fling his shoe into the ditch a mound might be raised by which the wall might be stormed" Stirling-Maxwell's *Don John of Austria*, Libr. edit., i, 366).

king, because all their provisions had to reach them from his country, wherefore they made peace together upon these conditions: That the Portuguese would live in their island according to their laws and customs, without encroaching in any way upon the lands or territories belonging to the said king, nor, in like wise, would he make any enterprise upon their island. Further, that the Indians in the island who are pagans (as a multitude in fact are, even to the number of more than 20,000) should live according to their own religion without constraint, observing indeed the Portuguese laws, whether of justice or police, but not being allowed to have any of their temples or pagodas in the island: and further, that they should pay for every male, of what young age soever, one perdo to the King of Portugal.

A rule is also observed between the two parties, that if a Christian or infidel of Goa, having committed some crime, happens to flee to the country of Dealcan, he cannot be followed by the officers of justice: nor, in like manner, a man of Dealcan at Goa. Yet it is exceeding difficult to win refuge at Goa, because one cannot pass over to the island without licence of the judge in writing, as I have said, and because of the guards that are at the passages and fortresses; nevertheless there are many that fly thither at all times. A great number of Portuguese and Christian Indians sojourn in these territories of Dealcan, and become residents there, living in all liberty, save for the exercise of the Christian religion, the which they cannot have, no more than the infidels can have theirs at Goa.

This King of Dealcan hath under him a very great extent of country, and many kingdoms, such as Decan, Ballagate, Hidalcan,[1] and others. These were anciently separate king-

[1] Pyrard is in the same hopeless confusion in regard to these names as his predecessor Linschoten. As has been shown, Hidalcan is really the name of the prince; *Dealcan* is a confusion of that name with *Deccan*; and *Ballagate* means simply the "Highlands", Pers. *bālā*, above, and Hind. *ghāt*, "a pass". Compare the old Scotch phrase, "abune the pass".

doms possessed by their own kings; but in process of time that of Dealcan hath subdued them all: it is at present very powerful and redoubted, and is bordered on the one side by the kingdom of Bengal, and on the other by the territory of the Grand Mogor. When I was about my departure from Goa, the news arrived there that this Grand Mogor had proclaimed war against the King of Dealcan, who was quite resolved to meet him, and it was said that this war was only to get a passage to march against the King of Bengala, which passage the King of Dealcan was resolved to prevent. The King of Dealcan is a Mahometan, as are a large part of his people: the rest are Gentiles and idolators, like the Canarins of Goa, the Nairs, and other Indians.

He is an amiable and peaceable prince—no tyrant, but a friend of all foreigners, and of his neighbours that are at peace with him. As for his power, it is such that he can put in the field 200,000 men, as he did at the last siege of Goa, which they say he would have taken at the last, but for the treason of two of the principal lords of his army, whom he afterwards beheaded on that account.

The viceroy has always an ambassador at the court of this king; there are also some Jesuits who are well received by him, and they make some use of their opportunities, but secretly. In all these countries there are great numbers of Portuguese, who are allowed to reside where they please in all assurance, but without the exercise of their religion: there are also there a goodly number of Christian Indians, but all these are men who have committed some crime and dare not return among the Portuguese, and therefore live there a reckless life. So, too, there are Dealcan subjects at Goa and elsewhere, living in the like liberty. As for the Portuguese that are about the king at Decan, or Ballagate, they can exercise their religion, because of the Jesuits and the Portuguese ambassador there.

This king also keeps an ambassador in ordinary at Goa;

he is a person of dignity and importance, and has the exercise of his religion in his own house. All the bodies of infidels at Goa are buried or burned in the Dealcan territories and not on the island. When this ambassador goes about the town he is accompanied by a power of men, partly his own domestics, and partly lords and merchants of the said kingdom. He has also a number of armed soldiers, as well before as behind him, carrying bows, arrows, arquebuses, pikes, swords, and Chinese bucklers. And though he has many fine horses yet most frequently he rides in a palanquin, followed by lords on horseback; and then he has his horses led by the hand, splendidly barbed and caparisoned, with a number of pages, one bearing his fan, another his silver box full of *betel*,[1] another a box containing *chunan*[2]—that is, lime for using with his betel—and two others with silver flagons or vases filled with water, one for drinking and washing his mouth, the other for washing the privy parts as occasion requires. His grand parasol is borne aloft, and a band of drums, flutes, hautbois, and other instruments of the country use, accompanies him. Thus do all the ambassadors and great lords of the country proceed.

It is now about forty years ago since, the King of Dealcan having two sons, the younger[3] came to Goa, became a Christian, and was baptised. Afterwards, his father being dead, he claimed a division with his brother, who refused to recognise him because of his religion, whereupon he sought aid of the viceroy, with whom he made war upon his said elder brother; the latter, partly under stress of war, and partly by advice of his council, at length gave him a share of the lands near Goa, viz.: the lands of *Bardes* and *Salcette*, which are in the vicinity of the Island of Goa, having only

[1] The Malayāl. *veṭṭila*, and Tam. *veṭṭilei* (*Piper betel*); see Yule, *Gloss.*

[2] Tam. *chuṇām*. The word is now in everyday Anglo-Indian use.

[3] The history of Meal-Khān, here inaccurately recorded from tradition, is given by De Couto, *Dec. V*, Liv. IX, cc. 8-11; Liv. X, cc. 1, 2, 6, 11: *Dec. VII*, Liv. I, cc. 10, 11; Liv. II, cc. 2, 7-10; Liv. IV, c. 9.

the river between, along with three or four other small islands. These two lordships are not part of the terra-firma at all, being separated therefrom by some streams that are easily fordable. The whole consists of about twenty leagues or more of country, very high, fertile throughout, with much trade, and the same people as at Goa. This Christian king, dying without children, left all his property and lands to the King of Portugal, who at this day possesses them under that title, and the Portuguese have built there fortresses, churches, and parish churches with colleges of Jesuits, who hold all the cures there, so that the faith waxes there daily. All these lands furnish the food of the Island of Goa.

To return to the King of Dealcan: he has a great number of elephants, whereof he makes presents betimes to the King of Spain, and these are kept at Goa for his service. He has also plenty of good horses, but these come from Persia and Mogor. As regards Arab horses, the viceroys of Goa give them to him; they are sent to his people young and fresh, and they break them, for there is no nation in all the Indies so handy with horses. The Portuguese themselves have no other grooms for breaking and training their horses but those from there; indeed also, after the Nairs, there are none who understand the management of elephants so well.

The country produces a vast number of tigers, which trouble them sore. The soil is fertile throughout, being watered by many rivers and streams. There are also serpents very thick and long. The finest and best diamonds come in quantities from the kingdom of *Ballagata:* they are among the principal sources of wealth to the king and country; for in the Indies the diamonds of Ballagata only are prized; plenty are found in Pegu and elsewhere, but not of like value. His people have also silk and cotton, whereof they make stuffs: they are exceeding well dressed, wearing trousers, and large coats of silk and cotton, with turbans on the head—straight, high, and pointed, and not round like those of the Turks and Arabs; their shoes are of the Turkish fashion, red, gilded and pointed in front, and open above; this is the dress as well of Gentiles as Mahometans. It is a marvel to see the throng of people that enters the island of Goa every day, as well men as women, laden with all kinds of provisions, with buffaloes, asses, and other beasts of burthen: thus is Goa fed.

It is now about fifteen years since there was at Goa a very near kinsman[1] of the King of Dealcan, who was not yet a Christian, but was nevertheless come with the intention of getting himself baptised. He was instructed every day, and so abode among the Portuguese two or three years in this hope, and was most desirous to get himself baptised, for there none are constrained thereto. At this juncture came to him some cheats from Dealcan, who made him believe that the king was dead, and that the crown belonged to him, as being the next heir, saying that they had the word of the chiefs for it, if he would go forth from Goa; all which he believed with simplicity, and conspired with them to depart secretly, so as not to be discovered by the Portuguese, who would have turned him back, and to whom he had given his word, having received much kindness at their hands; in such wise they so managed that they fled forth of Goa, and gained the country of Ballagata, where the king was. The poor prince being arrived there was fairly well received at the first; but was nevertheless closely watched. At length the king having assembled his council in his regard, was advised to put out his eyes, which is the punishment of all such as aspire to the crown, except the eldest son of the king: this is the custom among all the Indian and Mahometan kings, in imitation of the Turk and the

[1] The prince *Çufo Khan* (according to De Couto), son of Meale-Khan. He came to Goa in 1584 (see *Dec. X*, Liv. IV, cc. 7, 10, 11; *Arch. Port. Or.*, Fasc. 3, Doc. 23, § 14).

Persian. The king was afraid lest this prince should in course of time engage the Portuguese against him, as the other had done of whom I have spoken above.

Again, at the time I was leaving Goa, there was another prince of Dealcan, a kinsman of the king, who was residing there and was made a Christian, and even was married.[1] He draws a pension from the King of Spain, as do all the kings, princes, and great Indian lords who become Christians, and come for shelter to the Portuguese. This prince, after having been married five or six years to a pretty Metice lady, got tired of her and wanted to quit her, according to the custom of the Mahometan Indians, who thus quit one another when they think fit; and thinking to do the like he asked to be unmarried in the church; but this was not allowed. Seeing this he withdrew to the Moors' country and sent word to the Portuguese that he would never return unless they would unmarry him: whereupon they were advised that he being a man of consideration, it was more worth their while to permit it, and to let him be unmarried as his fancy was, than that getting a refusal he should renounce the faith. So it was that since then he has espoused a Brameny girl, with whom he lives quite peaceably.[2]

There was also a king of the Maldives that became a Christian at Cochin, and was baptised,[3] as I have already said in treating of the Maldives: he even brought his wife there and they were received in great honour. This king afterwards wished to constrain his subjects, who had revolted, to recognise him; to that end, he sent an army of Portuguese, who built a fort on those islands, and warred against them in such wise by the space of ten years, that they made

[1] This was the son of Mahmad Khan, a bastard of Meale-Khan. On becoming a Christian he was baptised by the name of Don João de Menezes Shâh (*Dec. X*, Liv. IV, c. 11).

[2] From a petition of this prince, given by Rivara, it appears that he was still resident in Goa in 1622.

[3] Under the name of Dom Manoel (see vol. i, pp. 245-249, and App. B.).

the majority of the islanders tributary. But at length the Portuguese were betrayed, and being surprised in their fortress were all slain. After that they have not been able to regain a footing, but the Mahometan king of the Maldives has agreed to pay a certain sum of money every year to this Christian king, and to his children and posterity. Under this treaty they are at peace, for no Christians reside amongst these people. I have seen at Goa the grandson of that Christian king, aged fifteen years, with his Portuguese mother; he is named Don Philippe.[1] The Portuguese give him the title of Majesty, calling him King of the Maldives, and honour and respect him greatly. The King of Spain gives a pension both to him and to his mother: they were lodged near the Jesuits' college, in a very handsome house. I have often been to see them, as indeed they begged me on account that I had lived at the Maldives, whereof they were glad enough to hear me gossip. I saw also in his house that gentleman named *Adrian de Gouya*, whom he had sent upon an embassy to the Mahometan king of the Maldives, as I have said[2]: he welcomed me with much courtesy, having been my warm friend. This little king has a suit against his uncle, named Don Pedro, who resides at Cochin, and is married there, for that he also calls himself king of the Maldives. This uncle is married to a Metice lady, nobly born and vastly rich, who maintains him in comfort; for without her he has only his pension from the king, which is small, and very often, indeed usually, but badly paid.

[1] See further App. B.

[2] See vol. i, p. 293.

CHAPTER X.

Voyage of the Author to Ceylon, and description of that Island.

Being then at Goa with the Portuguese, I was a soldier in many of their armies that they equipped during my sojourn there, chiefly beyond the coast where Goa is, to the island of Ceylon, to Malaca, Sumatra, Java, and other islands of Sunda and the Moluccas, and was paid like the rest.

For they are wont to equip many ships and galiots to send to Malaca, and as far as the Moluccas, to conduct their merchantmen in security; and also for an escort to such as traffic in China and Japan. Wherefore I shall describe here what I have observed in all those parts: where I have halted, sojourned, and fought.[1]

Ceylon is a very great island, towards the point of Cape Comorin; it extends north and south, and the southern[2] part is opposite Cape Comorin, between which and the island vessels cannot pass by reason that the sea is shallow. It is estimated to be three to four hundred leagues in compass. It is the richest island yet discovered, and is thickly set with many towns. Some Indians call it by the name of *Tenasirin*,[3] signifying land of delights or earthly paradise.

[1] He gives us no particulars of any engagement; indeed, at the close of this chapter he gives us to understand that at this period the Portuguese, when they met the Dutch, avoided fighting by striking.

[2] *Sic*, a mistake for "northern".

[3] The interpretation is right, but the application to Ceylon is erroneous. The name Tenasserim (Malay *tânah-sări*, the land of happiness or delight) was long ago given by the Malays to the Burma province, which still keeps it, the Burmese corruption being *Tanang-sâri*. Pyrard seems to be quoting Barbosa, the originator of the misapplication, who says of Ceylon that the Indians call it "*Tenarisin*, that is to say, land of delights" ("Tenarisin que quer dizer terra das delicias"). How this pas-

No words can express the richness, goodness, and fertility of this island. First as to its fruits: they have a taste and savour, such that none so excellent are to be found in all the Indies, though they grow wild in the woods and forests, and, among the rest, cinnamon. To name all would be impossible, but all those of the rest of India are to be found there in profusion and perfection; so that the Indians with no bad reason deem it to be the Earthly Paradise.[1] There are other trees, viz., palms, that bear the *areca*, which is chewed with the betel, and grows there in such abundance that all India is furnished thence, and a great traffic is carried on to all parts, for whole ships are laden with it for conveyance elsewhere.[2]

sage comes to appear in Lord Stanley's translation (p. 166)—"And the Indians call it Ylinarim. It is a rich and luxuriant land, etc."—is more than I can say.

[1] The Earthly Paradise of the middle ages is even more difficult to localise than the realm of Prester John. Its identification with Ceylon, which occurs also in Marignolli (see *Cathay*, pp. 326, 346) and elsewhere, is probably a confusion of the Christian legend, which seeks to localise the Garden of Eden, with the Mahommedan, which fixes Adam's Peak and its valleys as the place of Adam's retreat after his expulsion from Eden. What has been written on the terrestrial paradise would, as Col. Yule says, probably fill a respectable library. As developed by Christian fancy, "it is the old garden of Eden, which lay in the far east beyond the stream of Ocean, raised so high on a triple terrace of mountains that the deluge did not touch it. It is the residence of certain departed saints, and the pictures drawn of it are coloured with classical reminiscences of Elysium and the Islands of the Blest. How these outlines were filled up at different periods may be learned from Ephraem Syrus' poem on Paradise (4th century), from Cosmas Indicopleustes (6th century), from Dante (*Purg.*, c. 28 *et seq.*), and other mediæval sources." (*Encyc. Brit.*, art. "Paradise".)

[2] Ribeiro (i, c. 3) says that every year no less than a thousand *champanas* ("Sampan," a small boat; see Yule, *Gloss.*) of areca-nuts were loaded from the kingdom of Cotta. Legrand, followed by Lee, erroneously reads *arena* in this passage of Ribeiro, and makes this an export of *sand*. Tennent (ii, 27, *n.*) explains the mistake. Knox (p. 13) says there was great trade in these nuts with the Coromandel coast when he first went to Ceylon. It is still considerable.

The inhabitants are idolatrous folk, and worship idols, but of another sort than those of Malabar. They are all of great stature, very black and ill-favoured, but supple and ingenious; a people much given to their pleasures and delights; for the rest, very poltroons and cowards.[1] They go all naked, both men and women, save that they cover the private parts with rich silk cloths. The ears of both men and women are three or four inches long, and all pierced and laden with precious stones; they wear also many rings on the fingers, and girdles of fine gold. Their language is peculiar: they are called *Cingalla*.[2]

These *Cingalla* are very apt at manufactures, and have a very cunning and delicate hand for gold and silver, iron, steel, ivory, and other materials, which they work with excellent neatness. They make all sorts of arms, such as arquebuses, swords, pikes, and bucklers, which are the best and most valued in the Indies.[3] These people are very nimble, and good leapers: and all wear the hair long, like those of the Maldives. I never thought it possible they could show such excellence in fashioning arquebuses and other arms; more beautiful, indeed, are they in workmanship and ornament than those made here.

It is perhaps the most fertile region in the world for fruits: they are exceeding good and choice. The country is all covered with forests, fruit-trees bearing oranges both sweet and bitter, limes of a very sweet and delicious taste, pomegranates, cocos, pine-apples, and other Indian fruits.

Flesh of all sorts is abundant, nor is there any lack of fish; add millet, honey, canes, sugar, and butter in plenty; but there is grown no rice,[4] which is their principal nou-

[1] "The people of Seilan are no soldiers, but poor cowardly creatures" (*Marco Polo*, by Yule, Bk. III, ch. xiv).

[2] See vol. i, p. 266.

[3] Knox says they make good guns, but he does not praise them so highly as the author. Many existing specimens are of beautiful workmanship; but of course the art is dead now.

[4] Quite a mistake, though a large amount was then, as now, imported.

rishment: it is brought from Bengala. Moreover, all the cinnamon of the world comes from there only; there are whole forests of it. There are also vast numbers of elephants, whose teeth are much prized by them, and are a great article of traffic; also great quantities of precious stones, such as rubies, hyacinths, sapphires, topazes, garnets, emeralds,[1] cat's-eyes, etc., the best in the Indies; add to that, there is there the finest and greatest fishery of exceeding fine and beautiful pearls; but there are no diamonds.

The Portuguese have two fortresses in this island. The principal is called *Colombo*, and the other *Pointe de Galle*.[2] They are strong, and well garrisoned with soldiers, who are mostly criminals and exiles; and in the same way only women of ill-fame are sent thither. The general, or governor, of the country, who was there while I was at Goa, was named *Don Hieronimo Azebedo*,[3] a very good captain. The principal and greatest king of the island is called *Rachil*,[4] and there are many other kings.

[1] No emeralds are found.

[2] In orig. misprinted *Port de Salle*. These were the fortresses, but the Portuguese had then a number of small forts; *e.g.*, Mannar, Negombo, and Kalutara, on the west coast. About this time, too, after the visit of the Dutch to Batticaloa in 1602, they built forts there and at Trincomalee (Lee's *Ribeiro*, p. 50).

[3] Hieronimo Azevedo had been admiral at Malacca in 1585; he was eighteen years in Ceylon; became 20th viceroy Dec. 1612, and governed till Nov. 1617; he returned to Europe and ended his days in a dungeon at Lisbon. Faria y Souza says his reverses were a judgment from the Almighty for his barbarities in Ceylon. Pyrard was probably but a short time in Ceylon, and some soldier may have described this inhuman monster as a very good captain. His character may be estimated by his deeds, which included the tossing of Sinhalese to alligators, *to amuse his troops*, forcing mothers to pound their children, and other enormities (see *Faria y Souza*, by Stevens, iii, 72, 95, 98, 108, 167, 277; Monfart, *Trauailes*, p. 26; *Tennent*, ii, 23).

[4] Prob. *Raja*. The assumed title of Raja Sinha, "Lion King", the great usurper and tyrant, then not long dead, likely induced the notion that *raja* was part of the name. The king at this time was Seniwiratna, who reigned at Kandy (1604-16) after the death of Don Juan, who is next mentioned in the text.

There was one[1] seized and taken to Goa now twenty years ago; he then became a Christian, and was married, and had a good pension of the King of Spain for his maintenance, as have all the other kings and princes who are converted. This prince having resided a long while at Goa, well beloved of all, was so trusted that, by command of the King of Spain, and with the advice of the Council of the Indies, it was considered advisable to send him to Ceylon to rule there under the authority of the King of Spain, to the end that the people might obey him more gladly, as being a native of the country, in such wise that he was restored to the possession of all his country. But he was not there two years or so ere he abjured Christianity and returned to his first faith, and made war upon the Portuguese. This shows how perfidious and wicked these people are. The residence of this king was toward the port of Galla. He was called Don

[1] Kunappa Bandar, son of a prince of the royal house, whom Raja Sinha treacherously put to death, fled on that event to Colombo, whence he was sent to Goa. He was there during Linschoten's residence (*Linschoten*, i, 78), and was baptised as Don Juan, in honour of the victor of Lepanto. With great vigour and sagaci'y he led a successful revolt of his countrymen against the tyrant who had murdered his father, permitting the Portuguese to believe he was a tool in their hands. On being established on the throne (1592) he renounced Christianity, and took the name of Wimala Dharma. After several reverses he managed by a ruse to entrap a Portuguese army of 1,200 men, under Pedro de Sousa, in a mountain pass, where, deserted by their native allies, they were slain almost to a man. Donna Catharina, the Portuguese candidate, fell into the hands of the conqueror, who married her, and thus held the throne until his death in 1604. The end of his reign was signalised by his reception of the Dutch under Spilberg (1602), and the murder of Sibalt de Weer at Batticaloa (1603). Simple-minded Pyrard accuses him of perfidy in abjuring Christianity on gaining his throne; but what was his own royal master, Henry IV, about in the very same year, 1593? One act of the Sinhalese prince should go far to redeem him from the charge of perfidy. After the massacre above-mentioned, Sousa made a death-bed request that his son should be spared and sent back to Colombo. The conqueror promised and performed (De Couto, *Dec. XI*, xii; *Faria y Souza*, by Stevens, vol. iii; *Tennent*, ii, 21, *et seq.*; Pridham, *Ceylon*, ii, 95; Lee's *Ribeiro*, 26).

Jouan, and had been conquered, himself and his kingdom, by the captain, *André Furtado de Mendosa*, one of the bravest and most valiant captains that ever went to the Indies.

They used to worship a monkey's tooth, and when that was taken by the Portuguese they wished to buy it back at the price of great riches, but the Portuguese would not restore it, and it was publicly burned at Goa.[1]

[1] This sentence, which I have placed as a separate paragraph, is obviously out of place here. The story of the *Daḷadá*, or sacred tooth of Buddha, is too lengthy even to be sketched. Its earlier history is to be found in the *Dhâtuvansa* and the *Mahâvansa*; see also some interesting passages translated by Mr. Ievers in *J. Cey. As. Soc.*, vol. viii, art. "Beligala". The alleged capture of the *real* tooth by the Portuguese in 1560, has given rise to an infinity of notices and much controversy. That they captured, somewhere in the Jaffna district, a tooth or thing which they believed to be the historic relic, and that the viceroy Constantine de Bragança had it publicly pounded in a mortar and burnt to ashes at Goa, may be taken for fact (see De Couto, *Dec. VII*, passages from which, with all the authorities, are quoted by Mr. J. G. da Cunha in his *Mem. on the Tooth-Relic of Ceylon*, 1875). But as Mr. Rhys Davids points out (*Academy*, 1874, p. 341), it has never been shown how the tooth, though given to travel, got out of the Sinhalese into the Tamil country of Jaffna. To which objection I would add another, that the Sinhalese never seem to have mourned the loss of their palladium. The Portuguese heard in 1566 of the tooth cult going on at Kandy as of yore, and of course charged the King of Kandy with a fraud. They then bitterly regretted that they had not sold their captured ivory to the King of Pegu for 40,000 cruzados. The Sinhalese king was wiser. He sold a *real* relic to the King of Pegu, and, when the transaction was complete, discovered that the *most real* tooth was still in his possession. There need be no doubt that the relic now enshrined at Kandy, where I have seen it on two or three occasions between 1871 and 1873, is the same which has been worshipped at least since 1566. As to its material, nothing is known: in size and shape it is not of normal human dimensions; but this, in the eyes of its devotees, is rather proof of its genuineness. The best representation of it is that given by Forbes (*Eleven Years in Ceylon*), and copied by Tennent and by Yule (*Marco Polo*). The cut in Davy's *Ceylon* is, according to my recollection of the original, inaccurate. That the *daḷadá* was a monkey's tooth is of course only a Portuguese slander, in which Buddhism is confused with the Hindu worship of Hanuman.

This king, having revolted and abjured the faith, put to death all the Portuguese that were found in his borders; and so it was that afterwards the Hollanders passing the *pointe de Galla* with three ships, as their wont is to cast anchor and make a sojourn there, contracted a peace and alliance with this king; and such was the confidence reposed in one another, that the Hollanders used to go ashore in all freedom and assurance, and the Cingalla in like manner used to come aboard their ships. But upon this the king conceived a great treachery, assembling all the chiefs, principal soldiers, and most eminent men at his palace for a grand solemn banquet, which he gave to all the highest grandees of his court and of the Nairs.[1] The Hollander general went thither in good faith with sixty or seventy of the chief men of his three ships, chosen by himself, and arrayed in the bravest style possible. They were there received very magnificently, according to the custom of the country; but the poor Hollanders' dessert was after another fashion, for while they were at table thinking only to enjoy themselves and make good cheer, they were incontinently seized and massacred there and then by suborned villains.[2] The design of the king was at once to surprise all the ships, but God did not permit that, and saved them: for three or four mariners that were there waiting upon them escaped, and ran and flung themselves into their boats, to give word to those on board the ships of what had taken place. So it was they straightway

[1] His informants meant probably the Tamils of Batticaloa.

[2] The massacre of Sibalt de Weer and his comrades (1st June 1603) arose out of a difference between him and Wimala Dharma (Don Juan) as to the division of the Portuguese prizes, or, as some say, was brought about by the Dutchman's insulting language when drunk. The affair is involved in some obscurity. It took place at Batticaloa, and not at Galle, as Pyrard implies. Some say that it was done by the king's officers without his order: Pyrard's statement that it was done at the instigation of the Portuguese is uncorroborated, and may be dismissed as a Portuguese boast (see Van Warwyk's *Voyage* of 1602; Baldæus, *Hist.*, ch. vii; *Tennent*, ii, 36).

cut the cables, leaving their anchors there, and set sail, laying a course for Achen, whither God conducted them, for all their pilots had been slain. I have heard it said by the two Hollanders who came to the Maldives, and subsequently by others, that that general was one of the bravest and most valiant men that had come out of Holland this many a day, and that the rest of his comrades were of the same temper. The perfidious king that played them this sorry trick did it all to make his peace with the Portuguese; for I have heard them say themselves that this came about of their counsel, and that the king had promised to deliver up the ships to them, saving a part of the valuable cargo that he should retain. The general was not slain at the time,[1] nor were two or three others; but when the king saw that one part of his design had failed, he fell into such rage and choler, that he had their eyes put out, and practised a thousand other cruelties upon them. These kings of Ceylon are sometimes friends, sometimes enemies, of the Portuguese, changing thus in a thousand fashions.

The Portuguese are in continual war with these islanders, a great part of whom they have conquered and hold under their power, and little by little they are overcoming the rest. Many have been made Christians.

War is very difficult for the Portuguese, because the country is much covered and full of woods; and thus in going to war they must always have a bill and a hatchet in hand. Nor are the Portuguese so quick and nimble in marching through these woods as the islanders, who prepare ambuscades therein, and then escape in the thickest of them. Many a time have the Portuguese been besieged in their fortresses, but these have never been taken.

The war is very cruel between the two, and when the Portuguese take prisoners of war they make them slaves or put them to death. On the islanders' part, they do not put

[1] He was, according to the Dutch account.

the Portuguese to death, but merely cut off their noses and send them back; for they say they will not have their soil polluted with the bodies and blood of foreigners, so far as they can prevent it.

In this island is a point towards the south called "de Galla"; it is a cape advancing far into the sea. I shall tell what happened to three Hollander ships that were guarding it when they met those two large vessels, the one of Arabia, the other of Guzerate, whereof I have spoken in treating of the Maldives. These ships remained there about three months, during the time the east winds blow (which is also the time when the ships of India return from the South and from Bengala), and took sixteen or eighteen Portuguese vessels; for all the vessels coming from the coasts and shores of Bengala, Malaca, Sunda, China, Japan, and elsewhere must pass there, and sight this point or cape, as we did the Cape of Good Hope in going to the Indies. They also touch there in coming to all the rest of the Indian coast, that is, to the parts from Cape Comorin to Ormus. Those who will not go near it, without doubt will get entangled in the shoals of the Maldives, whence it is hard to withdraw without danger. Nevertheless, these captures incommoded the Portuguese more than they enriched the Hollanders, for most of the vessels carried only provisions for the ports. The Portuguese suffered in two ways: first, in losing honour and credit in the eyes of the Indian kings and peoples; secondly, in the necessity and lack of food which the people of the ports and havens to which the ships belonged sustained thereby; for if there is a failure of provisioning one year, the famine is very great. In these vessels were only some merchants and passengers, who are Portuguese or Metices and Indian Christians; for all the rest, as well officers as mariners, and even the merchants themselves, are Indians,—either Gentiles, Jews, or Mahometans. The Indian Christians habited in the Portuguese style are not deemed Indians, but Portuguese. The Hollanders gave more quarter and better terms of capitulation to these real Indians than to the Portuguese and Metifs; and none of the Indian ships, from whatsoever port, sustained any injury, but, on the contrary, got offers of aid and assistance, and this occurred to many that did not ask it. So it is that the Hollanders, English, and French, whom they rate all alike, are well received among these Indian kings and peoples, forasmuch as these nations do them no damage.

Now for the order observed by the Hollanders when they meet vessels, it is to fire a cannon-shot, whereupon the others strike at once, for they have no fancy to fight, being all private merchants, or Indian mariners and officers, to whom the Hollanders do no harm. But they seize the Portuguese and all their goods, and the ship also, if it belongs to the Portuguese, or they give it to the Indians. They put the Portuguese on shore without injury, giving them money for their support until they get into their own territories. When they meet Indian ships they search them to see if there be any Portuguese concealed therein; not finding any, they let them go without more ado. They merely ask if they are Mahometans, or of what other religion; being informed on this point, they make them swear on the book of their law, or on a biscuit (upon which oath they are believed), whether the cargo belongs to them or to the Portuguese. And when they are found mixed on a ship, the Hollanders do the like, setting apart and leaving the goods of the Indians, and seizing those of the Portuguese, that is, such as are their own property: and most often they set fire to the vessel or give it to the Indians, making them swear not to give what is left to the Portuguese; for if they came to know that they had given anything to them, they would treat them as enemies. It is impossible to count the ships that the Hollanders have seized in the Indies in this fashion, without firing a shot: for they are regarded as Kings of the sea by the Indians and by the Portuguese themselves. The latter, as soon as they sight the Hollanders afar off, even in lesser numbers, think of nothing but flight, and of abandoning their ship and all their merchandise, themselves escaping in some little boat.

CHAPTER XI.

Of Malaca, a description of it, and the memorable siege which the Hollanders laid thereto.

Departing from Ceylon, we steered our course to Malaca,[1] which is distant from Goa six hundred leagues, near the Equinoctial line, at one degree's elevation of the Arctic Pole's circle, very near the great island of Sumatra, and the kingdoms of Sian and Pegu. The Portuguese have built a very strong city there, which is of vast importance to them, seeing it is the key and staple of the trade of China, Japan, the Moluccas, and other islands in the neighbourhood of Sunda: so that, after Ormus, there is no captain thrives like him of Malaca, for there he is at the straits of Malaca and Sumatra, where all the ships must touch and pay their dues. Even the Portuguese vessels cannot pass without the acquittance of the governor of Malaca, both going and returning.

This place causes much trouble to the Hollanders, English, and French, by reason whereof the Hollanders have desired

[1] Thus spelt by the Portuguese, and more correctly than our *Malacca* (see Yule, *Gloss.*). It was a city of great importance before its capture by Albuquerque in 1511; Varthema, who visited it about 1505, saying, "Truly I believe that more ships arrive here than at any place in the world." Before the siege by the Dutch, which the author is about to describe, it had been several times invested by the leagued kings of Achin, Johore, and Java. The most notable sieges were three in the time of one governor—1573-76—described in the rare work, *Historia dos Cercos que em tempo de Antonio Monis Barreto Governador que foi dos estados da India os Achens & Jaos puserão á fortaleza de Malaca, sendo Tristão Vaz de Veiga capitão della Brevemente composta por Jorge de Lemos*; Lisbon, 1585, 4to., ff. 64.

to take it, and they laid siege to it in this wise:—The said Hollanders and the King of Jor had made a compact and treaty together to drive the Portuguese out of Malaca, and for this purpose the Hollanders had thirteen large vessels commanded by the Captain Corneille Madalif,[1] their general in the Indies. So, on the 29th day of April 1606, he cast anchor before Malaca, with full 1,500 Hollanders, who, being landed, invested Malaca. The town was much surprised, for the governor had had notice and orders from the viceroy of Goa to supply four ships of war to the merchantmen for an escort on the voyage from Goa to China and Japan. So there remained with him in the fortress no more than thirty soldiers, though he expected that the viceroy must full soon arrive, having had advice from Spain by the gallion which leaves Lisbon a month or two before the fleet of carracks, to go direct to Malaca, and not to the Indies. This gallion is of 700 or 800 tons burthen, and carries despatches, as well as loads cargoes in China and the islands of Sunda.

[1] Cornelis Matelief the younger left the Texel with eleven ships, 12th May 1605; met V. der Hagen at Mauritius on his way home, 1st Jan. 1606, and arrived before Malacca 30th April. During the siege he was joined by two more ships, making thirteen, as above stated. The account of the siege here given is nearly accurate. Matelief, a sea-captain, untaught in the art of war, proved himself in this siege, and in the two naval combats which followed it, to be a born leader of men. His enterprise was perilous in the extreme. He disembarked the great bulk of his small force and his cannon, leaving his ships undefended in the road, and exposed (should any mishap befall his scout) to the swoop of the viceroy's fleet, which throughout the siege was daily expected. He got little or no assistance from the Johore alliance; his own men were continually drunk, and fell an easy prey to dysentery and fever. These difficulties notwithstanding, Matelief re-embarked his men and guns with the precision of a veteran general. His own high courage at length animated his crews, and the Dutch never fought better than in the two desperate sea-fights before Malacca. For accounts of this voyage see *Rec. des Voy.*, vol. iii; *Grotius*, xvii, 792-800; Motley, *Un. Neth.*, ch. 44; and Matelief's own account, translated into English under the title, *An historicall and true discourse of a Voyage, etc.*, London, 1608, pp. 25.

Thus was the captain taken unawares, lacking provisions as well as men, and having no notice of this enterprise, nor that the Hollanders had as many vessels in the Indies. The attack was made with twenty-five pieces of cannon of ordnance, which they laid out on land. They were aided, as I have said, by the King of Jor and a number of petty kings, his vassals, who invested the place on the land side with 60,000 men: for he is a puissant king that holds all the territory and lands beyond Malaca. This siege lasted for the space of three months and nineteen days. The place was well defended by a very valiant Portuguese gentleman, named *André Furtado de Mendoza*, who happened to be there by chance.[1] For he looked forward to nothing in the Indies short of the post of viceroy, the which he soon after obtained.[2] He had with him but a hundred and fifty men under arms, including Portuguese and Indians.[3] But what was a good thing for the besieged was that there were there some merchant ships of Japan, manned by Japanese, who are the best soldiers in all the Indies: these helped to make up this number of a hundred and fifty men for the defence. It turned out happily, too, for the besieged that the viceroy of Goa, without knowing anything of the siege of Malaca, had put an armada to sea, whereof he himself took the command[4]; he was named *Don Martin Alphonça de Castro.* This armada consisted of seventy ships, and was in two divisions; the galleys, galiots, and vessels driven by oars went together,

[1] A mistake; he had been captain of Malacca nearly three years (*Liv. das Monç.*, i, 7).

[2] He became Governor of India on the 27th May 1609, but held office only three months.

[3] The Dutch account says that he had eighty Portuguese to start with, and that during the siege two vessels, one containing eighty more Portuguese, managed to run the blockade and reach the town.

[4] The viceroy was ordered to proceed in person to Malacca and the Moluccas by an *alvará* of the king, dated 15th March 1605 (*Arch. Port. Or.*, Fasc. 6, No. 46).

and the round sailing ships by themselves. This armada is considered to have been the finest the Portuguese ever put on the sea in the Indies, for it consisted of near 15,000 men well equipped.[1] He departed from Goa in the month of May 1606, having left the government of Goa and of Northern India in the hands of the archbishop of Goa, *Don Alexis de Melsio.*[2] A month after the viceroy's departure, the two armadas met and joined near Sumatra, as had been arranged. The intention was to take and conquer that island, because the king had given access to the Hollanders, and was a great enemy to the Portuguese; but they were valiantly repulsed and beaten by the King of Achen and his following, among whom were also some Hollanders who did him good service, both in action and in counsel. Meanwhile the viceroy, having news of the siege of Malaca, departed from Sumatra to go thither, thinking to surprise the Hollanders on land and burn their ships; but he did not make this out, for the said Hollanders were warned by one of their factors, that was at Sumatra, and promptly left to give them notice; but there was no need of him, for the Hollanders had always a pinnace seven or eight leagues out at sea to act as a sentinel, for fear of being surprised. As soon as this pinnace was aware of the armada, she went speedily and brought word to the Hollanders, who forthwith re-embarked themselves and their cannon, insomuch that the siege was thus raised the 19th[3] of the month of August. But this was the cause also that the Hollanders had an ill reputation and little credit among these Indian kings: for they had promised the King of Jor

[1] An exaggeration: the municipality of Goa, in their letter of 1606 to the king, state the force as 3,000 men (*Arch. Port. Or.*, Fasc. 1, Pte. ii, No. 11). Faria y Sousa says the fleet consisted of 12 gallions, 4 galleys, and 70 other vessels. Matelief's relation is 16 or 17 gallions, 4 galleys, and 15 or 16 fustas.

[2] Misprint for *Menezes.*

[3] Really the 17th; the battle which ensued was fought on the 19th.

and the others that they would without fail take Malaca, and drive the Portuguese thence; and, indeed, it was on their account all these kings made war upon the Portuguese, being aforetime very good friends with them. And, what was worse, the Captain Corneille raised the siege and re-embarked his men without giving notice to the King of Jor, whom he left to the mercy of the Portuguese, and at war with them.

The Hollanders, then, having raised the siege, set sail towards the viceroy, whom meeting, they fought with great fury for the space of two days. The Hollander captain was brave and valiant, and was esteemed as such by all the Portuguese and Indians, for he could not have done better than he did. He found himself in great difficulty one time, when a Portuguese vessel had come up with his, and seized her with iron grapples and hooks, in such sort that it was nigh impossible to get disengaged. Fire had already broken out in both vessels, which had like to have been burned there with all hands, had not the Hollander general called to the Portuguese captain that it was not the part of a brave cavalier to let themselves be burned so, and that it were better to separate the one from the other and stand off. The captain refused, having his orders under pain of death to get burned and lost himself, so as he destroyed an enemy's ship, rather than surrender; yet what at length made him consent was that the boats of the Hollanders were coming to take off their people, while none of the Portuguese were coming for theirs: wherefore they quitted their hold, and both were saved. But thereafter the Portuguese captain lost his head for this business.[1] A large number of men fell on both sides, but six Portuguese to one Hollander.

At the last the Hollanders remained victorious, without losing more than two ships, that were burnt, along with two

[1] A mistake; Dom Henrique de Noronha, the captain in question, was highly praised for his conduct, and afterwards became captain of Ormuz (*Liv. das Monç.*, i, 326).

other ships of the viceroy, who, now that the siege was raised, incontinently returned to Malaca with the remains of his fleet, and a month afterwards died there of dysentery.[1] The Hollanders also retired with their honour, as did the King of Jor and his allies. Thus Malaca remained free, and was afterwards very strongly fortified; indeed, they are still continually fortifying it.

The Portuguese lost a great number of brave and valiant captains, and much honour in this affair; and had great losses,[2] for their whole army was put to rout. Among others they lost two lords that were brothers and great captains, one called *Don Fernando* and the other *Don Petro Mascaregne*,[3] with two of their younger brothers. Never was there among the Portuguese so much regret for any men, a regret which lasts even to this day: it was even greater than for the viceroy, who died soon after of sorrow and melancholy; and a wonderful thing it was that thirteen vessels did such execution.[4]

The town is the richest and busiest in all the Indies, after Goa and Ormus, owing to the great cargoes from China, Japan, the Moluccas, and all the Sunda which are landed there. For all that, living is very dear.

[1] Only a few lines down he says that he died of sorrow and melancholy. The statement here is more probable, for the date of his death is quite wrong; De Castro did not die till the 3rd June 1607.

[2] The Dutch intercepted letters in which the loss of 521 Portuguese was acknowledged; no less than 6,000 are said to have perished in the siege.

[3] The brothers Mascarenha were on board the *S. Nicholas*, 800 tons, Dom Fernando being her captain. She was attacked by three Dutch ships, and taken. Out of her crew of 265 Portuguese, besides natives, only eight survived (Matelief's voyage, in *Rec. des Voy.*, vol. iii).

[4] He does not mention Matelief's further exploits. After cruising about for some weeks, he was again before Malacca on the 20th October, and he attacked the Portuguese ships in the very harbour. After some desperate fighting, the Dutch burnt three gallions, and next day the viceroy burnt three more, to prevent their falling into the enemy's hands. In this fight the Portuguese lost upwards of 400 men.

The inhabitants of the country are handsome men, well made and proportioned according to their stature, which is of the middle height, as also are their women. They are of a swarthy complexion, and go naked from the waist upwards, while below they have gowns of cotton and silk, the over-gown reaching only to the knees. They are girt with a rich girdle, and carry daggers exceeding richly garnished. As for the women, they are attired in silk cloths, and have their shifts full short: they wear their hair long, and well adorned with precious stones, and an abundance of flowers interlaced.

They are for the most part Mahometans, albeit there are nowadays a great number of Christians. The Jesuit Fathers have a very fine college there.

The air of this country is bad, intemperate, and sickly; even the natives are more subject to illness there than in any place in India. Few foreigners escape the sickness, and it is a great chance if they die not: at least notable marks of it remain; for instance, some lose their hair, others their skin—that is, such as have made a long sojourn. The soldiers there are almost all like those of Ceylon, that is, men exiled and banished for their misdeeds. As for the merchants, the desire of the great profits to be made causes them to hazard their lives; they return thence with a complexion of lead, and are never well again. The people of those parts are called *Malays*, as well in the land of Malaca as at Sumatra; they have a language that is spread over all the islands of Sunda: in all these parts it is the only one, and it is the most widespread and useful of all the Indian tongues.

CHAPTER XII.

Of the islands of Sunda—Sumatra, and Java,—and the towns of Bantan and Tuban; the islands of Madura, Bally, the Moluccas, and Banda.

The Portuguese call all the islands beyond Malaca, *la Sonde*, as one should say, "the sea and islands of the South".[1] Under this name are comprised Sumatra, Java, the Moluccas, and all the other islands of those coasts.

As for the island of *Sumatra*, I will not tarry to describe it, for I did not touch there, and merely passed in sight of it. It is situated under the Equinoctial line, which intersects it; it is of exceeding great compass, for it extends from the fifth degree on the north side to the sixth degree of southern latitude, that is, about the same as the Maldives, from which it is distant some six hundred leagues. As for the inhabitants, some are Mahometans, chiefly those that live by the sea-shore; the others are Gentiles. They are fond of traffic, wherefore all merchants are welcomed among them. The Arabs and other Mahometans resort thither and trade more than all other: the Portuguese go there too, but little, for they are not liked by the king. The Hollanders keep a factory there, and some factors. The country is very rich in pepper, which is larger than that of Malabar, but the latter nevertheless is more esteemed all over the Indies. But in this island there is such abundance that they can sometimes load thirty ships in one year. There is gold both in the mountains and the river-sands;

[1] They were called the Sunda islands, but not with this meaning, vol. i, p. 160. Sunda is the western part of Java, the people being distinct from the Javanese in race and language (Yule, *Gloss.*, s. v. "Sunda"). There is some confusion in the author's mind. The Portuguese called the Eastern Archipelago and the Pacific generally by the name *Mar do Sul.* Also in the East India Company's records, down to the early part of last century, those regions are always termed "the South Sea".

but this gold is very base, more so than any other found in India. They coin money of it, one side whereof has the figure of a pagoda, and the other that of a chariot drawn by elephants. This great island contains many kingdoms, but the most powerful is that of Achen.

When I passed by there, the reigning king was quite young; he had by force dispossessed his father of the kingdom, and made himself master of it, holding his father prisoner for a long time, and his mother too, even with irons on their feet.[1] His brother, whom he had driven forth, made war upon him, but at present they are agreed, for certain lands have been apportioned to him forty leagues beyond, and there he dwells. This king of Achen is very fond of the Hollanders, who have built there many houses; it is even the fixed place for all the ships of Holland that are in the Indies, where they have their staple for trading, and for the lading and unlading of merchandise; they keep there a number of factors, who drive a great trade. But he will not hear mention of the Portuguese, with whom he has had always, and has even now, war to the death.

Yet it is strange that this king has never been able to come to terms with the Portuguese, seeing that he agrees well with all other foreigners. Sometimes, indeed, some private Portuguese merchants are to be found there; but they have no favour with the king, and, indeed, never see him.

When the Hollanders first went to the Indies they had war with this king,[2] and for this cause sacked two Arabian ships laden with spices, wherewith they laded their own; but afterwards the Hollanders and he became good friends,

[1] Ali Maghayat Shah, son of Aladdin, a usurper, seized the throne in 1604.

[2] See the account of the Moucheron voyage of 1598-1600 in Davis's *Voy.*, Hak. Soc. The raja of Achen did not become friendly with the Dutch till about 1603.

and, indeed, he sent six ambassadors to Holland, the Hollanders leaving (as many of) theirs as hostages with him. These ambassadors were exceeding well received and honoured in Holland, and returned to Achen, but not all of them, for four died by the way, and I saw one of the two that got back at the island of Malé.

These Arabs that were pillaged at Achen by the Hollanders, seeing that the King of Achen and all the other Mahometan kings were in very good understanding with the Hollanders, and mortal enemies of the Portuguese, bethought themselves to send deputies to Holland to treat for peace and friendship with the Estates, and to demand satisfaction and justice for their stolen property: insomuch that they obtained their satisfaction and were reimbursed for their loss; though it was then about seven years after the seizure was made. And from that time the Hollanders have been at all times in good friendship with all the Indians.

But in truth what did us much harm at the first, and took away much of the good repute of the French, English, and Hollanders in this country (for in the Indies we are all considered alike, seeing that we are all friends among ourselves and enemies of the Portuguese) was, that there was brought to Sunda, or islands of the South, a quantity of false pieces of forty Spanish sols, which were made on board the ships. The Hollanders accused the English, and the English cast the blame on the others: however the fact was, the Hollanders paid dear for it, for the voyage after, a goodly number of them were killed at several places; and since then the Indians have not trusted them so much, and the rumour has spread over the whole of India that we are all cheats. But to return to the King of Achen, the Hollanders and he since their agreement have had always a good understanding; while he has always troubled the Portuguese as much as he could, as have also the kings of Jor, Bantan, and Java Major. All people in the Indies or on the other side the Cape of Good Hope, when they would go to Sumatra, merely say that they are going to Achen: for this city and port has acquired all the name and reputation of the island; and it is the same in Great Java with Bantan, so that only those two kings are spoken of.

The King of Achen has many times laid siege to Malaca, as also has the King of Jor. He is a formidable person, as he showed himself when he was attacked by the viceroy *Dom Martin Alphōça de Castro*, for he defended himself so well, and such a number of Portuguese were slain and drowned, that the viceroy had nothing for it but to retire with his loss of honour and men. That was a bad omen, for thereafter he went to Malaca to meet his end, as I have said. But this king had great service also of the Hollanders that were then at Achen, though they were few in number. For they gave him counsel as to intrenchments and fortifications after the fashion of Holland and France, and a good supply of cannon, whereof the king now has no lack, and I should never have believed there were so many cannon in the Indies as he has there. After this attack and skirmish, the Hollanders conducted themselves so well, and with such sincerity, that the king has begun to have a great affection for them.

The island of Java is at the southern end of Sumatra, turning away toward the east, and separated by only a narrow arm of the sea, whereof the beginning is under the seventh degree towards the south. It is a very great, rich, and wealthy island, containing many kingdoms. The most renowned is that of Bantan; also it is more resorted to than any other part. The Portuguese galiots going toward the Moluccas, as I did, sojourn there a while; this gave me an opportunity of seeing the country.

Bantan is a great city, thickly peopled, situate on the sea at the very end of the island, and near the strait (called the Strait of Sunda, which I believe has given its name to all this sea) that separates Java from Sumatra, from which it is distant only five-and-twenty leagues. On both sides of the town flows a river which bathes and surrounds it, and then falls into the sea. It is very broad there, but being only four fathoms in depth, is not navigable. The town is surrounded with brick walls, of not more than two feet in thickness. Every hundred paces near the walls are very lofty erections raised upon ship-masts, serving in the defence of the town, both as watch-towers and for firing at long range and with better command and view upon an enemy attempting to approach. These buildings are constructed of canes, the pillars being of wood, and are covered with palm-leaves. The rich and well-to-do have their houses hung on all sides with tapestries and curtains of silk, or of cotton cloth nicely painted. There are five large spaces, wherein every day is held the market of all sorts of merchandise and provisions, which are cheap, and living is therefore very good there. The fruits and animals are all similar to those of the other Indian countries whereof I have so often spoken, and are very cheap here. The town is situate on low and marshy ground, being between two arms of the river, so that for the most part of the winter the river is all overflowed throughout the town, and one cannot go through the streets but by boats. The streets are not paved: in nearly all parts of the town there are quantities of coco-trees. Outside the walled enclosure are a great number of houses for the foreigners.[1]

[1] On the arrival of the Dutch under Houtman in 1596, the Portuguese had a factory at Bantam, but were not on good terms with the king. Houtman ingratiated himself with the latter, and was enabled to establish a factory. The king, however, maintained his independence, and welcomed Lancaster in 1603, permitting the English also to found a factory. The English alliance was afterwards cemented by a treaty, and for many years Bantam was the chief presidency of the English in the East, the agencies at Madras, Bengal, and Surat being made subordinate. The Dutch meantime had taken the neighbouring town of Jacatra and built on its ruins the city of Batavia. By their greater

As for their religion, the most part are Mahometans: there are, however, great numbers of Gentiles and idolaters. There is a great mosque in the town where is practised the law of Mahomet; the lords and gentlemen have each his temple in his own house: the doctors or Cadis come thither from Arabia.

The inhabitants are of a yellowish colour; they are habited in a cotton or silk cloth, which they wear all around the body from the waist downwards; on the head they wear a little turban passed twice round.

Their arms are daggers or poniards, called by them *Cris*: the blade is waved, and is a dangerous weapon; the end of the haft is in the form of a demon, or some other hideous figure; the sheath is wooden, and of one piece. These daggers are finely adorned with gold and precious stones, and are worn at the side by all, high and low: it would be considered a disgrace not to wear it. When they go to war they carry swords and bucklers, and a sheaf of arrows, which they dart with the hand. They are a very stubborn race, also exceeding proud in their gait, and great liars and thieves.[1]

The men are exceeding idle; the slaves do the greater part of their business. The gentlemen and rich burghers have their gardens and country houses, where their slaves labour and till the soil, bringing in the fruits and revenues to their masters, who ordinarily busy themselves with nought, but sitting amid their wives—whereof each has a plurality—and constantly chewing betel; likewise their

energy and stronger naval force they engrossed the spice trade, and made the position of the English at times intolerable. Finally, in 1682, they fomented an insurrection of the son of the King of Bantam, and succeeded in forcing the English to retire (1683). The Dutch gradually annexed the whole of Java, while the English turned their attention to Sumatra, where they formed agencies at Achen, Priaman, Bencoolen, Fort Marlborough, etc.

[1] Lancaster says he traded there very peaceably, "although the Jauians be reckoned among the greatest pickers and theeves of the world" (*Voy.*, p. 100).

wives do nothing else. The female slaves play upon divers instruments before them, singing and striking basins melodiously; and to this music the wives dance one after another in presence of their husband, doing each the best she can, and striving to please him: for she that pleases him the most then, sleeps the following night with him. They also pass a great part of their time in washing and bathing, and remain long in the water: this renders the river unhealthful and bad for drinking, by reason of so many people washing and tarrying in it. For the rest, the women of quality are carefully guarded by the eunuchs, who are very numerous and are bought for the purpose. The beds are suspended, and they are rocked in them as are the residents at the Maldives. This town is thronged with many people, for there is great traffic and commerce there carried on by all sorts of foreigners, as well Christians as Indians; for instance, Arabs, Guzerates, Malabars, men of Bengala and Malaca. These come there chiefly in search of pepper, which grows abundantly in this island, and is usually worth only one sol the pound. I have seen many Chinese settled there and carrying on a great trade; and every year in the month of January come nine or ten great ships from China laden with silk stuffs, cotton cloth, gold, porcelain, musk, and a thousand other kinds of merchandise from their country. These Chinese have built there handsome houses for their lodging, till such time as they shall have finished their trading and become rich; to attain which end, there is no vile or disgraceful job they will not put their hands to—they are like the Jews in their manner of trading. Then, having filled their pockets, they return to China. On their arrival they buy women slaves, and on their return sell them back, taking away with them the children they have had. Also they observe a rule never to bury any of their dead either there or in any other foreign land; after salting and embalming them they carry them off.

The Hollanders have at present in this town many houses that they have built; they also keep there a factory and factors for managing their trade: for the king had an affection toward them, and the people love them. The king has his residence in the town. He is exceeding kindly and courteous. He has numerous wives, who are guarded with great rigour, for none are permitted to see them, or to enter their apartments; even should it be his own son, he could not see the king's wives nor enter where they are, else he would be put to death.

On the death of a man all his goods go to the king: his wife and children are his slaves, unless the latter were married and living apart from their father's house, or unless the king in return for some present, or to gratify the father, gives them their liberty, and sends them letters to that effect.

There is another great kingdom in the island of Java, whereof the principal town is called *Tuban*,[1] a town situate on the sea-shore, all surrounded and enclosed with walls. It is a very fine town, and a busy one too: pepper is very cheap there. They say that the King of Tuban is so powerful that when he wills to go to war, he can in four-and-twenty hours assemble 30,000 men, horse and foot. He is ever accompanied by a great number of his gentlemen, and keeps up a very gay court. You see there many elephants and horses.

We went thence to the island of *Madura*, which is on the northern side of Java, small, but fertile in rice, supplying some of the neighbouring isles therewith. There is a little town, very neat and well walled, called *Arosbay*. It obeys a king of its own. The inhabitants are equipped and armed in the Javan fashion: they are resolute, good soldiers, but great robbers, as well on shore as afloat.

From Madura we set sail, and stood out so as to reach

[1] On the north coast, in long. 112° E.

the Moluccas. We cast anchor at the island of *Bally*,[1] where we tarried some time, and thence completed our voyage to the Moluccas.

The island of Bally is situate quite near Java toward the east. It is fertile in rice, abounding with fowls and pigs, which are very good and delicate, and in vast numbers. Other animal food exists, but very lean and poor. There are many horses. Except foods, no merchantable stuffs grow there. The inhabitants are Gentiles and idolaters, but without any rule or fixed ceremonial, for one worships a cow, another the sun, another a stone—each what he wills. The women burn themselves when their husbands die. As for their dress, it is the same as at Bantan. Their arms also are poniards ; besides which they carry in their hands a pike and a *sarbatane*[2] two fathoms long, and in this behalf they have a case full of little darts to blow with the sarbatans; these weapons are exceeding dangerous when used against naked men. Moreover, they are very hostile to the Portuguese and

[1] Bâli, in which island, as the author seems to have some notion, Hinduism was maintained. The best scientific description of the island is that by Mr. R. Friedrich, translated in the *J. R. As. Soc.* (New Series), vols. viii and ix.

[2] "*Sarbataine*, a long trunke to shoot in; also the musicall instrument called a Sagbut" (*Cotgrave*). It is a very old weapon (see Ducange, *Gloss.*, s. v. "Zarabotana"). Among the less civilised races its use is localised in the Eastern Archipelago and in South America. As to the former, Varthema (p. 254) speaks of the *Zarabottane* in use in Java; Odoric describes it, but not by name (*Cathay*, p. 91). Barros mentions "armas de Zaravatanas hervadas"; and Houtman, also writing of Java, says, "Ils usent aussi des *Serbataines* par lesquelles soufflent fleschettes envenimez." See, too, a cut in Churchill (*Voy.*, vol. ii), showing its use by the natives of Macassar. As to South America, see Hans Stade (*Hak. Soc.*, p. 55). It is much used by the Indians of Guiana, the pipe being from 8 to 14 feet in length, the dart of 8 inches, barbed with the teeth of a fish, and poisoned. The certainty with which they take aim with this long weapon, supported only by one hand, is wonderful (Im Thurm's *Guiana*, pp. 245-7, 300-2). In modern times it has been reintroduced with us as the toy weapon, the "puff and dart".

to the Moors. This island obeys a king of its own, who lives with more magnificence than he of Bantan. His guards carry pikes pointed with fine gold; and when he goes forth it is in a chariot drawn by two white buffaloes.

As for the Moluccas, they are a number of islands fertile in spices. The following are the names of the islands which alone are comprised under this title[1]:—*Ternate, Amboin, Maquian, Bassian, Meau, Morigoran, Gilolo, Catel,* and *Tidor*; they are all, as it were, in the same canton, being quite close to each other. They are barren in food-products, which are scarce and very dear there, because they come from abroad. No kind of grain grows there. They make meal of the wood of a tree they call *Sagou*,[2] whereof all the people make certain pastry and cates, which are very good and very delicate when fresh made. There are some cocos and bananas, abundance of orange and lime trees, and very large almond trees: of the latter they make nice almond and sugar cakes which are sold in the markets.

But above all, there is there a marvellous quantity of cloves, which grow in no other part of the world but in these islands, and they are all covered with them: for which cause they are frequented by foreign merchants of all races, who come there from all quarters of the world to get that spice, both Christians and Chinese, Indians and Arabs. There are many parrots there of divers plumages, and exceeding beautiful.

In manners and customs, arms and dress, the inhabitants resemble those of Java and Sumatra: for all the people of the parts beyond Malaca, and called by the Portuguese *la Sonda*, differ nowise in features, colour, dress, language, or

[1] The name Moluccas is more properly restricted still further to the five small islands west of Gilolo, viz., Ternaté, Tidoré, Motir, Makian, and Bachian (see Yule, *Gloss.*, s. v., and authors cited in Middleton's *Voy.*, Hak. Soc., App. XVI).

[2] Sago, Malay *sāgū*, made of the pith of particular species of palm (see quotations in Yule, *Gloss.*, s. v.).

customs,—in fact, they are the same people. The religion is the Mahometan. They are a very simple folk, but courageous and valiant withal. *Ternate* is the chief Island[1]: it is full thirty leagues in compass, and grows more cloves than the others. It is ruled by a king of its own, and in former days the King of Ternate was king of all, but now each island has an independent king.[2] The Hollanders since a few years ago have occupied two, *Amboin* and *Tidor,* dispossessing the Portuguese.[3] As for Ternate, the king of that island drove the Portuguese from their fort there, but the Spaniards from the Philippine Islands or Manilla reconquered it,[4] and have now a treaty with him. So at the present day the Portuguese have no longer the disposal of the cloves: this vexes them much, and they have a plea of this matter against the Spaniards in the Council of the King of Spain. I have sojourned only at Ternate; as for the others, I have passed within sight of most of them.

In the same parts is another island, which I have visited, very celebrated for one sort of spice: it is *Banda,* distant four-and-twenty leagues from Amboin,—very fertile in nutmegs and mace. This place supplies the whole world with these products, for they grow nowhere else, save some trees

[1] And so immortalised with Tidoré by Milton, who, like Pyrard, makes them both dissyllables:—

> "Close sailing from Bengala, or the isles
> Of Ternate and Tidore, whence merchants bring
> Their spicy drugs," etc.—(*P. L.*, ii, 638.)

[2] Most early travellers, *e.g.*, Barbosa, dwell on the fact that each had its own king, and Col. Yule suggests as the probable origin of the name Moluccas, *Jazirat-al-Mulūk*, "the isles of the kings".

[3] Steven van der Hagen took the Portuguese fort at Amboyna on the 21st February, and that at Tidoré on 14th May 1605 (*Rec. des Voy.*, vol. iii). They never lost hold of Amboyna, but were driven from Tidoré by the Spaniards in 1611.

[4] In April 1606. For an account of this Spanish expedition, and for the consequent ill-feeling between the Portuguese and Spaniards, see De Morga's *Philippine Islands*, p. 249, *et seq.*

that are planted out of curiosity, as I have seen at Goa and other places. On this account many foreign merchants from all parts resort thither. It has an independent king; the inhabitants are Mahometans, brave and warlike, and of the same dress and customs as those of the other islands and the adjacent countries.

It would be impossible to mention in detail all the islands in this sea of Sunda—or "Southern Sea", as the Portuguese call it—by reason of their great number, small and great; making the navigation very difficult with their sands, shoals, and straits, so that you must have good and experienced pilots—natives of the islands if possible; and yet, with all that, you will often run aground and get wrecked. Further, none dare sail but by day only, for as soon as night approaches you must cast anchor somewhere; otherwise you may get wrecked in the night, and even while sailing by day you must always keep the lead in hand.

CHAPTER XIII.

Of the singular things that are brought from the islands of Sumatra, Java, Borneo, and from the Philippines and Manilla. Of China and Japan, and of the traffic carried on at Goa.

The three principal and largest of these islands are Sumatra, Great Java,[1] and Borneo, which are the largest of all that ocean, next to the island of *St. Lawrence,* which is deemed to be the greatest of all. All the peoples of these

[1] The Java Major of Barbosa (p. 197), of N. Conti (*India in the XV Cent.*, ii, 15), and of Ortelius, *i.e.*, Java proper. By Java Minor (originally applied to Sumatra), at a later time some seem to have meant Sumbawa, some Timor, and some Bali, but this need not concern us here (see Yule's *Marco Polo*, Bk. III, c. 9, and *Glossary*, s. v.).

islands in their disposition, manners, features, and language, approach those of the mainland of Malaca, which leads me to conjecture that these islands have been peopled by the Malays. The other islands are innumerable, lying quite near each other, all inhabited or but few not so, and each having a separate king, and some having more than one. They are fertile in peculiar fruits and merchandise, such as spices and other drugs that are found nowhere else; and excepting Sumatra and Java, which are fertile of all things, the rest abound only in one particular thing and are sterile of all else. So this one product wherewith they abound must furnish them with everything else; this is why all kinds of food are very dear, save their own product, which is cheap, and why these people are constrained to keep up continual intercourse with one another, the one supplying what the other wants.

In Sumatra and Java grow many things that are very good and valuable; the chief traffic is in pepper, theirs being larger than that of the Malabar coast, because, as I believe, these islands are farther toward the east and nearer the line, and the soil is moistened by more copious dews than the mainland. Banda yields mace and nutmegs; the Moluccas, cloves; Borneo, camphor and benjamin[1]; and so with the rest, all producing something peculiar. I content myself with speaking of them altogether, because they are inhabited by the same people, and lie under nearly the same parallel and climate, with the same temperature or intemperature. The air is not very healthy, but rather the reverse; and food is very dear—nay, very frequently cannot be got for money; for the supply by sea is not to be depended on. The people are treacherous, perfidious, and choleric, so that for a mere

[1] "A kind of incense derived from the resin of the *Styrax benzoin*; it got from the Arab traders the name of *lubān-Jāwī*, 'Java frankincense', corrupted in the middle ages" into the above and other forms (Yule, *Gloss.*, s. v.).

trifle they make no scruple to kill a man with the *cris* or poniard which they always carry. Traffic with them is carried on in fear and peril. The Hollanders, Portuguese, and other foreigners are obliged to run risks in trading with them, but those of their own faith do not, many of these having been cheated, and even some of the foreigners; but the greed of gain causes them to forget.[1]

The Portuguese of Malaca have clerks and factors in all the islands for trade. The inhabitants, too, are wont to go with their vessels laden to Malaca, which is the magazine and staple of all that merchandise, the commerce wherein is marvellously great, and carried on both by money and by the exchange of other products of all these islands from the Cape of Good Hope to China, with an infinite number of ships. They come there from the countries of the Abexis, from Arabia, Persia, Ormuz, Surate, Guzeratte, Cambaye, Goa, Malabar, Bengala, China, Japan, and all other parts of the Indian coasts. Now, too, the French and Hollanders also come thither for this same traffic in excellent fruits and drugs, whereof the flowers are very aromatic and odoriferous. For while the flowers are yet on the trees in their force and vigour, it is a marvel to smell the sweet scents which they exhale, wherewith the air is so full filled that the wind bears them six or seven leagues away.[2] But amongst all, the cloves bear off the prize; yet does it cost men dear to go for them,

[1] In original: "Les Holandois, Portugais et autres estrangers sont contraints de s'y fier pour le traffic, non pas ceux de leur loy, dont plusieurs y ont esté attrapez, et des estrangers mesmes, mais le desir de gaigner fait oublier tout."

[2] The "spicy breezes" of the poets and poetic travellers are a great annoyance to prosaic modern writers, *e.g.*, Tennent (*Ceylon*, i, 4); Milton fables his "Sabean odours from the spicy shore Of Araby the Blest" (*P. L.*, iv, 163), as being felt off at sea near Mozambique; Heber's spicy breezes only "blow soft o'er Ceylon's isle". The sensitive P. and O. passenger catches them quite six or seven leagues off Galle or Colombo; while the cynical old resident insists that they are only appreciable in the vicinity of a native bazaar.

seeing that sometimes they lose their lives or endure great sufferings in the quest.

The imports to these islands are cotton, cotton cloths, all kinds of silk cloth and stuffs, raw silk, rice, fish, butter, oils, munitions of war, arms, silver itself, and other things. The Hollanders and all others when they would go to these islands, go first to the coast of Guzerate, Saint Thomas, Massulipatan, and Bengala, to buy cotton cloths, upon which they make a double profit: for they gain on their own merchandise in the first instance, and then on their second cargo that they carry to these islands. But if these Malay islanders are cunning rogues, the Chinese are even more so, for all the silver that is brought to these islanders from all sides, the Chinese get into their own hands and carry off to China, giving them nothing in exchange but their worthless goods, bagatelles, and counterfeit gems. The Spaniards and Portuguese allege the same of the Flemings and Hollanders, who bring them nothing but baubles and toys, but will carry away in exchange from Spain only gold and silver, as they do also in France.

With regard to the Philippine islands that come next, not having been there I will say only in passing what I have been able to learn among the Portuguese. By them they are called *Islas de Manilla;* by the Castilians, the *Philippines;* and by the Indians, *Luçon,* from the principal island which is called Luçon. There are a great number more, each having a separate name. The Castilians have discovered and conquered them,[1] and have given them the name of their king. The Portuguese give them that of Manilla, from the principal town thus named, where the chief trade is carried

[1] They were taken by a Spanish expedition from New Spain in 1571. A full account of their conquest and government is given by De Morga, whose work, first published at Mexico in 1609, has been edited for the Hak. Soc. by Lord Stanley. From the opening chapter it seems that Spain proposed to give the name Philippines to the whole archipelago, including the Moluccas and Borneo.

on. It is at fifteen degrees north. The people are immigrants from China, as are also the people of Japan. The Spaniards possess them, and have there a viceroy and a bishop, both of whom have their residence at the town of Manilla, where Christianity is well advanced.

The Spaniards of Mexico, New Spain, and Peru come there by way of the South Sea. These islands are fertile in foods and fruits, but abound also with merchantable commodities. There is found there much civet[1]; also those tortoises whose shell is in such demand in the Indies, being found nowhere in all the Indies but there and at the Maldives, as I have said elsewhere; there is great traffic in this at Cambaye and Guzerate. So it is that the Spaniards hold these islands not for their own value, but solely in order to carry on trade and commerce with the Chinese; for as foreigners are not permitted to frequent the mainland of China, it is necessary to have some other place as a receptacle and staple for the merchandise brought by the Chinese. For this purpose the Portuguese hold the island of *Macao*.

The Spaniards have there a *Contretador* for the interchange of the goods of China and the East Indies. This renders these islands marvellously rich; but at the same time diminishes the commerce of Spain with the West Indies, for the cloth and silk fabrics of Spain are no longer carried thither as they were wont to be before this trade was established. The King of Spain also tried to prevent this result, permitting only certain ships to trade with Manilla, as he does at Goa. But the Chinese protested that if it were to be so they would have no intercourse with them either in the east or in the west, so that the king has been obliged to let the trade proceed in its natural course.[2] A

[1] "The natives have another means of gain, bringing much profit, for there are many civet cats, though smaller than those of Guinea" (De Morga, *Phil. Isl.*, p. 286).

[2] De Morga, who gives a full account of the trade of the Philippines (pp. 336-44), bears out all these statements. The King of Spain did

great quantity of silver is drawn from the West Indies to China. The Spaniards of the Manillas carry on a trade in the South Sea with the Portuguese of India, but pass not to this side of the Cape and Port of Malaca. I believe that more than thirty or forty ships come there every year from China and the Manilla islands. The Portuguese and Spaniards in their trading in this sea agree passably well. The Spaniards keep to themselves that fair and excellent island of the Moluccas called Ternate.[1]

From the city of Goa, where the merchandise from all parts of the Indies and Portugal is laden and unladen, the viceroy, in accordance with the king's standing order, despatches every year two or three vessels to China and Japan. Sometimes they go only to China; sometimes to both. By China is meant Macao only, which is an island and town inhabited by the Portuguese, with some number of Chinese. This place is the staple and emporium of all the merchandise from China and other parts of the world.

This Indian traffic is not allowed to all the Portuguese at all places; for that of China, Japan, Malaca, Mozembic, and Ormus is for none but the ships of the King of Spain, save sometimes in order to reward some lord, captain, or other officer, the king gives him leave to make one trading voyage with one or two vessels or more; but this is only for some signal service and in the case of a grandee. In these vessels go many private merchants for trade. These pay

not prohibit Chinese trade at the Manillas, but, in order to protect Spanish trade with Spanish America, he prohibited any persons of New Spain or Peru from trading with the Philippines, or from bringing Chinese goods to America. By thus protecting the trade of Spain he intended to conciliate the Spanish colony of the Philippines by giving them the monopoly of their island trade. But the result was that, the merchants of New Spain being interdicted, the Philippine trade largely fell into the hands of the Dutch, English, and Portuguese (De Morga, *u. s.*; Cocks' *Diary*, *passim*).

[1] See above, p. 166.

their ship expenses and the freight to the lord of the voyage, also the principal royal dues; for the king bestows these voyages free of everything, except some particular dues which must be paid to the *renderes*,[1] or farmers of the customs and tariffs.[2] They are, however, exempt from many exactions that are otherwise and elsewhere paid upon all goods. The principal cargo carried from Goa to Macao is silver; for in China silver is in great demand, and most of the silver that is taken from Europe by way of Ormus to the East Indies goes to China. So, too, that which comes from the direction of Japan, from the West Indies (by way of the South Sea), and from the Philippine Islands or Manillas, the last-named place being the staple for goods passing between the West Indies and China (by the said South Sea), as from Peru, New Spain, Mexico, Chili, and other places in those parts, insomuch that, as it is reckoned, there enters China every year more than seven millions worth of gold in silver. The Chinese, too, never let so much as a testoon[3] go out again, for they melt all this silver into ingots, and keep all their treasure in silver, and not in gold, which is vastly common and cheap there. The best silver in the Indies is that which comes from Persia by way of Ormus in (the form of) a long coin, called *larins*, which the smiths of India prize highly, and use to their great advantage, being a very pure, clean, soft, and ductile silver, and good for working. Next to it, that of Japan is the best, being also pliant. That from the West Indies is the worst, being hard, rough, and less purified than the former.

[1] Port. *rendeiros*, tax-gatherers or farmers.

[2] Fr. *Pancarte*, "papier affiché qui contenait le tarif de certains droits" (*Littré*); "a paper containing the particular rates of tolls, or customes due unto the king, etc." (*Cotgrave*).

[3] "*Teston*, a testoon, a piece of silver coin worth 18*d*. sterling" (*Cotgrave*). The English testoon of Henry VIII was worth only 6*d*., and latterly only 4½*d*.; the name is now obsolete, except in its slang corruption, "tizzy".

The ships leaving Goa are laden not only with silver, but with divers goods of Europe, such as wines, woollen fabrics, and among others, red scarlet, all sorts of glass and crystal wares, clocks (which are highly prized by the Chinese), much cotton cloth, precious stones cut and set in rings, chains, carkanets, tokens, ear-pendants, and bracelets; for the Chinese like vastly to get gems and jewels of all sorts for their wives. The ships leave Goa towards October, and touch at Cochin for precious stones and spices, such as pepper and cinnamon, leaving there the merchandise of Europe or of the northern parts of India. Thence they sail for Malaca: for they cannot make this voyage without touching at Malaca in order to get the Governor's passport, and also to purchase the merchandise of the islands of Sunda in exchange for cotton cloths and other goods of India and Europe.

Vessels making the voyage from Goa to Japan and back may reckon on taking three whole years; nor can they reckon on less by reason of the winds called by them *Monssons*, and by us *Muesons*, which prevail for six months and more, as I have said elsewhere. But this is no loss to them, for sometimes they double their money and goods, and sometimes treble them, and in some cases do even better still. From Malaca they go to Macao, and thence to Japan. At all these places they must await the Muesons; in the meantime while waiting they carry on their trade. At Macao they leave the greater part of their goods, and all their silver, relading with other goods of China, such as silks and Spanish white, which they as well as we call *aluya*[1]; it is dear, and much in request in Japan, where all the women whiten the whole body with it, even down to the legs. This white comes from the island of Borneo, whence it is carried to China; there they fine and mix it, making therein very great traffic and sales to all

[1] Ceruse, Spanish white, or as we say, whiting; Port. *alvayade.* No such word as in the text appears in the French dictionaries.

parts, but more to Japan than to all the world beside. Then they carry to Japan all those China goods and some others from Europe and India, which they sell exceeding well; they bring back only silver, which they get cheap, and return to Macao to re-sell all their silver, exchanging it for other merchandise. They make a long sojourn in all those places, and then return to Malaca, where they must call; there they make another exchange of goods for those of Malaca and the islands of Sunda. Thence they return to Goa, or whatever other place the master of the ship belongs to. It is impossible to tell all the great riches and all the rare and beautiful things which these ships bring back; among others they bring much gold in ingots, which the Portuguese call *pandoro*.[1] Some gold also they have in leaf, and some in dust; also great store of gilded wood-work, such as all sorts of vessels and furniture, lacquered, varnished, and gilded with a thousand pretty designs; then all kinds of silk stuffs, good store of unwrought silk, great quantities of musk and civet, plenty of the metal called *calin*,[2] which is much esteemed over all the Indies, and even in Persia and elsewhere. It is as hard as silver and as white as tin, and it gets whiter with use; money is made of it at Goa and in the other Portuguese territories, and in some of the Indian,—though rarely, for all their money is of gold or silver, which also they cut into pieces to make their purchases of goods. Of this metal they make all their utensils and ornaments as we do here of silver and tin; they even use it for rings and bracelets for girls and children. They import also from thence much porcelain ware, which is used throughout India, as well by the Portuguese as by the Indians. Besides all this, many boxes, plates, and baskets made of little reeds covered with lacquer and varnished in all colours, gilded and patterned. Among other things I should mention a great number of cabinets of all patterns, in the fashion of those of Germany. This is an article the

[1] Port. *pão de ouro.*

[2] See vol. i, p. 235, *note*.

most perfect and of the finest workmanship to be seen anywhere; for they are all of choice woods, and inlaid with ivory, mother-of-pearl, and precious stones; in place of iron they are mounted with gold. The Portuguese call them *Escritorios de la China.*

There is also imported a great quantity of sugar, the hardest, whitest, and finest I have ever seen; great store too of wax and honey, and paper, the whitest, finest, and smoothest in the world. Then all sorts of metals, save silver; among the rest much quicksilver, from which they make great profit by transporting it to all the places where there are silver mines, for this quicksilver purifies and refines silver. So much for the trade of Goa with China, Japan, Malaca, etc. As regards the retail trade in the island of Goa, it must first be noted that it is all done by the Banians, Canarins, and other foreigners, Gentiles and Mahometans, and rarely by Portuguese, Metifs, or Christian Indians. The wholesale trade is carried on in all quarters by rich men, whether Portuguese, Christians, or other. All sales, whether wholesale or retail, are conducted by sworn brokers, who are Gentile inhabitants of Goa and the neighbourhood.

All grains, seed, and other food-stuffs that come from abroad are discharged into the *Alfandeque*, and are there sold and distributed to those that want them, as well for their own use as for sale by retail in the town and island. As soon as they are discharged into this Alfandeque, the officers of police come and put a price upon the several goods, according to their value; this they do with every article of food and nutriment, whether it be in large or small quantities. If the goods are not sound and fit for food, whether cooked or raw, they are confiscated and given to the prisoners and other poor Christians of the town; and in addition the sellers are fined. For you must know that every day the magistrates and officers of police do nothing else but inspect all articles of food, and none durst sell anything ere the police have first fixed the price. Nor durst they sell aught wholesale or retail, whether food-stuffs or other thing, that have not paid tribute to the king. So it is that with merchandise of every craft, trade, or kind, however small, the power of dealing in it, making or selling it, is farmed out to the highest and last bidder. They call these farmers *Renderes;* sellers and dealers must have notes in writing from these Renderes, which cost them according to the value of the trade or craft. These Renderes or farmers are all Bramenis, Banians, and Canarins.

It is a wondrous sight, that of the vast crowd that is to be seen buying and selling from week's end to week's end at Goa, except on feast days, and in the island as well as in the town; the mighty traffic and commerce that is done there is such, indeed, that every day seems fair-day. Such as are here, severally, grocers, chandlers, apothecaries, and druggists, are there all of the same calling, which is practised altogether by men of the Brameny race, and no others. They keep all manner of drugs, as well for medicine as for food; for, excepting wine, flesh, fish, fruits, herbs, and cooked victuals, they sell all other things proper and necessary for human life, or for the food of men and horses, or for their health and healing; but they sell no cloth fabrics. At every corner of the streets and crossings there are always one or two shops.

All the Indians at Goa and elsewhere have a custom, strange and notable enough, viz., when they would make some bargain one with another, and there be some folks present whom they would not should hear the bargain and the price, nor should even have a suspicion of it, as might happen if they were to see them whispering together, they are wont to make signs under their silk or cotton mantles, which are worn like our cloaks: so touching the hands thus privily, they give one another to understand by the fingers at what price they are willing to buy or sell, without the others knowing or being aware of anything.[1]

But to return to the islands of Sunda, the Moluccas, Philippines, Japan and China; of them I could say much more, and of the excellent and strange things that are brought thence, but I content myself with having said so much in passing, leaving what remains to such as are more capable and curious than I.

Having then returned from the Sunda voyage, I remained another space at Goa, waiting an opportunity to get home. But before coming to my departure from the Indies, it seems fit, since I have given so minute a description of Goa and the other places of the Indies which I visited, that I should not omit what I observed and learnt with some study, while I was among the Portuguese, as well of their navigation, shipping, and trade, in divers parts of Africa and the Indies, as of many other singular things of the countries of Brazil in America, Angola, Mozambique, Sofala, Couesme, Melinde, Socotora, and other places on the African coast, and next of the remaining coasts of India from Ormus, Cambaye, Surat,

[1] The custom of silent bargaining exists throughout all the East, and is evidently of great antiquity. Mr. Tylor recognises in it a survival of the primitive method of counting (*Prim. Cult.*, i, 246). Varthema found it in use at Calicut (*Hak. Soc.* ed., p. 169). Tavernier describes it as general in India, and explains the method. A grasp of the whole hand signifies 1,000, and every additional squeeze another 1,000. A grasp of the five fingers only means 500; of one finger, 100; of half a finger to the middle knuckle, 50; of the finger-tip only, 10 (*Voy.*, Pt. II, Bk. II, ch. xi). M. Huc, with his usual humour, describes the chaffering on the sale of a camel in Tartary :—"They dispute by turns furiously and argumentatively as to the merits and defects of the animal, but as soon as it comes to a question of price the tongue is laid aside as a medium, and the conversation proceeds altogether in signs. They seize each other by the wrist, and, beneath the long wide sleeve of their jackets, indicate with their fingers the progress of the bargain" (*Travels in Tartary*, ch. v). A recent description of the practice will be found in the *St. James's Gazette*, 23rd March 1887.

Mogor, Diu, etc., on to China and Japan, and whatsoever memorable happened in all those places while I was in the Indies. All this I will relate briefly in the chapters following.

CHAPTER XIV.

Of the form and fashion of the Portuguese ships going to the Indies, and of their shipments, order, and police, as well going as returning.

First as to the Portuguese ships: in ordinary course three or four at most go out every year; these are the carracks, called by them *naos* "de voyage",[1] which are sent out with the intention that they shall return if they can. On extraordinary occasions, when the King of Spain wishes to send out an armada, or a viceroy out of the season, or some particular despatch, he sends other middle-sized ships, such as Biscay galions,[2] French, Flemish, or English ships, or caravels[3]; none of these ever returns to Portugal, except there should be need to bring some special intelligence out of the usual seasons; in such cases they despatch a caravel or other middle-sized ship. If peradventure the carracks leaving Portugal for Goa fail to arrive safely there or at some other Indian port, some Biscay galions are sent home laden with pepper and other goods. These galions are of 700 or 800 tons

[1] Port. *náo* or *nau*. They are generally called "naus de carreira".

[2] "Le Galion", says Jal, "fut dans l'origine un vaisseau hybride. C'était, à la bien prendre une nef allongée et plus étroite du fond et des flancs qu'une nef ordinaire. Quelques galions allaient à la rame, mais c'était le très-petit nombre. La poupe du galion, à la différence de celle de la nef qui était plate, était arrondie et avait deux lobes hemisphériques, séparés par l'étambot, fondement de l'arrière et support du gouvernail. Les galions ordinaires avaient deux ponts, les plus grands en avaient trois" (*Le Moyen Age et la Renaissance*, tom. ii).

[3] For a description of the caravel, see below, ch. xvi, and *note* there.

burthen or thereabouts, and are well equipped for war, and good sailers, better even than the carracks.

The carracks are all built at Lisbon, and not elsewhere, by reason of the harbour there, which is very suitable and convenient for shipment, more so than any other; this is by reason as well of the presence there of the officers and superintendents of these voyages, as of the goods, the utensils (or, as they are called, the "apparel"), the provisions (which they call "matelotage"), and the other commodities and necessaries.

These carracks are ordinarily of 1,500 to 2,000 tons burthen, sometimes more, so that they are the largest vessels in the world, so far as I have been able to learn; they cannot float in less than ten fathoms of water. There are some ships in the Indies, but very few, coming from Arabia, Surate, and other neighbouring parts, which nearly approach 1,000 or 1,200 tons, but they are none of them like the carracks, nor so strong, by reason that less iron is used in their fitting. On the other hand, they are not so liable to rot, nor so easily pierced by worms, because in the Indies they use no timber that has not lain three or four years after being cut: this renders it drier and harder. Moreover, their timber is by nature harder and better than ours. They can afford to wait this long while, because they have great store of timber, and build but few vessels, nor do they consume it as fuel, by reason of the heat of the country. Whereas, on the contrary, in Portugal there is but little timber, and many vessels are built, so that there they are constrained to use the timber quite green.[1]

[1] The smaller vessels used for the coasting fleet of India were built chiefly at Bassein (Baçaim). Such were *sanguiceis* (sing. *sanguicel*, q.v. Yule, *Gloss.*) and *fustas*, specially adapted for fighting the Malabar pirates, and corresponding in use to our gunboats. Thus, in 1598, six *sanguiceis* were built at Bassein for L. da Gama's expedition against Kunhâli (*Dec XI*). Owing to the lack of timber in Portugal, to which Pyrard alludes, and also to the success of the *Chagas* (see next note),

I have heard it said by the Portuguese, that no vessel ever made so many voyages from Portugal to the Indies as a certain carrack that was built at *Bassains*, which is between Goa and Cambaye: it made as many as six.[1] Those built in Portugal ordinarily make but two, or three at most, but the majority make but one. This place, *Bassains*, is to the Indies what Biscay in Spain is here, for all the vessels built for the King of Spain in the Indies are constructed there, because no country yields so much timber. True it is that in the kingdoms of *Pegu, Sian*, and in *Martabanne*, there is found even more and better; but these places are remote and less convenient.

These great carracks have four decks or stories, on each of which a man, however tall, can walk without touching his head against the deck above; indeed, he comes not within two feet of it. The poop and the prow are higher than the main-deck by the height of three or even four men, in such wise that it seems as if two castles were erected at the two ends. There may be thirty-five or forty pieces of bronze cannon; for they hardly ever use pieces of iron as we do. Their cannon is of the weight of four or five thousand

the King of Spain made every attempt to induce the India Government to build the carracks in India. A splendid carrack was built at Goa by Mathias de Albuquerque, and for good omen named a second *Chagas*. She sailed for Lisbon early in 1593, and, after a voyage of terrible misfortunes, was attacked by three ships of the Earl of Cumberland at the Azores, in June 1594. Her crew made a heroic defence, and finally blew her up, with her cargo of immense value (*Dec. XI;* Harris, *Voy.*, i, 688; *Purchas*, iv, 1147).

[1] The carrack alluded to is probably the *Chagas*, built in 1561, not at Bassein, but at the Goa arsenal, by the Viceroy Constantine de Bragança, at his own cost (*Dec. VII*, liv. ix, 17). She made nine or eleven voyages until 1587, when she was laid up as a hulk in the Tagus. On her last voyage to India, in 1585, she carried out the Viceroy Duarte de Menezes; she must have been a large, and even then a staunch ship, as she carried 900 passengers, besides a crew of 100, and did not touch land between Lisbon and Cochin, being seven months on the way.

pounds; the least is three thousand. Besides these, they omit not to carry some small pieces, such as *esperes*[1] and *perriers*, whereof they place some in the tops: for these tops are so large that they will hold ten or a dozen men. And the masts are so enormous that no tree is tall or thick enough to make a whole one,—I speak both of the mainmast and of the foremast. So, usually, all their masts are lengthened by splicing, and covered all round with "fishes",[2] which are thick pieces of timber, cleverly fastened, and of the required thickness. These timbers, being well adjusted, are firmly lashed with ropes, and well bound with iron braces, so as not to impede the yard in its rise and fall. The yard is of thickness proportionate to the mast, and four-and-twenty fathoms in length. It requires full two hundred persons to raise it aloft, and always with two big capstans.[3] They line not their ships with lead as we do ours; they only put it over the seams to keep fast the caulking. Then they cover the ship afresh with deal boards, and afterwards caulk it again, working it over with pitch, and then with sulphur and tallow. They are thus the tightest and staunchest ships you can see, and one is astonished at the number of stout timbers so well adjusted, and so much iron braced together. For all that, the sea sometimes shivers and shatters them

[1] Port. *espera* or *esfera*. De Couto (*Dec. VIII*) says they threw shot of 12 lbs. As to *perrier*, see vol. i, p. 23.

[2] Fr. *gaburons*,—"pièce de bois, nominée autrement *jumelle*, qu'on applique contre un mât, pour le fortifier" (*Littré*); *jumelle* = "fishes" (*Boyer*).

[3] A French engineer resident at Goa invented a machine for the purpose of saving this immense labour. The king, on being informed, instructs the viceroy (1st March 1594) to have it tested, and if effectual, used in the carracks. Before this despatch reached India the viceroy had, in fact, fitted it up in the carrack *As Chagas*, but as this vessel never reached Lisbon (see above, p. 182, *note*), the authorities there seem not to have seen the appliance even in 1596 (*Arch. Port. Or.*, Fasc. 3, No. 140, para. 46, and No. 204, para. 46). From the statement in the text, it may be concluded that the invention was a failure.

sooner than the smaller vessels; and verily I have observed that the larger and heavier a ship is, the more she labours. The smaller craft is lifted on the waves, whereas these cannot rise for their weight, and the waves strike and shiver them with the whole broadside of the storm, and break their masts and yards sooner than they would the others'. The more resistance the wind meets, the greater is its force and effect. The storm, however, must be a mighty severe one, for a little vessel would take for a storm what these big ones would consider a calm, so hard are they to shake. Moreover, they are very good sailers before the wind, but are worth nothing on the bowline,—that is, when the wind comes from one side or the other.

These vessels go for trade, and never for war. The other smaller ships, such as Biscay galions, Flemish hulks, caravels, and other French ships, remain in the Indies to make voyages to China, Japan, Malaca, Mozembique, Ormuz, and other parts of India. They serve also for war, or to bring despatches and attend the viceroy. They are indeed of service to the Portuguese in India; but their chief use is that the King of Spain sends them to accompany the carracks, and to convey men to the Indies; and if all the ships that go were to come back, there would not be found hands to man them, by reason of the great number that die on the voyages. Sometimes the hands of two ships are not sufficient to man one. Then, again, they obtain not enough cargo, that is, pepper, to fill them; and most often, for want of it, one or two of these carracks have to wait for the next year; and so, when the next year comes round, they send out from Portugal only one or two carracks, supported by some smaller vessels.

Note also that the soldiers in the Indies must not embark as mariners, nor the mariners as soldiers; so that the soldiers are forced to remain there, and the mariners to return. The latter dare not remain; and should there not be room for them in the returning ship, they wait for another opportunity. In the meantime they are paid every month at Goa, but they must not enter the ranks as soldiers; for if that were allowed, there would be none to man the vessels; and the soldiers there are held in the highest honour. For their soldiers they draw upon all classes; but they get not such good mariners as they could wish: from these they get their gunners and other officers. The soldiers have six perdos a month; the gunners and mariners, four. If a mariner wishes to return, he may do so, even if there is not a vacancy for one of his condition in the vessel; but not if there be at the time a lack of seamen, for then he is kept back till the next year, meantime receiving his regular pay. On board ship he would get his ordinary pay; but if he were to embark otherwise than as a rated mariner, he would be like a stranger, and would not get the bread-and-water ordinary, nor even a berth, unless he bought one. Wherefore they prefer in this case to wait a year, even two, if they have not the means to buy another mariner's place (which costs them about sixty or eighty perdos), or the means to buy a place to stow their baggage and goods. The condition of a man who has no berth on board is pitiful indeed: it is not as in our vessels, where the 'tween decks is common to all; in theirs there is not the smallest corner that is not given as a favour or sold, and the same on deck. A place on the poop must be got from the master, in the bows from the mate. Between the two masts—that is, on the orlop and on deck there—the space is at the disposal of the guardian.[1] This order and separation is observed in the vessels of the Indies only: in other voyages

[1] *Gardien.* Linschoten (ii, 231) says: "The guardian or quartermaster hath his cabin close by the great mast outward on the left hand, for on the right hand standeth the scullerie and kitchen"; and Ant. de Conflans (quoted by Jal, *Gloss.*, s.v.), 1515-20, speaking of the armament of the ship of Charles d'Amboise, writes: "Le Gardien avait soin de la Sainte-Barbe et de la soute aux poudres. La Sainte-Barbe avait alors le nom de *Gardiennerie*"; hence our "ward-room".

it is much the same as with us. In the smaller vessels they observe the same regulation as in the carracks, but the officers of the one do not in the least resemble those of the other: for the master of a galion who had made his voyage to the Indies would be mighty pleased on the return voyage to get the office of a guardian on board a carrack. These mariners and officers of the smaller vessels are all men impressed for service as mariners, masters, mates, pilots, etc., of these vessels. They can hope for but little gain, because their ships never come back, and for want of ship they have to wait a year or two, or return at their own expense. On their return, however, they are recompensed, for they get some office in a carrack, but of lower rank than they enjoyed in their galion. It is more honorable to be a mariner in the one than a mate in the other, wherefore a place in a carrack is sought after and purchased, being as well honourable as profitable.

These seamen on board the carracks resemble not any others that I have seen, nor even the Portuguese on other voyages. For true it is that all seamen while at sea are barbarous, cruel, and uncivil wretches, with no respect of persons, in short, very devils incarnate, while on shore they are very angels. These mariners of the Indian carracks, however, are exceptions, for they are courteous and well-mannered, both at sea and on shore, and seemed to be all men of honour and birth, bearing great respect to one another. Among the mariners of France I have never seen the like, as I shall describe more particularly hereafter.

As regards the order preserved by the Portuguese in these carracks during their voyages, I will say first of all that the "equipage" or crew numbers more than 1,000 or 1,200, or at least 800 to 900, who are ranked in manner following. There is a captain, who is absolute over the whole ship and the men on board; next there is a pilot, a second pilot, a master, a master's mate,[1] a guardian, two ropemakers,[2] some 60 mariners, 70 or more apprentices,[3] and a master gunner, whom they call the Constable, assisted by five-and-twenty other gunners (more or less, according to the vessel): he gives his orders to all below the captain, and submits to none but him: he has charge of the cannon, and the two great sheets.[4] There is also a chaplain-priest of the ship, who is rated, and obliged to say Mass on Sundays and Holy-days, without consecration (of the elements), however, for that is not allowed at sea. He is also obliged to confess, to preach, and to perform all other ecclesiastical functions and ceremonies. And though there be also other clerics of all orders on board, they are not obliged to do these things, except of their own will: they are not paid, and are merely embarked for the Indies, without leave to return to Portugal.

Besides these, there is a clerk[5] who is all-powerful, being

[1] In orig.: "un maistre, un contre-maistre". The English version of Linschoten designates the former as "master", and the latter wrongly as "boteson". The use of the French terms has changed with time, and *contre-maître* now means boatswain's mate. As according to the text the officer so named was next to the master in the general control of the crew, I prefer to render the term by "master's mate".

[2] Fr. *Trinquier*; Port. *Estrinqueiro*, from *estrinque*, rope (our "string"). Linschoten (i, 8) says, "two *strinceros*, those are they which hoise up the maine yeard by a wheele, and let it down againe with a wheele as need is." Mocquet mentions the officer as "*l'estrinquere* qui est celuy qui sert à mener la grande voile par une roue".

[3] Fr. *gourmet*; Sp. *grumete*; Du. *grom*; Eng. *groom*. They were the ship's apprentices, not necessarily boys. Below he calls them *sous-mariniers*, mentioning a grown man who so shipped; they would correspond to our ordinary seamen (not A.B.'s), formerly called "younkers".

[4] Fr. *écoutes*. This combination of duties may seem anomalous: but Adm. Brine informs me that even when he entered the navy, the gunner had charge of the guns and of the mainsail.

[5] *Escriuain*; Port. *escrivão*. The office of ship's clerk, now obsolete, was formerly of great dignity. "He is also called", says P. Fournier, "*commis, facteur*, or *agent*: the Italians call him *proveditore*; with them he holds the second place in the ship, being as it were the *Eye* of the prince, republic, burgher, or merchant, who has freighted the ship and sent her to sea" (*Hydrographie*, p. 143). In Holland he was called the

appointed by the king. Nothing is carried on behalf of the king or the private merchants that he does not take note of. He also registers all that comes in or goes out of the ship, and passes all bills and bonds whatever. For be it noted that all bills and bonds that are made at sea are good and lawful among the Portuguese, but among the French are null and void. This clerk also draws and preserves all informations and judicial writs, as in a Registry. When anyone dies, he makes an inventory of all his goods on board, and causes them to be sold by auction to the highest bidder. The money he gets thereby he puts out at interest, and when he arrives at Goa or Lisbon he delivers a copy of his inventory to the relatives and heirs, who pay him for his trouble. He has vast authority on the ship, and nothing takes place ere he has first given his advice and consent. All the ship's victuals are brought before him, and are distributed before his eyes, and he notes everything, even down to a pint (*chopine*) of water. He keeps the keys of the scuttles of the ship, and even when the captain would go below, he must have the clerk always with him; otherwise he could not, for the clerk represents the king on board. The captain has command over all, both the crew and the passengers, and for all they may be greater lords than he, yet must they obey him. Nevertheless, when something of importance has to be done, he takes the advice and counsel of all the officers, gentlemen, and merchants, and makes them all sign, in case of a future inquiry. He cannot condemn to death for crime, but must give the strappado[1] on

Fiscal, and presided at courts-martial, in which he was assisted by a council of war. In the Portuguese ships he had not judicial power, but only that of a registrar and notary. In this capacity we find the *scrivano* in the Ordinances of Trani (A.D. 1063), in the Statute of Marseilles, and in the Amalfitan Table, the last mentioned sea-law giving to his writing the same authority in a court of justice as that of a notary public. (See *Black Book of the Admiralty*, 1876, vol. iv, pp. 17, 532.)

[1] From the Ital. *strappata*, a pulling, wringing. In Eng. it was a

board (the French call this "passer par sous le navire", or "caler"), and other corporal punishments, also such as hanging under the forelocks. In civil causes he may award damages up to 200 cruzados, without appeal. He can also imprison a man in irons for the whole voyage: being arrived at land, he delivers him over to justice.

After the captain, the pilot is the second person of the ship, for the master obeys him, and acts only under his commands. He never leaves his place on the poop, ever observing his needle and compass; in this he has a second pilot to help him. Next is the master, who commands all the mariners, apprentices, and other ship's hands; he has a master's mate under him to assist him: all these are appointed by the king. The master's duty is to command from the poop to the main-mast, including that, as well in lowering the sails as in all other needful work. The master's mate takes charge from the forecastle to the foremast, inclusive of that mast, and has the same duties there as the master on the poop. The latter cannot give him any orders as to that part: each of them remains night and day on his own quarter, and it will happen that in six months they visit each other not four times.

The master's mate has charge of all the ship's cargo, both the lading and unlading thereof, and of other necessary jobs, both at sea and on arrival in port; for the master never leaves his poop. Next there is a guardian, who commands the apprentices, and is lodged with them night and day above on the deck, between the mainmast and the foremast: this part they call *Converso*,[1] and, wind or rain, they must be

form of the rack:—"Zounds", says Falstaff, "an I were at the strappado or all the racks in the world, I would not tell you on compulsion." The Fr. *estrapade*, as the text shows, was also applied to keel-hauling. Our sailors' version of the above French explanation was "under-going a great hard-ship".

[1] Pyrard seems to be the only authority for this form. The Port. is *convez* or *conves*, the deck of the "waist" or middle part of the ship, between

always there; they have nothing to cover them but ox-hides. This place is called *Converso* with good right, for it is the promenade of all on board, where they visit and converse with each other. This guardian commands the apprentices; and if at the second whistle one fails to answer and come quickly, he gives him in addition (to his task) heavy blows with a rope-end or a rod. These apprentices are rated lowest on board, and come after the mariners, serving only to give a hand with the ropes: they never go aloft, or leave the deck. They assist in all the hard work of the vessel, and are like valets to the mariners, who beat and chide them sore. Thus they are not allowed to manage the tiller or helm; so there is no sort of work, whether outside or inside the ship, that they are not obliged to do, such as cleaning ship, and working the pump which they alone do, except when, owing to accident, the ship is making more water than usual, and the pump has to be worked three or four times a day.

The mariners are highly respected; and there are few of them but can read and write, such being very needful to them for the art of navigation. For by this word mariner is to be understood one who is well instructed in navigation; but yet there are few good at it, although all bear the name: theirs is the work of steering the ship, each in his turn. In these great ships, that are difficult to handle, they take one or two apprentices to their aid. They do all the work that has to be done aloft, such as setting and reefing the sails,

the forecastle and the poop. Père Fournier (*Hydrographie*, 1643) borrows the word *converso*, and the explanation, with many others, from Pyrard. Aubin (1702) copies the passage from Fournier, and Jal (*Gloss. Naut.*) follows suit, suggesting that *convez* may be a corruption of *converso*, or may be from *convir*, to meet. As the word seems to be used by no Portuguese writer in this sense (Port. *converso* means a "convert" or a "lay brother"), I conclude that Pyrard has made a mistake, and therefore that *converso* may disappear from the dictionaries for the future.

handling the ropes, and so on. They are much honoured of the master and the pilot when they do their duty. They never clean the ship, nor work the pump, save when necessity requires. The guardian may not command them in anything. They are divided into three watches for the night: the pilot has one watch, the master another, and the master's mate the third; in like manner the apprentices are in watches with them; each party is on watch four hours, and each man is two hours at the helm. It must be noted here that in these large ships there must be three compasses: the pilot that is high up on the poop has one; under the deck there is another for the mariner who is there to hear the pilot, because he that is below at the helm could not hear him, so the one that is betwixt passes on to him the pilot's word.

There are two principal mariners, whom they call *Trinqueres*, that have the care of the ropes and sails, and when these require to be mended, they see to it. There are also four little boys called *Pages*, who serve only to call the whole company to their duty; they sing out from the foot of the mainmast, and even then all can hardly hear them. They summon the crew, both to come on their watch, and to go to the helm, etc. These boys also serve to look after the lamps, and to carry messages from the master and other officers; also, when the goods of a dead person are sold, it is they who make proclamation and call the bids. There is a sergeant to execute the commands of the captain in matters of justice; the prisons are at the foot of the pump; there they place the malefactors, most often with irons on their feet, and none can go near them but he alone. There are other smaller prisons, as for example on the deck, where are certain blocks of wood pierced with holes, whereinto they put the criminal's feet, which are then fastened with padlocks. This sergeant has also all the powder, ball, matches, and arms in his charge: all these are entrusted to him by tally. He has also charge of the fires, and no one, whosoever he might be, would dare to light or carry any fire without the sergeant gave it with his own hand. And for this purpose there are on the two sides of the ship at the place of the mainmast, two large kitchens, which they call *fougons*[1]; and when the sergeant lights the fire there, which is close upon eight or nine o'clock, there are always two guards or soldiers present, one at each kitchen, to see that no one commits any folly with the fire, as also to prevent any from taking a light and carrying fire about the ship. So if one has occasion to go down to the hold to inspect the goods, the sergeant, if he can trust him, comes and lights him a candle, by leave of the captain, and puts it in a lantern of white iron pierced all over, and fastens it with a padlock; if, however, he cannot trust him, he goes himself. Also he has the duty of seeing the fires put out, which is at about four o'clock.

In these vessels are also many necessary artisans, two of each office and craft; such as surgeons, carpenters, caulkers, coopers, etc. The most of the apprentices are made subject to them, each in his own place; for all the ship's officers have each his own station; and some are allotted to sleep always aloft in the top, and the rest each at his hatch, except the four that sleep in the top. All these artisans are liable to all work like the rest, when not occupied (at their craft). The master, mate, guardian, and master gunner have each a big silver whistle, hung at his neck with silver chains, wherewith they make known all their orders; that is, the master and mate to the mariners, the master gunner to the gunners, and the guardian to the apprentices and the four boys. There are also two stewards (*despenciers*), one for the mariners, and the other for the soldiers; but they can distribute nothing but in the presence of the clerk. These stewards are

[1] *Fougon*, a galley, or ship's kitchen: a Mediterranean term; Sp. *fogon;* It. *focone*, from Lat. *focus* (*Littré*).

also appointed by the king. In the ship there are great numbers of soldiers, gentlemen, merchants, ecclesiastics, and other passengers, of whom I say no more, having no concern with them here.

The King of Spain sends out these ships, armed and equipped at his own proper cost and expense, with his own goods, which consist of silver only. This he sends to help to pay the cost of the Indian government, and to buy pepper. So there is not a vessel that goes out but carries at the least 40,000 or 50,000 crowns in silver for him, besides the goods belonging to the private passengers. This silver is profitable to him, for on reaching the Indies it goes up in price one-third above the value in Portugal. In these ships are sometimes embarked from seven to eight hundred soldiers; the rest are the crew and passengers. But what causes these Portuguese ships to make so little resistance on occasions of fighting is, that all these soldiers are children of peasants and other folk of low estate, who are taken by force from the age of ten or twelve years: so that never having seen war, they cannot make a good fight of it. As for the gunners, they are mostly artizans, shoemakers, tailors, and others who, when the time arrives, know not how to fire a gun.[1] But for all that these fellows, notwithstanding their low estate, when they have passed the Cape of Good Hope, as we have already stated elsewhere, give themselves new names and call themselves gentlemen. Another thing that causes them to show so little fight is, that their enemies give them very good terms of capitulation[2];

[1] No wonder then that De Couto, in his severe indictment of Portuguese administration, exclaims, "Why, there is not a gunner in all India that could hit the hill of Cintra, unless he fired from the very foot of it!" (*Soldado Practico*, Dial. i, Scena 10).

[2] In orig. *leur font fort bonne guerre*. The terms of *buena guerra* were recognised as entitling the prisoners to their liberty without ransom (Hawkins' *Voy.*, pp. 320, 321).

all the loss is the king's, and they lose nothing, so say they.

When these great vessels are ready to start, the king furnishes them with all sorts of provisions, which are for the common use from Portugal to Goa, and no further. The steward for the soldiers gives them their commons first, then the steward for the mariners and the other officers and seamen serves out theirs; so all without exception get their ordinary day by day, one as another, viz., half a *canada*[1] of wine, and the same of water (a pipe contains three hundred canadas); of bread as much as they can eat. As for other things, such as salted meat, an *aroba* a month (the "aroba" weighs thirty pounds): everything else is given in the same proportion, such as oil, vinegar, salt, onions, and fish; all these are served out for a whole month, except the wine and water, which is for the day only, and all in presence of the clerk, who puts everything down in his accounts, with the names. If a man does not drink wine, he can sell it to the others, or keep it, leaving it in the hands of the purser, who keeps a score; being arrived at Goa or elsewhere, he can get the wine that is due to him, and do what he likes with it. But the evil that I find in all this is, that the provisions are given to them raw, and each man has to cook his own victuals; so that you will sometimes see more than eighty or a hundred pots on the fire at the same time; and when some are done, others are put on. So when any are sick, instead of being properly cared for, they are exceeding ill fed and maintained, and many die from this cause. The French and Hollanders have not the same practice, for they have one cook for all, and eat six off a dish. But among the Portuguese the eating and drinking is all a man's own affair; what is over of all the provisions and ship's utensils goes to the superintendents of ships residing at Goa; and when the vessels are about to return, they furnish them afresh at the expense of the king.

[1] A Port. measure equal to about three pints English.

The whole of the ship's utensils are delivered over to the master, and the provisions and goods to the clerk.

For the rest, the soldiers while on board have to keep a guard every night, but are not liable to any other work. Such as have refreshments in the ship sell to those that want: thus one has been known to sell a hen for twenty reals of forty sols the piece, that is, at forty livres, and he that bought it re-sold the soup or "bouillon" for as much as the hen had cost him, so as it left him free and quits: this was a sale to the sick.

With regard to the pay of the ship's officers, note that to the captain, pilot, master, and other men in command, the king gives them each a certain berth in the ship, and in like manner to the mariners. As for the soldiers, apprentices, mariners, artisans, and other officers, they are paid all alike; that is, for the voyage from Portugal to Goa, fifty cruzados each. The cruzado is worth fifty sols. The commanding officers and mariners, if they have the means, buy goods suitable each to his quality and rank, having to pay no dues for a certain amount of goods. Those who have not the means to buy make but little profit of the voyage. The others can make a profit of five for one; and though they take no silver with them, yet are they enabled to make purchases by selling their berths to passengers, as well gentlemen as soldiers and merchants. Certain berths are readily sold at three hundred cruzados, wherewith they buy some goods, the which the king permits them to stow in the hold: for the king retains to himself only two decks in each vessel, there being four in all, not counting the poop and the forecastle, which are equal to one and a half.

The soldiers are lodged under cover below the main deck, and the apprentices above in the open; and the same with the Jesuits, and other clergy, when there are any, saving the ship's chaplain, who has his berth as one of the officers. The soldiers have their berths in going to the Indies only, but not in returning. The navigating officers have their berths according to their quality.

These ships are mighty foul, and stink withal; the most not troubling themselves to go on deck for their necessities, which is in part the cause that so many die. The Spaniards, French, and Italians do the same; but the English and Hollanders are exceeding scrupulous and cleanly.

As for berths, a man that is without one is greatly pinched and pressed, for he will find no place to sleep under cover except he pays for one for a while. And so to put away his victuals and goods, he must buy a place of some one, otherwise he is constrained to leave them out in the open air, at the risk of being wetted, spoiled, or stolen; so that everyone is obliged to buy a place from the ship's folk, who have other places reserved for their own use.

Accordingly, one that would go to the Indies to advantage must have an appointment, which means a berth on board ship. If he does not get one from the king, he must buy it from some one else, or of some widow. These offices and berths, if the ship does not arrive safely in Portugal, will belong to the same persons in another ship that is to leave the year after; and if that does not make a safe passage, they wait again for the next, and so on till a ship arrives safely, which is the cause that all these offices are in great request, and the berths of widows and orphans bought at high prices. But with all that they must have something to take out with them, and they have a proverb, "He that takes nothing to the Indies will bring nothing home."[1] Again they have a saying that the first voyage is only to see, the second to learn, and the third to make money; and so if in three voyages a man does not make a fortune, he should not return.

As regards the Catholic religion, it is observed on ship-

[1] Port. "Quem nada leva á India, nada traz."

board as on land, saving the consecration (of the elements), which is strictly forbidden at sea. But all the other ceremonies are observed, such as Mass, vespers, holy-water, and procession; also Lent, and the annual holidays. There are chapels adorned with beautiful pictures, where everyone goes to say his prayers. When one dies, the master blows a whistle to advertise everyone to say prayers, but there is no firing of cannon as with us. As for their ordinary prayers, every evening at nine o'clock the master with his whistle summons everyone to say a *Pater* and an *Ave*. Then he gives another whistle to call all the seamen to keep their watch and ward, and all betake themselves to their several posts. At break of day all the ship's boys chant a sea-orison or prayer, which is for all sorts and conditions of men on board, each in his particular office, with special mention also of the ship, and all her apparel in order, making apt reference in the case of each article to every stage and thing in the story of the Passion: so that this prayer lasts a full hour: it is said with a loud voice.

These ships, thus equipped and ordered, depart from Lisbon at the end of February, or at latest at the beginning of March: they must not touch at any place this side of the Cape, except in case of urgent need. And if, peradventure, some accident should prevent them doubling the *Abrolles* or passing the Cape, they are forced to stand about straight for Portugal again, and so lose their voyage. But if the ships are not staunch enough to return, they have no ports where they can anchor except at *Angola*, on the coast of Guinea, or at Brazil, in the Bay of All Saints,[1] or else at Fernambour.[2] Also, when they can safely pass the Cape, and thence to India or Goa, they have no other places to land at and refresh themselves, except at Mozembique; and thither they go not but in direst extremity and necessity, sojourning there the least while they can, so their orders are.

[1] Bahia de todos os Santos. [2] Pernambuco.

Yet sometimes they arrive there so late that they are forced to remain a long time, by reason of the contrary winds and other accidents. The ships that go there leave at the same time that the Portugal ships are setting out to come home—that is, in the month of June or July. They arrive usually in September or October, unless fortune plays them false, and most frequently they arrive not at Goa, but go to Cochin or Couelan; but this is perforce, and by reason of the currents that carry them there, or of the calms and contrary winds.

When, then, they have passed the Cape of Good Hope, they come to the land of Natal or of the Nativity, where usually they meet with heavy storms. This land is on the coast of Ethiopia, about 150 leagues to the other side of the Cape. When the Portuguese find themselves at the altitude of this land, after passing it, they take counsel among themselves whether, according to the season, they have time enough to pass between the island of St. Lawrence[1] and the mainland; else, if it be too late, to take a course outside the island. For, in order to take the course between the island and the mainland of Africa, they must have passed the Cape early—that is, in the month of July: if it be later, they are obliged to follow the other course outside, and then they are not sure of making Goa, being more likely to make land at Cochin, or sometimes no further than *Couelan*,[2] as I have said. Whereas those that have passed the Cape early, can easily pass between the said island and Africa, and can go to Mozembique to refresh for ten or twelve days. Otherwise, if they put off too long on this course, they cannot easily arrive at Goa, because of the calms and contrary winds which ordinarily prevail at this season. Such as are too late in that sea have been full often forced to remain a long time at Mozembique, and thus have arrived very late at Goa, inso-

[1] *I.e.*, Madagascar. [2] Quilon, in South Malabar.

much that their voyage was retarded for another year.[1] As for those who have come—whether inside or outside the island of St. Lawrence, and have not touched at Mozembique—you must believe that they run grievous risks and have suffered wondrous troubles and labours, having been sometimes nine and ten months before they arrive at Goa; for, except Mozembique, there is no other port they could make: and those that will not make it when the season is too late, cannot fail to be grievously afflicted with the malady of the scurvy (*scurbut*), or as often even to die of thirst. While I was at Goa I saw some ships arrive there, in which, of the thousand or twelve hundred men that were in them at the setting out from Lisbon, there were left not two hundred, and well-nigh all these sick of the scurvy, which wears them in such sort, that after they are arrived they hardly recover.

I will say here in passing, that between the island of St. Lawrence and the mainland there are banks or shoals much to be feared, where many Portuguese vessels have been lost. They call these sands *baxos de Iudias*[2]—that is to say, "Judas banks." They are 50 leagues from the said island and 70 from the mainland; approaching them on the outward voyage they begin at the 23rd degree and end at the 22nd and a half. They are verily fearful and dangorous shoals.

But to return to our Portuguese ships. When they are

[1] The ordinary service of carracks was to leave Lisbon in February or March, and reach Goa (or Cochin) about September or October; and for the same ships, or such as survived, to leave India the following December or January. He has probably in his mind here the unfortunate fleet of the Conde de Feira, which left Lisbon in the spring of 1608. Mocquet, who was on board one of the few ships that reached India, did not get to Goa till May 1609. Thus a year was lost, for they ought by that time to have been nearly back to Europe.

[2] Port. *Baixos da Judia*; in the Eng. version of Linschoten (i, 22), "Flats of the Jewes", now the Europa shoals. A terrible account of the wreck on these shoals of the carrack *Santiago*, in 1585, will be found in Linschoten (ii, 176-82), and De Couto (*Dec. X*, Liv. vii, cc. 1-3).

arrived at Cochin they take in their cargo there, and go not on to Goa, because of the contrary winds and currents. They are laden there by command of the viceroy, whom they advertise forthwith of their arrival, and he sends them the King of Spain's officers to give the necessary orders: for in the other towns there are all manner of officers, and the same regulation in spiritual and temporal things as at Goa.

The navigation of these Portuguese vessels is carried on with exceeding bad order; for although they set out from Portugal all together and in convoy, and are expressly enjoined not to lose sight of one another, yet do they observe this order mighty ill, and make no account to obey their admiral, whom they call *capitaine major*. The cause of that is that all these captains are gentlemen of good houses, and are unwilling to yield in aught to one another. So each goes his own way, without having regard whether his companions are following or not. This is full often the cause of their loss, for, being alone, they may come up with some Hollander ships or other enemies that attack and take them, seeing that, as I said before, they make little resistance, the soldiers being only a mob of men, mostly taken perforce from among the villagers and poor artizans. Also, the captains have no great zeal to defend themselves, so little interest have they in the matter, for the Hollanders give them quarter and kill them not. It is only the King of Spain and some merchants, present and absent, that lose by it. When these ships are captured or lost they make among them an attestation of the loss of their goods, and of the office that each held in the ship, and when they get home they get recompensed for all, sometimes double. I must also note in passing, as I have said before, that all these soldiers and seamen, after they have passed the Cape, give themselves titles of nobility, otherwise they would be greatly blamed and despised by the other Portuguese resident in the Indies; for they bear to one another the greatest respect, even the highest to the lowest, and do greatly esteem one another, despising not only the Indians, but even all the other Christian nations of Europe, whom they call "white men"; the Indians call them *Faranquy* or *Franki*. But if an Indian have struck a white man, the law is that he has his hand cut off.

So much for the order observed by the Portuguese ships from their embarkment at Lisbon until their arrival at Goa or other place in the East Indies. And be it noted that in all these voyages it is only the poor soldiers and seamen that have a bad time of it and suffer poverty, because most often they do not get their wages and pay. I have sometimes seen them be four whole months without touching a sol, and all the time the King of Spain is paying. So from this it may be seen that the Indies are good and profitable only to the viceroys, governors, and some of the king's officers—not to the king, nor to the poor soldiers and mariners. Also all the presents that the Indian kings offer are all for the viceroy, while those that he gives in exchange are at the expense of the King of Spain, his master. But since the French, English, and Hollanders have begun to frequent the Indies, these viceroys have not made so great profits as theretofore, having lost most of their commerce, and not daring to navigate for fear of being taken by the English or Hollanders. I have myself knowledge of a vast number of ships that have been taken from the Portuguese or pillaged. And there were some of them, coming from China and elsewhere, that were valued at more than two millions of gold; and many others, coming from and going to Portugal and between all parts of the Indies. For all the strength of the Portuguese suffices not to keep the Hollanders from these seas; yet can the Hollanders not do them much harm on the mainland in their towns and fortresses, nor get the better of them by cabals, except a little in Sunda; but that is far removed from the territories and power of the Portuguese.

Before ending this chapter I must not omit a very notable peculiarity which all the Portuguese say they have observed in their Indian voyages, namely, that all the dead bodies which they cast into the sea on the northern, that is on this, side of the Equinoctial line, go not to the bottom, but float on the surface, the head always towards the west, and the feet towards the east; and if perchance the winds or waves turn them over to one side or another, they are seen incontinently to come back to their first position. But once the line is passed toward the south, then, as they say, all the bodies go to the bottom. I leave it to the more curious naturalists to find out the cause of this. We Frenchmen, indeed, have not observed it, inasmuch as to all the bodies we cast into the sea we attach a stone or cannon-ball, to make them go to the bottom. As soon as a man dies on board a French ship his body is wrapt in a winding-sheet or coverlet, with something heavy to make it sink. It is cast to leeward, with a (lighted) firebrand on the same side, while a cannon-shot is fired to windward, and everyone keeps his eyes on that side, and not on the side on which the corpse is thrown. This done, the master or captain calls out aloud to say prayers. But the Portuguese observe none of all that, as I have said. The master contents himself with giving a whistle, to warn the crew to say their prayers.

CHAPTER XV.

Of the traffic of the Portuguese throughout the Indies in general, and the order which they observe therein.

The principal traffic of the Portuguese is with the East Indies, where they will not permit any other nation to go and trade, not even the Spaniards; that is strictly forbidden by their king under pain of death[1]: for they have obtained this privilege of the King of Spain, otherwise it were ruin to their State. So it is seen that, since the other nations of Europe have taken to the same route and trade, they are greatly troubled thereby; and firstly, by reason of the war, wherein the English and Hollanders have far greater strength and advantage over them on the sea, of which the English in particular are said to be kings, as also in these days are the Hollanders. For the Portuguese are the poorest folk in sea-fight that are to be found in all Christendom, for all the reputation they have—that is, so far as I have been able to estimate them. They are merely good pilots and mariners, and nothing more. In their voyages their apprentices and sailors are not men for labour and fatigue, but careless, lazy, dirty fellows as can be; they would let themselves be wrecked and swamped often enough rather than work.

But the other disaster, and a greater, is to their trade and commerce, which is now much curtailed, as well by the prizes that are made of their ships as by the scarcity and dearness of goods, because the great number of merchant ships renders merchandise dearer among rivals in the trade. What formerly cost the Portuguese one sol, now costs them four or five,

[1] A law made by the King of Spain, 9th Feb. 1591, forbade all foreigners to go to C. Verd, Angola, Brazil, etc., without his licence, which was to be granted only to allies (*Arch. Port. Or.*, Fasc. 6, No. 49). In 1593 the king writes that he is informed from Morocco that an English merchant there was giving out that he was going to Sumatra, etc., and orders the viceroy to see that he is not allowed to set foot on land. The same letter shows that the king had heard of Raymond and Lancaster's expedition of 1591 (Fasc. 3, No. 127*a*). The particular instructions against the rebel Hollanders are too frequent to mention. On the 8th March 1605, the king amends the law of 1591, by prohibiting absolutely foreign trade with the above places or India, on pain of confiscation of ships, goods, etc. A further amendment (16th June 1606) excepts the Spaniards from this prohibitory law. Meantime, the municipality of Goa had been annually petitioning the king to prohibit even the Portuguese merchants, unless they resided in India, but he would go no further than to instruct the viceroy to report (Fasc. 1, Part II).

and even what they can bring in safety to Portugal they are obliged to get rid of at a less price than they were wont; nay, it is as much as they can do to get it sold at all, because the Hollanders sell at lower prices still, and do their business with much greater despatch.

Thus the Portuguese traffic in the Indies under conditions of continual dread of the foreigners there, and a great contempt of them is thereby engendered in the minds of all the kings and peoples of India, so that the latter now strengthen themselves with cannon, arms, and munitions more than formerly. They even go so far as to take part with men and vessels against the Portuguese, who were wont with truth to call themselves masters of the sea throughout all the Indies. For in past times they had none other competitors, save the Malabars, who carried on a continual war against them, as indeed they do still, and give them much trouble, as I have already said; but that did not disturb their vast shipping trade. The Portuguese used to tell these Indians that their king was the greatest in Christendom, that he had all the other Christian kings and princes for vassals, and that their nation was the most noble and valiant in all the West. This the Indians continued to believe until the English and Hollanders showed them the contrary: as also have we given them in those parts to apprehend the greatness and sovereignty of each of the other Christian kings and princes, and especially of our own.

The Portuguese established themselves in the Indies at the first partly by war, as in some places, and partly by friendly commerce, as in others. The latter was the most successful means, for they have with difficulty taken towns by force, as they did Goa and some others. They have contracted treaties of peace and friendship with most of the kings of India, calling them *Irmanos et Armes*,[1] that is

[1] The phrase *Irmãos em armas*, "brothers in-arms" (not "brothers-and-arms", as he has it), was in Europe used of kings between whom

to say, very arms, brothers, and allies with the kings of Portugal. By these treaties they are thus settled in their midst with their consent, and on these terms: that the traffic is to be only between these kings and the Portuguese, in the spices and other merchandises that are in demand in these parts, and that none of the enemies of the Portuguese are to be received of them. These kings have promised them neither to trade with, nor to harbour any others without their consent; while the Portuguese have reciprocally engaged to take all their merchandises at a certain price agreed between them for each kind, and to bring there those goods of Europe that are most needful to them, such as silver, cloth, and other things most in demand there. They have moreover warranted to these kings to guard all the sea of those coasts from corsairs and pirates, and to defend them at all points, and against all enemies that may appear in those parts. In this behalf, every year they equip for the six months of summer two armadas at Goa, the one for the North and the other for the South, all at the cost and expense of the King of Portugal: for there they speak of him only as King of Portugal, and not as King of Spain.

Thus have the Portuguese induced the said Indian kings to give them establishment at suitable places, and at the most convenient ports and harbours all along that coast, to live, settle, and trade there in all personal liberty and assurance. And for this purpose the Portuguese have built there towns, fortresses, and commodious houses, and at such places

existed an offensive and defensive alliance (Vieira, *Dict. Port.*). In India it was rather a title of honour conferred by letters patent upon the rajas who accepted the Portuguese alliance. The form of the patent, *carta de irmandade*, is given by De Couto, *Dec. XII*, cap. vii. It engages the recipient to treat the friends and enemies of Portugal as his friends and enemies, to assist in the spread of Christianity by all means in his power, and to carry out the Portuguese commercial monopoly. The royal envoy who presented it at the same time delivered a flag bearing the royal arms of Portugal.

are absolute masters, with the same power and authority as the kings themselves, the latter pretending to no power in these particular towns, and the Portuguese taking all the dues, tolls, and subsidies, whereof the kings take no cognisance at all. Nor do they make enterprises one against another; but all live in excellent peace together. But if perchance these kings have any quarrel with their neighbours, the Portuguese, in case they have not a treaty of peace and friendship with those neighbours, are obliged to succour and assist their allies with men, arms, and money; and the said kings are in the same manner engaged to them in like case. But if the kings that would go to war together are both friends of the Portuguese, then must the Portuguese take measures to settle their differences, or at least must not assist either party, otherwise than secretly. Thus have they done in the dispute between the King of Cochin and the King of Calecut, which they foster as far as they can, always, however, assisting him of Cochin more than the other. The King of Calecut holds himself aloof from both parties.

Under all these treaties and agreements the Portuguese have managed to become masters of the Indian seas; so that no Indians, whether of the mainland or of the islands, or of what country soever, durst navigate or make any voyage without a passport from them, which lasts but one year only. These passports, which they call *cartas*, permit them to navigate to certain named places only, but forbid them to carry pepper, arms, or munitions of war. They even specify what arms and men they may carry, and if more are found on board than are mentioned in the passport, everything is confiscated and deemed lawful prize, and the men are held prisoners. It is also mentioned of what port the ship is. But an exception is made in favour of the kings with whom they have treaties of peace: for these can send a certain number of vessels when they choose, and with any cargo of merchandise whatever, without any daring to say or do anything. They are not even bound to take a passport. Nevertheless, they take them for such ships as they fit out on their own behalf and are avowedly theirs. And this is the cause that many pass under their names, and carry pepper and other merchandise to Arabia, whither all these kings send every year a vast number of ships laden with spices and other drugs.

But there are plenty other kings in the Indies that are not at peace with the Portuguese, and yet cease not to navigate and traffic wherever they will, without troubling themselves about the passport of the Portuguese, whom they fear not at all. And when they meet there is a desperate struggle, and the booty is for the stronger. They that sail in this sort are all those from the coasts of Arabia, Guzerat, and Persia, the Malabars, those of the islands of Sumatra, Java, and other places—all these reck nothing of the Portuguese; no more, indeed, than do the English, Hollanders, and French[1] who in these days go to that country. For two or three ships can navigate and sail to and fro all the coasts of India in perfect safety, and all the Portuguese armadas would not dare to touch them or attack them: nay, they can even show themselves at the bar of Goa,[2] where six Hollander ships have sometimes had the assurance to cast anchor, remaining there

[1] The French had not done much to justify this boast. After the St. Malo expedition of 1601, in which our author took part, they sent out no ships till 1616, and then only two ships, under De Nets and Beaulieu. Of these only one returned home. Beaulieu started on his better known voyage in 1619, the year in which this edition was published.

[2] P. van Caerden arrived before Goa, fresh from the first siege of Mozambique, on the 17th Oct. 1607, and remained only three days (Van Caerden's *Second Voyage; Arch. Port. Or.*, Fasc. 1, No. 16, para. 13). On the 17th Sept. 1608, Verhœven arrived from the second siege of Mozambique and remained till the 27th (Verhœven's *Voyage; Arch. Port. Or.*, *ib.*, No. 17, para. 4). On this occasion they came close enough to see the new fort which the Portuguese had built at Bardes.

about three weeks at a time, during which time nothing can enter or leave Goa, while the Portuguese have not the boldness to attack them. They might do the same at all their ports and towns. Provided they keep out of cannon-shot they have nothing to fear. Even when there should be two or three Portuguese ships against one Hollander, if the Hollander fires a cannon-shot, they will incontinently strike, and will come and render themselves up to their mercy: which is the cause that the Hollanders generally give them quarter. They did not do so from the beginning, and got the worst of it; for on occasions when they assumed the defensive, the Hollanders punished them and slew them. But now they fight no more: for in these Portuguese ships there are for the most part only rich private merchants, who having wives and children, would much rather lose what little they have in the ship than be killed. This is the reason I have heard them allege sometimes when I spoke to them of it. The Malabars say that they never refuse fight, when there are two Portuguese ships or galiots against one Malabar vessel of the same size, which will go and attack them boldly. So it may be inferred from these facts, that nowadays the Portuguese, after all this talk about themselves, are the most wretched soldiers on the sea and the least to be feared.

But to return to their commerce and traffic in the Indies, a number of ships set out every year. These are the carracks; every year they despatch two, three, four, or more, of the burthen of 2,000 tons more or less, equipped with 1,000 or 1,200 men of all qualities, as I shall describe more particularly hereafter. All this is at the expense of their king; for no private person ever sends a ship or vessel to the Indies. But there are no people so unfortunate in their voyages; for they navigate so ill, and in such great disorder (as, indeed, they confess themselves), that none equal them in maritime dishonour. I have myself known of twenty-five ships, as well carracks as galions, and other large vessels, which left Lisbon on three voyages in three years for Goa: of these, fourteen left in one year, wherein was the Count *de la Fera*, who was sent out as viceroy: he died on his way on the coast of Guinea. In the two years following eleven started, and of the whole twenty-five, I am assured that there returned not four to Portugal.[1] The rest were wrecked, lost and sunk in the Indies, except three or four that were captured by the Hollanders. I omit all mention of the Indian-built ships, which are lost in all quarters in great numbers. It is not the fault of the vessels, which are very good; nor of their pilots, who are expert enough; but in truth it may be said that, though their ships are magnificent, yet do they encounter very heavy storms, also that their men are not capable of great fatigue, and that their officers (except the pilots) are rarely expert in their several offices. The reason is that most of them, nay all, captains, masters, master's mates, keepers, even the mariners, gunners, and others, get their offices by favour, or for money, or in recompense for their services or past losses; also that these offices are given to the widows or children of such as have died on voyages or elsewhere in the service of the king; then do these sell them to whom they will, without judging of his capacity or

[1] Above, at p. 86, *note*, the number of the C. da Feira's fleet is given as fourteen, on Pyrard's authority; but Mocquet (who was in it) and F. N. Xavier (*O Gabinete Literario*, Nova Goa, 1846, pp. 83, 109), who speaks from the Goa archives, give thirteen as the number. Xavier states that five left Lisbon in 1609 and three in 1610; but to those of 1609 must be added the extraordinary fleet of five ships which took out the viceroy, L. de Tavora (see below, ch. xxi). It is impossible to follow the fortunes of all the ships which left Lisbon, 1608-10, as the names are not always given; and sometimes ships remained at Goa for a season: but we do know that of the four which left with Pyrard, Dec.-Jan. 1609-10, three reached Lisbon; and that the two which left Dec.-Jan. 1610-11, under Vasconcellos, arrived safely (*Liv. das Monç.*, ii, 178). The statement in the text is, therefore, probably an exaggeration.

merit. Besides this, when their king wishes to send any additional or extraordinary fleets, he gets his officers and men, as well soldiers as sailors, wherever he can, such as poor householders having wives and children. But in addition to all that, I believe the principal cause that their voyages succeed so ill is the great severity and cruelty which they use toward their poor slaves, and the other sorts and races of men that are under their power and dominion. And what causes still more disorder among them is that the captains, being gentlemen, have a great ambition one with another who shall have the first place[1]; so they never await each other, and most often the last to arrive have to wait till the next year for pepper and other spices. All these things together cause the great loss of men, money, ships, etc., now suffered by the King of Spain in the Indies, nay, the loss of the Indies themselves. For the revenue of the Indies cannot at present be sufficient to pay and maintain the state, in spiritual as well as in temporal concerns, and the cost is greater than the value. It is indeed very certain that but for the reputation and interest of the Catholic faith (as they say) they would long ere this have abandoned all those lands. Some years ago he (the King of Spain) assembled his council upon this question, whether he should do so or no, because of the trouble and loss he was then incurring. The Portuguese made him this remonstrance, praying that, if he was of a mind to abandon everything, it might please his majesty to leave the Indies to them and hand over all his rights to them, engaging always to hold of him, and to govern and maintain the state in all propriety. Nevertheless,

[1] See *Linschoten*, ii, 235. The ship in which he came home sighted another of the same fleet, and made towards it to speak with it; but "for very pride and high stomacke they would not stay to speake with us againe: which our officers perceiving, did likewise winde from them, every one doing his best to get before the other. By this and such like signs of pride, the Portingales do often cast themselves away, etc."

the king did not agree thereto, and they have gone on as before.[1]

With regard to the goods exported by the Portuguese to the Indies for traffic there: in the first place, their king sends silver only; but the private merchants send (besides silver) woollen cloth, hats, swords, and all manner of arms and munitions of war, or the material for making the same; next, all kinds of the iron ware of these parts, paper, iron, lead, mirrors, all sorts of dried fruits, salt fish, wines, cheeses of Holland, oil, olives, vinegar, and other such things, that are in high esteem there; moreover, printed books, for there is no printing in the Indies.[2] White cloths they carry not out, for there is abundance of cotton there, as of all sorts of silk and gold stuffs. All these other merchandises are in great demand, and bring a profit of four for one, the provisions being as much as six and seven to one.

The order of Goa is that the viceroy is absolute in all things and in all places, so far as relates to the service of

[1] India was practically in the hands of the Portuguese. The King of Spain had the expense of fitting out the carracks at Lisbon, and all he got in return was the cargoes of pepper which they—or rather the survivors of the voyage—brought home; and to get even this supply of pepper he had to send out the silver for its purchase. In matters of administration he had the appointment of the governors and higher officers. All the lower offices were sold by the governors. F. y Souza and De Couto show that in every account against the king there was gross peculation, and that at this period Spain drew no revenue from India.

[2] A mistake. The *Colloquios da India* of Garcia de Orta was printed at Goa in 1563, apparently by a private printer, Joannes de Endem. Later, if not then, there was a press at the Jesuits' College, at which the books of P. de la Croix and Father Thomas Stevens were printed—of the former in 1634; of the latter in 1640. The first Malayālam type is said to have been made at Cochin in 1577 (Whitehouse, *Lingerings of Light in a Dark Land*, p. 154). In 1578, Father João de Faria cut Tamil types and printed on the Pescaria (Tinnevelly) coast in the same year the *Flos Sanctorum* and other works (see Burnell, *Elements of S. Indian Palæography*, 2nd edit., p. 44).

the king and the good of the state. And if he acquit himself not of his charge, they can only write to the king, making mention in articles of the matters wherein he has failed, and thereupon the King of Spain signifies his will. For Goa is ruled and governed like Lisbon itself, as I have described more amply above, and there are no Spaniards or *Castillanos* (as they call them), wherefore the Portuguese like to be there much rather than in Portugal, where the Castillanos domineer over them; at Goa they are the masters, and they would complain still more were it not for the fear they entertain of us and other Europeans. And but for the opinion they had that we were come to spy them out and to dispossess them, they would rather we had been among them than the Spaniards; but they are so jealous of their state that they desire that none should have any knowledge of it. And when they saw us there they spoke injuriously of us in the streets, with endless contumely: even saying to us that had come from France in our own ships that we ought to have had the permission of their king. They are a whit more gracious to foreigners who set out from Lisbon with them and in their fleets, yet they fail not to maltreat them and to suspect them, saying they have *enganado el Rey*, that is to say, deceived their king, and have passed for Portuguese. And true it is that one gets a passage only by great favour, and as a Portuguese; and further must have the licence and passport of the viceroy, and be registered in the roll of the *Casa d'India*. When they have news that any ships of the English, Hollanders, or other Europeans of these parts are coming, they seize incontinently all foreigners that are found in their towns, and make them prisoners. All the other strangers, such as Italians, and all those of the Levant, are far better received amongst them—indeed, like the Portuguese themselves.[1]

In short, their traffic is such that all the Oriental peoples

[1] See above, p. 6.

from the Cape of Good Hope, as far as China and Japan, bring their merchandise to Goa; while the Portuguese also go to seek it at the ports of all these people, at least of such as are in peace and amity with them. These places are China, which means the island of *Macao, Japan, Malaca, Pegu, Bengal, Ceylon, Comory,* and all the coast of Malabar, as for instance *Coilan, Cochin, Calicut, Cananor, Onor, Mangalor,* and the other places as far as Goa: thence to Mozembique, including *Bassains, Daman, Chaul, Dabul, Cambaye, Surate, Diu,* and so along the coast to Ormus, thence to Arabia, and from there to Mozembic. All the merchandise of these lands is brought to Goa and collected there; but the pepper remains always in the granaries, or cellars of the countries where it grows, until the ships of the King of Portugal are arrived at Goa. And if they cannot make Goa, they must make Cochin or Coilan, not any other port. And when they go there, it is due to the currents and winds that carry them thither, and prevent them getting up to Goa. Very often, too, though some ships have arrived at Goa, some nevertheless go to Cochin. After they have discharged the goods they have brought from Portugal, often the King of Cochin is unwilling to give the pepper, until the ships go there to load it; for his council represent to him that his country profits by this—as is true enough: for when the ships go there, there are sometimes on board them some four or five hundred persons from Portugal, all fresh comers to the Indies, most of them knowing nothing of the value of merchandise; they carry nothing but silver, wherewith the victuals of the ship are procured; and all this greatly enriches the country. But when the ships do not leave Goa, the Portuguese of Cochin go thither with their cinnamon and other goods which they have had at fair prices, or by barter of other merchandise. And when the ships are laden at Cochin they return not to Goa, but take the direct route to Portugal, passing at the head of the Maldive islands, which is to the north of the line.

For the rest, all the armies and fleets coming from the south towards Goa, at the conclusion of their voyages, as soon as they double a Cape, called *Capo de Ramos,* twelve leagues from Goa, fire all their cannon as a sign of rejoicing, as being then safe from the pirates—this Cape being the boundary separating Malabar from Dealcan. In like manner those that come from the north, when they have sighted *las Islas Quemados,* at twelve leagues from Goa, for then are they out of danger.[1]

[1] *Islas Queimadas*, or *Ilheos Queimados*, the "burnt islands", small desert islands off Goa, to the north. V. Le Blanc (i, 95) says the same, probably copying Pyrard.

A Carrack (*after Vandyck*).

A Caravel (*from a MS. at Havre*).

CHAPTER XVI.

Of the traffic to Brazil, the River de la Plata, Angola, Congo, St. Thomas, Mina, and the Slaves of Africa.

The Portuguese that carry on the sea trade to Brazil, the West Indies, Angola, and other places on this side the Cape of Good Hope, use not great vessels in this behalf, but only caravels,[1] whereof the largest are not more than six or seven score tons burthen; or else they use round ships, bought of

[1] The caravel, or carvel, was, according to Crescentio, first used by the Portuguese as a swift despatch vessel for the service of the fleets of carracks. At this time it was chiefly employed in the Brazil service, and but little in that of India, except in conveying extraordinary despatches. It was a round ship—that is, driven by sails only. It was four-masted, the foremast carrying two square sails and the other three each a lateen sail. These, with its curved keel, enabled it to tack very smartly and to sail very near the wind (Crescentio, *Nautica Mediterranea*, p. 526; Jal, *Le Moyen Age*, tom. ii).

the French, English, or Flemings. For the caravels have lateen sails, and are masted differently from those round vessels, which have square sails; also they are of greater burthen, viz., about two hundred tons. Thus do they steer a course for Brazil, setting out from Lisbon, laden with all manner of European merchandises necessary for the life or convenience of men, such as linens, woollen, and silk cloths, wines, oils, and other things, whereof they take in the greater part on their way at the Canary Islands and the Azores, among other things, wine, wheat flour, salt beef, oxhides, and salt fish. The Azores wine is much poorer than that of the Canaries and Spain; also the flour cannot be kept for long without difficulty. All these merchandises they obtain in exchange for others brought from Portugal. They carry out all these goods, because Brazil produces neither wheat nor wine; it grows no grain, nor even has any mills, wherefore they have to buy all the flour ready ground from Portugal; also the wheat would spoil on the sea during so long a voyage, seeing that that which is carried from France to Spain is liable to be spoiled, and to stink in such wise that only the common people will eat bread made of French wheat; the rich eat that made of country wheat, which also is dearer than the other.

So then the Portuguese, laden with all these merchandises, take a course for Brazil, so as to land at one of the ports of that country, and principally at Fernambucque,[1] where there is the greatest trade in sugars, and where grows the greatest quantity of Brazil-wood. Next there is the Bay of All

[1] Pernambuco, still vulgarly called Fernambouc by the French. Its trade, now insignificant compared with that of Bahia and Rio, was then the greatest in Brazil. "It is the greatest town in all that coast", says Lopez Vaz (1586), "and hath above 3,000 houses in it, with seventy *Ingenios* for sugar, a great store of Brasill-wood, and abundance of cotton, yet are they in great want of victuals: for all their victuals come either from Portugal or from some places on the coast of Brasill" (*Hakluyt*, iii, 787).

Saints,[1] and other places on this coast (of these we shall speak more particularly hereafter), where the same trade is carried on, but not to the same extent as at Fernambucque. On their arrival they sell and dispose of all their goods, partly for silver, and partly for the country merchandise. Then they return without prolonging their voyage, after waiting there three or four months to collect their silver and make their purchases, which consist only of sugars and preserves of all sorts. As for red wood or brazil,[2] they are forbidden to carry any of that under pain of death: the King of Spain keeps that for himself, and it is his only article of traffic, as is pepper in the East Indies. As for ginger, he prohibits that too, because the great quantity of it in those parts would prejudice the sale of his pepper. So none dare bring thence aught but preserves. Thus, laden with sugars they return straight to Portugal, setting out ordinarily in August or September, and arriving in November, for they are usually two months and a half on the passage.

All the wares brought by the Portuguese, as well from there as from other distant countries, on entering Lisbon pay thirty per cent.; and the Portuguese cannot depart out of Brazil ere they have given security and caution that they are going to Portugal, and that all their merchandise is registered. And though by stress of weather, or some other lawful cause, they should be constrained to make land elsewhere, whether on the territories of Spain or elsewhere,

[1] The full name was *S. Salvador da Bahia de todos os Santos*; then generally called S. Salvador, and now simply Bahia. (See further, ch. xxvi.)

[2] The original *brazil* was the sappan wood of India. On the discovery of South America the name was given to other species of *Cæsalpinia*, found chiefly at Pernambuco, and also affording a red dye; and hence the name of the country. The name "Brazil-wood" is now exclusively appropriated to the American wood (Yule, *Gloss.*). Brazil-wood was imported into England at least as early as Edward I:—"E si ceo seyt marchaundise qe seyt vendue e peysee par centeyne, com brasyl, alum, etc." (Domesday of Ipswich, in *Black Bk. of the Admiralty*, ii, 189).

and to pay dues for discharging their cargoes there, yet will they not escape paying the dues again in Portugal, the farmers of the customs having obtained the right to them. For the rest, no foreigners—that is, none but the Portuguese and Spaniards—durst traffic in this land of Brazil these ten or twelve years past.

Sometimes the Portuguese, willing not to return directly to Portugal, but to make a longer voyage, do sell there a part of their cargoes, such as they can to the best advantage, and relade their ships fully with meal of *Mandoc* (a root whereof I shall say more hereafter),[1] along with the rest of their merchandise wherewith their ships are already laden. Thence they take their course toward the kingdom of *Angole*,[2] in Africa, which lies due eastward from Brazil, distant thence about a thousand leagues or more, and also a Portuguese possession. It is at eight degrees from the line toward the south on the coast of Africa, between Guinea and the Cape of Good Hope. It is the poorest country in the world, and living is exceeding dear there, for it produces only some fruits. What costs ten sols in France will cost forty in Brazil, and one hundred there. No other traffic is carried on but in negro slaves; the Portuguese hold it solely for this, and would not otherwise inhabit it, for the land produces only some fruits and cattle, and but small store of these. Moreover, in Spain they but seldom put their malefactors to death as we do in France: they send them all to these desert countries to traffic there. The Mandoc meal that costs only forty sols the *alquera*,[3] a weight of about forty pounds, in Brazil, is

[1] See ch. xxvi.

[2] The coast of Loango, Congo, Angola, and Benguela was discovered in 1484 by Diogo Cam. It became the headquarters of the slave trade. The Portuguese still possess it, but their authority does not extend far inland.

[3] Port. *alqueire:* a measure for grain, of which 60 = 1 moio; also a liquid measure = 6 canadas or 12 pints. Ar. *alqueile:* from *cala*, to measure (D. Vieira, *Dict. Port.*).

worth sometimes eight francs there. As for the merchandise of Europe, it is twice as dear as in Brazil. They barter their merchandise there for slaves, whereof there is the greatest possible abundance; and they hold that this is one of the largest and clearest revenues of the King of Spain from all these coasts, for it is without expense or cost, and he takes ten cruzados a head on all slaves exported, old and young: and when they are landed in another country to be sold there, or to be kept there awhile, they pay another thirty per cent. on their value. Moreover, after their first purchase they cost nothing, depending only upon the ship for their sustenance; and sometimes a great number die.

As for the small money of this land of Angola, it consists only of little shells, somewhat like those of the Maldives, and little pieces of cloth made of a certain herb. These pieces are an ell in length, more or less, according to the price. And when they go to market to buy their goods they carry no other money. This country costs nothing to the King of Spain, and he draws large profits from it. Up the country there is a mine of silver, which the natives sometimes work. The Portuguese there, and those of Mozembique and *Sofala*, wish to join from the one side and the other to conquer it, and reach this mine to work it[1]: it will cost them twenty-five sols to get forty, and the silver is very good and pure. The cause that more ships go not to Angola is that the air is very intemperate and noisome; besides that, they fear the coast of Guinea, which is also intemperate and full of calms. This is the cause that makes living so dear and slaves so cheap there: when they are got away they become of great value by reason of the risks run.

Such as wish to return directly to Portugal, return laden with slaves; but they that would make a longer voyage take them to sell at the river *de la Plata*, where they obtain

[1] Referring to the mines of Monomotapa, as to which see next chapter.

much silver, and thence they betake them to Brazil to relade with sugars and preserves, and thence to Portugal. Others go directly from Angola to Brazil to sell their slaves, for vast numbers are required there to work their sugar-mills; the slaves of America not being capable of so hard work, nor so obedient as those of Angola and Cape Verd; therefore most frequently these latter are taken to the West Indies, and there sold at high prices. The River of La Plata is at 35 degrees toward the south in America, that is, at nearly the same altitude as the Cape of Good Hope. They that go thither go secretly and in fear, because the King of Spain has prohibited traffic on all that coast, seeing that they cheat him of his dues; and all the silver got thence is carried secretly, so as it cannot be discovered, because of the strict prohibition and penalty of death; wherefore, in order to win it, they lash the sacks full of silver to their anchors, and when the king's officers are withdrawn they weigh their anchors and haul the silver again on board; thus all the silver from that coast is gotten in fraud and robbery of the dues of the King of Spain. Nevertheless, they forbear not to carry away great store thereof—indeed, all the silver at Brazil and Angola comes from that place.

This river of *Plata*,[1] or "silver", is so called because it flows at the foot of the mountain of *Potosi*,[2] whence is gotten most of the silver that comes from the West Indies. There these merchants sell their slaves at good prices, and bring

[1] The Rio de la Plata is merely the estuary of the Paraná, the Uruguay, and other great rivers. It was first discovered in 1515 by Juan Diaz de Solis, and then called Rio de Solis. The name La Plata was given to it by Sebastian Cabot.

[2] The famous mountain of Potosi, in Bolivia, in lat. 19 deg. 36 min. S., 14 degrees at least north of the La Plata estuary; it is the water-shed of the Pilcomayo river, which feeds the Paraná and ultimately the Rio de la Plata. Potosi down to 1846 yielded no less than £300,000,000 sterling in silver. At this time (1611) the town contained 160,000 inhabitants, but now not more than 11,000. For its history, see D. Vicente Ballivian y Rojas' *Bolivian Archives*.

away only silver; then they go and fill up with sugars at Brazil. Throughout all the dominions of the King of Spain, especially on this side the Cape, slaves are in great demand—I mean in America, not in Africa, for those in Brazil have need of them for their sugars, and there is no mill but has more than a hundred of them at work; likewise they require them for their other works. They like one *Cafre* slave, that is, an African, better than three of Brazil, the latter not being so strong as those of Angola and Cape Verd, and willing rather to die than do aught contrary to their mind, albeit they are a cowardly and feeble folk. But the greatest profit that is made of these slaves is in taking them to the West Indies direct, for there they fetch high prices; and in exchange there are gotten gold, silver, or fine pearls or cochineal. The Portuguese have also another trade to Guinea and to *Congo*, where they obtain ivory (called by them *Morfie*[1]) in great abundance, also cottons and long pepper (called by them *Maniguete*[2]) and slaves. There the natives are exceedingly fond of iron and all sorts of hardware.

On the same coast are the islands of S. Thomas, of the Prince and Anabon,[3] where they (the Portuguese) carry on a traffic in ginger, sugars, cotton, and slaves. There is also *la Mina*,[4] where is a castle in their service, and a great trade

[1] Port. *marfim*.

[2] See Col. Yule's note in *Cathay, etc.*, p. 88, and G. de Orta, ff. 50-52, from which it appears that *manigueta* or *maligueta* was sometimes applied to species of cardamoms; at others, as here, to Ethiopic pepper. Col. Yule states that Columbus calls the Guinea coast *Costa de Manigueta*.

[3] All these islands were discovered in the voyage of João de Santarem and Pedro de Escobar (1470-1): St. Thomas on that saint's day (21st December 1470), Annobon on New Year's Day, and the I. do Principe on the 17th January 1471. The last, accordingly, was named after St. Anthony, but was afterwards called "Do Principe", because the king's eldest son had assigned to him, as his appanage, the duty on the sugars grown in the island (Major, *Discoveries of P. Henry*).

[4] Now generally called El-mina. It was discovered on the voyage last mentioned in 1470. The castle was called S. Jorge da Mina

is carried on with the country folk in gold and slaves. They have also the islands of Cape Verd, where they traffic in slaves, bartering for them iron and other cheap metals and hardware. It is the same all along the coast of Africa, on both sides of the Cape; the greatest wealth is that of slaves, whether at Mozembique, Sofala, or *la Mina*, where gold and ivory are also found. Insomuch that the vast number of slaves taken thence every year, and carried to America and Portugal, is a marvellous thing indeed, without counting those that remain in the country in the service of the Portuguese and the kings of that coast; moreover, within and about those lands the greatest tribute that is obtained of the people consists of these slaves. For of a certain number of children, the father and mother are bound to give some to their kings, who sell them. And even the fathers and mothers sell their offspring for their own profit; in such wise that there is a traffic in human beings there as in cattle here. These slaves are esteemed the strongest, most robust, courageous, faithful, and obedient in the world, so are they thus highly prized. They are all negroes, and the Portuguese call them *Cafres*. Such as are the issue of Portuguese and Cafres they call *Mulastres*. There are certain parts of the country where the slaves are better, and more esteemed for their good temper.

In all these foreign lands there is no Portuguese, however poor, whether man or woman, but has his two or three slaves, who win their master's bread, owing him a certain portion of every day's time, and supporting themselves to boot. It would be impossible for the Spaniards and Portuguese to inhabit those lands and to make them worth the possession but for the energies and service of the slaves; for

(Major, *P. Henry*, p. 200). It fell into the hands of the Dutch in 1638, and was long their headquarters on the Guinea coast. Recently (in 1872) it was transferred to Great Britain (*inter alia*) in exchange for her rights in Sumatra.

Spain is but small in extent, and poorly furnished with men in comparison of the territories she holds and the vast traffic she maintains with so much trouble and travail. The possessions of the Portuguese, as well on this side the Cape of Good Hope, at Angola, Guinea, and the adjacent islands, as in Brazil, are held in a different manner from the East Indies: for in the former places they are sovereign lords for the most part, like the Spaniards in the West Indies, without other competitors, having fortresses both on the coasts and within the country, which mostly belongs to them, or is being continually conquered by them. There are Portuguese lords that have their noble mansions there, and till and cultivate their domains, and manufacture sugar, just as they would here. Toward the River of S. Vincent[1] there are gold mines conquered by them, whence they already draw some profit. Wherefore, Brazil and Angola are vastly profitable to the King of Spain, with little cost and little hazard, the navigation being easy and safe; and, moreover, these countries relieve Spain of her fruits and merchandise: for the King of Spain permits none of the fruits of Spain to be planted or sown there.

CHAPTER XVII.

Of the traffic at Mozembique, Sofala, Coüesme, Melinde, Mombase, Socotera, and other places.—Of the siege of Mozembique, and what happened there.

With regard to the traffic of Mozambic, Sofala, Coüesme, and other places, I will speak first of *Mozambic*,[2] whence very

[1] A small river to the north of Sierra Leone, in lat. 9 deg. 30 min. N.

[2] Mozambique, discovered by V. da Gama, 1498. The first captain, Duarte de Mello (1505), built a fort, which was replaced by a more imposing structure in 1557. It was visited by Varthema (1507) and Barbosa (before 1517).

rich cargoes are brought to Goa, chiefly of slaves or Cafres, which are carried everywhere; but besides them, ivory, and ebony the blackest and most excellent in the world; and note that the Portuguese call it *pan de Mozambic*, meaning the wood of that country; there is also some ambergris. This place is of vast importance to the King of Spain, as well for the commodities which he draws therefrom, as that it serves him greatly in his government and navigation. For it is an island, a fortress, and a haven, well adapted for a refuge to ships on the outward voyage from Portugal to Goa, after they have passed the Cape of Good Hope. So that all that are afflicted by storm, disease, scarcity, or other ills take refuge there. You might call it a sentinel or a bulwark at the entering in of the Indies, or a kind of hostelry for the refreshing of the Portuguese, worn out with a long and toilsome voyage, when they have been for so long time at sea without touching land, sometimes spending seven or eight months amid such heat and calms as attend the passage of the line (especially about the coast of Guinea, which is exceeding intemperate and unhealthy); hence are produced the many ailments of scurvy and pestilential fevers, whereof full many die. Insomuch that it is no wonder they are glad enough to fetch some port for their refreshment, and there is none nearer than that of Mozambic, seeing they are under orders not to make land ere they get there: for their ships are so great and draw so many fathoms of water that they cannot touch at the nearer ports which are in their service. Wherefore, when they go to others, it is when they are forced thither by tempest against their will, and then most often they lose themselves, or at least their voyage.

Thus is it for them great joy to arrive there, after having doubled the tempestuous Cape of Good Hope and passed that dangerous land of Natal, which none do without meeting with storms and other accidents which dismast their ships, opening the seams, and breaking the yards or rudders, and sometimes both. At this favourable spot, Mozambic, the King of Spain keeps a hospital and a magazine to furnish necessaries to the fleets, and it is for this sole consideration that he has the place so well fortified and garrisoned, rather than for the profits which he draws from the trade. Without it, it would be exceeding difficult to make the outward voyage to the Indies. In like manner it is convenient for them on the homeward voyage to make the island of St. Helena.

The Hollanders having remarked[1] how profitable this place was to the Portuguese, and what trouble it would cause them to lose it, resolved to take it, and laid siege to it twice, once for the space of three months. The first occasion was in the year 1607, the second in 1609. The first siege[2] was carried on by eight large vessels; but they could not take it, and only lost a large number of men: albeit they took the island and the unenclosed part of the town, which they

[1] The Dutch had visited the place at least twice before the sieges, viz., in 1601 and 1604. Van der Hagen arrived on the 17th April 1604 with eight ships, and would have laid siege to the island but for the expected arrival of the Portuguese fleet. The soundings and notes of the fortifications taken on this reconnoitre were used for the two sieges.

[2] Paul van Caerden left the Texel with eight ships and 1,060 men on the 20th April 1606, and arrived before Mozambique on the 29th March 1607. He landed without difficulty, and entrenched a position at the Dominican convent. An attempt to effect a breach failed, owing to the strength of the walls and the weakness of the guns. Resort was then had to mining, but in this open working under screens was necessary, the soil being merely sand. They succeeded in getting within 15 or 16 feet of the walls, but the Portuguese destroyed the screens by grenades, and poured a deadly musketry fire upon the besiegers. During the siege, which continued to the end of May, the Portuguese suffered terribly from want of water, the population of the outer town having crowded into the fortress; as did the Dutch, from excessive heat and sickness. Van Caerden then demanded a ransom for the outer town, and a haughty reply being returned by the governor, D'Ataide, the Dutch proceeded to burn the whole outer town, including three churches, and to cut down the precious plantations of coco and other fruit trees. They also burnt three ships found in the harbour, and left the place on the 29th June.

burned on both occasions. The second siege[1] was by thirteen large vessels; but they fared no better. At the commencement they took a rich Portuguese carrack that was anchored before the fortress, and having pillaged it set it on fire. At that time the place was easy enough to take, but since then they have fortified it strongly, as they have all their other places in the Indies, since they have had the Hollanders and other foreigners there to disturb them. The Hollanders also lost there a big cannon, and a ship that was wrecked in setting sail out of the harbour.

Another misfortune also befell them during the siege, for

[1] Admiral Pieter Willemz Verhœven left Holland in Dec. 1607 with thirteen ships and 1,800 or 1,900 men. His instructions were to await and capture the outward-bound fleet of carracks, and the siege of Mozambique was entered upon, after a council of war, professedly *pour passer le temps*. On the 28th July 1608 he arrived in the harbour, and there found a carrack and two small ships. The carrack, with her crew of thirty-four men, surrendered to two Dutch yachts without striking a blow, and yielded a rich cargo of Spanish cloth, ivory, ebony, wine, and oil. Verhœven landed a force of 600 men, who took up a position, as before, at the Dominican convent, and used the same trenches by which Van Caerden had approached the fortress the year before. A demand for surrender was answered by Estevão d'Ataide with a sarcastic refusal: it would take better men than they to win his fortress, which was "not a cat that could be touched without mittens". The besieged again baffled the miners by their grenades and musketry, and on the 8th August made a sortie which inflicted serious loss on the advanced guard of the Dutch. A retreat was now ordered, and nothing remained but vengeance. Three deserters had joined the besieged, though the Dutch were aware of only one, whose surrender was demanded under threat of putting to death the whole crew of thirty-four Portuguese prisoners taken in the carrack. D'Ataide returned the spirited reply stated in the text below—the only one possible for a soldier and a man of honour. On the 17th August all the thirty-four (as the Dutch narrative admits, and not only six, as stated below in the text) were led out to the trenches in sight of the fortress and there shot down in cold blood. The outer town, or what remained of it, was then sacked and burnt; and on the 23rd Verhœven left the place, with a loss of thirty killed and eighty wounded, and with his own name tarnished by an act of ruthless barbarity.

three of their men, being malcontent, deserted them, and gaining the land, betook themselves to the Portuguese in the fortress, and gave the Hollanders vast trouble: for, but for these three traitors, they had infallibly taken the place, as I heard afterwards. The garrison were exhausted and were resolved to surrender, but these three bade them take courage, giving them to understand that the Hollanders were disposed to raise the siege for want of supplies both of munitions of war and provisions: and this was true enough. They said further that what had moved them to come over to them was their desire to become Catholics, and that they had been shipped against their will. This was false, for they were three good-for-nothing scoundrels, as I myself know, for I have since seen and spoken with them. The Portuguese made great ado about having won these three men, and especially the Jesuits thought they had done great things in the conversion of these knaves; but it was all a make-believe, for they had no devotion or affection for the Catholic religion. What had, in fact, caused them to desert was, that they could not endure fatigue, and were not good for any work; also they thought they would become somebodies among the Portuguese, who indeed took a great pride in the three rascals. The Hollanders, seeing they were betrayed by men that had informed their enemies of the straits wherein they were, resolved to raise the siege. They were also afraid of the coming of the carracks from Portugal, whose time was drawing nigh, for they could have burned their vessels; and in fact they did arrive seven or eight days after the siege was raised.

The Hollanders, before their arrival at Mozambic, had taken a ship coming from Portugal, the prisoners whereof they still had, and to get back their three men they bethought them of an expedient, and a cruel and barbarous one it was. They sent to ask a parley of the governor, who was named *Don Estevan*, a brave and gallant lord, offering to give up all the Portuguese prisoners they had, provided those three were surrendered to them; otherwise they would put six of the chief prisoners to death in his sight. The governor made answer that the ordinances of war forbade him to give up men that had come willingly to them in order to serve their king, or to expose them to the discretion of enemies that would put them to death; that he would rather be their executioner himself. As for the Portuguese that they had, they were prisoners of war, therefore they could put a price for their ransom, which for their part they would fully pay: should they, however, slay them in cold blood, that would not be the act of gallant men of war. They were for a whole day at this parley without coming to any conclusion. Seeing this, the Hollanders resolved to put to death the six Portuguese, who were all married men, rich, and some of the principal ship's officers, such as pilots, master, etc. So they bound them with ropes, their hands behind their backs, and led them outside their trenches, holding the rope's-end within the trench. The poor men cried for the mercy and pity of the governor to move him to relent; but he was contented to exhort them to die with resolution, saying that he could not surrender the three Hollanders, for that God and the king forbade it, seeing they had given themselves up to be converted; whereupon the Hollanders slew those six men with arquebuse-shots in the sight of their fellows, and then raised the siege and departed to Sunda.[1] As for

[1] The authorities for the sieges of Mozambique are:—For the first, the Voyage of Van Caerden, in *Rec. des Voy.*, tom. iii; *Arch. Port. Or.*, Fasc 1, pt. ii, No. 16. As to the second, the Voyage of Verhœven, *Rec. des Voy.*, tom. iv; *Arch. Port. Or.*, *ib.*, No. 17; and as to both, *Faria y Sousa*, tom. iii, pt. ii, ch. vii, and especially a full description by a Spaniard who served under the Portuguese, entitled, *Cercos de Mocambique Defendidos por Don Estevan de Atayde Capitan General y Gouvernador de aquella Plaça. Escritos por Antonio Duran, soldado antiguo de la India.* Em Madrid, 1633. This rare work is in the British Museum, and is noted by J. F. da Silva in his *Dicc. Bibliog.*

the three Hollanders, they were afterwards brought to Goa, where they were made but little of; on the contrary, they were subjected to a thousand insults, and were sent back to Portugal with us. One of them was in the same carrack with me, and was scolded and buffeted by all on board. He told me he was a native of Switzerland, and that he was with the late Monsieur de Mercure[1] when he died in Germany on his return from Hungary, and that one of his companions, after being taken by the Turks, came by land to Goa, where they joyfully met again.

But to return to Mozambic, it is a little island,[2] at the end and point whereof is the fortress which is toward the east and defends the harbour. The island is within a great bay full of shoals and banks, and the passage is very narrow and difficult of entrance, having these shoals and banks on either side, insomuch that you require pilots of the island, and to

The miserable condition of the place after the sieges is described by Mocquet, who arrived there a fortnight after Verhœven left (*Voy.*, p. 229, *et seq.*).

[1] Philippe, Duc de Mercœur (b. 1558). He was chief of the League after the death of the Guises in 1588, and submitted to Henri IV in 1598. In 1601 he commanded the army of Rudolf II against the Turks in Hungary. Returning from this campaign, he died at Nuremberg, 1602.

[2] The following description of Mozambique is given by Capt. W. F. Owen, who took part in the Admiralty Survey of Africa, 1821-4 :—"The harbour of Mozambique is formed by a deep inlet of the sea, five miles and a half broad and six long, receiving the waters of three inconsiderable rivers at its head. At the entrance are three small islands, which, together with reefs and shoals, render the anchorage perfectly safe in the worst weather. Of these islands, that of Mozambique, on which stands the city, is formed of coral, very low and narrow, and scarcely one mile and a half in length. It is situated nearly in the centre of the inlet, and just within the line of the two points that form its extremities. The other two islands, St. George to the northward, and St. Iago to the southward, lie abreast of one another, about 1,500 fathoms distant, and nearly three miles outside that of Mozambique. They are also of coral, surmounted by a rich mould covered with verdure and trees, but without inhabitants" (Owen's *Narrative*, i, pp. 187-8).

keep the lead continually in hand. The entrance is in a slanting course; but with a good pilot and in fair weather you can enter in all safety, and find good bottom. But there is no port or harbour in all the Indies where the Portuguese have lost so many vessels as in this bay. To enter it you must keep your head—that is, your prow—to the west, and thus you have the north on your right hand and the south on your left. On the north is the mainland, and toward the south are two small uninhabited islands side by side, at about a league from Mozambic. The one nearest is called *S. Jacques;* and the other, which you see but little of, as it is behind the former, is called *S. George.* Betwixt the island of Mozambic and the mainland there is only half a league of sea to cross. On the south side it is all shoals and sands, but on the north is the harbour, where there is good bottom. The island is very small, being no more than three-quarters of a league in length and half-a-quarter broad. It is equally peopled in all parts, not being in the form of an enclosed town, and having only the fortress, which is of fair proportions. The soil of itself is very sterile, and there is no fresh water save what is kept in some cisterns, and it is brought from the mainland in boats. Within the fortress there may be some five or six churches, chapels, and monasteries. Vessels can approach the island as near as they like, for the coast is quite safe, and has a good sandy bottom; but they cannot sail around the island, but only on the north side, for the south is beset with shoals and reefs.

This island is on the coast of Melinde, or Ethiopia, about 18 degrees from the equinoctial, toward the Antarctic Pole: it is distant from Goa about 900 or 1,000 leagues, and 600 or 700 from the Cape of Good Hope. It is low-lying and very sandy, and the air is very unwholesome. Provisions are brought from the mainland, where cŏco-trees, oranges, citrons, bananas, and other Indian fruits are grown. There are vast numbers of cattle, such as oxen, cows, sheep, pigs, goats, etc. All these animals are exceeding cheap, and like those of the island of St. Lawrence.

In Brazil and at Mozambic hog's flesh is deemed the most dainty and delicate of all; and the physicians order it for the sick, forbidding all other. There is also good store of fowls, very good and delicate, but all of black plumage; and the flesh is the same, whether cooked or raw.[1] This is strange to those who have not been used to see and eat it; it seems as if the flesh had been cooked with some black dye, and the soup is the same.

Before the Portuguese came to the island of Mozambic it was not inhabited,[2] as much on account of its small size as of its want of fresh water; and to this day it is inhabited only by Portuguese, Metices, and Cafres of the mainland, most of those being slaves of the Portuguese.

Of the neighbouring peoples of the mainland, some are their friends, others their enemies, with whom they wage a very cruel war continually. The Portuguese have no spot of ground in all the Indies so bad for victuals and residence as that, for all their provisions must come from Goa, and the viceroy allows no goods to be brought from elsewhere, save some petty commodities brought in barques from adjacent places. All sorts of merchandise are in request there, and every year the viceroy of Goa sends thither a number of vessels charged with Indian and Portuguese goods, which return laden with slaves, ivory, ebony, wood, and a quantity of purified gold that is found in the rivers. Nevertheless, were it not for the touching of the ships from Portugal there, they would never inhabit the place; but it is of vast importance to them in this behalf. They are also continually

[1] Only the bones are black, though Linschoten too says the same of the flesh. See Dr. Burnell's note in *Linsch.*, i, 25.

[2] Not so. When V. da Gama arrived, he found Mozambique a town of importance, under a sheikh, and the island of S. Jorge also inhabited.

increasing their conquests on the mainland.[1] From Mozambic they carry some vastly pretty mats to Goa, and all the merchandise that comes thence is exceeding cheap.

It would be difficult, nay impossible, for me to distinguish all the nations that are between the Cape of Good Hope and the Arabian Gulf or Straits of Mecca, by reason that they have divers names, and yet are all alike, resembling the negroes of Cape Verd or of Guinea. The people, as well of Mozambic as of the adjacent mainland, are all Cafres, albeit of divers kingdoms and languages. They carry on a cruel war among themselves, for they slay, kidnap, eat, and sell one another for slaves. They are without faith or religion, and should nowise be trusted, being all cheats and perfidious knaves. They go all naked, without even covering the privy parts: in disposition they are exceeding clownish and brutal, suited to labour like beasts; nor do they mind being slaves, even saying that their condition should be none other. Fathers and mothers sell their own children; they eat of everything like brute beasts; they are without ambition, yet passionate, disdainful, treacherous, and mischievous. They stink abominably, and even worse when they are heated.

On the same coast, about six score leagues from Mozambic towards the Cape, is the kingdom of Sofala,[2] where the Portuguese have a kind of fortress, but of little consequence. It is under the government of the captain of Mozambic, who keeps a factor and a merchant there to treat and traffic with the country people. The captain formerly resided at Sofala, and not at Mozambic, and even now bears the title of

[1] They made wars and expeditions, chiefly to get possession of the inland mines, but never to this day have they reduced the surrounding country to obedience.

[2] The fort of Sofálah was built in 1505, and is said to have been a good one in 1508 (*Varthema*, 290). For long the captain resided six months at Mozambique, and finally altogether there (João dos Santos, *Hist. d'Ethiope*, 1684, p. 15). For a modern description of the place (1823), see Boteler's *Voyage*, i, 346.

governor of Sofala, and not of Mozambic: the former being one of their ancient settlements, he has more pride in being called governor of the one than of the other. Some have held the opinion that this Sofala is Ophir,[1] whence Solomon drew his gold for building the Temple (though others will have it towards the golden Chersonese or Malaca, and China; others even at Peru), and there are manifest signs that great quantities were aforetime drawn from mines near the Portuguese fortress. The factor there collects good store of gold, which he sends to Mozambic; and all the gold the Portuguese have comes from trafficking with the kings and peoples of that land. For the Portuguese themselves fish not (*ne peschent*) for it in the rivers, but the people of the place only. There are factors, too, at other places than Sofala, both for the gold and for other merchandise. About thirty leagues from Mozambic, between Sofala and Mozambic, is a river in the country of Couesme,[2] otherwise called the "Black River", where they find much gold, purified, clean, and in dust: this they call gold sand; and it is held that the gold of Sofala and of the river of Couesme is the purest and finest in the whole world. These mines of Sofala and Monomotapa are indeed marvellous, being all of fine gold in dust or gold sand, which cannot be more refined. I have seen a branch of massive purified gold of a cubit's length, branched like coral, that was found thus in its natural state in the river of Couesme. This shows that gold is in veins in the earth, and has spread like water, and the hardest gold has remained compact in the form of the mould. That piece of gold was carefully preserved, and was sent in the ship wherein I embarked at Goa, to be taken to Portugal as a present to the Queen of Spain.

[1] So Milton: "And Sofala (thought Ophir)", (*P. L.*, xi, 400). Camoens (x, 124) says of the Chersonnese:

> "Aurea por epithéto lhe ajuntarão;
> Alguns que fosse Ophir imaginarão."

[2] Cuama, the Zambesi, also called Rio Negro by the Portuguese.

At the time of my departure from the Indies the Cafres round about Mozambic were in active warfare against the Portuguese; and the viceroy then in office at Goa, in passing by Mozambic, had left there his nephew and a number of men to carry on the war and to make conquests and discoveries. This young man, who was a new comer, wishing to show his gallantry, made attempt with some galiots and other vessels to go further up the river of Couesme than any Portuguese had yet been; but he never returned, and remained there with the most of his men, while the rest with great trouble got back. The viceroy hearing of this, was exceeding vexed, and resolving to be avenged, he employed the services of the captain and governor of Mozambic, who was the same that had the command during the two sieges, and was one of the bravest and gallantest lords to be met with among the Portuguese, a friend of God and man, and especially of foreigners. He was called *Don Esteuan de Zaida.*[1] He had won a marvellous fame among his countrymen, and even the Indians, for having sustained the two sieges with the small forces at his command, taken unawares as he was: for which services he looked for conspicuous reward at the hands of his king, inasmuch as captains after three years' service usually return rich, with a hundred thousand cruzados, more or less, in their pockets, gotten

[1] D. Estevão d'Ataide, for his services rendered and great personal loss incurred during the sieges, had his term of office prolonged, with the title of Capitão Mór. On making the expedition up the Zambesi, referred to below, d'Ataide effected an arrangement with the viceroy, L. de Tavora, whereby he was to have for himself a considerable share in the traffic of the forts he was to establish and in the produce of the mines. This contract, on being reported, was annulled by the King of Spain, as being beyond the powers of a viceroy. D'Ataide was ordered to Goa, where an inquiry was instituted, with directions that he should make restitution of all profits made by him. The result does not appear. Probably it ended in nothing (*Livro das Monçoes*, vol. ii). D'Ataide died at Goa, and was buried in the church of St. Paul (Botelho, *Africa Oriental*, 1855, p. 322).

as well out of their dealings and traffickings as by means of their larcenies and underhand practisings; but he through these two sieges had spent all his own fortune instead of making any profit. Wherefore he was continued for another year in this government beyond the ordinary three years.

The viceroy then advised his council that an enterprise must be made upon these Cafres, and a naval armament sent thither, whereof this *Don Esteuan* should be general, as he was experienced in those parts, having made this long sojourn of four years there. Their intention was to go far up this river of Couesme, then to land and to get possession of these gold and silver mines that are between Angola and Sofala, and that the Portuguese of Angola should be warned of their coming and should join them at a rendezvous, and that they should proceed together thence to the conquest. For this purpose the drum was beaten in Goa for all to come that would. To these a year's pay—that is, 72 perdos (each worth 32½ sols, or 25 sols of France)—was advanced. I was greatly importuned to go, for all foreigners are permitted. But I feared lest they should leave me there to guard their mines without being allowed to touch the contents. They started the same day on which we embarked on our return: for they set out from Goa for Mozambic at one time in the year only, viz., about January, February, or March, sooner or later, because of the *Muesons*, or Monsons, whereof they have to take good heed. On returning to Goa they set out about the month of August or September. From Goa they carry to Mozambic all sorts of European and Indian merchandise, such as wheat, rice, silks, cotton cloth, spices, etc. But this commerce is not free to all the world: the viceroy and captain alone can take into partnership whom they will. This trade is one of the best and most useful in all the Indies, for they sell what they like and all they bring, and carry back other good merchandise, as I have said above.

On the coast of Melinde the Portuguese have another fortress, called *Bombasse* or *Mombase*,[1] where they carry on a great trade; but they consider not this fort to be of great importance: it is between Mozambic and the Straits of Mecca. Then, at the entering in of this strait, toward the coast of *Abexis*, otherwise of Prester John,[2] at twenty leagues from the mainland—that is, the Cape of *Gardafunt*—is an exceeding great and fair island, named *Socotera*.[3] The Cape of Gardafunt is the nearest to it, advancing far into the sea, forming on one side the Strait of Mecca, which is the limit of the coast of Africa and Melinde. This island is at the entrance of the gulf, but leaning toward the *Abexis*. It is about fifty leagues in circuit, well peopled, and has a king of its own, who holds it of the Cherife King of Arabia. The people are Mahometans, and a mixed race of Abexis and Arabs, but they call themselves Arabs, and preserve the manners, customs, and language of that people. The land abounds with cattle and fruits, and the people trade at Goa, where they are well received—better indeed than the Arabs proper, who durst not come thither without a passport, and that they rarely seek. These Socoterans traffic all along the coast of Arabia, and thence to Goa and elsewhere, with passports from the Portuguese like the other Indians. They are habited in the Arab fashion. They carry back the merchan-

[1] Mombasa, discovered by Vasco da Gama in 1498; yielded up to D. Alvarez Cabral in 1500; attacked and burned by F. de Almeida in 1505; besieged by Nuno da Cunha, 1528; surrendered to the Turks in 1586. Again taken and burnt by the Portuguese in 1588; retaken by the tribes in 1589, and again by the Portuguese in 1596. Their possession lasted till 1720. It was held by the British from 1824 to 1826, but is now nominally subject to Muscat. (For description, see Burton's *Zanzibar*, ii, 28.)

[2] For the history of Prester John, see Col. Yule's article in *Encyc. Britannica*.

[3] Socotora has never been a coveted possession. Albuquerque built a fort upon it, but this was soon abandoned. It has been recently annexed to our Indian Empire.

dise of India to Arabia. Their island produces a marvellous quantity of dates, which they bring to Goa, selling a pound of the finest and best in the world for a liard: a pound of the dearest at Goa is worth only two liards. They have also much rice; they bring also very pretty *Esteres,* or mats made of palm leaves; large quantities of incense, which is so common at Goa that they cover the outsides of their vessels with it, as we do here with tar or pitch. They possess also good store of aloes wood.[1] They are a very courteous people, but not to be trusted. Two English ships[2] had once cast anchor there for refreshment and traffic, and had been well received of them, and had been for nine or ten days on friendly terms; but at length the king had a fancy to play them a bad turn, and feigned to give a feast in their honour, as he had before this done to others, in order to entrap and slay them, and seize their ship: so the said Englishmen told me afterwards at Goa.[3] But the English, whether out of distrust or on what other ground I know not, were advised of it in time, and full speedily withdrew. This island produces also some horses, so that on the whole it is in great estimation in the Indies. All that come thence to traffic at Goa are either Arabs, or at least have the same manners and dress, both men and women.

[1] The best aloes is known by the name *Aloe Socotrina* (see Yule, *Gloss.*). Aloes-*wood* is a mistake of Pyrard's. That is an entirely different thing, *Aloexylon agallochum*, or "eagle-wood", the aloes of the Old Testament. Bluteau, in his *Vocabulario*, makes the same confusion.

[2] The *Dragon* and *Hector*, in April 1608. See journal of the *Hector*, Capt. Wm. Hawkins (Hawkins, *Voy.*, 383).

[3] They had been captured by the Portuguese at Surat. See further, ch. xx.

CHAPTER XVIII.

Of the kingdom of Ormus: a description of it, and of the punishment of a Prince of Ormus at Goa.

Next, at the commencement of the coast of India, is Ormus, a very great kingdom, distant from Goa 500 leagues, near Persia, at the entrance and over against the straits of the Persian Sea. In that sea is a little island (under the altitude of 26 degrees or thereabouts to the north of the equinoctial) of only three leagues circuit, called Ormus, from the town, for the island used to be called *Gerun*.[1] It is distant about three leagues from the mainland of Persia, and some ten from that of Arabia. The island and town are held and possessed by the Portuguese,[2] who have built a fortress there, good and well garrisoned. This island after Goa is the richest, and has the largest revenues of any in the Indies possessed by the Portuguese, for it is a great mart

[1] The ancient city of Ormuz was on the mainland. Owing to repeated Tartar invasions, it was removed to the opposite island, *Jerún* (old Persian form *Garún*; the Gerum of Camoens, and Gerun of the text). On this trachytic rock, as unpromising a site as the lagoons of Venice, arose and flourished (from the end of 13th to the 17th century) a city whose fame in the East almost rivalled that of Venice in the West.

The relative positions of Old and New Ormuz are seen in Col. Yule's map, *Marco Polo*, i, 108. The ruins of the ancient city are described by Sir L. Pelly (*ib.*, p. 105). As to the aspect of the island city at the present day, see Palgrave (*Cent. and East. Arabia*, ch. xiii).

[2] Ormuz was possessed by the Portuguese from 1507 to 1622, when it was taken by Shah Abbas, with the aid of the English E. I. Company, William Baffin, the navigator, losing his life in the operations. On its re-annexation to Persia, the insular site was no longer required, and a new emporium was built at Gombroon, on the opposite shore—thenceforward also named Bunder Abbas; but this place never equalled in prosperity the famous city, founded upon an absolutely sterile islet, which was to Milton the type of Oriental splendour.

of merchandise where all goods are landed, principally the wealth of Persia; and besides that, the merchandises of India are brought thither in great quantity for the furnishing of Persia, Syria, and all the Levant.

The merchandises that come thither are all valuable, for it is the staple and landing-place for all goods from Persia, Arabia, Armenia, Turkey, Europe, etc., which are brought thence overland by caravan; likewise all Indian goods are landed there. From Ormus to Goa come, firstly, the fine pearls from the fishery at an island of the Gulf, called *Baharen*,[1] toward the coast of Arabia beyond Ormus. They are the fairest, biggest, and cleanest of any found in the East Indies. The fishery produces a vast quantity; hence comes the name given to these of "Oriental pearls". Secondly, there comes thence much of that silver money that is called *Larins*,[2] the finest silver in the world: these are called larins of Ormus. Thither, too, are brought quantities of Persian silks, both in the piece and worked, and in other forms. Next, what we here call Turkey carpets, and the people of those parts Persian and Ormus carpets, the most exquisite and the best made in the world. Then there are horses of Arabia, Persia, and Ormus, the handsomest and most beautifully caparisoned possible; being all covered with gold, silver, silk, and pearls, in the Persian and Ormus mode, as also in the Portuguese: they fetch a high price at Goa.[3] Then come all

[1] *El-Bahrayn*, the "two-sea island" (as Burton explains); the seat of the pearl fishery of the Persian Gulf.

[2] See vol. i, pp. 232-4.

[3] All the best horses at Goa, as now at Bombay, came from the Persian Gulf, and were shipped at Ormuz. Cæsar Frederick travelled in a vessel from Ormuz, carrying eighty horses to Goa. After the Portuguese conquest, and for the greater part of the 16th century, horses paid a heavy import duty at Goa. This duty was afterwards remitted, and in order further to stimulate the trade, all goods brought in ships carrying twenty horses (*C. Frederick*, p. 4), and latterly ten (*Wm. Barret*), were allowed to come into Goa free of duty.

kinds of sugars, conserves, marmalades,[1] raisins or dried grapes of Persia and, Ormus, and much big dates which are very excellent. Next, many watered camlets[2] of Persia and Ormus, of all colours, made of the wool of large sheep that have not curled fleeces like ours. Of it they make also good store of cloaks and capes, called by the Indians *Mansaus*, and by the Portuguese "Ormus *cambalis*":[3] they are made of the same wool, in bands of different colours, each four inches wide. Everyone takes these to sea for a protection from the rain. The tissue is the same as of cloth. They make also other cloaks, capes, and mantles of felt, like our hats, which resist the rain well.

As for the drugs, aromatic, medicinal, and others, it were difficult to specify all that come from Ormus, whither so many are brought from elsewhere, nor to tell all the merchandises brought from the Indies and Europe. In short, it is the common proverb in those lands, that if the world were an egg, Ormus would be the yolk[4]; for it is the best place in the world, whether for its fertility (that is, of the rest of the kingdom, for the island itself is desert and barren of all produce) or for the convenience of its situation for the traffic of all parts. The merchandise and goods of all the world must pass there and pay tribute to the Portuguese, who search all the ships to see if any merchandise is being carried

[1] Port. *marmelada*, *i.e.*, made of quinces, from *marmelo*, a quince; in France, about this time, or later, also used of various *entremets*. Thus we have in *Le Patissier François* (Amst., 1655), "Marmelade ou œufs brouillez au verjus sans beurre"—"avec beurre"—"à la crême"—"au fromage", etc.

[2] So called because originally made of camel's hair. Fr. *camelot*.

[3] *Kambala*, the modern Anglo-Indian "cumbley", a coarse woollen wrapper or blanket. About this period it was Anglicised as *camball*, but this form did not survive.

[4] Another proverb made the world a ring and Ormuz the gem:—

"Si terrarum orbis, quâquâ patet, annulus esset,
Illius Ormusium gemma decusque foret."
(Sir T. Herbert, *Travels*, p. 105.)

that is contraband and prohibited by their king. But that is the place where the governors fill their pockets, inasmuch as they will for money let everything pass. These governors aspire to no other dignity than that of viceroy, and they go there solely to that end. For they enrich themselves in marvellous wise in the three years of their office from the heavy dues and tolls they exact upon all things: to do which with impunity, they make great presents to the viceroy. He that was governor there while I was at Goa was called *Don Pedro de Coustigno,*[1] a Portuguese lord of a very great house. He had a brother at Goa, also a great lord, that had made a very wealthy marriage, and was called *Don Diego de Coustigno.* He had bought the government of Cochin for his life—for that is the only office in all the Indies that is for life, the captain there having no other profit but his pay and his honour, because there is a *Viador de Fasienda,* as at Goa, who is general overseer of all that belongs to the king, and is changed every three years, so that the captain touches nothing.[2]

But to return to this governor of Ormuś: it was said at the time that he was returning from his three years worth more than 600,000 crowns. He returned to Portugal with our fleet. At Goa, with his benefactions, liberality, and alms, he made

[1] From the *Livro das Monçoes* it appears that Pedro Coutinho was captain of Ormuz from 1604 to 1607. He was succeeded by Henrique de Noronha (*v. s.*, p. 78). As stated below, he remained at Goa till the end of 1609, living with great display—probably in the hope of succeeding to the government of India in case of a casual vacancy.

[2] This is a mistake as regards Diogo Coutinho, who was both captain and *vedor da fazenda* at Cochin (*Liv. das Monç.*, ii, 119). This officer was among the few at this day whose public spirit rose above personal aggrandisement. In 1604 his services at the bar of Goa against the Dutch are warmly commended to the king by the municipality of Goa (*Arch. Port. Or.*. Fasc. i, No. 13). He remained captain of Cochin throughout the governments of De Tavora and Azevedo, freely expending his private wealth in the equipment of ships, etc. He won the respect and confidence of both these governors, and is highly eulogised by the historian Bocarro (*Dec. XIII, passim*).

a show like the viceroy, but not in dignity and honour: for the viceroy *Don André Furtado de Mendosa* and he were on any but good terms. Don André, holding the office of viceroy, had asked him to lend 50,000 perdos for the king's service, promising to pay him back in Portugal or in the Indies, whichever he wished; the other refused, and when the viceroy replied that it was to provide pay for a naval armament against the Malabars, this governor said that he was a man to equip an army and lead it himself for the king's service, and not to give his money to another. This was the cause that on their return these two embarked not in the same ship: the viceroy went first, intending to arrive before the other in Portugal, to get the better of him and thwart his designs; but he died on the way, as I shall tell hereafter. When these governors return they carry no large cargoes of merchandise, but only pearls, precious stones, ambergris, musk, gold, silver, and other rare and precious things. When I left Goa, the son of the viceroy *Don Loyso Lorencio d'Establo,* who was aged only twelve or thirteen years, was already appointed to the government of Ormus, and was entering upon it.[1]

This island is exceeding sterile, having no fresh water: it is all the same as the island of Mayo, on the Cape Verd coast—for it is all rock-salt, which they use as salt. There is also saltpetre there.

The Kings of Ormus pay tribute to the King of Persia, and are in peace and friendship with the Portuguese. They are Mahometans, like the Persians, and they cause the eyes of their successors to be put out, like the Kings of Dealcan.[2]

[1] See above, pp. 78, 81.

[2] As to the Deccan, see above, p. 137. This barbarous practice is most frequently related of the kings of Ormus, *e.g.*, by Varthema (p. 96), Barbosa (p. 44), Linschoten (i, 46), and Teixeira (*Relaciones*; 1610, p. 40). The last named states that the eyes were scorched to blindness, not actually put out.

The people of Ormus are almost as black as the Moors of Ethiopia, and nowise resemble the Persians, who are fairer.

When some men of authority die at Ormus, their wives are obliged to mourn for them once a day, by the space of four consecutive weeks; there are also women paid to bewail the dead.

The inhabitants wear long shirts, girding them at the waist with a broad band of taffetas, as do many of the Indians and all the Arabs. On their heads they wear white turbans, diversified with many colours. Many of them wear rings in their noses. They speak Persian, and are much addicted to fornication, and above all to the unnatural sin. They love music and instruments of music.

Their arms are gilded Turkish bows, the strings whereof are of fine silk; they are of a very strong and well-set wood or of buffalo horn, and their arrows are neatly made of gilt canes. They are exceeding adroit in the use of the bow. They carry also iron clubs, well made and damascened.

It is now about ten or twelve years since the brother of the King of Ormus came to the Portuguese at Goa, in a ship laden with great wealth, to become a Christian, as he said: he had also some quarrel with his brother. He was received with all the honours possible, and had one of the finest houses in the town allotted to his use.[1]

After being some time at Goa, he asked the Portuguese to aid him to recover his share of the inheritance, giving a promise to transfer to them all he could recover, if they would give him a pension. The Portuguese sent a powerful army to the kingdom of Ormus, and made terms with the king

[1] Turun Sháh, the prince referred to, a younger brother of the reigning King of Ormus, for some years resided at Goa, where he petitioned the King of Spain to support him against his brother. The cause was referred to the High Court, with special instructions to decide the matter according to the best policy (*Liv. das Monç.*, i, 14, 15, 50).

that he should give up certain lands to his brother, which was done.

But it happened that this prince at Goa, who every day promised to become a Christian, and never did, committed sodomy with a young scholar, a Portuguese Metice; for which crime he was condemned to be burned by the office of the Inquisition at Goa. This sentence was carried out some four or five years since,[1] although the prince before his execution was converted, and baptised by the Jesuits; and notwithstanding that he offered 500,000 crowns to be spared, and, further, to build some churches in expiation of his sin. But all these promises were of little avail to move the Portuguese, who had in their possession already all he promised them.[2] Besides, he had been already rebuked and repri-

[1] *I.e.*, before 1611, the date of the first edition.

[2] The execution of this prince for the crime mentioned probably seemed to the King of Spain to be impolitic, and Pyrard has previously said (*supra*, p. 91) that the king was greatly incensed against Menezes for his conduct in the matter. In the Life of Menezes by Fr. Agostino de Santa Maria, prefixed to the latter's *Hist. da Fund. do Real Conv. de Sta Monicá* (Lisb., 1699), it is admitted that the High Court and all the notables of Goa were against the execution, and that slander attributed the archbishop's resolution to a desire to annex the prince's property. The biographer states that when the king wrote, the archbishop was able to show that the whole of the prince's property was in the Treasury. In his despatches, however, he nowhere openly reprobates the sentence; but in 1610, apparently with the policy of playing off claimants against those in possession, he issued letters patent reinstating the sons of Turun Sháh in all the rights and titles of their father (*Arch. Port. Or.*, Fasc. 6, No. 105).

The death of Turun Sháh is described by the Jesuit Guerreiro (*Relaçam, etc.*, 1609, f. 135*b*), and by the Carmelite Philippus a Sanct. Trinitate (Lat. ed., 1649, lib. v, c. i). Both these writers say that he was beheaded, not burnt. Guerreiro's account (curtailed) is as follows:—"On the sentence being communicated to him, a Father of the company went to speak to him of his soul's salvation. On a subsequent day he sought holy baptism. The Father obtained from the governor and the royal courts a respite of three days for his catechising, during which by day and night our Fathers were with him continually, and by turns catechising and instructing him in the matters of our faith. On the day

manded many times for this heinous vice, to which he had promised never to return: albeit he again fell thereinto, and so met with well-deserved punishment. As for the poor young Portuguese, he was put in a barrel and cast into the sea, for fear of scandal.

CHAPTER XIX.

Of the Kingdoms of Cambaye, Surat, and of the Grand Mogor; Diu, and the rest of the coast of India; Malabar, and the King of Tananor and his perfidy.

Having spoken of Ormus, I come in their order to Cambaye and Surat, whence comes the greatest and cheapest traffic of Goa, from which it is distant about 100 leagues to the north. This traffic is such that two or three times a year there come together from 300 to 400 vessels, called *Cafiles*,[1] of Cambaye, like the caravans of Aleppo. At Goa the whole city looks out for these Cafiles and fleets, as in Spain they await those from the Indies. And when they arrive not at their due season, every one is in apprehension of the Hollanders, or the Malabars, or the Cambayans themselves, who frequently stop them when ready to set out, as happened the year I left

fixed for the execution he walked forth from the prison with his eyes fixed upon the crucifix, the Misericordia following behind. The Padre Preposito and four other Fathers marched by his side. On reaching the place where he was to suffer, the Padre Preposito baptised him by the name of Sebastian, first putting to him all the requisite interrogatories, whereto he replied with the warmth of conviction. So he who could not attain an earthly kingdom, for which he had striven for the space of five or six years, in a moment attained the kingdom of heaven for his eternal possession."

[1] Port. *cafila*, the Ar. *kāfila*, a body or caravan of travellers; regularly used in Portuguese documents, as here, for a fleet of merchantmen under convoy (see Yule, *Gloss.*, *s. v.*; also in latter sense, *Liv. das Monç.*, i, 3, 334; iii, 228, 440).

Goa, and on many previous occasions: the fleet had been ready for more than two months, but was not allowed to proceed to Goa, insomuch that all were already crying famine. This was for a grievance the King, or Bascha, of Cambaye had against the viceroy of Goa, who had refused him something: for although this king holds of the Grand Mogor, as lord of all those lands, yet is he absolute in all things that prejudice not the Mogor's service.

When this fleet does arrive the joy of the merchants and the whole people is marvellous; and in truth it is a very pretty and pleasant sight to see so many sail together: but it is seldom that the Malabar corsairs fail to capture some of them. Every ship or galiot is worked by oars, so as to keep the coast, and to speed against the wind: they have all their own ensigns, and the livery of their several lords on their flags; and the merchants to whom they are consigned recognise them afar off. They have some war galiots for their escort, and when they arrive at Goa there is much cannonading from the town, the fortresses, and the viceroy's palace, before which they come to anchor, as do all the other vessels, for there is the *alfandeque*, and the warehouse and the royal steelyard. There are but few of the inhabitants of Goa, whether Christians or other, that have not a share in this fleet, or at least in some of the ships at Goa and the other ports of the Portuguese; for along with this fleet come many ships from Cambaye, Surat, and other places.

As for the merchandise which they bring, it consists in the first place of *Anil* or *Indigue*,[1] which is a violet-blue dye, obtained at Cambaye and Surat, whither it is brought from all the neighbouring country, and prepared in those two towns alone. This merchandise is greatly dealt in, and much prized even by the English and Hollanders; and the principal cause that they keep their factors there is to get

[1] Port. *anil*, from Ar. *al-nil*, "the blue", Sansk. *nila*, *i.e.*, indigo; the latter being the Greek Ἰνδικόν, (see Yule, *Gloss.*, under both heads).

these dyes. Secondly, they bring good stores of precious stones, not of the fine sorts, such as diamonds and rubies, but other kinds, which they know how to cut skilfully, and to work into a thousand pretty things. Next, much rock-crystal, iron, copper, rock-alum, a vast quantity of the best wheat in the world, which is reaped twice in the year: and they say that if it were not for the Portuguese they would not sow it at all, because they are not used to eat bread. This is the cause that bread is eaten so cheap at Goa; for the Metices and most of the Portuguese prefer to eat of the rice that is grown in great abundance in Cambaye, and thence exported to Goa. Besides these, they bring vegetables of endless variety, such as peas, beans, lentils, and others of all kinds and colours, even peas from China, which are eaten there like the rest. Next, medicinal drugs, butter, oils of divers sorts, as well for eating as for perfume, and for rubbing the body withal; white and black soap; sugars and conserves, paper, wax, honey, much opium or poppy-juice, wherein is great traffic and sale among the Indians, as well Moors or Mahometans as Christians.

But the principal riches consist chiefly of silk and cotton stuffs, wherewith everyone from the Cape of Good Hope to China, man and woman, is clothed from head to foot. These stuffs are worked, the cotton also made into cloths of the whiteness of snow, and very delicate and fine, and is also woven of a medium and of a thicker stoutness for divers uses. Others are bespangled and painted with various figures. The silk-work is the same of all these kinds, the articles imported being pillows, counterpanes, and coverlets, pinked with much neatness, and cleverly worked: these they call *colches*.[1] Then there are quilts stuffed with cotton, painted and patterned exceeding prettily. Next, they bring couches and bedsteads, that are painted and lacquered with all

[1] Port. *côlchas*, coverlets or quilts; *v. s.*, p. 4, *note*.

manner of colour and design; and other domestic furniture of the same use. Then bands, which they call *Parcintes*,[1] for the sacking of beds, chairs, stools, joint-stools, and other seats: they are made of fine white cotton. They make also cotton beds in the form of nets, like those of Brazil; not, however, used for sleeping o' nights, but when they go to the country they are borne therein by two or four men as in a palanquin or litter, and much at their ease: they are used all over India. Also they make carpets of the fashion of those of Persia and Ormus, but not so fine or so dear, for they use the rougher and longer wool; the patterns are, however, the same; they also make small cotton carpets with bands of many colours.[2] They also make cabinets in the German style, inlaid with pieces of mother-of-pearl, ivory, gold, silver, and precious stones, the whole neatly fitted. Also other little cabinets, coffers, and boxes of tortoise-shell, which they polish so clear that nothing can have a prettier effect, the shell being patterned by nature.

In short, I could never make an end of telling such a variety of manufactures, as well in gold, silver, iron, steel, copper, and other metals, as in precious stones, choice woods, and other valued and rare materials. For they are all cunning folk, and owe nothing to the people of the West, themselves endued with a keener intelligence than is usual with us, and hands as subtle as ours: to see or hear a thing but once, is with them to know it. A cunning and crafty race: not, however, fraudulent, nor easy to defraud. And what is to be observed of all their manufactures is this, that they are both of good workmanship and cheap. I have never seen men of wit so fine and polished as are these Indians: they

[1] This word is not in Vieira or Roquete; nor can I find it used elsewhere than in Linschoten (i, 61): "*Persintos*, that are stringes or bands, wherewith the Indians bind and make fast their bedsteddes, thereon to lay their beds." The Hindustani is *newár*, and these bands are still used to form the flat of a bed (*charpoy*).

[2] The *dari* ("durry") or *sittrinji* of modern India.

have nothing barbarous or savage about them, as we are apt to suppose. They are unwilling indeed to adopt the manners and customs of the Portuguese; yet do they readily learn their manufactures and workmanship, being all very curious and desirous of learning. In fact the Portuguese take and learn more from them than they from the Portuguese; and they that come fresh to Goa are very simpletons till they have acquired the airs and graces of the Indies. It must then be understood that all these countries of Cambaye, Surat, and others (in the region) of the river Indus and of the Grand Mogor, are the best and most fertile of all the Indies, and are, as it were, a nursing-mother, providing traffic and commerce for all the rest: so, too, is the kingdom of Bengal, where their manners and customs are the same. The people, both men and women, are there more cultivated than elsewhere; those countries are the mart of all the ships of India, and there living is better than anywhere else.

Cambaye is a great kingdom, giving its name to the metropolitan city, where the king hath his residence. The town is in the altitude of twenty-three degrees this side of the Equinoctial. The Gulf is twenty leagues broad at the mouth, and the town is at the farther end of the Gulf. This country has its own king, who is a vassal of the Grand Mogor, and a Mahometan by religion, though most of his people are Gentiles. But every man lives according to his own religion, by reason whereof one sees here men of all laws and sects. After Goa, I have never seen in the Indies any city so famous and opulent as is Cambaye, chiefly for its commerce and traffic. The principal nation and race there are the *Banianes*, who are in such numbers that one speaks only of the Banians of Cambaye: they are to be found in every port and market in India, along with the Guzerates, who are Mahometans of Surat and other (neighbouring) lands. The Banians, on the other hand, observe the same manner of life as the Bramenis, albeit they wear not the cord. These people are better versed in the sciences, above all in mathematics and astrology, than any other; for the rest, honourable men, well habited, and of good conversation. No people in the world know so much about pearls and precious stones; and even at Goa the goldsmiths, lapidaries, and other workmen occupied with the finer crafts are all Banians and Bramenis of Cambaye, and have their own streets and shops.[1]

The town of Cambaye is one of the greatest and richest of all the coast of India, where merchants resort from all quarters of the world. The language of all those countries, as also of all others belonging to the Grand Mogor, and of Bengala and those neighbouring thereto, is the Guzerate language, which is the most widespread and useful, being understood in more places than any other Indian tongue. The men and women of Cambaye, Guzerate, and Surat are in colour somewhat olive; but handsome, and well-proportioned. The women, who take care of their complexions, are also pretty, fair, neat, and well-bred, more so than the women of these parts.

But having spoken of Cambaye and Surat, countries appertaining to the great King of Mogor,[2] methinks I must say something of this prince, according to what I heard in those parts. This Grand Mogor, whom they call the great *Achebar Pachat*,[3] that is, "Great Sovereign King", is the most puissant king in all the Indies that I had knowledge of, and wondrous stories are told there of his grandeur and magni-

[1] "There is also another street where the Benianes of Cambaia dwell, that have all kinds of wares out of Cambaia, and all sortes of precious stones, and are verie subtill and cunning to bore all kinds of stones, pearles and corrals" (*Linschoten*, i, 228).

[2] Here used, as frequently by the Portuguese, of the country (Yule, *Gloss.*, *s. v.* "Mogul").

[3] "The Great Pádsháh." Akbar the Great died in 1605, and was succeeded by his son Selim, under the name of Jehanghir, the emperor referred to in the text. There is no ground for applying the name Akbar generically to the Mogul emperors.

ficence. He resides chiefly at three cities; one is called *Dirly*,[1] the second *Agra*, and the last and greatest of all, where he more usually lives, as being the capital of his empire, is *Lahor*,[2] which is more than 120 leagues from the coast of Cambaye. He can put in the field 30,000 elephants, 80,000 horse, and 200,000 foot. His ordinary guard is 10,000 men, who are ever stationed for seven leagues round his person. When any would come, whether to speak with him or for their private concerns, the first guard they meet conducts them like ushers to the next, and so on from one to another, until they are arrived at the city, where they are handed over to those who have the charge of them: and note, that the first guard that delivers them to the second are obliged to get a ticket of the deliverance for their discharge, and so with the other corps of guards, and so do they know all that have come and gone. These soldiers of the guard are paid every week. They say in these Indian countries that this king is the Great Tartar, as he is called; but it would seem that the Great Cham of Tartary, so renowned these 300 years, is another more remote, towards the north and east, beyond China and towards Cathay. These Tartars are the best soldiers, the strongest, most powerful, and skilled in war to be found in the world. They carry thick bows of iron, which the strongest among us could hardly bend even a little. The riches of this prince are inestimable; for he has divers houses and stores apart for his pearls, gold, silver, precious stones, and other things of price. A Baschat once came to his court to render account of the tribute he had brought; but he had nine whole months to wait ere he that had the office to receive it had time and leisure to count it, because of the great number of other

1 Delhi.

2 Agra had been the chief city of Akbar. Jehanghir preferred Lahore, but also kept court at Agra, where about this time Captain William Hawkins visited him (*Hawkins' Voy.*, 436).

vassals that were arrived before him to render their like accounts. Hence may be understood the extent and riches of the territories of this prince.

He likes the Jesuits much, and has them always about him, respecting and honouring them greatly. None of all that come to his presence does he rise to salute, except them; for when they enter any place where he is, he rises from his place and makes them be seated. There are Jesuit Fathers at the towns of Lahor, Dirly, and Agra, though but few in each place. They have built churches, and have the liberty to preach and to convert as many as they can, so long as it be voluntarily. Nevertheless, hardly any are converted. All the Jesuits in the Indies also say, "It is more easy to convert fifty—nay, a hundred—Gentiles or Idolaters than one Mahometan." The late King *Achebar*, or Grand Mogor, who died six or seven years ago,[1] promised and gave hope that he would become a Christian,[2] making but one request, viz., that he should be permitted to keep all his wives, as his religion allowed; and pending solution of this question he died. His son and successor drove out the Jesuits, and even the other Christians, and treated them roughly; but this he did to get himself settled on his throne: for afterwards, two or three years ago, he recalled the Christians to his court, as they were in the lifetime of his father.

When this prince Achebar died all India was in disquietude and alarm, for the war that was feared would ensue in those parts: for that king was greatly dreaded and feared of all the other Indian kings. And it can be said with assurance that he is lord of the fairest and best countries, and

[1] Probably dated from 1611, the year of the author's first edition.

[2] The Jesuits confidently hoped that they were effecting his conversion, and afterwards insinuated that he had died a Christian, though without open confession; P. Manouchi relating that he saw in Akbar's tomb images of the Virgin and of St. Ignatius (Catrou, *Hist. of the Mogul Dynasty*, p. 135).

of the most valiant people in the world, as the Tartars are. Many of his people, too, are exceeding rich and cultivated. None speak of the Turk in all the Indies, but only of the great Achebar; and when his subject-kings themselves speak of him, they bow their heads in token of respect. He is on good terms with the King of Persia, and oftentimes sends him presents and embassies as his ally. He gives assistance to this king or *Sophy*,[1] who is called the Great *Chaa*, against the Turk. He that is at present the grand *Achebar* had a son[2] that rebelled against him, but was taken and brought to the king, who, not willing to put him to death, is content to hold him prisoner. He has great affection for strangers, and there was at one time at his court an agent or ambassador of the King of England.[3] This prince is so curious, that when any ambassadors or other sorts of persons come before him, he questions them who they are, and of what quality in their masters' courts; and so he did to those sent by the Grand Turk. And so it is, when he knows all, he despises them and their masters, and keeps them about him, giving them money, offices, and dignities, indeed, all that they can desire, in such wise that these ambassadors quit their office of embassage and tarry there, as did the Englishman, according to what I heard from the English at Goa.[4] In the

[1] From *Sūfī*, *Safavī*, or *Safī*, the name of the dynasty which reigned over Persia for more than 200 years (1499-1722). (Yule, *Gloss.*, *s. v.*) The Persian king was always known as "The Sophy", in distinction, as in the text, to "The Turk" and "The Mogul". Colonel Yule quotes *Twelfth Night*, iii, 4: "They say, he has been fencer to the Sophy."

[2] Khuzru.

[3] Captain William Hawkins, from 1609 to 1611; he was succeeded by Sir Thomas Roe in 1615, but, as appears below, the reference is to the former.

[4] Hawkins was induced to remain, after presenting his letters and obtaining the Mogul's answer; and also to marry a daughter of Mubarik Khan, a Christian Armenian, who afterwards accompanied him to England (*Hawk. Voy.*, p. 404).

services of his table and chamber this prince is waited upon by the fairest girls and women that are to be found.

In connection with Cambaye, Surat, and other territories of the Grand Mogor, it remains to speak of Diu,[1] an island that was aforetime a dependency of the kingdom of Cambaye, and is still inhabited by the same races, viz., Banians, Bramenis, Gentiles, and Mahometans. When the Portuguese went there first they made a treaty of peace and friendship for the purpose of trade with the King of Cambaye, as with the others; in such wise that the king permitted them to reside in the island, which, as time went on, they fortified so strongly that they became absolute masters of the place, and rule there to the present day. They have built two fortresses, and made the town strong with bastions. The King of Cambaye has besieged them on two occasions, but saw no prospect of success, and so at present they are good friends.

[1] The Portuguese had factors at Diu from the time of Albuquerque, but had no fortress till 1535. Then Bahádur Sháh of Guzerat, being attacked by the Emperor Humáyun, made a defensive alliance with the Portuguese, whereby the latter were allowed to build a fortress at Diu. Between the parties, however, there was but little confidence, or even good faith, and in the next year Bahádur Sháh was killed in a scuffle on landing from a Portuguese ship. This led to the first siege of Diu in 1538, by Muhammad III, assisted by 7,000 Turks, the fort being successfully defended by Antonio de Silveira. The same king conducted the second siege in 1546; this was ended by the celebrated relief of Dom João de Castro, who achieved a brilliant victory over the besiegers, and reduced the whole island, which to this day remains a Portuguese possession. It has a population of over 10,000, and some of its great buildings still remain. The authorities for the sieges are:—For the first, *Diensis oppugnatio*, by Damião de Goes; *Prim. Liv. do Cerco de Dio*, by Lopo de Sousa Coutinho, Coimbra, 1556, fol.; for the second, *Commentarius de rebus a Lusitanis in India apud Dium gestis anno* 1546, by Diogo de Teive; *V. de João de Castro*, by F. Andrada; and for both, Barros, *Decada V*, and F. y Sousa. The inscriptions of Diu have been published by Mr. J. H. de Cunha Rivara (*Nova Goa*, 1865). There is a plan of the fortress (as of the others mentioned below) in the Resende MS. (Sloane Coll., No. 197).

This island of Diu is very near the mainland of the Cambaye coast, twenty leagues north of the entering of the Gulf, and thirty leagues from the great town of Cambaye. It is of great renown, and brings in good revenues to the Portuguese in consequence of its good port and haven, wherein vessels ride in complete safety, by reason of the protecting fortresses. It is the mart and staple for all the vessels coming from Cambaye, Surat, the Red Sea, the Persian Sea, Ormus, and other places in the Indies. The merchants land there willingly enough, as well for the good haven as for the cheapness of commodities; also because they fear to enter the Gulf, where contrary winds often prevent them coming out; but the chief cause is that the Portuguese constrain them to touch there, so as to reap the dues and customs, and thus to make the place more prosperous. It is worth much to the King of Spain. The people there carry merchandise to and from Cambaye in great barques of fifteen to twenty tons burthen each, with a full cargo each way. The Malabar corsairs make their profit out of these, for they seize as many as they like; and I have seen them while I was there seize at one swoop forty or fifty of them, and that was no uncommon occurrence. This island of Diu is passing fair, rich, and fertile; innumerable vessels touch there, and render it the most wealthy place in the Indies after Goa: for you live there very cheaply, and with all the conveniences and luxuries imaginable; and nowhere in all the Indies is there greater freedom with women than there. Even the soldiers in the Indies go to spend the winter there with great pleasure. All nations and religions meet there freely; but the Portuguese are masters. Indeed, there is more liberty of conscience than at Goa, where there is exercise of none but the Christian religion. The country abounds in beasts, fowl, and other food-stuffs, while everything else is brought from the mainland in great plenty. The climate is very good and healthy, so that the place is of the highest importance and profit to the Portuguese, and they are at pains to guard it well.

From Cambaye and Diu the course is along the coast of Goa, and thence to the Cape of Comori. This is what is properly called the coast of India, that is, from Cambaye to Goa some 100 leagues, and from Goa to Cochin another 100, and from Cochin to Comori 60, so that the whole coast is about 260 leagues. The whole region between the Cape of Good Hope and China is not properly called India, but only this coast[1]; the other parts have separate names. So, when one is making a voyage from Goa, one says to which quarter one is going, whether to the south or the north coast. "The north" is from Goa to Cambaye, "the south" from Goa to the Cape of Comori; but when one is at any other place, and wants to go (for instance) from Cambaye to Comorin, you say that you are going along the coast of India. On that coast between Cambaye and Goa the Portuguese hold but three fortresses, and those not so great nor so important as the others. Starting from Cambaye, the first town and fortress you come to is *Daman*, then *Bassains*, and then *Chaul*. Beyond Chaul is another fortress called *Dabul*,[2] but it is not in the service of the Portuguese, and they have only a factor there. All this coast is good country, fertile and salubrious, and supplies much wealth and commodities to Goa and other parts. But these three fortresses held by the Portuguese are held at the pleasure of the kings of the country, who are vassals of the Grand Mogor. Daman[3] furnishes much rice

[1] See vol. i, p. 334, *note*.

[2] Taken by Almeida in 1509, but lost to the Portuguese in 1526. A very ancient and flourishing mart (*Barbosa*, 71; *Varthema*, p. 114; *India in XV Cent.*, iii, 20); it sadly dwindled under the adverse influences of the Portuguese monopoly, until at the end of the 17th century its commerce was a thing of the past (*A. Hamilton*).

[3] Sacked by the Portuguese in 1531, rebuilt by the natives, and afterwards, in 1558, taken by the Portuguese. They hold it still, with a small district, under a governor subordinate to the Governor of Goa. There

to Goa; from Bassains[1] comes all the timber for building houses and vessels; indeed, most of the ships are built there. It also supplies a very fine and hard freestone, like granite; and I have never seen columns and pillars of single blocks so large as what are produced there. All the magnificent churches and palaces at Goa and the other towns are built of this stone.

The town and fortress of *Chaul*[2] is quite different from the other two, because the country there is vastly rich, and

is a good account of Daman, as it was in 1634, in the *Chron. de Tissuary*, iii, p. 217, from A. Bocarro's *Liv. das Plantas*.

[1] Bassein (*Wasāi*, in Port. Baçaim), twenty-six miles north of Bombay. The city was ceded to the Portuguese in 1536, in the government of Nuno da Cunha. It became the favourite resort of the wealthier Portuguese, the place being noted for handsome villas and pretty gardens. As a city of fashion it was called *a côrte do Norte*. It had a splendid cathedral, thirteen churches, five convents, and a Misericordia. Bassein was taken by the Mahrattas in 1739, after a siege of three months, in which the Portuguese, for the last time in India, fought with stubborn courage. Forty-one years later (1780) the town was captured by the British. In 1782 it was restored to the Mahrattas, and in 1818 retaken on the overthrow of the Peshwás. Bassein is now a sub-division of Tanná district. The population, which even in the decadence of the place before the siege exceeded 60,000, has now dwindled to about one-tenth of that number. A full account of the history and antiquities of Bassein will be found in Mr. J. G. da Cunha's *Chaul and Bassein*, Bombay, 1876.

[2] Chaul is famous for many Portuguese exploits. Here Dom Lourenço, the chivalrous son of the Viceroy D. Francisco d' Almeyda, lost his life in a naval engagement in 1508. After some severe fighting, the previous factory was in 1516 converted into a fort. Other attempts to dislodge the Portuguese failed, and in 1570-1 the fortress sustained a long siege, simultaneously with that of Goa. The Portuguese were not, however, secure so long as the *Morro*, or hill of Korlé, on the opposite side of the estuary, remained in possession of the enemy, and this position was captured, after an obstinate resistance, in 1594. Both fortresses were surrendered to the Mahrattas in 1741, after their capture of Bassein, and in 1818 fell into the hands of the British. Chaul is now an insignificant village, though many of its fine old buildings remain to testify its former greatness. For a full account of the place, see Mr. da Cunha's *Chaul and Bassein*.

productive of all kinds of valuable merchandise, which the merchants from all parts of India and the East come to seek. But the chiefest are the silks, which are obtained there in such quantity that alone they almost supply Goa and all India. They are of a different quality from those of China; and at Goa no account is made of any but Chaul silk, whereof very pretty stuffs are made; it also largely supplies choice cotton fabrics.

At Chaul are two towns; one belongs to the Portuguese, and is very strong. In former days they had a great war with the king of the country, but now they are at peace together. The other belongs to the natives, where is carried on a great manufactory of silk, as also of a vast number of coffers, boxes, cases, and cabinets in the China style, all very rich and elaborate. They make also couches and bedsteads, lacquered in all colours; in this work the people are very adroit and industrious. The king is a Mahometan, very puissant and much feared: they call him the *Malic* of Chaul. He is a vassal of the Grand Mogor, like the rest. All this coast is very rich and the climate healthy, and it has very good ports; living is very cheap, and most of the inhabitants are Gentiles and idolaters. The king has a great number of elephants, and when he takes his meals he causes to come about him a number of beautiful women, who sing and play instruments of music; others take a piece of coloured taffetas, and tear it into pieces so small that they are good for nothing, were it not that those present pick them up each a shred as a kind of badge. After these amusements the king dismisses everyone, and betakes himself to the contemplation of the vanity and uncertainty of life, to such effect that incontinently he falls asleep.

All the kings of India near the Mogor, who cannot resist him, disdain not to be his vassals; indeed, they are considered all the stronger in consequence, and are the more honoured among their neighbours.

Beyond Chaul, and toward Goa, is another fine town and port called *Dabul,* where the Portuguese have only a factor or agent: it sends many commodities to Goa.

Between Goa and Comorin, that is to say along the Malabar coast, are many fortresses, such as *Onor*, at the 14th degree toward the north; *Barcelor* at the 13th; *Mangalor* at the 12th; *Cananor* at the 11th; *Crangenor* at the 10th; and Cochin at the 8th; then comes *Coulan* at the 7th. All these places[1] are in the service of the Portuguese, who have fortresses there, and all that coast supplies Goa with pepper and spice. Cochin and Calecut I have amply described above. At the time of my departure from Goa, on my return home, the fortress of Coulan was besieged on the land side by the king of the country, whereupon the Portuguese were equipping an army of succour; but I know not what ensued.

Before finishing this chapter, I have to tell of that great ship of one of the kings of this coast, to wit, of *Tananor,* that came laden with rice to the Maldives while I was there; which occurrence I have already described.[2] This vessel went on to *Achen* to traffic there, and picked up a friendship with the Hollanders, who having aforetime cast anchor at Tananor, had some acquaintance with this king. It was agreed between the captain and chief men of this ship and the Hollanders that the latter should be permitted to trade freely at Tananor, and should send two factors and some merchandise, and a present for the king, in his vessel. This was ratified; the two Hollanders embarked in this vessel with much merchandise, and the present was well received

[1] Onor (*Honāvar*), Barcelor (*Basrūr*), and Mangalūr are (or were) ports of Canara. Cannanore, Cranganor (*Kodungalūr*), Cochin, and Quilon are Malabar ports. All are very ancient seats of commerce, and described by the early travellers on this coast, whose works are already cited in these volumes. See also authorities quoted as to each in Colonel Yule's *Glossary*. Plans of the Portuguese fortresses are given by Resende (Sloane MS. No. 197.).

[2] See vol. i, p. 266.

by the king. He was, nevertheless, highly disgraced in the eyes of all the other kings and the lords and merchants of India; for it is held for truth that he sent and gave word at Cochin that the two Hollanders were with him, and that if the Portuguese would send to fetch them he would deliver them up—as, indeed, most vilely and treacherously he did. But to give some colour to his treachery, and to the end that this thing should not be deemed to have come from him, and so he should lose his reputation among the other Nair kings, of whom he was one, as well as for fear of falling into a war with the Hollanders and their allies, he bade those at Cochin (which is twenty leagues off, Tananor being between Calecut and Cochin) come in strength, that so he might say he had been constrained to this thing by force. In short, these Hollanders were given up, they and their merchandise, and conveyed to Cochin, where, as I heard, they were afterwards hanged. The King of Calecut has been ever evilly-disposed toward this king, seeing he takes the side of the King of Cochin. When the Hollanders pass by there, all they can do is to fire much cannon-shot over this king's land, for they have never been able to take their revenge otherwise.

This is all I have been able to learn of these divers countries of the coasts of Africa and India while I was with the Portuguese. They have a very particular knowledge of all, seeing they are in possession of some of them, and drive a regular trade with all those others which are not under their dominion and power.

CHAPTER XX.

Many captures of Portuguese ships, and other occurrences in the Indies during the sojourn of the author at Goa.

Having returned to Goa after my voyage to Malacca and Sunda, I remained there another space of six months to pass the winter. But, before I come to my embarking for Portugal, I must tell of some remarkable occurrences that happened in the Indies while I was there. First I will refer to an engagement between the Hollanders on their way to the Indies and a large and powerful Portuguese vessel on her way from Ormus to Goa. It was a great calm at the time, which was the cause that the Hollanders could not at once board the vessel, which they looked upon as their own the moment any wind should get up. At nightfall, however, the Portuguese let down two boats and made their escape, carrying with them all that was most precious in the ship, such as gold, silver coined in larins, Oriental pearls in large numbers, and other riches; so that when the Hollanders were about to make their attack they found no resistance, for all had escaped except one old merchant. To him the crew would not give time to embark his goods, so he said that he recked not of death since he was losing all his wealth, and preferred to await the arrival of the Hollanders. The latter, enraged to find themselves baulked of so fair a prize, pillaged what remained, and set fire to the ship, which contained a good number of Persian and Ormus horses. She was also laden with sweetmeats, to wit, conserves, dates, and raisins, called by them *Passes*,[1] which are like our Damascus raisins. The most excellent quince preserves come from Persia and Ormus; these the Portuguese call *Marmelades*,[2] and we *Cotignats*. The loss of this vessel was a vast misfortune for them; nor did it come alone, for the Hollanders burned

[1] See above, p. 73. [2] See above, p. 240.

many others afterwards. That vessel belonged to the above-mentioned lord, named *Don Diego de Coustigno*, who resided at Goa.

Another time a great ship of Cochin, belonging to the Portuguese, and laden with merchandise of Bengala, whence she hailed, was met by some *pados*, or galiots of Malabar corsairs, who wanted to attack her, but, seeing they were not strong enough to take her, they, against the grain, left her there. But as their good luck, and the Portuguese ill luck would have it, whilst they sped off they met a Holland ship, which they hailed, giving word of that Portugal vessel, and offering to show the Hollander captain where she lay, as well as to aid in taking her. To this the Hollander agreed, and the Portuguese surrendered at the first shot. The Malabars would have slain the crew to a man, but the Hollanders prevented them. The Malabars first made a preliminary sack of the ship, taking all the stuffs and light goods on the upper and main decks only; which done, they said they laid no claim to more. But the Hollanders told them that they intended them to have a third of the whole, and this division was carried out, though the Hollanders retained the ship, which they gave as a present to the King of Cananor. They did ill, however, in leaving seven poor Christian prisoners in the hands of the Malabars, the captain giving them over that the Malabars might profit by their ransom, and promising them that they should be ransomed. But the Malabars, notwithstanding this promise, slew one of them, and the captain of the vessel was himself one of the seven. This was the vessel of which I have spoken that came to the Maldives while we were wrecked there.[1] These Malabars

[1] See vol. i, pp. 78, 239. It is difficult to identify this story in the Dutch journals. After all, it is only gossip which the traveller picked up in India long after the events. It is probably a combination of two occurrences: (1) the capture of a Portuguese frigate by Steven van der Hagen, off Cannanor, in October 1604; and (2) the dealing with the

cruelly entreated those men. Afterwards, too, arose a great dispute between two of the chief Malabars because the Hollanders gave two pieces of cannon from this ship to one named Marcaire, whom also I have mentioned above, and who held himself out for the chiefest man among these robbers. But the captain of the galleys said that as the galleys engaged were his, so the prize belonged to him, seeing his ships had borne the hazard of the enterprise. So this quarrel waxed hot between them, and the King of Calecut was every day expected during his journeying in his territory to bring them to an understanding. These two lords were always well escorted when they went abroad from their houses; they resided only four leagues apart, with a single town between them.

Then, about a year before we left Goa, arrived an English ship[1] in the river of Surate and Cambaye, whither she came with a view to trade. A gentleman of her company landed there, and went as ambassador on behalf of the King of England to the Grand Mogor, by whom, as I heard afterwards, he was exceeding well received. And forasmuch as great ships cannot approach close to the towns and territory of Cambaye and Surate, where these Englishmen came to trade in Anil or Indigo for the manufacture of their violet scarlet, they unfortunately sent ashore two of their boats, laden with merchandise, and manned by seventeen hands: these were cut off by a number of Portuguese galiots that stole up between the land and the ship, out of reach of cannon-

Bom Jesus, taken by Verhœven's fleet at Mozambique. The Dutch chronicler does not say that in the former any assistance was given by the Malabars, nor that the captured ship was given over to the Raja of Cannanor. The two guns alluded to below were from the *Bom Jesus*. (See *Second Voyage of S. van der Hagen*, and *Voy. of Verhœven.*)

[1] The *Hector*. The English Ambassador referred to was William Hawkins. For an account of the capture of the two English boats, see *Hawkins' Voyages*, p. 392 *et seq.* The *Hector* arrived at Surat 24th Aug. 1608.

shot. They were thus captured and taken off to Goa by a certain *Don Fernando de Sylva de Menessez*, who was general of the ordinary galiots of the North. This general embarked in the same ship in which I had my passage to Portugal, and paid me great attention, as I shall relate hereafter. These seventeen Englishmen were taken prisoners, and were full soon reduced to six or seven, for the rest died. As for their ship, she forthwith weighed anchor and sailed off for Achen. There were, in fact, two English ships[1] that went off together; the one took her course to Achen, and the other to Cambaye.

Six months, too, before I embarked, there came another English vessel[2] to traffic in the East Indies. While she was on the coast of Melinde, and near *Bombase*, the captain sent her boat to the *Zanzibar* islands to sound and reconnoitre the coast; but it was surprised by the natives, and the Portuguese, who made a pretence of going a-fishing there, slew nine or ten of the boat's crew. I saw one of the survivors brought a prisoner to Goa, named Seigneur Richard,[3] a man of proud and noble bearing, like a captain. He was

[1] The *Hector*, Captain Hawkins, and the *Dragon*, Captain Keelinge, the latter being admiral. Abstracts of *Keelinge's Journal* are given by Purchas (iii, ch. vii, p. 206), and in the *Lancaster Voyages* (Hak. Soc.), p. 108. Concerning the *Dragon* an interesting fact may be repeated here (see *Lanc. Voy.*, Introd., p. ix), viz., that when off the Guinea coast, in Sept. 1607, her men performed the "Tragedie of *Hamlett*".

[2] The *Union*, Captain Rowles, sailed from England with the *Ascension*, Captain Sharpeigh, in 1608 (see further, vol. i, p. 45). The event at Zanzibar took place early in 1609, and the prisoners would be brought to Goa about May or June, *i.e.*, about six months before Pyrard's departure from India.

[3] Richard Wickham; he had been the merchant of the *Union*. The account of his capture by the Portuguese is given above (i, 45, *note*), from the letter of S. Bradshaw, in Purchas (i, p. 232). With four other English captives, he sailed from Goa to Lisbon, in the same carrack with Sir Robert Sherley, arriving there in Aug. 1610. He was much patronised by Sherley, and at first stayed in his house at Lisbon, but soon afterwards made his escape to England. Subsequently he proceeded to Firando, in Japan, as a factor for the Company, and is frequently referred to in Cocks's *Diary*. After vexing the soul of Richard Cocks

long in prison, in company with us, and it was intended to put him on his trial for having been taken in the act of sounding. He said they had slain his cousin in cold blood, as I have already related, and had raised his head on a pike for a trophy. His misfortune was to have been taken with the lead in his hand, that being a dangerous implement on a Portuguese coast. At length he embarked for Portugal in one of the carracks that started when I did.

Four months later the same English ship,[1] on her voyage from Surate to Achen, and while 60 leagues off the coast abreast of Chaul, a territory of the Grand Mogor, who is friendly to the English, ran into some banks and shoals, and was lost; but her crew, to the number of about eighty, had time to lower her two boats, and embark on these with all their money and the better part of their other goods. They reached Chaul, in the realm of the Grand Mogor, and took their journey by land to Surate and Cambaye, where they were exceeding well received because of the money they spent, and then took resolution to go to the court of the Mogor, thence to return home overland by way of Tartary. This they did, and got passports from the king, who likewise gave them money, horses, arms, buffaloes, and oxen to carry them and their baggage and provisions, and so furnished they set out. Some fifteen of them would not be of this party, and tarried there awaiting the grace of God at some other season. There were then at the Mogor's court some Jesuit Fathers, one of whom made friends with these Englishmen,

in many ways, and striking for higher pay, he threw up his position and left Japan, in 1618, worth £5,000 or £6,000.

[1] Not the *Union*, but her sister ship, the *Ascension*. The loss of this ship, and the adventures of some of the survivors, are related by T. Jones, in Purchas (ii, 228). This man and three others were deluded by a Jesuit at Surat, to put themselves in his hands. They were taken to Daman and Chaul, and thence to Goa, where they arrived 18th Nov. 1609. They were sent to Lisbon in the *N. S. de Piedade* (*v. i.*, ch. xxi), arriving there Aug. 1610. Jones does not mention Pyrard in his story, though, as appears below, they made friends at Goa.

who were Protestants. This was about the time when the great fleet called *Cafile* was coming from Surate and Cambaye to Goa. These English had plenty of money, and this Jesuit Father made four of the chiefest of them with all assurance believe they could go to Goa and live there without any harm. This they did, believing in his word, and came to Goa, where at first they were well enough received, having a lodging given to them among the servants, and being well treated. I saw them many a time, for we were very good friends. But, after they had been there some time, they were as badly treated as the rest of us, as I shall relate in the next chapter.

CHAPTER XXI.

The author's taking ship at Goa.—Condition of the Indies at that time.—The author's imprisonment and deliverance.—Arrival of carracks, and other matters on this head.

Having thus passed the winter at Goa, after my return from Sunda, when the season came round again my two companions and I resolved to be off and to take ship home.

The state of Goa was then as follows.

The viceroy was none other than the archbishop, whom *Don Martin Alphonce de Castro*, who died at Malacca, as already related, had left as governor in his absence, and he held that office for three years. One appointed by the viceroys or by election[1] is called only *Gouernador de la India*,

[1] A double mistake: viceroys did not nominate their successors, nor was there any election of governors. On both the occasions alluded to, when Archbishop Menezes and A. Furtado respectively became governors, recourse was had to the *vias de successão* (*Arch. Port. Or.*, Fasc. 1, No. 15, para 5, and Rivara's *Pyrard*).

DOM ANDRÉ FURTADO DE MENDOÇA

37th Governor of India 1609.

(From the LIVRO DO ESTADO DA INDIA of P. Barretto de Resende.

Sloane Collection No. 197.)

that is, Governor of India, and such was he; nevertheless, he was absolute in the absence of the other, and governed with great wisdom. But the enemies of the Portuguese, to wit, the Malabars, Hollanders, etc., glad to find they had to deal only with a man of the Church, took more courage, and daily made raids and prizes even at the very bars and roadsteads of the Portuguese ports. This archbishop, named *Don Alexis de Mexiosa*,[1] would not have been in power so long, but that a viceroy was expected full soon from Portugal; and, indeed, the King of Spain, on hearing the news of the viceroy's death, had sent one out, by name the Count *de la Fera*, who, as I have elsewhere recorded, died on the Guinea coast. Thereupon an assembly was called at Goa of all the nobility, the clergy, and the third estate, to take counsel what should be done, seeing that affairs were then in so sorry a condition.[2] It was then resolved that the archbishop should quit his office, and that *Don André Furtado de Mendoza*,[3] the greatest and most renowned captain then amongst

[1] *Sic*, for *Menezes*.

[2] The assembly met, not for an election, but merely to open the *vias*, which were brought in the same ship in which Mocquet (see below) reached Goa.

[3] F. y Sousa, who always has Tacitus in his mind, thus writes of Furtado: "Most men appear fit for public employments before they have them, and afterwards wholly incapable of them. It was not so with A. Furtado, for everybody esteemed him fitter to govern after he was placed in that power than they had done before, and yet there was none before but wished to see him in that post." This great captain had begun his military service at the age of 16, when he accompanied King Sebastian in his ill-fated expedition to Morocco. A year or two later he embarked for India, and already in 1582 made his name by his relief of Barcelor. From 1590 until his succession to the governorship in 1609 he was employed in every enterprise of moment, and on every occasion justified the confidence of his countrymen. He fought the Malabar pirates in several pitched battles by sea, defeated and slew the King of Jaffna, and raised the siege of Colombo. In 1600 he restored the Portuguese reputation by his capture of Kunhali's fort (*supra*, vol. i, pp. 354-6), where F. da Gama had suffered so severe a reverse. He was then appointed Captain of Malacca, and, after various encounters with the

them, should be elected. He had been thirty years in India, and never wished for the government, but only to be captain and general of the army; he was very liberal to his soldiers. He was accordingly elected, and was received with the same ceremony as in the case of those that come from Portugal. Without loss of time he commenced to reform the state, and by new ordinances to put the administration on a good footing. All the Indian kings that were allied with the Portuguese rejoiced that he had the office, and sent their ambassadors with presents to greet him. He raised great armies and fortified many places; in short, this lord was beloved of God, of the king and the people, as well as of the captains and soldiers, but not of the nobility, for he was neither robber nor ambitious, nor would he see others rob the king. He was not married, and withal was continent and devout. In less than three months he equipped armadas to despatch in all directions, and did more in that time than the others in the course of years.

This viceroy, or governor, had a nephew named *Don Diego Furtado de Mendoza*, that was appointed general of an armada then preparing for the North. He was one of the four lords already mentioned who supplied the soldiers with food during this winter: for it is then the work is afoot of pre-

Dutch, sustained, with a very inferior garrison, a siege of four months against their forces under Matelief (*supra*, p. 151). His appointment to the governorship of India seems to have aroused enthusiasm, and by his personal influence he seems to have got men to work, instead of defrauding their royal master. In two months' time he had a great fleet equipped and manned. At the end of his third month arrived De Tavora to reap the benefit of his labours. Furtado's portrait, as copied by Resende from the gallery in the Viceroy's palace, shows us a man grave and keen, modest and determined, of whom Faria probably speaks truly when he says that, on his elevation, he was "courteous to his inferiors, and lifted himself not above those who had been his equals. As a private captain he dressed costly, now as governor plainer than a private captain. The workshops were his rooms of state, the arsenal his garden." (Stevens' *Faria*, iii, 162.

paring the armada to sail at the beginning of summer.[1] During this winter at Goa my companions and I used to go, like the Portuguese, and eat at the house of this lord, who bade us come, and had our names put upon his rolls, for he was resolved to take us with him upon his expedition, and I, like the rest, had given him my promise. But the viceroy was minded to make us all prisoners, together with some Englishmen that were at Goa, viz., the survivors of the seventeen taken at the bar of Surate,[2] and the other four brought by the Jesuits from the court of the Grand Mogor,[3] with the other Englishman called the Seigneur *Richard*,[4] also some Hollanders or Flemings that were there: so were we all thrown into prison together. The pretext was that we were there to spy them out and report upon all we saw, and that the season was at hand when the Hollanders were wont to cast anchor at the bar of Goa. Thus did they to all the other foreigners, saving such as had come to the Indies in Portuguese ships, so that the Jesuit Fathers had again to exert themselves for our deliverance. Four or five of them assembled, including the Christians' Father,[5] by name *Père Gaspar Aleman*,[6] a Castilian; an English Father, named *Thomas Estienne*,[7] rector of a college in the Salsete territory,

[1] The commencement of the fine weather following the close of the S.W. monsoon, *i.e.*, about the end of August.

[2] *V. s.*, p. 263. [3] *V. s.*, p. 266. [4] *V. s.*, p. 264.

[5] One of the Jesuits was appointed to look after the converted natives and foreigners in distress, with the title of *pai dos Christãos*.

[6] Fathers Gaspar Aleman and De la Croix had been most instrumental in obtaining Pyrard's release from prison in the previous year (see above, p. 22, where, after the words "Jesuit Father", read "by name Gaspar Aleman," the latter words being omitted by an oversight.

[7] Father Thomas Stevens, of all Englishmen *primus in Indis*. The Jesuit authorities say that he was from *Buston*, in the diocese of Salisbury, a place which may be identified as Boscombe, a village a few miles N.E. of Salisbury. Hakluyt says he was "sometime of New College in Oxford", but his name cannot be found in the books there. One of his name is entered of St. John's College, in 1577, but by this time our Stevens had joined the Jesuits. At an early age he fell

called *Margon;* the Fathers *Jan de Cenes,*[1] a Lorrainer of Verdun; *Nicolas Trigaut,*[1] a Walloon of Douay; and the good

in with Thomas Pounde, and was by him sent to Rome, where, on Oct. 20, 1575, Stevens was enrolled as a novice at S. Andrea. The persecutions of the Catholics by Elizabeth necessitated a life of deception, if not conspiracy, and this was not to Stevens' liking. While at Rome he probably read the life and work of Francis Xavier, and in a petition to the Father-General he besought the favour of being sent to the East Indies (Foley's *Records of the Eng. Jesuits*, vol. iii).

His wish was fulfilled, and he sailed from Lisbon in 1578. On arrival at Goa he wrote to his father a long and interesting account of his voyage, which is preserved to us in *Hakluyt.* Well for our countrymen was it that the first Englishman to set foot in India was a man of Stevens' calibre, who united learning, warmth of heart, and diplomacy, and who, in his attachment to his Church and order, never forgot that he was an Englishman. During his long residence at Goa he was on occasions able to use his influence on behalf of Englishmen. Fitch and Newbery, and their friends, in 1584, owed their liberation to his intercession. "The two good fathers of S. Paul", says Newbery, "who travelled very much for us, the one is called Father Marke, who was borne in Bruges, in Flanders, and the other was borne in Wilshire, in England, and is called Padre Thomas Stevens. James Storie went into the monasterie of St. Paul, where he remaineth, and is made one of the companie, which life he liketh very well" (*Hak.*, i, 211).

Stevens went out to India at the age of twenty-six, and laboured there for forty years, during thirty-five of which he was rector of the college at Salsette. In 1619 he died at Goa. He was the first to make a scientific study of Canarese: "Primus Canarinum idioma in regulas ordinemque digessit," says Ribadaneira. Three of his works survive, all printed after his death: (1) the *Arte da linguoa Canarim*, em Rachol, 1640; one example of it is in the National Library at Lisbon, and perhaps another is at Goa, as the book was reprinted there 1857, 8vo.; (2) *Doutrina Christã em lingua bramana-canarim*, em Rachol, 1622, 8vo.; (3) *Discurso sobre a vinda de Jesus Christo*, etc., Goa, 1626, 1649, and 1654.

Much more might be written of Stevens. The fullest account of his early life is in Foley; bibliographical and other notices, however, appear in all the Jesuit authorities, Ribadaneira, Backer, Southwell, Parsons, More, and Oliver. See also articles by Mr. Rivara in the Lisbon *Archivo Universal*, vol. iv, No. 13 (Jan. 1861); by Professor Monier Williams in the *Contemp. Rev.*, April 1878; and by F. M. Mascarenhas in the *Ind. Antiquary*, vol. vii, p. 117.

[1] See above, p. 36, where "Jean de Seine" is described as a Lorrainer from Nancy.

Father *Estienne de la Croix*,[1] a Frenchman of Rouen, who all worked together with such effect that we were set free after an imprisonment of nigh three weeks. The English also got out by the means of that good Father Thomas Estienne, who took much pains therein. Four of them became Catholics at Goa; but of these two died there. And in truth those good Fathers heartily wished us all in our own countries because of the trouble we were raising, and they assisted us in all things as though we were their own brothers. But what chiefly consoled us, and vexed and annoyed all the people of Goa, was that at the end of three months after this viceroy had been instituted there arrived from Portugal a new viceroy named *Don Loys Lorencio d'Establa*,[2] who found in readiness all that his predecessor had been at such pains to prepare, and himself took all the honour and profit, giving the appointments to men of his own choosing. He had set out from Portugal with an extraordinary fleet of carracks, and spent a long winter at Mozambic, waiting for the wind. The Government of India had sent petitions to the King of Spain that he should grant the title of viceroy to *Don André Furtado*, which he would willingly have bestowed, but that the other had left Portugal ere the news from Goa arrived in Spain.[3]

1 See above, p. 36.

2 Ruy Lourenço de Tavora assumed the government as 19th (or, according to Faria, 21st) viceroy on the 5th Sept. 1609, and held office till Dec. 1612, when he was succeeded by Jeronimo de Azevedo (as to whom see above, p. 143). De Tavora's period was uneventful; Faria sums him up thus: "He had more inclination to peace than war, which produced concord with all the kings of India; of stature tall, his complexion fair, aged, and a good Christian, a rare thing among men of quality."

3 That is, the news that Furtado had succeeded to and assumed the government. The King of Spain might, and probably did, put the names of the best men in the *vias* or sealed orders, but (his mails arriving never less than six months after date) he never knew which of them would be alive and in India at the time a vacancy should occur.

Two months after the coming of this viceroy four great carracks arrived at Goa, each of 2,000 tons burthen or thereabouts; the general, or captain *Mayor*, was *Don Manuel de Menaica*. Five had left Lisbon, but they had lost sight of the fifth in a storm at the Cape of Good Hope. Each carrack had had on board upwards of a thousand men, including soldiers and sailors, Jesuits and other clergy, merchants and gentlemen; and when they arrived at Goa they had but 300 aboard each, and half these were sick by reason of the great calms, the great fatigue, and the want of fresh water they endured at sea, for they were eight months without touching land.[1] They brought an edict from the King of Spain, forbidding the viceroy to permit any French, Hollanders, or Englishmen to be amongst them, and commanding him to compel any that might be there, under pain of death, to take ship and be off, forasmuch as they only went there to become acquainted with India, and to spy out the land.

Wherefore, as it was not permitted to any but Portuguese to embark without permission, we besought these good Jesuit Fathers to get us the viceroy's licence to return to Europe, and to get us provisions. The which we easily obtained, because the viceroy had the express commands of the King of Spain to that effect. But we required to have it in writing and signed by his hand. This, however, was by no means easy to get, less so, indeed, than food. All the while, too, the captains at Goa wanted to take me with them, some to China and Japan, others to Mozambic and Sofala; but these good Fathers counselled us to return home and get quit of these fellows, who in the end would do us an ill turn.

[1] The English letter from Lisbon, dated March $\frac{18}{28}$, 1609 (cited above, p. 119), affords a truer reason for the terrible mortality in the voyage of this fleet. The greater part of each crew of 1,500 were boys from the age of ten and upwards, who were totally unfit for the perils of an Indian voyage.

So at length we three Frenchmen were taken before the viceroy, who was greatly astonished to hear who we were, seeing that no French ship had hitherto come to the East Indies; but seeing the plight we were in, and the long time we had spent there, he promised to give us leave to go, and victuals for the coming voyage.

For four months the carracks were being refitted, during which time an armada of galiots was sent to convoy ten ships to Cananor, Bacalor, Barcelor, and Onor, on the Malabar coast to the south of Goa, in order to bring pepper for a cargo to the carracks.

This was because the King of Cochin would not give his pepper unless the Portuguese sent the carracks themselves for it. Be it noted here that only the King of Spain can buy and possess pepper: the merchants cannot buy even a pound of it, nor export a grain of it, while in all the other Indian merchandise they can traffic freely. Wherefore the king reserves in each of these ships room for 500 casks of pepper: the rest is left for the goods of the merchants and mariners, who pay no other freight, but thirty per cent. at Lisbon.

When these ten ships returned to Goa with the pepper the carracks were laden and fitted for the home voyage. *Don André Furtado de Mendoza*, who had three months before yielded up the office of viceroy, was appointed general and commander-in-chief for the voyage to Portugal.

We then got our licence from the viceroy; but he gave us no provisions, as he had promised, saving only that he put in our passport an order to the ship's officers to let us embark with our clothes and *matelotage*, which is the food that every one takes with him, and to give us the regular commons of biscuit and water, as they give to the sailors. For, as I said before, their king supplies all commodities on the outward journey, but on the homeward none except to the ship's officers, and then only biscuit for the whole voyage (though, in fact, it doesn't last three months), and nothing else. This is done of design, and for fear lest, if he should supply provisions for the homeward as for the outward voyage, most of those would return who are now constrained to remain in India.

Thus, while the vessels were being laden, every one got ready his *matelotage;* but it must be noted that when a viceroy, archbishop, or other great lord goes from Goa to Portugal all the poor soldiers and such others are exceeding glad, for these grandees then promise to provide victuals for a certain number of men, a hundred or so. The Archbishop of Goa also was intending to embark in one of these carracks, but he changed his mind afterwards, and remained at Goa for that year. He had promised us our provisions on the voyage; but when it was known that *Don André Furtado* was to go, every one went to him to get his name upon his roll, for he had made provision for well-nigh 200 persons, including his own domestics.[1] The Jesuit fathers and we ourselves did all we could to get enrolled in that list, but it was impossible, because of the great number of Portuguese who were going with him; and also because the Jesuit fathers, who had brought these four Englishmen from the Mogor, had engaged places for them, and even they got their passage with great trouble.

With him also embarked a Frenchman named *Jean Moquet,*[2]

[1] The *Arch. Port. Or.* (Fasc. 6, No. 104) contains the order of the viceroy to the king's factor, dated 22nd Dec. 1609, to pay to the captain of Furtado's ship the sum of 3,500 xeraphins (about £250) for the hospitalities of the ex-governor on the homeward voyage.

[2] Jean Mocquet, born near Vienna, 1575. His family had been adherents of Henri IV in his adversity, and young Mocquet became the king's apothecary. Having a great desire to travel, he obtained permission, on condition that he collected curiosities for the king's cabinet at the Tuileries, of which he was appointed custodian. He started in 1601, and in the space of twelve years had made no less than five long and hazardous voyages: (1) West Coast of Africa; (2) Guiana; (3)

who had come to Goa from Lisbon with a viceroy, by name Count *de la Fera*, that died by the way, as already described. I saw him often at Goa; he had as much reason to praise the Portuguese as we had, for he had his share of good treatment, as you may read more particularly in the book of his voyages to India.[1] He embarked at Lisbon in the household of this viceroy, in the capacity of an arborist and apothecary, as he did again on his return with *Don André Furtado,* who gave him the place. While he was at Goa he was some time apothecary to the Royal Hospital; then he returned, as I have said, with Don André Furtado, who is rumoured to have been poisoned.[2] He was ailing a long time; and in India they give slow poisons, to act after such interval as they desire. Thus did we strive to get aboard his ship, but we could not, for the reasons stated,

Morocco; (4) Goa; (5) Holy Land. When he was at Paris, in the intervals of his voyages, Henri IV took much pleasure in hearing the traveller's gossip. In 1614 he was minded to make a tour of the world, and went to Spain, but there was refused leave to proceed to America. He then returned to Paris and published the entertaining volume of the voyages above mentioned. His account of the voyage to India is a terrible picture of misery, though his medical knowledge enabled him to battle with the scurvy, with which he, as well as nearly all on board, was stricken. As stated above, he was apothecary to the Conde de Feira on the voyage out, and to A. Furtado on the voyage home, and it was his melancholy duty to embalm the bodies of both. Mocquet, after acknowledging the kindness shown to him by his countryman, Father de la Croix, adds: "J'eu vy aussi trois autres qui s'etoient sauuez des Maldiues, entre lesquels estoit un nommé François Pirard, Breton, qui a fait l'Histoire de ses Voyages."

[1] The *Voyages en Afrique, Asie, Indes Orientales et Occidentales, etc.*, was first published at Paris, 1617, 1 vol. in-12; other issues were at Rouen, 1645 and 1665, and again at Paris, 1830. It has been translated into Dutch (Dordrecht, 1656, 4to), into German (Lüneburg, 1668, 4to), and into English (London, 1696, 8vo).

[2] This is mere gossip. He died of jaundice (*F. y Sousa*). Before he left Goa he was seriously ill of liver and spleen disease, for which he was treated by Mocquet. After thirty arduous years in India his condition was by no means abnormal.

and also because our passport bore the name of another vessel. And well was it for us, although, in sooth, we endured in that voyage every possible hardship and suffering; for we were distributed four in each vessel, and French, English, and Hollanders mixed. These poor Englishmen were fairly astonished when, as soon as they got on board, they got irons clapped on their feet, which was no more than we had at Goa. In fact, all the foreigners that were shipped in the three carracks which left before us were all made prisoners on arrival at Lisbon, as I heard afterwards. We, however, were more fortunate, notwithstanding all the ills we suffered; but of that anon.

The carrack upon which Don André embarked was called *Nossa Senora de Peigna de Francia*, that is to say, Our Lady of the Coast of France, to whose name there is a church at Lisbon. She was the first laden and equipped, and set sail the 26th December 1609. At his departure all Goa cried for sorrow, because he had been thirty years in India, having gone out full young and been successful in his wars. He was so beloved by the clergy, the nobility, and the common people, and even by the Indian kings, that every one said he had never seen any viceroy or general that was so great a captain, so valiant, so pure, and so beloved as was this Seigneur Furtado. When he went aboard to set sail it was one of the prettiest sights in the world, for all the town went to escort him and see him depart as far as the bar, with their covered *manchoues*, like galiots, full of bands of music, gifts of fruits, and other presents. And though the people thus displayed great joy and gaiety, yet were they indeed sore at heart, and grieved to see this lord depart.

Such was his character; and the King of Spain, being desirous to see and know him, had sent for him to come.[1] At his departure he promised the people of Goa that he

[1] Probably gossip: the regulations required that no ex-governor should remain in India.

would return after seeing the king; but he did not survive the voyage, for he died at sea near the *Açores*, as I heard in Spain after my return.[1] Inasmuch as the four carracks did not set out together and at the same time, not being all ready and laden, it was arranged that they should tarry at the island of St. Helena for the space of twenty days, and after that a letter should be left in the chapel giving news of their voyage and departure.

The second carrack, called *Nostre Dame des Carmes*,[2] set sail the 8th January 1610: in her was embarked *Don Manuel de Menaiça*, who was general of the five carracks when they left Portugal. But when they return with the viceroy he is general of the fleet, as was *Don André Furtado* now.

The third carrack, called *Nostre Dame de Piedade*, set sail the 15th of the same month, and she had for her captain *Don Pedro de Coutigno*, who had just quitted the government of Ormus, and had also on board the Persian ambassador,[3] who came on behalf of his master to induce the King of Spain to make war against the Turk: he was bringing rich presents.[4] Of the fourth carrack, whereon I was embarked, I shall speak in the following chapter.

Before, however, closing this, I will tell how, when we

[1] He was buried in the church of Our Lady of Grace at Lisbon. His funeral sermon, by Fr. Antonio de Gouveia (author of the *Jornada* of Archbishop Menezes), is published under the title *Sermão nas exequias de A. Furtado de Mendonça Governador que foi da India.* Lisboa, por Vicente Alvares, 1611, 4to. (Da Silva, *Dicc. Bibliogr. Port.*).

[2] Her full name was N. S. do Vencimento do Monte do Carme.

[3] This ambassador was sent by the King of Persia for the above purposes, and also to counteract and check the diplomacy of Sir Robert Sherley, who had proceeded to Lisbon and Spain the year before. The *N. S. de Piedade* arrived at Lisbon in August 1610, and the conduct of the rivals at the Court of Spain is described in English letters from Lisbon (*Cal. St. Pap. E. I.*, i, 487, etc.).

[4] He is said to have brought 250,000 ducats' worth of silk and jewels (*op. cit.*, i, 487).

were ready to start, there arrived at Goa one of these Englishmen, who, as I said before, took the land route to England from the court of the Grand Mogor. He told us that in all the countries of that prince, which are of vast extent, they had experienced no harm or discomfort, by reason of the passport they had of him, and that they had brokers day by day for payment. But when they got further into Grand Tartary they could pass no farther, for they were set upon and undone in such wise that but a third part of their company escaped, and these were forced to return to the place whence they came; and as for the rest, whether they were dead or in prison, they knew not.

I must not forget to mention that whilst I was at Goa I had the acquaintance and friendship of a Portuguese gentleman, a soldier, by name *Don Francisco de Caldera.* He spoke very good French, having resided at the court of France for the space of ten or twelve years, and having also been in the service of *Don Antonio,*[1] King of Portugal, who died at Paris. This gentleman was for more than a year and a half in prison at Goa, or rather in sanctuary in a church in Goa, where he took refuge after slaying a man in a quarrel; for there, as in Spain, a church is an asylum and a franchise for such as have slain a man, provided it be not by assassination or ambuscade, but in battle defending with his own body. I sometimes went to see and speak with him at the door of the church and of the parsonage, for he could not go abroad for fear of being seized by the officers of justice. He told me, among other things, that he had

[1] Don Antonio, natural son of Louis, Prince of Portugal. He had accompanied King Sebastian to Morocco in 1578, and was made prisoner at the fatal battle of Alcaçar-Quivir. He managed to escape, and was proclaimed King of Portugal, but was completely overthrown by the Duke of Alva at the battle of Alcantara, which secured the Portuguese throne for Philip II. Don Antonio took refuge in exile, and, after many endeavours to raise combinations against the Spanish domination, at length died at Paris in 1595.

seen at Goa a French gentleman, who called himself the *Comte de Monfar*, otherwise the *Sieur de Feines*,[1] who had come from Venice by sea to Alexandretta, thence by land to Aleppo, thence with the caravan to Babylon, then to Persia to the king's court at Spahan, where he sojourned a while; next he came by land to Ormus, and thence to Goa, where he was some time a prisoner, like the rest, and at length was returned to Portugal in a Lisbon galion with a *viador de Fasienda*, by name *Bras Courayge*.[2] I afterwards heard

[1] This is a somewhat mysterious personage. Nothing is known of him, except what appears in two accounts of his voyage, in Pyrard's notice above, and in a similar notice by Mocquet. Curiously, the first edition of his voyages was in English—*An exact and curious Survey of all the East Indies, etc.*, by Monsieur de Monfart, London, 1615, 4to. This was written by a French resident of London, who states that he made his acquaintance on a visit to Paris, and made up the book from the notes and conversation of the traveller, who, though "a right French gentleman . . . . cannot very well write." The second edition was published at Paris, 1630, under the title *Voyage faict par terre depuis Paris jusqu'à la Chine*, par Sr. de Feynes. Owing to the name Monfart being used in the English edition, and Feynes only in the French, none of the bibliographers seem to have been aware that the traveller was the same, although the English edition begins, "I, Henry de Feynes, commonly called by the name of the Mannor of Monfart." Dr. Burnell, even, in his copy of the English book, notes that he does not find Monfart in any biographical dictionary (he appears in the *Biog. Univ.* under the name Feynes), and rather hastily concludes, "He was, it is plain, a swindler." Much suspicion has been cast upon the French (or Feynes) voyage, owing to its absence of dates, but the English (or Monfart) book, confirmed by the notices of Pyrard and Mocquet, settles the general truth of the voyage. The English edition states that he started on the overland journey in 1608. Mocquet, who arrived at Goa 26th May 1609, heard that Feynes had been there three months before. He probably arrived at Lisbon about the end of 1609, and was kept a prisoner in the castle of Xativa till 1613. In the English edition he acknowledges that his liberation was due to the good offices of the Duc de Mayenne. It seems that before his voyage he had been in the household of the Cardinal de Joyeux, and that after his return to France he was taken into the household of Louis XIII.

[2] Bras Correa had a career of great adventure. De Couto describes him as "a captain of experience, a good soldier, and a great mariner."

that as soon as he arrived at Lisbon he was cast into prison without his knowing why, and remained there four whole years, until *Monsieur de Mayenne*, proceeding to Spain for the marriages in 1613, got him set free by his interest and favour.

In April 1592 he went out as captain of the *Nazareth*, and arrived at Goa in Sept. of the same year. Early in 1593 he left Goa in the same ship, and with five others, one only of the six reaching Lisbon. Correa with great difficulty got the *Nazareth* to Mozambique, where she was abandoned. The *Santo Alberto* had been wrecked on the coast of Natal, and the survivors of her crew and ladies, after terrible misery, had made their way to Mozambique. Here also had arrived the *Chagas* (*v. s.*, p. 182) of the same fleet, the fine new ship lately built at Goa. The crew and passengers of both the *Nazareth* and *S. Alberto* were taken on the *Chagas*, with as much as she could carry of the cargo of the *Nazareth*. She was greatly overladen, and with difficulty made the Azores. Here, off Fayal, she fell in with three ships of the dreaded Earl of Cumberland, under Captains Cave, Anthony, and Downton. A terrific combat ensued, the Portuguese captains, especially Correa, behaving with the greatest heroism. Several attempts at boarding her were repulsed with loss. Anthony was killed, and Cave and Downton both wounded. At length the carrack took fire, but her brave defenders fought on to the bitter end. The few survivors cast themselves into the sea, those from whom ransom might be expected were saved by the English boats, others (to the disgrace of England) were shot as they swam for their lives. The fire on the carrack had now reached the magazine, and she blew up and went to the bottom with a cargo of priceless value, including the gems (*pedraria*) of three ship's companies. Correa and another captain, Nuno Velho, were saved and brought to England, where they remained more as guests than prisoners of the Earl for a year. Their ransom of 3,000 cruzados was paid by Nuno Velho for both. On their return to Spain they received the thanks of the king for their splendid defence. Some years afterwards Correa returned to India and was *Vedor da fazenda* at Goa in 1606, until he left at the beginning of 1609. From a dispatch in the *Liv. das Monç.* (ii, 250), it seems that he died about 1611.

CHAPTER XXII.

Departure from Goa.—Manner of embarking.—Provisions on board.—Treatment of the author.—Vermin in India.

The fourth carrack was one named *la nau de Nuestra Senora de Jesus*, that is to say, "Notre Dame de Jesus," whereon we were shipped by order of the viceroy. We numbered three Frenchmen and one Hollander, but he was so ill that he had to be put on shore again and left at Goa. We had also one of the three men who, as I have said, deserted from the Hollanders at Mozambic. On the voyage he was rated as an apprentice, or "under-mariner", and had his wages as such; but it was pitiable to see how ill he was dealt with during the voyage; for there was no man, great or small, but treated him despitefully and wished him ill; and in truth he did nothing to get himself liked, being an idle fellow and a parlous glutton. He said he was Swiss by race. He was the cause of the poor Portuguese being shot at Mozambic, as already related; and as several of their kinsmen were on board, that was one of the chief reasons that he was so hated. The captain of this carrack was *Antonio Baroso*, a man of fifty years of age or thereabouts.

Seven or eight days before our going on board we bade our adieux and took leave of our friends, thanking those that had assisted and been kind to us, amongst others the good French Jesuit Father, *Estienne de la Croix*, who a week before our departure had chanted his first mass. I begged him to write to his kinsmen at Rouen, promising him to deliver his letters faithfully, but he made excuses, saying he did not wish his relatives and friends to have news of him. The other two Fathers, *Nicolas Trigaut* and *Jean de Seine*, were then no longer at Goa, for Father Trigaut had gone to Cochin and Cape Comory with the armadas of the South, with the design when the armadas returned at the conclusion of their voyage to make his way thence to *Macao*, in China, and not to return to Goa; all this he did, as may be seen in his history of China. Father Jean de Seine had gone with the armadas to the northern coast to take up his residence at Chaul.

The viceroy, the archbishop, and some other great lords and wealthy men of our acquaintance dispensed to us liberally of their means when we went to take our leave of them, and what with that and with such of the allowances given to us by the King of Spain as we had saved, we had accumulated enough to supply ourselves with linen and other necessary clothing for the voyage. We took no thought for food, believing that we were to be fed on board at the king's expense, but in this we were mightily deceived, as you shall hear anon. Nor must I forget to mention a great insult I suffered before our departure, viz., that as my two companions and I were walking about the town buying what we had need of, I had the misfortune to have my pocket picked of the purse that contained all my money. This caused me the greatest possible inconvenience during the whole voyage, for I was without the means of purchasing many things; my companions who had money of their charity supplied me with the best clothes they could afford, although they had no more than they needed. Thus did ill fortune, that had accompanied me from the commencement of my voyage, pursue me through this last stage of it, and even to the end; nay, has pursued me since, and with the same constancy to the present moment, but God be praised who has given me grace to endure with patience.

At length arrived the time for our taking ship, which we did on the 30th January 1610. We went on board by night on account of the tide; but this is a dangerous time by reason of the robbers then abroad who lie in wait for the poor folks that are going aboard with their baggage and merchandise, and rob and plunder them, nay, sometimes maim and murder them. We were four days on board before we set sail, which was on the morning of the 3rd February.

It is a marvel to embark on one of these vessels, that seem like castles, with the vast number of people on board and the amount of merchandise they carry. Ours was so laden with goods on the deck that they reached almost half-way up the mast; and outside on the chain wales, which are the ledges on each side, you saw nothing but merchandise, provisions, and bunks,[1] which are the little cabins wherein the mariners and others lie, covering them over with fresh ox and cow hides. In short, the whole place was so obstructed that one could hardly get about. The second day after we got aboard, being still at anchor, and the officers of the ship still on shore, a man named *Manuel Fernando* (the same who had the sword-cut at Goa, and was like to die, having gone to visit a soldier's wife, as I have described elsewhere), while some work was being done about the ship, came and gave me a box on the ear, saying if we would not work he would fling us all into the sea, and that we were Hollander *Luteranos*. He had indeed been badly treated by the Hollanders, as I heard: afterwards on the voyage he was exceeding kind and courteous to me; that was, I believe, when he learnt that we were Frenchmen, though they hate us as much or more than any other nation. I submitted to the indignity with the best grace I could, fearing worse treatment or to be put back on shore.

When our captain came on board more than thirty galiots or "manchoues" surrounded the vessel with all kinds of instrumental music; this armada of galiots gave salutes with volleys of muskets and cannon, and friends all bade their farewells. At the same time we set sail also set out the

[1] In orig. *renches*, from the Sp. and old Ital. *rancio*, "chambrée, plat, logement des matelots dans un navire du commerce" (Jal, *Gloss. Naut.*).

armada for the conquest of Couesme, between Sofala and Mozambique. On leaving the bar of Goa, at twelve leagues to the north, you see some desert islands, like as if burnt, which the Portuguese call the *Islas quimados;* they are very dangerous reefs. It is the first land sighted by ships coming from Lisbon to Goa. One of the four carracks that had come out was left behind, because it had arrived too late, and there was no time to refit her; so in place of her another was taken that had remained behind from the preceding year, there not being enough pepper then to load her (the others even had not full cargoes). It is the officers' loss when ships arrive too late, for they have to wait a whole year, spending their substance the while; on the other hand they are the first selected for the year after. In our vessel we were about 800 persons, including the slaves, and about sixty Portuguese and Indian women. Two Franciscans also embarked with us without leave of the archbishop or their superior. They had got on board secretly, and had money enough for their provisions, for which I think they paid the master pilot at Goa, as he got a half-share of their "matelotage" or victuals. These cost a single man 300 pardos, which must be paid at Goa in advance. These two Franciscans were afterwards put ashore as prisoners at Brazil when we landed there, and sent thence to Portugal. Any that will may go to India, but not return —a rule applying more strictly to the Jesuits and religious persons, except for some good and lawful cause.[1]

[1] In Jan. 1598 the king wrote to the viceroy: "He (the late viceroy) also tells me that it will be for the service of God to recommend the Franciscan, Dominican, and Augustinian prelates of this realm to send out to India professed clergy of a better stamp, because those who take the frock there are deficient in such education and qualities as are requisite for the improvement of society by their example and conversation. Wherefore I have caused letters to be written to the prelates of the said orders that the professed clergy who go out to India are not to return thence, informing them of the evils which result from their doing so. This you will communicate to the prelates in India" (*Arch. Port. Or.*, Fasc. 3, No. 304).

When we were embarked we were greatly surprised at the custom in use in these ships from Goa to Lisbon, viz., of giving the seamen but one small portion of bread and water, as I have already remarked; whereas we thought to have had an ordinary as in our own ships, and so had failed to lay in store of provisions, as we had easily done with the aid of our friends and rich acquaintance; and what is more, they had promised to feed us, and so we had come on board with provisions for no more than four or five days only. Having set sail, the following day we presented ourselves to the captain and the clerk, and showed them our passport, which we had already, after our coming on board, shown to the ship-guards, two men set by the king to watch all that come and go from the ship, both men and merchandise. The captain was astonished to find that we were on board; for you may be there five or six months without knowing of each other, so vast are the ships and so great the company. When he heard that we had no provisions, he told us we were mighty ill-advised to make so bad arrangements, and was much annoyed at the viceroy and the *Viador de Fasienda* (as usual), for that when one was shipped by order of the king he should be provisioned at the expense of the king; and that these fellows were robbers, seeing they would not fail to enter it in the king's accounts, just as if they had supplied the victuals; and that furnishing us with bread and water would be to that extent diminishing the rations of the mariners. This did nevertheless raise in them such compassion for us that throughout the voyage they were both kind and courteous toward us, and forbade any to address or treat us in ill sort. This command was well obeyed, but in respect of food we suffered the greatest possible privations; for though so little bread and water was due to us, the ship ran so short that we could not be supplied with it for more than fifteen days' journey from the place we then were; insomuch that they were constrained to borrow, from some on board, our rations for a month, viz., thirty pounds of biscuit and a barrel of water for each, containing some twenty-four pints; but the mischief was, that, as we had no place under lock to put these stores, some were stolen by night, notwithstanding that corporal punishment was the penalty for that offence; and when it rained we had nowhere to put them under cover.

There was also great and general inconvenience throughout the whole ship by reason of certain animals like May bugs (*hanetons*), called by them *brato*,[1] which are very numerous, and are vastly annoying to all that come from the Indies, but not to those that go thither. These vermin come from India; and when you kill them in your hands they send forth the most abominable stink, like bugs (*punaises*). Our ship was full of them, and they got into all the boxes, casks, and other wooden vessels, so that they leaked, and the wine and water were lost. They also ate the biscuit and made sad havoc therein. The biscuit served out on board is made at Goa, and is as white as our chapter-bread.[2] To make it they take the whitest bread and cut it in four flat portions, heating these in the oven twice: this biscuit is very good to the taste. We got water so long as it lasted, like the mariners and officers of the ship, and so with biscuit, but at the end of three months the pittance failed. Sometimes the voyage lasts eight or nine months, more or less. Thus did we suffer many hardships in this voyage from Goa to the Bay of All Saints, which took us about six months. At times, but rarely, some good man bade us to eat with him, or sent us something. But a greater rarity was drink, which they gave us very seldom, and then it was a little *eau de vie* or raisin wine. The worst of the victuals on board is that they are all salted in order to keep better, and that changes their quality in such sort that full often I durst not eat at all,

[1] *I.e.*, cockroaches (*Blatta Orientalis*).

[2] *Pain de chapitre*, "pain qu'on distribuait chaque jour aux chanoines dans quelques chapitres" (*Littré*).

having so small a daily allowance of water in such a time of heat and calm. And what caused the water to run still more short was that the chief article of food was rice, which has to be cooked in water, and this made away with much. For the rest, we were fairly well off, and those on board treated us respectfully; for had any malapert knave said or done anything insolent he would have been summarily punished, more promptly indeed than if he had offended one of his own countrymen.

When we got to sea the captain took the names of all on board. He then appointed the captains of the night and day watches, giving particular directions to the day watch to see that none carried fire about the ship, this being strictly forbidden for fear of accidents. For you must know that justice is so strictly administered by the captain that he can without appeal give the strapado, or in a civil suit cast a defendant in damages to the extent of a hundred crowns.